VOLUME 1
Economic Principles

VOLUME 2
Institutional Issues

The Economics of Regulation:
Principles and Institutions

The Economics of Regulation:

Principles and Institutions

VOLUME 2
Institutional Issues

ALFRED E. KAHN

Cornell University

JOHN WILEY & SONS, INC.

New York · London · Sydney · Toronto

Contents

VOLUME 2

Introduction   xi

1. Monopoly and protectionism   1
   The association of regulation with monopoly   1
   Protectionism and conservatism   11
      Transportation   14
         The Motor Carrier Act of 1935   14
         The problems created by exempt carriers   18
         Price cutting by the railroads   21
         The orientation of regulatory policy   24
      The tendency of regulation to spread   28
      Community antenna television   32
      A few warning notes   46

2. Incentives and distortions   47
   The A–J–W effect   49
   Incentive plans   59
   The problem of intercompany coordination   64
      The imperfect adaptation of business structure: Electric
         power   70
   Regulatory planning   77
   The adjudicatory role and its consequences   86
   Conclusion: The inherent limitations of regulation   93

3. Positive influences on public utility performance   95
   Evidence of good performance   95
   Internal motivations   101
      The profit motive   101
      Managerialism   101
   Technological factors   102
   Market factors   102
      Elasticity of demand   102
      Competition   103
   The threat of government enterprise   104

The A–J–W effect   106
The role of regulation   108

4. The role and definition of competition: Natural monopoly   113
Economies of scale   116
Evolution of the natural monopoly concept   117
The essential prerequisite of natural monopoly   119
Cases of apparently increasing costs   123
Competitive certification versus centralized planning and
responsibility   126
The national telecommunications network   127
The above-890 decisions   129
The MCI cases   132
The communications satellite   136
Alien attachments   140
If competitors want to enter, how natural can mon-
opoly be?   146
Natural gas transmission   152
Economies of scale   153
Coordinated investment planning   157
The role of competitive considerations   158
Competition for existing business versus protectionism   165

5. Destructive competition and the quality of service   172
The theory and prerequisites of destructive competition   173
The theory applied   178
The case of trucking   178
Does trucking pass the tests?   178
Would quality standards suffice?   185
The effect on industry performance   186
Stock exchange brokerage commissions   193
The regulation of nonprice competition: Air transport   209
The issue of cream-skimming   220
The economic case for unrestricted cream-skimming   221
Possible cases against cream-skimming   223
The imperfections of competition case   223
The discrimination problem   224
The promotional case   233
Externalities, option demand and the tyranny of
small decisions   236
Offsetting imperfections and the problem of second
best   241
Noneconomic considerations   243
Conclusion: The benefits and dangers of discriminatory
competition   246

6. The role and definition of competition: Integration   251
Financial integration   256
Combination companies   264
Transportation   268
Electric and gas   276
Horizontal and geographic integration   281

Vertical integration in communications 290

Financial integration: the problem of judgment 306

Intercompany coordination 307

Piggyback service 309

Power pooling 314

7. The institution of regulated monopoly: reprise 324

Integration, coordination, and competition as partial alternatives 324

The imperfections of regulated monopoly 325

The choice among imperfect systems 327

Selected Bibliography 331

Index for Volumes I and II 337

Introduction

Most of our Volume 1 was devoted to developing rules for the efficient pricing of public utility services. The length of that treatment is itself instructive: the economist, like anyone else, spends most of his time doing the things that he is trained to do. In this, he is like the man who, having dropped a coin on the sidewalk on a dark night, looks for it under the street-light, not necessarily because he thinks that is where it probably has come to rest but because that is the only place he has any hope of finding it. The rules for efficient pricing flow out of the main stream of microeconomics as it has developed during the last century or two; that is our street-light, and we make such use of it as we can. We urge society to make use of it, too, because we are convinced of its usefulness.

But there is also a long tradition in economics of dissent from the "conventional wisdom" of normative microeconomic theory and a recognition of its limitations even as a purely economic guide to policy—although to read Mr. Galbraith one would think that his was the first and only pair of hands trying to strike matches over some of the darker parts of the sidewalk.[1]

These limitations are of two quite different kinds. First, there are the limitations of the rules and of the goals they are intended to achieve, even as statements of economic rules and goals. We obviously want our industries to achieve a lot more than such allocational efficiency and distributional equity as can be achieved by the mere equating of prices and marginal costs; and we are prepared, if need be, to make very large sacrifices of static allocational efficiency to the extent necessary to serve these other purposes. Specifically, we want industry:

1. To be efficient in the technical sense, that is, to keep the costs (social as well as private) to which price is to be equated as low as possible.

2. To improve its efficiency as rapidly as is economical—perpetually to devote efforts to improvements in efficiency so long as the incremental costs of those efforts are exceeded by the (discounted current) value of the cost savings thus achieved.

---

[1] Compare his *The Affluent Society* (Boston: Houghton Mifflin, 1958) and *The New Industrial State* (Boston: Houghton Mifflin, 1967) with almost any book by Thorstein Veblen or J. M. Clark.

3. To engage in product or service innovation with an intensity subject to the same economic test.

The listing of these additional goals suggests the second major limitation of any mere exposition of the normative rules of economic behavior and performance: they tell us absolutely nothing about *how to achieve* these results. This is what we mean by the *institutional* problems of regulation or of the ordering of the economy generally: by what kinds of institutional arrangements can we obtain the maximum assurance (compatible with such noneconomic values as security, freedom, due process of law, and so on) that the goals will in fact be achieved? How do we *get* prices down to marginal cost, services extended as widely, and the efficiency of production and quality of service kept as high and improved as rapidly as the pure theory of markets tells us is economically desirable? When we turn from the normative question of *what we want* to the institutional question of *how we get it*, we find ourselves launched into the baffling arena of social and political as well as economic behavior and organization, into the real world of ignorance, error and corruption, where all institutions are in varying degrees imperfect.

In that world, compromise and balance must be embodied in all the plans that are formulated. Entirely apart from the need for compromising economic and noneconomic objectives, there is an inescapable problem of choice and trade-offs even among the economic goals, and no simple blueprint can point the way to maximizing along all fronts simultaneously. Economies of scale create an immediate necessity for balancing off the requirements of the smaller number of sellers compatible with efficiency, on the one hand, and necessary for pure competition, on the other. The optimum rate of innovation requires a balance of pressures of competition on the one hand and protections against immediate competitive replication and appropriation of the fruits of innovation on the other, of maximum profit incentives for innovating, on the one hand, and maximum speed in passing on its benefits, on the other. The patent system and infant industry protection are two illustrations of the kinds of imperfect compromises that have to be made.

Problems like these are far less tractable to economic or indeed any other kind of analysis than the ones that concerned us in Volume 1. There are no clear-cut principles or proofs, no answers that are demonstrably right or wrong; the only available analytical tool is judgment informed by economic theory and experience.

And to even this modest statement of qualifications, the economist must attach a caveat. Experience is useful in forming judgment only to the extent that it is transferable. But the very decision to regulate, to withdraw an industry from the general rules that govern most markets, reflects a determination that the industry is in some essential respect peculiar. To the extent that determination is justified, the experience of unregulated industry, generally, or of other regulated industries is less applicable to any particular regulatory situation than it is within the more or less competitive and unregulated sectors of the economy. This consideration suggests that this part of our study, which addresses itself to institutional problems in the public utility industries taken as a group is seeking a level of generalization broader than the varying and peculiar characteristics of the individual industries falling within this group would justify. In view of this great diversity of the regulated industries, we obviously cannot hope to supply authoritative solutions to any of the numerous specific issues to which we shall allude in these chapters.

But there are major features general to the regulatory experience; there are common problems, even though the socially appropriate answers may differ from one context to the next. The various combinations of institutional arrangements—for example, market structures and regulatory policies—tend to yield predictable economic results. It is these common problems, these generally observable causal relationships that we attempt to expose and to illustrate in this volume, as they bear on the formulation of regulatory policy.

The two principal institutions of social control in a private enterprise economy are competition and direct regulation. Rarely do we rely on either of these exclusively: no competitive markets are totally unregulated, and no public utilities are free of some elements of rivalry. The proper object of search, in each instance, is the best possible mixture of the two. This is the central institutional issue of public utility regulation, and it is therefore the central theme of our remaining chapters. The theme has three separate, though closely interrelated aspects. First, there is the multifaceted question of how much competition it is appropriate to continue to permit, encourage, and rely on in the regulated sectors of the economy. The second concerns the kinds of policies—for example, with respect to integration, mergers, entry, price discrimination, and interfirm collaboration—that will be promotive of workable competition, to the extent that this is a feasible goal. These are the subjects of our Chapters 4 to 6. But if the search for the proper mix of competition and regulation is to be made intelligently, it can only be in full recognition of the inherent characteristics and problems of the regulatory device itself, as such. It is to the latter that we turn first: What are the competencies and incompetencies of the regulatory device? What kinds of incentives and distortions does it introduce? What are the main institutional influences on public utility performance? These are the subjects of Chapters 1–3.

In searching for answers to these questions, it is useful to remind ourselves that the scope of government regulation extends far beyond what we have, with some degree of arbitrariness, defined as the public utility area. If this technique has certain inherent or common characteristics, we should expect to find them exhibited also, therefore, in such disparate ventures as the framing of building codes, the licensing of doctors, electricians, and television stations, setting production quotas for oil or sugar; and we should not hesitate to draw on these experiences as well. Good reasons can be adduced for and against each of these policies. What will differ from one case to the next is the particular *balance* of need for regulation on the one hand and limitations and dangers on the other.

CHAPTER 1

Monopoly and Protectionism

If the decision to regulate were nothing more than a decision that competition was in some way or other inadequate to serve the public interest, and if regulation itself merely *supplemented* such competition as prevailed, there would still be problems of making those decisions but there would be no general regulatory dilemma. The general dilemma arises from the fact that the decision to regulate is, typically, a decision also to restrict competition, not just to supplement it in one way or another, but to *supplant* it. Whether this essentially competitive rather than complementary relationship between these two alternative systems of social control is inescapable or is the result of bad policy, the fact remains that as it has evolved historically, regulation has consisted largely in the imposition and administration of restrictions on entry and on what might otherwise have been independent and competitive price and output decisions.

THE ASSOCIATION OF REGULATION WITH MONOPOLY

There are several interrelated reasons for this association of regulation with restrictions on competition;[1] all of them help to define the major institutional issues in this field.[2]

---

[1] We alluded briefly to some of these in the first chapter of Volume 1.

[2] The word "reasons" has two, quite distinct meanings. In one sense, it refers to the *reasoning* by which particular courses of action are supported, the rationalization of policies. In its other meaning, it refers to the "real" reasons, the historical *forces* explaining why particular courses of action have been adopted. The former meaning embraces arguments and justifications; the latter, such operative factors as group interests and pressures in the political arena. There is no need to distinguish the two explicitly in this discussion. For one thing, the two categories are not mutually exclusive: surely most professors must believe, for example, that "ideas are weapons"

(see the book of this title by Max Lerner, Viking Press, New York, 1940) that is, that arguments do have real historical efficacy. Public policies usually are enacted in response partly to pressures of interested parties and partly because some more or less disinterested people become convinced by arguments that the policies will serve the public interest. That such arguments are typically proffered by privately interested parties does not make them wrong any more than the fact that "public interest" considerations likewise motivate some disinterested legislative decisions necessarily makes them right.

Our principal concern, of course, will be with the arguments and their merits, rather than the real historical reasons. But it is often impossible

1

One reason is the conception of *"natural monopoly"*: that the technology of certain industries or the character of the service is such that the customer can be served at least cost or greatest net benefit only by a single firm (in the extreme case) or by a limited number of "chosen instruments." In such circumstances, so the argument runs, unrestricted entry will be wasteful and productive of poorer service, with cycles of excessive investment followed by destructive rivalry (spurred by the wide spread between marginal and average costs). If the pressure of excessive capacity leads to rate wars—as are said to have characterized United States railway history periodically in the nineteenth century, or the maritime shipping industry in the absence of effective government regulation or collusive price-fixing—the effect may be to push rates down so close to short-run marginal costs as to impair the ability of the surviving companies to maintain their plant in good working order, to introduce needed renovations, or to continue to give good service. If, on the other hand, as may well occur when sellers are few, the parties refrain from vigorous price rivalry, customers continue to be poorly served because there exists no reliable mechanism for driving out the excessive number of firms, concentrating production in the hands of the "natural monopolist," and bringing costs and prices down to the minimum, technologically feasible level. In either event, the required policy is, allegedly, one of licensing only such entrants as are required by the "public convenience and necessity."

The character and applicability of the natural monopoly rationalization will, of course, vary from industry to industry. A particularly specialized version applies to the case of radio and television. The natural monopoly in this instance is the width of the radio-frequency band required for effective transmission of signals and the geographic area to which those signals reach, encroachment on which by competitors results in excessive interference and deterioration of signal quality.

We reserve for Chapters 4 and 5 all assessments of these rationalizations for regulatory restrictions on competition. It is worth pointing out, however, that some economists and historians have taken violent exception to the concept of natural monopoly, whether as an explanation of the way in which public utility monopolies have actually emerged or as a justification of the "unnatural" acts that conferred monopoly on them. An outstanding critic has been Horace M. Gray:

"The public utility status was to be the haven of refuge for all aspiring monopolists who found it too difficult, too costly, or too precarious to secure and maintain monopoly by private action alone. Their future prosperity would be assured if only they could induce government to grant them monopoly power and to protect them against interlopers. . . .

"The obvious conflict between the traditional ideology and the public utility concept was resolved by resort to rationalization. It was said that enterprises supplying gas, electricity, street transportation, water, and telephonic communication were 'inherently' or 'naturally' monopolistic;

---

to assess the arguments for a particular course of regulatory action without understanding also the political forces that will help to determine how the proposed policy will work out in actual practice. And it is precisely such inherent tendencies that regulation may exhibit in the real world that must be understood if one is to evaluate the institution itself. The same, obviously, can be said for such institutions as "competition," "private enterprise," or "socialism."

that they had certain 'natural characteristics' which distinguished them from other enterprises . . . that, because of this 'natural' force, they tended 'inevitably to become monopolies. . . . Thus, the fiction of "natural monopoly" was invented to explain the centripetal tendencies then observable. . . .

"'Franchises, way-leaves, contracts, charters, patents, secret agreements, injunctions, dummy corporations, cut-throat competition, newspaper and banking influences, and political corruption are the institutional ingredients from which monopoly was forged by skillful and unscrupulous manipulators. A critical evaluation of these elements might have shed considerable doubt upon the "naturalness" of this and similar monopolies.'"[3]

A second reason has been *the need for franchises*: in most of the public utility industries it would be infeasible for companies to operate without government permission. Railways, turnpike companies, electric companies, and pipelines have ordinarily (some more consistently than others) required access to the right of eminent domain in order to construct their various facilities. Distributors of gas, water, and steam have to have the right to dig up city streets; telephone and electric companies to put up poles and wires along the sidewalks, highways and across the country. That governments have been unwilling to dispense these privileges freely to all applicants is a reflection in part of natural monopoly—why let several companies tear up the streets to lay competing gas or water mains or build their own telephone or electricity poles when one would suffice? To these technical considerations must be added the political influences dictating a restrictive policy—the possibility of *selling* exclusive franchises as a means of rewarding favorites or raising money, whether for the government itself or for the officials dispensing these favors; and the self-interest of the applicants, anxious to enlist the support of the government in ensconcing them in monopolistic positions.[4]

Governments have exercised this licensing authority in a restrictive manner also for *promotional reasons*. As our patent system itself recognizes, one way of

---

[3] "The Passing of the Public Utility Concept," reprinted in American Economic Association, *Readings in the Social Control of Industry* (Philadelphia: The Blakiston Company, 1942), 283–284.

"One of the most unfortunate phrases ever introduced into law or economics was the phrase 'natural monopoly.' Every monopoly is a product of public policy. No present monopoly, public or private, can be traced back through history in a pure form." James R. Nelson, "The Role of Competition in the Regulated Industries," *The Antitrust Bulletin* (Jan.–Apr. 1966), XI: 3.

The historical fact, if it is a fact, that none of our present so-called public utilities would have enjoyed a monopoly had it not been for the intervention of government does not, of course, necessarily invalidate the natural monopoly thesis as a rationalization for that intervention, as Nelson's own ensuing analysis makes clear (see his pp. 5–10). See also pp. 117–126, Chapter 4, below. On the other hand, even where the

natural monopoly argument is valid, governmental licensure of entry is not necessarily called for. With respect even to the seemingly irrefutable case for licensure of radio stations, Coase argues that the courts were already well on the way to establishing property rights in the radio spectrum, which could have been bought and sold in such a way as (a) to avoid excessive interference and (b) to ensure the most economical allocation and utilization of that scarce resource, before Congress intervened and imposed the system of administrative allocation that we have today. R. H. Coase, "The Federal Communications Commission," *Jour. Law and Econ.* (October 1959), II: 25–35. See also note 2, Chapter 4 of Volume 1.

[4] "As for monopoly in general: to this day, clues must be sought in the nature of Charles I as well as in the nature of things." Nelson, *op. cit., The Antitrust Bulletin* (Jan.–Apr. 1966), XI: 3. The same is true of the origins of our modern patent system. On the franchise as the legal basis for regulation, see note 21, Chapter 1 of Volume 1.

inducing private investment in unusually risky fields—the East India trade at the end of the sixteenth century, the building of turnpikes or railroads into as-yet insufficiently settled areas in the nineteenth century, or the development of commercial air transport in the twentieth century[5]—is to offer the investors some protection against subsequent competition. Again as in the case of the patent, the exclusive franchise may, by assuring to the initial investors the opportunity to reap the full rewards of their innovational or promotional endeavors, internalize benefits that would otherwise be external from their standpoint; without such assurances economically desirable investments (whose benefits exceed total costs) might in fact not be made. Where, as in the case of the American airlines, the promotional purposes are achieved in part, as well, by the grant of subsidies, an additional consideration inducing governments to restrict entry is the desire to minimize the burden on taxpayers, by limiting the number of potential recipients and assuring to each the maximum opportunity to cover costs with ordinary revenues. Restrictive licensing might, of course, discourage development of the industry more than the subsidies might encourage it; we are not at this point assessing the wisdom of these policies.[6]

The all-embracing reason for the close association of regulation with monopolization or cartelization is, of course, the fact that society invokes the former process whenever and wherever it believes that unregulated competition produces unsatisfactory results. In the natural monopoly cases it takes the view that competition conflicts with the technological requirements for maximum efficiency. But in many other instances in which competition is

---

[5] According to Edgar Gorrell, president of the Air Transport Association of America,

"Hitherto, when we have approached questions of government regulation, we have thought largely in terms of protecting the public from abuse of economic power in private hands. . . . [But] the need for [aviation] legislation springs . . . rather from the need to assure the industry itself opportunity for vigorous growth."

"The Civil Aeronautics Act of 1938 and Democratic Government," *Jour. Air Law* (October, 1938), IX: 705, 708. See also Lucile S. Keyes, *Federal Control of Entry into Air Transportation* (Cambridge: Harvard Univ. Press, 1951), 59–105.

[6] On the possibility that methods of subsidization could have been devised that would have permitted more competition without necessarily imposing a greater burden on the American taxpayer, see note 182, Chapter 5, below. See also pp. 233–235, on the promotional case for restricting competition.

The historic link between subsidies and restriction of competition is an ancient one. In 1690 Louis XIV officially adopted and began to subsidize the theatrical company that he named the *Comédie Française*. He gave it the exclusive right to perform all plays by authors no longer living. Many independent ventures were formed,

but as they expanded their offerings, the *Comédie* complained and induced the Crown to impose various restrictions on them:

"Some could let their characters faint or bleed, but not die. Some could let their performers do only acrobatics or pantomime. Two small establishments . . . were forced to hang a gauze curtain between actors and audience. One amateur theater . . . could open only at seven, over an hour after the others, and so on."

All the familiar criticisms were heaped on the favored company—excessive admissions charges, conservatism in its productions.

Not surprisingly, the onset of the French Revolution was accompanied by attacks on the royal monopolist. At the news of the storming of the Bastille, the director of one of the aforementioned restricted theaters, "[t]earing down the curtain of gauze the police had required on his stage . . . threw himself onto the forestage, shouting, 'Long live Liberty!' The battle for freedom was launched." The ascendancy of Napoleon brought a return of licensing, censorship, and a reservation of the repertoire of the Comédie to that subsidized company; the same favored treatment was accorded the Opéra and the Opéra-Comique. See Marvin A. W. Carlson, *The Theater of the French Revolution* (Ithaca: Cornell Univ. Press, 1966), Chapter 1 and especially pp. 12, 16.

technologically entirely feasible, regulation is invoked because it is believed that competition would be characterized by intolerable imperfections.

One such imperfection is *buyer ignorance*—the inability of buyers readily to judge the quality of what they purchase. In one trade after another, entry is controlled and methods of doing business subjected to a variety of restrictions in the belief that unregulated competition leads to serious deterioration of the quality of service. Building codes and the licensing of doctors, tree surgeons, public accountants, barbers, undertakers, and plumbers are only a few of the almost limitless reflections of this kind of reasoning. In principle, we have already observed, regulation of this kind need not substitute governmental fiat for the competitive process in making the basic economic decisions, about what shall be produced and sold, by whom, of what dimensions, at what price. It might be confined, for example, to requiring disclosure of the ingredients of the product or the qualifications of the supplier. As others have observed, mere registration or certification could conceivably, in most cases, provide customers with the necessary information and the government with sufficient means of enforcing ethical behavior, without being as subject to monopolistic abuse as licensure. On the other hand, the belief that customers are unable to judge quality in advance and could therefore suffer irreparable damage from poor service has resulted in much more direct regulation—minimum product specifications, standards of cleanliness or safety, and admitting into the field only those with specified qualifications. Such considerations provide a conceivable justification for licensing plumbers, tree surgeons, veterinarians, and even beauticians, not to mention drug manufacturers. By means of licensing, applicants can be forced to meet tests of qualification; and if they face the penalty of forfeiting the right to practice if they prove unworthy of their trust, they can perhaps be held more effectively than otherwise to high standards of performance.

Even licensing could in principle be compatible with reliance on competition as the prime economic regulator, in determining the number of sellers, price, and even the quality of service over and above the legally prescribed minima. But in practice these controls, and particularly occupational licensure, have all too often been perverted into an instrument for raising barriers to entry and brazenly protecting practitioners in a wide variety of trades from unwanted competition.[7]

Moreover, in some industries believed to be inherently subject to *destructive*

---

[7] See note 5 of Chapter 1, Volume 1. For elaborations and documentation, see Milton Friedman, *Capitalism and Freedom* (Chicago: Univ. of Chicago Press, 1962), Chapter 9; Walter Gellhorn, *Individual Freedom and Governmental Restraints* (Baton Rouge: Louisiana State Univ. Press, 1956), Chapter 3; Thomas G. Moore, "The Purpose of Licensing," *Jour. Law and Econ.* (October 1961), IV: 93–117; and, for a specific instance, Reuben A. Kessel, "Price Discrimination in Medicine," *Jour. Law and Econ.* (October 1958), I: 20–53. According to Gellhorn's survey, 75 percent of the occupational licensing boards were composed exclusively of practitioners with a direct economic interest in the decisions made. *Op. cit.*, 140.

"GOTTA LICENSE? A growing number of jobs require you to have one.

"Occupational licensing by Federal, state and local bodies increases sharply. The Labor Department estimates that 550 occupations are licensed by at least one governmental jurisdiction, double the number 25 years ago. Recent additions to the list: Pest-control experts, nuclear materials handlers and fund-raisers. Licensing often results from public outcries against unqualified or dishonest practitioners.

"But Labor Department officials worry that the licensing power is sometimes used to keep qualified workers out of certain occupations. In one small community, a licensing board dominated by plumbing contractors rejected seven of

competition, the asserted purpose of maintaining the quality of service has been used to justify quite explicit substitution of thoroughgoing public utility regulation for competition. In these situations, competition is believed to be infeasible because it tends to be excessively keen and ultimately destructive of the ability of the industry to offer good service. In common carrier trucking, for example, restrictive licensing was imposed on entry not merely into the industry but, with some specific exceptions, into every single one of its submarkets—each individual route, each kind of freight—with the Interstate Commerce Commission deciding in the case of each applicant whether his proposed service is *economically* justifiable, on the ground that excessively easy entry had produced unreliability of service, unacceptable instability and unreliability of published rates, inadequate protection of shippers against damage, loss or disappearance of their cargoes and a breakdown in the ability of the regulatory authorities to enforce standards of safety and financial responsibility on the carriers.[8]

A similar argument has been offered by the Bell companies to justify their historic policy of prohibiting "foreign attachments" to telephones—independently produced accessories and equipment of one kind or another, like devices to muffle conversations or to permit conversations between the telephone instrument and parties at the other end of private communications systems. To permit independent equipment manufacturers this free competitive access and subscribers such free choice would, they have asserted, lead to deterioration in the quality of the telephone service. That this rationalization, like the others that we have been listing thus far, must be taken seriously becomes quite clear when it is recognized that the alleged threat is not merely to the quality of the service enjoyed by the customer who chooses to install the equipment—in which event there would seem little justification to abandon the protection of *caveat emptor*—but also to the service of innocent, third parties, whose reception might be subjected to all sorts of obscure interference. What we really have in this case is a variant of the natural monopoly rationalization, and we therefore consider it in Chapter 4.[9]

---

eight applicants for a license required to set up a plumbing business. Despite its large Spanish-speaking population, New York City gives its licensing exams only in English.

"Prostitutes, rainmakers, tatoo artists, beekeepers and lightning-rod dealers are among today's licensed practitioners." *Wall Street Journal*, August 5, 1969, 1.

[8] See, for example, U. S. House of Representatives, Committee on Interstate and Foreign Commerce, 74th Cong. 1st Sess., *Report of the Federal Coordinator of Transportation, 1934*, House Document No. 89, Washington, January 30, 1935, 113–114, 119–120. For a similar rationalization underlying the Civil Aeronautics Act of 1938, see W. K. Jones, *Cases and Materials on Regulated Industries* (Brooklyn: Foundation Press, 1967), 735–738. For a brief historical summary of the main judicial and economic contributions to this general line of argument for regulation, see pp. 7–10, Volume 1; for a fuller evaluation of it, see Chapter 5, below.

An interesting variant on this rationalization for limiting competition is applied mainly in various financial markets, where it is felt that excessive competition can have harmful effects on the operation of the economy at large. It is on grounds such as these that limitations are imposed on the ability of banks to compete with one another, for example by offering higher interest rates on deposits—the fear being that this kind of competition will, via its effect on credit policies, contribute to macroeconomic instability. A similar rationale is offered to justify self-regulation by the stock exchanges, including the right to prevent competition among their members in the commissions they charge for effecting security transactions (see pp. 199–200, Chapter 5, below). Analogous justifications apply in the field of insurance.

[9] One interesting example of the possible deterioration in service consequent on unrestricted entry and unregulated rivalry is provided by the electricity supply industry in

A related justification is the fact that even within individual industries the degree of monopoly power will differ greatly from one market to another. In consequence, competition tends to be highly selective and *discriminatory*, hence not merely unfair but injurious to the disadvantaged customers. This case is strengthened in the public utility industries, as we have already seen, by the fact that in many, perhaps most of their markets, suppliers have no direct competition at all; that effectively regulated monopolists have strong incentives to expand their markets and rate bases, even by taking on unremunerative business; and that this combination of circumstances creates the possibility of certain customers being forced to subsidize their supplier's competition for the patronage of others. This was the prime original justification for the institution of railroad rate regulation at the federal level. It remains the central issue today, after several decades of increasingly intensive and pervasive intercarrier competition have cast doubt on the continued necessity for any residual regulation of competition in the transportation field at all: the question remains whether a sufficient percentage of shippers, of particular commodities and between particular points, enjoy a sufficient range of competitive alternatives to prevent excessive discrimination among them. Considerations such as these constitute a case for the regulatory fixing of specific prices—both maximum rates, to protect customers inadequately protected by competition, and minimum rates, to prevent either undue preference to particular shippers or destruction or predation at the primary level.[10]

Regulatory agencies frequently intervene also to prevent the practice known as *cream-skimming*. The contention is that if entry is free, competitors will naturally choose to come into only the lucrative markets, "skimming the cream" of the business, negligently leaving to the established common carriers the burden of providing continuing service to the poorer and thinner markets—the isolated communities generating only small volumes of traffic, the off-peak business, and the like. The same kind of reasoning is used to oppose free price competition, which would likewise be expected to focus on the creamy markets. The alleged threat is that the common carriers, finding themselves either losing or suffering reduced returns on the profitable part of the business, forced increasingly to subsist on a diet of skimmed milk, will be unable to carry on in the thinner geographic and seasonal markets, with consequent destruction of service to large areas of the country and bodies of customers.

The phenomenon and the corollary case for restricting competition are not confined to the public utility arena. All businesses are in some measure and in some respect conglomerates: they operate in more than one market, supply more than one service, or supply a given service at more than one point in time. And, because the conditions of supply and demand, and particularly

---

Great Britain, where the profusion of separate companies resulted in a corresponding profusion of qualities and specifications of service. The result was that the institution of a national interconnecting grid was seriously delayed by the incompatibilities of the various separate systems. The development of the electrical manufacturing industries was similarly retarded: since it was necessary to produce appliances and equipment of varying specifications for use with different frequencies and voltages, it was impossible to standardize products sufficiently to exploit fully the potential economies of large-scale production. See *Statist*, Supplement (Dec. 17, 1938), 1–2, 4, 7.

[10] See note 85, Chapter 2, and Chapter 6 in Volume 1; also note 64, pp. 26–27, below.

the intensity of competition, will inevitably vary from one of these markets to the other, all companies will find, inevitably, that the profitability of these various operations (by *some* meaningful measure) will vary correspondingly. If competition prevails, it will tend naturally to concentrate on the lucrative markets. That is how it is supposed to operate—to erode away supernormal returns, to equalize returns in various markets except for differences in risk. But here again objection may be raised and legal restrictions on competition advocated, if in some way the creamy business was "carrying" the others, with the result that intensified competition in the former threatens curtailment of supply to the latter. This kind of case has been made, for example, for resale price maintenance: that unrestricted price competition on popular, fast-moving brands (best-selling books, whiskeys, toothpastes, or appliances) would drive out of business the small, conveniently situated, low-volume retailer, the merchandiser who offers service, the diversified bookstore, the neighborhood pharmacist, all of whom, it is alleged, survive in part because of the protected margins on the former items.[11]

But it is in the public utility arena that the issues are most sharply posed. Public utility companies have, typically, been given exclusive or partially exclusive public franchises, in return for which they are asked to assume the obligations of common carriers or of public callings; and implicit in these obligations is, usually, at least a general conception that the company has a responsibility to extend supply as broadly as possible, and to continue to provide service even where it may not be economical for it to do so. This view clearly reflects extraeconomic considerations—notably the possible benefit to national security of preserving financially strong common carrier transportation and communications systems, with greater and more widespread capacity to serve than would be justified by purely market tests; and the desire to assure service even to segments of the country unable to pay the long-run marginal costs of serving them. But there are possible economic arguments of an institutional character as well, as we shall see. In these circumstances, it could well be considered the function of public policy to protect firms that assume such obligations, against the competition that might impair their abilities to continue service in good seasons and in bad, in thick markets and in thin.

The cream-skimming argument was an important part of the rationale for the Motor Carrier Act of 1935, which imposed on the industry the pervasive controls briefly described above.

"The contract carrier may differ from the common carrier only in the fact that he undertakes to skim the cream of the traffic and leave the portion which lacks the butterfats to his common-carrier competitor. Obviously such operations can have very unfortunate and undesirable results."[12]

"Prior to regulation, a very important factor in railroad rates was 'what

---

[11] See my "The Tyranny of Small Decisions: Market Failures, Imperfections, and the Limits of Economics," *Kyklos* (1966), XIX: 34–39. The reader may recognize that the case for restricting competitive cream skimming thus far presented is a case for preserving a pattern of internal subsidization, a practice that we demonstrated was economically indefensible in Volume 1 (pp. 143, 190–191). And so it is, in the usual presentation. But, in fact, some defenses can be erected on economic grounds. We analyze and appraise the issue more systematically on pp. 223–243, below.

[12] *Report of the Federal Coordinator of Transportation, 1934, op. cit.*, 17.

the traffic will bear.' . . . The result of this . . . has been that in general the higher-valued commodities and the shorter hauls pay higher rates, relatively, than the lower-valued commodities and the longer hauls. . . .

"It will be readily seen . . . that this deviation from cost of service favored truck competition, since it made the traffic vulnerable on which the relatively higher rates are charged. This is what the railroads mean when they say that the trucks are taking the 'cream of the traffic' . . . ."[13]

"A broader aspect of responsibility also deserves mention. This relates to the maintenance of truck or bus service on which the shipper or traveler has come, perhaps entirely, to depend. Certainly no responsibility is felt by the motor-transport industry today to maintain unprofitable or relatively unprofitable service, such as the railroads have maintained, frequently voluntarily, although sometimes by order of public authorities. The highway operator assumes a lesser degree of responsibility for a complete coverage of the transportation needs of the area he sets out to serve. Truck and bus operators tend commonly to concentrate their efforts on the profitable avenues of traffic."[14]

Similar arguments have been used to justify the limitations on entry imposed by the Civil Aeronautics Board.

"It is clear that, if there had been no regulation, the quantity of service and the extent to which service has been provided to different and less populated areas of the United States would have been curtailed substantially Or, to put it differently, an overwhelming majority of the cities to which the airlines provide service just do not generate enough traffic to warrant operations if air transport were not regulated and was subject only to the rules of the 'free' market place. . . .

"It is surprising to some that trunk carriers as well as local service carriers provide service to the smaller cities in the United States. The trunklines are able to do this because the losses sustained at these marginal cities, *which also deserve the advantages of air transportation*, are compensated for by the revenues developed at the greater traffic-producing areas. . . . [Stress supplied.]

"A most effective way to illustrate the specious nature of this doctrine of freedom of entry is to imagine the situation which would doubtless result if there were no regulatory limitation on entry. . . .

"On the day that concept was introduced, every airline would tear up its timetables, disregard its certificates, forget that it has franchise responsibilities, and do what business it pleased in the interest of greater profits and not public convenience. . . . The industry, in such a chaotic struggle for survival, would then have to abandon service to roughly some 500 of the cities to which it is now certificated, and operate only between the 50 most profitable pairs of points."[15]

---

[13] *Ibid.*, 114–115.
[14] *Ibid.*, 120. See also Ernest W. Williams, Jr., *The Regulation of Rail-Motor Rate Competition* (New York: Harper & Brothers, 1958), 8–9.
[15] Stuart G. Tipton and Stanley Gewirtz, "The Effect of Regulated Competition on the Air Transport Industry," reprinted from the *Jour. Air Law and Commerce* (1955), XXII, No. 2 in U. S. Senate Select Committee on Small Business,

84th Cong. 2d Sess., *Materials Relative to Competition in the Regulated Civil Aviation Industry, 1956*, April 18, 1956, 204, 217.

Similar supports for this position may be found in D. Philip Locklin, *Economics of Transportation*, 6th ed. (Homewood: Richard D. Irwin, 1966), 827–828 and Daniel Marx, Jr., *International Shipping Cartels: A Study of Industrial Self-Regulation by Shipping Conferences* (Princeton:

As we shall see in Chapter 4, the issue has come to be keenly contested in the field of communications as well, where such technological developments as microwave radio and communications satellites have opened up the possibility of large users bypassing the major common carriers. The latter have in turn sought to induce Congress and the Federal Communications Commission to block this emergent competition on cream-skimming grounds.

Another rationalization for regulation of competition in industries that could not, by any stretch of the imagination, be termed natural monopolies is interestingly related to some of the ones mentioned so far. This is the argument that, at least in certain circumstances, there is a danger of *excessive nonprice rivalry*, producing not deterioration but unduly costly inflation of the quality of service. The phenomenon has been encountered in recent years in air passenger transportation, where the International Air Transport Association and the American Civil Aeronautics Board have found it necessary to specify maximum distances between seats and maximum quality of free meals and beverages served on tourist flights, to require a charge for motion pictures, and to consider restricting the competitive scheduling of flights. As we shall point out more fully in Chapter 5, this kind of regulation is or ought to be the inescapable consequence and counterpart of restrictions on price rivalry. If members of a cartel agree on minimum prices, they may well find it necessary, if there remains any spark of independence and rivalry among them, to enforce corresponding ceilings on quality of service.[16] Restrictions of this type cannot be lightly dismissed; the possibility must be confronted that in some circumstances competition may take on a destructive character not only in price cutting but in service inflating, to the ultimate detriment of customers.

The reader will recognize here the counterpart of the case we set forth in Chapter 2 of Volume 1 for regulating the quality of service provided by public utility companies. If a monopolist can exploit buyers by charging excessively high prices, he may do so also by providing excessively poor service. If competitors may compete "destructively" by cutting prices they may do so also by improving the quality of service. In each case if the government wants to prevent the first practice it may well have to try to prevent the second.

Two concluding words: What we have done so far is merely to list some of the outstanding historical reasons and theoretical justifications for the association of regulation with the imposition of restraints on competition. We have not yet appraised them, either in general terms or in specific contexts. That is the first word. The second is that the merits of the policies implied must, in the nature of the case, be constantly changing over time. For example, technology is perpetually developing: so the natural monopoly of yesterday may no longer be natural today.[17] Again, the economic case for

---

Princeton Univ. Press, 1953), 4, 56–57, 187–198. In the case of ocean shipping, it should be noted, the argument is used to justify not governmental licensure or entry, but shipping conferences— private organizations of shipping companies setting minimum rates. Many conferences also give shippers substantial discounts if they use the services of conference members exclusively. These exclusive patronage refunds have the same tendency to restrict the entry of price-cutting

independents, who, it is alleged, skim only the heavily traveled routes in the busy seasons, leaving it to the "reputable" conference members to maintain reliable schedules, in thin markets as well as thick, in and out of season.

[16] See pp. 209–220, Chapter 5, below.

[17] The converse may also be true: technology may spawn new "natural monopolies." But it seems to be in the nature of modern technology that it tends on balance to increase rather than

promotional policies, like patent protection, is inherently self-limiting in time, as far as specific applications are concerned: either the infants grow up to a point where they no longer need protection or they ought to be permitted to die. Again, market structures that are conducive to destructive competition in periods of depression may not be so in periods of general economic expansion. When we come to examine some of the issues raised in this section, we will want particularly to do so in the context of the technology and the general economic environment of the 1970s, not that of the 1930s or the 1890s.

PROTECTIONISM AND CONSERVATISM

The close two-way causal association of regulation and restraint of competition is in turn closely linked to another set of characteristics that the regulatory process exhibits in practice—protectionism and conservatism. Generalizations of this kind are of course always dangerous when applied to such a variegated set of social and political institutions. There have been wide differences between commissions and in their legislative mandates, and changes over time in the political environment in which they operate. Both the differences and changes on the one hand and the common core are illustrated, for example, in the oversimplified but illuminating generalization that regulatory commissions tend to go through a life cycle, setting out as vigorous, imaginative, and enthusiastic protagonists of the public interest, reflecting the public concern and ferment that had to be mobilized to legislate them into existence in the first place, defining their responsibilities broadly and creatively, then gradually becoming devitalized, limited in their perspective, routinized and bureaucratized in their policies and procedures, and increasingly solicitous and protective of the interests of the companies they are supposed to regulate, resistant to change, wedded to the *status quo*.[18]

We leave to historians and political scientists the task of deciding to what extent developments such as these are reflections of a tendency for regulatory agents to be "captured" by the industries they were set up to govern. There are certainly many factors that tend to have this effect—the disparity in the quality of personnel and the amount of financial resources available to each side; corruption, including the subtle corruption that may affect administrators whose hope for future advancement may lie in working for the private companies they are supposed currently to be regulating; the fact that

decrease the range of alternatives, developing additional ways of satisfying old needs, and new wants to compete with old ones. The connection between technological progress and monopoly is of course a complex one, particularly when one turns to the question of what is the best form of market organization for the generation of such progress. But if one looks only to the results, one must conclude that—at least in the dynamic sense and probably statically as well—technology is far more often the enemy than the promoter of monopoly. If the invention of the automobile resulted in the displacement of a competitive carriage industry with a monopolistic automobile industry, in one dynamic sense the invention could be said to have introduced additional competition—added choices for consumers. But by producing a change in consumer tastes, it would in this event have left the economy, statically, with more possibility of monopolistic exploitation than before. On the other hand, clearly, even if automobile manufacturers have a great deal of monopoly power, they have increased competition in the interurban transport of people and commodities.

[18] See, for example, Marver H. Bernstein, *Regulating Business by Independent Commission* (Princeton: Princeton Univ. Press, 1955), especially Chapter 3, "The Life Cycle of Regulatory Commissions."

producing interests are typically better organized than consumer interests to exert pressure, either directly on commissions or indirectly on legislatures, when it comes to public policies that bear directly on them. All of these factors have undoubtedly been influential.[19]

More subtle and, the economist might say—betraying his parochialism—more fundamental, is the inherent consequence of substituting regulation for competition as the prime instrument of social control. When an administrative commission is invested with authority over the central economic decisions of an industry, it finds itself invested also with a heavy responsibility. The decision to regulate usually takes for granted the strength and financial health of the industry and seeks to introduce a counterpoise, to control abuses and protect the public. But the regulatory commission soon finds, in framing its policies, that it cannot take the health on the supply side of the market for granted. For one thing, it has to reckon with legislative injunctions on it to be fair to investors, and with judicial warnings that it cannot, consistent with the Fourteenth Amendment (and corresponding injunctions in state constitutions), deprive them of a fair return on the fair value of their investment. Then there are the wearily predictable protestations of company witnesses and lawyers that any regulation will immediately dam up the flow of capital into the industry and thereby bring down on the commissioners' heads the wrath of the consuming public, Congress, and the courts. But the commission cannot in any event escape recognizing its responsibility for contentment on *both* sides of the market. Responsible for the continued provision and improvement of service, it comes increasingly and understandably to identify the interest of the public with that of the existing companies on whom it must rely to deliver these goods.

The virtues of the competitive market are many. One major one is that no one company or coherent, identifiable group of companies can be said to bear direct responsibility for industry performance.[20] Another, and related one, is that each individual investor or businessman can therefore afford to be irresponsible, to take the risk of large losses in the hope of large gains, to experiment, to upset the status quo, to destroy existing equities. Indeed, competition *forces* businessmen to behave in this "irresponsible" fashion if they are to prosper, even to survive.[21]

---

[19] See, in addition to the above, James M. Landis' excellent *Report on Regulatory Agencies to the President-Elect*, December 1960, published as a Committee Print by the U. S. Senate Committee on the Judiciary, 86th Cong. 2d Sess., Washington, 1960, 13–15 and 71.

[20] "It is because of this basic dissimilarity between the automobile industry and the natural gas industry, for example, that regulation must be 'protectionist' to the extent that it must assure the continued financial integrity of the industry in order that the consumer will have continued reliable, adequate utility service. If an automobile dealer goes out of business there are others to sell automobiles; but if an interstate pipeline goes out of business, many of its customers will have no source of supply. Because of this basic distinction, regulation must as a matter of social policy intrude at some point to stifle the impersonal forces of competition and perform the role of a 'protector' of the regulated industry." Carl E. Bagge, Federal Power Commissioner, "Regulated Competition: An Alternative to Anti-trust," an address before the Independent Natural Gas Association of America, San Francisco, September 4, 1967, mimeo., 3.

[21] This picture of competition is of course an idealized one. The reader might have difficulty recognizing in it any resemblance to, let us say, the American steel industry. The implied contrasting picture of the functioning of regulation is, in the author's opinion, at least equally overdrawn. But there remains an important difference in the impact of these two alternative systems of organization.

But these very virtues of competition are its defects from the regulatory standpoint. If the commission is responsible for the proper performance of industry, how can it permit that responsibility to be diluted by the independent, competitive maneuvering of a bunch of irresponsible firms, known and unknown, which are not subject to its control? If it is responsible for the financial health of the regulated companies, from whom it is thereby enabled in turn to exact certain guarantees with respect to the continued provision and quality of service and on whom it can force a reduced return on investment, reflective of the security that regulated monopoly conveys, how can it afford to have that security subject to the vagaries of unregulated competition?[22] Regulation necessarily places a high value on predictability and continuity: how else can the commission proceed on the basis of evidence respecting some past, test year to set rates or pass on investment plans that look to the future—especially in view of the legal restraints, the complicated rules and procedures that govern administrative proceedings, enacted to assure fair treatment of all contesting parties, which often stretch the decision making process over hundreds of volumes of testimony, exhibits, and "briefs," and many years? Competition introduces strong elements of unpredictability—unpredictability about prices, instabilities of market shares. Industry planning is one thing, competition quite another, and there are strong incompatibilities between the two.

It is extremely difficult to *plan* for *change*, for the kind of flux and disruption that competition entails, for one supervising agency to program the types of results that are produced when the sources of initiative and responsibility are dispersed.[23]

It is for reasons such as these, apart from the more obvious political influences, that regulation itself tends to be conservative. This conservatism is enhanced when, as is typically the case, regulators cannot themselves initiate or force the companies under their supervision to undertake risky investments, to embark on new and unproven ventures, because they too are dealing with "other people's money."[24] Because planning requires stability, regulators are apt to be tolerant if not positively enthusiastic about rate bureaus and similar devices by which potential competitors post prices and agree to adhere to them. They are likely to be hostile to new entrants and prone to adopt policies that assure a "fair sharing" of contested business among the inside parties rather than to leave its determination to the warfare of competition.

This is not to conclude—at this point, at least—that the purposes of improving service and protecting competitors, or the interests of consumers and the owners of regulated companies, are necessarily in conflict. The point is, only, that regulation typically chooses to serve the one by serving the other. That the companies pressing for the legislation and for a protectionist interpretation of it are doubtless interested primarily in the latter goals is relevant as a historical fact, but does not resolve the question of whether the methods chosen are socially the best ones available.

---

[22] For an interesting illustration of this attitude, in which the "chosen instrument," insulated from competition, is given direct responsibility for regulation as well, see the case of the organized stock exchanges, in Chapter 5, pp. 194–200, below.

[23] See, for example, David McCord Wright, *Democracy and Progress* (New York: The Macmillan Company, 1948), Chap. 1.

[24] See note 20, Chapter 2, Volume 1.

The evidences of this conservatism and protectionism on the part of regulatory agencies are so numerous that it would be impossible to cite even a small fraction of them; we postpone the detailed appraisal of these tendencies and of the specific decisions in which they have been manifested for later chapters. We set forth some major examples in considerable detail at this point, however, partly because concrete illustrations are always more informative than broad generalizations, partly to demonstrate the wide variety of regulatory circumstances in which these tendencies manifest themselves, and partly to describe a few of the major regulatory issues and policies that we shall more fully analyze at a later point.

Transportation

It should not be surprising that the leading examples of these tendencies can be found in the transportation field; it is there, above all the so-called public utilities, that the possibilities of competition are so great and the consequent necessity for the choice between regulation and competition so pervasive.

The Motor Carrier Act of 1935. The two principal operative provisions of this statute extended the authority of the Interstate Commerce Commission to include licensure of entry and regulation of rates charged in intercity operations by common and contract carriers by truck (the former offer their services to the public at large, the latter limit themselves to serving the needs of particular, individual shippers.) We have already cited the major consideration motivating the imposition of this comprehensive set of public utility-type controls on a highly dispersed and competitive industry—the belief that unregulated entry and price competition had resulted in poor service. The other side of the coin is that the Act was passed and has been enforced with the explicit purpose and effect of protecting railroads against the intensified competition of motor carriers and protecting motor carriers from one another.[25]

It is not a contradiction but a fuller explanation of this protectionism that it was in turn motivated largely by a desire to protect the discriminatory pricing structure of the railroads from being undermined by competition. Indeed, one important reason for the deep inroads of trucking into the freight business was that the rails had clung unimaginatively for decades to a "value of service" rate structure that involved extreme price discrimination against more valuable commodities, on the theory that their demand for transportation was inelastic. This assumption may well have been appropriate when railroads had a virtual monopoly. It became irrelevant once trucks were available to compete for that business. The common carrier truckers, in general, merely matched the rail rates; and because of the superiority of their service (greater speed and door-to-door delivery, without need for intermediate loading and unloading) they were able in this way to take away the bulk of this more valuable business.[26]

---

[25] See, for example, U. S. Senate, Committee on Interstate Commerce, 74th Cong. 1st Sess., *Report to Accompany S. 1629*, Senate Report No. 482, Washington, April 11, 1935, 2 3; *Report of the Federal Coordinator of Transportation, 1934, op. cit.*, 127.

[26] See pp. 64, 155, and 171 (note 23) of Volume 1, and especially Wilson, "Effects of Value-of-Service Pricing Upon Motor Common Carriers," *Jour. Pol. Econ.* (Aug. 1955), LXIII: 337–344. Once the trucking alternative was available, defining value of service (or demand inelasticity)

One consistent thread that runs throughout the entire history of the Interstate Commerce Act is the desire on the part of Congress and the ICC to keep freight rates low on the large-volume, low-valued agricultural commodities—a preferential treatment made possible in part by the traditional discrimination against the high-valued manufactured products. If this pricing pattern was to be preserved, the railroads clearly had to have some protection against the competition by trucks for the latter traffic. The Motor Carrier Act of 1935 filled this need.[27]

In its licensing provisions, the Act places on the applicant for common carrier authorization the burden of proof that the service he proposes to offer is "required by the present or future public convenience and necessity. . . ."[28] It does not suffice that a trucker is willing to take the risks of going into the business himself; he must convince the Commission that his services are required. When the service he proposes would compete, directly or indirectly, with that offered by an existing carrier, the latter may enter a protest. And in any event the Commission has pursued an extremely restrictive policy with regard to the issuance of new licenses. The possibility that the applicants would take business away from existing carriers has been an important consideration in inducing it to refuse them. Time and again, it has turned down applications that enjoyed the support of shippers, on the ground that the service provided by existing carriers either was in its judgment sufficient *or could become so.* In short, even an admittedly poor performance by existing carriers is not necessarily a sufficient justification for permitting more competition.[29] Moreover, the licenses that the ICC does

---

in terms of the value of the commodities being shipped became highly illogical. As Joel Dean has pointed out:

"If the value of commodities should be recognized by the rate structure at all, exactly the opposite treatment would be the most effective in competing against trucks. This is because trucks reduce the time merchandise is tied up in transit. The higher the value of the merchandise, the larger the cost saving from fast delivery; hence, to compensate for the railroads' slower and more erratic service, rail rates per 100 pounds should be lower, relative to trucks, on high-value commodities than on low-value commodities. . . ." As quoted in U. S. Senate, Committee on Interstate and Foreign Commerce, 87th Cong. 1st Sess., *National Transportation Policy,* Preliminary Draft of a Report prepared by the Special Study Group on Transportation Policies in the United States (John P. Doyle, Staff Director), Washington, January 1961 (hereinafter referred to as the *Doyle Report*), 662–663.

See also pp. 8–7, above, and 97, below.

[27] For a challenging documentation of this argument, describing the especially great opposition during the depression to the rails' effort to make good some of their revenue losses on high-valued commodity freight by increasing rates on agricultural products, see Robert A. Nelson and William R. Greiner, "The Relevance of the Common Carrier Under Modern Economic Conditions," in Universities–National Bureau Committee for Economic Research, *Transportation Economics* (New York: National Bureau of Economic Research, 1965), 352–374. This means that the purpose of the restriction was to preserve a pattern of internal subsidization—holding rates to some customers above the ATC of serving them alone (by truck) in order to hold the rates to others closer to marginal costs. Contrast this purpose with the rules for acceptable price discrimination set forth at pp. 142–143, Volume 1, above; see also the discussion of this alleged cream-skimming by the trucks at note 154, p. 226, below.

The exemption of the carriage of agricultural commodities from the provisions of the 1935 Act was of course entirely consistent with this basic purpose. See also Ann F. Friedlaender, *The Dilemma of Freight Transport Regulation* (Washington: The Brookings Institution, 1969), 10–27.

[28] 49 U. S. Code 307 (a), 1964 ed.

[29] It is always hazardous to attempt general characterizations of Commission policy, when that policy is laid down over a great number of years in thousands of individual cases. When faced with an application for permission to extend service to areas or for the carriage of products in which, according both to shipper

complaints and its own findings, existing service was inadequate, the Commission has insisted on first giving existing carriers the opportunity to improve their service. It has done so with sufficient frequency to lead a District Court to find, in 1967, that this was its "invariable rule":

"The invariable rule of the Commission is and has been for a long time that no certificate affecting the area of another carrier will be issued until that other carrier has been furnished an opportunity either to improve or to correct his service to such route or decide whether he wishes to or can furnish the added service sought by the applicant carrier." *Dixie Highway Express, Inc. v. United States*, 268 F. Supp. 239, 241 (1967).

In support of this finding, the same District Court referred to the following declaration by the Commission itself, issued in 1965.

" 'We have repeatedly stated that existing carriers normally should be accorded an opportunity to transport all of the traffic they can handle in an adequate and efficient manner without the added competition of a new operation.' " *Dixie Express Inc. et al. v. U. S.*, 242 F. Supp. 1016, 1021 (1965).

The ICC attitude on this specific point contrasts interestingly with the policy of the CAB.

"There is still another way in which the Board's handling of route cases tends to furnish a continuous incentive for carriers to maintain the quality of service, even in monopoly market segments or those where the number of carriers has not changed recently. Decisions in route cases often note that existing carriers have moved to rectify the inadequacies in their service after a route proceeding has been opened. If the Board would accept such improvements as a basis for not adding competitors, the carriers would have a relatively easy time of neutralizing the Board's efforts to promote the quality of service through point-to-point competition. However, the Board does not operate in this way. Rectifying service inadequacies to deter a competitive route award has in no significant case caused the Board to stay its decision to add competing service. A carrier which fears that one of its markets may attract would-be competitors cannot skimp on service until the threat is actually in sight." Richard E. Caves, *Air Transport and Its Regulators* (Cambridge: Harvard University Press, 1962), 240.

On the other hand, in the *Dixie Express* case itself—and in others, as well, in recent years (*Wall Street Journal*, December 19, 1967)—the Commission obviously had departed from that rule, finding,

"in considerable detail . . . . that shippers and receivers were hampered by the inadequacy of existing service, and . . . that, despite numerous complaints, existing carriers had not demonstrated that they could be depended upon to furnish adequate service,"

and therefore authorizing another carrier to extend service to the points in question. On complaint by competing motor carriers, the District Court twice returned the case to the Commission, the second time on the ground of the alleged "invariable rule" and on the ground too "that carriers have a property right to such opportunity [that is, to improve their service] before a new certificate may be issued. . . ." *United States et al v. Dixie Highway Express, Inc., et al.*, 389 U.S. 409, 410, 411 (1967).

The Supreme Court concluded that "no such limitation has been established by the Commission's own decisions or by judicial determinations," holding, instead, that:

" 'the Commission may authorize the certificate even though the existing carriers might arrange to furnish successfully the projected service.' *ICC v. Parker*, 326 U.S. 60, 70 (1945); see *Schaffer Transportation Co. v. United States*, 355 U.S. 83, 90–91 (1957)." *Ibid.*, 411–412.

No doubt the Supreme Court itself deserves considerable credit for this partial relaxation of ICC policy in recent years. In the *Schaffer* case, just cited, the Commission had refused to issue a license to a trucker to provide service between points previously served only by rail, on the ground that:

"The evidence indicates that the witnesses' main purpose in supporting the application is to obtain lower rates rather than improved service. It is well established that this is not a proper basis for a grant of authority. . . ." As quoted 355 U.S. 83, 89 (1957).

But the Supreme Court pointed out, in overruling the Commission, the ICC itself had found that the lower truck rates on less-than-carload service would permit shippers to avoid the delays and expense of accumulating full carload shipments, as they had hitherto done because of the much lower rail rates on that service; and that shippers had asserted they were at a disadvantage in competing with suppliers from other areas who did enjoy the benefit of truck service.

"The ability of one mode of transportation to operate with a rate lower than competing types of transportation is precisely the sort of 'inherent advantage' that the congressional policy requires the Commission to recognize." *Ibid.*, 91.

So it quoted with approval the statement of the ICC's own Division 5 that:

"no carrier is entitled to protection from competition in the continuance of a service that

grant are extraordinarily detailed in their limitations,[30] permitting carriage of only specified commodities over only specified routes, in specified directions: licenses that permit carriers to offer service between points A and B

---

fails to meet a public need, nor, by the same token, should the public be deprived of a new and improved service because it may divert some traffic to other carriers." *Ibid.*, 91.

The U. S. Senate Select Committee on Small Business held hearings in 1955 in order

"to examine the validity of the many and bitter complaints received from small truckers and small shippers directed at the policies and practices of the Interstate Commerce Commission. No better summary statement of the charges . . . has come to the attention of your committee than those contained in a letter from an attorney accustomed to representing small trucking clients in proceedings before the Commission. This concise yet comprehensive summary of allegations is as follows:

"'It seems to me and to my clients that the basic problem confronting Congress and the country with respect to the ICC is not simply that the decisions are long delayed and expensive. The basic problem is that the ICC takes such a narrow and restrictive view of the motor carrier authority that should be authorized that even when a small carrier is willing to run the gantlet [sic] of an ICC procedure, it has very little hope of being able to secure any significant extension or addition of authority. The ICC seems to take the same view of the economy that is taken by reactionary business and labor unions when they seek to prevent the entry of any new enterprises into their respective fields. This view seems to be based on the assumption that there is only a limited amount of business and that it is to be the interest of those in the business to get the biggest slices of the pie that they can by keeping everyone else out of the field.

"'When such conduct is engaged in by private business or by labor unions, it is prosecuted as a violation of the antitrust laws and regarded as highly improper. It seems to me that the effects are just as baneful and antisocial when they are caused by a Government agency. . . .

"'It is respectfully submitted that any careful analysis of an examination into the ICC administration of the Motor Carrier Act will indicate that the Commission has acted principally to prevent the entry of new enterprises or the expansion of old ones and that this is an unwise, unreasonable, and improper method of administering the transportation policy of this Nation and is an extremely poor method of encouraging the economic growth and expansion of the

Nation.'" *Competition, Regulation, and the Public Interest in the Motor Carrier Industry, Report*, 84th Congress, 2d Session, Senate Report No. 1693, March 19, 1956, 2.

As the Committee itself concluded,

"the Commission tends to ignore shipper needs and to show an inordinate concern for the protection of truckers already possessing operating authority. . . .

"The Commission's own testimony in this regard is both revealing and alarming. Commissioner Mitchell, chairman of Division 1, stated the Commission's views on 'public convenience and necessity' as follows:

"'If I was convinced that one carrier was capable of giving good service to a shipper, I do not believe I would authorize another one. . . .

"'All I am interested in is the evidence of the proof of the need. I believe that if you put a lot of transportation companies in a certain territory that we are going to destroy many of them and the public is not going to get the kind of service they should. . . .'

"Given this economic orientation, the Commission is not likely to approve operating authority for a potential competitor over a specified route, even though the applicant may demonstrate that he can provide cheaper, more efficient, or more effective service to the shipping public. Under the circumstances, public convenience tends to be subordinated to public necessity, and public necessity interpreted in a narrow, physical sense rather than a meaningful, economic sense. . . . As long as service over a given route is physically adequate, the Commission seems satisfied, even though such service could be improved and costs reduced through the certification of additional competitors." *Ibid.*, 9–10.

See, also, the illuminating case study, David M. Welborn, "Trucking Service for Pittsburgh Plate Glass," in Edwin A. Bock, ed., *Government Regulation of Business, a Casebook* (Englewood Cliffs: Prentice-Hall, 1965), 412–448; also Jones, *op. cit.*, 505–558.

[30] This is true also of the ones it issued, after proceedings involving some 90,000 applications and over a decade of litigation, under the Act's "grandfather clause"—that is, to carriers already conducting operations at the time the law was enacted. See John B. Lansing, *Transportation and Economic Policy* (New York: The Free Press, 1966), 254.

and B and C do not necessarily convey the privilege of going directly between A and C, when all three are not on a straight line, or of picking up cargo for the return hauls.[31]

The important point is not that the ICC is typically right or wrong in its determinations of whether there is a "need" for additional service in these cases. It is that it is the *Commission* that decides whether existing service is so *inadequate* as to justify granting competitive authorizations; that *it* has to be convinced of their desirability; that in so deciding it feels it must give heavy weight to the interests of existing carriers; that it understandably places a heavy burden of proof on those who wish to compete, even when potential customers actively support those efforts; and that it places little value on competition as such as a force for providing a performance that is more than "adequate."[32]

As for the rate-making authority, it is perhaps a sufficient indication of the legislative intention that it is schedules of *minimum* rates that contract carriers are required to file and adhere to. And, as to its application in practice, of the 173,248 tariffs filed with the ICC in 1962, the Suspension Board considered 5,170; of the latter, approximately 95% involved rate *decreases*.[33]

The Motor Carrier Act was passed in the middle of the Great Depression. We shall have occasion, below, in assessing the feasibility of freer competition in trucking, to ask to what extent the apparent evils of excessive competition during that period, which played an important role in inducing Congress to cartelize the industry, were a temporary phenomenon, reflecting the general state of the economy. We have already remarked, in Volume 1, on some of the other, similarly anticompetitive regulatory policies introduced during the same period—NRA, farm price supports, production control in crude oil, the Civil Aeronautics Act of 1938, a federal fair trade law and so on; recall, too, that the Supreme Court's *Nebbia* decision was handed down in 1934.[34]

The Problems Created by Exempt Carriers. The difficulties of the railroads, however, persisted and intensified during the extremely prosperous

[31] See for example the case described in the Senate Small Business Committee Report, *op. cit.*, 7; Jones, *op. cit.*, 559–576. For a survey of these restrictions and of ICC policy in this regard see Charles A. Taff, *Operating Rights of Motor Carriers* (Dubuque, Iowa: Wm. C. Brown Company, 1953); also Carl H. Fulda, *Competition in the Regulated Industries, Transportation* (Boston: Little, Brown and Co., 1961), 71–105 and Alexander Volotta, *The Impact of Federal Entry Controls on Motor Carrier Operations* (University Park, Pa.: Pennsylvania State Univ., 1967). Lansing cites evidence developed by James C. Nelson indicating that many motor carriers have as many as 200 certificates covering specific permissible kinds of business, and a statement by an Interstate Commerce Commissioner pointing out that the 244 grants of operating authority held by one carrier filled a 124-page volume, and reporting also that the Commission receives "upwards of 30,000 requests each year as to whether or not a particular carrier holds the right to transport a particular shipment." *Op. cit.*, 256. See also

pp. 187–188, below.
[32] "We are of the opinion that applicant has failed to establish any substantial inadequacy in the service which Dugan is authorized to provide from Sioux Falls. . . . As for applicant's contention that protestant's service is monopolistic in character, the mere existence of monopoly, standing alone, is not a sufficient justification for the establishment of a new operation in the absence of a showing of some inferiority or inadequacy in the transportation service of the existing carrier." *Transport, Inc., Extension—Sioux Falls, S. Dak.*, 81 M.C.C. 751 (1959), as excerpted in Jones, *op. cit.*, p. 552.

The question is: without competition to show the way, how can it be determined whether existing service is as good as it could possibly be?
[33] Merton J. Peck, "Competitive Policy for Transportation?" in Almarin Phillips, ed. *Perspectives on Antitrust Policy* (Princeton: Princeton Univ. Press, 1965), 257.
[34] See pp. 8–10, Volume 1, and 180–182, below.

fifteen years or so after the end of World War II.[35] And the common carrier trucks, too, continued having their competitive problems. Although the ICC's policy of restrictive licensing and discouragement of price competition (see the following section of this chapter) under the Motor Carrier Act helped to preserve the value-of-service rate structure, it also had the effect of leaving the door wide open for the growth of exempt motor carriage. The 1935 Act had established two major exemptions from regulation—carriers of agricultural commodities and private carriage (that is, in trucks owned and operated by the shipper). Shippers could therefore escape from the noncompetitive common-carrier rates by using their own trucks; and farmers applied sufficient political pressure to keep the truckers serving them similarly free of ICC-enforced operating limitations and rate minima. Moreover, the exempt carriers were under strong temptation to invade the common carriage market. Agricultural, private, or contract carriers with a preponderance of freight in one direction—from the farm or company plant, for example—solicited customers for the return trip at cut rates, reflecting its negligible incremental cost.[36] And when, as it consistently did, the Commission sought to close these loopholes,[37] the exempt carriers sought various ways of escaping. They would lease out their trucks at cut rates to common carriers for the return trip, often by highly circuitous routes—wherever the business took them; or engage in the fiction of nominally purchasing the goods at the point of origin and reselling them at the destination.

All of these moves and countermoves provide illuminating case studies in the economics and politics of cartellike restrictions on competition, illustrating these inherent tendencies: (1) a tendency of the cartels themselves to hold prices above the marginal costs of at least some producers; (2) a tendency for such producers to try in one way or another to take advantage of the profit opportunities thereby created—by entering the cartelized market, if they are outside it, by soliciting business at cut rates, if at all possible; (3) a consequent pressure on the cartel managers or regulators to limit or control these competitive incursions; and (4) the exertion of political and economic pressures by the various parties affected, the "spoilers" to keep free of cartel controls, the companies already regulated to extend the controls to the intruders and price cutters.[38]

---

[35] See pp. 52 note 76, 64, and 170, Volume 1.

[36] See the similar situation involving railroads in note 8, p. 164 of Volume 1. And for an appraisal of the economics of competition in these circumstances, see pp. 182–184, Chapter 5, below.

[37] For example, by attempting to deny the agricultural exemption to farm products that had been subjected to any processing at all; by imposing strict limitations on the practice of trip-leasing; by limiting what agricultural cooperatives could bring back to the farm on return hauls; and by vigilant efforts to keep contract carriers from soliciting business generally and thereby encroaching on the common-carriage market. These attempts were sometimes overturned by the Courts, then sometimes later confirmed by Congress. See Louis B. Schwartz, "Legal Restriction of Competition in the

Regulated Industries: An Abdication of Judicial Responsibility," *Harvard Law Rev.* (January 1954), LXVII: 456–460; Jones, *op. cit.*, 507–520, 535–540; Walter Adams, "The Role of Competition in the Regulated Industries," *Amer. Econ. Rev., Papers & Proceedings* (May 1958), XLVIII: 535–537. See also the footnote immediately following.

[38] See the section of this chapter, "The tendency of regulation to spread," below. Consider, for example, the history of the agricultural cooperatives exemption—49 U.S.C. 303 (b) (5), 1964 ed.—itself, obviously, the consequence of successful political pressure by the farm block in Congress and one that is estimated to have saved farmers one-fifth to one-third in their trucking costs (see note 58, pp. 190–191, below). In principle, the purpose of none of the farm-related exemp-

tions was to permit the carriers thus favored to engage without restriction in common carrier trucking. The exemption (from all but the Act's safety provisions) of a farmer's own trucks was specifically confined to their use "in the transportation of his agricultural . . . commodities . . . or in the transportation of supplies to his farm"; the exemption of "motor vehicles used in carrying . . . agricultural . . . commodities" explicitly applied only "if such motor vehicles are not used in carrying any other property, or passengers, for compensation. . . ." But the exemption of "motor vehicles controlled and operated by a cooperative association," in contrast, contained no such limitation. 49 U.S.C. 303 (b), 1964 ed.

In consequence, farm cooperatives began extensively to haul nonfarm-related products for the account of nonmembers. The ICC complained, in 1964:

"the number of groups and organizations claiming exemptions as agricultural cooperatives . . . has grown considerably in the last 10 to 15 years . . . . these exemptions are being used by various groups and organizations as a guise to perform general transportation services and to divert substantial amounts of tonnage from regulated motor carriers and freight forwarders." *Annual Report, 1964,* 76–77.

Confronted with the unqualified exemption in the Motor Carrier Act, the Commission sought redress in an interpretation of the Agricultural Marketing Act, which provides that cooperatives not deal in *farm* products, supplies, or business services with or for nonmembers in amounts greater in value than with or for members. 12 U.S.C. 1141j (a), 1964 ed. This provision, the ICC asserted, implied that cooperatives could not deal in *nonfarm* products or services at all; and in a leading case it sought to apply this interpretation to the Northwest Agricultural Cooperative Association's haulage of nonexempt commodities for nonmembers.

This, the Circuit Court of Appeals held, was an unreasonably and unjustifiably strict interpretation. The obvious purpose of the provision, it said, was simply to require that cooperatives do at least half of their business with members. As long as the carriage of nonfarm commodities was necessary and incidental to the essential business of buying, selling and transporting farm and farm-related commodities on behalf of their farmer members, the defendants retained the essential character of a cooperative and were thus entitled to complete exemption from the route and rate regulation of the ICC.

"On the uncontradicted facts, Northwest's transportation of nonfarm products and supplies was incidental and necessary to its farm-related transportation . . . incidental because limited to otherwise empty trucks returning from hauling member farm products to market, and producing a small return in proportion to Northwest's income from trucking farm products and farm supplies; necessary because it is not economically feasible to operate the trucks empty on return trips and because the additional income obtained is no more than that required to render performance of the cooperative's primary farm transportation service financially practicable."

The Court therefore concluded that the

"trucking operation, viewed as a whole, is a farm service performed jointly by Northwest's members 'for themselves.' The return hauls enjoined are 'connected with farm operations,' for they are incidental and necessary to the effective performance of Northwest's trucking operation." *Northwest Agricultural Cooperative Association, Inc. v. Interstate Commerce Commission,* 350 F. 2d 252, 255, 257 (1965).

As a result of this decision, advertisements soon appeared in various business journals, in which agricultural cooperatives offered their services to haul goods of all kinds at reduced rates; several actually signed contracts with the Department of Defense. The ICC, in turn, went to Congress, with the support of representatives of the common carriers, to close the flood gates. See the United States Senate, Committee on Commerce, Subcommittee on Surface Transportation, 90th Cong. 1st Sess., *Agricultural Cooperative Transportation Exemption,* Hearings, July 1967 and Senate Report 1152, May 28, 1968. The outcome was, understandably, a compromise: PL 90–433, signed by the President July 26, 1968 (82 Stat. 448) provided that a cooperative might carry nonfarm-related commodities for the account of nonmembers only insofar as this was "incidental to its primary transportation operation and necessary for its effective performance," only in tonnages up to 15 percent of the total and subject to full access by the Commission to the records of such operations. This account is in large measure a summary of a paper prepared for me by my student William C. Van Dam.

Similarly, the statute exempting from ICC regulation the carriage of commodities in bulk by barges sets three commodities as the maximum number that barge lines may carry on a single tow, and forbids the mixing of exempt and nonexempt cargo. Following the lure of economic opportunity created by the development of increasingly powerful towboats, barge operators petitioned the ICC to permit them to put together large convoys mixing exempt cargo with freight subject to ICC route and rate authority. The Commission ruled against them, and its prohibition was sustained in the courts.

In any event, the consequence was a continuing competitive handicap imposed on the common carriers. It was estimated that in 1964 only 33 percent of all intercity truck ton-miles were carried by holders of ICC operating licenses; the other two-thirds were handled by exempt motor carriers.[39]

Price Cutting by the Railroads. The railroads and common carrier truckers were understandably unhappy at this competition. They argued with some justification that they were unfairly disadvantaged by the ICC controls, which limited their ability to reduce rates while leaving the exempt carriers free to quote whatever charges they pleased. The rails, in particular, began, belatedly and with widely varying degrees of aggressiveness,[40] an attempt to regain some of the lost traffic, by introducing modern equipment and proposing sharp rate reductions. They showed a salutary disposition to abandon the discriminatory and increasingly unrealistic value-of-service rate schedules and to bring prices down more nearly to long-run incremental costs.

It is excessively easy to oversimplify in characterizing the ICC's response to these efforts.[41] Perhaps the most important characterization is, as Ernest

---

Gulf Canal Lines, Inc. v. United States, 386 U.S. 348 (1967). In 1967, however, recognizing the immense cost-savings of long, mixed tows, the ICC granted the barge companies a temporary exemption and both parties asked Congress to relax the restrictions. The companies estimated that the temporary exemption had produced cost-savings of about 30 percent. But the railroads opposed the requested liberalization, and as of January 1970 Congress had not acted. *Wall Street Journal,* October 11, 1967, 2, and *Business Week,* January 10, 1970, 104, 106.

[39] Lansing, *op. cit.,* 254. According to the 1963 *Census of Transportation,* U. S. Department of Commerce, Bureau of the Census, Vol. IV, 3, 42,986 of the 57,800 motor carriers in the U. S. in that year were exempt from ICC regulation. It is not clear that regulated motor carriers have suffered a persistently declining share of the business. The percentage of total intercity *truck* traffic (ton-miles) handled by regulated carriers was 37.2 percent in 1939 and fluctuated roughly around that level for the next 25 years; their share was 36.1 percent in 1965. Jones, *op. cit.,* 521 and ICC, *81st Annual Report,* 1967, 57. See also *Business Week,* November 10, 1962, 82, reporting a study by the Northwestern University Transportation Center that showed no appreciable difference in the rates of growth of regulated and unregulated motor carriers between 1939 and 1959.

But, of course, the continued decline during these years in the share of total traffic carried by the rails resulted in a corresponding decline in the market share of all regulated as compared with all unregulated carriers. See Friedlaender, *op. cit.,* 100–103.

In the United Kingdom, railroad freight traffic declined from 22 to 15 billion ton-miles between 1952 and 1965, while licensed motor carriage rose from 10 to 16 billion, and private road carriage from 9 to 25 billion ton-miles. A. A. Walters, "Subsidies for Transport?" *Lloyd's Bank Rev.* (January 1967), 22.

[40] "The traffic downturn of 1954 . . . may some day be recorded as the beginning of a series of events which may perhaps bring the rail carriers to a reluctant recognition that their industry has been bankrupt in the matter of effective policy for coping with intercarrier competition.

"The Commission's exercise of its regulatory powers must bear a share of the responsibility, but the result has been shaped more, perhaps, by carrier policies than by any policies generated by the Commission. For the Commission has played its essentially passive role case by case. . . . Meanwhile, if there has been any railroad policy, other than sheer expediency, we have been unable to detect it. That railroads have fought a delaying action against motor-carrier competition is clear, but they have not developed and put forward a plan for reshaping the vulnerable areas of their rate structure in a way designed to prevent diversion where the cost advantage is with the railroads.

". . . railroads appear to have lost one opportunity after another to establish under regulation a basis for rates in the competitive area which would give scope to their cost advantage." Williams, *op. cit.,* 219–222. For a similar verdict, see Edward T. Thompson, "What Hope for the Railroads?" *Fortune* (February 1958), 137–139 and ff., especially 148.

[41] "One of the difficulties in generalizing in this field is that ICC decisions are like the Bible; textual support can be found for any position." Peck, *op. cit.,* 251 note 11.

Williams makes quite clear in his study, that it never did formulate a general policy. The only reasonably consistent pattern discernible is one of conservatism and protectionism. As far as rate competition between regulated carriers is concerned, this attitude is reflected in a fairly consistent resistance by the Commission to reductions that would threaten the general principle of "rate parity"—the principle that the rates ought to be either equal or unequal only to the extent necessary to reflect differences in the quality of service. The general tendency is to eliminate rates as a factor in competition, with the ultimate purpose of preserving for all existing regulated carriers a "fair share" of the business. Both the operating rule and the goal are, of course, in flat contradiction to the economic principles enunciated in our Chapter 6, which would require that the rates of competing carriers reflect their own respective long-run marginal costs and that the business be apportioned purely on the basis of those costs. As Williams observes:

"With respect to the relationship of rail to motor-carrier rates the Commission seemingly has been moved by a desire to preserve both types of transportation in virtually the whole range of service they had come to occupy at the time its jurisdiction was broadened. Consequently it has given large emphasis to the preservation of the opportunity to compete and to secure a 'fair' share of the traffic. . . . [P]roposed rail rates which the Commission feared would impair motor-carrier service have been disapproved, and the Commission's concept of meeting competition through rate parity has left the motor carriers in possession of advantages of lower minimum weights, lower costs to shippers for packaging, loading, and unloading, and faster, more complete and flexible service. . . .

"In contrast to this indirect effect of rate relationships, the principle of rate parity can and does, immediately and directly, deprive one type of carrier of its cost advantage over the other in so far as its bid to the market is concerned, in apparent disregard of the national transportation policy . . . . It is difficult to avoid the conclusion that regulation has consistently, over the twenty years since the Motor Carrier Act, deprived the low-cost carrier of its cost advantage, a result often tantamount to depriving it of all opportunity to compete for traffic. . . .

"This result is consistent with a point of view which concerns itself primarily with what must be done 'in fairness' to the carriers which have actually been competing for the particular traffic in issue. . . . It does not, however, contribute to the development of a more economic division of the traffic, to coordination of the services, or to the development of economy in the handling of the available business. And it extends great encouragement to the growth of private and exempt trucking to the detriment of all common carriers. . . ."[42]

[42] *Op. cit.*, 210–215. For other, similar assessments, see James C. Nelson, *Railroad Transportation and Public Policy* (Washington: The Brookings Institution, 1959), Chapter 5 and pp. 431–435; Jervis Langdon, Jr., "The Regulation of Competitive Business Forces: The Obstacle Race in Transportation," *Cornell Law Q.* (Fall 1955), XLI: 57–92; Presidential Advisory Committee on Transport Policy and Organization, *Revision of Federal Transportation Policy* (Washington, June 1956: "carriers, notwithstanding demonstrated lower costs, are permitted to do no more than to meet the competition facing them which, with some exceptions, means to name the same rate regardless of cost relationships." 5); David Boies, Jr., "Experiment in Mercantilism: Minimum Rate Regulation by the Interstate Commerce Commission," *Columbia Law Rev.* (April 1968), LXVIII: 599–663.

In fairness to the Commission, it should be pointed out, as we shall presently observe more fully, that the laws under which it operates contain the same bias. On the other hand, it has had an important role in writing those laws and in their interpretation. The persistence of the financial difficulties of the railroads during the 1950s and the growing recognition of the unfairness and economic irrationality of the ICC's cartellike policies[43] finally led Congress in 1958 to amend the law in order to permit freer rate competition on the basis of the respective costs of the competing transport media. But the ICC exerted its influence to soften the amendment and interpreted it thereafter as enjoining it to continue protecting the trucks and water carriers from rail competition. We have already told part of this story in Chapter 6: how the proposed amendment would have enjoined the Commission to look only to the costs and traffic of the railroads proposing rate reductions; how, in its final version, it contained the added, qualifying clause, "giving due consideration to the objectives of national transportation policy," and how the ICC thereafter, on the basis of that qualification, continued not only to weigh the costs of all carriers concerned but to apply the test of fully distributed rather than long-run marginal cost in determining which carrier had the "inherent advantage" and whether therefore the proposed rate reduction should be permitted.[44] What remains to be added is that it was the Commission, along with the carriers with which the rails compete, that "objected strongly" to the original formulation of the amendment, precisely on the ground that "the ICC would be unable to protect the 'inherent advantages' enjoyed by the competing carriers on the traffic to which a rate reduction was to be applied"[45] and that the altered language was specifically introduced to cover cases in which railroads might establish rates below their own fully distributed costs.[46]

So, not surprisingly, the ICC continued its protectionist policies after 1958 as far as regulated carriers were concerned. In its *New Haven* decision of 1960, subsequently overturned by the Supreme Court, it refused to permit railroads to set a rate that was above even their fully distributed costs on half of the traffic simply because, it decided, the proposed rates would in time destroy the coastal shipping industry.[47] In its first *Southern Railway* decision, in 1963, the ICC rescinded part of a 60 percent rail reduction that still left the rates above incremental costs, in order to protect competing barge lines.[48] Ironically, the railway had spent $13 million for more than 500 new, oversize aluminum cars to carry the grain, precisely in order to get its costs down, an innovation that the Commission itself hailed as a "major break-through in the control of costs and a notable advance in the art of railroading."[49] This decision was reversed by the courts and on reconsideration the Commission permitted the full cut.[50]

But its reasoning on reconsideration was instructive. It justified its willing-

[43] See, in addition to the authorities already cited, the 1957 *Economic Report of the President* (Washington, 1957), 51.

[44] See notes 9 and 12, pp. 164 and 165, Volume 1.

[45] *American Commercial Lines, Inc., et al. v. Louisville & Nashville R. Co. et al.*, 392 U.S. 571, 580 (1968).

[46] *Ibid.*, 581–582, 585–586.

[47] *Interstate Commerce Commission v. New York, New Haven & Hartford Railroad Co. et al.*, 372 U.S.

744 (1963). For a more defensible aspect of this decision, however, see p. 249, Chapter 5, below.

[48] See note 12, Chapter 6, Volume 1.

[49] *Grain in Multiple-Car Shipments—River Crossings to the South*, Second Report and Order of the Commission on Reconsideration, 325 ICC 752, 759–760 (1965).

[50] *Ibid.*

ness in this instance to use "long term out-of-pocket costs"[51] as a test of whether the proposed rates were compensatory only because the competition in question was primarily with *unregulated* truckers—for the preservation of whose "inherent advantages" it had no statutory responsibility. Nor, obviously, did it feel any other kind of responsibility. The Commission made it perfectly clear that it proposed still to use fully distributed costs if the competition were with another regulated carrier.[52] And so it did, just a few months later, in the *Ingot Molds* case, as we have already seen. In this instance, the Supreme Court sustained the Commission's refusal to permit the railroads to reduce their rates to a point above their estimated long-term out-of-pocket costs, in order to save the business for the trucks and barges. The statutory language and legislative intent, the Court reasoned, clearly gave the ICC authority to use fully distributed costs as its measure of "the inherent advantages" of the various carriers; and the Courts were obliged in those circumstances to defer to the expert judgment of the regulatory agency. The only ray of hope was the Court's observation that the ICC then had under way a broad examination of the cost standards to be used in making intermodal comparisons; that it was not itself insisting that the Commission cling to fully distributed costs, but that it was particularly reluctant in these circumstances to prejudge the outcome of those deliberations.[53]

The Orientation of Regulatory Policy. At least the Commission was reasonably consistent in its policies—on the one hand suppressing price competition and protecting "fair shares" in the business, on the other interpreting the exemptions from its authority narrowly and attempting continuously to bring more exempt carriage under its cartel umbrella.[54] The Report issued in April 1955 by the Presidential Advisory Committee on Transport Policy and Organization, which President Eisenhower had constituted in recognition of the growing plight of the railroads,[55] provides an amusing illustration of a more schizophrenic attitude.

The principal emphasis of the Committee's report was on the enormous increase in competition that had occurred in transportation during the preceding thirty years and the desirability of giving much freer play to these competitive forces, in order to assure the most efficient distribution of the business. On the other hand, another strong underlying theme was the desirability of protecting the common carriers, with a corollary hostility to unregulated competition:

"regulated common carriers today encounter large and growing competition by exempt for-hire carriers or pseudo carriers whose operations are

---

[51] As we have already pointed out, this measure includes a return on a portion of allocated investment, and therefore exceeds true long-run marginal costs. See note 6, p. 162, Volume 1.

[52] 325 ICC 752, 772; see also 758–759—where it identifies this as the controlling consideration—770, 773–776. It seems reasonable to conclude that the willingness of the Commission in 1962 to sanction railroad rates close to extremely low, incremental backhaul costs on the carriage of coal from Kentucky to Florida—see note 8, p. 164, Volume 1—was attributable to the fact

that the competition was with unregulated water carriers, as it specifically pointed out.

[53] 392 U.S. 571, 578, 590–591 (1968). Justice Harlan concurred only with this explicit understanding and, obviously, only with great reluctance. *Ibid.*, 594–597.

[54] The Commission's *Annual Reports* provide a convenient summary of these efforts. See especially the reports of 1967, 95–96; the report of 1968, 110–114 and 129.

[55] *Revision of Federal Transportation Policy, op. cit.*

largely opportunistic in character. These operations are conducted without the necessity to publish rates[,] with freedom to discriminate in rates and service, and with no obligation to serve the general public. The continuing growth of this exempt for-hire carriage would seriously impair the maintenance of a strong and healthy common carrier industry, which by contrast is generally obliged to serve all of the public without discrimination."[56]

Along, then, with strong recommendations

"to reduce economic regulation of the transportation industry to the minimum consistent with the public interest to the end that the inherent economic advantages, including cost and service advantages, of each mode of transportation, may be realized in such a manner so as to reflect its full competitive capabilities,"[57]

the Report asks also for a tightening of exemptions: for example.

"Redefine a private carrier by motor vehicle as any person not included in definition of a common or a contract carrier who transports property of which he is the owner, provided that the property was not acquired for the purpose of such transportation. . . .

"A primary problem in transportation at present concerns the infringement of private carriers upon the field of common carriage and the need for remedial action in the form of more effective regulation of private carriers. . . .

"Redefine motor and water contract carriage as being that transportation providing services for hire but otherwise equivalent to *bona fide* private carriage and require that actual, rather than minimum, charges be filed.

"The definition of contract carrier by motor vehicle and contract carrier by water . . . should be sharpened to make clear that such carriers are of a specialized nature, and that they should be so regarded only if they clearly substitute for a feasible private carrier operation and do not perform common carrier services which would ordinarily be undertaken by common carriers."[58]

The Kennedy administration made a conscious attempt to achieve a greater degree of consistency. The *Presidential Message on Transportation* to Congress, dated April 4, 1962, took as its major theme the desirability of freeing management from the "excessive, cumbersome, and time-consuming regulatory supervision that shackles and distorts managerial initiative," and of leaving the allocation of transportation business to "reliance on unsubsidized privately-owned facilities, operating under the incentives of private profit and the checks of competition to the maximum extent practicable."[59] As to the problem of exempt carriage:

---

[56] *Ibid.*, 3.

[57] *Ibid.*, 4.

[58] *Ibid.*, 7–8. There were other recommendations along similar lines, including a request that Congress reexamine and limit the agricultural commodity exemptions. See the review of the Committee's report by James C. Nelson, "Revision of National Transport Regulatory Policy," *Amer. Econ. Rev.* (Dec. 1955), XLV: 910–918. Nelson specifically underlines the inconsistency between these two aspects of the

report, pointing out that, for all its references to the feasibility and desirability of enhanced competition, the Committee has no criticisms to offer of the tight restrictions on entry into the common-carrier business by road and waterway, and asking

"Why do common carriers need protection from competition of private, contract or unregulated transportation if common-carrier organization is inherently more efficient?" *Ibid.*, 917.

[59] Mimeo. version, 2–3.

"the transportation of bulk commodities by water carriers is exempt from all rate regulation under the Interstate Commerce Act, including the approval of minimum rates; but this exemption is denied to all other modes of transportation. This is clearly inequitable both to the latter and to shippers—and it is an inequity which should be removed. *Extending to all other carriers the exemption from the approval or prescription of minimum rates* would permit the forces of competition and equal opportunity to replace cumbersome regulation for these commodities. . . . While this would be the preferable way to eliminate the existing inequality, Congress could elect to place all carriers on an equal footing by repealing the existing exemption—although this would result in more, instead of less, regulation and very likely in higher though more stable rates."[60]

Similarly, with respect to the exemption of the carriage of agricultural and fishery products by motor carriers, the President recommended:

"*This exemption from minimum rates should also be extended to all carriers.*"[61]

These two proposals would have exempted from ICC minimum rate control freight accounting for 44 percent of total rail revenues and 70 percent of total tonnage.[62]

It should be noted, parenthetically, that the President did not recommend elimination of ICC regulation even over these commodities. The burden of his recommendations was to free competition by taking away the Commission's authority to fix *minimum* rates,

"while protecting the public interest by leaving intact the ICC's control over maximum railroad rates and other safeguards (such as the prohibition against discrimination, and requirements on car service and common carrier responsibility)."[63]

It is an interesting question, which we need not however try to settle here, whether the continuous concern of the ICC with protecting the common carriers has been the result of an administrative hardening of the arteries (as is suggested by the "life cycle of the administrative commission" theory, mentioned above), a historical shift in the thrust of its policy, or has been reflective of the legislative intent from the very outset—that is, back in 1887.[64] But it would, in any event, be a misreading of that history to see the

---

[60] *Ibid.*, 3–4.

[61] *Ibid.*, 4.

[62] Peck, *op. cit.*, 252.

[63] *Ibid.*, 4. See the general argument along lines similar to those of the Kennedy *Message* in the 1970 *Economic Report of the President* (Washington, February 1970), 108–109.

[64] The traditional view has been that the entire corpus of railroad legislation, beginning with the state granger laws of the 1870s, was the response above all else to public outrage at the monopolistic exploitations by the railroads; that the roads themselves bitterly opposed this legislation and exerted themselves continuously and with almost complete success during the first twenty years of the Commission's life to hamstringing its regulatory efforts; and that it was the combined pressures by shippers, the public at large, and the ICC that finally produced the Hepburn Act of 1906 and Mann–Elkins Act of 1910, which gave the Commission the authority it needed to protect the public. See, for example, the monumental study by I. L. Sharfman, *The Interstate Commerce Commission, A Study in Administrative Law and Procedure* (New York: The Commonwealth Fund, four volumes, 1931–1937), Vol. I, 14, 23–24, 39–40, 71–72. According to this view, the Commission emerged from these struggles "almost universally accepted as an essential arm of the government," with "its many fruitful accomplishments . . . generally accorded unstinted recognition," (*Ibid.*, Vol. I, 12) and it was only many decades, indeed almost a half-century, later that the Commission became the

great cartelizer. See, for example, Clair Wilcox, *Public Policies toward Business*, 3rd ed. (Homewood: Richard D. Irwin, 1966), 401.

Recently, Gabriel Kolko has presented a great deal of convincing historical evidence in many respects fundamentally contradicting the traditional conception.

"the railroads, not the farmers and shippers, were the most important single advocates of federal regulation from 1877 to 1916. . . .

"From the 1870's until the end of the century. . . . railroad freight rates, taken as a whole, declined almost continuously. . . . In their desire to establish stability and control over rates and competition, the railroad executives often resorted to voluntary, cooperative efforts involving rate agreements and the division of traffic. When these efforts failed, as they inevitably did, the railroad men turned to political solutions to rationalize their increasingly chaotic industry. . . .

"The crucial point is that the railroads, for the most part, consistently accepted the basic premises of federal regulation since only through the positive intervention of the national political structure could the destabilizing, costly effects of cutthroat competition, predatory speculators, and greedy shippers be overcome." *Railroads and Regulation, 1877–1916* (Princeton: Princeton Univ. Press, 1965) 3–6. Copyright 1965 by Princeton Univ. Press.

It is not feasible here to summarize the evidence that Kolko adduces. The interested reader should consult also the empirical study by Paul W. MacAvoy, demonstrating that:

"The regulation of the structure of rates . . . tended to make more effective the cartel's control of the level of long-distance rates. . . . Rates were 'stabilized,' and 'increased,' for long-distance transport of bulk commodities [in the carriage of which competition would otherwise have prevailed]. Rates were 'destabilized' when regulation was weakened by the Supreme Court in the later 1890's." Reprinted from *The Economic Effects of Regulation, The Trunk-Line Railroad Cartels and the Interstate Commerce Commission before 1900*, 1965, v, by permission of The M.I.T. Press, Cambridge, Massachusetts. See also George W. Hilton, "The Consistency of the Interstate Commerce Act," *Jour. Law & Econ.* (October 1966), IX: 87–114.

So far as the legislative *intent* is concerned, there is evidence also on the other side. For example, many of the original state granger laws fixed *maximum*, not minimum rates; contrary to the interest of the railroads, the original Interstate Commerce Act did explicitly forbid pooling; the Commission began by specifying rate

reductions; the Hepburn Act finally gave it specific authorization to fix *maximum* rates; and it was not until the Transportation Act of 1920 that the Commission was given explicit authority to fix minimum rates and to encourage combinations, pooling, and consolidations of railroads. See, for example, Wilcox, *op. cit.*, 388–395. Also see the review of the Kolko book by Louis Galambos, *Econ. Hist. Rev.* (April 1967), XX: 200.

The one thing we can be sure of is that, while there are important differences between these two interpretations, the conflict can easily be overdrawn. The farmer and shipper interests who most loudly emphasized the necessity for protection placed heavy emphasis on the evils "of destructive competitive warfare, of fluctuating and discriminating rate adjustments" (Sharfman, *op. cit.*, Vol. I, 14), which the railroads were equally interested in stopping. One of their central complaints was that the intense rivalry among railroads, under the pressures of big shippers, proved to be highly discriminatory; it is not surprising, therefore, that the interests of both smaller shippers and the railroads to some extent converged. Nor does the fact, noted by Sharfman and Kolko alike, that the Elkins Act of 1903, which greatly strengthened the power of the Commission to prohibit rate rebates to powerful shippers, "was enacted on the initiative of the railroads themselves, as a means of conserving their revenues" (*ibid.*, Vol. I, 36; compare Kolko, *op. cit.*, 94–101) necessarily vitiate the former's further observation that the measure

"was generally regarded, from the public standpoint, quite as much a necessary instrument for curbing the unconscionable tactics of the so-called trusts in extorting special favors from the carriers as a desirable extension of federal authority over the railroads. . . .

"The Elkins Act . . . proved from the very beginning to be 'a wise and salutary enactment.'" (Vol. I, 36–37.)

The more important point, for us, is that it is unnecessary and perhaps not even sensible to try to choose between these conflicting interpretations. What we would emphasize, instead, is the inherent tendency for even a predominantly "public-minded" commission to betray a hostility toward intense price rivalry, which tends— inevitably, in highly imperfect markets—to produce instability and discrimination among buyers. This is a consequence of neither stupidity nor venality, but of the resort to regulation, the case for which can not be lightly dismissed merely by pointing to the virtues of an unattainable perfect competition. On the other hand, it does not follow that this tendency should not be resisted.

Commission's philosophy as resulting from either historical accident, perversity or a subversion of the regulatory process. It is not a matter of the ICC having become excessively "railroad-minded," or untrue to its legislative mandate; these policies are just as protective of the interests of existing regulated motor carriers (and of the Teamsters Union) as of the railroads[65]; and they have been applied at a later date just as much to discourage competitive rate reductions *by* railroads, in an effort to retrieve their lost business, as to insulate the rails from truck competition. Rather, these developments reflect the inherent thrust of regulation itself, which confides to the expertise of an administrative agency the responsibility for ordering the affairs of industry; to such a planning venture, competition is troublesome and disruptive.[66]

The Tendency of Regulation to Spread

The story of the ICC illustrates another kind of historical principle as well: the necessity for limitations on competition to become ever more extensive and thorough if they are to succeed. So long as regulation imposes restraints on competition, it will have continuously to widen and deepen its scope. The economics of this is quite simple. If regulation limits competition, it must be because some competition would otherwise be feasible: the ability and will to compete are therefore present. And, if the regulation is effective, price will be held above at least some producers' or potential producers' marginal costs. In these circumstances, controls over price competition are subject to evasion by accentuated quality and service rivalry, limited only by the ingenuity of businessmen in seeking new methods of enticing customers. They will be impelled to exercise such ingenuity so long as price is held above marginal cost. Similarly, the elevation of price—above the marginal cost of insider firms, above the average total cost of potential entrants, using the newest possible technology—sets up persistent temptations for new businessmen to come into the market, in turn creating the necessity for regulatory limitations on entry, and for extension of controls to unregulated firms.[67]

---

[65] See Robert D. Leiter, *The Teamsters Union* (New York: Bookman Associates, 1957), 135–139. Of the contested applications for rate reductions, many more are proposed by motor carriers than by railroads—probably reflecting the potentially more competitive nature of trucking. Merrill J. Roberts, "Transport Costs, Pricing and Regulation" in *Transportation Economics, op. cit.*, 18–20.

[66] See the violent attack by Samuel P. Huntington, "The Marasmus of the ICC: The Commission, The Railroads, and The Public Interest," *Yale Law Jour.* (April 1952), LXI: 467–509; the response by Charles S. Morgan, "A Critique of 'The Marasmus of the ICC: The Commission, The Railroads, and The Public Interest,'" *ibid.* (December 1952), LXII: 171–225; "The ICC Re-examined: A Colloquy," *ibid.* (November 1953), LXIII: 44–63; and the comment in Louis L. Jaffe, "The Effective Limits of the Administrative Process: A Reevaluation," *Harvard Law Rev.* (May 1954),

LVII: 1107–1108.

[67] See Kahn, "Cartels and Trade Associations," *International Encyclopedia of the Social Sciences* (The Macmillan Co. and The Free Press, 1968), II: 321–322. Also, for example, our discussion at pp. 194–197, Chapter 5, below, of some of the consequences of the fixed minimum brokerage commission schedule imposed by the securities exchanges: a tendency for the protected brokers to bid for the business by "give-ups"—surrenders of large portions of their commissions by one subterfuge or other—and various reciprocal deals, all to get round the exchanges' prohibitions of rebates. This in turn led the New York Stock Exchange to attempt to prohibit such deals; and this in turn subjected it to demands by institutional investors for the right to membership on the exchange in order to get around the monopolistically high commission rates they were being charged. "Both exchanges have asked the SEC to declare a moratorium on such further memberships until the commission produces a

These tendencies are clearly illustrated by the history of the American oil industry. Under the rule of capture, every landowner is entitled to whatever oil or gas he can draw up from the reservoir that lies under his own land and that of his neighbors. The result has been an irresistible temptation to terrible waste; no one landowner can afford to hold underground oil that his neighbor can suck up from under him. As a result, the several major producing states have instituted systems of direct production control, assigning specific quotas to each individual well (though exempting the majority of wells, which produce in relatively small volume). In addition, the provisions of the federal income tax law provide various special stimuli to encourage the exploration for and production of oil. The combination of these two circumstances has been to hold price far above the marginal cost of the large-capacity wells, whose output has been curtailed in the manner just-described. It has also apparently been for long periods of time below the ATC of new, successful explorers.

As a result, for ten to fifteen years after World War II, exploration continued apace and—until 1956—expanded rapidly. In addition, the sustained price gave rise to an artificially enhanced incentive to drill additional wells, on which one could then demand a production quota. The resultant expansion of capacity required a continuous tightening of production controls: wells were held to a lower and lower rate of production. The higher costs thus imposed on producers—with more and more investment in wells, with lower and lower production quotas—then clearly forced the extension of regulation to the control of well-drilling also. Finally, the resulting high costs and diminished profitability of domestic production encouraged producers to go into the foreign field. In time this—along with the natural expansion of low-cost foreign output—in conjunction with the artificially sustained domestic price threatened to drown the domestic market with a flood of imports. So once again the scope of regulation had to be extended: in 1959 mandatory controls were imposed on imports. And so it goes: one interference with competition necessitates another and yet another, and an industry of "rugged individualists" becomes more and more tightly enmeshed with the government to which they originally turned in hope of protecting themselves from competition.[68]

Technological progress—which may itself be stimulated by the monopoly pricing of the regulated service—tends likewise to break down cartels. And it confronts regulatory commissions with the dilemma of seeing their charges

set of guidelines." *Wall Street Journal*, June 10, 1969, 4. Fortunately for the economy, the cartel-man's lot is not a happy one, as Gilbert and Sullivan almost put it.

For a general explanation of the tendency of regulation to spread, see Lee Loevinger, "Regulation and Competition as Alternatives," *Antitrust Bull.* (Jan.–April 1966), XI: especially 117–123.

[68] This account is of course extremely sketchy. See, for a fuller analysis, Melvin G. de Chazeau and Alfred E. Kahn, *Integration and Competition in the Petroleum Industry* (New Haven: Yale Univ. Press, 1959), Chapters 6–10; Kahn, "The Depletion Allowance in the Context of Carteliza-

tion," *Amer. Econ. Rev.* (June 1964), LIV: 286–314, and "The Combined Effects of Prorationing, the Depletion Allowance and Import Quotas on the Cost of Producing Crude Oil in the United States," U.S. Senate, Committee on the Judiciary, Subcommittee on Antitrust and Monopoly, 91st Cong., 1st Sess., *Government Intervention in the Market Mechanism*, Hearings, *The Petroleum Industry*, Part 1 (Washington, 1969), 132–140; Paul T. Homan and Wallace F. Lovejoy, *Economic Aspects of Oil Conservation Regulation*, published for Resources for the Future by Johns Hopkins Press, Baltimore, 1967, and the forthcoming volume by Stephen L. McDonald on this subject.

lose business and the regulated price structure threatened with undermining —or trying to bring the new suppliers as well under the regulatory tent. The case of trucking is an obvious illustration; so, as we have seen, has been the development of new technology by the railroads—the unit train, the "Big John," piggybacking—in their effort to regain business from their competitors. This impact of new technology and the dilemmas it creates for a protectionist regulatory commission are nowhere more clearly illustrated than in the field of communications.[69]

But before we turn to that field, it is necessary to observe that cartelization is not the only reason legislatures and commissions find it necessary to spread the regulatory net wider and wider over time. A quite different but equally pervasive occasion, and one that has no necessary connection with protecting the interest of the regulated companies themselves, is to be found in the ingenuity of businessmen in seeking new and alternative ways of exploiting their monopoly power, when regulation has blocked certain paths to that goal.

For example, as the progress of technology in the 1920s and 1930s made increasingly feasible the interstate transmission of electricity and natural gas, local and state commissions found an increasingly large component of the cost of service of the companies under their jurisdiction—namely, the electric current or the gas imported from out of state—falling outside their reach.[70] This growing gap was filled by the Federal Power Act of 1935 and the Natural Gas Act of 1938, which conferred on the Federal Power Commission regulatory authority over those wholesale rates.[71]

The Public Utility Holding Company Act of 1935 represented a regulatory response to a similar kind of problem. As, during the 1920s, local gas and electricity distribution companies came under the control of the rapidly spreading network of holding companies, the local regulatory authorities found themselves, once again, unable to exercise jurisdiction over a large portion of the cost of service—in this case, the prices paid by the operating companies to their holding company affiliates, not only for power and gas but also for various technical, managerial, and financial services. The 1935 Act met this difficulty by vesting in the Securities and Exchange Commission authority to break up and to simplify the structure of the holding company

---

[69] See Walter Adams and Joel B. Dirlam, "Market Structure, Regulation, and Dynamic Change," in Harry Trebing, ed., *Performance under Regulation* (East Lansing, Mich.: MSU Public Utilities Studies, 1968), 131–144.

[70] See *State of Missouri v. Kansas Natural Gas Company*, 265 U.S. 298 (1924).

[71] See Chapter 17, "'Gaps' in the Regulatory Process and the Federal Dentist," in A. J. G. Priest, *Principles of Public Utility Regulation, Theory and Application* (Charlottesville: Michie Co., 1969), II: 523–556. On the important extensions of the FPC's authority over virtually all wholesale sales of electricity after 1961, on the ground that electricity generated and sold intrastate is "comingled" with electricity sold interstate— increasingly the case as the nation's electric utilities become more and more interconnected

(see pp. 64–65 and 314–323, Chapter 2 and 6 below)—see the leading *City of Colton* case, *FPC v. Southern California Edison Company*, 376 U.S. 205 (1964) and Louis Lister and Paul T. Homan, *Energy Industries and Public Policies in the United States*, draft ms. (Washington: Resources for the Future, 1968), Part IV, Chap. 2, 20–23. On the great importance of the *Colton* decision in safeguarding the competitive opportunities of publicly owned distributing companies, see pp. 322–323, Chapter 6, below. For similar developments in gas, see *FPC v. East Ohio Gas Co. et al.*, 338 U.S. 464 (1950), retracted by the so-called Hinshaw Amendment of 1954 to the Natural Gas Act (15 U.S.C. 717c, 1964) and the extension of the comingling doctrine in *California et al. v. Lo–Vaca Gathering Co. et al.*, 379 U.S. 366 (1965).

systems, reorganizing companies on functional and geographic lines, and also to regulate the charges made by parents to subsidiaries.[72]

Since these extensions of regulation were clearly necessary to close off newly developed avenues for the monopolistic exploitation of consumers, their necessity has not seriously been questioned by impartial observers. For the same reasons, they are, at least in retrospect, far less controversial than the extensions of regulation whose purpose has been to forestall or to restrict newly emergent *competition*.

This observation can certainly not be made, however, about the extension of the FPC's authority from control over the rates charged by interstate natural gas transmission lines to the prices those lines are charged for the natural gas that they purchase in the field from producing companies. The rationalization of this step was similar to the ones just described. The Natural Gas Act of 1938 had given the Commission jurisdiction over "the transportation of natural gas in interstate commerce" and "the sale in interstate commerce of natural gas for resale for ultimate public consumption," and had explicitly stated that its provisions were not to apply "to any other transportation or sale of natural gas or to the local distribution of natural gas or . . . to the production or gathering of natural gas."[73] Until 1954, the Commission had assumed, though not without dissent, that the explicit exemption of the "production or gathering of natural gas" was intended to deny it authority over the prices charged by producers or gatherers *to* pipelines, even though these too were "sales in interstate commerce for resale." Then, in its controversial *Phillips* decision of 1954, the Supreme Court instructed the FPC to see to it that the prices paid for natural gas in the field by pipeline companies were likewise "just and reasonable," holding that the statutory exemption of "production and gathering" did not extend to *sales* of gas by producers and gatherers. The Court justified this finding on the ground that it had been precisely the purpose of the 1938 Act to close the gap in regulation created by the inability of the local and state regulatory commissions to control the prices paid by local distribution companies for supplies purchased interstate, and that the price paid by interstate pipelines for gas purchased in the field was an important component that could not be neglected if regulation were to be effective.[74]

This particular extension of regulation has been much more controversial than those contemplated originally in the 1935 and 1938 Acts cited above, not only because it was by no means clear that this was the original intent of Congress but also because it was not established that the producers of natural gas had the kind and degree of monopoly power sufficient to justify extension of public-utility-type regulation to them. Effective regulation of local electricity rates has not typically been construed, for example, to require public-utility regulation of the prices charged electricity generating companies by sellers of residual fuel oil or coal, even though these constitute an important part of their total cost of service. The assumption has been that the industries supplying these important inputs have been sufficiently competitive to protect the consumer; and that as long as they remained financially independent, the regulated monopolists had no incentive to pay more than

---

[72] See also, on this topic, pp. 70–73, Chapter 2, below.

[73] 15 U.S.C. 717b, 1964 ed.

[74] *Phillips Petroleum Company v. Wisconsin et al.*, 347 U.S. 672, 681–685 (1954).

the competitive price. Whether the same is true of the field market for natural gas has been the subject of intense controversy.[75] In any event, the purpose and economic effects of this extension of regulation, like those involved in the Federal Power, Public Utility Holding Company and Natural Gas Acts of 1935 and 1938, were quite different from the cartellike, widening restrictions on competition that we have traced in the field of transportation.

Community Antenna Television

The Federal Communications Commission has the responsibility of licensing radio and television stations, as well as other users of the limited radio spectrum.[76] For television, there is room for only 12 channels on the very high-frequency (VHF) band, and the Commission had set aside 552 channels in this range for commercial stations in the contiguous 48 states as of June 1, 1967; 518 of those channels were actually occupied by authorized stations as of June 30, 1968.[77] In consequence principally of the physical limitation but partly also for economic reasons, approximately two-thirds of the country's communities receive only two or fewer signals.[78]

Into this breach stepped a new industry in the 1950s, community antenna television (CATV). These systems, by use of large receiving antennae, pick television signals directly off the air, amplify them and transmit them directly to subscribers by cable; they may also use microwave radio relay to bring the signals into the wire distribution system. Their contribution is to bring as many as twelve (and it may soon be twenty) signals, of high quality, into homes that could otherwise receive only one or two; their original success was therefore mainly in small towns.[79] In the 1960s, however, CATV entrepreneurs began to tap a much richer market in large cities, where their principal contribution is to offer signals of a far superior quality, free of interference from airplanes, electric motors, and reflection off buildings and other obstacles; but here, too, they have been able to offer the possibility of bringing in additional programs from the outside. In either event, CATV systems are direct competitors of local stations, which had theretofore

---

[75] See, for example, the masterly summary and survey in Lister and Homan, *op. cit.*, Part II, Chap. 6, 3–20; also the discussions in our Volume 1, at pp. 40 note 49, 42 note 55, and 68 note 14.

[76] The relevant legislation has been the Radio Act of 1912 (37 Stat. 302), conferring limited regulatory authority on the Department of Commerce, the Radio Act of 1927 (44 Stat. 1162), and the Communications Act of 1934 (48 Stat. 1064). See 47 U.S.C. 151–609, 1964 ed.

[77] FCC, *34th Annual Report, Fiscal Year 1968* (Washington, 1969), 110.

[78] According to a 1965 study, only 95 of the 265 television markets in the continental United States had three or more stations, 172 had one or two—more than half of the latter only one. Martin H. Seiden, *An Economic Analysis of Community Antenna Television Stations and the Television Broadcasting Industry*, a Report to the Federal Communications Commission, Washing-

tion, February 12, 1965, 82. The total number of stations authorized increased from 668 to 835 between mid-1964 and mid-1968 (FCC, *Annual Reports*). But since by far the greater number of the entrants were in the UHF band and most of them in the larger cities, the situation in the smaller markets remains essentially the same, as far as the presence of local stations is concerned. FCC, *Annual Reports*, 1968, 110; 1964, 78. Also Leland L. Johnson, *The Future of Cable Television: Some Problems of Federal Regulation* (Santa Monica: The Rand Corporation, Memorandum RM–6199–FF, January 1970), 1–7.

[79] Of the 377 CATV systems established or franchised in the period from January 1960 through August 1964, 77 percent were located in areas that were not within 40 miles of two network signals and 91 percent in areas more than 40 miles away from three network signals; the majority of the remainder were in places with special terrain problems. Seiden, *op. cit.*, 82.

enjoyed virtual monopolies (or oligopolies) in their receiving areas.[80]

Set up to prevent physical interference between competing users of the radio spectrum, the FCC now found its wards subject to *economic* competition. Its response was to extend its authority over the CATV systems—regardless of whether they actually used the limited spectrum.[81]

These initial regulations, promulgated in 1965 and 1966, have since been largely superseded. But they remain instructive, as illustrations of the protectionist bias of the regulatory institution. In its 1966 ruling, the Commission required, first, that all[82] CATV systems carry the signals of all local television stations in their vicinity. Although this rule, like the others,

---

[80] Between January 1, 1960 and January 1, 1969, the number of CATV systems increased from 640 to 2260, their subscribers from 650,000 to 3,600,000. Annual data from Television Digest, Inc., *Television Factbook*, reproduced in Johnson, *The Future of Cable Television*, 11. For a summary of a study concluding that:

"(1) CATV's economic impact on station revenues is substantial. (2) A significant percentage of existing stations, particularly in small markets, cannot withstand a relatively small increase in CATV penetration in their audience area without concomitant cost reduction. (3) A substantial percentage of potential new station entrants, particularly UHF, are likely to be discouraged from entry by a relatively small increase in CATV penetration in their potential audience area," see Franklin M. Fisher and Victor E. Ferrall, Jr., in association with David Belsley and Bridger M. Mitchell, "Community Antenna Television Systems and Local Television Station Audience," *Q. Jour. Econ.* (May 1966), LXXX: 250.

On the other hand, both Seiden (*op. cit.*, 5, 84–86) and the President's Task Force on Communications Policy (*Final Report*, Washington, 1968, Chapter VII, 10–11) have deprecated this competitive impact on existing stations and potential entrants. And while Johnson persuasively argues that unregulated CATV does indeed pose a serious threat to marginal broadcasters, he also emphasizes that, with proper safeguards, the relationship between the two can be complementary and mutually supportive. *The Future of Cable Television*, 68–73; see also note 111, below.

Although the immediate impact of CATV has been to introduce direct competition with television broadcasters, it offers the opportunity also for an exciting variety of quite different communications services—fire and burglary alarm systems, facsimile duplication of newspapers in the home, facsimile mail, linkage to computers, to video tape libraries, in short providing the communications link for a broad

spectrum of a city's mercantile and banking operations. Jack Gould, *New York Times*, October 15, 1967, Section 2, 25; and FCC, *In the Matter of Amendment of Part 74, Subpart K, of the Commission's Rules and Regulations Relative to Community Antenna Television Systems etc.*, Docket No. 18397 (hereinafter referred to by the docket number), Notice of Proposed Rule Making and Notice of Inquiry, December 12, 1968, par. 8–9, 60. See also the analysis by H. J. Barnett and E. Greenberg, "On the Economics of Wired City Television," *Amer. Econ. Rev.* (June 1968), LVIII: 503–508 and the proposal for community use of CATV advanced by Stephen White in "Toward a Modest Experiment in Cable Television," *The Public Interest*, Number 12 (Summer 1968), 52–66.

[81] The Commission had, as far back as 1956, successfully asserted its authority to impose certain engineering standards on CATV systems, in order to eliminate electrical interference between their signals and those of the regular broadcasters. FCC, *22nd Annual Report, for the Fiscal Year 1956*, Washington, 1956, 99–100. In its first attempt to assert economic jurisdiction, in 1965, the FCC confined its attention to the smaller portion of the industry that employed microwave relay service from communications common carriers to carry signals from their master antennae to their local cable distribution systems. *In the Matter of Amendment of Subpart L, Part II, To Adopt Rules and Regulations to Govern the Grant of Authorization . . . for Microwave Stations to Relay Television Signals to Community Antenna Systems*, First Report and Order, 38 FCC 683 (1965) (hereinafter referred to as *Microwave CATV*). In 1966, the Commission promulgated general rules covering all CATV systems, whether microwave-served or operated exclusively via antennae and cable. *Microwave CATV*, Second Report and Order, 2 FCC 2d 725 (1966). This final assertion of authority was upheld by the Supreme Court in *U.S. et al. v. Southwestern Cable Co. et al.*, 392 U.S. 157 (1968).

[82] Specifically exempted were systems serving less than fifty customers, or serving only as apartment house master antennae.

illustrates a tendency to protect the regulated companies from competition, it is difficult to take exception to it. A CATV system is itself a natural monopolist, within any given geographic region, subject to the familiar increasing returns with increasing intensity of use; it would obviously be inefficient to have more than one antenna and system of cables serving any particular locality. Moreover, the quality of the signal and service it provides is typically superior to that received by the set that takes its programs directly off the air; where cable service is available, therefore, many or most households attach themselves to it, and most of them give up their own antennae. If, then, this franchised monopolist were to refuse to carry the programs of local stations over its facilities, it could well deprive them of a market and drive them out of business. This would be in its own interest because it would deprive householders of their one alternative source of television programs and thereby force anyone who wished to enjoy television at all to enter the lists of its subscribers. It would enhance its monopoly power in dealing with local advertisers as well.[83] Finally, it would have the indirect effect of completely depriving of television service people in nearby rural areas too sparsely inhabited to justify extension of the cable. Here is an example of a situation in which it may be necessary to compel regulated companies to cooperate.[84] It illustrates the fact, also, that none of the institutional issues we confront in these chapters can intelligently be posed as a simple, once-and-for-all choice between competition and regulation, since either system is subject to imperfections of varying intensity and mischievousness.

Second, the Commission forbade CATV operators to duplicate programs broadcast by local stations during the same day. The earlier version of this rule, adopted in April, 1965, had forbidden duplication of local broadcasts within a much greater period—15 days before and 15 days after. This second restriction on competition was clearly more questionable than the first, as is indicated by its considerable modification in the 1966 as compared with the 1965 order. A rule prohibiting precisely simultaneous duplication, it would seem, would have been unobjectionable: for a CATV system, required in any event to carry the programs of the local stations, to bring the identical programs to their subscribers on more than one channel at the same time would serve no purpose but diversion, with a consequent threat to the continued viability of the local station. But it clearly limits viewers' choices to deny them the opportunity of seeing the same program at some other time during the same broadcast day.

Still, there was some justification in principle for this protectionist policy as well, tracing back to the fact that the fundamental conditions for effective

---

[83] Station operators had, in fact, complained to the FCC that their CATV competitors were refusing to carry their programs. FCC, *32nd Annual Report for the Fiscal Year 1966*, Washington, 1967, 85.

[84] CATV carriage of the programs of a local station is not costless; it would ordinarily have to be at the expense of carrying the programs of some other, outlying station. In most instances, however, it would appear that the programs in question would be those of one of the three national networks, and the choice would therefore merely be one of bringing in identical programs from the local or from the outlying station. It would appear in such instances that forcing the CATV operator to transmit the programs of the local station would have no cost to the viewer—since the programs sacrificed would be identical—and would preserve an important alternative source of broadcasts and possible program origination.

competition, large numbers of sellers and freedom of entry, are physically impossible in this industry.[85] Since the justification is a rather complicated one, it will be helpful to outline its major components, before proceeding to explain each. They are:

1. Unregulated competition in these circumstances can not produce economically optimal results;
2. One possible cure is to impose on broadcast licensees certain obligations with respect to programming that may conflict with their self interest;
3. In return, it may be necessary to protect them from the competition of CATV companies that merely import programs originated by others without paying for them.

The competition among the limited number of stations and networks that can reach homes in any one locality is competition for an audience that does not, as such, pay for the programs it views. The goal of each competitor is to deliver the attention of a maximum number of viewers to advertisers, who are the ones who foot the bills and whose interest is, of course, in getting the largest and most receptive audience possible for their commercial messages. Where broadcasters compete in this way for audience, they necessarily aim their programs at the "least common denominator," at the mass market; this produces a high degree of similarity in their programming. And this has the result that commercial broadcasters make less than optimum use of the limited channels available *even in the purely economic sense*—that is, taking as the test of optimality whether the limited spectrum is employed to generate the maximum of viewer satisfaction over cost of production and transmission, taking consumer or viewer preferences as they are, not as they would be if consumers had better taste.

With free entry, no block of demand for a particular variety of product that is willing to pay the costs of serving it need or will go unsatisfied. When, instead, the number of sellers is limited, there may be a conflict between the self-interest of each on the one hand and the interest of all their customers, taken together, on the other. Each one may feel himself forced to come as close as possible to duplicating the service of the other, in hope of getting a share of the mass market, even though most of the sales he gains in this manner are merely diverted from his competitors.[86] What happens in television, thus, is that the mass audience is spread among all competing stations by minor differences in the programs they offer, while other viewers with more specialized tastes go unsatisfied entirely. If, instead, the firms were jointly owned or pooled their revenues, it would be in their collective interest to make a composite offering of greater variety, in order to maximize their

---

[85] This limitation was particularly intense until at least the late 1960s, when commercial broadcasting was virtually confined to the very-high frequency (VHF) range. The technical progress that opened up the ultrahigh-frequency range (UHF), coupled with the passage of the all-channel television receiver law in 1962 (76 Stat. 150)—which required that all television sets manufactured thereafter be equipped to receive UHF and so promised in time to eliminate the principal obstacle to entry of new UHF stations,

the fact that very few receivers were equipped to receive their signals—opened up the possibility of a substantial expansion in the number of competitive stations in any given place.
[86] On this general tendency of competing sellers to cluster, with the result that "buyers are confronted everywhere with an excessive sameness," see the historic article of Harold Hotelling, "Stability in Competition," *Econ. Jour.* (March 1929), XXXIX: 54.

aggregate audience. The latter course could well produce more total viewer satisfaction than the former. The mass audience, that is to say, might still be retained with little loss in satisfaction by an offering that contained one fewer typical commercial program at any given time, leaving the single, released station free, then, to program for a very different kind of audience. But this is something that the individual commercial station would be unwilling to do as long as it could hope by conventional programming to attract away from other commercial competitors a larger number of viewers than it could obtain by radically different programming.[87]

The FCC's historic response to these problems was certainly not illogical. It has placed its major emphasis on encouraging the entry of additional stations, particularly in the still largely vacant UHF spectrum: the major step in this program was passage of the all-channel receiver law, which promised in a few years to assure that almost all sets would be equipped to receive UHF programs.[88] And it has proclaimed—though unfortunately hardly enforced[89]—a policy of pressing local stations to generate their own local, public service programs, as a condition of keeping their valuable franchises. Given this orientation, its desire to keep local stations alive in the face of CATV competitors importing mainly national commercial programs was understandable. (On the other hand, it is difficult to reconcile this reasoning with the Commission's historic hostility to program origination by the CATV companies themselves—a theme of FCC policy to which we shall turn presently.)

The Commission's protectionist policy may be justified, also, on grounds of externalities. We have already had one example of this—the loss of television service to inhabitants of rural areas, which cannot economically be reached by CATV, if competition by the cable in town drives the local station out of business or discourages the entry of another. The CATV customers, naturally, do not take this external cost into account in deciding whether to subscribe. In fact, those customers might, by subscribing to an unrestricted CATV service, be imposing a similar external cost *on themselves*: they too might place considerable value on the continued operation of the local station, as the sole possible source of locally originated programming, even though each willingly subscribes to the cable service when it is offered to him. The effect of a general acceptance of that service in forcing the local station out of business would be an external cost of those individual subscription decisions; it would pay no one viewer to refuse to subscribe in hope of keeping the local station alive, because the effect of his individual abstention in this respect would be miniscule; it would take collective action or

[87] See, for example, Peter O. Steiner, "Program Patterns and Preferences, and the Workability of Competition in Radio Broadcasting," *Q. Jour. Econ.* (May 1952), LXVI: 194–223; Jerome Rothenberg, "Consumer Sovereignty and the Economics of TV Programming," *Studies in Public Communication*, No. 4 (Autumn 1962), 45–49; and Joel B. Dirlam and Alfred E. Kahn, "The Merits of Reserving the Cost-Savings from Domestic Communications Satellites for Support of Educational Television," *Yale Law Jour.* (January 1968), LXXVII: 514–518. See on the other hand the argument by John J. McGowan, "Competition, Regulation, and Performance in Television Broadcasting," *Washington Univ. Law Q.*, Fall 1967, 499–520, especially 507–513, to the effect that the individual broadcasters are under considerable pressure to differentiate their offerings during any programming period and will therefore come closer to maximizing their aggregate audience and profits than is suggested by the foregoing exposition.

[88] See note 85, above.

[89] See pp. 89–90, Chapter 2, below.

regulation to prevent the disappearance of this alternative source of supply. The market does not give viewers a separate, effective opportunity to express the intensity of their desire to keep this alternative option available.[90]

The fact remains that the FCC adopted a protectionist approach to ensuring optimal use of the limited airways; it sought to encourage the entry of new, commercially marginal stations (particularly in the opening-up UHF spectrum) *by protecting them as well as existing local stations from competition.*[91] Its reaction to CATV was clearly affected by the threat that this innovation posed to its own regulatory program, as well as to the survival of the many local stations who hastened to complain about this new competition. The fact remains, moreover, that CATV, too, offered viewers increased alternatives, though in a manner different from the one envisaged by the Commission. It was obviously providing a new service that subscribers were anxious to have. The FCC reaction, therefore, though moderate and measured, was a typical regulatory reaction. When considered in conjunction with its almost complete failure in practice to hold local stations to its proclaimed standards of performance, as we shall see in Chapter 2, the essentially protectionist character of its policies becomes even more manifest.

It would be impossible on economic grounds to quarrel with the Commission's purpose of encouraging the maximum number of economically viable stations and sources of programming, consistent with physically good signals. But if that effort was limited by the economically marginal character of many stations (both those in existence and those on the margin of entry), the better solution, it would seem, would have been not to impose restraints on the CATV alternative, but to broaden the geographic coverage of the

---

[90] Much of this reasoning is developed by Franklin M. Fisher, "Community Antenna Television Systems and the Regulation of Television Broadcasting," *Amer. Econ. Rev., Papers and Proceedings* (May 1966), LVI: 320–329. For a general analysis of this particular kind of market failure, in which the disappearance of facilities available to satisfy "option demand"—the desire to have certain services *available* for use, even though one does not necessarily use them sufficiently to keep them economically alive—is exposed as an external cost, see Burton A. Weisbrod, "Collective-Consumption Services of Individual-Consumption Goods," *Q. Jour. Econ.* (August 1964), LXXVIII: 471–477.

I have characterized these market failures as issuing from the "tyranny of small decisions": the decision by each subscriber whether to take CATV service is a "small" decision; neither individually nor collectively do subscribers and rural nonsubscribers ever have the opportunity to cast their dollar votes with respect to the "large decision" of whether the local stations should be kept alive. *Op. cit., Kyklos* (1966), XIX: 23–47.

[91] This protective attitude is in interesting contrast to the Commission's traditional position with respect to radio that "under the Communications Act economic injury to a competitor is not a ground for refusing a broadcasting license," *FCC v. Sanders Brothers Radio Station*, 309 U.S. 470, 472 (1940), a view upheld by the Supreme Court:

"We hold that resulting economic injury to a rival station is not in and of itself, and apart from considerations of public convenience, interest, or necessity, an element the petitioner [the FCC] must weigh, and as to which it must make findings, in passing on an application for a broadcasting license. . . .

"The sections dealing with broadcasting [in the Communications Act] demonstrate that Congress has not, in its regulatory scheme, abandoned the principle of free competition, as it has done in the case of railroads. . . .

"the broadcasting field is open to anyone, provided there be an available frequency over which he can broadcast without interference to others, if he shows his competency, the adequacy of his equipment, and financial ability to make good use of the assigned channel.

"The policy of the Act is clear that no person is to have anything in the nature of a property right as a result of the granting of a license. . . .

"Plainly it is not the purpose of the Act to protect a licensee against competition but to protect the public." *Ibid.*, 473–475. For other examples, see Jones, *op. cit.*, pp. 1094–1105.

television markets each is licensed to serve.[92] Such a course of action, too, would have diminished the competitive attractiveness of CATV, whose primary appeal was that it brought into markets theretofore served by less than three stations the additional signals available from a distance; but it would have done so by loosening the restrictions on existing suppliers rather than tightening the controls over the threatening competitors. If the Commission's purpose was merely to encourage local programming it could have imposed requirements to this effect on the CATV operators as well—rather than restricting their right to originate their own programs and to sell advertising.[93] And if the still necessarily few stations serving any particular area do not provide optimum program variety, far more effective than the restriction on CATV and the exertion of feeble pressures on every small community in the United States to generate it own programs would be direct public subsidies to public television,[94] the exertion of powerful pressures on the major networks to expand their efforts in this direction, and, above all, a far more strenuous insistence that the local franchise holders accept more of the excellent public service programs that the networks already make available to them.[95]

The core of monopoly power in this industry is in the local, franchised station. It has the exclusive right to a portion of the spectrum, which it sells off to the highest bidder. Not surprisingly, it is here that the highest profits[96]

---

[92] This was the recommendation of Seiden, *op. cit.*, 7, 89–90.

[93] For reference to some relatively limited local programming by CATV operators and their promise in this regard, see Edward Greenberg, "Wire Television and the FCC's Second Report and Order on CATV Systems," *Jour. Law and Econ.* (October 1967), X: 185–186. As of 1968 or so, about 10 percent of the CATV systems originated some of their own programs. *Fortnightly Corporation v. United Artists Television, Inc.* 392 U.S. 390, 392, note 6 (1968). On the later shift of FCC policy in these respects, see pp. 43–45, below.

[94] See, for example, Carnegie Commission on Educational Television, *Public Television: A Program for Action*, New York, 1967; Sidney S. Alexander, "Public Television and the 'Ought' of Public Policy," *Washington Univ. Law Q.*, Winter 1968, 35–70.

[95] It is my impression that the local network affiliates exercise their rights of program selection far more often to refuse the public service than the commercial programs proffered by the networks, precisely because this is what it would be in their financial interest to do. In his justly famous "vast wasteland" speech, Newton M. Minow, then chairman of the FCC, referred to this practice and expressed the opinion that local stations should be required to explain all such refusals. *The New York Times*, May 10, 1961, 79. The failure of the Commission to adopt such a policy, imposing entirely proper conditions on its free gift of valuable franchises to broadcaster applicants, provides yet another illustration of pusillanimous regulation.

For this failure Congress must share a large portion of the blame: the speed with which it responds to the complaints of broadcasters when the Commission moves to regulate them more effectively, accompanied by irrelevant outcries against "public censorship," borders on the scandalous—particularly when it is recognized that many Congressmen themselves have financial interests in broadcasting stations. For a particularly flagrant example, as well as a discussion of the censorship issue, see pp. 91–92, and note 129, p. 90, below.

[96] Strictly speaking, these represent not monopoly profits but economic rents, the scarcity value of the nonreproducible natural resource the disposition of which the franchisee controls. As we have suggested in Volume 1 (p. 88, notes 2 and 4), if this resource were sold off at auction, bidders would have to pay a price that reflected the marginal opportunity cost of their having it— that is, the value of that portion of the spectrum to the next-highest bidder. If this were done, it would have not only the attraction on distributional grounds that the rents would accrue to the taxpayer rather than to private parties, but also that the spectrum would be allocated in the most efficient fashion (that is, to those to whom it was the most valuable, by the test of the competitive market) and users would be under strong pressure to use it economically. See Coase, *op. cit.* On the other hand, as Harvey J. Levin has suggested (most thoroughly in a manuscript

are earned: in the four-year period 1964–1967, the VHF stations as a group earned an extraordinary average of 75.3 percent before taxes on the depreciated value of their investment in tangible broadcasting property. (True, the three major networks earned even more—148.9 percent; but this figure represents a lumping together of the much higher returns from their own stations and the much lower return on their networking operations as such.)[97]

The third restraint that the FCC imposed on CATV in its 1966 order was the most flagrantly protectionist of all. We have already referred to the tendency of the cable systems to move into the larger television markets, in part because of their ability to bring in sharper signals, in part because subscribers have appreciated their ability to bring in additional "foreign" programs not otherwise available locally. Because the Commission has its highest hopes of inducing the entry of UHF stations in these relatively rich markets it was particularly anxious to prevent the spread of CATV there. It was also, apparently, concerned lest the CATV systems begin to provide for pay-television—something that is most likely to be feasible in concentrated urban areas. Accordingly, it proclaimed that

"Parties who obtain state or local franchises to operate CATV systems in the 100 highest ranked television markets . . . will be required to obtain FCC approval before CATV service to subscribers may be commenced. . . .

"An evidentiary hearing will be held as to all such requests for FCC approval. . . . These hearings will be concerned primarily with (a) the potential effects of the proposed CATV operation on the full development of off-the-air television outlets (particularly UHF) for that market, and (b) the relationship, if any, of proposed CATV operations and the development of pay television in that market. . . .

"the Commission will entertain petitions objecting [also] to the geographical extension to new areas of CATV systems already in operation in the top 100 television markets."[98]

---

on spectrum management, to be published around 1970 by Resources for the Future), society might instead choose to demand those rents "in kind"—demanding from the broadcasters standards of performance—that is, of programming—that would, because of their external benefits, otherwise justify taxpayer subsidization. An outstanding example would be the provision of free air time for political candidates.

[97] Computed from figures in FCC, *Annual Reports*. For figures for the period 1958–1966 and supporting references for these conclusions, see Dirlam and Kahn, *op. cit., Yale Law Jour.* (January 1968), LXXVII: Table 1 and 497–499. Of course, the high *average* profits of television stations conceal an extremely wide spread. The UHF stations as a group have lost money every year since 1965 (*ibid.*, 509n and FCC, *Annual Reports*; the 1968 figures are the latest ones available as of this writing).

So the FCC's concern that CATV might discourage the entry of new UHF stations was not necessarily groundless—see notes 80, above, and 98,

below—though it may have been misguided.

[98] FCC, Public Notice, "FCC Announces Plan for Regulation of all CATV Systems," Washington, February 15, 1966, mimeo., 2. No such hearing was to be required for proposed CATV systems or operations in markets ranking below the top 100. "However, the Commission will entertain, on an *ad hoc* basis, petitions from interested parties concerning the carriage of distant signals by CATV systems located in such smaller markets." *Ibid.*

In 1968, by a 4–3 vote, the FCC overturned the opinion of its hearing examiner and found in the experience of CATV companies bringing Los Angeles signals into San Diego a competitive threat to local UHF stations great enough to justify its imposing limitations on the former companies. *In the Matter of the Petition of Midwest Television, Inc. et al.*, Decision, Docket No. 16786, 13 FCC 2d 478 (1968). These findings in turn provided the justification for its proposals later that year to continue restrictions on CATV entry into the top 100 markets. See p. 44, below.

When the Commission requires CATV systems to carry the signals of local stations and forbids their duplicating those programs within a short time period it does not subject viewers to appreciable deprivation. But when, in its zeal to protect local stations, it forbade the cable systems bringing in entirely different programs, indicated that it would subject any such applications to the test of whether they might impede the entry of new stations, and announced that it would ask Congress for a "prohibition of the origination of programs or other materials by a CATV system with such limitations or exceptions, if any, as are deemed appropriate,"[99] it unmistakably set out on the same well-marked path as the ICC has been following for at least the preceding thirty years.

One theme that runs through the FCC's 1966 opinion and order is a suspicion if not outright hostility toward pay or subscription TV; the Commission was at least tentatively aligning itself with the other interested parties battling to "save free TV."[100] First of all, "free TV" is hardly free. Viewers themselves buy their seats and pay for repairs and electricity; advertisers pay billions of dollars to television networks and stations and no one has suggested that this comes out of the profits of their stockholders; and the industry makes free use of a crowded spectrum from which other potential users are excluded—and we have already seen that the opportunity cost of using a congested facility is certainly not zero.[101] True, the viewer as such does not pay for the costs of programming and transmission. But it is not clear what virtue there is in having this particular price held to zero—rather than, say, the price of food or medicine—particularly when poor people pay it, willy-nilly, when they buy the products that are advertised on television.

The present system of financing television programming has the one, major economic virtue of conforming to the fact that, as Samuelson has pointed out,[102] television is in one important respect a public good—that is, one whose marginal cost is zero. This is the case when the dimension of output is taken to be the supply of programs to additional viewers: it adds nothing to aggregate costs if more rather than fewer people turn on their sets. It makes economic sense from this standpoint, therefore, that the price is zero: other than the costs of electricity and a more rapid wearing out of the receiver (both of which are, of course, incremental costs and quite properly borne by the viewer), the viewer pays no charge for tuning in a program.

On the other hand, when the dimension of output is the production of programs, there are very definite, positive marginal costs: it is obviously possible to expend fewer or more resources on program quality. And in as

---

[99] *Ibid.*, 3.

[100] "CATV is a form of pay-TV. . . . there are substantial numbers of people who either cannot afford to or do not wish to pay for television. If then the CATV blocks development of UHF broadcasting, it would again mean that some people would be getting additional service at the expense of those who cannot afford or are unwilling to pay for such service." 2 FCC 2d 725, 775 (1966); see also 787, where the Commission recommends that Congress prohibit program-origination by CATV systems.

[101] See the references in note 96, above, and especially Levin, "The Radio Spectrum Resource," *Jour. Law and Econ.* (October 1968), XI: 433–501.

[102] Paul A. Samuelson, "A Pure Theory of Public Expenditure," *Rev. Econ. Stat.* (November 1954), XXXVI: 387–389; "Diagrammatic Exposition of a Theory of Public Expenditure," *ibid.* (November 1955), XXXVII: pp. 350–356, and "Aspects of Public Expenditure Theories," *ibid.* (November 1958), XL: 332–338.

much as viewers do not have to pay prices for programs of varying qualities reflecting those varying incremental costs, the economic propriety of those production outlays is not subjected to the familiar market test. There *is* a market test, of sorts, which does to some extent serve as a proxy for the market's directly ascertaining what viewers would be willing to pay for programs of varying qualities: the charges are borne by advertisers, and they undoubtedly do compare marginal costs of more expensive programming with the value of the additional audiences that it is expected to attract. But since much of the advertising conducted in a monopolistically competitive economy is not informational but hortatory and mutually offsetting —with advertiser A forced to devote resources to this purpose merely in order to prevent diversion of sales to advertiser B, and B operating under a similar pressure, but with both able in imperfect markets to pass on all or part of the costs to buyers of their products—it seems a fair conclusion that this particular method results in an overallocation of resources into television transmission and programming—more, that is, than would be justified if the viewers themselves were confronted with prices correctly reflecting the marginal costs of increasing output along these dimensions.[103]

Moreover, the interests of advertisers must be a very imperfect representative of the tastes and desires of viewers. The former are interested in maximizing the net monetary value (over cost) of the television programming they sponsor measured in terms of the response of viewers as purchasers of their products, rather than the maximum net satisfaction of their audience as viewers of the programs.

"To take a simple-minded example, suppose that the more intelligent (or better-educated) the viewer the more impervious he is to advertising messages. Then, to the extent advertisers are rational, the interests and tastes of the more intelligent potential viewers will carry less weight in program selection than those of the more gullible purchasers of the advertised product."[104]

"In the 'Golden Age' of television drama, the advertisers believed that the ideal play for television must not be too boring or the viewer would switch to another channel, nor too interesting or the viewer would resent the commercial break."[105]

Pay or subscription television is, in a sense, the other side of this coin. It has the disadvantage of imposing a positive charge, with the result that some families are deterred from viewing from which they would derive positive satisfaction, even though the marginal costs of supplying them are zero. On

---

[103] On the tendency toward an excessive allocation of resources to advertising, see Nicholas Kaldor, "The Economic Aspects of Advertising," *Rev. Econ. Studies* (1949–1950), XVIII: 1–27; compare Lester G. Telser, "Supply and Demand for Advertising Messages," *Amer. Econ. Rev., Papers and Proceedings* (May 1966), LVI: 457–466, and especially the comments by Harold J. Barnett and Peter O. Steiner, *ibid.*, 467 and 472–474.

My student, Keith Anderson, has pointed to an offsetting consideration. The marginal revenue (to the advertiser) of (additional) expenditures on programming is probably a function predominantly of the additional viewers it will attract. But the marginal satisfaction thereby generated from the social standpoint is the additional enjoyment thus conferred on *all* viewers, including those who would have tuned in even to less expensive programs. This consideration suggests a tendency to *under*allocation of resources to programming, since the benefit to the advertiser (who pays for it) is less than the total social benefit.

[104] Dirlam and Kahn, *op. cit., Yale Law Jour.* (January 1968), LXXVII: 517–518.

[105] Gore Vidal, "Classy TV," *New York Review of Books*, December 7, 1967, 25.

the other hand, it has the major advantage of affording a market test with respect to both the appropriate quantity of resources to put into television and their proper distribution between different kinds of programs.[106] Neither system, therefore, is ideal; but it would seem that the closest approach to the ideal would be to permit both to coexist, in competition.[107]

Another consideration influencing the FCC's decision to impose restrictions on CATV systems was its feeling that their competition with regular broadcasters is unfair, since the CATV operators do not have to pay for the programs that they pick out of the air and transmit, at a rental, to their subscribers.[108] This issue was raised in an intriguing manner in 1966, when on the complaint by a company that owned copyrights to motion pictures, a U. S. District Court held that such CATV operations involve "performing" the works in question and therefore infringe the copyright if done without a license.[109] In consequence of this unfavorable decision, CATV operators began negotiations with the broadcasting industry, and it appeared that a compromise settlement might emerge in which the broadcasters would waive their claim for royalties in exchange for an agreement by CATV companies not to originate any programs of their own.[110] Like the FCC's own 1966 decision, this would surely have protected the regular broadcasters from competition.

This particular threat to competition was at least temporarily forestalled in 1968 when the Supreme Court reversed the lower court opinion, holding that the operations of the CATV systems were analogous not to performance of the copyrighted works but to the mere viewing of them.[111] But, as will

---

[106] See the exchange between Jora R. Minasian, "Television Pricing and the Theory of Public Goods," and Paul A. Samuelson, "Public Goods and Subscription TV: Correction of the Record," *Jour. Law and Econ.* (October 1964), VII: 71–83. Minasian, ignoring the tendency for an excessive allocation of resources to advertising, concludes that more rather than fewer resources would probably be drawn into the industry under a system of pay-television. It is not necessary, for our purposes, to decide whether his prediction or ours is correct, although it is difficult to imagine the average American family being willing to have its television set going five or six hours a day if it had to pay more than the present zero charge. More important is our agreement that the present system does not produce the appropriate allocation.

[107] On the presence or absence of an unsatisfied demand for pay-television, see David M. Blank, "The Quest for Quantity and Diversity in Television Programming," *Amer. Econ. Rev., Papers and Proceedings* (May 1966), LVI: 452–454, and the comments by Harold J. Barnett, Hyman H. Goldin and Peter O. Steiner, *ibid.*, 467–475.

[108] *Microwave CATV*, First Report and Order, 38 FCC 683, 704–705 (1965).

[109] *United Artists Television, Inc. v. Fortnightly Corporation*, 255 F. Supp. 177 (1966).

[110] *New York Times*, June 18, 1968, 96.

[111] "Essentially, a CATV system no more than enhances the viewer's capacity to receive the broadcaster's signals; it provides a well-located antenna with an efficient connection to the viewer's television set. It is true that a CATV system plays an 'active' role in making reception possible . . . but so do ordinary television sets and antennas." *Fortnightly Corp. v. United Artists Television*, 392 U.S. 390, 399 (1968).

The economic merits of the issue are complicated. As far as network programming is concerned, it is difficult to see that the claim for copyright protection has any validity. Broadcasters sell the attention of viewers to advertisers. Anything that increases their audience increases the value of their service. So it is the networks that pay the local stations to induce them to carry their programs—not the other way around—by sharing advertising revenues with them. By the same token, the networks justify their expenditures on programming in terms of the audiences that the programs promise to attract. The larger the audience, the greater the value to them of such programs—and the larger a price a copyright owner of a program could expect to get from them. When CATV operators pick up the broadcast signals and bring them to a larger number of viewers, they are obviously increasing the value of what the networks sell to advertisers

appear presently, the FCC promptly demonstrated once again that it was not dependent on the copyright laws to protect stations from CATV competition.

Fortunately, the persuasive power of a rapidly developing technology is extremely difficult to resist. Within two and one-half years of its 1966 order, the FCC issued a proposed notice of rule making for CATV that was practically ecstatic about its vast and versatile potential for offering a previously undreamt-of variety of communication services, while saving on use of the limited radio spectrum.[112] In this statement, the Commission seemed also to recognize how much more richly CATV promised to achieve the very goals it had previously sought by protecting local stations from its competition—to increase the number of alternative programs offered to the householder and, in particular, the possibility of catering to minority tastes and the opportunities for local and public service programming.[113] Accordingly, it now proposed actually to *require* CATV operators to originate their own programming as a condition of being permitted to operate at all, and to encourage them also to lease channels to others for the same purpose.[114]

---

and the value of the films and programs sold to the networks. It is difficult to see any justification, therefore, for charging them royalties. In a competitive market, it would seem, they too, like the local stations, might successfully claim compensation from the network for their contribution; broadcasters would compete to induce them to accept and retransmit their programs.

To some extent these same considerations should apply to programming that originates with the local station. It too can charge advertisers more or less—and afford to pay more or less for the films or other programs it rents—depending on the size of its audience; and CATV increases the number of viewers it can reach. But much of the local station's revenue comes from the sale of time to local advertisers, who may not find it any more valuable because CATV systems carry their messages into other localities: to this extent CATV does the station no favor; but neither does it do it any injury.

None of this is to deny that CATV competes with the local station into whose territory it carries programs from the outside—the very competition that the FCC was trying to curb. What it denies is that the stations whose signals it carries have any legitimate economic complaint against them worth honoring.

On the other hand, the independent program producer may actually be injured in these circumstances, in such a way as to diminish the value of his copyright. He obtains a large part of his revenues by selling programs to individual stations for subsequent runs, after the network showing. Here it is the station that pays, receiving its reimbursement directly from national and local spot advertisers. Many of these, as just suggested, are interested only in the local audiences. To the extent this is the case, the

CATV systems increase neither what the advertiser is willing to pay to the originating station nor what the latter is willing to pay the copyright owner, when they carry those programs into other cities. But in so doing, they reduce what local stations in those other cities will either at that time or thereafter be willing to pay for the program: they have reduced its value for those showings in the other cities. (I am indebted to A. Frank Reel for pointing this out to me.)

So in effect CATV does diminish the ability of a copyright owner to parcel out the privilege of showing his property in separate markets in such a way as to maximize his return. But that is what competition does, too.

For a careful analysis of the merits of requiring cable systems to pay for the programs they import, concluding that on balance such a requirement would provide a desirable stimulus to additional and more diversified programming, see Johnson, *The Future of Cable Television*, 14–40.
[112] See the reference to its discussion of this potential at note 80, this chapter, above.
[113] Docket No. 18937, Notice of Proposed Rule Making and Notice of Inquiry, December 12, 1968, pars. 4–10.
[114] *Ibid.*, par. 15.

"We believe that the public interest would be served by encouraging CATV to operate as a common carrier on any remaining channels not utilized for carriage of broadcast signals and CATV origination. This would provide an outlet for others to present programs of their own choosing. . . . It might also provide a low cost outlet for political candidates, possibly advertisers, programs on a subscription basis, and various modestly funded organizations and entities in the community who may be unable to afford time on or obtain access to broadcast

It expressed a willingness also to consider wider use of CATV as an instrument for introducing pay-TV, that is, by a per program or a higher monthly charge (Par. 17). In late 1969, it put the first of these proposals into effect, ordering all CATV systems with 3500 or more subscribers, as a condition of being permitted to carry the signals broadcast by others, to operate "also to a significant extent as a local outlet by cablecasting," and it encouraged smaller systems to do the same.[115]

But the FCC was not prepared, as of December 1968, entirely to give up its protectionist policies. In the *Notice of Proposed Rule-Making*, issued that month, it announced that it was ready to consider prohibiting CATV stations from selling time to advertisers, giving no justification other than that otherwise CATV competition might impair the viability of competing stations (pars. 17–18). Still concerned that the "unfair" competition by CATV operators importing signals into the largest (100) markets[116] could discourage the entry of new UHF stations there, it proposed not, as before, to deny licenses in these cases but to require the CATV operator to obtain the consent of the originating stations for that retransmission (pars. 32–43).[117] In this way, the Commission in effect proposed to hand back to the broadcasters the opportunity that the Supreme Court had taken away from them in the *Fortnightly* decision just six months earlier, to suppress CATV competition in the very markets in which the most extraordinarily profitable stations are located.[118] It had no intention of giving up the responsibility for

---

facilities. And it might further provide a means for municipal authorities to fulfill any of their communications needs. . . ." *Ibid.*, par. 26. For an intriguing discussion of some of the problems and prospects of CATV systems operating as common carriers, see Johnson, *The Future of Cable Television*, 54–61.

At the same time, properly recognizing the naturally monopolistic character of CATV service, the FCC proposed to limit the number of program originations by the CATV operator himself as well as to consider various possible regulatory controls to prevent concentration of control over alternative communications media, excessive rates, and to assure "reasonable opportunity for the discussion of conflicting views on issues of public importance." Pars. 20 and 19–25, passim.

[115] *In the Matter of Amendment of Part 74, Subpart K, of the Commission's Rules and Regulations Relative to Community Antenna Television Systems, etc.*, Dockct No. 18937, First Report and Order, October 24, 1969, 20 FCC 2d 201, Appendix; see also pars. 19–20, 26–28.

[116] "both the CATV system and the broadcast station are . . . competing for audience—yet the one pays for its product and the other, without any payment, brings the same material into the community by simply importing the distant signals. . . ." *Ibid.*, par. 35. But see note 111, above.

[117] It made this proposal for the large markets only, on the grounds that these were the ones in which new UHF stations were most likely to be able to enter and that the smaller markets have a clear need for the additional signals that CATV brings in. But the Commission promised to keep its eye on the smaller markets as well, and

"to take such action as may be appropriate . . . where there is a substantial public interest showing, e.g., that . . . the cumulative effect of existing and proposed CATV operations . . . would jeopardize the likelihood of [an independent station's] obtaining or retaining a network affiliation or of maintaining audiences large enough to attract needed advertiser support." Par. 55.

[118] That this danger was not purely hypothetical is indicated by the resumption of negotiations between the National Association of Broadcasters and representative of the cable companies. Out of these emerged a tentative agreement to be recommended for FCC approval that would have permitted cable companies to carry up to six commercial channels, including imported signals from distant cities, but would on the other hand have prohibited them from making interconnections such as might eventually produce a new and competitive national network. So once again the FCC seemed ready to deliver into the hands of the broadcasters a weapon that they could use to exact agreements restricting the competitive threat of CATV. The agreement fell apart, however, in mid-1969. *New York Times*, June 21, 1969.

deciding, itself, whether CATV operators were "importing signals from *unnecessarily* distant centers or in such quantity as to *unduly fractionalize* the . . . potential audience of stations in these . . . markets."[119] As Commissioner Bartley pithily summarized the issue in his dissent:

"The interim procedures, are, I believe, contrary to the public interest because they deny to the people of the United States a communications service for which they have shown a demand in the market place."[120]

But even these protectionist reservations were doomed to continued erosion by the new technology. By October of 1969, persuaded that the CATV systems might not be able to initiate their own programs without additional revenues, the FCC was ready to permit them to sell advertising, provided they presented the messages only at natural breaks and only in connection with their own original programming.[121] And in May of 1970, by a 4 to 3 vote and in an almost complete turnabout, it instructed its staff to bring in proposals that would free CATV systems to import programs into the 100 largest cities as well as all others.[122]

See the attack on the proposed agreement and the implied criticism of the FCC in the *Comments of the U.S. Department of Justice*, FCC Docket 18397, September 5, 1969, processed, 2-3, 10, 13-14, 17-18, and the later repudiation by the Commission of any limitations on the ability of CATV systems to interconnect on a regional or national basis—a development that it recognized could offer new competition with the three major networks. First Report and Order, *op. cit.*, 20 FCC 2d 201, pars. 7 and 17 (1969).
[119] Par. 56. Stress supplied. In this particular statement the Commission is explaining the basis of its continued attention to the impact of CATV operations in the smaller markets.
[120] The Antitrust Division, speaking for the U.S. Department of Justice, endorsed the FCC's proposed liberalizations of the controls on CATV operators but called for giving them even greater opportunity to compete with local stations:

"We . . . believe that CATVs should not be prevented from . . . accepting advertising. . . . Permitting CATV systems to accept advertising is significant because it provides not only a financial means of supporting program origination, but also provides a new advertising outlet for smaller local firms which may not be able to afford the rates of existing TV stations.
"The Commission . . . should relax its rules on program importation." FCC, Docket No. 18397, *Comments of the U.S. Department of Justice*, April 7, 1969, processed, 13-14, 29.
[121] First Report and Order, *op. cit.*, 20 FCC 2d 201, Appendix and pars. 17, 31-32 (1969):

"(1) it would permit CATV to derive additional revenue to help defray the costs of origination; (2) it would provide the public with a new type of service— one where commercials did not interrupt program material . . . (3) it would afford advertisers a new and different type of outlet in terms of size and selectivity of audience . . . and (4) it would be less apt to affect the advertising revenue available to local broadcast services to the same degree that the alternative of unlimited CATV commercials might." *Ibid.*, par. 38.
[122] It proposed also to require the cable operators to carry the commercials of the local UHF stations, without charge, in place of those of the out-of-town broadcaster, at the commercial breaks in the imported programs:

"The theory here is that most CATV viewers would have been stolen from the UHF stations— but the stations would still be able to sell advertising on the basis of a new combined audience" ("A new FCC tune elates cable-TV," *Business Week*, May 23, 1970, 38)—an interesting confirmation of the argument in note 111, above, to the effect that a CATV system can help a broadcaster when it "steals" his programs and brings them to additional viewers.
In addition, the Commission tentatively decided (1) to ask Congress to enact a tax on the gross revenues of CATV systems, in order to remunerate copyright owners; (2) to require the CATV operators to turn 5 percent of their gross revenues over to the Corporation for Public Broadcasting, as a subsidy to educational television; (3) to require them to carry all local signals, and to set aside channels for the use of city governments and local community groups and for lease to other would-be program originators; and (4) to permit them to use one channel for pay-TV. *Ibid.*; also *Wall Street Journal*, May 19, 1970, 8, and June 26, 1970, 5;

A Few Warning Notes

It would be inaccurate to suggest that regulatory commissions uniformly come down on the side of policies protective of the interests of existing regulated firms, although we shall encounter other illustrations of this tendency as we go along. We have already alluded to the FCC's opposite policy in granting licenses to new radio stations;[123] and to its reversal, in 1968–1970, of most of the earlier rulings that had been so restrictive of CATV competition with licensed broadcasters. In Chapter 4 we shall see several important instances in which the Commission permitted serious competitive encroachments on the theretofore exclusive position of the Bell System in voice and record telephony. The tendencies we have described are real ones; but there are important exceptions. That is the first warning.

The second is that we have made no concerted effort, in this chapter or in those that follow, completely to expunge all pejorative rhetoric in our characterizations of the regulatory process. The economist has certain biases; and the very words that he uses to characterize the inherent tendency of regulation to substitute monopoly for competition and to protect the status quo inevitably disclose that he regards these tendencies at least with suspicion, even if he tries to supply a purely objective account.

In fact we do not pretend to have made a fair or definitive appraisal of the many specific issues that we have described in illustrating these tendencies. The issues are complex; the decision to regulate suggests that uncontrolled competition would not work perfectly in these situations either.

But the objective fact and tendencies remain. When a commission is responsible for the performance of an industry, it is under never completely escapable pressure to protect the health of the companies it regulates, to assure a desirable performance by relying on those monopolistic chosen instruments and its own controls rather than on the unplanned and unplannable forces of competition. And society must take into account this inherent tendency of regulation when it chooses among alternative systems of industrial order.

New York Times, May 18, 1970, 1, and May 20, 1970, 83. The proposals appeared formally in FCC Docket No. 18397-A, *op. cit.* note 80, above, Second Further Notice of Proposed Rule Making, June 24, 1970.

[123] See note 91, p. 37, above. Another example was the decision of the Commission to authorize Mackay Radio and Telegraph to operate a direct radio telegraph circuit between the United States and The Netherlands in direct competition with a similar service offered by RCA and a cable service furnished by Western Union. See *Federal Communications Commission v. RCA Communications, Inc.*, 346 U.S. 86 (1953). The certification policy of the Civil Aeronautics Board has fluctuated from one attitude to the other, reflecting partly its changing membership and partly the fluctuating financial condition of the airlines already certificated. So, in the *Air Freight Case* (10 CAB 572, 1949, affirmed *American Airlines, Inc. v. Civil Aeronautics Board*, 192 F. 2d 417, 1951), the CAB

"certified a number of applicants to engage exclusively in transporting air freight, although existing certified carriers engaging in transporting both passengers and freight showed that their freight capacity was adequate to handle foreseeable traffic and that the air freight business was already being conducted at a loss which would be aggravated by dispersing the business among additional carriers." Louis B. Schwartz, *op. cit., Harvard Law Rev.* (January 1954), LXVII: 441. Copyright 1954 by Harvard Law Review Association.

On the other hand, the Board has reached the opposite conclusion when confronted by arguments precisely the same as those cited by opponents of the certification in the *Air Freight Case*. The discussion in this footnote is based on the description of these cases by Schwartz.

CHAPTER 2

Incentives and Distortions

Regulation has an inherent tendency to place its principal reliance on (1) the decisions of its monopolist chosen instrument and (2) its own controls. In this division of responsibilities, it is also inherent in the institution that management proposes and the commission disposes. It could hardly be otherwise. The decision-making unit is the private corporation itself; it is private management, using private capital, that must initially determine the quality of service, the level of capacity, efficiency, and the rate at which all of these are improved. Typically—but by no means universally, as we shall see—the initiative must be private.

In these circumstances, the central institutional questions have to do with the nature and adequacy of the incentives and pressures that influence private management in making the critical economic decisions. The subsidiary question is: how much scope is there, really, for regulation itself to exert a significant influence? These matters are the subject of this chapter and the next.

Regulation in a private enterprise system almost inevitably operates only at the periphery of the decision-making process. Regulators can presumably exert a considerable influence on the level of profits. They almost certainly can and do control discrimination in rates and service. But for the preponderant portion of the cost of service, they can at most disallow individual components that are flagrantly inflated; and as for quality, they can set minimum standards, and impose limited penalties when service is obviously bad.[1] They are essentially incapable of assuring that performance will be positively good. Probably the most obvious and important manifestation of this weakness has been their inability to force public utility companies to experiment with rate reductions, as long as their overall rates of return were not excessive. The most familiar case is that of electricity rates, where elasticities of demand and economies of scale seem clearly, with the wisdom of hindsight, to have justified bold rate reductions, but the only way in which the government could achieve them was by introducing publicly generated and distributed power.[2] As far as explicit interventions are concerned, regulation itself necessarily operates mainly as a restraining influence.

---

[1] See pp. 22–25, 29–32, Volume 1.   [2] See pp. 105–107, below. Richard A. Posner

This negative character of a regulatory process that concentrates mainly on the rate of return on aggregate company investment entails several inadequacies or adverse consequences. It means that regulation as such contains no built-in mechanism for assuring efficiency. To the extent that it effectively restrains public utility companies from fully exploiting their potential monopoly power, it tends to take away any supernormal returns they might earn as a result of improvements in efficiency, thereby diminishing their incentive to try. And if it permits them to earn only the cost of capital, it creates a situation in which any inefficiencies can simply be passed on in higher rates without injury to existing stockholders.[3] Indeed, it creates strong incentives on the part of the companies to pad their expenses—with management voting itself higher salaries and other emoluments at no cost to stockholders, and stockholders as well benefiting to the extent that the company can succeed in buying its services, raw materials, and other inputs at inflated prices from financially affiliated suppliers.

But, in practice, regulation can never be completely or instantaneously "effective," in the foregoing sense. Indeed, if effectiveness were defined, as it obviously ought to be, with an eye to the institutional requirements for efficiency and innovation, public utility commissions ought not even to *try* continuously and instantaneously to adjust rate levels in such a way as to hold companies continually to some fixed rate of return; and they probably ought not to try either to hold the rate of return down to the bare cost of capital. The *regulatory lag*—the inevitable delay that regulation imposes in the downward adjustment of rate levels that produce excessive rates of return and in the upward adjustments ordinarily called for if profits are too low[4] —is thus to be regarded not as a deplorable imperfection of regulation but as a positive advantage. Freezing rates for the period of the lag imposes penalties for inefficiency, excessive conservatism, and wrong guesses, and offers rewards for their opposites: companies can for a time keep the higher profits they reap from a superior performance and have to suffer the losses from a poor one. A similar function is served by the Commission's following the explicit policy of holding permitted profits not to a fixed percentage, but within a range or "zone of reasonableness," with adjustments in rates permitted or imposed only when returns fall outside that range.

cites another interesting example:

"The outcome of the FCC's investigation of Western Union is revealing in this connection. The investigation resulted in a staff report that advised the company to reduce telegram prices selectively in order to recapture business from the telephone companies. Western Union's management disagreed with the staff's diagnosis. They claimed, and still claim, that to reduce telegram rates would be to throw good money after bad. They have not implemented the staff's recommendation—but they have persuaded the Commission to authorize further rate increases." "Natural Monopoly and Its Regulation," *Stanford Law Rev.* (February 1969), XXI: 618. Copyright 1969 by the Board of Trustees of Leland Stanford Junior University.

[3] This will not be so to the extent that the permitted return exceeds the marginal cost of capital. If demand has any elasticity, higher costs and prices will mean lower total sales and a smaller total investment on which the permitted rate of return may be earned, hence lower aggregate profits. And if the permitted return exceeds the cost of attracting new capital, stockholders will be better off with a larger investment than a smaller one. See notes 64 and 69, in Chapter 2, Volume 1, and pp. 49–59, below.

[4] The required rate adjustments for excessive or inadequate returns are stated as they are on the assumption, almost certainly justified, that demand for a sufficient portion of the company's services is inelastic, so that rate changes will ordinarily produce profit changes in the same direction.

Permitting a rate of return above the bare cost of capital, while by no means free of danger, as we shall see, offers similar possible advantages. It causes the interest of a vigorous, growth-oriented management in aggressive expansion of sales and investment to coincide with that of the stockholder: existing stockholders pocket the difference between the cost of raising additional capital and the return they are permitted to earn on it. It is therefore an offset to public utility monopoly itself—to the familiar discrepancy between marginal revenue and average revenue under monopoly, which counsels higher than optimal prices and lower than optimal levels of output and investment. Combined with the presence of incompletely exploited monopoly power, which means that any losses resulting from mistaken or excessive investments or rate reductions may be recouped from existing customers, it encourages the undertaking of risky investments, expenditures on research and development, or efforts at sales promotion that monopoly might otherwise unduly restrict. Considering also the inevitable uncertainties in commission efforts to estimate the cost of capital, it mini mizes the danger that an unduly restrictive policy will make management reluctant to raise new capital, for fear of causing a dilution of stockholders' equity.[5]

THE A–J–W EFFECT

As we have already pointed out, the combination of incompletely exploited monopoly power and a rate of return in excess of the marginal cost of capital, both of which regulation is likely to entail, also involves certain dangers.[6] The very incentives to expansion of investment and output to which they give rise may instead be regarded as distortions, tending to produce inefficient results. As Averch, Johnson, and Wellisz, among others, have pointed out, this combination of circumstances may induce public utility companies to make investments the social benefits of which fall short of their social costs, because (1) such investments will expand the rate base on which the companies are entitled to a rate of return in excess of the cost of capital and (2) to the extent that the net revenues directly generated by such incremental investments fall short of yielding the allowed rate of return, they can recoup the revenue deficiencies by raising their rates in markets in which they have thitherto been prevented from pricing at profit-maximizing levels. These considerations could induce them (1) to adopt an excessively capital-intensive technology and (2) to take on additional business, if necessary, at unremunerative rates.[7]

---

[5] See note 64, Chapter 2 of Volume 1; James C. Bonbright, *Principles of Public Utility Rates* (New York: Columbia University Press, 1961), 254–256, and pp. 106–108, below.

[6] See p. 147, Volume 1.

[7] Harvey Averch and Leland L. Johnson, "Behavior of the Firm under Regulatory Constraint," *Amer. Econ. Rev.* (December 1962), LII: 1052–1069; Stanislaw H. Wellisz, "Regulation of Natural Gas Pipeline Companies: An Economic Analysis," *Jour. Pol. Econ.* (February 1963), LXXI: 30–43. See the development of the hypothesis by Arnold F. Parr, *Theory of the Capital Decision in the Regulated Firm,* Ph.D. Dissertation, University of Oklahoma, University Microfilms, 1967, and Eugene P. Coyle, *The Theory of Investment of the Regulated Firm in the Special Context of Electric Power,* Ph.D. Dissertation, Boston College, University Microfilms, 1969. See the review of the literature and important modifications of the hypothesis by William J. Baumol and Alvin K. Klevorick, "Input choices and rate-of-return regulation: an overview of the discussion," *Bell Jour. Econ. and Mgt. Science* (Autumn 1970), I: 162–190.

The "A–J–W effect" (after Averch, Johnson, and Wellisz) undoubtedly describes a real tendency, although demonstrating that it has in fact prevailed over offsetting forces and produced inefficient investments in specific instances or determining whether it has on balance done more harm than good (I incline to the latter view)[8] would take more intensive research than has so far been done. It might be reflected in[9]

1. The resistance of many public utility companies to full peak-responsibility pricing, which would tend to hold down the expansion of demand at the peak and the consequent justification for capacity.[10]
2. A willingness to maintain a large amount of standby capacity, in excess of peak requirements.[11]
3. Some considerable resistance by electric utility companies to the thoroughgoing regional planning of investment that represents the most highly integrated form of power pooling.[12] The more usual practice, in which the various members of the pool take turns in installing capacity, and the corresponding typical requirement that over the long run each member possess capacity of its own sufficient to meet its peak requirements doubtless have numerous explanations;[13] but, like the resistance to

---

[8] See pp. 106–108, below.

[9] On some of these, see Harold H. Wein, "Fair Rate of Return and Incentives—Some General Considerations," in Trebing (ed.), *Performance under Regulation*, 42–53; and for a careful and critical appraisal, see the "Comment" of William R. Hughes, *ibid.*, 73–87.

[10] See note 34, p. 99, Volume 1. Shepherd characterizes the failure of gas and electric rates to follow this principle as "the most glaring instance" of inefficient pricing. William G. Shepherd and Thomas G. Gies, *Utility Regulation: New Directions in Theory and Practice* (New York: Random House, 1966), 265 n. Also his "Marginal-Cost Pricing in American Utilities," *South. Econ. Jour.* (July 1966), XXXIII: 61–64; Ralph K. Davidson, *Price Discrimination in Selling Gas and Electricity* (Baltimore: Johns Hopkins Press, 1955), 150–151; and Wellisz, *op. cit.*, *Jour. Pol. Econ.* (February 1963), LXXI: 35–36. This contention is not necessarily refuted by the tendency of natural gas pipeline companies to press for peak responsibility cost allocations in opposition to the FPC's *Atlantic Seaboard* formula. They have done so primarily because loading capacity costs on the commodity charge often made it impossible for them to quote off-peak rates for industrial customers low enough to get that business. They have also had the special incentive to do so arising from the fact that the more of the costs that they can get incorporated in the demand charge, the greater is their jurisdictional cost of service. See pp. 98–100, Volume 1.

[11] See, in addition to the citation of this example by Wein and the criticism by Hughes (note 9, above), the partial rebuttal by Irwin M. Stelzer,

"Rate Base Regulation and Some Alternatives: An Appraisal," a paper delivered at a Brookings Institution Symposium on the Rate-Base Approach to Regulation, June 7, 1968, and in *Public Utilities Fortnightly*, September 25, 1969, 3–11. The decline in the late 1960's in this margin of safety in the country at large for electricity—which produced a near-crisis in New York City during the summer of 1969—is apparently attributable to unexpectedly long delays in the delivery of nuclear generating plants and successful opposition by conservationist groups to various proposed installations. Similar congestion in local telephone service clearly reflects gross underestimation of the rate of demand increase. See also note 12.

[12] On both of these, see Shepherd, *op. cit.*, *South. Econ. Jour.* (July 1966), XXXIII: 61, and pp. 64–65, this chapter, below. The FPC's Bureau of Power has clearly implied that the power shortages in New York City, alluded to in the preceding note, would have been less severe had the local supplier been prompter in following the Commission's earlier recommendation that it substantially expand its interconnections with neighboring utilities. *A Review of Consolidated Edison Company 1969 Power Supply Problems and Ten-Year Expansion Plans*, Washington, December 1969, 73–76. See esp. note 57, below.

[13] Among these may be the desire to exclude from membership in the pools smaller, especially municipally owned distribution companies; see pp. 316–323, Chapter 6, below. Other factors explaining the unwillingness of electric companies continuously to purchase their power from others, even when this would produce the lowest cost, are the desire to escape federal juris-

completely integrated pooling itself, they probably reflect the fact also that when a distribution company purchases power from one of its partners, it receives nothing more than reimbursement for those actual expenses, whereas if it generates the power itself it has an expanded rate base on which it is entitled to a return.

4. A resistance to the introduction of capital-saving technology. One public utility engineer has insisted to this writer that the natural gas transmission companies have insufficiently developed underground storage in the Northeast, preferring instead to expand the more capital-intensive pipeline capacity as the principal means of meeting peak winter demands.[14] This same problem has been posed with particular urgency in recent years in the field of communications, where satellites seem to promise very great capital savings over ordinary terrestrial (and underwater cable) facilities.[15]

5. A reluctance to lease facilities from others. The Communications Satellite

---

diction, which extends to interstate sales, and the fear that they would have lesser assurance of continued availability of supply in time of shortage than if they were more nearly self-sufficient. See Hughes, in Trebing (ed.), *op. cit.*, 84 87. Some of these obstacles to the truly integrated planning of investment could be offset by joint ownership of pooled facilities, no matter where located; but some states do not permit their companies to include facilities outside their service areas in their rate bases; and the companies may be reluctant to participate in such joint ventures for fear of coming under the jurisdiction of the Securities and Exchange Commission as holding companies (see pp. 72–73, below).

[14] The winter heating demand creates an extreme seasonal peak in this part of the country. The larger the available storage capacity near the points of consumption, the less the needed pipeline capacity: smaller pipelines could approach capacity operations the entire year-around, bringing up much more gas than was being consumed in the summer months and placing it in storage, and drawing on those stocks to supplement their reduced carrying capacity during the winter peaks. Alternatively, they could serve the same end with a larger pipeline capacity, sufficient to meet the peak requirements with currently flowing gas, and attempting to fill in the summer troughs by developing large off-peak markets at rates relatively unburdened by capacity charges. The charge is that pipeline companies have been influenced, in making their choice between these two alternatives, by a preference for the larger rate base entailed by the second—the inflated costs of which can be passed on to the ultimate consumer while yielding larger aggregate profits. See also p. 100, Volume 1.

[15] See Merton J. Peck, "The Single-Entity Proposal for International Telecommunications," *Amer. Econ. Rev., Papers and Proceedings* (May 1970), LX: 199–201. This contention is not uncontroverted. When in 1968 the Federal Communications Commission responded favorably to a request by AT&T that it be permitted to apply for authorization to lay a submarine cable between the United States and Spain, it did so because, among other considerations, a majority of the commissioners believed that, at least for the next several years, submarine cable would be the more economical means of providing the international communications service. See note 89, this Chapter, below. Whichever of these views is correct, it is nonetheless instructive that it was the Bell System that wanted to construct the cable—the cost of which would go into its rate base—while representatives of Comsat argued that the demand should be met by an expanded communications satellite system. For indications that similar motives have influenced the (negative) attitude of not only the terrestrial carriers but Comsat as well toward the possibility of direct broadcasting from satellites to receiving sets, see Lawrence Lessing, "Cinderella in the Sky," *Fortune* (October 1967), LXXVI: 131–208. It quotes the President of Comsat as contending that

"Retransmission through established ground channels and TV stations . . . is 'more natural, logical, and economical,' because it allows greater channel capacity and flexibility, and is *less disruptive of the vast investment in ground facilities.*" (Stress supplied)

Lessing observes that

"Comsat is predisposed for its domestic system toward the higher capital-cost distributive system, for it would add more to its rate base than the direct-broadcasting system. . . ." *Ibid.*, 198.

Corporation (Comsat), which was set up in 1962 as the United States' chosen instrument for installing and operating an international satellite communications network in cooperation with other countries, is essentially a carriers' carrier: the only ultimate consumer authorized thus far to deal directly with it is the National Aeronautics and Space Agency (NASA).[16] The possibility of its taking over an increasing share of the communications business is therefore dependent on the patronage and decisions of the common carriers, who would have to lease channels from it and use them in turn to take care of their customers' demands. But the carriers, it seems generally conceded, have less incentive to use the Comsat facilities than to construct their own, the cost of which would go into their rate bases: to the extent that they took the former course, they would make no profit on that portion of the communications operations; all they could do would be to include the rental charges in their own cost of service and get them back dollar for dollar. The latter course, in contrast, would mean greater aggregate profits. This lack of incentive to use leased facilities[17] would seem to be a clear manifestation of the A–J–W distortion and could well, given the peculiar institutional arrangements of the satellite part of the industry, result in overinvestment in economically less efficient facilities and a serious retardation in the development of satellite technology.[18]

---

[16] See the discussion of its constitution and the FCC's decision with respect to its authorized users at pp. 136–139, Chapter 4, below.

[17] For another illuminating example, see "Utilities' Embrace of Nuclear Fuel Stalled by its Classification as a Current Asset," *Wall Street Journal*, November 12, 1968, 4:

"The biggest decision facing the electric companies is whether to purchase their fuel cores or lease them from a supplier or third party. . . .
"There are some unquestioned advantages to leasing. . . . [It] could relieve utility executives of a host of technical problems. . . .
"Many utilities, however, contend that the benefits of leasing are questionable. . . .
"More important . . . many utilities fear that leasing fuel could force them to reduce electric rates at the same time they are undertaking heavy expenditures to switch to nuclear fuel. The reason is that in determining electric rates, state utility commissions allow the generating companies sufficient revenues to recover their operating costs and earn a return . . . on their invested capital.
"By leasing their fuel, however, a utility wouldn't be able to include this substantial investment in its rate base." But see note 29, below.
The FPC in 1970 proposed that electric and gas companies be permitted to capitalize a portion of their research expenditures, in hope that including these in their rate bases would encourage the companies to mount a greater

research effort. *Wall Street Journal*, January 28, 1970.

[18] See the interesting paper by A. Bruce Matthews, Vice President of Comsat, "Problems Posed by Current Regulatory Practices to the Rapid Introduction of Communications Satellite Technology," presented at the Brookings Symposium on the Rate-Base Approach to Regulation, June 7, 1968. A vice-president of AT&T indirectly conceded these possibilities when he posed the question:

"Does it [that is, rate base regulation] make the ownership of property so important that a utility has little or no incentive to lease or make other arrangements for the use of facilities it does not own (e.g., satellite circuits), even if this will result in savings to the users of service?"

"there are . . . situations in the telecommunications field where investment should play only a minor role in regulation. This might well be so where large volumes of business can be carried on with only a small investment being involved. Moreover, it is possible that over the coming years, because of leased plant or other factors, there may well be an increasing number of such situations. In all such situations a method, or methods, of regulation might be used, giving primary weight to the nature and quality of the service performed and little weight to the investment involved." John J. Scanlon, "Is Rate Base-Rate of Return Regulation Obsolete?" presented at the same conference, mimeo., 1, 17.

6. A tendency for public utility companies to adhere to excessively high (because excessively costly) standards of reliability and uninterruptibility of service, with correspondingly high and costly specifications for the equipment they employ. The alleged tendency described briefly under point 2, above, is clearly a special case of this one. It is, of course, extraordinarily difficult to demonstrate. Conceivably, the costs of interruptions in service to users of electricity are so extraordinarily great that the demand for continuity is completely inelastic;[19] or, conceivably, telephone subscribers are so annoyed by any delay whatever in completing their calls or by wrong numbers or misconnections that they, too, would pay whatever is necessary to obtain the very maximum of service that it is physically possible to provide. But the need for an economic calculus in matters such as these is inescapable: electric and gas companies sell services of varying degrees of interruptibility, at correspondingly varying discounts below the price for firm energy; and telephone companies do not place all calls instantaneously and correctly, nor do they devote unlimited resources to research into methods of improving their performance in these respects. It is entirely conceivable, therefore, that the economic calculations they do make are, consciously or unconsciously, influenced by the A–J–W consideration, particularly since it would have a tendency to reinforce their other motivations to do the best possible job—pride, an instinct of workmanship, a desire to minimize public complaint, and so on.[20]

7. A tendency to bargain less hard than they otherwise would in purchasing equipment from outside suppliers. Fred M. Westfield has cited complaints that the electric utility companies were insufficiently perceptive of the electric equipment manufacturers' price conspiracy of the late 1950s and insufficiently vigorous in pressing suits for damages as the basis for his theoretical demonstration that the A J–W effect could have made these companies not only susceptible to such exploitation but eager for it.[21] It is perhaps significant that that famous conspiracy was broken by the

On the general problem that he raises, see also note 25, below.

The FCC has, in certain decisions, recognized the desire of common carriers to participate in the ownership of facilities they use and the possible disincentive to such use if they do not—for example, in requiring AT&T to share ownership of authorized new cable facilities with competing carriers [*In the Matter of American Telephone & Telegraph Co., et al.*, Memorandum Opinion and Order, 37 FCC 1151 (1964)], and in requiring Comsat to share ownership in its various ground stations (for the transmission, receipt and retransmission of signals from satellites) with the other international carriers. *In the Matter of Amendment of Part 25 of the Commission's Rules and Regulations With Respect to Ownership and Operation of Initial Earth Stations in the United States etc.*, Second Report and Order, 5 FCC 2d 812 (1966). See also Herman Schwartz,

"Comsat, the Carriers, and the Earth Stations: Some Problems with 'Melding Variegated Interests,'" *Yale Law Jour.* (January 1967), LXXVI: 443–453, 457–458.

[19] So the Federal Power Commission observed at the outset of its report on the great Northeast power failure of 1965:

"The prime lesson of the blackout . . . was that 'the electric utility industry must strive not merely for good but for virtually perfect service.'" *Major Power Failure Investigation, an Interim Report*, as quoted in FPC, *1966 Annual Report*, 42.

[20] For an observation that the Bell System may err in this direction, see John B. Sheahan, *Competition Versus Regulation as a Policy Aim for the Telephone Equipment Industry*, unpublished Ph.D. dissertation, Harvard University, 1951, 90–91.

[21] "Regulation and Conspiracy," *Amer. Econ. Rev.* (June 1965), LV: 424–443.

complaints not of a private company but of the Tennessee Valley Authority.[22]

"the analysis suggests that the capital-goods suppliers of other rate-of-return regulated industries may turn out to be fertile hunting grounds for antitrust law violations."[23]

8. A tendency to reach out for additional business, inside or outside the sphere of their franchised public-utility operations, if need be at rates below incremental costs. As we have already observed, this kind of behavior is most likely to be encountered in competitive situations, because it is there that the elasticity of demand may require unremunerative rates if the regulated company is to obtain the business and in this manner to increase its rate base [24]

It has been suggested that dangers such as these—in particular the reluctance of regulated companies to lease facilities from others—could be forestalled by using some method of determining permissible profits other than one based on allowing a maximum rate of return on a rate base. For example, the ICC makes some use of an operating ratio method for regulated motor carriers; under this method, overall revenue requirements are set at some percentage markup above operating expenses. If this method were applied more generally, a regulated company would be permitted a profit margin on its leasing or labor expenses rather than or in addition to a return on investment in its own facilities. The quick answer, as far as the A–J–W problem is concerned, is that the operating ratio method would substitute a new distortion, or add it to the other: since profits would be a fixed percentage markup over expenses, the regulated companies would now have an incentive to inflate those expenses, rather than (or in addition to) their capital investment.[25]

[22] Clarence C. Walton and Frederick W. Cleveland, Jr., *Corporations on Trial: The Electric Cases* (Belmont, California: Wadsworth Publishing Company Inc., 1964), 29–32.

[23] Westfield, *op. cit.*, 442.

[24] See p. 159, Volume 1.

[25] Actually, the operating ratio method is usually advocated only for industries or operations where capital–sales ratios are low. And the major justification proffered is that, in such situations, profits that are held to some fixed percentage of capital investment will involve only a small percentage of sales and can therefore quickly be wiped out by even slight unfavorable developments. Consider the following example offered by Charles Alan Wright of a "typical utility" and a "typical bus company," with the same level of revenues but widely divergent capital requirements, and both permitted a 6 percent return on investment.

	Typical Utility	**Typical Bus Company**
Annual income	$10,000,000	$10,000,000
Net investment	25,000,000	4,000,000
Operating expenses	8,500,000	9,760,000
Return (6% of investment)	1,500,000	240,000

A 2.4% decline in sales (operating expenses remaining constant) or a 2.5% increase in costs would reduce the latter's profit to zero. An operating ratio of about 93%, permitting revenues of not quite $10,500,000 and profits of $740,000, would give it a fairer margin of protection. "Operating Ratio—A Regulatory Tool," *Public Utilities Fortnightly* (January 1953), LI:

24–26. Also Lawrence S. Knappen, "Transit Operating Ratio—Another View," *ibid.* (April 1953), LI: 485–497.

But, as Stelzer points out, this is only another way of saying that the investment in bus operations is the more risky of the two and requires a higher rate of return ($18\frac{1}{2}\%$ in the above example) on its investment for this reason. There is still no way of determining the proper operating ratio except by ascertaining the appropriate rate of return on investment, whether measured by cost of capital or comparable earnings. *Op. cit.*, Brookings Institution symposium, June 1968.

True, to paraphrase advocates of this method, when capital–sales ratios are low, "investment is not the primary factor in determining revenue needs." But when they proceed then to say something such as "the principal risk is attached to the substantially greater amount of expense," they are being very imprecise. The risk continues to be borne by the owners, and the risk is that they will lose their invested capital. The ratio of expenses to revenues does have an important influence on that risk, by increasing the likelihood that small percentage changes in costs or sales will result in revenues that do not cover that part of operating expenses that cannot readily be sloughed off, that is, that does not represent variable costs in the very short run. But the size of such expenses relative to the probable range of net revenue fluctuations provides a measure of the risk that earnings on capital will fluctuate; and the proper remuneration must therefore be in the rate of return permitted on that investment. The CAB achieved this result in 1960, directly, without recourse to an operating ratio technique, by setting a maximum allowable return at 12.75% (permitting 21.35% on equity alone) for local service airlines and 10.5% for domestic trunk lines. *Re: Rate of Return, Local-Service Carriers Investigation*, Docket No. 8404, Opinion, 31 CAB 685, 690 (1960) and *Re: General Passenger-Fare Investigation*, Docket No. 8008 et al., Opinion, 32 CAB 291 (1960). See also the recent ICC decision rejecting a request by truckers for a general rate increase based on a purported need for an operating ratio of 93% (that is, roughly a 7% profit markup over operating expenses), on the ground that

"The respondents in this proceeding have not attempted to show by any objective measure what amount of money they need over and above operating expenses. . . .

"Some analysis of the capital costs of the carriers' business must be presented to establish a need for additional revenue, and to measure such need." *General increase, Middle Atlantic and New England Territories*, 332 ICC 820 (1969), 837–838.

The reasoning of the Commission is supported and the limitations and possible usefulness of the operating ratio method further spelled out in the following conclusions of a study by National Economic Research Associates of *Methods for Testing the Reasonableness of Motor Carrier Earnings* (processed, New York, April 17, 1967, 1–2). (We have no opinion about the appropriateness of the particular *level* of return that they tentatively recommend.)

"1. Fair and reasonable rates for motor carriers can be meaningfully defined *only* in terms of return on invested capital.

"2. Whether a given operating ratio will provide adequate return cannot be determined without knowing something about the amount of invested capital.

"3. The allowable return on invested capital should be adequate to (1) attract required capital, and (2) match the return earned in industries of comparable risk. Preliminary analysis indicates that the required rate of return should be in the neighborhood of 15–20 percent on equity and 11–13 percent on total capitalization.

"4. For any given rate of return on invested capital there can be found a corresponding operating ratio. Thus, it is possible to apply an operating-ratio standard as a matter of administrative convenience, although return on invested capital would be the ultimate standard.

"5. Because of the short period over which investment is depreciated, the net investment "rate base" may be subject to short-term fluctuations which make the selection of a "test year" extremely difficult.

"6. Therefore, over short periods of time, fluctuations in the operating ratio may more accurately reflect true changes in the cost-revenue relationship than changes in the rate of return on rate base.

"7. Thus, the Commission should select as its standard an operating ratio which, on average, will yield the desired rate of return on invested capital. The Commission should periodically— every five or seven years—review the cost structure of the industry to see whether any change in the operating-ratio standard is required. But in the interim, the operating-ratio standard should be applied in setting rates which are reasonably responsive to changes in cost. This highly flexible approach is necessary in order to minimize regulatory lag which, when profit margins are narrow, can create extremely serious problems for the regulated industry."

Does this solution apply without limit—that is, no matter how low the capital–output ratio? What if the preponderant contribution of a regulated company is the services of a team of professionals—research chemists, management

There just is no easy way of eradicating these possible distortions of incentives, within the regulatory context; all the commission can do is to supervise, prod, and subject proposed investments, promotional prices and the like to economic tests. If, for example, the communications common carriers are truly reluctant to lease circuits from Comsat, on which they are permitted no profit, preferring instead to add uneconomically large owned facilities to their own rate bases, one remedy is for the FCC to refuse to certificate such uneconomic investments: this would force the carriers to use Comsat.

But, by the same token, these dangers can be drastically attenuated or eliminated to the extent that regulated companies can be exposed to the same incentives and pressures as apply *outside* of the regulatory context—the incentive of higher or lower profits depending on individual performance, and the pressures of competition. An automatically effective solution to any reluctance of the above-mentioned carriers to use lower-cost but less capital-intensive satellite facilities would be direct competition between Comsat and them: this would ensure that the business went to the lowest-cost instrumentality. We reserve consideration of this kind of solution for Chapters 4–6 below,[26] confining our attention here to the tendencies and solutions *under regulation.*

Observe that the A–J–W tendency prevails only to the extent that regulation approaches instantaneous effectiveness in holding realized rates of return to a single, legally prescribed level. Only in these circumstances could regulated companies, without fear of loss, undertake investments the marginal product of which fell short of their cost of capital: only if the rate of return that they were previously earning was already at the legal *minimum* and only if, after these investments were made, rates could instantaneously be raised on the inelastic portions of the business to hold the return to that minimum would there be no losses to offset the benefit of the expanded rate base. Only if, to look at it from the opposite direction, all reductions in cost were instantaneously accompanied by equivalent rate reductions, so as instantaneously to take those cost-savings away from them, could regulated companies afford to have no compunctions about adopting excessively capital-intensive, hence cost-inflating methods of production.

But in fact regulation is far from instantaneously effective. The consequence is that the profits of public utility companies would, for longer or shorter

---

or economic consultants—as in the case of a research or consulting contract with a government agency? Suppose, to take the extreme case, the government needs only a research organization, to put to work on a military problem in a government-owned laboratory? If it is unwilling to conscript the scientists—by no means an unthinkable proposition, as long as it conscripts soldiers—and wants to induce companies to bid on the contract, how is it to compute the required profit inducement? Clearly, no company would bid if the contract provided only for reimbursement of the salaries plus some return on the zero company investment. The answer would presumably have to be some measure of the opportunity cost to a bidding company like General Electric. And this would clearly be only the salaries only if G.E. could instantaneously replace all the scientists it supplied to the government, with no loss in productivity or contribution to its overall profit. So, to put it positively, the necessary profit component of this regulated price would have to be the estimated contribution that the required team of scientists would otherwise make to company profit over and above their salaries and over and above the contribution G.E. might be expected to obtain by using that salary money for other purposes—an easier concept to describe than to measure!

[26] See in particular pp. 137–138, Chapter 4.

periods of time and with a considerable margin of uncertainty about the speed of recoupment, suffer from the undertaking of investments that do not themselves return the cost of capital. Moreover, regulatory commissions seem, typically and understandably, to be much more generous about the rates of return they are prepared to permit in a context of stable or declining rates than when faced by company requests for rate increases. In these circumstances, regulated companies may have a stronger incentive to reduce costs, which enables them to earn a gently rising return for substantial periods of time on a rate base that grows only to the extent justified by comparisons of marginal returns and marginal cost of capital, than to make uneconomic investments in the expectation of being permitted rate increases on inelastic portions of their business sufficient to increase their total profits.[27]

It is with arguments such as these that public utility executives indignantly deny that there exists any such tendency as suggested by the A–J–W hypothesis. In the planning of new investments, they present their engineers with estimated loads and the other relevant constraints—such as minimum service standards—and ask them to compute various alternative ways of meeting that anticipated demand; and their invariable rule, they assert, is to select the lowest-cost alternatives, applying a uniform cost of capital to the capital component of those cost estimates. As long as the engineers do not apply a discount rate that is too low, that is, that underestimates the true cost of capital, this procedure could not lead systematically to the selection of inefficiently capital-intensive methods of production.[28]

They frequently argue, also, that they have found extremely onerous the necessity they have faced since World War II of going regularly to the capital markets to finance the constant additions to capacity required merely to meet their ever-increasing demands. These circumstances, they assert, have forced them assiduously to economize in their use of capital. This assertion might be translated into a contention that these companies can typically raise capital only at increasing costs—that is to say, that the cost of capital to a given company at any time is higher, the larger the amount to be raised.[29] Such a tendency would not only limit the scope of the A–J–W distortion;

---

[27] By the same token, of course, as the rate of return gently approaches what management thinks is the maximum its commission will allow, the A–J–W incentive should become increasingly powerful. It seems doubtful that companies can consciously turn their attention to cost cutting on and off, depending on where they find themselves with respect to the regulatory lag; but there seems no reason to doubt that the vigor with which management insists on saving paper clips, using the mail instead of the telephone and tourist rather than first-class air service does in fact vary as profits are easy and hard to reap.

[28] See the generally corroborative observations of Hughes, in Trebing, *op. cit.*, 74–80, to the effect that the use of redundant capital or paying excessive prices for equipment are likely to be much less attractive outlets for A–J–W tendencies than expanding service and improving

its quality.

[29] It might mean also that, with the generally rising long term interest rates of the late 1950s and 1960s, the cost of additional capital has *over time* approached the permitted average rate of return; such a development would at the limit eradicate the A–J–W tendency. So, in interesting contrast with the attitude expressed in note 17, above, many electric utility companies were reported in late 1969 as planning to *lease* rather than buy nuclear fuel cores, because "[b]uying the fuel entails a sizeable capital outlay of up to $50 million, in an era of sky-high interest rates." *Business Week*, December 27, 1969, 17. With rates on high-grade bonds running well above 8% and permitted rates of return still reflecting the much lower average embedded cost of debt, this shift in attitude was entirely consistent with the A–J–W hypothesis.

it could conceivably produce a distortion in the *opposite* direction.[30]

Another piece of evidence suggests that the alleged tendency toward overly capital-intensive technology has not, in fact, materialized. According to the estimates by John W. Kendrick the margin of superiority of productivity advances in public utilities over American industries generally, during the period 1899 to 1953, is just as great in capital and total factor productivity as in labor productivity alone.[31] If the industry had a tendency to use excessively capital intensive methods of production (and it would be reasonable to assume that the tendencies would be progressive over the 54-year period studied by Kendrick, particularly since public utility regulation almost certainly became increasingly effective over this period), one would have expected it to show up in a more rapid relative rate of increase in labor productivity than in either capital or total factor productivity.[32]

---

[30] A monopsonist faces a rising supply function of whatever it is he is buying: he will have to pay a higher unit price the more he tries to buy. So a labor market monopsonist, for example, will find that the marginal cost of labor to him exceeds the average cost or wage rate, because in addition to the wage for the added worker he must pay higher wages for all the other workers as well. And because of this he will cut off his hiring at the point at which that marginal cost equals the marginal value product of labor; and this will be short of the socially efficient point—which would be where the (average) wage equalled that marginal value product. So here, the firm that faces a rising capital supply function, because of its monopsonistic position in capital markets, might refuse to undertake socially desirable investments, the (average) capital cost of which was less than their marginal product, because raising the additional capital would increase the average cost of all the capital the firm would otherwise have to raise. See Richard S. Bower, "Rising Capital Cost *Versus* Regulatory Restraint," *Public Utilities Fortnightly*, March 4, 1965, 31–33. Shepherd uses a rising marginal cost of capital function in his exposition of the A–J–W tendency. "Regulatory Constraints and Public Utility Investment," *Land Econ.* (August 1966), XLII: 350.

[31] See his *Productivity Trends in the United States* (Princeton: Princeton Univ. Press, 1961), 136–137, 152–153, 166–167. See some of these and later data at pp. 99–100, Chapter 3, below.

[32] Stelzer supplies several additional considerations and pieces of evidence that would appear to be incompatible with the A–J–W tendency. Among these are the general failure of electric and gas companies to take advantage of the mounting public concern with environmental quality as a justification for rapidly expanding their investment in underground transmission and distribution facilities or for installing air and thermal pollution control equipment; the fact that the extension of telephone, electricity, and

gas services to rural areas, at rates that may not even cover long-run marginal cost, is probably explicable more generally by the pressures of regulatory commissions and the threat of government competition than by an avid quest by the reluctant companies for additional rate base; and that, similarly, the publicly owned TVA keeps at least as large a reserve of generating capacity as the private part of the industry. *Op. cit.*, Brookings Institution symposium, June 1968. On the similar, at least equally great reluctance of public power companies and tough regulatory commissions to follow or to permit full peak responsibility pricing, see p. 98, Volume 1, and pp. 107–108, Chapter 3, below.

Also in apparent conflict with the A–J–W hypothesis is what appears to have been the typical practice of regulated companies in recent decades to urge regulatory commissions to permit them to depreciate their investment at more rapid rates. If, in fact, it is in their interest to inflate the rate base, it is difficult to understand why they would generally try so hard to get capital out of the rate base faster than commissions have allowed. The companies usually offer in justification a fear of technological obsolescence and their need for capital funds. See, for example, the strong argument by William J. Crowley, "The Management Factor in Accounting Policy," *AGA Monthly*, February 1968, 24. This kind of argument might be interpreted as involving the proposition that the cost of capital is not constant regardless of the life of the equipment in which it is embodied, but increases with equipment longevity because of the increasing uncertainties of recoupment the longer the planning time horizon. Since the A–J–W distortion applies only to the extent that the cost of capital is less than the rate of return, it would in this event not necessarily conflict with the desire of regulated companies to get their capital rapidly out of long-lived equipment subject to rapid obsolescence. The contention by Crowley that "a company that is allowed a realistic

Finally, it should be recognized that the A–J–W distortion is an entirely static one. Its tendency is to produce an overallocation of capital to regulated industries. But the principal institutional deficiency of regulation is dynamic —the absence of a spur to progressive performance comparable to and as reliable as that of competition. Instead, these industries are subject to the restrictive and conservative influences of monopoly. These influences are likely, if anything, to be reinforced by regulatory surveillance, by the necessity of submitting proposed prices, promotional campaigns, and investments to the possibility of veto by a politically appointed commission. The almost inescapable cumbersomeness of administrative procedures, the expense and delay involved in clearing major policy changes with a governmental commission almost certainly tend to breed conservatism in the companies themselves, and an unwillingness to make changes, to take chances.[33] And it is precisely with respect to the dynamic probing of demand elasticity and to risk-taking innovation that the possibilities of earning a return in excess of the cost of capital and of recouping losses from an incompletely exploited fund of monopoly power would seem a desirable offset to monopoly, as we have already suggested. That is why we suggest (at greater length in Chapter 3, below) that the A–J–W tendency, to the limited extent it exists, could well be a more important influence for good than for poor performance.[34] Still, the dangers remain as well; and they call for continuing attention.[35]

INCENTIVE PLANS

Certainly to some extent commissions can devise explicit incentives for dynamic and efficient performance in an attempt to induce managements to overcome the inertia of monopoly, bureaucracy, and regulation itself. The most promising are simply the aforementioned regulatory lag and "zone of reasonableness" rate of return, both of which tend to offer the same sort of automatic stimuli as operate in the unregulated sectors of the economy. Some observers have proposed that these devices be institutionalized, that is, explicitly adopted as a policy, thus assuring to companies the rewards and penalties they provide.[36] This might create more problems than it solves.

---

depreciation expense provision would be more willing to adopt new methods, new labor-saving and cost-cutting ideas and equipment" (*ibid*) seems to reflect the consideration discussed at pp. 118–119, Volume 1, as well.

The attempt of companies with large annual capital needs to finance a larger proportion of their investment internally might be explicable also in terms of the possibility mentioned at p. 57, above—which would, again, be entirely compatible with the A–J–W analysis, but would diminish its practical importance.

[33] For a brief allusion to some of these political-administrative influences and problems, see pp. 87–88, below.

[34] See p. 49, this chapter above; see also Sidney Weintraub, "Rate Making and an Incentive Rate of Return," *Public Utilities Fortnightly,* April 25, 1968, 30–31. So we have pointed out that the effectiveness of regulatory lag in

stimulating continuing attention to cost cutting presumably diminishes, and the A–J–W danger grows, as the rate of return approaches the legal maximum and/or the next cost-of-service computation (see note 27). But in those same circumstances the power of the A–J–W tendency for good as well as evil would likewise be enhanced in inducing a greater willingness to take risks, or to cut prices experimentally in hope of increasing sales and justifying a larger investment.

[35] See, for example, our discussion of the need for commissions placing an LRMC floor (or an even higher one) under discriminatory rate reductions, particularly in competitive situations, in Chapters 5 and 6 of Volume 1.

[36] On the regulatory lag, see William J. Baumol, "Reasonable Rules for Rate Regulation: Plausible Policies for an Imperfect World," in Almarin Phillips and Oliver E. Williamson, *Prices: Issues*

After the rate of return reached its ceiling or the period of regulatory lag drew to its preannounced close, the incentive for improved performance would be exhausted and could indeed be reversed: the company would now be tempted to construct a high cost of service for the new test year. Paradoxically, the same would tend to happen when profits approached the floor: the company's attention would shift to constructing the strongest possible case for a rate increase. This has led others to propose that the period of the lag and the limits of the zone of reasonableness be left purposely uncertain—which is not far from where we are now.

Of course, if the regulatory lag is on balance helpful, attempts to make regulation "more efficient" in limiting the rate of return to the prescribed levels not just from one major rate case to another but year to year are likely to be on balance harmful. This is the concern one might have about the FCC's proclaimed practice of "continuous surveillance" over telephone rates, even though this device, involving reliance on continuing informal conferences rather than long, drawn-out major rate investigations, has proved fruitful in forcing a prompter translation of the benefits of tax reductions and technological progress into lower prices than would otherwise have been possible.[37] This possible objection could perhaps be eliminated if the surveillance of realized profit rates were conceived of—as in part the FCC evidently has—as a device for reducing not so much *profits* as *prices*. The latter is obviously the more important part of performance.

Suppose the commission found that a company's realized return exceeded the allowable level by a certain number of dollars. If its primary focus were on those dollars, it would regard its efforts as frustrated if the company responded to the order for rate reductions by cleverly choosing those services whose demand is most elastic and production most subject to decreasing costs—as it would be in its interest to do. Indeed, if they took such a narrow view, the regulators might press the company instead to reduce rates in the markets with inelastic demand or subject to increasing costs, or, indeed, *raise* them in markets of elastic demand, because this would most reliably reduce profits. But this would manifestly not be in the public interest. The proper focus would be on getting the maximum reduction in *rates* consistent with the required profit reduction. This suggests that if there is to be continuing surveillance, the corrective orders should run in terms of eliminating a certain number of dollars of test-year profits, *on the assumption that sales would continue at test-year levels*, leaving it to the company to design the optimum structure of rate reductions from its standpoint (within limits of LRMC). This would give it the opportunity and incentive to experiment by trying to make the cuts in areas of the greatest demand elasticity and cost reducibility.

in *Theory, Practice, and Public Policy* (Philadelphia: University of Pennsylvania Press, 1967), 108–123. On the zone of reasonableness:

"I would favor ratemaking based on a relatively wide range of permissible rate of return as providing efficiency incentives which would better serve the public interest in securing efficient service at minimum charges." Commissioner Loevinger, concurring opinion in FCC, *In the Matter of American Telephone & Telegraph*

Co. et al., Docket No. 16258, Interim Decision and Order, 9 FCC 2d 30, 121 (July 1967).

The Commission explicitly adopted the same principle, for the same reason, *ibid.*, Memorandum Opinion and Order on Reconsideration, 9 FCC 2d 960, 963 (September 1967).

[37] William Haber, "Forward: An Introductory Note," and Gies, "The Need for New Concepts in Public Utility Regulation," in Shepherd and Gies, *op. cit.*, vii and 107–111.

True, such cuts in the rate level would be most likely to "fail" by the standard of holding down total profits. But it would have the maximum likelihood of success in terms of the ultimately important standard—cutting rates and extending service within the limits of LRMC.[38]

Of the more specific incentive plans employed or proposed, most involve varying the permissible rate of return (r) according to some indicator of ultimate performance. Most familiar are the various sliding scale plans, in which r is inversely related to comparative rate levels or to changes in rates over time.[39] These plans have typically been short-lived, being usually modified or abandoned when rates of return under them became unacceptably high. Under the famous Washington (D.C.) plan, which was in effect continuously from 1925 to 1955, if earnings rose above $7\frac{1}{2}$ percent, rates were to be reduced in subsequent years in such a way as to eliminate half of the remaining excess; if the return fell below the minimum, the commission was supposed to raise rates sufficiently to restore the deficiency entirely. Since demand grew rapidly in this period and may also have been elastic, returns kept rising during the first two decades; what broke down the plan was the inflation after World War II. It also had the defect of providing no penalty for inefficiency.[39a] A similar device by which corporations would be permitted to retain some percentage of incremental profits while sharing their gains with the rate payers was proposed by Irston R. Barnes. While retaining the feature of the Washington plan that involved rate reductions in a succeeding year by a percentage sufficient to eliminate 50 percent of any excess of earnings actually realized over r, it added the provision that any excesses actually earned be divided, with half of them going into the accumulation (up to 20 percent of the rate base) of an earnings-equalization reserve and the other half going into trust for rate payers. The former reserve could be used by the utility to make good any future deficiencies in earnings; and once the equalization reserve came to exceed 20 percent of the rate base, the company could use the excess for whatever corporate purpose it chose—"an extra dividend to stockholders, a bonus to management, or a profit-sharing agreement for the benefit of the workers." The other half, held in trust for the consuming public, would be used in effect to reduce the rate base; or, if used, for example, for capital expansion, the property thus acquired would not be included in the rate base. In effect, thus, consumers would obtain an equity interest in the company, a share in ownership of the assets, income from which they would receive in the form of an exclusion from the rates charged them of a return on that capital sum.[40]

---

[38] See pp. 142–145, Volume 1. If, then, the cuts proved the following year to have "failed" by the first test, the commission could come back and order another reduction—set, once again, in terms of the number of dollars by which net revenues would have been reduced if sales remained at base-year volumes.

[39] See the extensive survey of these plans in Charles Stillman Morgan, *Regulation and the Management of Public Utilities* (Boston: Houghton Mifflin Company, 1923), 154–187.

[39a] See Harry M. Trebing, "Toward An Incentive System of Regulation," *Public Utilities Fortnightly*

(July 18, 1963), LXXII: 22. Trebing points out that the price of utility services in the District of Columbia fell compared with the United States average in this period and that during the 1925–1940 period rates of return were well above average: the overall rate never fell below 8.8 percent and the return on equity averaged 14.4 percent. For a survey and analysis of such plans see Irvin Bussing, *Public Utility Regulation and the So-Called Sliding Scale* (New York: Columbia Univ. Press, 1936).

[40] *The Economics of Public Utility Regulation* (New York: F. S. Croft & Co., 1942), 529–599.

In his classic study Charles Morgan emphasized above all the necessity of providing incentives for efficient performance directly to management, rather than in the corporate rate of return.

"The principal conclusions reached as a result of this study are that public necessity requires, in the case of public utilities, the establishment of conditions which will specifically conduce to the maximum utilization of the agencies or means of production, and that these conditions shall be such as to stimulate and reward management, rather than capital as such, for superior efficiency."

". . . to reward capital as such through allowing added returns for a show of increased efficiency of operation is both gratuitous and impracticable. So to reward capital would be gratuitous, for capital would thereby receive a return for a contribution which it itself did not make. It is to management and not to capital that we must look for increased efficiency, and it is to management, the human, personal force and that which alone is able to respond to the offer of a special reward for especially meritorious effort, that the appeal of a reward for efficiency should be directed."[41]

His point is well-taken, though probably exaggerated. While higher corporate profits do of course accrue to the current stockholders, they almost certainly benefit managers as well—giving them higher returns on the stock they hold, permitting and justifying the payment of higher salaries and bonuses, increasing the demand for their services by other public utility companies, making it easier for the company in question to justify raising new capital,[42] hence to grow, and in this way as well giving successful managers additional satisfaction and approbation.

In either event, the difficulty with plans such as these or with unplanned regulatory lag is that the levels and trends of rates and earnings reflect a vast complexity of factors in addition to management efficiency and enterprise. Merely permitting companies to earn higher rates of return does not necessarily reward good performance; it may unnecessarily reward good luck and other favorable external developments. Similarly, other companies may be penalized for unfavorable developments in costs and demand that are no fault of their own; and, whatever the cause, commissions will be loath to penalize them if the consequence is to diminish their ability to attract the capital that may be necessary to improve their service. Still, it remains true that sliding-scale rates of return or rewards to management *do* provide one useful and, at least in many circumstances, promising incentive. Regulatory commissions need not be incompetent to identify situations in which the rewards prove to be unnecessarily high and to make the necessary downward adjustments. Or to provide the opposite kind of correction when profits turn out persistently undeservedly and harmfully low.

A fully effective incentive system would require that commissions be able to make direct assessments of the performance of the companies under their supervision, as a basis for rewarding good management and penalizing bad. In view of the diverse and ever-changing factors determining the costs and profits of each, and in view of the numerous, partially conflicting criteria of good performance—low costs, intensive promotion, expanding sales, the

---

[41] *Op. cit.*, vii–viii, 315–316. Morgan's proposals, set forth in his Chapter 7, include various non-pecuniary devices as well as pecuniary rewards.
[42] See note 64, Chapter 2, Volume 1.

taking of market and technological risks—devising rating scales capable of general acceptance is an extremely difficult task. The fact remains that commissions can and do make such judgments and could do more—if need be with the help of management consultants. For example,

"the Commission has found the reasonable rate of return to which utilities should be entitled to be from 7 to 8 percent of the fair value of the property and business. We believe that in the present case . . . the latter rate of return is fully justified. . . . We cannot escape notice of the fact that the Milwaukee exchange of the Wisconsin Telephone Company has been and is managed with an exceedingly high degree of efficiency. . . . the investment in Milwaukee is very low for an exchange of its size and nature, and . . . the operating expenses appear to be very conservative. . . . As far as we can determine, the officials of the Milwaukee exchange and of the company have been continually on the alert to discover means of conducting the business economically and maintaining desirable relations with the public."[43]

In the most ambitious effort of this kind to date, William Iulo has attempted, by the use of multiple regression analysis, to determine quantitatively the major objective factors determining the individual costs of a sample of approximately 170 electric companies. Selecting his independent variables to exclude those that might themselves be heavily influenced by managerial efforts, he assumes further that any remaining significant differences in costs, unexplained by these external factors, can be attributed in significant measure to managerial efficiency or inefficiency.[44] Obviously if such identifications could be made with confidence, they would permit introduction of a system of direct rewards and penalties for superior or inferior management.[45] At the least, they could identify situations calling for more detailed regulatory scrutiny.[46]

---

[43] From a decision of the Wisconsin Railroad Commission, quoted in Charles S. Morgan, *op. cit.*, 292–293. For examples and for a discussion of the need, the difficulties, and the possibilities, see *ibid.*, 293–300, 323–327, and pp. 30–31, 53–54, in Volume 1. Shepherd is a leading proponent of commissions conducting management audits—making direct appraisals of the efficiency and innovation performance of regulated companies. See his "Regulation, Efficiency and Innovation," a paper presented at the Brookings Institution Symposium on The Rate Base Approach to Regulation, June 1968, unpublished. Also p. 85 and note 119, below.

[44] His analysis enables him to estimate the influence on cost of each of his independent variables (for the most important of these see note 45). Using these data, he is able to derive an estimated cost for each company, depending on the values of these external determinants in each case. He then assumes

"that an efficient utility is one that operates within the historical, operating, and market conditions reflected by the independent factors in such a way that its actual unit electric costs

are substantially less than its unit costs estimated on the basis of the factors included in the regression analysis. Conversely, an inefficient utility will operate, subject to these conditions, in such a manner that its actual unit costs are substantially higher than its unit costs estimated on this basis. . . .

"a utility whose actual unit electric costs are either substantially higher or substantially lower than its estimated unit costs can tentatively be characterized as being relatively inefficient or relatively efficient." *Electric Utilities—Costs and Performance* (Pullman: Washington State Univ. School of Econ. and Business, 1961), 140, 142.

[45] As my student John William Wilson has demonstrated, Iulo's analysis is seriously undermined by the fact that his selected independent cost-determining variables are not truly independent of managerial efficiency or enterprise. Surely, his two most important determinants, consumption per residential customer and the distribution of sales among different classes of customers, could be importantly influenced by rate levels and structures and promotional efforts, as could such other "independent" variables as capacity utilization, consumption per industrial

THE PROBLEM OF INTERCOMPANY COORDINATION

Technology does not necessarily respect the ownership patterns and boundaries that happen to prevail in industry. This is particularly true among the public utilities, where those patterns and boundaries are rigidly prescribed by the government, and businesses are not always free to adapt to the requirements and opportunities presented by a constantly changing technology.

In these circumstances, there are often important cost savings that can be achieved by intercompany coordination. If local entrepreneurs develop community antenna television services, it is likely to be most efficient for them to string their wires from the receiving tower to subscribers' homes along the poles belonging to telephone or electric companies. The most efficient method of making a particular shipment of freight will often require that it make use of the facilities of several carriers—several railroads, or some combination of truck, rail, barge, and ship for different parts of the trip, either consecutively or simultaneously, as in the carriage of truck trailers ("piggyback") on railroad flat cars, or railway freight cars on barges. This calls for intercarrier agreements to fix joint rates, to coordinate their schedules, and to divide the joint revenues. Similarly, because of the prohibitive costs of unloading and reloading boxcars, railroads have to make cooperative agreements for accepting and using each other's cars on shipments going over more than one line—agreements for returning boxcars to their owners and compensating them in the interim.[46a] Electric companies can take fullest advantage of the economies of scale and of diversification—opportunities for both of which have grown enormously in recent decades[47]—only by interconnecting their transmission networks and entering into elaborate power pooling and interchange agreements. These arrangements enable them (1) to build much larger generating units (staggering their separate construction programs over time, taking turns in building very large increments to capacity and selling the surplus among themselves), and to

---

and commercial customer, and the typical size of the steam-electric generating stations. The implication of such interrelationships on Iulo's proposed measurement of managerial efficiency may be best illustrated by an example. Suppose an enterprising management succeeds, by vigorous promotional efforts, in increasing average residential consumption. The latter factor would be included among the (cost-reducing) variables that are assumed to be independent of managerial efficiency; so management would get no credit for its own efforts that produced this result. Indeed it would show up as inefficient, because the promotional expenses would cause actual costs to exceed those estimated by application of the independent variables. See *Residential and Industrial Demand for Electricity*, unpublished Ph.D. dissertation, Cornell University, 1969, 231 246.

[46] On the general problem of direct incentives see Wein in Trebing (ed.), *op. cit.*, 54–67.

[46a] And when the carriers cannot agree on the

division of revenues or transfer prices, the regulatory commission has to decide. See, for example, the Civil Aeronautic Board's threat to rescind a 6.35 percent airline fare increase approved in the fall of 1969 if the carriers could not agree on a new plan for the division of joint fares giving a disproportionate share to the local service airlines, on the ground that their costs per mile are higher than for the trunk carriers. *Wall Street Journal*, December 19, 1969, 4, and February 2, 1970, 3; also note 69, p. 153 of Volume 1. And see the tortured history of the ICC's efforts to find a formula for freight car rental fees that would strike an acceptable balance between the interests of the Western roads, which own most of the cars, and the Eastern, which are car-borrowers. *Boston & Maine Railroad et al. v. U.S. et al.*, 297 F. Supp. 615 (1969), and *Union Pacific Railroad et al. v. U.S. et al.*, 300 F. Supp. 318 (1969), affirmed 396 U.S. 27 (1969).

[47] See page 128, Volume 1.

achieve also (2) lower operating costs (by taking power continuously, as total demand fluctuates from instant to instant, from the lowest-cost sources in the entire, interconnected system)[48] and (3) higher load factors, that is, a higher average utilization of capacity, by virtue of interregional diversities of demand,[49] than any of them could do individually.[50] There may prove to analogous advantages in setting up a more nearly national grid system interconnecting long-distance natural gas pipelines.[51]

The beauty of the free market is that it achieves collaborations of this kind by private contracts freely entered on, wherever they are economically beneficial. If there is a demand to be served, and if A refuses to cooperate with B in serving it, it is reasonable to infer that A feels it can do the entire job itself at lower incremental cost than in collaboration; in this event, it is socially efficient to permit A to do so.[52] If, instead, the collaborative device is the more efficient alternative, one would think that A or B would find it financially possible to offer the other a large enough bribe or participation in the joint benefits to enlist its cooperation.[53] For example:

---

[48] The economist will appreciate the rule that the engineers follow in order to achieve this purpose: with the help of computers, the system operator adjusts output from each source in such a way as to equalize their respective marginal costs of delivered power. See Wallace E. Brand, "Northeast Electric Bulk Power Supply," *Public Utilities Fortnightly* (June 9, 1966), LXXVII: 68, 74–78; Fred M. Westfield, "Marginal Analysis, Multi-plant Firms and Business Practice: An Example," *Q. Jour. Econ.* (May 1965), LXIX: 253–268. See the more formal demonstration of the economics of this at pp. 264–266, Chapter 6, below. As Brand points out, under the most advanced coordination, the location of each investment project will be similarly planned, to minimize system-wide costs; as a result some partners might never build a plant but always purchase from others. *Op. cit.*, 79 and 65–88, *passim*.

[49] If the daily or seasonal peaks of the various interconnected members of the pool do not coincide—that is, if their coincident (or combined, simultaneous) peak is smaller than the sum of their individual noncoincident peaks—clearly they can meet their respective peak demands with a smaller aggregate capacity if they can exchange power than if each must supply its own at all times. (If system A's and B's peaks do not coincide, A can make fuller use of its capacity by meeting some of B's demands at the time of the latter's peak and conversely; in consequence neither has to have the full capacity necessary to supply its own peak requirements. See page 96 of Volume 1, where this principle is shown to justify levying demand charges on the basis of purchases at the time of the coincident, system peak.)

Similarly, pooling permits reduction in the total amount of reserve capacity that has to be carried against the possibility of power failure; if, for example, the worst possible contingency is the loss of the single largest generating unit, one reserve unit of this size will provide full protection against power failure for two interconnected systems, whereas if the two were not connected each would have to have a reserve unit of this size to protect itself. Another way of describing the latter saving is that the chances of simultaneous outages at two or more plants are obviously less than a single outage at any one plant; as a result the same spare capacity can serve to back up many plants, if they are interconnected.

[50] U. S. Federal Power Commission, *National Power Survey, 1964*, I, Washington, October 1964, Chapters 11–16 and *passim*. Closer coordination over wider geographic areas is an important precondition for the $11 billion of savings in annual electricity costs (involving a reduction in average unit costs from the 1962 level of 1.68 cents to 1.23 cents per kwh) that the Commission estimated were achievable by 1980. *Ibid.*, Chapter 17.

[51] See Harry Thomas Koplin, *Natural Gas Certification Policy of the Federal Power Commission*, unpublished Ph.D. dissertation, Cornell University, 1952, 403–417; and Resources for the Future, *U. S. Energy Policies, An Agenda for Research*, RFF Staff Report (Baltimore: Johns Hopkins Press, 1968), 62.

[52] A might, of course, be mistaken. The defense of the free market would be a defense of letting individuals make mistakes and suffer the consequences, as they will in competitive markets.

[53] Suppose, for example, the service could sell at a price of 10, the marginal cost to A of doing the entire job itself were 7, the MC to A of permitting B to use its facilities for this purpose instead were 3 and the separate MC to B for

BARGE LINES PUSH JOINT RATE PLEA
Initiate a New Approach in Courtship
of Railroads
The love-hate relationship between those two arch rivals for hauling bulk cargoes, the barge lines and the railroads, goes back well over a century. . . .

The water carriers have for many years courted the cooperation of the railroads in setting joint water-rail rates, pointing to the better deal this would mean for shippers. . . . Every branch of the Federal Government has looked with favor on such arrangements. . . .

The Water Transport Association has now begun a new approach. . . . it has started offering examples of freight savings that could bring new profits to railroads as well as barge companies.

Floyd H. Blaske, chairman of American Commercial Lines. . . . underlined that these figures of savings were not necessarily entirely for the benefit of the shippers, hinting that "It may well be, on some of these movements, that the right economic decision is to share these savings between the shipper and the connecting railroad."[54]

Or, where even greater efficiency advantages can be achieved if the co-ordination is effected under the management of a single company, one would expect such companies to emerge or existing companies to consolidate.

So one would think that separate public utility companies could be relied on to see their mutual interest in working out joint rates, or the use of one another's facilities, or pooling arrangements, if and to the extent that coordination were economic. And to a large extent they can and they do.[55] And one might expect public utility companies to combine various operations under the management of a single, integrated enterprise, whether by an individual company taking on additional functions or by merger, where financial consolidation promises additional efficiencies. And, of course, they have.[56]

But voluntary coordination is likely to be incomplete, and has in fact been so, as we shall see. So an important task of regulation is to compel cooperation. The problem illustrates many of the limitations of the institution of regulated monopoly—the inadequate or distorted incentives of regulated companies and the inadequacy of the results when regulation plays only a passive or negative role. It illustrates also certain important problems of preserving the competitive opportunities of individual firms and prescribing the proper mix of intercompany cooperation and rivalry. Our discussion here will therefore overlap to some extent with the consideration of competitive issues in Chapter 6.

It is difficult to be certain of all the reasons for the failure of regulated companies to cooperate to the fullest extent required for optimum performance. The following must be the among the most important:

1. Pressed only sporadically or partially by competition, public utility companies are all too often simply excessively relaxed about seeking out

---

performing the service, using A's facilities, were 3. If the two collaborated, their total MC would be only 6, leaving a profit of 4, whereas if A did the entire job itself its profit would be only 3. In these circumstances, it would certainly seem that a bargain could be struck, with B giving A something between 6 and 7 and keeping for itself something between 3 and 4, thus leaving both of them better off than if A did the entire job alone.
[54] *The New York Times,* June 9, 1968, Sec. 5, 25. Copyright 1968 by the New York Times

Company. Reprinted by permission.
[55] See, for example, William R. Hughes, "Short-Run Efficiency and the Organization of the Electric Power Industry," *Q. Jour. Econ.* (November 1962), LXXVI: 592–612; Curtis A. Cramer, "Interconnection and Peak Responsibility in the Natural Gas Industry," *Land Econ.* (May 1968), XLIV: 229–234.
[56] See pp. 70–75 and 79–80, this Chapter, and Chapter 6, below.

and availing themselves of all possible opportunities for cost reduction or service improvement.[57]

2. This is particularly likely to be the case when the cost savings can be achieved only by sharing revenues with others, and the alternative is for the company to do the business entirely by itself, at rates that exceed its own incremental costs. In purely static terms, this kind of consideration would be irrational for an unregulated, profit-maximizing firm: as we have already suggested, if a joint operation would either reduce costs or increase revenues, both firms can be better off if they share the business. But this would not necessarily be the case for a public utility company, for A–J–W reasons: if one company's handling all the business itself means a larger rate base, it can earn greater total profits (over and above the cost of capital) by keeping it all to itself.[58]

3. This last obstacle might be removed by financial integration. If the two potential collaborators were to merge, it would be a matter of indifference whose rate base were expanded. Or, if individual regulated companies could integrate freely, performing the various functions under one financial umbrella, then each would find it more nearly in its interest to perform each function with the least-cost combination of media. But, as we shall more fully discuss in Chapter 6, below, financial integration might in some circumstances conflict with the preservation of competition; in consequence this route to coordination is often closed. Nor would it completely eliminate the possibility of an A–J–W distortion: if the Bell System were permitted to operate both communications satellites and underwater cable, it might still have the same irrational (from a social standpoint) preference for the more capital-intensive communications medium, though in less extreme form than when, as at present, it can use the former method only by leasing circuits from Comsat, with no contribution whatever to its own rate base.

4. Obstacles of these kinds are likely to be reinforced by dynamic considerations. When a company feels that it is in a position to hold or to take over a growing market, it may on this account forego the reductions in cost or short-term increases in revenue it might achieve by cooperating with others, if it feels that it might in this way lessen their ability to compete for that business. Telephone companies have apparently been unwilling at times to rent use of their poles at reasonable rates to other

---

[57] For an analysis attributing the recent difficulties of the electric power industry in large measure to its failure to set up regional grids as urged by the FPC and blaming that failure on the ineptitude, conservatism, and lack of imagination of managements "grown complacent on private monopoly and regulated profits," see Jeremy Main, "A Peak Load of Troubles for the Utilities," *Fortune*, November 1969, 116–119 and ff. For similar explanations of noncooperation on the part of the railroads, see pp. 81–82, this chapter and pp. 271 and 310, Chapter 6, below.
[58] See in particular the discussion of the resistance to thoroughly integrated power pooling and lack of incentive to lease facilities at pp. 50–51

and 51–52 (points 3 and 5), above, and the numerical illustration involving joint railroad carriage of traffic, at note 101, p. 81, below. On the need for electric power pooling over wider geographic areas and particularly single-area planning of additions to capacity (locating them always on the basis of cost considerations alone, rather than having the partners simply take turns), see also FPC, *National Power Survey*, I, 3, 5, 14, 30, 169–171, 199–200, and 273; Hughes, *op. cit.*, *Q. Jour. Econ.* (November 1962), LXXVI: 608 note 8; Twentieth Century Fund, *Electric Power and Government Policy* (New York: Twentieth Century Fund, 1948), 33; and notes 48 and 50, above.

communications media, such as CATV companies;[59] and electric companies have been reluctant to exchange power nondiscriminately with, or to deliver power to, cooperatives or municipal electric systems.[60] Railroad companies have often been unwilling to make their facilities available to other kinds of common carriers on reasonable and nondiscriminatory terms—for example, to offer joint rates with barge or shipping companies that did not discriminate against the latter in favor of all-rail shipment; or to develop joint rates with truckers for piggyback service fully reflecting the cost and service advantages of that integrated operation as compared with the use of all-rail facilities.[61] The possibility of hampering a competitor and taking over more of the business oneself could outweigh the attraction of a temporarily mutually profitable collaboration.

5. In circumstances such as these, companies are likely to be selective in deciding with which other firms they are prepared to cooperate; and the basis of selection need not coincide with criteria of social efficiency. Railroads, for example, have notoriously been more willing to publish attractive joint rates for all-rail shipments—involving two or more rail carriers—than for trips involving a combination of rail and water, as we shall see. One explanation would seem to be the greater mutuality of interest in the first case than in the second. Railroads are more likely to run end-to-end; and if one railroad is willing to collaborate in this fashion with another, it may expect a return of the favor for shipments in the opposite direction. Water carriers are more likely to be directly competitive. They are more likely also to be at the mercy of the railroad initiating the shipment, to let them have a share of the joint trip, and

[59] For example, the TeleCable Corp. complained to the FCC in 1969 that the General Telephone Co. of Illinois had refused to negotiate pole attachment contracts with it, in order to favor a CATV subsidiary of its own, and the Commission, in ordering a hearing, recognized the possibility that the phone company might be trying to monopolize the CATV business. *Telecommunications Reports*, May 12, 1969, 33. See also pp. 308–309, Chapter 6, below. In consequence, the FCC in 1970 prohibited telephone companies offering CATV service themselves within their (telephone) operating territories and required them to offer pole line attachment rights to others at reasonable rates and nondiscriminatorily, where space could be offered without injury to the telephone service. *In the Matter of Applications of Telephone Companies, etc.*, Docket 18509, Final Report and Order, January 28, 1970.
[60] This reluctance to cooperate has been accentuated by ideological conflicts between proponents of private and public, subsidized and unsubsidized power. See, for example, the FPC, *National Power Survey*, I, 273, 275. But the ideological rift would surely have less influence on business policy were it not that the two systems are in competition (see pp. 105–106, Chapter 3,

below); and it may be a questionable business practice to help your competitor, even if he is prepared to pay a price for your services that covers your long-run marginal costs. See, on these controversies, pp. 316–323, Chapter 6, below. On July 14, 1969, the Department of Justice filed an antitrust suit against the Otter Tail Power Co., an integrated power system in Minnesota and the Dakotas, accusing it of monopolizing the sale of electric power to more than 400 towns in that area. It allegedly did so by refusing and threatening to refuse to sell power at wholesale to towns that proposed to substitute another local distribution system—privately or municipally owned—for Otter Tail, and by refusing and threatening to refuse to carry power from other wholesale suppliers (including the Bureau of Reclamation) over its transmission lines to such towns. *U. S. v. Otter Tail Power Company*, Civil Action No. 6–69 Civil 139, U. S. District Court, District of Minnesota, 6th Division. The President of the company admitted it had established a policy of refusing to transmit federally generated power from the Missouri Basin development over its lines. *Wall Street Journal*, July 15, 1969, 6.
[61] See pp. 271–272 and 310–311, below.

less able to deny the railroad its share in the traffic they originate, for the inland part of the journey. Similarly, large, vertically integrated electric utility companies are more likely to be willing to pool power with each other, because each has something important to contribute to the pool, than to let in on equal terms small, nonintegrated distribution companies that have very little to contribute except their patronage, which they are in any event not free to take elsewhere (either because they are themselves prohibited from engaging in generation of power, or because their requirements are so small that any plant they could themselves construct would be uneconomically small in scale). In such cases, it has taken regulatory intervention to control what might otherwise be a form of predatory or unfair intermedia competition, and to impose the requirement of coordination on nondiscriminatory terms, in the interest of efficiency or of the preservation of competition. We consider some of these interventions in Chapter 6, below.

There is another, quite different kind of reason for regulatory intervention that is, however, closely related to the last: the regulated companies may "coordinate" their activities with excessive enthusiasm. The institution and division of joint rates, the arrangement of power pooling, or joint use of facilities requires constant communication between firms that are in important respects also competitors or potential competitors. It is very difficult to encourage companies to cooperate in such delicate matters as setting joint rates, the sharing of business, and the planning of investment while insisting that they compete vigorously in other respects, especially where there is a strong, general consensus among their managers that unrestricted competition tends to become destructive. So there is a strong tendency for these collaborative efforts to turn into instruments for the collusive suppression of competition among the participants and the collective exclusion of nonparticipating competitors. In consequence, regulatory commissions and antitrust agencies must try to see to it that railroad rate bureaus do not interfere with the right of individual railroads to set their own rates as they choose;[62] or that shipping conferences—associations of shipping companies that fix rates to which the members agree to adhere—are prevented from employing predatory or exclusionary practices with respect to nonmembers.[63] It will not be surprising, in light of our discussion in Chapter 1, that the

---

[62] See *U. S. v. Ass'n of American Railroads*, Civil Action 246, U. S. District Court, District of Nebraska, Complaint filed August 23, 1944, 4 F.R.D. 510, CCH 1944–45 Trade Cases par. 57,417; *Georgia v. Pennsylvania R. R. Co. et al.*, 324 U.S. 439 (1945); and the ensuing Reed–Bulwinkle Act, which exempted ICC-supervised, common-carrier rate bureaus from the antitrust laws, though still nominally insisting that the right of carriers to act independently be preserved. 49 U.S. Code 5b, 1964 ed. Also Locklin, *op. cit.*, 254, 305–306; note 1, Chapter 4, and pp. 255–307, below.

[63] See note 15, Chapter 1, above. In 1959, 63 of the 113 shipping conferences in the foreign trade of the United States employed a dual rate system, charging preferentially lower rates to shippers giving their patronage exclusively to conference members. Daniel Marx, Jr., "Group or Conference Rate-Making and National Transportation Policy in the United States," *Law and Contemporary Problems* (Autumn 1959), XXIV: 600. See *Federal Maritime Board v. Isbrandtsen Co. Inc., et al.*, 356 U.S. 481 (1958), outlawing the practice, and the 1961 amendment to the Shipping Act of 1916, in which Congress legalized dual rates if approved by the FMC and subject to other restrictions. 46 U.S.C. 813a, 1964 ed. See also *Federal Maritime Commission et al. v. Swedish American Line et al.*, 390 U.S. 238 (1968), and Charles Peter Raynor, "Ocean Shipping Conferences and the Federal Maritime Commission," *Cornell Law Rev.* (July 1968), LIII: 1070–1093.

enthusiasm of the commissions for this kind of effort is not typically great, that the antitrust agencies try harder—since preserving competition is *their* responsibility—and that neither is outstandingly successful.

The Imperfect Adaptation of Business Structure: Electric Power

The problem of intercompany coordination among public utilities, then, springs basically from disparities between the requirements and opportunities of technology, on the one hand, and the ways in which these industries are organized, on the other; and from limitations imposed on the ability of the latter to adapt to the former. It is compounded by the deficiencies of the institution of regulated monopoly—the lesser exposure of such companies to the test and pressure of competition; the possible conflict between letting them pursue their own interests and preserving competition; the A–J–W tendency; and by the limited capacity of regulation itself to require the necessary modifications of business policy—conceiving capacity in the sense both of its ability to envisage all the opportunities and its political power or legal authority to force regulated companies to grasp them.[64]

This inhibiting influence of the institutional structure that the industry has inherited from its past is well illustrated in the failure of the electric industry to take full advantage of the opportunities for power pooling. We have already enumerated both the potential advantages and the obstacles.[65] On the other hand, changing technology has been a powerful influence forcing modifications of business organization and practice over time; it would be highly misleading to imply that the latter have been utterly unresponsive.

In the early days of the industry, economies of scale in generation were slight and transmission of power over long distances uneconomic. It therefore consisted in its first decades of a very large number of self-sufficient, local operators: before 1900, indeed, it was not uncommon to have several competing distribution companies in each locality. By 1900, the pattern had emerged of local, franchised monopolists—to what extent as a result of a recognition of the superior economy of distribution monopoly, to what extent of a quest for monopoly privilege is unimportant to the present argument.[66] Rather than rely on private monopolists, many municipalities set up their own generating and distributing systems: there were 700 to 800 of these at the turn of the century.

With increasing opportunities for economies of scale in generation and the feasibility of transmission over greater distances, a growing national concentration of generating plants was, in any event, inevitable; and this alone would have required some financial consolidation and cooperation among previously separate companies. The rise of the public utility holding company, extending financial control over increasing numbers of operating

---

[64] Some of these deficiences are peculiar to the public utility arena, others more marked there but by no means absent in unregulated industry generally. It would be an interesting exercise for the reader to consider to what extent they apply outside of the regulated industries.

[65] See pp. 50–51, 64–65, and 66–69 above. On the inadequately integrated planning in the New England region, see *Municipal Electric Ass'n of Massachusetts et al. v. F.P.C.*, 414 F. 2d 1206, 1208 (1969).

[66] See pp. 2–3, Chapter 1 and pp. 117–119, Chapter 4, below.

companies, was undoubtedly motivated in part by the quest for such economies, including also providing the member companies with more efficient management than they could muster on their own and the advantages of technical assistance, and of centralized, large-scale purchasing of supplies and equipment and raising of capital.

To these inducements the booming stock market of the 1920s added immense opportunities for promotional profits and financial manipulation. The organizers could vote themselves large blocks of stock as compensation for their promotional efforts. By vesting in the holding companies the voting common stock of the operating companies, by raising the preponderant portion of the required capital by sale of bonds, preferred stock and non-voting common, and by pyramiding holding companies on top of holding companies, the promoters could with comparatively small investments control vast empires of subsidiary companies.[67] Exercising this control, they could then exploit the operating companies and through them the ultimate customers, by selling equipment and technical, managerial and financial services to them at inflated prices. They could bid up the prices of operating company assets by exchanging them for securities of the acquiring company —securities that the investing public gobbled up at inflated prices; and they could then write up the book value of the assets acquired in this fashion. With *Smyth v. Ames* still controlling, the result could be a higher rate base for purposes of rate level determination. And by trading so heavily on equity, they could enormously increase the returns on the relatively small amount of invested capital represented by their own investment in common stock and thus also increase its saleability to the avid, investing public—as long as the industry prospered.[68] As a result, the frenzied building of holding

---

[67] Suppose the operating companies that are to be acquired have a total capitalization of $1 billion, $\frac{3}{4}$ financed by sale of senior securities— bonds and preferred stock—and $\frac{1}{4}$ by common stock. Assume for the moment all of the common stock carries voting privileges and that it takes ownership of $\frac{1}{2}$ of it for effective control. In this event, it would take an investment of only $125 million to acquire control over the $1 billion system. But suppose, instead, the acquisition of the required $125 million of operating company stock is made by one or a number of first-level holding companies—perhaps by exchange of holding company securities for operating company stock—themselves financed in the same proportions. These companies—whose assets will consist entirely of the $125 million of operating company common stock—can themselves be controlled, similarly, by a purchase of only $\frac{1}{8}$ of their securities, or only $15,625,000. Assume, finally, that this stock is to represent the total assets of a single, peak holding company, financed in the same proportions, and add the other device: assume that only $\frac{1}{2}$ of *its* common stock carries voting privileges. Then it can be controlled by an investment only $\frac{1}{16}$ as large, or just under $1,000,000. So by a minimal, three-layered pyramid total assets of $1 billion

come to be controlled with an investment of only $\frac{1}{16}$ of $\frac{1}{8}$ of $\frac{1}{8}$, or $1/1024$ of that total. And to the extent that the promoters take any of the voting stock at one or another level for themselves as their promotional fees, the required investment on their part drops to an even smaller fraction.

The $1/1000$ is not at all fanciful. See James C. Bonbright and Gardner C. Means, *The Holding Company* (New York: McGraw–Hill Book Company Inc., 1932), 113–116. The Standard Gas and Electric Co. system, with a total investment of $1.2 billion, was controlled by $23,000 of common stock. Twentieth Century Fund, *op. cit.*, 36.

[68] Suppose the senior securities of all the companies in the example in the preceding footnote carry an interest of 4% and the operating companies earn 5% on their invested capital. Of their total earnings of $50 million, thus, $30 million go to the senior securities' holders (4% of $750 million) and $20 million belongs to the common stock, $\frac{1}{2}$ of which is owned by the first level holding companies. This represents an 8% return on their total invested capital ($10 million on $125 million). Of this $10 million, $3,750,000 goes to the bond and preferred stock holders (4% on the $\frac{3}{4}$ of the $125 million financed in this way), leaving $6,250,000 for the $31,250,000 of

company empires and the resulting consolidation of financial control of the industry went far beyond the dictates of economy or efficiency.

The state regulatory agencies were in large measure powerless to prevent this exploitation of their customers—to disallow the inflated service charges, to write down the inflated rate bases of the operating companies. They were powerless because they lacked the competence to make the necessary evaluations, the financial resources and the political strength to stand up to the powerful holding companies, and the authority to do so unless they could prove "bad faith" or "abuse of discretion" before the courts, to which they were certain to be dragged. Least of all could they strike at the heart of the problem by blocking the spread or requiring the dissolution of these vast and intricate holding company systems that created virtually unlimited opportunities for financial manipulation, overcapitalization, cost of service padding, and concealment—for "prestidigitation, double shuffling, honeyfugling, hornswoggling, and skullduggery," in the words of William Z Ripley.[69] By 1929, seven such systems controlled some 60 percent of the electricity generated in the United States.

Recognition and dissatisfaction with the emergent state of affairs grew during the 1920s. But it was the financial collapse of the major systems after the 1929 crash that set the stage for the ultimate reform. The assets of the holding companies consisted, after all, of little more than the common stock of the operating companies at the base of the pyramid. And since at each layer a very large portion of their capital was raised by debt-financing, it took only a comparatively slight deterioration in the fortunes of the operating companies to convert the enormous rates of profit higher up in the pyramids to equally enormous losses; leverage works downward as well as upward.[70] Widespread defaults on debt and the subsequent revelation of the rich record of financial manipulation and exploitative practices[71] led to the passage of the Public Utility Holding Company Act of 1935.

---

their common stock—a return of 20%. Since the peak holding company owns ½ of that common stock, its total earnings on this account are $3,125,000. Of this amount only $468,750 is needed to pay the holders of its senior securities (4% of the $11,718,750 they have contributed to the entire $15,625,000 investment), leaving $2,656,250 for the common stockholders—a return on their $3,906,250 investment of approximately 68%. If, in this example, the operating companies' return on investment were not 5% but 6%, this would produce a return to their common stockholders of 12% and a return to stockholders of the peak holding company of over 130%. Further pyramiding, such as did in fact occur, would provide even more striking examples of leverage, and these too would not be fanciful. See the clear illustrations of both pyramiding of control and leverage of earnings in Eli W. Clemens, *Economics and Public Utilities* (New York: Appleton–Century–Crofts, Inc., 1950), 491–493.

[69] *Main Street and Wall Street* (Boston: Little, Brown & Co., 1927), 303, as quoted in Clemens,

op. cit., 499.

[70] Let the return of all the operating companies in the example in note 68, above, fall from 5% to 4% and the return on all the common stock, up and down the pyramid, drops to 4% too. Let the former return decline only to 3½% and the common stockholders in the peak holding company suffer a loss—after paying the $468,750 they owe on their senior securities, if they can—of $1,093,750, or about 28% of their total investment in that single year. A drop in operating company return to 3% gives their common stockholders a return of precisely zero and common stock of the peak company earnings of minus 60% on investment.

[71] Notably in the *Final Report* of the Federal Trade Commission's investigation of electric and gas utilities, undertaken in 1928 at the direction of Congress and summarizing some 70 volumes of testimony and exhibits. *Utility Corporations*, 70th Cong., 1st Sess., Senate Document 92, Part 72A (1935). See also Bonbright and Means, *op. cit.*, especially Chapters 5–7.

The Act decreed a "death sentence" for the third and higher levels of holding company pyramids. It directed the Securities and Exchange Commission to effect a simplification and reorganization of the entire structure, to refashion the industry into a number of geographically compact systems each composed of functionally interrelated operating companies, with holding companies being permitted to retain control of more than one such integrated system only on demonstration that dissolution would involve "the loss of substantial economies."[72] In addition, it empowered the SEC to institute pervasive controls over the operations of holding companies and their relationships with subsidiaries.

"By 1951 the Commission had undertaken the reformation of corporate structures including more than 200 holding companies and nearly 2,000 other companies. In 1952 it reported that 85 percent of the job was done."[73]

By 1964, the proportion of electricity generation controlled by holding companies had been cut to 21%.[74]

There seems to be little dissent from the conclusion that the job the SEC did in dismantling the jerry-built holding company structures needed doing and was well done.[75]

But it began to appear, 25–35 years after the passage of the enabling act, that the SEC's discouragement of new holding company systems was increasingly incompatible with the dramatic technological developments that became manifest in the decade after World War II.[76] The sharply increasing economies of scale in generation and long-distance transmission at high voltages counselled integration of the industry over wider and wider areas. Largely because of the traditional, localized structure of the industry, a tradition intensified by the unhappy experience with the holding companies and by the 1935 Act, the necessary coordination was achieved principally by voluntary collaboration among operating companies. The collaboration typically fell considerably short of achieving the full possible advantages of complete integration, and particularly the integrated planning of investment.[77] So, paradoxically, Lister and Homan observe:

"The problems to which the Holding Company Act was directed have almost entirely disappeared, a tribute to the Act and its administration. The great problem of the future for the electrical utilities is that of integration and interconnection of systems."[78]

---

[72] Even in this event, continued affiliation was to be permitted only for geographically contiguous systems and only if "the continued combination . . . is not so large . . . as to impair the advantages of localized management, efficient operation, or the effectiveness of regulation." 15 U.S. Code 79k (b) (1), 1964 ed.

[73] Wilcox, op. cit., 368; see 362–369. For a more detailed discussion of the Act's enforcement, see Robert F. Ritchie, Integration of Public Utility Holding Companies (Ann Arbor: Univ. of Michigan Press, 1954).

[74] Lister and Homan, op. cit., IV, Chap. 2, 41; see 30–48.

[75] See, in addition to the others already cited,

A. J. G. Priest, op. cit., II, 515. "[P]erhaps," writes Priest, "in Victor Hugo's phrase, God was bored with non-integrated holding companies. He could have been forgiven for that sentiment." Ibid., 520. It is a mildly amusing footnote to a footnote that Professor Priest had not included the qualifying adjective "non-integrated" in an earlier published version of this remark, "The Public Utility Holding Company Act Revisited," Public Utilities Fortnightly (August 1, 1968), LXXXII: 31.

[76] See p. 128, Volume 1.

[77] See pp. 50–51 and 66–69, above, and the sources cited there.

[78] Op. cit., IV, Chap. 2, 48.

And so they pose some challenging questions:

"Might a fundamentally different organization of the electric power industry best serve the interests of efficiency? . . . The ways of achieving an efficient production structure are no longer bound to local distribution systems.[79] The existing integrated corporate structures, however, still reflect the local origins; and so far as the corporate entities operate in a self-contained way, they tend to nullify the results of advancing technology. When the advantages of inter-corporate collaboration are recognized, it becomes a matter of public interest that the advantages should materialize; and the question arises, whether this should happen solely at the discretion and convenience of separate corporate managements. This poses a new type of regulatory problem.

"Like the corporate structure of the industry, the authority and procedures of state regulatory commissions also reflect the local origins of the industry. As the generating and transmission systems progressively transcend local and intrastate limits, state authority is not only curtailed, but becomes increasingly ill-defined. If generation and transmission were organized in regional networks separate from distribution functions, the lines of regulatory authority would be clear-cut as between state and federal agencies. With the present corporate structure, they can hardly fail to become confusingly intermingled and overlapping.

"These problems of structure and regulation, it must be recognized, are relative. They have not prevented much of the industry from making striking technical progress. But they do define a fundamental difficulty or anomaly: a striking lack of compatibility between the corporate structure of the industry, its emerging technical imperatives, and the procedures by which it is regulated."[80]

The electric utility industry consisted in 1965 of 3,614 companies in all. Some 3,000 of these were local distribution systems owned by municipalities or rural cooperatives, the majority of which did not generate their own power, but purchased it from the 42 federal projects and from the 243 privately owned systems, preponderantly fully integrated (in generation, transmission, and distribution).[81] The central issue today is whether those 243 are not too many or too incompletely coordinated to take full advantage of the potential economies of scale. The answer seems definitely in the affirmative—as far as the bulk supply of power (in contrast with its local distribution) is concerned. William R. Hughes has concluded that if the private sector of the industry were organized into a maximum of twenty to thirty major systems of roughly equal size it could not only more fully achieve the

---

[79] See the suggestion by Leland Olds, ten years earlier, that planning for mass production of electric power at minimum cost required the separation of local distribution from generation and vesting the latter in huge regional grids, jointly owned by the distribution companies served. "The Economic Planning Function under Public Regulation," *Amer. Econ. Rev., Papers and Proceedings* (May 1958), XLVIII: 553–561.

[80] *Op. cit.*, IV, Chap. 6, 6–8.

[81] The 243 private companies generated 75% of the power sold for public use, the federal projects an additional 14%. The publicly but not federally owned companies and cooperatives accounted for another 11% of the power generated but served perhaps 20% of the retail customers. Figures from the U. S. Department of Commerce, *Statistical Abstract of the United States, 1967*, 526, with more detailed breakdowns, for 1962, in the FPC, *National Power Survey*, I, 17.

available economies of scale—he estimates the efficiency loss from the actual, suboptimal system at four to ten percent of the total cost of power—but it could also pioneer more effectively in extending the "scale frontiers," that is, in promoting technological progress along lines that would further increase the advantages of size. Others have argued that an even greater consolidation of the industry is desirable.[82]

The industry's response has been a renewed merger movement, which, together with an increased resort by smaller distributors to wholesale purchases of power, has resulted in a sharp decline in the population of small companies, public and private, with their own generating facilities.[83]

As the Lister–Homan observation suggests, it was not just the structure of the private industry that had become outmoded by technological progress; the same was true of its regulatory apparatus. The deficiency to which they refer resides in the federal system, with its division of responsibility between the state and federal governments. One consequence of this has been to increase the reluctance of local electric companies to interconnect and pool with others across state lines, because it would bring them under the jurisdiction of the federal agency.[84] Another has been the imposition of restrictions on such coordination by the various state laws and commissions, for fear that it would make the local companies dependent on outside sources of supply, the reliability of which the individual states are less capable of guaranteeing. From the opposite standpoint, there is the problem that the authority of the responsible agencies to compel companies to take full advantage of the opportunities for integration is frequently inadequate.

The Federal Power Commission has only limited powers along these lines. It lacks authority to license construction of interstate transmission facilities; it can compel interconnection of systems only on the petition of others and it cannot in any case do so if this requires one of the parties to enlarge its generating facilities;[85] and it cannot force the separate systems to adopt a

---

[82] Hughes, "Technological Change, Scale Frontiers, and the Organization of the Bulk Power Industry," to be published in a volume of papers delivered at the Brookings Institution Conference on Technological Change in the Regulated Industries, 1969, processed, Charles River Associates, 15, 42, 52–53. See also p. 281, below.

[83] Between 1955 and 1965, the number of private electric supply systems with generating plants declined from 315 to 243 while the total number of such systems dropped from 581 to 472. In the same period the total of publicly but nonfederally owned systems increased from 2,060 to 2,114, but those with generating plants declined from 913 to 813. *Statistical Abstract of the U.S., 1968,* 513.

[84] See p. 30, above.

[85] "Whenever the Commission, upon application of any state commission or of any person engaged in the transmission or sale of electric energy . . . finds such action necessary or appropriate in the public interest it may by order direct a public utility (if the Commission finds that no undue burden will be placed upon such public utility thereby) to establish physical connection of its transmission facilities with the facilities of one or more other persons engaged in the transmission or sale of electric energy, to sell energy to or to exchange energy with such persons: *Provided,* That the Commission shall have no authority to compel the enlargement of generating facilities for such purposes, nor to compel such public utility to sell or exchange energy when to do so would impair its ability to render adequate service to its customers. The Commission may prescribe the terms and conditions of the arrangement to be made between the persons affected by any such order, including the apportionment of cost between them and the compensation . . . reasonably due any of them." 16 U.S. Code 824 (b), 1964 ed.

The Commission's authority is similarly limited with respect to natural gas pipelines. 15 U.S. Code 717f (a), 1964 ed.

In any event, the FPC availed itself of the above authority in the landmark *City of Shrewsbury*

completely integrated planning of the construction and utilization of their facilities. In consequence, as we have already observed, the degree of coordination actually achieved falls considerably short of the optimum. The efforts of the FPC to obtain such powers[86] and the development of pooling on a voluntary basis, as well, are both complicated by continuing controversies over the Commission's authority over the wholesale rates charged by pool members[87] and the terms, if any, on which publicly owned generating or distribution companies are to be admitted to such pools. Since these issues concern the appropriate role and definition of competition in the industry, we reserve consideration of them for Chapter 6, below.

There is another potentially effective way in which regulatory commissions can force coordination on reluctant companies: to the extent that they have the authority to certificate (or refuse to certificate) proposed new investments, or to decide what investments they are prepared to permit a company to include in its rate base, they can disallow those commitments of capital that reflect insufficient integration. Thus, as we have already suggested,[88] the Federal Communications Commission has it within its power to overcome any possible reluctance of established common carrier companies to lease facilities from the Communications Satellite Corporation, and any corresponding bias in the direction of constructing their own terrestrial (or submarine) facilities, by refusing to certificate the latter investments. This very issue was presented in the application of AT&T in 1968 to lay additional submarine cable (the TAT–5) between New York and Southern Europe, a request strongly contested by Comsat. The Commission may or may not have made the correct decision in giving the applicants a green light,[89] but there was no question that it had the opportunity here of

---

case, in which it ordered the New England Power Company to interconnect with the facilities of that city's municipal distribution company and in this way to give the city the opportunity of getting its power at a lower rate. *Shrewsbury Municipal Light Department v. New England Power Co.*, 32 FPC 373 (1964), upheld in *New England Power Co. v. F.P.C.*, 349 F. 2d 258 (1965). A number of other small systems responded to that decision by filing similar complaints with the Commission. Charles R. Ross, "An Alternative to Small-Scale Generation and Transmission," an address before the Legal Seminar of the American Public Power Association, Atlanta, Georgia, November 14, 1966 (mimeo), 10–11. For a later example, see the FPC's Opinion 550, November 5, 1968, *Gainesville Utilities Department et al. v. Florida Power*, E–7257, ordering the latter company to interconnect with and to serve the former on terms prescribed by the Commission. The order was sustained by the Circuit Court of Appeals, 5th Circuit, in *Florida Power Corp. v. F.P.C.*, May 1, 1970. See, similarly, *Otter Tail Power Co. v. F.P.C.*, 429 F. 2d 232, (1970).

[86] It has recommended passage of the Electric Power Reliability Act of 1967 (S. 1934, H.R. 10727), which would, among other things, authorize establishment of regional planning

councils, including all segments of the industry, "to review, test and coordinate plans for bulk power facilities throughout a region"; would give it power to review the construction of extrahigh-voltage transmission lines "to insure their consistency with high standards of reliability, usefulness, efficient utilization of land and conservation of historic sites and other limited resources"; and to "authorize the Commission to require interconnections between bulk power suppliers. . . ." FPC, *Annual Report, Fiscal Year 1967*, Washington, 1968, 5. This Report also summarizes the several cases in which the Commission ordered integrated private utility companies to interconnect with publicly owned distribution systems, and to supply them with wholesale power at reduced rates. *Ibid.*, 19–20; see also note 85, immediately preceding.

[87] See the discussion of the FPC's successful assertion of expanded authority along these lines, at note 71, Chapter 1, above, and of the industry's attempt to reverse it, pp. 322–323, Chapter 6.

[88] See pp. 51–52 and 56, this chapter, above.

[89] Its decision has the flavor of an effort to keep both contending parties happy by assuring them "fair shares" in the expanding international communications business. In granting the application of AT&T, IT&T, RCA, and Western

correcting for any possible biases in the investment decisions of the companies subject to its jurisdiction. The burden of the argument of this chapter is that regulatory commissions have too seldom had either the competence, the willingness, or sufficient authority to substitute their judgments for those of private management in this fashion.[90]

REGULATORY PLANNING

As the preceding discussion has demonstrated, regulatory intervention neither need be nor should be confined to the passive offer of inducements to private management. On the contrary, the more competent the commission and its staff and the broader and more clear-cut its legislative mandate, the greater are the possibilities of its assuming the initiative in influencing the performance of the companies under its jurisdiction.

An appropriate place to begin is with the Federal Power Commission

---

Union to participate in the project, it attached a condition that the parties

"use satellite circuits . . . in numbers sufficient to insure that the unfilled portion of the TAT–5 cable and of new satellite facilities (i.e. Intelsat III–1/2 or IV) provided within the 1970–72 time frame . . . will each be filled at the same proportionate rate. . . ." *In the Matter of American Telephone and Telegraph Company et al. Applications for authorization to participate in the construction and operation of an integrated submarine cable and radio system etc.*, Memorandum Opinion, Order and Authorization, 13 FCC 2d 235, at par. 10 (iii) (May 1968).

It is difficult to decide whether this sort of compromise—uncomfortably reminiscent of ICC policy in regulating the competition between different transportation media (see pp. 21–22, Chapter 1, above)—was likely to result in as seriously an inefficient distribution of the business as it has in the field of transportation. The majority of the Commission seemed to feel that there was an immediate prospective need for additional capacity that only the cable could supply, that for that need the cable was the lowest-cost alternative, and that the uncertainty about the future state of the art in both cable and satellite technology justified giving both media an opportunity to grow together and probe the possibilities of improving their respective technologies. On Commissioner Johnson's dissent concerning the relative economy of the two alternatives, see p. 122 of Volume 1 and especially note 98. As he remarked at one point in the proceedings,

"If ATT wants to invest in an uneconomic cable why not let them? If a manufacturer invests in uneconomic plant he will suffer competitive disadvantage, may lose money, and may even go out of business. ATT, however,

suffers no such risk. ATT's investments, once approved by the Commission, go into its 'rate base.' Forever after its charges for telephone service will be fixed by the Commission at levels adequately high to provide a 'rate of return' on that investment. Thus, unless uneconomic capital investments are challenged by the Commission they will be unchecked. . . ." FCC, Letter of February 16, 1968 to Richard R. Hough, Vice President, AT&T, FCC 68–212 12514, Dissenting Opinion.

[90] This is the conclusion, also, of Clemens, *op. cit.*, 127–131. One would have thought that the comparative costs of cable and satellite would have played a major role in the FCC's TAT–5 decision. And, in fact, in its earlier invitation to AT&T to submit that application, the Commission did conclude that the cable would be the more economical expedient for the near future (see note 89, above). Perhaps because of the vigorous dissent on this question by Commissioner Johnson, it is instructive that in its final decision the Commission simply retreated from cost comparisons.

"[W]e do not believe that any useful purpose would be served by going over relative costs. . . .

"[W]e do not feel it necessary to make definitive findings on the relative merits of TAT–5 and present . . . satellites.

"[T]here are difficulties in making comparisons between cable and satellite costs. . . ." As cited by Posner, *op. cit.*, *Stanford Law Rev.* (February 1969), XXI: 617 note.

For another example of a regulatory commission passing up the opportunity to take a strong initiative at the investment planning stage, an initiative strongly proposed by its own staff and presiding examiner, see the discussion in Chapter 4, pp. 154–155, below.

itself, since we have just been commenting on the inadequacy of its powers to impose true integration on the electric industry. Given these limitations, the Commission did take an important and creative step forward, in 1964, under its statutory mandate to:

"divide the country into regional districts for the *voluntary* interconnection and coordination of facilities for the generation, transmission, and sale of electric energy. . . . It shall be the duty of the Commission to promote and encourage such interconnection and coordination. . . ."[91]

Its *National Power Survey*, published in that year, represented the first effort to carry out that mandate on a national level. As the statutory language indicates, the Commission has no power to enforce its recommendations, and there remain difficult problems in securing the necessary cooperation from the industry. Still, this initiative—involving in its preparation the cooperation of all portions of the industry, and serving as a stimulus to industry-conducted efforts, as a goal, and a model—was a laudable and successful effort to overcome the inherent limitations of the regulatory process.[92]

Regulatory commissions may be able to play a creative role of this kind mainly indirectly—by actively refashioning the structure of the industry—or directly, by framing comprehensive rules for the conduct of the regulated companies and specifying the results they are to achieve. The outstanding example of regulatory intervention along both these lines was the one we have already briefly described—the complete reconstitution of the financial superstructure of the electric power industry and pervasive regulation of dealings between parent companies and subsidiaries, carried out by the SEC under the Public Utility Holding Act of 1935.

In contrast, the comprehensive and systematic reorganization of the railroads called for in the Transportation Act of 1920 never took place. (A comprehensive restructuring did take place in the 1960s, but as we shall see in Chapter 6, it was hardly systematic and hardly a reflection of active regulatory planning.) The roads emerged from World War I, during which period they were actually under government ownership, amid widespread concern about their financial strength, credit worthiness, and ability to provide adequate service. In consequence, whereas regulation before 1920 had been essentially restrictive and negative, designed essentially to prevent abuses, the revision of 1920 directed itself primarily to the promotion of a strong railroad industry. To this end it specifically instructed the Interstate Commerce Commission to make valuations of railroad property and adjust rates to permit a fair return. It conferred on the ICC for the first time the power to fix minimum as well as maximum rates, reflecting the further shift in emphasis from the prevention of exploitation to the curtailment of competition.[93] More directly relevant, it directed the Commission to take a more active role both in influencing the industry's structure and controlling its performance. The ICC was, for the first time, given authority to establish

---

[91] 16 U.S. Code 824 (a), 1964 ed., stress supplied.
[92] See Hughes, "Regulation and Technological Destiny: The National Power Survey," *Amer. Econ. Rev., Papers and Proceedings* (May 1966), LVI: 330–338. Also Leland Olds, *op. cit.*, whose proposals of eight years earlier the FPC was in part following in making its survey.

[93] This is not at all to disavow the Kolko, Hilton, or Boies thesis that this had always been an essential purpose and inherent tendency of the Interstate Commerce Act. But the novel provisions of the 1920 Act do support our own qualification of that thesis. See note 64, Chapter 1, above.

rules for the exchange of freight cars (this one happened in 1917), to require joint use of terminals, to control the building of new lines and abandonments of service, to compel a railroad to extend its lines where required "by the public convenience and necessity," and to permit or disallow pooling (which had previously been forbidden) and mergers (which had previously been systematically and successfully attacked under the antitrust laws).[94]

Most dramatically emphasizing the shift intended by the framers of the 1920 Act from negative controls to positive planning, from a primary reliance on competition and antitrust to coordination and consolidation, was the directive to the ICC to prepare a plan for the consolidation of the nation's railroads into a limited number of systems of roughly comparable efficiency, financial strength, and profitability. The primary intention here, as in the rest of the Act, was to improve the financial position of the railroads as a group, while avoiding conferring unnecessarily high returns on the strong companies. The conception was, accordingly, that the reorganization of the industry would involve the joining of strong and weak roads, with the effect of equalizing profitability, permitting such rate increases as were required to improve the financial health and credit attractiveness of the entire system, forestalling abandonment of service by unprofitable lines, and permitting improvement and extension of service generally.[95]

This ambitious legislative effort was an almost total failure. As early as 1921, the Commission boldly published the comprehensive reorganization plan prepared for it by Professor William Z. Ripley of Harvard; but the plan came under such bitter attack, from such a variety of sources within and without the industry, that it lost heart, concluded by the mid-1920s that the task was infeasible, and asked Congress to relieve it of the responsibility. Only after Congress had failed several times to act did the ICC, finally, publish its own plan, in 1929.[96] Partly because of this delay and partly because of the long depression that followed, no consolidations were carried out by plan between 1920 and 1940, in which year the provision was abolished. As a matter of fact, numerous railroad acquisitions and consolidations took place, notably by long-term lease and by the use of holding companies—the latter being uncovered by the Commission's new authority over mergers—but

---

[94] This account of the Act of 1920 and the experience under it draws heavily on Stuart Daggett, *Principles of Inland Transportation*, rev. ed. (New York: Harper & Brothers Publishers, 1934), 584–606 and Chapter 39, and Locklin, *op. cit.*, 226–252, 296–304, 392–404.

[95] It was hoped that the same purpose could be achieved, in the interim, by the Act's so-called recapture clause, which provided that if in any year a carrier earned in excess of 6 percent on the value of its property, it was to turn over one-half of the excess to the ICC, which could use the proceeds to make loans to needy carriers, or to acquire equipment which it would in turn lease to them. (The other half was to be retained by the successful roads and accumulated in a reserve fund that would enable them to maintain dividends, interest, and rental payments in poor years.) This provision was almost totally in-

effective, because of the inability of the Commission to work out a system of railroad property valuation (on which the 6 percent cutoff rate of return was to be computed) acceptable to the Supreme Court [see *St. Louis & O'Fallon Ry. Co. v. United States*, 279 U.S. 461 (1929), overturning the Commission's valuation for failure to give consideration to reproduction cost]. It was destroyed by the great depression of the 1930s, and was given a decent burial in the Emergency Railroad Transportation Act of 1933. See Locklin, *op. cit.*, 231–232, 248–249, 392–395, 400–401; Sharfman, *op. cit.*, Part III, Vol. B, 221–255.

[96] See the comprehensive account by William Norris Leonard, *Railroad Consolidation Under the Transportation Act of 1920* (New York: Columbia Univ. Press, 1946), Chapters 4 and 5.

"judged in the light of the major object which Congress sought to accomplish when it enacted the consolidation laws, that is, the combination of weak and strong roads into a limited number of systems balanced as to size, competitive strength and earning power. . . . the results were negligible."[97]

We cannot here appraise the purposes of the consolidation clause of the 1920 Transportation Act. Its basic approach of having profitable roads acquire unprofitable ones was economically questionable[98]—involving as it did an implicit intention of fostering internal subsidization, of protecting some companies from deserved extinction and uneconomic services from abandonment. This was not the way to increase the efficiency of the entire system or to equip it to meet the only-just-beginning competition of the motor carrier. On the other hand, there seem to have been significant economies that could have been achieved by a well-designed system of consolidation, including important economies of compulsory coordination;[99] and to a considerable extent all three goals—efficiency, protecting weaker roads, and the preservation of competition—were entirely compatible.

The point is that some of the disadvantages of the smaller roads were purely strategic, rather than a reflection of either inefficiency on their part or an inability of the territories they served to support continued service. And these disadvantages could have been eliminated by an appropriate program of mergers, with the consequence not only of strengthening the smaller roads but also cutting transportation costs. As Daggett stated:

"Some strategically located systems use their exclusive control over certain terminal facilities or their ability to divert traffic from one to another of their connections to extort a species of monopoly profit, which enriches them while keeping other railroads poor. This practice has a two fold result upon the

---

[97] *Ibid.*, 261; see Chapters 6 and 7 and pp. 257–267.

[98] Daggett pointed out it was impossible to achieve the asserted purpose of permitting such rate increases as might be required to raise profits of the railroads, taken together, to reasonable levels, while avoiding the injustice of conferring excessive returns on the already profitable roads—except by concealment. The reason is that the terms of the consolidation would presumably involve the stockholders of the separate companies obtaining participations in the new, merged company more or less in proportion to the earning power of the predecessor railroads. Stockholders of the profitable roads could be expected to acquire stock in the successor company in disproportionately large amounts, and the stockholders of previously unprofitable companies in disproportionately small amounts, compared with their original investments. Raising or holding the return of the successor company to reasonable levels would still have the effect of conferring supernormal returns on the former and subnormal on the latter. *Op. cit.*, 596–597.

[99] Leonard concluded:

"It is safe to say that the failure of the railroads

to consolidate has meant a financial loss to them and the nation running into billions of dollars." *Op. cit.*, 267.

And he criticizes both the Transportation Act and the ICC for their failure sufficiently to have emphasized this purpose, rather than the mere support of weak roads by the strong. *Ibid.*, 281–283. (We will have occasion in Chapter 6 to consider these possibilities and whether the ICC did a more successful job of planning the substantial restructuring of the industry that took place in the 1960s.) These advantages could conceivably have been achieved by coordination alone, without need for financial consolidation. This was the major purpose of the Emergency Railroad Transportation Act of 1933 (Public Law No. 68, 73rd Cong.), creating the office of the Federal Coordinator of Transportation:

"Congress apparently contemplated such things as pooling of equipment, joint use of tracks and terminals, and cooperative effort of many sorts." Locklin, *op. cit.*, 246.

This hope, too, was disappointed: the initiative in working out these plans was to be taken by committees of the railroads themselves, and managements simply could not agree. *Ibid.*

public. That is to say, it tends to hamper railroad development in the territory of the less favorably situated carriers, and it causes deflections of traffic and consequent wastes of transportation that are disadvantageous to shippers and consumers as a whole. The underlying purpose of the Ripley plan was to minimize these practices by giving to each of the great systems of the country easy access both to sources of traffic and to destination points in large selected territories, a result which would be of undoubted advantage to railroad transportation as a whole."[100]

That is to say, consolidation plans could have overcome the handicap of small lines stemming from their lack of direct access to points of traffic interchange or origination. Under unregulated competition this meant their competitors had the first shot at such traffic, even in situations in which the disadvantaged lines might conceivably have been the more efficient carrier for their portion of the journey.

"Too often this factor is overlooked, and consolidation is considered as contributing to the solution of the weak-and-strong-road problem only through saddling weak and unprosperous lines upon the stronger."[101]

In any event, the call for bold Commission planning brought no effective response, mainly because the Act gave the ICC no power to compel such reorganizations as it felt were required. Its only authority was to reject mergers submitted for its consideration that did not, in its judgment, conform to the overall plan. Leaving the initiative entirely to the railroads, the plan failed because railroad managements did not respond to the opportunity— partly because no executive was willing to "consolidate himself out of a job,"[102] and partly because of their ingrained hostility to collaborating in so

---

[100] *Op. cit.*, 601–602. See also 597 ff.

[101] Locklin, *op. cit.*, 396.

The reader will recognize here another illustration of the problem of intercompany coordination, discussed earlier in this chapter: two roads may perform the transportation function more efficiently in combination, but one of them, in a position to do the entire job itself, chooses not to take on the other as a partner. The question may, again, be asked: if B (the weaker line) could do its portion of the haul at lower marginal costs than A, why would it not pay A to turn to B for that portion of the task? It would seem there ought to be a price for the service, somewhere between the incremental costs of A and B, respectively, at which both would profit from such an arrangement—B would make money and A would save money (see note 53, above). Suppose, for example, A originates some X to Z traffic at point X, but for the second part of the trip, between points Y and Z, it could be carried either by A's circuitous route, at an MC of 3, or B's more direct route, at an MC of 2. Clearly both A and B would be better off if A let B do the carrying in exchange for a share of the joint rate anywhere between 2 and 3. But what if the published rate for the YZ trip is 5? If that is the price B charges on traffic originating at Y and if it would be illegally discriminatory for it to take any less as its share of any joint X to Z rate that it sets in collaboration with A, A would be better off keeping all the traffic and pocketing the difference between its MC (3) and the fare for the Y to Z portion of the trip (5). If, that is, the quoted tariff for the business in question (Y to Z) exceeds the marginal cost of both high- and low-cost carriers, and they are not in a position to negotiate a lower price *between* their marginal costs, it will pay the higher-cost carrier to keep the business rather than share it. A's incentive to do so might be increased, too, by the possibility that, denied the opportunity to participate in such collaborative arrangements, B might eventually have to go out of business, or might be induced to sell out to A at a favorable price. A financial consolidation of the two would eliminate such obstacles to having each portion of the business handled by the physical facility with the lowest incremental cost.

But compulsory coordination, imposed by the regulatory agency, could produce the same result and preserve the competition between A and B. See 273–275, 285–287, below.

[102] Leonard, *op. cit.*, 269 note, quoting the president of the Baltimore and Ohio Railroad.

thoroughgoing a fashion.[103] Finally, some of the blame must go to the ICC itself: it was not to be expected that a commission, with some 40 years behind it of passive and negative regulatory experience, would be prepared to undertake so bold and controversial an initiative.[104]

Interestingly, it was an ICC examiner, John S. Messer, who, 40 years later, tried unsuccessfully to induce the Commission to take a bold new initiative, this time by directly prescribing certain aspects of railroad performance. Messer's radical suggestion was that the ICC for the first time assert the authority to impose on all railroads in interstate commerce certain minimum (and improved) standards for passenger service.[105] The recommendations issued from the first investigation of the adequacy of passenger service in the Commission's 81-year history: it had been generally assumed previously that the ICC had no authority in this area—an assumption that the Commission reaffirmed in 1969 when it overturned the Messer decision.[106]

---

[103] The economist is naturally reluctant to accept explanations of business behavior that run in terms of suspicion and "irrational" attachment to independence. It is conceivable that the proponents of consolidation exaggerated the opportunities for cost reduction; and that the principal reason for the failure of strong lines to merge with weak was that there were no mutually acceptable terms on which the former could have been expected to take on the burdens of the latter. But the institutionalist will recognize that men are motivated by considerations other than maximizing the profitability of the companies they manage; and that they cannot necessarily be counted on to seize all opportunities for pursuing their own goals, whatever they may be.

[104] See *ibid.*, 271–281; Sharfman, *op. cit.*, Vol. 3A, 482–483; Williams, *op. cit.*, 199 ff.; and for a general appraisal, the *Doyle Report, op. cit.*, 249–272.

[105] He proposed, among other things, that:

"Trains operating over a line of railroad in excess of 250 miles must include in their consist facilities for meal service of no less a standard than that provided by an automat car as previously described.

"Every train engaged in transporting passengers . . . between the hours of 10 P.M. and 8 A.M. must include in its consist adequate sleeping-car accommodations.

"Trains whose transit-time is 12 hours or more must include in their consist adequate sleeping-car accommodations and a diner-lounge car as well as additional meal service when required.

"All cars used for the transportation of passengers must be equipped with air conditioning and heating facilities, lighting, rest rooms, and drinking water, all in good operational order. These cars must be maintained in clean and sanitary condition, both interior and exterior.

"The average speed of passenger trains must not be less than that of the carrier's most expedited freight train." *Adequacies—Passenger Service—Southern Pacific Company Between California and Louisiana*, Report and Recommended Order, Interstate Commerce Commission, No. 34733, served April 22, 1968, mimeo (hereinafter, Messer, *op. cit.*), 44.

[106] *Adequacies—Passenger Service—Southern Pacific Co. between California and Louisiana*, Report of the Commission, 335 ICC 415 (1969). It was generally accepted that before passage of the Transportation Act of 1958 authority over passenger train service had been left entirely to the states. The 1958 Act gave the ICC authority only with respect to proposed discontinuations of passenger service and only where the operations in question were subject to state regulation: (1) with respect to interstate service, to suspend any proposed discontinuations for one year if it found the continued operation "required by public convenience and necessity" and not unduly burdensome on interstate or foreign commerce and (2) with respect to intrastate service, to *overrule* any state agency's order *prohibiting* discontinuation, on petition by the carrier and on a finding that "the present and future public convenience and necessity permit of such discontinuance . . . and . . . the continued operation or service . . . will constitute an unjust and undue burden upon the interstate operations of such carrier or carriers. . . ." 49 U.S. Code 13a, 1964 ed. See also note 107 immediately following and Locklin, *op. cit.*, 256–257, 578–580.

The Hearing Examiner concluded that the ICC did have the power to regulate the quality of passenger service, on the basis of the provision of the Interstate Commerce Act that imposed on common carriers the duty "to provide and furnish transportation upon reasonable request therefor" and "to provide reasonable facilities." 49 U.S. Code 1 (4), 1964 ed. He justified the

Equally striking is the fact that the recommended decision came ten years after enactment of the Transportation Act of 1958, which made it much easier for railroads to discontinue unremunerative passenger service;[107] during the decade, they had availed themselves of the opportunity in increasing measure, and passenger service had, in fact, been severely constricted in quantity and deteriorated in quality.

The Examiner's proposal reflected a widespread conviction that the railroads were abusing the privilege—pursuing a deliberate policy of downgrading passenger service, in order then to justify its discontinuation. The Commission itself had on this basis refused a few years earlier to permit a requested discontinuation.

"The evidence in this proceeding makes it abundantly clear that Southern Pacific has continued to discourage use of these trains by passengers. In fact, it has intensified its efforts in that direction. Whenever it appears, as it does in this proceeding, that a carrier has deliberately downgraded its service in order to justify discontinuance of a train irrespective of the actual or potential needs of the travelling public, the Commission will order the service to be continued. See *Pennsylvania R. Co. Discontinuance of Passenger Service*, 320 ICC 319, 323 (1963). The Commission will not find burdens on interstate commerce within the meaning of Section 13a of the act to be 'undue' if those burdens are voluntarily created by carriers for the purpose of obtaining a favorable decision from the Commission."[108]

So, in this later *Southern Pacific* case, on the basis of similar findings—

"The evidence . . . justifies the conclusion that the S.P., and other railroads, has downgraded its passenger-train service and that this has contributed materially to the decline in patronage"[109]

Examiner Messer took the next logical step, requiring that the quality of service be positively improved.

---

novel assertion of authority on the ground, first, that the Commission had in the past abstained in deference to the wish of state commissions to control passenger service themselves, whereas in the Southern Pacific proceeding it was five states that had petitioned it to intervene, and second, that it had not been as necessary in the past for the ICC to step in to protect passengers in this way:

"Humans were certainly not excluded from such humanitarian considerations out of callousness or indifference, but rather because the human creature was being treated with deference and accorded every consideration. . . . Today, we are confronted with an entirely different situation. While we still have laws to protect the treatment of dumb animals, the human beings riding the involved passenger trains are provided marginal eating and no sleeping facilities on a 2,033 mile run which takes 45 hours and 15 minutes to complete, if the train is on schedule." Messer, *op. cit.*, 8; see 3–11.

[107] See note 106, immediately preceding. Congress passed the law because it believed that state regulatory commissions had unduly obstructed abandonments, with the consequence that the freight business was forced to subsidize passenger traffic. For other provisions of the Act, see note 12, Chapter 6, Volume 1, and pp. 23–24, Chapter 1, above. As far as interstate service is concerned, the Act gives carriers the right to discontinue any portion thereof, entirely on their own volition, merely by giving 30 days advance notice, subject only to the above-mentioned authority of the ICC to suspend the proposed discontinuation for a year. On intrastate service, the carriers must, as before, apply to the state authorities for permission to discontinue, but the Act for the first time permits them an appeal to the ICC. The latter agency may then overrule any state restraining order under the conditions cited above—that is, where it finds that continued provision of the service does in fact impose a financial burden on the interstate operations of the carriers.

[108] As quoted by Messer, *op. cit.*, 31.

[109] *Ibid.*, 41.

To some extent he was probably trying to force the railroad company to do something that was not to its advantage—that is, to carry on a noncompensatory passenger operation at the expense of its stockholders and other classes of customers. This purpose is betrayed by his references to the public service obligations of the railroads and to the past favors conferred on them by society, giving rise in turn to an obligation to serve that, the Supreme Court had earlier declared, "cannot be avoided merely because it will be attended by some pecuniary loss."[110] This explicit intention to preserve a system of internal subsidization is suggested also by the Examiner's recognition that the increases in freight rates that had been permitted in the past "would not have been as large as they were if there had been no passenger deficit," and by his observation that decisions to abandon certain passenger services were "motivated on the principle that profitability was the only criterion, with total disregard of the social and economic needs of the public."[111]

But in other respects the proposed decision both recommended and reflected a more active assumption of responsibility by the ICC for producing a more efficient performance of the railroad industry in strictly economic terms. First, following the lead of the Commission's own comprehensive 1959 report on the *Railroad Passenger Train Deficit*,[112] as well as the various Congressional and Presidential reports on national transportation policy (alluded to in Chapter 1), it pointed out the numerous ways in which the passenger revenues and costs *of the railroads* understate the total benefits and exaggerate the economic costs of travel by rail relative to other media. Among the externalities and distortions listed were the benefits to local communities at large of continued availability of passenger service, the congestion of roads and airways, the flagrantly discriminatory burden of state property taxation, and the inflation of railway labor costs by unreasonable union contract provisions.[113] So, Messer made wide-ranging recommendations for corrective action by local and state governments, Congress, and the railroads themselves. He recommended, for example, that local governments purchase the railroad depots (thereby removing the property from the tax rolls), maintain them at public expense and rent them back to the roads at reasonable rents; he suggested, further, that carriers be authorized to abandon service to communities refusing to enter into such arrangements.[114] The failure of legislatures to eliminate or correct these many market

---

[110] *Alabama Public Service Commission et al. v. Southern R. Co.*, 341 U.S. 341, 353 (1951).

[111] *Op. cit.*, 39, 29, respectively.

[112] 306 ICC 417 (1959).

[113] On some of these distortions see pp. 130, 161 note 2, 165–166 note 12, and 199, all in Volume 1, and notes 199 and 200, Chapter 5, below.

[114] Messer, *op. cit.*, 45. He summarizes the recommendations of the ICC report on the *Railroad Passenger Train Deficit*:

1. Repeal of the 10 percent federal excise tax on passenger fares;
2. Reduction of federal taxes;
3. Reduction of state and local taxes;
4. Provision of state and local subsidies;
5. Greater use of passenger-trains by various government agencies. All these involve government-imposed distortions or corrections of market imperfections. The remainder call for corrective action by the railroads themselves:
6. Elimination of duplicate services by railroad management;
7. Experimentation with new types of equipment;
8. Improvement in the attractiveness of passenger service, as a means of stimulating more traffic;
9. The undertaking of management studies of possible fare adjustments, schedule

distortions cannot fairly be cited as evidence of the defects of regulation by administrative commission.

Second, and even more challenging, the Examiner did not hesitate to substitute his own judgment for that of the railroad's management in deciding whether passenger service was or could be made to be financially remunerative. He revised the company's proffered revenue and cost figures, which produced a purported operating deficit of over $4 million in the test year (1966)—primarily by excluding from allegedly "out-of-pocket" costs expenditures for such things as maintenance of equipment and of right-of-way and structures on the ground that these would not be "eliminated as a result of discontinuance. These are fully allocated costs and are not of a savable nature."[115] These revisions converted the loss into an estimated $700,000 annual profit. This profit, he asserted, would more than offset the expenses of the sleeping-car and diner-lounge car that he wanted to require the railroad to restore. As for the future, he rejected the company's projections of continued decline in demand for passenger train travel, asserting, instead, that

"If the defeatist attitude of the rail carriers could be overcome and reasonable efforts be made to improve the passenger service, a considerable portion of the lost patronage could be recovered."[116]

Setting aside, for the moment, the fact that it was eventually aborted, what are we to make of this attempt on the part of a regulatory commission to tell private management how to pursue its own interest? To the extent that this last interpretation of the recommended decision is appropriate, a regulator was not here proposing quality standards in order to prevent a monopolist from exploiting consumers by poor service; rather, he was arguing that improvement in service would be in the interest of both company and customers. If the passenger service in question either did or could be made to cover its incremental costs, why would not a profit-maximizing company, monopolist or otherwise, see and pursue its own interest in cultivating it? The question is obviously an institutional one, and cannot be answered within the framework of an assumption of perfectly rational, profit-maximizing behavior by regulated companies.[117] In view precisely of the institutional deficiencies of regulation, an important one of which is the danger that a conservative management may respond to competition by retrenchment rather than by risk-taking innovation, the economist probably should applaud this kind of initiative on the part of regulators. The possible benefits of a more dynamic, competitive performance probably outweigh the economic waste that would occur if the commission's appraisal of the market prospects proved to be incorrect.[118]

---

changes and improved promotional activities. *Ibid.*, 41–42.

These suggestions are more fully discussed also in the *Doyle Report*, 445–491. In the fall of 1969 the Department of Transportation announced that it would shortly propose legislation for upgrading the nation's railroad passenger service. *Wall Street Journal*, September 26, 1969, 3.

[115] *Op. cit.*, 17–18, 37–38, and Appendixes D

and E. On the governing economic principles and the nature of the ICC's measurements, see pp. 150–155, Volume 1.

[116] *Ibid.*, 41.

[117] See the similar observation in note 103, above.

[118] Since the full Commission's rejection of the trial examiner's recommended decision turned on the legal question of its authority to require railroads to improve passenger service, it is not of substantial economic interest. In fact, the ICC

Perhaps the greatest opportunity for regulatory commissions assuming a more active role in the direct planning of industrial performance is offered by the general and growing discontent with traditional rate-base, rate-of-return regulation among regulated companies and public alike. We have already detailed its limitations: its concern with the minor portion of total costs and with a comparatively unimportant aspect of total performance. The question inescapably presents itself: could not commissions instead focus directly on, and specify standards with respect to the major aspects of performance—the level and trend of prices, the extent, quality, variety and reliability of service? These could, most of them, be formulated in quantitative terms; and it could only be helpful to all parties for commissions to monitor and publish their measurements of performance in these various dimensions. Conceivably, commission and companies might concentrate their efforts on striking a bargain specifying what would constitute a reasonable performance in some predetermined period of time, with the former agreeing to permit the latter a rate of return that would vary in proportion to achievement of the agreed-upon goals. Both parties might work toward translating the bargain into an estimate of the company's total financial requirements, and the proportion that it would be allowed to recover in its rates. The emphasis would in this way be shifted from the costs of existing levels of service in some past year to the estimated costs of producing *desired* or *projected* levels of service in the future.

There are obvious problems in designing an acceptable list of performance goals properly related to what is economically achievable and in devising a system of rewards neither too great nor too small to elicit the desired results, and to be payable only upon delivery. But the effort would be in the right direction.

THE ADJUDICATORY ROLE AND ITS CONSEQUENCES

But such examples of Commission initiative—apart from the more informal and continuous advice and prodding, whose intensity, frequency, and effectiveness are difficult to characterize[119]—remain the exception rather than the rule. And, apart from the SEC's enforcement of the Public Utility Holding Company Act, their accomplishments have been limited. Pre-

---

had earlier supported Messer's substantial conclusions, when it refused to let the Southern Pacific drop the service in question on the ground that the company had "deliberately downgraded the service" in order to discourage passengers. See p. 83, above. When, therefore, in overturning the Messer decision, the Commission later decided it lacked authority to regulate the quality of service, it recognized that the petitioning states were powerless, too, and therefore specifically asked Congress to give it that power:

"What we have in mind are requirements for the restoration of reasonable standards of service, equipment, and facilities, giving due regard to the carrier's resources and the willingness of the public to provide its support and patronage. . . .

"Within the framework of these standards . . . we believe the quality of service offered by the Nation's railroads can be significantly improved." 335 ICC 415, 433, 435 (1969).

For another striking example of regulatory initiative, in which an examiner proposed that his Commission rise above the mere choice between competing applicants or mere approval or disapproval of applications before it, see the discussion of the *El Paso* gas case at pp. 154–157, Chapter 4, below.

[119] See Morgan's reference to the "endless cases" in which active commissions have given engineering advice and assistance, *op. cit.*, 242–247, and insistence that much more could be done along these lines, *ibid.*, Chapter 7, "Elements of a Constructive Program."

ponderantly, regulation has been a negative process, with the initiative coming from the companies themselves; private parties act, and commissions react. From this fact follows most of the other severely criticized characteristics of the regulatory process: it proceeds on a case-by-case basis, on issues usually framed and a record made up by contesting parties, rather than on occasions and issues formulated by the government itself in terms of its own, independent judgment of the public concern.[120]

The function of the regulator therefore becomes primarily adjudicatory rather than executive or legislative. Commissions come to be set up as courts, constrained by elaborate rules of evidence designed, principally, to protect the interests of the private litigants rather than for the formulation of general policy by expert bodies. This leads in turn to vexatious restrictions that deny commissioners the right to consult informally with industry representatives or with their own staff, who are treated in the same way as other litigants, when such *ex parte* contacts would be conceived of as prejudicial infringements on the impartiality of the commissioner-judges. Another consequence of this "overjudicialization of procedures"[121] is that Commission decisions typically must be confined to rulings on written records developed by litigants in adversary proceedings; outside evidence may not be considered.

This case-by-case adjudication tends often to degenerate into pragmatic, timid compromises between the contending private interests. The result is all too often a decision to keep existing competitors alive and to permit each to enjoy its "fair share" of the business, rather than one embodying well-formulated general considerations of the public interest.[122] And this of course

---

[120] So, for example, the Circuit Court of Appeals overturned a Federal Power Commission decision licensing the Consolidated Electric Company to install pumped storage facilities on the Hudson River over objections raised by conservationists that the project would destroy scenic values, in the following terms:

"In this case as in many others, the Commission has claimed to be the representative of the public interest. This role does not permit it to act as an umpire blandly calling balls and strikes for adversaries appearing before it; the right of the public must receive active and affirmative protection at the hands of the Commission." *Scenic Hudson Preservation Conference v. Federal Power Commission*, 354 F. 2d 608, CA2d (1965).

As Commissioner Ross interpreted this instruction, the Court was telling the Commission that it

"had a duty to independently advance its own position and not just rely on the position advanced by the utilities, to put on a case that it considered in the public interest." Richard Hellman, *Government Competition in the Electric Utility Industry of the United States*, processed, unpublished Ph.D. dissertation, Columbia University, 1967, 99/12 note.

[121] Harry M. Trebing, "A Critique of the Planning Function in Regulation," *Public*

Utilities Fortnightly (March 16, 1967), LXXIX: 24. See this article, 21–30 and his "Toward Improved Regulatory Planning," in the same journal, March 30, 1967, 15–24, for an excellent summary and survey of these criticisms of regulatory procedures and functions.

[122] "The inability of social organization to adapt quickly and with foresight is illustrated well by the FCC. Despite the vast changes in both technology and the market circumstances of those using the spectrum, the Commission retains the criteria for spectrum allocation developed at the outset of regulation. There is no evidence that it has ever seriously considered revision of its methods of assigning uses of the spectrum in any way which would take directly into account alternative social benefits, though this consideration must implicitly enter into many of its decisions. . . .

"The most disturbing evidence that the Commission is unlikely to lead in the establishment of a new regulatory scheme for communications is its continued practice of separating rather than joining inseparable problems. The Commission has separate inquiries and issues separate rules with respect to STV [subscription television], CATV, telephone rates and earnings, domestic satellite communication, international satellite communication, telegraphy, UHF frequency

reinforces the tendencies to restriction of competition and protectionism
already discussed in Chapter 1.[123]

---

allocation, multiple station ownership, broadcast advertising, computer time-shared operations, etc. As is true of many other organizations, it appears to do little in studying broad aspects of its own *raison d'être* and the public interest therein." Almarin Phillips, "Television and New Communications Technologies: An Overview of Problems of Public Policy," address at the annual meeting of the Southern Economic Association, Nov. 16, 1967, unpublished ms, 26–27.

The criticism of the FCC must surely be tempered by a recognition of the extraordinary difficulty of planning for spectrum allocation in the face of so rapidly changing a technology— and of the limitations of relying on a free market to achieve a more efficient result. But it is instructive that President Johnson felt it necessary to set up a special Task Force on Communications Policy to attack all these interrelated issues in coordinated fashion; the regulatory commission was really not suited for providing this kind of overview. See *Global Communications System, Message from the President of the United States Transmitting Recommendations Relative to World Communications*, House of Representatives, 90th Cong. 1st Sess., Document No. 157, August 14, 1967. See also note 135, below.

According to W. N. Leonard, the deficiencies of this kind of quasi-judicial, case-by-case proceeding have been particularly glaring in the ICC's supervision of the mammoth merger movement among American railroads during the 1960s (see also pp. 288–290, Chapter 6, below).

"The ICC sits as a quasi-judicial body considering each application brought before it by rail managements, limiting its judgment to a determination of issues present in the record. This procedure has numerous drawbacks, namely:

"1. Certain self-interested corporate and financial groups may set the pattern of mergers rather than have it come about as a deliberate expression of public interest.

"2. The ICC cannot go outside the record to promote mergers which might be more in the public interest.

"3. It fails to take into account the fact that one important merger in one section of the country affects all competitive relations in this area, and that where several mergers are pending in one area, the cases inexorably shade into each other requiring a rearrangement of competition on a regional basis.

"4. The ICC can be entrapped into approving merger No. 2 because it has approved merger No. 1, and so on. . . .

"5. It leaves the raising of basic issues to the opponents of the merger, and if the opposition withdraws, as in the case of the Norfolk & Western-Nickel Plate-Wabash merger, there may be an inadequate record." "Issues of Competition and Monopoly in Railroad Mergers," *Transportation Journal* (Summer 1964), III: 8.

"It has been a stereotype of political wisdom that the bureaucrat is ever ready to exercise authority arbitrarily. But there is the far greater danger that the second-rate, insecure personality who often finds his way into bureaucracy will become uncomfortable at having to exercise authority and will anxiously seek to placate as many interests as possible. This fear to offend, complaisance, and readiness to listen and be 'fair' and 'reasonable' clog the muscles of the will, and what begins in amiability can end in corruption." Louis L. Jaffe, "The Scandal in TV Licensing." Copyright 1957, by Harper's Magazine, Inc. Reprinted from September 1957 issue of Harper's Magazine by permission of the author (CCXV: 77).

[123] A logical corollary of "fair-shares" is "don't rock the boat," a particularly inappropriate policy in the face of the rapid technological changes that have occurred in many of these industries.

"They now act more as arbiters of disputes between the modes than as the instigators of industry practices which are designed to keep pace with rapidly changing conditions and techniques. Very much like industry leaders, they subscribe to the principle of: 'Don't rock the boat.' . . . The only trouble with this philosophy of Government is that technical advances and rapid changes in industry do not likewise subscribe to a philosophy of gradualism. 'Fair and impartial regulation of all modes of transportation,' as provided in our national transportation policy, does not mean the disallowance of new methods and business practices based upon technical advances because it is believed one mode will benefit rather than another if permission is granted. There is every reason to believe that the Interstate Commerce Commission's early views upon piggyback, for instance, may have been based upon such apprehensions. This 'Don't rock the boat' philosophy leads to pusillanimity in the regulatory agencies. . . . For instance, in 1958, when

Another result of the case-by-case approach—along with their usual solicitude for the interests of the regulated companies—is the failure of commissions to lay down and enforce clear guidelines of permissible performance. An outstanding example has been the failure of the FCC to make its grant to private broadcasters of exclusive franchises for portions of the precious radio spectrum conditional on adherence to strict standards of quality—with respect, for example, to the length, frequency, and intensity of sound of their commercials or their allocation of time to educational or other public service programming. The Commission does purport to take into account proposed programming, in choosing between applicants for broadcasting licenses, but it has not typically seen to it that successful licensees kept their promises. Except in a few cases of flagrant abuse, involving, for example, continuous attacks on minority groups, or taking of extreme political positions, or the purveying of misleading advertising, the Commission has almost universally and automatically renewed licenses of existing broadcasters.

"The actual programming bears no reasonable similitude to the programming proposed. The Commission knows this but ignores these differentiations at the time when renewal of licenses of the station is before them."[124]

Under strong internal and external pressures (see notes 124 and 126), the FCC began to make threatening gestures during the course of 1969, suggesting it might not renew the licenses of particularly glaring offenders. Although the major cases turned mainly on allegedly excessive concentration of control over communications media in the locality (notably the ownership of TV and radio stations by local newspapers),[125] there were some in which the Commission reluctantly[126] entertained competing applications from parties

---

the rail carriers were urging Congress to permit them to engage in motor and water operations, the position of the expert body, the Interstate Commerce Commission, upon this crucial question was:

'This proposal involves extremely broad policy questions which only the Congress can resolve. . . . Whether this policy should be reversed or modified is a most important question on which the Commission is not prepared to express an opinion at this time.'

"If the expert body was not in a position to express an informed opinion upon this grave question, no one was. As a matter of fact, the members of the Commission could not help but have a strong opinion upon the matter; they simply did not choose to express that opinion individually or as a commission." The *Doyle Report, op. cit.*, 218–219.

[124] Landis, *op. cit.*, 54. For a more thorough survey and indictment see especially the devastating *Broadcasting in America and the FCC's License Renewal Process: An Oklahoma Case Study*, a statement by Commissioners Kenneth A. Cox and Nicholas Johnson on the occasion of the FCC's renewal of the licenses of Oklahoma broadcasters, released June 1968. This study

prompted the *New York Times* to remark, editorially:

"Of all the regulatory agencies in Washington, the Federal Communications Commission is the one with the biggest rubber stamp." June 11, 1968, 42M.

See also a strong earlier dissent by FCC Chairman E. William Henry, joined by Commissioner Cox, on the renewal of licenses of eight stations in Mississippi, Louisana, and Arkansas on July 22, 1964. FCC, Public Notice—B, July 24, 1964, Report No. 5173.

[125] See note 9, p. 254, Chapter 6, below, on these developments.

[126] See the case involving its withdrawal of an earlier renewal of the license of WPIX–TV, in New York—a renewal granted without investigation of charges that the station had been distorting news broadcasts and without considering the competing application by a group of community leaders. *New York Times,* June 19, 1969, 1 and Daniel Zwerdling, "FCC Impropriety," *The New Republic* (June 21, 1969), CLX: 10–11. Also, the opinion of the Circuit Court of Appeals excoriating the Commission for its hostility to intervenor witnesses represent-

who complained that the programming of the incumbent licensees were unusually poor or objectionable—advocating racial segregation, or inadequately representing the interests of minority group viewers, or featuring excessive violence or insufficient public service programming.[127] In one case, involving KHJ–TV in Los Angeles, its examiner, in a 111-page report, recommended stripping the license from a particularly offensive licensee on the ground that it had "miserably failed to serve the public interest," dedicating most of its air time "to the service of the young, the congenitally gullible and those not very bright." He cited surveys that ranked the station first only in showing movies and another that found in one week it had depicted 181 murders, 98 attempted murders, 55 "justifiable killings," 18 shootings, and eight kidnappings.[128] It was generally expected that President Nixon's 1969 appointees to the FCC could be counted on to restore the Commission to its former sanity.[129]

---

ing the United Church of Christ and the National Association for the Advancement of Colored People, who opposed the renewal of a license for WLBT–TV in Jackson, Mississippi on the ground of allegedly racially biased programming. So angered was the Court by the FCC's handling of the case that it voided the licenses itself and ordered the Commission to invite competing applications. *United Church of Christ v. FCC*, CCA for the District of Columbia, June 20, 1969.

[127] See the survey of pending cases in the *New York Times*, April 27, 1969, 72.

[128] *New York Times*, August 18, 1969, 71.

[129] One hopeful sign was that it was the new President's appointee as Chief Justice of the Supreme Court, Judge Warren E. Burger, who had written the condemnation of the Commission's handling of the WLBT–TV, Jackson, Mississippi, license renewal (see note 126, above).

One favorite argument used by broadcasters to resist any kind of consideration or control of their program content has been the statutory prohibition of censorship and the protections of the First Amendment. Holders of these valuable public franchises, which enable them to exclude others from the right to speak over the limited airways, professed to see a violation of the rights of free speech and press in FCC requirements that, for example, they provide fair coverage of opposing political viewpoints and opportunities for reply to persons subjected to personal attacks in their broadcasts. The Supreme Court has unanimously rejected such self-serving defenses, holding that requirements such as these enhance rather than abridge freedom of speech. Significantly, the American Civil Liberties Union intervened on the side of the Commission, not of the broadcasters. Since the argument of the broadcasters has at least superficial plausibility, it is worth reproducing the Court's reasoning.

"Where there are substantially more indivi-

duals who want to broadcast than there are frequencies to allocate, it is idle to posit an unabridgeable First Amendment right to broadcast comparable to the right of every individual to speak, write, or publish. . . .

"as far as the First Amendment is concerned those who are licensed stand no better than those to whom licenses are refused. . . . There is nothing in the First Amendment which prevents the Government from requiring a licensee to share his frequency with others and to conduct himself as a proxy or fiduciary with obligations to present those views and voices which . . . would otherwise, by necessity, be barred from the airwaves. . . .

"It is the purpose of the First Amendment to preserve an uninhibited market place of ideas in which truth will ultimately prevail, rather than to countenance monopolization of that market, whether it be by the Government itself or a private licensee." *Red Lion Broadcasting Co., Inc. et al. v. Federal Communications Commission et al.*, 395 U. S. 367, 388–390 (1969).

See, along similar lines, the decision of a Circuit Court of Appeals upholding against a similar defense, and equally convincingly, an FCC requirement that broadcasters carrying cigarette advertising "devote a significant amount of broadcast time to presenting the case against cigarette smoking":

"The cigarette ruling does not ban any speech. . . .

"Even if some valued speech is inhibited by the ruling, the First Amendment gain is greater than the loss. A primary First Amendment policy has been to foster the widest possible debate and dissemination of information on matters of public importance. . . .

"where, as here, one party to a debate has a financial clout and compelling economic interest in the presentation of one side unmatched by its

The virtual absence of regulatory guidelines of acceptable performance extends also to certification policies. The FCC and the CAB often choose among competing applicants on the basis of informal considerations inadequately disclosed, leaving it to their staffs to write the supporting decisions developing the requisite rationalizations. As a result, certification decisions of these two agencies are said to defy all efforts to trace out a consistent policy.[130]

For these weaknesses, the legislatures must themselves bear a large share of blame. First, they typically lay down only the vaguest policy guidelines, enjoining the commissions to make "reasonable" decisions, to serve "the public interest," or to be guided by the "public convenience and necessity." Second, even more reprehensibly, any commission that decides to take a bold stand in the public interest can be certain that it will be called to account and threatened with reversal by a Congress—or, even worse, by the influential chairman of a congressional committee—that has been aroused to action by complaints of interested parties, including, all too often, the legislators themselves. It would be impossible here to cite more than a fraction of the examples. But this is what happened to the Federal Trade Commission in 1965, when it moved, under its mandate to stop false or misleading advertising, to require cigarette advertisements to carry clear warnings of the hazards to health involved in smoking;[131] to the FCC when it undertook its

---

opponent, and where the public stake in the argument is no less than life itself—we think the purpose of rugged debate is served, not hindered, by an attempt to redress the balance. . . .

"We do not think the principle of free speech stands as a barrier to required broadcasting of facts and information vital to an informed decision to smoke or not to smoke." *John F. Banzhaf, III* (the private party who was almost singlehandedly responsible for the FCC ruling) *v. Federal Communications Commission and U. S. v. WTRF–TV, Inc. and National Association of Broadcasters*, 405 F. 2d 1082, 1101–1103 (1968).

[130] Such procedures give rise also to the suspicion that political connections are more important than economic merit in the awarding process. For a recent example, see the major decisions involving the Trans–Pacific air route awards, in which White House favoritism was widely rumored to have played a role. Since the final decision on international route awards rests with the President, Mr. Nixon stayed the enforcement of these portions of the decision by his predecessor and instituted a reexamination shortly after taking office. *New York Times*, February 27, 1969, 81. For further reference to these inherent dangers of licensing see note 15, p. 177, below.

For a survey of the policies of the FCC and CAB, see especially Henry J. Friendly, *The Federal Administrative Agencies, The Need for Better Definition of Standards* (Cambridge: Harvard Univ. Press, 1962), Chapters 4 and 5.

"In broadcast license cases no criteria for decision have evolved. True, criteria of various

different kinds are articulated but they are patently not the grounds motivating decision. No firm decisional policy has evolved from these case-by-case dispositions. Instead the anonymous opinion writers for the Commission pick from a collection of standards those that will support whatever decision the Commission chooses to make." Landis, *op. cit.*, 53.

See also William K. Jones, *Licensing of Major Broadcast Facilities by the Federal Communications Commission*, a study done for the Administrative Conference of the United States, reprinted in U. S. House of Representatives, Subcommittee No. 6, Select Committee on Small Business, 89th Cong. 2d Sess., *Activities of Regulatory and Enforcement Agencies Relating to Small Business, Hearings*, Part 1, A103–A112, A165–A174; Jaffe, *op. cit.*, *Harper's Magazine* (September 1957), CCXV: 77–84; Harvey J. Levin, "Regulatory Efficiency, Reform and the FCC," *Georgetown Law Jour.* (Fall 1961), L: 1–45.

[131] Congress stepped in to preempt the field for four years, with its Cigarette Labelling and Advertising Act, which vetoed the FTC's proposed action and itself imposed only the very modest requirement that a mild health warning be printed on the cigarette packages. 79 *U. S. Statutes at Large*, P. L. 89–92 (July 27, 1965). In 1969, when the foregoing Act neared expiration, the House of Representatives once again passed a bill that would prohibit any agency requiring a health warning in cigarette advertising and itself proposed a reworded warning on the package. *New York Times*, June 19, 1969, 1.

first limited venture of authorizing a local test of pay-television,[132] again in 1963 when it proposed to set rules covering the length or frequency of broadcast commercials[133] and, later, in response to its timid steps, described above, to examine critically applications for renewal of broadcast licenses.[134]

Finally, Congress must bear principal responsibility for the vast diffusion of regulatory authority in many of these areas. The outstanding illustration of divided, conflicting, and overlapping jurisdiction is provided by transportation, where responsibility is distributed among the ICC, the CAB, the Federal Maritime Commission, the FPC (for natural gas pipelines), the Bureau of Public Roads, the Military Transportation Service, the Army Corps of Engineers, and the Department of Commerce, a defect only very partially and imperfectly eliminated by the constitution of the new Department of Transportation.[135]

---

[132] Wilcox, *op. cit.*, 461.

[133] This example and many others are described in William L. Cary, *Politics and the Regulatory Agencies* (New York: McGraw–Hill Book Co., 1967), 35–59. The FCC effort to limit commercials is a particularly apt illustration because it represents an obviously justified and laudatory effort on the part of a regulatory agency to move away from ad hoc determinations and to set forth general guidelines under its responsibility to issue or renew licenses on the basis of the "public convenience, interest or necessity"; and because it produced the following Congressional gem of rationalization for obstructing more effective regulation.

"In the final analysis, it is the judgment of the community which determines whether a broadcaster meets community needs. . . .

"Self-regulation by industry is an accepted and valuable supplemental regulatory tool, the effective use of which should be encouraged rather than discouraged.

"The adoption by rule of compulsory standards, on the other hand . . . would substitute Commission judgment for individual licensee judgment regarding the licensee's day-to-day responsibility of serving the community which he is licensed to serve. . . .

"Therefore . . . it is necessary for the Congress to limit explicitly the scope of the Commission's powers in this respect. . . .

"The instant rulemaking proceeding constitutes an outstanding example of a regulatory agency arrogating to itself the right to legislate." From U. S. House of Representatives, Committee on Interstate and Foreign Commerce, 88th Cong. 1st Sess., *Lack of Authority of Federal Communications Commission to Make Rules Relating to the Length or Frequency of Broadcast Commercials*, House Report No. 1054, 5–7, as cited in Cary, *op. cit.*, 46–47. The Commission did, however, warn radio stations in 1970 that it would expose them to license renewal hearings if they carried more than 18 minutes of commercials in more than

10% of their weekly broadcast hours. *Wall Street Journal*, March 13, 1970, 28.

[134] In this case Senator Pastore introduced a bill in 1969 that would prohibit the FCC from considering competing applications for broadcast licenses up for renewal unless it had first determined that renewal of the existing licensee "would not be in the public interest." S. 2004, 91st Cong. 1st Sess., April 29, 1969. In this instance the Commission evidently satisfied its Congressional critics without giving up the fight entirely. It issued a *Policy Statement on Comparative Hearings Involving Regular Renewal Applicants* declaring that in confronting competitive applications at renewal time it would give preference to existing licensees who could demonstrate that their programming had "substantially" served the needs and interests of its area. In so doing, it emphasized that by "substantially" it meant a "solid" or "strong" performance, not one "minimally" serving those interests. Commissioner Johnson asserted he could not go along with this compromise solution because it limited the possibilities of competition and denied the public the opportunity of being served by the *best possible* station, as long as the existing licensees' performance was "substantially" in the public interest. But he conceded that the Policy Statement promised a genuine improvement over the previous practice of renewing licenses in cases of all but the most outrageously bad performance.

"I have considerable sympathy and respect for my colleagues' commendable and good faith effort to resolve this conflict between formidable political power and virtually unrepresented public interest. . . . And it is not at all clear to me that more than they have done would have been politically possible, or could have withstood political appeal. It is not even clear that today's effort is secure." *Public Notice*, FCC 70–62 40869, January 15, 1970—B.

[135] See, for example, the *Doyle Report*, 94–97. For similar problems in the field of communi-

Conclusion: The Inherent Limitations of Regulation

There is an enormous body of literature, in the general area of administrative law, addressing itself to these many inadequacies of the regulatory process and proposing procedural, organizational, and substantive reforms. The question is raised, for example, whether the administrative commissions ought to retain as much of their traditional formal independence or whether they ought not, instead, be more closely integrated into the executive branch of the government and subjected more directly to the control and responsibility of the presidency. Some observers have called instead for greater control by the legislature, whether by fuller and more precise declarations of intent in the controlling legislation or by more competent scrutiny and surveillance of commission policies as they evolve. Others have recommended constitution of an ombudsman or a consumers' counsel office in the administrative commissions, to serve as a forum for consumer complaints and as an active and aggressive representative of consumer interests—an ironic suggestion considering that one might naively have assumed that this was the function of the commissions themselves, but perhaps a good one nonetheless.[136]

The extent to which the substantive, policy determinations of regulatory commissions ought to be subject to judicial review is a historic theme in American constitutional law. The courts at certain times in effect have substituted their judgment for that of the regulators in reviewing the compatibility of their decisions with the Fourteenth Amendment or with the legislative intent, and, at others, deferred almost without question to the commission's presumed "expertise." There has been much consideration of the appropriate degree of separation between the administrative, policy-making function, on the one hand, and the judicial functions, on the other, involving a great variety of correlative questions about commission organization, procedures, rules of evidence, and standards of ethical conduct. An inescapable subject has been the problem of reconciling and synchronizing the policies of the various agencies of government exercising responsibility in such fields as transportation, communications, and energy. One pervasive set of interrelated issues concerns the extent to which legislatures should be presumed to have called for a continued reliance on competition except where they have explicitly decreed otherwise; and the corresponding distribution of authority in these fields between the antitrust agencies, operating through the courts, and the regulatory agencies.

We offer no pretense even of adequately characterizing these political, administrative, and legal issues, let alone resolving them, although they

---

cations and energy see Landis, *op. cit.*, 24–30 and note 122, above. The President's Task Force on Communications Policy concluded that as a result of the fragmentation of governmental authority in that field, "policy has evolved as a patchwork of limited, largely *ad hoc* responses to specific issues, rather than a cohesive framework for planning," (*op. cit.*, Chapter 9), and, partly following its recommendations, President Nixon in 1970 established an Office of Telecommunications Policy to help make for a more coherent administration policy. *Telecommunications Reports* (September 14, 1970), XXXVI: 1–4.

[136] See, for example, the *Utility Consumers' Counsel Act of 1969*, S. 607, sponsored by Senator Lee Metcalf. Also, the responses of the administrative commissions and especially by members of the FCC in the U. S. Senate, Committee on the Judiciary, Subcommittee on Administrative Practice and Procedure, 91st Cong. 1st Sess., *Responses to Questionnaire on Citizen Involvement and Responsive Agency Decision-Making*, Committee Print, September 9, 1969.

obviously have a close bearing on the economic substance of regulation. Nor do we underestimate their importance when we observe that whatever the administrative or statutory arrangements, the tendencies and problems we have described in these two chapters are inherent in the institution of regulated monopoly and inescapable as long as we retain that as our instrument for the governance of industry. Obviously, divided authority and conflicting or unclear statutory mandates must make for an inefficient performance of the regulatory function; but attempts to centralize the responsibility and clarify the mandate cannot in themselves resolve the diverse and often-conflicting purposes that these various public interventions attempt to serve. Making commissions more independent or less, more closely tied to the executive or the legislature, more or less subject to judicial review, will serve the public interest better or worse depending on how one defines that interest, the identity and composition of these various agencies, and what kinds of influences are brought to bear on the decisions of each. There is no way a priori to determine the proper mix of regulation and competition valid for all times and places: that is why regulation is introduced here and not there. But the decision to introduce it cannot be made intelligently except with a full recognition of the inherent tendencies and limitations suggested in these chapters.

CHAPTER 3

Positive Influences on Public Utility Performance

Chapters 1 and 2 consisted, essentially, in a description of the limitations of regulation in the presence of monopoly as an institutional device for assuring good economic performance Were the performance of the public utility industries in fact unrelievedly bad and incapable of improvement under regulation, we could stop at this point and go on to happier matters. But, in fact, neither of these two conclusions would be justified. What, then, have been the positive influences? It is important to ask this question not only if we are fully to understand the objective, historical record but also if we are to find ways of improving it—because, presumably, the way to do so would be first to identify the positive influences, then to strengthen them or give them fuller play.

Evidence of Good Performance

The question of whether the performance of American public utility industries has been good or bad is almost meaningless. For one thing, the category is too broad and embraces far too heterogeneous a group of companies and industries, places and times for successful generalization. But even if we were to break the question down into separate investigations of more nearly homogeneous groups of companies, in single industries, at some particular place and time, certain major difficulties would remain. Presumably, the main relevant aspects of performance would be the following:

1. Efficiency—the level of cost.
2. The relationship of prices individually and collectively to cost—to marginal cost in the short run, to average total cost in the long run.[1]
3. Improvements in efficiency over time and the passing on of the benefits to consumers, as reflected in cost and price trends.
4. The quality of service.
5. Service improvement and innovation over time.

What objective yardsticks could we use for these five criteria, against which to measure the performance of individual companies or industries?

---

[1] The latter on the assumption that private utilities must cover ATC over time, though MC may be less.

There would seem to be only two possibilities: the record in each of these respects of *other* industries in the same area, and the record of the *same* industries in other regions or countries. As far as the first possibility is concerned, interindustry comparisons could meaningfully be made only with respect to criteria (2) and (3) above. One could compare, for example, patterns of price discrimination or rates of return or cost-price trends over time in, say, gas distribution with other industries. But such comparisons would be meaningless with respect to criteria (1), (4), and (5); it would make no sense to compare the cost of producing a ton of steel with the cost of delivering a thousand cubic feet of natural gas, or to compare the quality of the former with that of the latter. And even where arithmetic comparisons can be made, the result can be only vaguely illuminating at best and positively misleading at worst. Suppose we find, for example (as in fact we would), that the price of a day's stay in a general hospital or of a 15-minute appointment in a doctor's office (or even of an economically more meaningful service, such as the cure for a case of influenza, of a given variety and intensity) has increased sharply in the last three decades while the cost and price of a long-distance telephone call between two particular cities has gone down dramatically. This does not permit us to conclude that the performance of the health industry has been poor and that of the telephone industry good, or even that the one has been worse than the other. Obviously, the behavior and composition of the respective demands and, even more important, the character of their respective technologies and potentialities for improvement are utterly different. These same results could therefore have been compatible with the former industry doing an extremely good job and the latter an extremely bad one, considering the character of their problems and the means available to each for meeting them.

To some extent, the same kind of observations would apply to inter-country performance comparisons of the same industries. Any differences in these records might be attributable more to differences in the general conditioning circumstances of the two countries—the character and education of their labor forces, the motivations of their managers, their natural resource endowments, and so on—than to the organization and policies of the specific companies and industries in question. One way of eliminating this problem would be to develop indices of performance for particular public utility industries in, for example, the United States *relative* to that of all other American industries, and compare those ratios with corresponding indices for foreign countries. A little reflection will convince the reader of the immensity of any such task, although it could be worth trying.[2]

In any event, efforts like these could at best produce only rough approxi-

---

[2] Setting aside the question of whether it were, in fact, statistically feasible, such a comparison would presumably eliminate the effect of national differences, insofar as they operated to produce differences in the *average* performance of all industries in the two countries. It would still not eliminate national differences—for example, in the endowment of particular, required raw materials or technological resources—that operated specifically to alter the *relative* performance in each country of the particular industry in question. Yet these industry-specific differences too would have to be eliminated if one were to be left only with differences in performance attributable solely to differences in the controlling institutions, which it would be the purpose of these comparisons to measure. And, of course, the institutions would have to be substantially different among the countries being compared: otherwise the whole comparison would not shed much light on which institutions work well, which badly.

mations of answers to the only relevant question about the performance of any particular industry at any particular time and place: how does its record compare with what *might have been achieved*—by that *same* industry, at that *same* time and place—under some alternative system of control.[3] Since only one of these two records has objective existence, the task must, in the last analysis, always be one of judgment: objective, statistical comparisons can never do any more than help to inform that judgment [4] So, the few pieces of evidence that we proceed now to offer suggesting that the performance of the public utility industries in the United States along the five dimensions listed above has been "good"—or at least, obviously, not all "bad"—cannot be definitive.

It is probably fair to say that the quality of service provided by the U. S. telephone industry and in communications generally, and by the electric and gas utility companies has been good, in terms both of reliability, uniformity of quality, and the speed and courtesy with which they are provided and maintained.[5] In transportation, the verdict on this score would undoubtedly have to be more mixed. But in all these fields, it must be conceded, service is generally good, also, in terms of the variety of alternatives available to customers. In transportation and communications, particularly, there have also occurred commendable service innovations, to which we have from time to time referred—though it is questionable that the rate of innovation has in all cases been the best achievable.

As for the relationship of price to marginal cost: the elaborate value-of-service freight schedules developed by the railroads and imitated by the trucks certainly represented an effort, in principle sound, to reconcile an approach to marginal cost pricing for large-volume, low-value commodities with the coverage of joint and common costs. On the other hand, as we have already seen, the clinging by the railroads to long-outmoded, excessively discriminatory rate structures made it possible for competing carriers to take over great chunks of the business that should on grounds of efficiency have stayed on the rails, with a high resultant cost to society.[6] Although we have

---

[3] See Jesse W. Markham, "An Alternative Approach to the Concept of Workable Competition," *Amer. Econ. Rev.* (June 1950), XL: 349–361, reprinted in American Economic Association, *Readings in Industrial Organization and Public Policy* (Homewood: Richard D. Irwin, 1958), especially 94–95.

[4] See, for example, Corwin D. Edwards, "Public Policy and Business Size," *Jour. of Bus.* (October 1951), XXIV: 280–292, and Alfred E. Kahn, "Standards for Antitrust Policy," *Harv. Law Rev.* (November 1953), LXVII: 28–54, both reprinted in Amer. Econ. Association, *Readings in Industrial Organization and Public Policy*, especially 343–344 and 363–364, respectively.

[5] This verdict is offered in full recognition of the lamentable power failures, shortages, and congestions that have from time to time appeared in these industries. It seems, once again, fair to recognize that the inconvenience and indignation occasioned by these breakdowns reflects in major part the high level and rapidly increasing volume of service to which we have become accustomed—and addicted.

[6] See John R. Meyer, Merton J. Peck, John Stenason and Charles Zwick, *The Economics of Competition in the Transportation Industries* (Cambridge: Harvard Univ. Press, 1959), 187–195, 243; and pp. 14–15, Chapter 1, above. Some of these discussions are couched in terms of opposition to all value-of-service pricing. But, apart from the possibility of distorting effects at the buyer level, such price discrimination is, as we have seen in Chapters 5 and 6 of Volume 1, not objectionable in principle. The error lay not so much in the principle itself as in its misapplication, and specifically in the assumption that the value of the commodity shipped was an accurate measure of the elasticity of demand for the transportation service. See George W. Wilson, "The Effect of Rate Regulation on Resource Allocation in Transportation," *Amer. Econ. Rev., Papers and Proceedings* (May 1964), LIV: 165–166; Baumol *et al.*, "The Role of Cost in the Minimum

pointed to serious inadequacies in the rate design of the typical electric and gas utility,[7] it could still be true, as Bonbright states, that

"Along with improved engineering technology and with the development and promotion of electrical appliances, it shares the credit for the amazing success of the industry in reducing rates or keeping them from rising materially during a prolonged period of price inflation."[8]

The simplest reflection of the generally satisfactory long-run relationship between price and cost in the public utility industries is to be seen in the comparative profit rates set forth in note 76, page 52 of Volume 1. As these comparisons show, rates of return on stockholder equity have run somewhat below the levels in industry generally during the comparatively prosperous years since World War II—only slightly lower in the case of electric and gas utilities, and markedly below in the case of the telephone companies. Significantly, the profit rate of Western Electric, the manufacturing subsidiary of the Bell System, runs much lower than those of manufacturing companies generally and other electrical equipment manufacturers in particular.[9] Since public utility companies rely disproportionately heavily on debt financing, their returns on total invested capital have run even more markedly below those in manufacturing than profit rates alone.

Whether these rates of return may nonetheless still be too high is very hard to say. That they considerably exceeded the cost of capital during most of these years is suggested by the fact that the common stocks of these companies sold during the 1960s at prices markedly above their book value.[10] Still, they suggest at least a moderately satisfactory long-run relationship of prices to cost.

The much lower returns of the railroads are a good deal more difficult to cite as evidence of satisfactory economic performance. On the contrary, they reflect a combination of intensified competition, on the positive side, and, on the negative, a sluggish response by the rails and by the ICC and an

---

Pricing of Railroad Services," *Jour. of Bus.* (July 1963), XXXVI: 348–351.

It is, of course, possible that neither the rails nor the common carrier truckers were entirely irrational, from their own point of view, in clinging to value-of-service pricing, even though the former lost a large share of the business to the latter and both were forced in consequence to share their markets with unregulated motor carriers. Following the familiar monopolistic calculus, they might conceivably have been better off with high rates on the high-value freight, at the cost of a considerable loss of volume, than with lower rates and a larger share of the business. On the other hand, the recent awakening by the railroads to the deleterious consequences of their value-of-service pricing and their intensified efforts, after careful study, to reduce rates in order to regain a larger share of the traffic suggests that the previous practice was irrational from a private as well as from a social point of view. See also, on the same point, note 103 of Chapter 2 and p. 85, above.
[7] See pp. 96–100, Volume 1.

[8] *Principles of Public Utility Rates*, 315–316. See these pages also for a favorable comparison of the electric utilities in this respect with transportation companies and a quotation from a gas-company executive to the effect that "perhaps no other one factor has contributed so much to the success of the electrical business as the study of the rate problem." *Ibid.*, note 22. The success of the natural gas pipeline companies in wearing down the FPC's *Atlantic Seaboard* formula (see p. 99 and especially note 35, Volume 1) and the profusion of promotional campaigns by both electric and gas companies (see pp. 177–180, Volume 1), whatever their imperfections, similarly contrast favorably with the sluggishness of the railroads until the mid-1950s. On similar improvements by the airlines see pp. 75–76, 149–150, and 153, note 69, Volume 1.
[9] See pp. 291–292, Chapter 6, below. The profit rates of the non-Bell companies have been generally lower than of the Bell System. See Shepherd, in Shepherd and Gies, *op. cit.*, 42–43.
[10] See p. 48, note 69, Volume 1.

unhealthy financial situation that probably impairs the ability of the former to render service for which they would be the most efficient carriers.

Profit rates are, of course, only the minor indication of the appropriateness of the level of price. The major one is the level of the costs to which the profits are added (and against which the allowable rate of return is applied). As we have already suggested, there is no easy way of comparing the costs of public utility with other companies. It is worth noting, however, that the comparatively modest returns on total invested capital are not offset by unusually high rates of executive compensation. On the contrary, an analysis of 1965 data found that the great majority of electric and gas companies paid their chief executives less than companies of the same size in unregulated industries generally, and the discrepancy was even slightly greater in the case of the second and third-highest-paid executives.[11]

table 1 Average Annual Rates of Increase in Total Factor Productivity (Percent)

	1899–1953	1948–1966
Communications and Public Utilities	3.6%	...
Telephone	2.0	
Telegraph	1.8	3.8
Electric utilities	5.5	
Manufactured gas	4.7	3.7
Natural gas	2.0	
Transportation	3.2	...[a]
Railroads	2.6	...[a]
Local transit	2.5	...
Residual transport	4.0	...
Manufacturing	2.0	3.0[a]
Private domestic economy	1.7	2.4

Source. Comparisons of 1899–1953 from John W. Kendrick, *Productivity Trends in the United States*, National Bureau of Economic Research (Princeton: Princeton Univ. Press, 1961), 136–137. Comparisons of 1948–1966 from Kendrick, "Productivity Trends in the U. S. Private Economy and in the Public Utilities, 1948–1966," *Public Utility Valuation and the Rate Making Process Conference, Conference Proceedings*, April 24–26, 1968, Ames, Iowa, C–12, C–14.
[a] For comparisons of labor productivity trends alone, see note 24, this chapter, below.

The most striking indicators of good public utility performance are the long-run comparative trends in their costs and (since there have been no substantially offsetting trends in profits) their rates as well. The data in Tables 1 and 2 show this very dramatically. According to the estimates of Kendrick, the average annual rate of increase in total factor productivity (output per unit of labor and capital, combined) in communications and public utilities was more than twice as great as in the private economy

[11] "Executive Compensation in the Utility Industry" (New York: National Economic Research Associates, 1967). Of course, the public utility executives might still be relatively overpaid, in terms of merit!

generally, and 80 percent higher than in manufacturing alone, during the period 1899–1953. Their margin of superiority in the shorter period 1948–1966 was less, but still notable. The performance of the railroads in this respect was, likewise, markedly better than in industry generally and in the economy at large.[12] Roughly reflecting these favorable relative cost trends, though for a more recent time period, are the price changes set forth in Table 2. The most dramatic reductions have been in long-distance communications; but the rates for local telephone service, for electricity, gas and passenger air transportation (but not railroad freight rates) have all risen far less than the general price level. The comparative stability in these prices in a period of general inflation reflects rapid improvement in efficiency, both in absolute terms and relative to the economy at large.

table 2 Percent Change in Price, 1940–1968

Telephone rate, 3 minutes, daytime, station-to-station, New York to San Francisco	− 58
Cable and radio-telegraph, New York to Tokyo	− 53
Cable and radio-telegraph, New York to London	+ 5
Index, interstate telephone rates	− 24
Index, local telephone rates	+ 51
Index, total telephone rates	+ 10
Revenue per passenger-mile, domestic trunk airlines	+ 8
Railroad freight rates	...a
BLS indexes (% increases)	
Retail price of electricity	+ 5
Retail price, gas	+ 42
Consumer price index	+ 148
Wholesale price index	+ 153

Source. Telephone rate index numbers from AT&T statement on S. 607, to U. S. Senate, Subcomm. on Intergovernmental Relations, *Consumers' Counsel Act of 1969*, April 30, 1969; airline per mile revenues from CAB, *Handbook of Airline Statistics*, updated figures supplied by courtesy of the Board; railroad freight rates from ICC, Bureau of Economics, *Transport Economics*, June 19, 1969, 9. All others from *Statistical Abstract of the United States, 1969*.

a These were increased 36 percent, 1947–1968. The comparable percentage increase in the BLS wholesale price index was 34.

It bears repeating that these impressive accomplishments must reflect, above all, the enormous potentialities of the technology with which these industries work—potentialities for technological progress and for the economies of scale described in Chapter 5 of Volume 1. Whether the public utility industries took the best possible advantage of these opportunities cannot be disclosed by interindustry comparisons.

---

[12] See also Edwin Mansfield, "Innovation and Technical Change in the Railroad Industry," in *Transportation Economics, op. cit.*, 169–197. It must be recognized that in many of these industries the innovations that made the dramatic improvements in productivity possible were developed not by themselves but by their equipment suppliers. See, for example, Richard J. Barber, "Technological Change in American Transportation: The Role of Government Action," *Virginia Law Rev.* (June 1964), L: 845–852. For calculations producing a much lower estimated rate of advance of total factor productivity in communications than the Kendrick data, see Shepherd, "Communications: Regulation, Innovation and the Changing Margin of Competition," a chapter to appear in a Brookings Institution symposium on *Technological Change in the Regulated Industries*, ms. pp. 42–43.

The fact remains that technology does not develop unassisted by human hands, nor do the benefits of long-run decreasing costs fall as rain from heaven. The data presented do inescapably support a judgment that there have been favorable institutional factors operating in these areas of the economy. What would these be?[13]

Internal Motivations

The Profit Motive. Profit maximizers, even if monopolists, have an incentive to reduce costs, to cut rates if they think demand is sufficiently elastic, to engage in product or service innovation whenever the prospective incremental returns exceed the costs. And, we have suggested in Chapter 2, regulation is sufficiently loose to offer regulated companies an opportunity to retain any additional profits generated in this fashion—all of them for a considerable period of time, some of them (if added rate base is justified) permanently.

Managerialism. To the extent that the interests of managers and stockholders diverge, the divorce of ownership and control can produce worse results rather than better.[14] But tending in the latter direction are the exposure of public utility executives to public scrutiny and criticism, their desire to be associated with growing and progressive companies,[15] to enjoy the approbation that comes from giving good service, and to avoid unpopular rate increases—motives that are reinforced by the presence of regulation.[16]

---

[13] The following discussion draws heavily on my chapter "Inducements to Superior Performance: Price," in Trebing, *Performance under Regulation,* 88 102. Reprinted by permission of the publisher, the Bureau of Business and Economic Research, Division of Research, Graduate School of Business Administration, Michigan State University.

[14] See, for example, pp. 28–29, Volume 1, and 71–72 of this Volume.

[15] On the possible conflict between the interest of stockholders in profits and of managers in sales maximization, and the likelihood of the latter producing a more nearly competitive performance, see Baumol, *Business Behavior, Value and Growth* rev. ed. (New York: Harcourt, Brace & World, Inc., 1967), 73–75 and *passim*.

For demonstrations of the ways in which the performance of regulated companies may be expected to differ depending on the various possible motives of managers, see Milton Z. Kafoglis, "Output of the Restrained Firm," *Amer. Econ. Rev.* (September 1969), LIX: 583–589, and E. E. Zajac, "A Geometric Treatment of Averch-Johnson's Behavior of the Firm Model," *ibid.* (March 1970), LX: 117–125.

The substitution of sales for profit maximization is not unqualifiedly desirable in economic terms. In particular, it might, like the A–J–W tendency, lead to overinvestment and overproduction, with companies undertaking price reductions or promotional campaigns to produce additional sales the value of which to buyers is less than the additional costs that they entail. That is to say, it could cause production to be carried beyond the optimal point, where $MC = AR$; as long as MR is still positive at this point, total revenues could in this way be maximized. On the other hand, this tendency could merely offset undesirable monopolistic restriction of output (since of course producing only up to the point where $MR = MC$ falls short of the optimum when $MR < AR$) and, in dynamic terms, a closer approximation to competitive performance in expanding output, developing new services, and so on.

[16] Here, for example, are some of the observations made in private correspondence by a perceptive executive of a public utility company.

"I think the whole trouble is with the concept of economic man, and especially the assumed characteristics of this construct: perfect intelligence and thorough venality (at least within the limits of the law).

"An instance of the distance between economic man and real man is to be found in the fact that utility people work like mad cutting costs and benefiting consumers despite the fact that the industry is essentially a cost plus industry. . . .

"Despite what I see around me every day, and have seen for decades, some economists 'prove' that since regulation is a cost plus system the management has no incentive to cut costs. . . .

"A second example of the error of the intelligence-cum-venality hypothesis is in the article

Technological Factors

Long-run decreasing costs, in the static sense, and the dynamic *potentialities of their technologies* have already been suggested by the comparisons in Tables 1 and 2, above, and documented in Volume 1 (pp. 124–130). As we pointed out in that latter discussion, these two factors are intertwined in practice: rapidly growing demand both permits suppliers to move down along static, decreasing cost functions and impels them to more rapid technological progress. These conditions create unusually attractive opportunities for both profit and other managerial satisfactions from a progressive and efficient performance.

Market Factors

Elasticity of Demand. The more elastic industry demand, the greater is the incentive for even a profit-maximizing monopolist to set his price at the purely competitive level. The decision to regulate the public utilities undoubtedly reflects the assumption that at least large portions of the demand for their services are inelastic, and that is why consumers need protection; and the assumption is almost certainly more correct than incorrect. The demand for electricity for lighting, the basic residential and commercial demand for telephone service[17] are almost certainly quite inelastic. But in view of the fact that an estimated 47.8 percent of residential usage for electricity in 1966 was for water heating, house heating, clothes drying, and cooking—for all of which there is keen competition with other fuels[18]—there is room for considerable skepticism about the showing of econometric studies that total residential demand is inelastic.[19]

---

by Averch and Johnson. . . .

"when you look at the actual behavior of the utility companies you will quickly see that they go to great lengths to avoid capital investments. For example, the resistance to the undergrounding of electric lines; the resistance to the construction of cooling towers at generating plants . . . the vigor with which we try to buy our land as cheaply as possible despite the 'adverse' effect on our rate bases. We fight zoning cases in order to have a lower capital investment. We try hard to place our gas mains in the locations where the required capital will be less, rather than more. We risk the charge of ugliness in order to save capital by not enclosing our generating stations. . . . In example after example I can demonstrate that the management of an electric and gas utility company is positively stinky stingy in the making of capital investments despite the fact that in almost all situations r [the allowed rate of return] exceeds k [cost of capital].

"I believe it is because the real joy in this industry comes from rendering good service at low rates. . . ."

It is probably not a sufficient answer to the foregoing protestations that the behavior described is fully compatible with profit-maximization, given a sufficient regulatory lag.

There seems to be no reason whatever to doubt that managerial pride and an "instinct of workmanship" represent a separate and additional force operating in the same direction. By the same token, managerial inertia, a common attribute of public utility monopoly, operates in the other direction. See, for example, note 57, Chapter 2, and p. 81, above.

[17] See Carl Stern, "Price Elasticity of Local Telephone Service Demand," *Public Utilities Fortnightly* (Feb. 4, 1965), LXXV: 24–34.

[18] Stelzer, "Impact of Competition on Regulation: Utility Rate-Making," paper presented at a Conference on Public Utility Valuation and the Rate-Making Process, University of Iowa, April 25, 1968 (New York: National Economic Research Associates, 1968), 1–6, 18–20. One electric company reports that the average annual consumption of its customers using electricity for home heating was 22,000 kwh, compared with 5,800 for its other customers. In view of the sharp competition with other fuels for this market, this suggests a high elasticity of total residential demand. Stelzer and Bruce C. Netschert, "Hot War in the Energy Industry," *Harv. Bus. Rev.* (November–December 1967), XLV: 15.

[19] Franklin M. Fisher and Carl Kaysen, *A Study in Econometrics: Demand for Electricity in the United*

The Tennessee Valley Authority was constituted and run on the opposite premise—that sharply reduced retail rates would tap an enormous potential market. The conclusion of most students is that those optimistic predictions were proved correct, at least for that time and that area;[20] and that private power companies were moved in part by that lesson to reduce their own rates on the basis of the same expectation.[21] It is impossible not to be impressed, similarly, by the apparently enormous response of the use of long-distance telephoning to reduced rates in general and particularly to reduced night-time rates in recent years; and the sharp increase in air travel that has attended fare reductions.

"The main reasons for rapid growth in this market . . . have been lower fares and improved service resulting from intensified competition. . . . Traffic on this route appears to be elastic with respect to fares, and the staff study shows that declines in average fares bring more than proportional increases in traffic."[22]

Of course, to the extent that public utility services compete with one another, or with services supplied by outsiders, the elasticity of demand for each and the consequent likelihood of low-price policies is enhanced. This suggests the next market influence—competition.

Competition. We have already alluded at some length to the pervasive and growing competition to which the public utility companies have been subject in recent decades and to the probability that the rapid and ever more diversified progress of technology has increased its variety and intensity.[23] The effectiveness of that competition has, of course, been uneven and the results would, in the absence of regulation, be highly discriminatory. But it has been a powerful influence on at least important segments of these industries in enforcing attention to reducing rates and otherwise promoting

---

States (Amsterdam: North-Holland Publishing Co., 1962), 2–9, 134–135; H. S. Houthakker and Lester D. Taylor, *Consumer Demand in the United States, 1929–1970* (Cambridge: Harvard Univ. Press, 1966), 88, 153–154. See also Damodar Gujarati, "Demand for Electricity and Natural Gas," *Public Utilities Fortnightly* (January 1969), LXXXIII: 3–6. The Fisher-Kaysen study estimates elasticity by relating price (and other variables) to estimated stocks of various electrical appliances in users' hands. They identify electric ranges and water heaters as "two striking exceptions" to their findings. For these appliances, they assert, "the price of electricity may have a definite influence." *Op. cit.*, 5. My former graduate student, John W. Wilson's own cross-sectional studies show residential demand with an elasticity of around −1.5, and very high responsiveness of the percentage of homes with electric water heaters, furnaces, and ranges to the price of electricity. *Op. cit.*, 11–73. Compare John R. Felton, "Competition in the Energy Market between Gas and Electricity," *Nebraska Jour. Econ. and Bus.* (Autumn 1965), IV: 3–12.

[20] The Fisher-Kaysen and Houthakker-Taylor studies do suggest a considerably higher elasticity of demand in low-income areas, both within the United States and abroad. Of course, the elasticity of *industrial* demand for TVA power would be expected to be greater than that of total national demand for electricity, because, as Wilson also shows, the location of heavy electricity-using industries is highly responsive to relative price. *Op. cit.*, 172–174, 184.

[21] See, among others, Ben W. Lewis, in Leverett S. Lyon and Victor Abramson, *Government and Economic Life* (Washington: The Brookings Institution, 1940), II: 733–743; Joseph S. Ransmeier, *The Tennessee Valley Authority, A Case Study in the Economics of Multiple Purpose Stream Planning* (Nashville: Vanderbilt Univ. Press, 1942), 167–168; Gordon R. Clapp, *The TVA, An Approach to the Development of a Region* (Chicago: Univ. of Chicago Press, 1955), 93–95; Bonbright, *Public Utilities and the National Power Policies* (New York: Columbia Univ. Press, 1940), 45–47.

[22] From a CAB press release describing a staff report, *Traffic, Fares and Competition, Los Angeles–San Francisco Air Travel Corridor*, September 20, 1965.

[23] See pp. 64–65, Volume 1, and note 17 of Chapter 1, this volume.

sales, cutting costs, improving old services and offering new and more attractive ones—as our discussions in Chapter 6 of Volume 1 will partially attest.[24]

The Threat of Government Enterprise

Governments conduct an enormous variety of businesslike activities even in the United States; and the motives and circumstances have been almost equally diverse.[25]

We do not consider here whether public enterprise is superior or inferior to private enterprise as an instrument for getting the world's work done —although we allude to this question in our concluding chapter: in our judgment the question is too broad and too vague to have any meaning at least in purely economic terms. But there is strong evidence in the public utility arena that *competition between* the two systems of organization, like competition among private businesses, is highly conducive to improved performance. It may take the form of direct rivalry (for the patronage of the same customers in the same market); or of competition-by-example (where comparisons may be drawn between the performances of private and public enterprises in serving their respective customers, in different markets); or by threat of total displacement (where the management of each is aware that voters are examining its performance with the possibility of substituting one system of control for the other). When governments are willing to say to private insurance companies, for example: "if you will not design—and find low-cost ways of selling—simple, reliable, cheap, and nondiscriminatory policies, we shall," the probability of improved performance is surely enhanced[26]—either because the private companies may rise to the challenge or because, if they do not, the government may make good its threat.[27]

---

[24] It would be superfluous to add illustrations at this point. We shall also see, in Chapters 4 and 5, how unregulated competition has contributed to reduced rates and costs in trucking, air transport, and communication and provided large investors with an escape from the discriminatorily high brokerage commissions set collectively by the organized security exchanges.

It is difficult to doubt that intense intermodal competition has made an important contribution to the good record of technological progress in railroads compared with industry generally, demonstrated by the Kendrick estimates in Table 1, p. 99, above. Kendrick presents no estimates of changes in total factor productivity between 1948 and 1966 for transportation, but his figures show railroad output per unit of *labor* input rising no less than 5.1% a year in that period compared with 3.7% in transportation generally and 3.0% in manufacturing. (The source is indicated in Table 1.) This especially favorable showing is no doubt partly the accidental consequence of technological developments elsewhere—notably the introduction of the diesel locomotive and of the computer, which railroads have adopted for operations control. But along with the price and service experi-

mentation, which we have already described, it probably reflects also a delayed competitive response to the long shrinkage in their share of the total freight business. See also Barber, *op. cit.*, 824–895 and especially 836–853.

[25] See, for example, Wilcox, *op. cit.*, Chapter 20.

[26] In response to a series of insurance abuses uncovered in 1905, Louis D. Brandeis initiated a plan for mutual savings banks to sell life insurance policies at favorable rates in competition with private companies. This competition is said eventually to have forced the private carriers to reduce their rates. See Alpheus Thomas Mason, *Brandeis: Lawyer and Judge in the Modern State* (Princeton: Princeton Univ. Press, 1933), 28–30.

[27] Sometimes, of course, private companies fail to provide the service demanded because it is uneconomical, and the government can do "better" only because it subsidizes it. In that event, the government "yardstick" is inaccurate and produces a poorer rather than a better performance. The fact remains that where, as is almost inevitable, the private performance falls short of the ideal, this kind of actual or potential competition between the two systems can play an important role in improving it.

The most familiar illustration of this kind of competition in the United States has been in the field of electric power. There has been endless controversy over whether the numerous municipally owned and operated distribution companies (many of which do their own generation of power as well)[28] or the cooperatives that have been organized to supply power in rural areas, with the aid and encouragement of the Rural Electrification Administration, or the various Federal power projects like those in the Tennessee Valley are really fair "yardsticks" for determining whether private power rates are as low as they might be. Direct comparisons of rates do not, in fact, provide a fair test of relative economic efficiency: the taxes and costs of capital for public and private companies differ in material respects.[29]

The fact remains that there is intense rivalry between these public and private systems, far less in the form of direct competition in the market for the same customers than at the political level, along the lines already suggested.[30] It is clear that the public power companies—most notably TVA— were able to take the risks of setting rates low and thereby to test their assumptions about the high elasticity of demand on the one hand and the downward slope of their long-run cost curves on the other—risks that private companies either could not take or, at any rate, could not be forced by regulatory commissions to take.[31] To what extent it was the example of TVA's experience, demonstrating that it was in their private interest in any event to reduce rates, and to what extent the fear that if they did not do so there would be other TVA's set up to take over their business, is not important. The fact is that the competition-by-example or by threat of displacement

---

[28] See the statistics at p. 74, above.

[29] See, for example, Twentieth Century Fund, *op. cit.*, 436–437, 650–651, 718–720, and Ransmeier, *op. cit.*, 154–169.

[30] For a comprehensive survey and analysis, see Hellman, *Government Competition, op. cit.* There were, as of 1966, 62 cities in the United States with populations over 2,500 served by both publicly and privately owned electric utilities; and in 38 of these there was actually some degree of direct competition, some paralleling of lines, offering some customers a choice of suppliers. The residential customers served by these 38 city plants were only 0.4 percent of the national total; and even in these 38 instances the direct, competitive overlap was minor, frequently limited to some part, usually the oldest part, of the city. In contrast, there were some 1,900 municipalities, with 13 percent of the nation's total residential customers, served by municipally owned monopolies. *Ibid.*, 70–72, 76–77, 102–103.

The Federal Public Works Administration (PWA), which contributed greatly during the 1930s to the expansion of municipally owned electric power plants and distribution systems, gave most of its financial and other assistance to city plants already enjoying a monopoly. Eighty-three of its 319 allotments of funds to such companies did go to entirely new municipal systems, where a private monopoly already existed; but in the great majority of these cases, as well as in an even larger number in which the municipalities had merely made applications for PWA assistance, the application or the grant served the purpose of inducing the private companies to reduce their rates to levels satisfactory to the cities or to sell out to them—in either event avoiding an overlapping of private and public systems. The larger proportion of PWA power allotments went to Federal and State generating and transmission projects. The major contribution that projects such as these made to competition was by offering a supply of cheap, reliable power to cooperatives and municipals; but the latter distributors did not for the most part engage in direct, duplicative competition with private companies. *Ibid.*, 42–51. It has been the deliberate policy of the TVA, similarly, to avoid direct, duplicative competition in its service area; and as far as rural areas are concerned, the TVA Act directed the Authority to bring cheap electricity to rural areas not already served (at the time, only 11 percent of the farms in the country were served by electricity and in the TVA states the percentage was lower), and the Rural Electrification Act of 1935 has a similar restriction. *Ibid.*, 36–40.

[31] See note 36, below.

by public enterprise has greatly improved the performance of this industry.[32] The competition of public with private power has probably been a much more powerful influence than regulation in this respect, and particularly in bringing about dynamic price reduction, sales promotion, and extension of service.[33]

The A–J–W Effect

We have already alluded in various contexts to the tendency of regulation to encourage an uneconomic expansion of company investments, in order to inflate the rate base. As we have already pointed out, regulatory lag greatly diminishes the danger of this distortion. To the extent that it remains, it would seem to manifest itself mainly in the possible tendency for public utility companies to charge less than full marginal cost on some business in order to justify expanded investments. But, it is important to observe, the monopoly power that most public utility companies possess tends to produce the opposite result. Given the unwillingness of any profit-maximizing firm to expand output beyond the point where MR and MC are equated, the gap between MR and AR under monopoly results in a failure to produce up to the optimum level, where MC and P would be equated.

In other words, the circumstances of incompletely exploited monopoly power, regulation, and a return in excess of the cost of capital—all necessary for the A–J–W tendency—make the marginal private return on investment greater than the marginal social return, because to the net revenues directly generated by incremental investments, if they fall short of yielding the allowed rate of return, can be added the revenues the company can recoup by raising rates on other parts of its business. So it tends to produce over-investment. Monopoly has the opposite tendency; it makes marginal private return on output-expanding investments *less* than marginal social return, because it makes marginal revenue less than average revenue; so it tends to result in underinvestment.[34]

If regulation were instantaneously effective, it would eliminate this restrictive effect of monopoly; and that is precisely what it is supposed to do. The economic purpose of holding price to average total cost, including only a competitive return on investment, is to produce the competitive level of investment and output. In principle, regulated companies do not have the choice of restricted output with higher-than-competitive rates of return, on the one hand, and competitive levels of output with competitive rates of return on the other. If they expand investment and output from the monopoly to the competitive level, this will not, in contrast with the unregulated monopoly situation, reduce their *rates* of profit; instead they can only benefit by undertaking the expansion, as long as the price at which they sell the additional output covers marginal cost.[35]

[32] Twentieth Century Fund, *op. cit.*, 404, 431–437, 718–720, and *passim*; also the references in note 21, p. 000, above. For an example of the fear that "they might propose another TVA over in the Southwest" inducing a private company to keep its rates low, see Aaron Wildavsky, *Dixon-Yates: A Study in Power Politics* (New Haven: Yale Univ. Press, 1962), 9.

[33] The most thorough exposition and docu- mentation of this thesis is by Hellman, *op. cit.*

[34] This discussion draws heavily on my "The Graduated Fair Return: Comment," *Amer. Econ. Rev.* (March 1968), LVIII: 170–173.

[35] Or, to put it another way, effective regulation makes the *marginal revenue* product of the utility company's investments (the added output multiplied by MR) the same as the *average* revenue product (the added output multiplied

But the fact is, as we have seen, that regulation is not instantaneously effective. Public utility companies therefore do have some opportunity to choose between higher and lower rates of profit, at correspondingly lower and higher respective rates of output. More important, merely holding the overall rate of return to competitive levels does not suffice to assure competitive levels of capacity and output. The reason for this is that regulators can never be certain about the elasticity of demand and the behavior of unit costs with increased sales. In the face of these inescapable uncertainties, commissions are powerless to order rate reductions as long as the regulated companies are earning no more than the permissible return on their rate bases, even though the reductions could well prove justified after the fact, if only there were some means of putting them into effect.[36] Competition automatically probes the elasticity of demand and the long-run behavior of costs; regulation cannot.[37]

As an offset to monopoly, the A–J–W distortion probably does more good than harm. It encourages risk-taking and output-expanding investment. We have earlier suggested that one possible manifestation of the A–J–W effect is some reluctance of public utilities to adopt thoroughgoing peak-responsibility pricing:[38] if peak users can be charged less than the full capacity costs for which they are (marginally) responsible, this "justifies" a greater capacity and a larger rate base, the costs of which can then be recouped partially from off-peak users. But it is precisely with respect to such investments that monopoly has heretofore been accused of producing excessive conservatism.[39]

It is significant that the main agencies whose purpose is to offset this conservatism, public power authorities and "tough" regulatory commissions, have been, according to Shepherd's survey, as a group, markedly worse than

---

by AR or price), thus eliminating the tendency to monopolistic restriction that exists when the former is less than the latter.

[36] This is graphically illustrated by William Vickrey, "Some Objections to Marginal-Cost Pricing," *Jour. Pol. Econ.* (June 1948), LVI: 228. Suppose, he suggests, demand and *LRAC* have

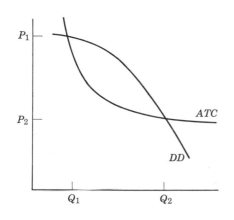

the slopes shown in the accompanying figure, but there is no way of being sure, and price is at P_1. Since the company is earning only *ATC* there is no way of forcing rate reductions to P_2, which would be the optimum level if revenues had to cover total costs and no discrimination were possible. Competition provides a means of getting from P_1 to P_2; regulation may not.

[37] It is this circumstance that lends attractiveness to government yardstick competition. TVA was able to do what regulatory commissions could not require private companies to do: to set low rates and see what happened to demand and cost. See, for example, Lewis, in Lyon and Abramson, *op. cit.*, II: 733–743; Twentieth Century Fund, *op. cit.*, 493–494, 651–652.

[38] See p. 50, above.

[39] H. M. Gray, "Transportation and Public Utilities, Discussion," *Amer. Econ. Rev., Papers and Proceedings* (May 1958), XXXVIII: 485–487; John Bauer and Peter Costello, *Public Organization of Electric Power, Conditions, Policies and Program* (New York: Harper & Bros. Publishers, 1949), Chapter 2; Robert F. Bryan and Ben W. Lewis, "The 'Earning Base' as a 'Rate Base,'" *Q. Jour. Econ.* (February 1938), LII: 339, 342–345; and M. G. de Chazeau, "Reply," *ibid.*, 346–359.

average offenders against such marginalist practices as peak-responsibility pricing.[40] These agencies have regarded it as their function to promote an expanded use of electricity: this was TVA's explicit purpose and, according to Shepherd, it practices no marginalist pricing at all.

The Role of Regulation

This is a formidable list of favorable influences. But it is the assumption of most economists that they are is not adequate, in the presence of monopoly; and this view probably accords with the political preferences of Western societies as well. We are generally unwilling to rely solely on the benevolence or even the enlightened self-interest of profit-maximizing monopolists or of their managers. We tend to prefer good results that are forced on industries by objective, external constraints such as regulation or competition. So the foregoing influences are not necessarily sufficient to elicit optimum performance—though, obviously, the more powerful they are, the less the need for government intervention. We still have to face the difficult question: what has been the impact of regulation itself? And what light does the foregoing list of favorable circumstances cast on the appropriate emphasis and direction of regulatory policy?

No healthy-minded person would devote large amounts of his time to the study of some institution that he thought had no importance. By this limited, double-negative test, the present writer is healthy-minded. I believe that regulation *does* make some difference. And that by thinking and trying, it can be made to make more of a difference—or, more importantly, a *better* difference.

The assumption that regulation does or can have an important effect is widely shared by practitioners in the field. They, better than anyone else, can observe the tremendous amounts of time, energy, and money devoted to the effort, and can clearly feel the heat with which issues in particular cases are contested. It is their function to argue the cataclysmic effects of legislators or commissions neglecting to follow their advice.

The result can be an occupational myopia. All this tumult and emotion does not prove that regulation does really make a difference, other than the difference of enriching lawyers and economists and using large quantities of resources. Economists have directed astoundingly little attention to this question,[41] and there is little convincing evidence that the performance of regulated industries differs significantly from what it would be in the absence of regulation. Or, even more important, that the benefits of regulation outweigh the costs.[42] Or, to state the proper test precisely, that regulation is carried on only to the point where marginal costs equal marginal benefits.

It may astound the reader to learn that many economists question whether regulation makes any major difference at all; others, that it makes

---

[40] See p. 98, Volume 1; see also the other references there in note 30, and the description thereafter of the similar effects of tough FPC regulation of natural gas pipelines.

[41] See, for example, any of the standard text-books on utility regulation.

[42] Richard E. Caves, "Direct Regulation and Market Performance in the American Economy,"

Amer. Econ. Rev., Papers and Proceedings (May 1964), LIV: 172–181. See also Paul W. MacAvoy, *The Effectiveness of the Federal Power Commission*, Working Paper, Alfred P. Sloan School of Management, Massachusetts Institute of Technology, undated; a revised version appears in *Bell Jour. Econ. and Mgt. Sciences*; (Autumn 1970) also note 1, Chapter 7, below.

performance better. As one of them summarized a symposium on the subject:

"The views expressed in the papers presented in this session seem, where they overlap, to be broadly in agreement. What the regulatory commissions are trying to do is difficult to discover; what effect these commissions actually have is, to a large extent unknown; when it can be discovered, it is often absurd."[43]

Probably the most influential examination of this question has been the study of electricity rates through 1937 by Stigler and Friedland.[44] They found that interstate differences in average rate levels were explained principally by such factors as the size and density of the respective markets, per capita income and the proportion of power from hydroelectric sources. Introducing the additional consideration of the effectiveness of regulation in each state—as measured by the presence or absence of a special state commission with power to regulate rates—added nothing significant to the explanation of interstate differences. The results were likewise negative when they introduced the effectiveness of regulation, measured in the same way, into equations attempting to explain the relative treatment of small (relative to large) and domestic (relative to industrial) customers in the several states. They surmise:

"The ineffectiveness of regulation lies in two circumstances. The first circumstance is that the individual utility system is not possessed of any large amount of long-run monopoly power. It faces the competition of other energy sources in a large proportion of its product's uses, and it faces the competition of other utility systems. . . . The second circumstance is that the regulatory body is incapable of forcing the utility to operate at a specified combination of output, price, and cost. . . . [R]ecognize that the cost curve falls through time, and recognize also the inevitable time-lags of a regulatory process, and the possibility becomes large that the Commission will proudly win each battlefield that its protagonist has abandoned—except for a squad of lawyers."[45]

The results of the Stigler–Friedland study are sufficiently striking to suggest, at the very least, that the question with which they begin is a meaningful one. Whether their answer will prove to be definitive is still subject to various doubts. First of all, the interstate comparisons are undoubtedly weakened by spillover effects from state to state: it could be, for example, that effective regulation in one state influences rates in adjoining states, by competition or imitation. Second, it is almost certainly true that the statistical indicator they use for the effectiveness of regulation is insufficiently precise; the presence of

---

[43] Coase, "The Regulated Industries—Discussion," *ibid.*, 194.

[44] George J. Stigler and Claire Friedland, "What Can Regulators Regulate? The Case of Electricity," reprinted from the *Jour. Law and Econ.* (1962), V: 1–16, in Shepherd and Gies, *op. cit.*, 187–211.

[45] *Ibid.*, 200–203. A more recent study, using entirely different techniques, reached a tentative conclusion not far different. On the basis of direct estimates of marginal costs, on the one hand, and elasticity of demand, on the other, Thomas G. Moore concluded that the actual rates of the Detroit Edison Company were approximately the rates one would have expected an unregulated, profit-maximizing monopolist to charge. "The Effect of Regulation on Electrical Power Prices," unpublished paper delivered at North American Regional Conference of the Econometric Society, San Francisco, December, 1966.

commissions has been no guarantor of effective regulation;[46] and several of the states that lack commissions to this day leave regulation to their municipalities and to the control of government enterprise.[47] Moreover, regulation was hamstrung during most or all of the period their investigation covers by the holding company and by the restrictions imposed by the Supreme Court. But finally, it could well be that the impact on electricity rates of such alternative "regulatory" devices as municipal distribution companies and public enterprises for the generation and transmission of power is greater than that of regulation of the traditional type. These possibilities are suggestive only.[48]

It is difficult to read the record of the regular and only partially successful requests of Bell System companies for rate increases in the decade after World War II; or their regular and only partially successful requests for rates of return on equity more nearly comparable with those allowed other regulated companies; or their continuous and largely unsuccessful argument that Western Electric ought to be allowed rates of profit comparable with unregulated electrical equipment manufacturers;[49] or the succession of reductions in long-distance telephone rates introduced in considerable measure under the pressure of the Federal Communications Commission— which in the summer of 1967 required AT&T to put into effect some $120 million of rate reductions after explicitly denying the company's plea for higher earnings than $7\frac{1}{2}$ percent on total invested capital[50]—without concluding that regulation has had some significant influence here in the direction of holding rates down.[51] It is impossible to emerge from discussions of rate making with electric company executives without the very strong impression that most of them *think* major portions of their demands are highly inelastic; and without a great deal of skepticism, therefore, about the Stigler–Friedland hypothesis that "the individual utility system is not possessed of any large amount of long-run monopoly power." The history of

---

[46] On the wide variation from state to state and from one time to the next in the efficacy of state commissions, see Lewis, in Lyon and Abramson, *op. cit.*, II: 642–643.

[47] See note 36, p. 10, Volume 1.

[48] Richard Hellman contends that the authors' use of gross revenue per kilowatt-hour as their measure is likewise defective. Where electricity is sold under block rate schedules, with the applicable rate varying from one bloc of purchases to the next, the average rate in each state will be determined preponderantly by the composition of the market—that is, by the relative importance of customers using power in different quantities. The influence of this factor could well conceal much of the effect of regulation in determining the level of the entire rate schedule. Review of Shepherd and Gies, *op. cit.*, in *Amer. Econ. Rev.* (March 1967), LVII: 308–309.

[49] See pp. 291–292, Chapter 6, below.

[50] *In the Matter of American Telephone and Telegraph Co. et al.*, Memorandum Opinion and Order on Reconsideration, 9 FCC 2d 960, 971, 979 (September 1967). This followed cuts of $100

million in 1965. As a result of continuing surveillance, the company agreed in the fall of 1969 to further reductions totaling $150 million annually in long-distance rates. *New York Times*, November 6, 1969, 1.

[51] See the careful study of the rate increase requests by the Michigan Bell Telephone Company during the period 1948 through 1961 by Troxel, with the conclusion:

"No one can look at these facts, I think, and deny that the Michigan Commission puts strong constraints on telephone prices and revenues."

"Telephone Regulation in Michigan," in Shepherd and Gies, *op. cit.*, 154; see 151–162 and *passim*. Troxel rejects the possibility that the rate increase requests were inflated, so that in the end the company got pretty much what it wanted. But that possibility is by no means entirely eliminated: he recognizes that the company "has been quick to return to the Commission when it did not get all that it requested in a current decision." (157)

the railroads contradicts the notion that grossly discriminatory exploitation of these inelastic demands would represent no significant danger in the absence of regulation.[52]

Transportation offers a quite convincing demonstration that regulation makes a difference: consider the significance of the single fact that a taxi medallion—symbolizing the license to run a taxicab in New York City— sells for approximately $25,000. Here is market proof that licensing cuts down the number of taxis and increases the profitability of the business, either by raising rates or by keeping the cabs more fully occupied, hence harder to find when needed.[53]

As this last example suggests, if the first proper question is whether regulation has any effect at all, the second is: does it do more good than harm? The second question is inescapably posed by the record in transportation, to which we have already alluded many times.[54] Many students would answer it in the negative, agreeing with the very first sentence of Walter Adams and Horace N. Gray's chapter on "Regulation and Public Utilities" in their book, *Monopoly in America, The Government as Promoter*:

"Among all the devices used by government to promote monopoly, public utility, or public interest, regulation is in some respects perhaps the worst."[55]

In my judgment, regulation does do a great deal of good—notably in providing a public forum for continuing scrutiny of the performance of companies that do still have too much monopoly power, in too large a proportion of the markets in which they sell, to be left unregulated; in providing a check and a goad; in preventing unacceptable discrimination between customers.[55a] The FCC's ruling requiring television stations to give "equal time" to agencies that wished to warn viewers of the dangers of cigarette smoking was a major step in the direction of wiping out a stain on the good name of a market economy.

Regulation also does a great deal of harm—mainly because of its association with restraints on competition. It is this fact, rather than corruption, senility, or "industry-mindedness," as we have suggested, that is fundamental to the many complaints about the regulatory process that we have detailed in Chapters 1 and 2. To take one specific example: we have alluded to the complaints that the FCC and CAB have developed no general guidelines for

---

[52] On the question of whether regulation makes a difference in transportation, see the thoughtful appraisal by Wilson, *op. cit.*, *Amer. Econ. Rev., Papers and Proceedings* (May 1964), LIV: 160–171.

[53] The equilibrium price for the privilege of operating a taxicab is the price that will just ration the number of available licenses among the people who would like to enter the field. Taxicab rates and revenues must be sufficient to provide an acceptable livelihood for the driver plus a return on the $25,000 investment. Such rates and returns would therefore be excessive if it were not necessary to make that investment; or, to look at the matter from the other end, manifestly many more drivers would wish to enter the field if they could do so without paying so high an entrance fee.

[54] See, for example, pp. 161–166, Volume 1, 14–28, above, and 178–193, Chapter 5, below. See, for a specific illustration, Paul W. MacAvoy and James Sloss, *Regulation of Transport Innovation, The ICC and Unit Coal Trains to the East Coast* (New York: Random House, 1967).

[55] The Macmillan Co., New York, 1955, 39. "In terms of economic efficiency alone, a policy that ended all rate regulation and common carrier obligations [in transportation] would create benefits far in excess of costs." Friedlaender, *op. cit.*, 164. For further consideration of whether regulation is worth what it costs, see p. 326, below.

[55a] For similar views in the field of transportation, see the recommendations cited in note 63, Chapter 1, and note 216, Chapter 5.

certification policy to which their decisions may in any sense be said to conform. Economic logic would suggest that by far the more fundamental determinant of the performance of these industries is the fact that entry is certificated in the first place. Any defects in their subsequent performance would flow more from the fact of entry restriction and fewness of sellers than from remediable deficiencies in the way in which the licensees are selected. If private parties are to have exclusive access to particular radio frequencies for the transmission of radio and television programs, it may be predicted that they will use the privilege to make the most money possible for themselves; and this suggests in turn that it makes relatively little difference whether applicant A is preferred to applicant B or the other way around:

"If there are going to be only three airlines operating between New York and Atlanta, does it really matter to the public whether the third service is rendered by Braniff or Delta?"[56]

None of this is to deprecate the importance of making regulation more intelligent and more effective in those circumstances in which competition is simply infeasible. If, in fact, technical conditions require the restriction of entry into broadcasting, it does become important that the FCC take into account opportunity costs in devising its allocation of the spectrum, set forth intelligent guidelines for certification policy, and make vigorous attempts to define and assert the public interest in the character of programming. More thoroughgoing policy formulation by regulatory commissions, more active planning in the public interest, a more direct scrutiny of industrial performance—efficiency, progressiveness, quality of service, rate structures—are surely necessary, to the extent that motivations of company managers and competition are inevitably inadequate.[57] Improvement of the stimuli and incentives offered regulated companies must also, clearly, be high on the agenda of regulatory improvement.

But, when all is said and done, the critical decisions have to do with the proper role and definition of competition. If we consult our list of favorable factors operating on public utility performance, we cannot help noting that the profit motive, managerialism, decreasing costs, and elasticity of demand are all strengthened by the force of competition. Competition is far more powerful than regulation in forcing businesses to explore the slope of their cost functions and elasticity of their demands, and to push down costs, if they are to prosper. In those situations in which competition is feasible, regulatory commissions clearly should welcome it rather than rush to restrict it.[58]

So we find ourselves face to face with the complex and omnipresent problem that constitutes the subject of the next three chapters.

---

[56] Roger C. Cramton, "The Effectiveness of Economic Regulation: A Legal View," *Amer. Econ. Rev., Papers and Proceedings* (May 1964), LIV: 185.

[57] See, for example, Trebing, *op. cit., Public Utilities Fortnightly* (July 18, 1963), LXXII: 22–35; Morgan, *Regulation and The Management of Public Utilities*, 242–269; and Chapter 2, above.

[58] For a fuller development of this argument, particularly with respect to public utility pricing, see my paper in Trebing, ed., *op. cit.*, 88–102.

CHAPTER 4

The Role and Definition of Competition: Natural Monopoly

The decision to regulate never represents a clean break with competition. No regulatory statute to the author's knowledge completely abandons reliance on competition as one guarantor of good performance.[1] The determination of the proper mixture of competitive rivalry and government orders in the

---

[1] The following examples are taken mainly from the important article by Louis B. Schwartz, *op. cit., Harvard Law Rev.* (January 1954), LXVII: 436–475.

With respect to the certification of natural gas pipelines, the Natural Gas Act provides that

"a certificate shall be issued to any qualified applicant . . . if it is found that the applicant is able and willing properly to . . . perform the service proposed . . . and that the proposed service . . . is or will be required by the present or future public convenience and necessity. . . ." 15 U.S. Code 717 f (e), 1964 ed.

"Nothing contained in this section shall be construed as a limitation upon the power of the Commission to grant certificates of public convenience and necessity for service of an area already being served by another natural-gas company." 15 U.S. Code 717 f (g), 1964 ed.

The Civil Aeronautics Act of 1938 directs the CAB to

"consider the following among other things as being in the public interest. . . .

"Competition to the extent necessary to assure the sound development of an air-transportation system properly adapted to the needs of the foreign and domestic commerce of the United States, of the Postal Service, and of the national defense. . . ." 49 U.S. Code 1302d, 1964 ed.

Section 7 of the Clayton Act, which prohibits intercorporate stock and asset acquisitions and mergers "where . . . the effect . . . may be

substantially to lessen competition, or to tend to create a monopoly" (15 U.S. Code 18, 1964 ed.), applies to the regulated industries as well as the unregulated, with enforcement authority vested in the ICC, the FCC, the CAB, and the Federal Reserve Board for the industries within their respective jurisdictions. 15 U.S. Code 21a, 1964 ed. And, correspondingly, the Interstate Commerce, Federal Communications, and Federal Power Acts all require that proposed mergers of the regulated companies be subject to approval or disapproval by the corresponding regulatory commissions, and the Federal Aviation Act specifically prohibits mergers

"which would result in creating a monopoly . . . and thereby restrain competition or jeopardize another air carrier. . . ." 49 U.S. Code 1378b, 1964 ed.

The Reed-Bulwinkle Act of 1948, which authorized the Interstate Commerce Commission to approve agreements among carriers for the joint consideration and establishment of rates and gave such approved agreements exemption from the antitrust laws, specifically required that they accord

"to each party the free and unrestrained right to take independent action either before or after any determination arrived at through such procedure. . . ." 49 U.S. Code 5 b (b), 1964 ed. See also pp. 161–165, below.

Of course, such competition as the regulatory statutes permit with or among locally franchised

formula for social control is or ought to be the central, continuing responsibility of legislatures and regulatory commissions.[2]

The question is not simply one of *how much* competition to allow—how much freedom of entry or independence of decision making with respect to price, investment, output, service, promotional effort, financing, and the like. It is a question also of what, in the particular circumstances of each regulated industry, is the proper *definition*, what are the *prerequisites*, of effective competition. The effectiveness of competition cannot be simply measured along a single linear scale running from pure monopoly at one end to pure competition at the other—the latter characterized by an infinite number of sellers, complete independence of action, perfect standardization of products, zero governmental intervention, and zero monopoly power. (Or to "perfect" competition, which includes all the attributes of pure competition and requires, in addition, perfect mobility of factors and perfect knowledge and foresight.) The main reasons why pure competition is in fact not ideal are familiar: (1) economies of scale in production and distribution will typically require that sellers (and buyers) be larger in size and fewer in number than would be consistent with an utter absence of monopoly (or monopsony) power; (2) consumers want variety in product and service qualities and characteristics, which means that there cannot always be a large number of sellers of the same (standardized or undifferentiated) product; (3) effective innovation may, similarly, require firms too large and, hence, too few in number for monopoly power to be completely absent, and may require monopoly profits to finance the necessary innovative effort and to reward the successful innovator; (4) competitive structure may, in the presence of serious imperfections of competition, be too pure in other respects—entry too free and rivalry too intense—for optimum performance. All of these considerations make the determination of what kinds of policy will produce the most effective competition difficult enough in unregulated industry generally;[3] they make it even more difficult in the public utility arena, which has been subjected to more direct regulation precisely because of the presence there of unusually strong circumstances making unrestrained competition both infeasible and undesirable.

In making complex judgments like these, the anticompetitive bias of the regulatory mentality has ample opportunity to manifest itself. The essence of the regulatory approach, we have observed in Chapter 1, is the acceptance of a single company (or selected group of existing companies) as society's *chosen instrument* for performing the service in question. It vests in that chosen

---

telephone, or electric and gas distribution companies is typically only peripheral in character—in wholesale markets only, or only among competing fuels or communications media, or, by example, between public and private or Bell and non-Bell companies.

[2] "regulation as a general systematic alternative to competition is literally inconceivable. We do not have the conceptual foundation to construct or operate a completely regulated economic system. . . . At most, regulation is a supplement or partial alternative to competition, resorted to on a largely *ad hoc* basis to secure particular

objectives which it is thought cannot be obtained by competition." Lee Loevinger, "Regulation and Competition as Alternatives," Reproduced with permission of *The Antitrust Bulletin*, from Volume XI (January–April 1966), 139, © 1965 by Federal Legal Publications, Inc.

[3] For a survey of these problems and of the rich literature on the subject, see Dirlam and Kahn, *Fair Competition, the Law and Economics of Antitrust Policy* (Ithaca: Cornell Univ. Press, 1954), especially Chapter 1. See also the brief reference to some of these problems at page 44 of our Volume 1 and the introduction to this volume.

instrument, by license, explicit responsibility for providing good and economical service to all comers; it imposes obligations on it that go far beyond obligations imposed on private companies in the economy generally; and it subjects it to all sorts of controls. In return, it protects it from competition. In brief, it places society's principal reliance on conscious and explicit planning, by monopolists or a limited number of selected companies on the one hand and regulatory commissions on the other, under cover of a complicated pattern of privileges, public duties, and responsibilities.

The competitive approach, in contrast, places reliance on the market mechanism itself. Good results are expected to flow from the interplay of independent companies, under conditions of unrestricted entry, independent competitive endeavor, and free contract. Neither government agencies nor any particular private companies need assume explicit overall responsibility for the results that issue—the price and quality of service and so on. The only government planning required is of the antitrust kind—directed at preserving the competitive market *mechanism*—and related efforts to make that mechanism work as well as possible. The only privilege conferred on private companies is the opportunity to compete; and their only responsibility is for each to look to its own interests.

The marriage (perhaps the better term would be miscegenation) of these two approaches in the public utility context is inevitably an uneasy one. But the almost universal conception is that the mixed marriage is better than none: that such competition as can be permitted, consistent with efficiency, can contribute to improved performance; yet unregulated competition is infeasible—provided, that is, that the industry is properly treated as a public utility in the first place!

As we have already suggested in our Introduction, the proper institutional structure for the regulated industries—in particular, the economically optimum mix of competition and regulation and the definition of optimum competition itself—will clearly vary from one to the other: each is in important degree *sui generis*. There are no simple, scientific rules; in each context the formulation of good policy calls for informed judgment—a judicious balancing and appraisal of often conflicting considerations and predictions. But if that last sentence is to mean anything at all—if by "judicious balancing" we are to mean something more than utter pragmatism, or simple compromises of all conflicting views and interests—the judgment must be informed by *something*. That something is presumably experience, from which emerges an ability to discriminate between correct and incorrect, relevant and irrelevant, logical and illogical arguments and considerations—an understanding of whatever generalizations can be drawn from the regulatory experience generally. Chapters 4–6 are an attempt to contribute to that understanding, by defining and analyzing the major aspects of this central institutional question and by describing a few illustrative cases in detail.

The three chapters correspond respectively to the three major facets of the problem. The first and simplest rationalization of the public utility institution is the concept of natural monopoly. Its corollary is the need for restriction of entry—the most decisive limitation of competition. Chapter 4 is devoted to an examination of this concept, of the entry control that it purports to justify, and of the extent to which even natural monopoly may properly be subjected to competition.

Chapter 5 examines the other major justification:[4] the alleged threat of excessive competition and consequent deterioration of service, giving rise to the necessity for restricting competition from both the outside (via entry) and inside. This rationalization is quite different from the first. Although competition among "natural monopolists" will likewise have some tendency to be destructive, the remedy there is to prohibit entry, rely on a single chosen instrument and impose upper limits on his price and minimum standards of service. Here, instead, there is no suggestion that monopoly is technologically desirable. Reliance is placed, rather, on competition, constrained partly by restrictions on entry, partly by price *floors*, and partly by the setting of *ceilings* on service rivalry. (To be sure, maximum prices and minimum specifications of service may likewise be imposed.)

Chapter 6 considers the main aspects of the problem of integration in the public utility industries—the question of the extent to which regulated companies should either be permitted or required to integrate horizontally, geographically, vertically, or conglomerately, by financial consolidation or by collaboration among themselves. Whereas Chapters 4 and 5 are concerned with the two major rationalizations for limiting competition, this Chapter is basically concerned with its proper definition. The question is, in part: to what extent will integration make for more or less effective *competition* in the public utility context? But the question is not limited to the bearing of integration on competition; the fundamental question is what combination of integration, interfirm collaboration and rivalry will make for the best possible performance in these industries.

ECONOMIES OF SCALE

The possibility of competitive entry is the principal limitation on monopoly power in a market economy. Etymologically, the prime characteristic of monopoly is the presence of a single ("mono") seller of a differentiated product; and economists have demonstrated that joint monopoly power may be exercised also when sellers are few ("oligo") or act in concert. But how badly a monopoly can in the long run perform (relative to the performance that could be achieved under competition) depends on the height of the barriers to entry into its market.[5]

No barrier to entry is more absolute than one imposed or enforced by the sovereign power of the state. All others are potentially subject to hurdling, erosion, or circumvention. So our study of the proper role of competition in the regulated industries properly begins with a consideration of the fact and

---

[4] We have, in Chapter 1, pp. 1–11, above, identified a longer list of reasons for the association of regulation with restraint of competition. There is no need for us to engage in a systematic effort at this point to reconcile the two lists. A perceptive reader will see, however, that all the other reasons except possibly the promotional one reduce in one way or another to the two broad categories set forth here; and even the promotional one can, as we shall see, be regarded as a special variant of the destructive competition case—the belief being that excessively intense

rivalry will retard or abort the development of a desired service.

[5] See Joe S. Bain, *Barriers to New Competition* (Cambridge: Harvard Univ. Press, 1956). The United Supreme Court has defined monopoly power under the Sherman Act as the power "to raise prices or to exclude competition when it is desired to do so." *American Tobacco Co. et al. v. United States*, 328 U.S. 781, 811 (1946). But these two conditions are not alternatives, as the Court implied; the first is in the long run dependent on the second.

major rationalization of governmental restriction of entry, the concept of natural monopoly. Whatever its validity as a historical explanation of how these monopolies in fact emerged, this remains the most generally accepted justification for confining at least some aspects of the supply of communications, electricity, gas, water, and perhaps urban transportation to single, chosen instruments.

The essence of the natural monopoly concept can be illustrated by a recent example. In 1968, the President's Task Force on Communications Policy recommended that all United States international communications media be placed under the operating control of a single company.[6] One important basis for this recommendation of monopoly, which we shall elaborate in Chapter 6 (see pp. 264–267, below), is the advantage of permitting a communications company to operate all the available media, so that it can select whatever combination—cable, satellite, radio—will most efficiently perform the function. But these advantages of conglomerate integration do not themselves justify closing the field to *all but one* such conglomerate enterprise. This additional step requires a demonstration that monopoly is the most efficient mechanism for providing international communications services. And this must mean that the potential economies of firm size are so great that only a single firm, capable of supplying the entire market, can take the fullest possible advantage of them.

Evolution of the Natural Monopoly Concept

Until around the turn of the twentieth century, the typical public policy toward the public utility industries was one of local competition rather than monopoly—not of completely unrestricted entry, to be sure, but one of chartering numerous suppliers in the various localities. (This statement is insufficiently precise, since individual cities might themselves be composed of separate marketing areas, for each of which a separate company might be the sole supplier. But, in fact, overlapping franchises were likewise frequent.) Between 1882, when Edison opened his Pearl Street station in New York, and 1907, nonexclusive, competitive electric franchises were granted freely, often as a means of forcing down rates that cities considered too high.[7]

Burton N. Behling cites several reasons for this practice. First, there were technical factors: the use of direct current at low voltages made it impossible to distribute electricity over an area greater than one square mile. Second, it was difficult, at the early stages of the industry, for small, local companies to raise large quantities of capital such as would have been required to serve entire areas exclusively. Electrical equipment manufacturers, competing with one another, would each set up its own generating and distributing company. But the most important explanations were institutional. Competition, or at least laissez-faire, represented the general national policy and there had not yet emerged a general acceptance of the notion that in certain industries regulated monopoly might produce a better performance. And regulatory

---

[6] *Final Report*, Chapter 2.

[7] "The haphazardness of franchise-giving is illustrated by Chicago. During 1882–1905, it granted 29 franchises. Towns it absorbed gave 18. The grants were for such small areas as 'one block each way', or 'a few blocks on the north-' west side', or 'old twelfth ward.' Sixteen were competitive, only one was exclusive. Three covered the entire city: one of these in 1897 was hawked about the streets until in self-defense the Chicago Edison Company bought it up." Hellman, *Government Competition*, 9.

institutions themselves were still in an embryonic state: so, municipalities tended instead to charter competitive companies when they were dissatisfied with the rates being charged by existing suppliers. The experience was similar in the supply of gas and in local telephone service, after the original Bell patent expired, in 1893.[8]

It is not surprising, therefore, that there is no trace of the concept of natural monopoly in the landmark constitutional cases delineating the category of businesses "affected with a public interest."[9] Although *Munn v. Illinois* cited the alleged monopoly power of grain elevators in Illinois in partially justifying regulation of their rates, there was no conception that monopoly in these industries was positively desirable, on grounds of efficiency. Nor was it; grain storage is simply not a natural monopoly.[10]

But competition in the public utility industries typically proved ephemeral and ineffective. While it lasted, it

"favored the public for a time with low rates, but invariably at the expense of a deteriorated service. Financial exhaustion of one or more of the companies eventually brought about a complete consolidation, or an agreement as to rates or territory."[11]

The issuance of competitive franchises was, with discouraging regularity, followed by combination among the franchisees, despite the efforts of legislatures to prevent it. Some promoters took out these licenses merely to sell them to other companies, for whom they might be expected to have at least a nuisance value. In city after city, as a result, one company would emerge with almost all the franchises issued. The policy of competition, it seems generally conceded, was a failure.[12]

It was out of this experience that the concept of "natural monopoly" gradually emerged, as an attempt on the one hand to explain the persistent tendency of competition to produce inferior results and to disappear and, on the other, to justify its abandonment.[13] The logical corollary was the

[8] Behling summarizes a special census report of 1902, covering the 1,002 incorporated cities in the United States with population in excess of 4,000 that had telephone facilities: independent companies had a monopoly in 137 and Bell companies in 414 of these; 451 had duplicated service. *Competition and Monopoly in Public Utility Industries* (Urbana: Univ. of Illinois Press, 1938), 20; see also 18–19. In most states, Behling points out, granting of exclusive franchises was either unconstitutional or contrary to statutory law on into the twentieth century. *Ibid.*, 23. See also Martin Glaeser, *Public Utilities in American Capitalism* (New York: The MacMillan Co., 1957), Chapters 4–5.

[9] See pp. 3–8, Volume 1.

[10] "On *political* grounds, grain elevators were particularly vulnerable in the Granger era. They sufficed to raise the essentially ideological issue of the warrant for *any* government price regulation of *any* industry. Yet, in a transportation center the size of Chicago, there is no technical or economic reason why numerous companies

should not operate grain elevators. In short, *Munn v. Illinois* involved a representative industry from the standpoint of establishing the *right to regulate*, but its industrial background was singularly inappropriate as a source of answers to questions about *types of regulation*." James R. Nelson, *op. cit.*, *The Antitrust Bulletin* (January–April 1966), XI: 8.

[11] Behling, *op. cit.*, 20.

[12] See *ibid.*, 21–22; Glaeser, *op. cit.*, 16; Hellman, *Government Competition*, 9–11.

[13] The reference here is to direct, duplicative competition between private companies. As Hellman is at pains to point out and document at length, the advocacy and practice of government enterprise as an alternative device, directly competitive with private enterprise in only a small minority of the cases, but providing competition-by-example and by threat of displacement remained very much alive. See pp. 104–106, above. In 1913, for example, Cleveland undertook direct competition with a private company for the residential market, at the same

constitution of independent regulatory commissions; the first were set up in New York and Wisconsin, in 1907. There remains to this day a widespread consensus that at least some part of these businesses is, in truth, a natural monopoly, in the sense that direct competition is likely in most instances to involve unbearably great inefficiencies. This agreement does not, however, exclude the possibility that the *potentially* superior efficiency of monopoly might in fact not be achieved, whether because of monopolistic inertia or because of the inadequacies of regulation; and, as a corollary, that the inefficiencies introduced by even direct, duplicative competition could, in principle, be less important than its positive stimulus, particularly to a dynamically superior performance.[14]

The Essential Prerequisite of Natural Monopoly

The critical and—if properly defined—all-embracing characteristic of natural monopoly is an inherent tendency to decreasing unit costs over the entire extent of the market. This is so only when the economies achievable by a larger output are internal to the individual firm—if, that is to say, it is only as more output is concentrated in a single supplier that unit costs will decline.[15]

The principal source of this tendency is the necessity of making a large investment merely in order to be in a position to serve customers on demand.[16]

---

time specifying that the 10-cent per kwh company rate be reduced to a flat 3 cents; the eventual compromise was 5:

"Thereafter, both systems prospered under duplicative competition. The company had one of the lowest rates in the country. The competition received wide publicity, and was a thorn in the side of the private industry." *Op. cit.*, 26; see also 11–27 and *passim*.

[14] The following summary statement by the distinguished staff of economists that prepared the 20th Century Fund's factual findings, *Electric Power and Governmental Policy*, back in 1948, may be taken as still summarizing the consensus (p. 29):

"It is well known that in the power industry local monopoly is more economical than competition. If a number of systems compete for a single group of customers, there is duplication of investment. Each system can carry an additional load without a proportionate increase in costs. If they compete, each will take additional business so long as it can be obtained at a price exceeding the added costs; prices will then tend to cover output costs but not capacity costs. Sooner or later they are likely to agree to eliminate competition, or one will drive out the other. While costs *can* be lower under local monopoly than under competition, they may not be. The monopolist, protected from competition, may not operate efficiently, and his waste may be as great as that of competition. Hence prices may be

lower under competition than under monopoly."

Hellman minimizes the purported inefficiencies of competition in the local distribution of electric power, surveys the experience of several cities with direct duplication of municipally owned and private systems, and praises the results. But for the most part his argument is based on the fact that actual duplication is typically slight. The government competition that he strongly supports is far more side-by-side competition by example or by threat than of the direct variety. See *op. cit.*, 70–77, 83–98, and the various city case studies in his Chapter 2; also note 30, Chapter 3, above.

[15] Economies of scale might instead be *external* to the individual firm. It could be, for example, that as an entire industry grows it can acquire some of its inputs at decreasing average costs, because its growth enables the suppliers of those inputs to take advantage of potential economies of scale internal to *their* industry. Increasing returns of this kind are compatible with a competitive organization of the first industry: all firms in it could benefit equally from these emergent external economies, no matter what the scale of their individual outputs. See Howard S. Ellis and William Fellner, "External Economies and Diseconomies," in Amer. Econ. Ass'n, *Readings in Price Theory* (Chicago: Richard D. Irwin, 1952), 242–263.

[16] On the question of whether this fact makes for only short-run rather than long-run decreasing costs, see p. 126, Volume 1.)

The railroad has to construct a roadbed and lay a track before it is in a position to carry any passengers or freight at all; water, gas, electricity, and telephone companies have to dig up the streets and lay down pipes or build poles and string wires from the point of production to every single point of potential consumption and install meters before a single drop, cubic foot, or kilowatt hour can be sold or a single call placed. Those costs may be absolutely fixed and unchanging no matter how many units are sold; to the extent that this is true, average costs per unit decline in inverse proportion to the number of units sold. This tendency is created or accentuated by certain common and interrelated characteristics of many public utility services: that they involve a *fixed* and essentially immovable *connection* between supplier and customer or locality (true even of trains, but not of trucks); that the services are largely nonstorable (true of transportation, electricity, and communications, not of gas and water); that the company is under an obligation to supply instantaneously, on demand—at the flick of a switch, the click of a thermostat, the lifting of a telephone instrument; and that the demands, both of individual customers and on the system as a whole, fluctuate widely from one point in time to the next: for urban and commuter transportation it is concentrated in the rush hours; for almost all of these services it is much larger during the day and possibly early evening than during the night; for gas it is concentrated in the winter; for electricity in the northeast, where the heavier usage is for airconditioning, in the summer. For all these reasons, there has to be a heavy investment in capacity sufficient to meet the peak demands; and it is most efficiently provided by a single supplier, with a single fixed connection to the customer.[17]

Even where the investment in capacity is not totally predetermined and fixed—where, that is, a larger investment will be required if demand is large rather than small, or as demand grows over time—technological economies of scale may still make monopoly the most efficient form of organization. This will be true as long as plants constructed for higher levels of output will have lower average costs than smaller plants, or where it will cost less for an existing supplier to add a given amount of capacity to its existing plant than for a new supplier to provide it. The railroad may have to lay down a second track; gas, electricity, and telephone companies may have to build larger or additional transmission, generating, or exchange capacities; but they will typically be able to do so at lower incremental costs than a competitor starting afresh.[18]

---

[17] The wide divergence between peak and off-peak demand does not in itself contribute to economies of scale or natural monopoly. As far as this factor alone is concerned, the requisite capacity could be provided just as efficiently by a large number of suppliers, with an average load factor corresponding to that of the single one. Nor is the consequent prevalence of excess capacity off-peak a sign of short-run decreasing costs. Peak and off-peak service are two distinct, joint products. As our discussion at pp. 79–83 and 90–95 of Volume 1 demonstrates, the sum of their marginal costs need not on this account be less than their combined average total costs—and it will not be, unless the joint production is itself subject to increasing returns. Compare C. F. Phillips' assumption to the contrary, when he contends that the prevalence of excess capacity off-peak makes competition inherently unstable. *The Economics of Regulation*, rev. ed. (Homewood: Richard D. Irwin, 1969), 24–26.

[18] Paul J. Garfield and Wallace F. Lovejoy's discussion of the possibility that a monopoly may be able to "take full advantage of the economies of large-scale production" has mixed in with this factor another whose relevance is not nearly so clear:

"Once public utilities were able to serve an entire market under the protection of monopoly,

Clearly, these tendencies are related to the fact that fixed or capacity costs bulk unusually large among total costs in most public utility industries.[19] And it is these fixed costs that might be wastefully duplicated if two companies tried to serve the same markets. But heavy fixed costs do not themselves necessarily make for natural monopoly.[20] An industry's technology might be such that all of its costs were fixed—its output produced in fully automatic plants, drawing their energy from the sun and their raw materials from the air—yet in the absence of internal economies of scale over a sufficient range of supply, it might be equally efficient to have that production carried on by a large number of separate firms, each with its own wholly automatic, completely fixed-cost plant. The tendency of agriculture to suffer wide fluctuations in prices is correctly attributed in part to the importance of fixed costs in that industry, a large proportion of a farmer's costs being the return on his own investment in the land and its improvements, in his equipment, and on his own labor. This has the effect of making supply highly inelastic, so that even slight changes in demand result in sharp fluctuations in price.[20a] But since economies of scale in agriculture are very limited relative to the size of the market, the industry is clearly not a natural monopoly.

Obviously, then, the phenomenon of natural monopoly is in some way related to the wastes that would arise if, in the presence of competition, certain facilities would have to be duplicated. But here, as with the phenomenon of heavy fixed costs, it is not the fact of duplication alone that makes for a natural monopoly, but the presence of economies of scale or decreasing costs in the provision and utilization of these facilities.[21] We may have

---

it became feasible for many utilities to concentrate their production in the larger and more efficient plant and equipment units made possible by technological advancement." *Public Utility Economics* (Englewood Cliffs, N.J.: Prentice-Hall, 1964), 18.

But competition, too, has the effect of concentrating production in the "more efficient plants" —that is, in those with the lowest short-run marginal costs (see pp. 264–266, Chapter 6, below). Nor is competition incompatible with firms taking the fullest advantage of technological progress, to the extent that it is economical to do so, on the basis of a comparison of the average variable costs of existing plant and average total costs of new (see p. 118, Volume 1, above). Technological progress contributes to natural monopoly only to the extent that it is of a type that increases the importance of economies of scale relative to the size of the market. For evidence that developments in electricity generation and transmission have been of this character, see p. 128, Volume 1, and 74, Chapter 2, above. For a similar confusion see note 39, p. 12 of Volume 1.

[19] See pp. 35–36, Volume 1.

[20] Compare Garfield and Lovejoy:

"Part of the explanation of this decreasing-cost tendency is found in the fact that public utilities require a relatively greater investment in plant

and equipment than other principal industries . . . Because public utilities must have greater investment in plant and equipment than other industries, their cost structure is dominated by the costs related to that fixed investment. It is most important to note that plant-related costs are constant in amount and do not fluctuate with variations in production, assuming constant plant size." *Op. cit.*, 17. © 1964. Reprinted by permission of Prentice-Hall, Inc., Englewood Cliffs, N.J.

Fixed costs do, of course, make for a condition of decreasing costs within the limits of the capacity of a given plant; but they do not in themselves give rise to the long-run decreasing costs—that is, the economies of scale—that are the essential condition of natural monopoly.

[20a] See pp. 173–174, below.

[21] Compare Behling's statement to the contrary:

"Even when it is observed that decreasing cost does not extend without limit in public utility enterprise, the conclusion does not follow that monopolistic organization should be abandoned. . . . Whether increasing or decreasing cost applies, a given area can be served more economically by a single enterprise than by rival companies operating in the same territory. Competitive duplication results in a larger total investment and a higher cost per unit. Combined capacity is greater than the market requires, and neither "competitive duplication" in the form of thousands of farms all producing the same product, scores of doctors practicing in the same locality, and great numbers of salesmen, representing competing manufacturers of the same product, combing the same market territory. None of these "duplications" is necessarily inefficient, as long as the market has need of all these suppliers and none of them is too small to take full advantage of the available economies of scale. It is only when the entire demand can most efficiently be supplied via a single set of telephone poles and gas mains that it becomes inefficient to duplicate them, to have two companies digging up the streets at various times rather than one. So, duplication is inefficient—indeed, one might prefer to say that only in this event does it in fact constitute duplication —only in the presence of the economies of scale that make for natural monopoly.[22]

An additional source of these potential economies of scale is to be found not on the supply but on the demand side. We have mentioned the effect of variability in demand in imposing on a public utility company the burden of maintaining capacity sufficient to supply however much service is demanded at the peak. This variability tends, other things being equal, to make it more efficient to supply many customers and regions than few; that is to say, it gives rise to economies of scale when the dimension along which output is measured is not the quantities taken by some given number of customers but the number and diversity of customers and markets served. The greater the latter, the greater is the likelihood that the variations in their separate demands will tend to cancel one another out; the more diverse the markets, the greater the possibility that the maximum requirements of some will fall at times different from the maximum requirements of others. In consequence, the firm that covers the entire market is likely to have a better relationship (that is, a lower ratio) between total investment costs (which are determined

---

competitor is likely to reach maximum efficiency in terms of cost and economical use of capital resources. Public convenience also dictates the minimum of pipes, poles, and other distribution equipment necessary for service." *Op. cit.*, 36.

[22] The argument here is not merely semantic. If one chooses to characterize the provision of the same services by competitors as duplicative only in the presence of decreasing costs, it remains true that it is the presence of such economies of scale that is the necessary and sufficient condition for converting mere replication into (wasteful) duplication.

Garfield and Lovejoy are guilty of some fuzziness on this score as well:

"Electric and telephone company poles and underground conduits and cables occupy choice and strategic land sites in metropolitan areas and along our highways. Gas and water mains run under our streets. It is not hard to imagine the obstructions which would be presented by a duplication of utility company facilities. . . . The same, of course, holds true for gas and water companies, which occasionally dig up city streets to repair or enlarge their mains. In light of the

automobile traffic situation, it is apparent that more than one bus or streetcar line on a street is disadvantageous." *Op. cit.*, 16.

These considerations sound conclusive; in fact, they are not. The critical question is: *how many* holes, conduits, mains, and buses, how many diggings up of the streets are necessary to serve a city? And are these most efficiently supplied by one company or by many? Suppose, for example, that the provision of water required two separate underground pipes, each of maximum efficient size, in some portion of the city: it would not necessarily require more digging up of the streets, in order, for example, to repair a leak, if each pipe were owned by a separate company rather than both by one. The monopoly is natural only when one pipe, or common ownership of numerous pipes, with a correspondingly minimized number of diggings, is the most efficient method of supply. Similarly with buses and street congestion: the presence of competing bus *companies* does not necessarily mean an excessive total number of *buses*. It is only if one company can supply the same aggregate service with fewer buses than two that monopoly becomes natural.

by the total demand placed on it at the system peak) and total dollar sales over the year, hence lower average costs, than two or more separate firms, each supplying some portion of the total market.[23]

Cases of Apparently Increasing Costs

There are cases of natural monopoly that would seem at first blush not explicable in terms of long-run decreasing costs. We have already observed, for example, that as the number of telephone subscribers goes up, the number of possible connections among them grows more rapidly; local exchange service is therefore generally believed to be subject to increasing, not decreasing unit costs, when the unit of output is the number of subscribers.[24] And yet, it seems clear that this service is a natural monopoly: if there were two telephone systems serving a community, each subscriber would have to have two instruments, two lines into his home, two bills if he wanted to be able to call everyone else.[25] Despite the apparent presence of increasing costs, in short, monopoly is still natural because one company can serve any *given* number of subscribers (for example, all in a community) at lower cost than two.[26]

In fact, however, this example is not necessarily an exception to the general principle that long-run decreasing costs are an indispensable condition for natural monopoly. The rise in the exchange cost *per subscriber* as their number

---

[23] We have already seen that this is one possible advantage of power-pooling. See note 49, p. 65, Chapter 2, above. The diversity factor is the ratio of the sum of the (noncoincident) maximum demands of the various subdivisions of a firm's customers to the maximum (coincident) system demand. The higher that ratio, the greater is the total quantity of services that can be supplied over some period of time with a given capacity. A single supplier need have capacity only sufficient to meet the sum total of demands at the time of the system's peak. If, instead, there were separate companies supplying each of these subdivisions of the market, each would have to have a total capacity equal to the peak requirement of its own class of customers; and the sum of those noncoincident peak demands calls for a greater total capacity than if they were supplied by a single monopolist.

Economies of diversity of demand do not, however, necessarily require monopoly. An airline whose peak winter demand is on the New York to Miami route may find it economical to operate also New York to Europe, in order to use its equipment on the transatlantic route during the summer. But this fact does not mean it would be most economical to have only such company. The economies of scale might be equally fully exploited by several such companies, each with a similar diversity of routes with noncoincident peaks. Diversity of demand is thus an argument for geographic integration of operations—not necessarily for monopoly.

[24] See note 4, Chapter 5 of Volume 1; also

Garfield and Lovejoy, *op. cit.*, 198–200.

[25] It is possible to imagine alternative arrangements that would avoid these duplications while having more than one company serve a community, but all would in effect involve monopoly. Each company could serve a separate geographical portion of the community, while interconnecting with the other: in their respective territories all would be monopolists. If their market territories overlapped, each could have its own exclusive set of subscribers (once again with interconnections); but this would obviously involve higher cost unless they used common poles and cables—that is, joined together in a single operation for the naturally monopolistic part of the business.

[26] So, for example, Bonbright takes great pains to refute

"what seems to be a widespread assumption that a public utility *must* be producing on the declining-cost segment of a unit-cost curve in order to justify its claim to acceptance as a natural monopoly. This assumption is quite unwarranted. It ignores the point that, even if the unit cost of supplying a given area with a given type of public utility service must increase with an enhanced rate of output, *any specified* required rate of output can be supplied most economically by a single plant or a single system." *Principles of Public Utility Rates*, 14–15. The point is not one of great urgency, but I believe he is mistaken, for reasons that I proceed to develop in the text immediately following.

increases is the counterpart of an improvement in the quality of service rendered: each telephone is thereby enabled to reach more and more customers. The fact that the dollar cost of a unit of service rises as its quality improves is not a proof of decreasing returns. Increasing or decreasing returns can be measured only by the behavior of costs when there is an increased *quantity* of service of an *unchanging* quality. By that test local exchange service, too, is subject to increasing returns: the same subscriber plant (the phone instrument and the drop-line into the house) can handle additional calls at zero additional costs; and the cost of increasing the capacity of the exchange for this purpose is likewise less than the average.[27]

A different kind of apparent concomitance of long-run increasing costs and natural monopoly is illustrated by the case of an electric utility able to generate most of its power in hydroelectric plants at a low cost, but forced then, if it is to meet the additional demand, to shift to higher-cost steam plants. In this event, its marginal cost will exceed the average. But it might still be a natural monopoly, Bonbright observes,

> "For, on the one hand, the single company can secure the maximum advantages of economies of scale and of density, while on the other hand it is no more subject to the diseconomies of enhanced output resulting from scarcity of water power and of other natural resources than would two or more companies if called upon to supply the region with the same total output."[28]

But all this example shows is that certain portions of an industry—those subject to decreasing costs—may be natural monopolies while other portions may not. The point is that the *generation* of electric power is not necessarily a natural monopoly at all—that, to turn Bonbright's observation around, two or more companies in this part of the business might have no higher costs than a single one.

Moreover, as we have already emphasized, the critical factor in the naturalness of monopoly is the presence or absence of economies of scale *internal* to the firm. As Bonbright points out, the rising average costs that are attributable to the exhaustion of choice hydroelectric sites would be a reflection of *external* diseconomies to which the entire industry would be subject, whether composed of one firm or many. In itself, therefore, this upward slope of the industry's LRAC function tells us nothing about whether it is a natural monopoly. The same observation would apply to the apparent tendency for municipal water supply to exhibit long-run increasing costs, evidently because, among other factors, a city has to go farther and farther away—both extensively (geographically) and intensively (for example by resorting to increasingly costly water treatment)—to get additional supplies.[29] And yet water supply, too, is evidently a natural monopoly, because of tendencies to long-run decreasing cost *internal* to the firm.

Moreover, the divergence between marginal cost (of the steam plants for

---

[27] The same observation applies to the apparent tendency to increasing unit cost (that is, per subscriber) as electricity or gas distribution are extended to additional, less sparsely populated areas (see p. 125, Volume 1, above). The reason is that the unit of service is changing in these cases: it is not just the number of kwh or Mcf that is being increased but also the average mileage of transmission service (that is, of "place utility") accompanying each unit of current or gas.

[28] *Ibid.*, 15–16.

[29] See Priest, *Principles of Public Utility Regulation*, II: 751–761.

electricity or desalination plants for water) and average cost is in fact apparent only, and would disappear in perfectly functioning markets. Once the available hydroelectric sites (and nearby fresh water supplies) are exhausted and it becomes necessary to turn to more costly sources of supply, the rental value of the former scarce resources rises sharply. If those scarce inputs (falling and fresh water, respectively) were not owned by the public utility company but were purchased by it in the open market, those rising rents would be incorporated in their purchase prices, and (to confine ourselves to the first illustration) the average unit costs of hydroelectric generation would be increased to those of steam generation. It is the scarcity of certain strategic inputs that is responsible for the external increasing cost tendencies. Payment of their economic rents, reflective of their (growing) scarcity value, would raise the average total costs of all intramarginal output to the long-run cost of the marginal output. And whether, in these circumstances, marginal costs were higher or lower than average total cost would reflect only the presence or absence of internal economies of scale.[30]

In summary, as long as the tendency prevails for unit costs to decline with an increasing volume of business, because of economies of scale internal to the firm, it is more efficient, other things being equal, to have one supplier than several. This does not exclude the possibility that the gains introduced by competition would outweigh the inefficiencies that it entails. But competition in these circumstances has at least a tendency to become (1) destructive: marginal costs are below average cost, and since wholehearted price rivalry means that firms will push prices down to the former level (and even below, if there is hope of driving out a rival), total costs may not be covered for long periods of time, with possible consequent deterioration in the quality of service; and (2) rankly discriminatory—with prices cut to marginal costs in those markets where competitors meet and held at monopolistic levels where they do not.

The first task of public policy, then, is to ascertain for each of these industries the proper scope of natural monopoly, that is, to define the parts of the business where internal economies of scale constitute a strong case on efficiency grounds for permitting only a single supplier. The decision need not be an all-or-nothing one for the entire industry. It may be feasible to permit competition in those branches that are not naturally monopolistic along with, for example, joint ownership or joint utilization of the facilities that are—as when the several railroads crossing the Mississippi River into and out of St. Louis organized themselves into an association to operate bridges and terminal facilities, while yet (at least in principle) continuing to compete in other aspects of their business.[31] In the same way, separate electric distribution companies may take fullest possible advantage of the economies of scale in generation and transmission by participating jointly in the construction of large new generating plants,[32] and private communi-

---

[30] See the references in note 25 on p. 74 of Volume 1.

[31] *U. S. v. Terminal Railroad Association of St. Louis et al.*, 224 U.S. 383 (1912) and 236 U.S. 194 (1915).

[32] See pp. 64–65 and 73–76, in Chapter 2, above. This case is a complicated one, involving natural monopolies of differing geographical scope at the two levels—the locality in distribution and the multistate region in generation. That joint participation in the latter ventures can be conducive to certain important kinds of competition at the distribution level is indicated in our further discussion of power pooling at pp. 316–323, Chapter 6, below.

cations systems may hook up with the Bell interstate switched network monopoly in order to have access to every telephone in the United States (see note 60, p. 133, below).

There is, of course, no general definition of these respective areas valid for all public utility industries or even for any one of them at all times and in all places. The clearest case of natural monopoly is in local distribution, where a single investment in distribution network and plant, a single hook-up with the ultimate user, a single periodic reading of meters and billing can handle an expansion of sales within all foreseeable limits at incremental costs far below average and in important respects at zero cost. A familiar illustration of the way in which the proper definition changes over time is provided by the technological changes of recent decades in electricity generation and transmission, which, by vastly extending the economies of scale, have correspondingly extended the geographic scope of natural monopoly in that part of the business.

COMPETITIVE CERTIFICATION VERSUS CENTRALIZED PLANNING AND RESPONSIBILITY

The most intriguing and actively contested issues involving the proper definition of natural monopoly center not on the desirability of single local distribution systems but on the proper regional, national, and even international structures of the public utility industries. Particularly in communications and the generation and transmission of electricity, but also in the long-distance carriage of natural gas, in the devising of airline schedules and in the operation of railroads, the difficult questions of the 1960s and 1970s have to do with the economies achievable by integration of investment planning and scheduling of operations over wide regions and the proper residual role of competition.

An economist might wonder what it can possibly mean to attempt to preserve competition if the relevant markets are local and in those markets monopoly is natural. Whether a series of local monopolists are linked together financially or retain their separate existence, it would seem, could have no effect on the degree of monopoly power each of them possessed at its point of contact with the ultimate purchaser. The answer will vary from industry to industry; but the general answer is that the relevant markets are not solely local. True, the individual purchaser of electricity, telephone service, and gas will ordinarily have only one local source of supply, and will receive no direct benefit from the presence of separate companies providing the same services in other markets. But there are also wholesale and bulk-sale retail markets, in which the separate local distributor-monopolists and large business customers frequently have the opportunity of choosing among alternative suppliers. In electricity and gas there is also competition-by-example and by threat of takeover, between public and private companies. And in communications, as in transportation, there are possibilities of competition for different parts of various journeys between separate companies, and in almost all the regulated industries large users have the alternative of serving their own needs, as well.

The National Telecommunications Network

It has been the accelerated technological progress of recent decades that has brought these issues to the fore; and nowhere have they been more intense than in the field of communications. We have already alluded to the technological explosion in communications after World War II and discussed some of the numerous competitive issues that it has generated—most prominently the proper role of private microwave relay systems, of communications satellites and transoceanic cable,[33] of community antenna television systems,[34] and the proper pricing of communications services in these circumstances.[35] In the presence of such rapid change, the natural monopoly of yesterday may be transformed into a natural arena of competition today; and vice versa.

That the provision of local telephone service is a natural monopoly is generally conceded. The Bell System makes a powerful argument that the same is true of the entire national telecommunications network. The argument, as all others for natural monopoly, can be embraced under the familiar rubric of decreasing costs over the entire relevant range of production. But it has so many facets in addition to the familiar one of progressive economies of scale in the production of a standardized service that it is worth examining in detail.

The case for a national telecommunications network monopoly has the following interrelated aspects:

1. Simple economies of scale in the provision of a standardized service. The cost per circuit-mile of capacity seems to have a tendency indefinitely to decline, the larger the number of circuit-miles provided for.[36]

2. Aggregate investment costs can be minimized, it is argued, if the planning for the installation and expansion of capacity is done with an eye to the requirements of the entire system. The essence of the service is the provision of physical connections and interconnections—300 million to 400 million calls daily—between the 102 million telephones in the country. Since any of the 5 million billion possible connections that the system must stand ready to make at any point in time may be performed over an almost infinite variety of routes, ranging from the most direct to the most indirect, and since the demand placed on any single portion of a route will fluctuate widely from one moment and one season to the next, the clue to providing instantaneous connections with any given probability of delay, at minimum total investment cost, is the provision for automatic rerouting of calls from one circuit to another in the event that the preceding one is occupied. This means, ideally, that the addition of any individual links of capacity can most efficiently be accomplished only in consideration of the extent to which the particular link will provide backup capacity for all other parts of the system, on the one hand, and, on the other, the extent to which the particular connection being provided for may, in case of need, be provided instead by existing capacity along alternative routes. The principle is the same one as justifies interconnection of electric power companies, because, in the

---

[33] See pp. 65, 122 note 98, Volume 1, and pp. 51–52, Chapter 2, above.
[34] See pp. 32–45, Chapter 1, above.

[35] See pp. 121–122, 134, 156–158, 173–174, Volume 1.
[36] See pp. 125–129, Volume 1.

presence of diversities of demand for the services of each, they can jointly provide for their markets with a smaller total investment than if each were at all times completely dependent on its own resources alone.[37]

3. The higher the standards of service demanded, the greater, it is maintained, is the need for centralized responsibility and control. Specifically, to provide virtually instantaneous connections, automatic switching and high standards of intelligibility of the signals, one company has to be responsible for all the parts whose interaction determines the level of performance.[38] This contention has traditionally provided the support for the Bell System's historic insistence that it alone provide, install, and continue to own and service all equipment hooked up in any way with the telephone network:

> "At any one time, during the busy hours, there may be five or ten million simultaneous conversations going on over the network, and thousands of them may be going through a single cable or radio relay system.

> "This concentrated use of switching and transmission facilities means that, in order to avoid mutual interference, there must be careful control of the character of the signals used to activate the switching system, and of the level of signals which carry speech or other forms of intelligence."[39]

These high standards of performance, on the one hand, and the inescapable interdependence of all parts of the system, on the other, it is contended, impose extraordinary requirements of compatibility among all parts of the plant, of reliability in the functioning of the millions of its separate components, in the planned availability of repair, maintenance, and backup capacity. And all of these require that a single company have the full and sole responsibility.[40]

4. If the network is to be truly national, if (almost) everyone is to be able at any moment to reach (almost) everyone else, then service must be extended to (almost) everyone, rich and poor, over routes extending to the most isolated parts of the country. It is burdensome to stand ready to serve all users, on demand, on routes that are rarely used, with backup capacity sufficient for almost any emergency (consider the demand on the telephone system imposed when the President was assassinated). No company is likely to assume such responsibilities unless it is given a

---

[37] See note 23, this Chapter, above. To what extent the investment process for the entire Bell System is in fact systematically planned in this fashion, the writer is unable to say; he has heard skepticism expressed on this score.

[38] AT&T describes its network as

"A web of millions of intricate and complicated mechanisms, all of which must work reliably and compatibly at a moment's notice to make any of five million billion possible connections. It is an ever-changing and delicately balanced machine, designed and nurtured to meet the System's responsibility to the public to provide a first class nationwide service—and it

does just that." "Vertical Integration in the Bell System: A Systems Approach to Technological and Economic Imperatives of the Telephone Network," President's Task Force on Communications Policy, Staff Paper 5, Part 2, Appendix C, PB 184 418, June 1969, 2.

[39] "Competition Situations Faced by the Bell System," Company Memorandum, mimeo., December 26, 1968, 6.

[40] These various arguments for a single integrated operation extend also to the necessity for vertical integration: manufacturing, installation, and service functions are all held to be part of the natural monopoly. See pp. 297–302, Chapter 6, below.

monopoly on the lucrative routes as a quid pro quo and as a means of assuring it the ability to cover all the costs of its readiness to serve. The reader will recognize here the argument against competitive cream-skimming (see pp. 7–10, in Chapter 1, above). Since this argument applies not only to the protection of natural monopoly but also to the more general case against competition in regulated industries, we reserve its further consideration for Chapter 5.

This position has been subjected to increasingly intense challenge in recent years, especially in the market for private or bulk communications, which provides large users with circuits of their own for continuous point-to-point communication.

The Above-890 Decisions. The occasion for the first major challenge was the development of microwave radio transmission, which made it possible for such users to set up their own facilities—provided the Federal Communications Commission would allocate to them the required portions of the radio spectrum.[41]

Because the costs of microwave for such purposes promised to be much lower than the common carrier rates, numerous large commercial, industrial, and governmental entities applied to the FCC for the necessary authorizations. Supporting their petitions were various manufacturers of electronic equipment, who were anxious to get into and develop that rich market, from which they would have remained essentially excluded if the field were left entirely to the common carriers and their own, financially affiliated, virtually exclusive manufacturing subsidiaries such as Western Electric. Prominent among the former were representatives of utility companies, the oil industry, railroads, truckers, the National Association of Manufacturers—speaking, among others, for the automobile, air frame manufacturing, chemical and steel industries—state highway officials, state turnpike authorities, municipalities, chiefs of police, and newspaper publishers. The common carriers intervened to oppose the applications.[42] Arguing that (1) the limited capacities of the radio spectrum and (2) the naturally monopolistic character of communications both required that the spectrum be reserved for themselves, they contended that if large users were permitted to build their own facilities the result could only be congestion in the airwaves and higher cost and poorer service for all. The fact remained, the private applicants pointed out, that if permitted to construct their own facilities, they could provide for their needs at much lower costs than the carriers' tariffs.[43]

For a time, the Commission accepted the natural monopoly philosophy, issuing licenses for private systems only on an interim basis, when the

41 On much of the following see Manley R. Irwin, "The Communication Industry and the Policy of Competition," *Buffalo Law Rev.* (Fall 1964), XIV: 256–273.
42 They raised no objection to the applications for public safety organizations (police and fire protection) and right-of-way companies—railroads, oil and gas pipelines, and power companies—which need communications facilities along routes generally not served by common-carrier systems. *In the Matter of Allocation of Frequencies in the Bands Above 890 Mc.*, Report and Order, 27 FCC 359, 367–379, 386 (July 1959).
43 On the reasons for this discrepancy, see pp. 146–149, below. On the record of this controversy as it developed in the area of television network interconnection services, see FCC, *Network Broadcasting*, Report of the Network Study Staff to the Network Study Committee, published by the U.S. House of Representatives, Committee on Interstate and Foreign Commerce, 85th Cong. 2d Sess., House Report No. 1297, 1958, 542–549.

applicants could demonstrate that common-carrier facilities were not yet available to them, and only until such facilities did become available. But the pressures by private users for a liberalization of this policy continued to mount during the 1950s[44] and finally, in its famous "above 890" decisions of 1959 and 1960, the Commission capitulated. Pointing to the demonstrated need for private point-to-point communications systems, and concluding that there were adequate frequencies above 890 megacycles to take care of present and reasonably foreseeable future needs of both the common carriers and private users, it deprecated the threat to the common carriers and emphasized the advantages of competition in spurring the development of communications technology.[45]

All the major issues confronted by the FCC in these proceedings involved in one form or another the question of whether the public would be better served by free competitive entry, on the one hand, or by a common-carrier monopoly on the other. In response to the carriers' contention that the highest quality and minimum cost would be assured by vesting the responsibility exclusively in them, the Commission instead accepted the views of the applicants that private systems could provide service of a quality and at a cost better tailored to their individual requirements:

"In many cases, the operation of the private users is such that it is not convenient or practicable for common carriers to provide such service (e.g., remote or isolated business operations). . . . Even in areas where common carrier facilities and personnel are readily available, there appears to be a need for private systems. In the first place, the private users do not require, in all cases, the high quality of service provided by the carriers to meet the varied needs of the public. Also, such private systems would provide for better control and flexibility for meeting their own hour-by-hour operational and administrative needs."[46]

The Commission recognized, too, the possibility that the availability of this competitive alternative could contribute to a superior dynamic performance:

"it may be observed that certain of the private users now licensed endeavored to get the common carriers to provide such service initially and constructed their private systems only when the carriers refused to do so."[47]

"There is yet another consideration which impels us to our determination. We feel that the expanded eligibility will afford a competitive spur in the

---

[44] The reader can imagine, from our earlier discussion of the FCC's solicitude for the viability of small television broadcasters, how difficult it must have been for it to resist the claim of these companies that they could not afford AT&T's charges. *Ibid.*, 547–549.

[45] "We stated that the liberalized licensing policies would provide an impetus in the manufacturing of microwave equipment, which, in turn, would result in improvements in the communications art. The evidence in the record shows that the manufacturers of microwave equipment for private users have been reluctant in the past to develop microwave equipment to any substantial extent due to the fact that the

licensing of private microwave systems has been on a developmental basis except in the aviation services. With the opening of a new market for microwave equipment, it seems quite clear that the resultant competitive situation among manufacturers will provide the incentive for developing better equipment for meeting the needs of private users and a concomitant improvement in the communications art." *In the Matter of Allocation of Frequencies in the Bands Above 890 Mc.*, Memorandum Opinion and Order, 29 FCC 825, 854 (1960).

[46] 27 FCC 359, 413 (1959).

[47] *Ibid.*

manufacturing of equipment and in the development of the communications art."[48]

It made its endorsement of the freely competitive approach even more complete when it rejected the position of the common carriers that it should not license private users if common-carrier facilities were available or would be made available "within a reasonable length of time," and that any licenses it grant be subject to the condition that the private system be "amortized when common carrier service becomes available."[49]

"we are of the opinion that the public interest would not be served by a policy of restricting or denying the licensing of private point-to-point systems solely because common carrier facilities are available or may become available in the reasonable future. It follows that the Commission should not consider the availability of common carrier facilities as a condition of eligibility for private users."[50]

This attitude contrasts interestingly with the policy followed by the ICC in deciding whether the public convenience and necessity justify its authorizing additional motor carrier service.[51]

On the other hand, the Commission was by no means prepared to authorize additional competition in the common-carrier communications business itself, or to commit itself to a policy of unrestricted competitive entry without regard to the possibility of an unfavorable impact on the carriers and their other customers. On the first point, it refused to permit the private users to share frequencies on a cooperative basis, thus making it clear that it was opening the door only to individual users who wished to supply their own individual needs:

"While it is recognized that such [cooperative] use may, in some cases, result in a better and more effective utilization of frequencies, this argument is, at least, equally persuasive in support of a conclusion that service should be afforded by communication common carriers. Further, although such an arrangement may make it economically feasible for smaller firms and organizations to utilize microwave for their operations, it must be observed that such shared usage is inconsistent with one of the principal justifications urged by private users for their own systems; viz., exclusive control of their own facilities because of special communications problems. Finally, we have some concern with the fact that creation of extensive point-to-point co-operative facilities may lead to undesirable situations where the cooperatives have many of the attributes of communication common carriers without assuming the responsibilities of service and the burdens of regulation which apply to common carriers."[52]

On the latter point, the Commission rejected the objections of the common carriers that a free licensing of private systems would amount to cream-skimming, but only on the ground that no showing of such an adverse effect had yet been made:

"Of course, this matter requires continued surveillance, and, if future

---

[48] *Ibid.*, 414. See also note 45, above.   [51] See pp. 15–18, Chapter 1, above.
[49] *Ibid.*, 387.   [52] *Ibid.*, 407–408.
[50] *Ibid.*, 412.

conditions warrant, appropriate consideration will then be given to the problem."[53]

When, then, in the *Comsat Authorized Users* litigation, the Commission determined that there would be such an adverse effect on the general users, it reached a decision that greatly restricted the possibilities of genuine competition, as we shall shortly see.[54]

Any account of the competitive impact of microwave would have to describe AT&T's vigorous reaction to the threat of competitive entry sanctioned by the *above-890* decision. To hold its large customers it offered a new set of private line services at much more favorable rates—several classes of Telpak, Wide Area Telephone, Wide Area Data (WATS and WADS), and Dataphone services.[55] Western Union and Motorola (a leading manufacturer of microwave equipment) promptly charged that the Telpak rates were unduly discriminatory, and the FCC eventually held that they were.[56] The Commission has been almost continuously engaged since 1956 in investigating rates charged by AT&T and Western Union for private line and other business services, examining the possibility that they were (1) injurious to competition and (2) a burden on—that is, subsidized by—the users of ordinary long-distance (message toll telephone—MTT) service.[57] Obviously, these two aspects of the proper role and nature of competition in public utilities—how much freedom of entry and how much freedom to price competitively—are closely interrelated; we consider them together presently. The shift in AT&T strategy in this instance, from an attempt first to exclude competition spawned by technological progress or to subject it to tight licensing, to a demand for greater freedom to engage in selective competitive price cutting is clearly the story of the railroads revisited.

The MCI Cases. The *above-890* decisions opened the door only to private communications systems. An even more direct competitive threat to the common carriers appeared several years later, when a tiny newcomer, Microwave Communications, Inc. (MCI), applied for FCC certification for public, common-carrier, point-to-point microwave radio communications service between Chicago, St. Louis, and intermediate points, with a direct duplication of Bell and Western Union services and facilities.[58] The service MCI proposed to offer was barebone in character: it would simply operate the radio path between its specified points;[59] subscribers would have to

[53] *Ibid.*, 412.
[54] See pp. 137–139, below.
[55] See C. F. Phillips, Jr., *op. cit.*, 677–678.
[56] *In the Matter of AT&T Co. Tariff FCC No. 250, TELPAK Service and Channels*, Memorandum Opinion and Order, 37 FCC 1111 (1964). For a later negative decision, see FCC, *In the Matter of TELPAK Tariff Sharing Provisions of American Telephone and Telegraph Company and the Western Union Telegraph Co.*, Docket No. 17457, Decision, June 10, 1970.
[57] *AT&T and Western Union Private Line Cases*, 34 FCC 217 (1963). This was the principal issue in phase 1B of Docket 16258; see pp. 156–158, and 173–174, Volume 1, and pp. 227–233, Chapter 5, below. Pursuant to the stipulated settlement that terminated Phase 1B, AT&T

undertook long-run incremental cost studies to determine whether its various business service rates were compensatory. On the basis of those studies, in 1969 it put into effect increased rates for television program transmission, and filed new tariffs also for TELPAK and TWX service, all of which it estimated would bring in $87,000,000 of added revenue at 1969 volumes; and indicated its intention to introduce corresponding reductions in MTT and WATS rates. *Telecommunications Reports* (October 6, 1969), XXXV:1–7.
[58] FCC, *In re Applications of Microwave Communications, Inc.* Docket No. 16509, Initial Decision of the Hearing Examiner, mimeo., October 17, 1967. See also note 60, below.
[59] The principal use, it was anticipated, would

acquire and maintain their own terminal equipment and build their own
connections with the MCI stations—something they were evidently not
expected to be willing to do. It hoped to be able to negotiate for interconnection with the common carriers; but in view of the hostility and scorn
the latter showed for its proposed operation in their interventions before the
FCC, the prospects for this were hardly rosy until the Commission indicated
in 1969 it was virtually prepared to order them to interconnect.[60] Its construction quality would be minimal, as were its proposed provisions for
service, maintenance, for protection and guarantee against all conceivable
types of interference, outage, failure, and other acts of man and God.

And yet MCI offered two things that the Bell companies and Western
did not: first, low rates—its proposed charges were less than half those of the
established carriers—and second, far greater freedom and flexibility in use
of the service: customers could attach such equipment as they saw fit and up
to five of them could share the use of a single channel, thus further reducing
the cost of each. And it was this proposed contribution that, in the last
analysis, induced the FCC to approve the application.[61] MCI had, the
Examiner concluded, given sufficient demonstration of a market for its
services:

"The specific 'need' which on this record it can be concluded that MCI

---

be for simple interoffice and interplant communications, for voice, teleprinter, facsimile,
data transmission, and time-shared computer
facilities.

[60] "The Hearing Examiner does not go as far as
the Common Carrier Bureau in assuming 'that
MCI will be able to negotiate appropriate
interconnection arrangements with existing
carriers. . . .' The carriers' intransigence, manifested in this case, can hardly be expected to
abate. . . . But there is no need to anticipate at
this stage. . . . It may be that on full consideration
the Commission will refuse to compel interconnection. After the hearing and pleadings, it
should come as no surprise to MCI that it will
in all likelihood be faced with another round of
litigation to enable it to complete its system."
Ibid., at par. 107.

"Since they [the common carriers] have
indicated that they will not voluntarily provide
loop service we shall retain jurisdiction of this
proceeding in order to enable MCI to obtain . . .
a prompt determination on the matter of interconnection. Thus, at such time as MCI has
customers and the facts and details of the
customers' requirements are known, MCI may
come directly to the Commission with a request
for an order of interconnection. We have already
concluded that a grant of MCI's proposal is in
the public interest. We likewise conclude that,
absent a significant showing that interconnection
is not technically feasible, the issuance of an
order requiring the existing carriers to provide
loop service is in the public interest." FCC,
In re Applications of Microwave Communications, Inc.,

Docket No. 16509, Decision, August 13, 1969,
par. 36.

By 1970, compulsory interconnection of common carriers with any and all competitors on
reasonable and nondiscriminatory terms had
become a general, clearly enunciated FCC
policy:

"If access to local facilities is requested and
needed by the applicants, we would expect the
local carrier—Bell or other carrier—to permit
interconnection or leased channel arrangements
on reasonable terms and conditions to be negotiated with the new carriers. In other words,
where a carrier has monopoly control over
essential facilities we shall not condone any
policy or practice whereby such carrier would
discriminate in favor of an affiliated carrier or
show favoritism among competitors. Customers
of any new carrier should also be afforded the
option by the local carrier to obtain local distribution facilities under reasonable terms set forth
in the tariff schedules of the latter." *In the Matter
of Establishment of Policies and Procedures for Consideration of Applications to Provide Specialized Common Carrier Services in the Domestic Public Point-to-
Point Microwave Radio Service etc.*, Docket No.
18920, Notice of Inquiry to Formulate Policy,
etc., July 15, 1970, par. 67. On the general
principle, and for similar examples in other
regulatory situations, see pp. 307–323, Chapter
6, below.

[61] A sharply divided Commission upheld the
Examiner's recommended decision in all substantial respects, by a 4 to 3 vote, on August 13,
1969. See the note immediately preceding.

has established that it will fulfill is for a cheaper communications service." (par. 109)

"It may be found that there is a market for common carrier service of acceptable quality at a cost substantially lower than results from rates in filed tariffs."[62]

Conceding "no pretense . . . that MCI . . . is other than a shoestring operation," the Examiner found it had "sufficient money in hand and reasonable expectation of procuring more to stamp it financially qualified."[63] Recognizing that "from the lofty viewpoint of the carriers, MCI's system is jerry-built," that "the sites are small; the architecture of the huts is late Sears Roebuck toolshed," he concluded nonetheless that "there is no reason to believe that the system will not work."[64]

In endorsing these conclusions, the Commission did not really confront the critical economic question: would MCI's entry and others like it result in injury to the common carriers and hence a higher-cost, lower quality communications service to all other users? Its decision makes the clear case for competitive entry: a new firm, seeing a market not thus far tapped, is willing to risk its capital to bring in a new, lower price-quality combination. But if the telecommunications network is really a natural monopoly, the indirect costs and inefficiencies imposed on the entire system by such entry could outweigh its direct benefits. This was the real burden of the carriers' opposition: they claimed that MCI proposed to engage in mere cream-skimming, throwing on them and their other customers the costs thereof. We consider the merits of this objection in our general discussion of the cream-skimming problem, in Chapter 5.

It is nonetheless difficult for an economist to find fault with the Examiner's and the Commission majority's general disposition to adopt a "wait and see" attitude with regard to those possible injuries and to incline on the side of letting a small, would-be competitor probe the possible existence of a market for lower-cost service:

"Any such grant [of certification] should not be construed as indicating that the Commission would favorably regard similar proposals between other major markets by MCI or others. The instant proposal should be given a reasonable opportunity to become established and thereby afford the Commission an opportunity to observe the results and consequences of its operations in terms of the demand generated for its services, its ability to operate efficiently and profitably, and its effect upon petitioners' [that is, AT&T and Western Union's] operations."[65]

Nor can the economist but applaud the Examiner's suggestion that the effect of this experiment, because of the price-elasticity of demand, could well be beneficial rather than injurious to the regular carriers as well:

"The record may not be sufficient to warrant a definite conclusion that . . .

---

62 *Op. cit.*, par. 66. The Examiner did qualify this finding by recognizing that persons expressing an interest in MCI service had assumed it would be interconnected with the facilities of the admittedly hostile common carriers; but decided it was not his function, in this proceeding, to decide whether MCI would indeed succeed in

obtaining interconnection. See *ibid.*, par. 67, 69, and note 60, above.

63 *Ibid.*, par. 94.

64 *Ibid.*, pars. 96, 97.

65 *Ibid.*, par. 103. The Commission's opinion makes essentially the same observation (par. 37).

there is a 'sub-market' of potential users not able to afford existing service but who could be exploited by MCI. Nevertheless, one can speculate, with justification equal to that underlying the carriers' assumptions about their vulnerability, that there would be an addition to their revenues through interconnection for MCI customers expanding communications usage."[66]

Probing the elasticity of demand is another thing competition can do much more reliably than monopoly, natural or otherwise.

The promise of microwave radio and a burgeoning demand soon proved too powerful to permit the FCC the luxury of following the cautious and tentative policy it had adopted in accepting the modest initial MCI proposal. Within a year it was confronted with no fewer than thirty-seven applications by companies (ten of them associated with MCI), proposing to establish themselves as specialized common carriers. The proposals involved construction of 1713 microwave stations, more than one-third the number in the entire Bell system. The most dramatic of these, submitted by Data Transmission Co. (Datran), was for a $350,000,000 nation-wide switched network solely for the transmission of data, providing end-to-end service in direct competition with the Bell System.[66a] And so, also, within the year, the FCC staff was calling for a radical generalization of the *above-890* and *MCI* decisions into a bold policy of free entry into the field of specialized communications services, within the limits of radio spectrum availability. The logic of its argument was simply that competition could far more effectively than monopoly develop and exploit the varied potentialities of the new technology, particularly in satisfying the specialized requirements of business users:

"In proposing a policy favoring the entry of new specialized common carriers, we look toward a degree of competition oriented toward the development of new communications services and markets and the application of improvements in technology to changing and diverse demands. Thus, we are not faced with the question of whether we should increase the number of carriers which are to serve a fixed market with the same services. . . . Rather we anticipate that the new carriers would be developing new services and would thereby expand the size of the total communications market."[66b]

---

[66] *Op. cit.*, par. 113. The FCC had suggested exactly the same possibility in its *above-890* decision, 27 FCC 359, 388 (1959).

[66a] FCC, *In the Matter of Establishment of Policies*, *etc.*, Docket No. 18920, *op. cit.*, note 60, above, pars. 6, 10–11 and Appendix; and information from AT&T. All the other proposals (besides Datran) were for specialized, private line service from one geographic point to another; none would offer switched, message service, end-to-end (i.e., directly interconnecting subscribers).

[66b] *Ibid.*, par. 29. According to Datran,

"Full realization of the public interest in computer technology requires achievement of appropriate specialized communications services. The users of computer technology are not obtaining adequate service from communications facilities constructed for, and dedicated to, meeting voice and record transmission needs. Effective utilization of existing data processing technology is constrained by present common carrier communications services and facilities, and the design and development of new computer applications requiring data transmission is constrained by high cost as well as unreliable and inflexible service." *Ibid.*, par. 9.

According to the FCC staff,

"In order to realize large scale economies, a single supplier must conglomerate diverse functions and provide general standardized services, thereby foregoing potential economies of specialization that could be derived by serving a specialized portion of the market . . . .

"The sheer size of the AT&T organizational structure, its enormous financing requirements, its vertical integration, and near monopoly

As the foregoing comment indicates, the Staff deprecated the threatened diversion of business from the Bell System and consequent loss of the benefits of scale economies, arguing that only 2 to 4 percent of Bell's existing business would be subject to the competition, that the entrants would mainly be developing new, specialized markets rather than competing for existing business, and that the expanded total sales of communications services to which they could be expected to contribute could well produce a net increase in demand for Bell services, for interconnection and local distribution.[66c]

The Commission itself split 3 to 3 on the question of openly endorsing the Staff's proposals, but its notice scheduling hearings left the strong impression that it was highly receptive to them.[66d]

The Communications Satellite. From the very outset, the intense political struggle over who would be authorized to put up and operate the satellite system was clearly envisaged as determining whether this new communications medium would develop as an integral part of the operations of the existing common carriers or whether, instead, it might develop independently of, and in direct competition with them. Proponents of the latter position argued strenuously that if the carriers, and preponderantly AT&T,[67] controlled the satellite system, they would restrain its development in order to protect their huge investments in existing facilities. They also made much of the Bell System's expressed skepticism about the commercial feasibility of the new techniques and of its preference for the low-level, random, moving satellites, which would (and in fact did) prove to be much more expensive than the 22,300-mile high synchronous satellites now being used.[68] The result was a compromise: in 1962 Congress entrusted the

---

position . . . may make it slower to perceive and respond to individual, specialized requirements and to initiate market and technical innovations. Competition in the specialized communications field would enlarge the equipment market for manufacturers other than Western Electric, and may stimulate . . . the introduction of new techniques." *Ibid.*, pars. 33, 34.

[66c] *Ibid.*, pars. 39–40.

[66d] For example, some of the applicants claimed that their proposals were mutually exclusive on economic grounds. The FCC nevertheless declined to hold comparative hearings on such claims, asserting that the market potential seemed great enough to support more than one applicant in the same area, and that users ought to have the benefit of a choice of competing services:

"We are not confronted here with applications which seek to duplicate all or even a major portion of the services provided by the existing carriers or to enter a static market. Instead, the applicants seek to develop a relatively new and potentially very large market . . . .

"Various systems may develop along different lines, each offering something of value to the public which would attract sufficient customers for viable operations. The number of successful operations may well depend on the ingenuity, enterprise and initiative of applicants and equipment manufacturers over a period of years in taking advantage of changing circumstances and in coming up with the types of services and equipment that will attract sufficient business to support the particular system." *Ibid.*, pars. 48–49; see also 50–50b.

[67] In the international field, AT&T has the monopoly on message telephone and voice-grade channel service. ITT World Communications, RCA Communications and Western Union International operate in the transmission of recorded messages.

[68] Because the synchronous satellites remain in a fixed position in the sky, they can be fewer in number and can be served by far more simple ground (receiving and transmitting) stations. The stations required for tracking moving satellites across the horizon and shifting automatically from one to the next would have been much more costly. See U.S. Senate, Committee on Foreign Relations, 87th Cong., 2d Sess., *The Communications Satellite Act of 1962, Hearings*, 1962, and the debates in the *Congressional Record*, 87th Cong., 2d Sess., CVIII (1962), particularly the speeches of Senators Morse, Long, Yarborough, and Kefauver.

international field to the Communications Satellite Corporation, a separate, newly established company whose ownership was to be divided equally between the common carriers on the one hand and the investing public on the other, with only six members of its Board of Directors to represent each of these two constituencies and another three to be appointed by the President, and with the further provision that no stockholder could elect more than three directors.[69] The issue of who would be authorized to set up a domestic system was not resolved at that time.[70]

The mere constitution of a quasi-independent corporation did not, however, resolve the question of the extent to which Comsat was to be permitted to compete directly with the established carriers, or whether it was, instead, to serve entirely as their own instrument. The issue was most dramatically posed when, during 1965, the Federal Communications Commission received requests from several companies—including press wire services, a newspaper, a television network, and an airline—about the possibility of their obtaining satellite telecommunication services directly from Comsat. When the Commission set this question down for hearing, a great number of private companies and trade associations (for example, the American Petroleum Institute, the American Trucking Association, the Associated Press, the American Newspaper Publishers Association, Dow Jones) and the United States government intervened to press their interest in being able to deal directly with the satellite corporation, rather than through the common carriers alone. The latter intervened to press the case for confining Comsat to the role of a "carriers' carrier," thus forcing all ultimate customers to depend on them for any communications services using the satellite. While the FCC rejected the latter view, it nevertheless handed down a decision that restricted very severely the circumstances under which noncommon-carrier companies might be authorized to deal directly with Comsat—rejecting even the the contention of the General Services Administration that the United States Government, at least, had the right of unrestricted direct dealings. As for nongovernmental users, the Commission concluded:

"Comsat would be authorized to deal directly with the users in only those instances where the requirement for satellite service is of such an exceptional or unique nature that the service must be tailored to the peculiar needs of the customer and therefore cannot be provided within the terms and conditions of a general public tariff offering."[71]

---

[69] 47 U.S. Code 701–744, 1964 ed. These arrangements were slightly amended in 1969. Public Law 91–3, 91st Cong. 1st Sess., 83 Stat. 4. See also John McDonald, "The Comsat Compromise Starts a Revolution," *Fortune* (October 1965), LXXII: 128–131; Harvey J. Levin, "Organization and Control of Communications Satellites," *Univ. of Penn. Law Rev.* (January 1965), CXIII: 315–357; and Herman Schwartz, "Governmentally Appointed Directors in a Private Corporation –the Communications Satellite Act of 1962," *Harvard Law Rev.* (December 1965), LXXIX: 350–364.

[70] This question was raised in 1965, when the American Broadcasting Company asked FCC permission to do so. The Commission thereupon invited suggestions from other interested parties. FCC, *In the Matter of the Establishment of Domestic Non-Common Carrier Communications Satellite Facilities by Non-Governmental Entities*, Docket No. 16495. While the matter has not been decisively resolved as of this writing, it appears that development of the domestic system is likely to be more highly competitive. See note 77a, below.

[71] *In the Matter of Authorized Entities and Authorized Users Under the Communications Satellite Act of 1962*, Memorandum Opinion and Statement of Policy, 4 FCC 2d 421, 431 (1966); Memorandum Opinion and Order, 6 FCC 2d 593 (1967).

What was at issue here, clearly, was the right of Comsat to enter the communications market on its own behalf. As long as it remains almost exclusively a carriers' carrier, those companies control the flow of business to it; it is they, therefore, who will determine to what extent this alternative communications medium will in fact be developed—except to the extent that the FCC limits their discretion.[72] And, as we have already pointed out (p. 52, Chapter 2, above), the carriers would presumably not have the same incentive as a competitive Comsat to push the development of this far less capital-intensive technology, when the alternative is to use their own facilities, and thereby justify their own rate bases. The one sure remedy for any A–J–W distortion is of course competition; and the FCC decision on authorized users severely limited the potential scope of that competition— unfortunately in the very situation in which, because of the widely divergent capital intensities of the alternative technologies available, the A–J–W danger seems particularly serious.[73]

On the other hand, as the FCC pointed out, unrestricted competition between Comsat and the other carriers is infeasible. The governing statute limits the former company to the international satellite portion of the service; and it would presumably be intolerably inefficient for it to attempt to duplicate the domestic facilities of the common carriers. Therefore even if the Commission permitted any and all customers to deal directly with Comsat, it would be only the large users that could hook up directly with its ground stations and lease circuits from it. So the only feasible competition would be for these customers alone; only they would receive the full cost savings of satellite transmission.[74] Whether this would produce optimal results

---

[72] On the condition the FCC attached when it authorized the common carriers to lay another transatlantic cable (the TAT-5) in 1968, see note 89, pp. 76–77, above.

[73] Considerations such as these were clearly relevant, also, in the disputed issue of who would be permitted to own the ground stations serving and served by the satellite, which the FCC resolved in 1966 by conferring joint ownership on the Communications Satellite Corporation on the one hand and the common carriers on the other, at least as far as the six initial earth stations in the United States were concerned. *In the Matter of Amendment to Part 25 of the Commission's Rules and Regulations with respect to Ownership and Operation of Initial Earth Stations* etc., Second Report and Order, 5 FCC 2d 812 (1966). Herman Schwartz has an interesting criticism of this decision: while recognizing that participation in the ground station investment will make the common carriers more inclined than they otherwise would be to make use of the satellite facilities, he points out that this investment would be very slight compared with their stake in cable and conventional radio facilities, and criticizes the decision on the ground that it increases the likelihood of common-carrier control over the development of the satellite system. It seems difficult to reconcile his position here, however, with his approval of the *Authorized*

Users decision, which, he feels, properly forestalled the threat of cream-skimming. (On this point, see our Chapter 5, pp. 227–233, below.) *Op. cit., Yale Law Jour.* (January 1967), LXXVI: 444–453, 457–459, 471–473. As long as few users can deal directly with Comsat, it would seem that the common carriers are in any event in a position to control the rate of its development, which is precisely what Schwartz fears.

[74] The FCC argues that the possibility of unrestricted competition is similarly limited by the inability of the *other* carriers to go into Comsat's exclusive field of operations: if Comsat could deal unrestrictedly with all ultimate customers, it could use its statutory monopoly on the space segment of international communications to deny the other carriers a fair opportunity to compete. *Op. cit.,* 4 FCC 2d 421 (1966), pars. 20, 26. The Commission's reasoning here is somewhat cryptic. What it seems to mean is that Comsat might deny the other carriers access to its international satellite facilities on fair terms, or might divert to its own facilities exclusively whatever traffic it originated. The FCC's opinion does not consider whether such dangers could be forestalled, as in transportation, by requiring Comsat to serve all carriers fairly and nondiscriminatorily and to set joint rates with them. See pp. 273–275, 307–323, below.

is a question we consider once again in our separate discussion of cream-skimming.[75]

The satellite does not eradicate the case for natural monopoly in communications: like microwave radio, it merely redefines its proper scope. There is no question of the specialized microwave systems or whatever carrier operates the satellite directly duplicating the intricate exchange-switching service of the Bell System, although Datran proposes to do exactly this for one specialized market. The question is mainly one of the extent to which the System's transmission facilities are properly subjected to competition where that is commercially feasible. The ideal arrangement would seem to be for the maximum feasible competition among alternative media for those portions of the service for which they do represent viable coexisting alternatives.[76] The satellite is one such; microwave apparently another.[77] Any attempt to deny these competitive media a full and fair opportunity to compete ought properly to bear a substantial burden of proof that their entry would be truly injurious to the common carrier service, causing its quality to deteriorate unjustifiably or its real costs to increase.[77a]

---

[75] See pp. 227–233, Chapter 5, below.

[76] There is another possible "ideal": that "competition" between the alternative communications media be achieved not by market rivalry between companies utilizing only one or the other exclusively but by diversified companies free to use *either*, choosing among them on the basis of which medium or combination of media would do the job best. On the general principle, see pp. 264–267, Chapter 6, below. The choice becomes a difficult one, when the economies of scale are so great, relative to the extent of the market, as to leave room for only one such company, as the President's Task Force on Communications Policy concluded was the case in the international arena (see p. 117, above; note 102 of this chapter; and note 32 of Chapter 6, below).

[77] Direct satellite-to-receiver radio and television broadcasting could bypass the existing communications network entirely (see note 15, p. 51, Chapter 2, above) just as long-distance telephoning completely bypasses the Post Office and the electronic transmission of written messages would do even more effectively. But for most services, the competition would be partial only; for those portions in which a continued Bell monopoly remained "natural," that monopoly could remain inviolate.

[77a] One factor limiting the competitive impact of the satellite is that Comsat was given exclusive jurisdiction in this field, as far as international communications are concerned. This was done evidently on the assumption that a single chosen instrument was required by the economies of scale and that it would be most conducive to the exploitation and development of this as yet unexplored technology. (See our discussion of the promotional case for restricting competition on

pp. 3–4, above). Therefore, it was natural to think of Comsat as essentially a carriers' carrier, rather than, primarily, as their direct competitor.

But since the potential domestic U.S. market for satellite service is so much greater, relative to the available economies of scale, competition is believed to be feasible domestically. Leland L. Johnson, "Technological Advance and Market Structure in Domestic Telecommunications," *Amer. Econ. Rev., Papers and Proceedings* (May 1970), LX: 208. Possibly this is also so because the commercial feasibility of the new technology has now been much more clearly demonstrated. In these circumstances, the possibility is opened up of far more direct and pervasive competition between satellite and terrestrial facilities.

So the FCC appeared ready, in 1970, to consider initiating a test of free entry and competition in the domestic satellite field. The lead was provided by a policy statement by the White House, proposing a three- to five-year test of such a policy:

"In the absence of clear economies of scale and overriding public interest considerations to the contrary, the American economy has relied on competitive private enterprise rather than regulated monopoly to assure technical and market innovation. . . .

"At this stage of domestic satellite planning, it is not possible to identify major economies of scale. Rather, it appears that a diversity of multiple satellite systems as well as multiple earth stations will be required to provide a full range of domestic services.

"Further, we find no public interest grounds for establishing a monopoly in domestic satellite communications. . . .

"Subject to appropriate conditions to preclude

Alien Attachments. The process of defining and redefining the area of natural monopoly is nowhere more clearly illustrated than in the evolving policies of the Bell System with respect to the kinds of equipment it permits customers to attach to the telephone receiver or to hook on to the network and the circumstances, if any, under which it permits interconnection between other communications systems and its own. The original rule was one of complete noncooperation, a rule implying the widest possible definition of the natural monopoly. Until 1913, for example, AT&T refused to interconnect in any way with the numerous independent local telephone companies that had sprung into existence on expiration of the Bell patent; in that year, however, following on the threat of an antitrust suit, it agreed thenceforth to connect its system for toll service purposes with the lines of independent companies whose equipment satisfied its quality specifications.[78] Similarly whereas the independent telephone companies generally have permitted unrestricted interconnection between their facilities and private microwave systems, the Bell companies have historically done so only in very special circumstances.[79]

As far as customer-owned and supplied equipment or attachments were concerned, the Bell rule was unequivocal:

"No equipment, apparatus, circuit or device not furnished by the Telephone Company shall be attached to or connected with the facilities furnished by the Telephone Company, whether physically, by induction or otherwise. . . . In case any such authorized attachment or connection is made, the Telephone Company shall have the right to remove or disconnect

---

harmful interference and anti-competitive practices, any financially qualified public or private entity . . . should be permitted to establish and operate domestic satellite facilities for its own needs; join with related entities in common-user, cooperative facilities; establish facilities for lease to prospective users; or establish facilities to be used in providing specialized carrier services on a competitive basis. . . . Common carriers should be free to establish facilities for either switched public message or specialized services, or both.

"The number of classes of potential offerers of satellite services should not be limited arbitrarily." The White House, *Memorandum for the Honorable Dean Burch, Chairman of the Federal Communications Commission*, mimeo., January 23, 1970.

The FCC is not, as of the time of writing, prepared to go quite so far. It did, in March 1970, invite applications from any and all interested parties, but reserved judgment on whether it would permit any financially qualified applicant to set up and operate a domestic satellite system. Still, its announcement was widely acclaimed, and it elicited statements from AT&T, the broadcast networks, and the University Computing Company's subsidiary, Data Transmission Co. (see p. 135, above) that

they were studying the possibility of applying. *Wall Street Journal*, March 18, 1970, 6, and March 25, 1970, 11.

[78] This agreement was provided in the Kingsbury Commitment, so called because it was contained in a letter to the Attorney General from a company vice-president. On the consequences of this kind of mandatory interconnection, see note 149, p. 308, Chapter 6, below. In that same letter, AT&T agreed also to dispose of a large interest that it had acquired in Western Union in 1909 and also not to acquire control of any additional competing independent phone companies. The controlling legislation now permits telephone companies to merge with the approval of the relevant regulatory agency. 47 U.S. Code 221 (a), 1964 ed.

[79] "where, according to Bell System witnesses, considerations of safety of life and property are involved, and, under certain circumstances, with right-of-way companies." *Above-890*, 27 FCC 359, 409 (1959).

Both of these exceptions, it should be noted, are for private systems that are essentially noncompetitive with those of the Bell System itself. *Ibid.*, 396.

As of Jan. 1, 1969, AT&T's general tariff permits interconnection service with private microwave systems generally. See p. 144, below.

the same; or to suspend the service during the continuance of said attachment or connection; or to terminate the service."[80]

So, for example, the Bell companies have consistently refused to connect up with switchboards and associated facilities manufactured by others and furnished by the private users themselves. An extreme example of this policy was its application against the Hush-A-Phone, a purely mechanical attachment to the telephone itself manufactured by an independent company of that name—a cuplike device that could be simply snapped on to the instrument and that, by confining the speaker's voice within its enclosure, provided some privacy for his conversations and quiet in the room and kept room noises out of the transmitter. The Bell companies justified their insistence that this innocent device be removed in familiar terms—it is they who are responsible for the quality and price of their service; if they are to bear and exercise that responsibility, they must have reasonable discretionary control over the kind of equipment used:

"it would be extremely difficult to furnish 'good' telephone service if telephone users were free to attach to the equipment, or use with it, all the numerous kinds of foreign attachments which are marketed by persons who have no responsibility for the quality of telephone service but are primarily interested in exploiting their products."[81]

The rationalization is a powerful one. But there are offsetting considerations. Regulated monopoly is not necessarily the ideal device for ensuring a zealous, continuous quest for improved quality and variety of service. At a very elementary level, the Hush-A-Phone demonstrated this. From 1921, when it was introduced, through 1949, 126,000 of them had been sold; and there was no lack of evidence that many subscribers felt it met a need. The Bell companies contended, in the face of this objective market evidence, that there was "no appreciable public demand for a voice silencer such as the Hush-A-Phone"; they pointed out that they supplied certain devices that fulfilled a similar function (notably the addition of "push-to-talk" and "push-to-listen" switches) and that, if users wanted privacy, "it may be obtained without the use of any attachment to the telephone, as by cupping a hand around the transmitter and talking in a low tone of voice." Finally, it added, "if a general public demand for a handset type voice silencer were encountered, the defendants would undertake to meet that demand!"[82] Big Brother said he would provide best—even in the face of clear evidence that 100,000 people thought he did not.

The FCC sustained the position of the Bell companies in this case, on the ground that the Hush-A-Phone had been shown to "impair telephone service":

"when the device is used for maximum privacy, there is a noticeable loss of intelligibility . . . which means that the person to whom the Hush-A-Phone user is speaking hears a lower and somewhat distorted sound."[83]

[80] FCC, *In the Matter of Use of the Carterfone Device in Message Toll Telephone Service*, Decision, 13 FCC 2d 420, 427 (1968).
[81] *In the Matter of Hush-A-Phone Corporation et al.*, Decision, 20 FCC 391, 415 (1955).
[82] *Ibid.*, 397.
[83] *Hush-A-Phone Corporation et al. v. United States of America and Federal Communications Commission, et al.*, 238 F. 2d 266, 268 (1956). See the FCC decision, *op. cit.*, 405.

Who should decide whether an improvement in product quality in one respect is worth the cost of some possible deterioration in another? The question is not an economic one. But the only answer consistent with the efficiency criteria of a private enterprise economy is the buyer—unless he is illinformed, *or* his independent purchase decisions impose costs on others. But, as the Circuit Court of Appeals pointed out in overturning the FCC in this case, the only parties affected were the two parties to the conversation:[84]

"The question, in the final analysis, is whether the Commission possesses enough control over the subscriber's use of his telephone to authorize the telephone company to prevent him from conversing in comparatively low and distorted tones. . . . [I]ntervenors do not challenge the subscriber's right to seek privacy. They say only that he should achieve it by cupping his hand between the transmitter and his mouth and speaking in a low voice into this makeshift muffler. This substitute, we note, is not less likely to impair intelligibility than the Hush-A-Phone itself. . . . In both instances, the party at the other end of the line hears a comparatively muted and distorted tone because the subscriber has chosen to use his telephone in a way that minimizes the risk of being overheard. . . . The intervenor's tariffs, under the Commission's decision, are in unwarranted interference with the telephone subscriber's right reasonably to use his telephone in ways which are privately beneficial without being publicly detrimental."[85]

The upshot of the Hush-A-Phone decision was a softening of the flat prohibition of alien attachments:

"The provisions . . . shall not be construed or applied to bar a customer from using devices which serve his convenience in his use of the facilities of the Telephone Company . . . provided any such device so used would not endanger the safety of Telephone Company employees or the public; damage, require change in or alteration of, or involve direct electrical connection to the equipment or other facilities of the Telephone Company; or interfere with the proper functioning of such equipment or facilities; or impair the operation of the telephone system or otherwise injure the public in its use of the Telephone Company's services."[86]

But the Bell companies continued to interpret this exception as narrowly as possible and continued their general refusal to interconnect. The next major complainant-victim was the Carter Electronics Corporation, which had, from 1959 through 1966, marketed some 3,500 of its Carterfones, devices which make it possible to conduct two-way conversations between ordinary telephones and the individual units of private mobile radio systems. The device involves no wire-to-wire connection with the telephone network, but only placing a telephone handset, at the office of the mobile radio system's

---

[84] The FCC attempted to stretch the possible annoyance to the party *without* the attachment to his telephone into a threatened impairment of the entire telephone service:

"the use of the Hush-A-Phone affects the quality of telephone service not only to the Hush-A-Phone users but also to all other subscribers who are connected with the same nation-wide telephone system and who may call or be called by Hush-A-Phone users." *Ibid.*, 424.

Surely a grotesque extension of the concept of externalities; all the aggrieved party has to do is say "what"?

[85] *Op. cit.*, 238 F. 2d 266, 269 (1956).

[86] FCC, *Carterfone* decision, *op. cit.*, 13 FCC 2d 420, 427 (1968).

base station operator, in a cradle specially designed to receive it; this device transmits the telephone signals automatically via radio to the private mobile units and amplifies the sounds coming in from the radio field units so that the telephoner can hear them.[87]

The telephone companies had by now elaborated the justification of their policy on foreign attachments into what they termed the "systems concept":

"the network as a whole is regarded as a single system with the effect of every part on each of the other billions of parts being calculated before it is introduced into the system. If this is not done, so goes the theory, the introduction of a single disruptive piece could have an ever widening effect on every other piece in the system and ultimately impair or even destroy the efficacy of the whole. For this reason the telephone companies contend that they must control every element of the system if they are to accept responsibility for its operation."[88]

The Commission found no fault with this basic principle: the common carrier must, indeed, be able to exercise responsibility for the quality of the service and all equipment affecting it:

"This argument is reasonable, plausible and persuasive. If the issue in this proceeding was whether users should have a right to attach anything they choose to the system at any time without restriction or consideration of the consequences the record would not sustain a favorable finding. However, that is not the issue here."[89]

But the Examiner found

"no reason to anticipate that the Carterphone will have an adverse effect on the telephone system or any part thereof. It takes nothing from the system other than the inductive force of the electrical field in the earpiece of the handset, which force is dissipated into the atmosphere in any event. It puts nothing into the system except the sound of a human voice into the mouthpiece of the handset, and that is the precise purpose for which that portion of the system is engineered."[90]

In the circumstances, the FCC found that the tariff provision itself was unreasonable, as well as discriminatorily applied against the Carterfone:

"our conclusion here is that a customer desiring to use an interconnecting device to improve the utility to him of both the telephone system and a private radio system should be able to do so, so long as the interconnection does not adversely affect the telephone company's operations or the telephone system's utility for others. A tariff which prevents this is unreasonable; it is

---

[87] The conversations can be initiated from either end, and must be connected through the radio system's central operator. The operator then contacts the called party, using either the radio system or a telephone connection, depending on where the call was initiated. When both parties are ready, the operator places his own telephone handset into the cradle. The Carterfone cradle essentially merely amplifies the signals—the telephone signal that is then broadcast over the radio transmitter and the radio signal coming in. The description taken from FCC, *In the Matter of*

the *Use of the Carterphone Device in Message Toll Telephone Service*, Initial Decision of the Hearing Examiner, 13 FCC 2d 430, 432–433 (1967).

[88] *Ibid.*, 434.

[89] *Ibid.* (This statement was by the Hearing Examiner but its purport was endorsed by the FCC.)

[90] *Ibid.*, 434–435. The Examiner's decision also convincingly discusses and dismisses other possible dangers asserted by the telephone companies, 435–437.

also unduly discriminatory when, as here, the telephone company's own interconnecting equipment is approved for use. The vice of the present tariff, here as in *Hush-A-Phone*, is that it prohibits the use of harmless as well as harmful devices."[91]

Far more than *Hush-A-Phone*, *Carterfone* forced the Bell System into a fundamental reexamination of its interconnection and alien attachment policies. In December of 1968 the FCC permitted AT&T to put into effect greatly liberalized tariffs for its business customers (the liberalization does not apply to the residential subscriber). These permit the direct connection of a wide variety of customer-provided terminal devices and communications systems, for the transmission and reception of data and voice signals from computers, facsimile machines, teletypewriters, and so on, subject only to the reservation that the telephone company is to provide protective devices at the "interface" between the private equipment and the telephone network in order to control the quality of the signal. The latter proviso was not acceptable to various independent equipment manufacturers and customers, who complained that they could provide such protective and transmitting devices equally capable of preserving quality and at lower cost; in this they were supported by the Antitrust Division of the Department of Justice. In permitting the tariffs to go into effect, the FCC left open the question of whether customers should be permitted access to the public system through their own network control signalling equipment.[92]

In any event, it was widely anticipated that this liberalization of the tariffs would open up a greatly expanded market for independent equipment manufacturers. Business users of communications facilities, it was widely predicted, would soon have available to them an increasingly rich variety of services, at reduced cost; among such possible attachments now available are fire or burglar alarms that automatically dial police or fire departments and transmit prerecorded calls for help; devices that automatically transfer calls to another number; and so on.

---

[91] 13 FCC 2d 420, 424 (1968). Similarly, although in its *above-890* decisions the Commission did not issue any orders to interconnect with the private systems, it did point out the discrepancy between the Bell companies' policies of refusal to interconnect with private communications systems and the policies of the independent telephone companies and Western Union, concluding

"It is clear from the record that, from a technical standpoint, interconnection of private systems with the common carrier systems is feasible where compatible and adequate transmission standards are maintained." *Op. cit.*, 27 FCC 359, 397 (1959).

Another incident in the controversy over the Carterfone was a $1.35 million antitrust suit that its manufacturer brought against AT&T and the General Telephone Company of the Southwest; the suit was settled out of court in 1969 with the plaintiff accepting $375,000 in damages. *The New York Times*, April 4, 1969.

[92] The Bell companies maintain that the instruments (like the ordinary dial telephone) that control the setting up, disconnecting, and charging for calls "are not mere attachments . . . [but] an integral and essential part of the service," which must, if quality of service is to be guaranteed, be supplied, installed, and maintained by the telephone companies themselves. AT&T, "Network Control Signalling," a statement submitted to the FCC, November 15, 1968. They therefore retained in the revised tariffs a requirement that "network control signalling in the furnishing of long distance message telecommunications service shall be performed by equipment furnished, installed and maintained by the Telephone Company." The Commission permitted retention of this provision pending the institution of technical conferences to assess its merits. *In the Matter of American Telephone and Telegraph Company "Foreign Attachment" Tariff Revisions etc.*, Memorandum Opinion and Order, 15 FCC 2d 605 (1968) and August 13, 1969 (the latter rejecting petitions for reconsideration).

So ended one phase in the continuous process of defining the natural communications monopoly. The enthusiasm expressed by the Chairman of AT&T's Board toward the much more modest definition implicit in the new tariffs contrasts amusingly and hearteningly with the company's attitude in *Hush-A-Phone*, some 10 to 15 years earlier:

"We believe that new regulations will open up new communications potentialities for our customers and afford new opportunities for the many fine companies that are making and marketing information-handling devices. . . .

"First, we welcome the use of our switched network for communications between customer-owned information generating and using equipment. The more the merrier.

"Second, we want to make the connection of such equipment as easy as possible, and the rules and regulations as few as possible. . . .

"We want to find more ways to say, 'Yes' to our customers—to approach these things imaginatively and flexibly."[93]

---

[93] H. I. Romnes, *195 Magazine*, September 16, 1968, as supplied in an internal company memorandum. Mr. Romnes also asserted the continuing responsibility of the Telephone Company for the overall quality of the service, its continued insistence therefore on treating "the network control device as an integral part of the switched network," and its opinion that it could best assure that "energy is not put into the network at such levels and frequencies as to interfere with other users" by "providing for the connection of customer-provided equipment to the network through an inexpensive protective device." *Ibid.*

For a good, general statement of the position of the Department of Justice on the side of maximizing the opportunities for competition in the redefinition of the network monopoly, see Lionel Kestenbaum, "The Limits of a Regulated Monopoly—Telephone Attachments, Interconnection and Use of Circuits," *The Antitrust Bulletin* (Fall 1968), XIII: 979–989.

Another closely related and rapidly developing aspect of this problem has to do with the proper relationship of the communications industry to the burgeoning computer service industry—in particular, the shared use of remote access computers, with the access achieved by wire or radio communications. The complicating factors are that, on the one hand, this use of the computer depends on the provision of communications facilities and, on the other, that the computer itself can perform many of the services now performed by communications common carriers—receiving, storing, and forwarding messages.

So, on the one hand, computer service bureaus are attempting in effect to go into the communications business, providing their customers with message switching services. See, for example, the description of the Datran application at p. 135, above, and the Bunker-Ramo Corporation's Telequote IV service offering, which permitted stock brokers to place, execute, and confirm stock orders between their offices. Manley R. Irwin, "The Computer Utility: Market Entry in Search of Public Policy," *Jour. Ind. Econ.* (July 1969), XVII: 240–243. And the question has been raised of whether these computer-communications services have sufficiently monopolistic characteristics to justify subjecting them to regulation: the consensus is that they do not. See, e.g., the President's Task Force on Communications Policy, *op. cit.*, Chapter 6, 29–30, and the other sources cited in this note.

On the other hand, it follows equally that the communications companies have the facilities and the talents to move into the entire computer field. Western Union has begun to offer data-processing services, in direct competition with computer service bureaus. The Bell System is prohibited from doing so by the terms of the 1956 Antitrust Consent Decree, which limits its operation to regulated industries; but it is in any event the principal source of the communications services on which this new industry depends, and can by its tariff provisions and rates exert a powerful influence on the nature and speed of its development. The FCC in 1966 scheduled hearings on these complex interrelationships (*In the Matter of Regulatory and Policy Problems Presented by the Interdependence of Computer and Communications Services and Facilities*, Docket No. 16979, Tentative Decision and Notice of Proposed Rate-Making, April 1, 1970) in order to determine, among other things, to what extent such computer operations should be subject to regulation (which step, incidentally, would open the field to the Bell companies, under the 1956 decree) and to what extent the provision of data-

If Competitors Want to Enter, How Natural Can Monopoly Be?
The assertion of natural monopoly is that a single, chosen instrument can achieve lower costs and better service than can a number of competing suppliers. Yet competitors are successfully challenging the telephone company and customers are choosing to serve themselves. These numerous competitive challenges obviously raise serious doubts about the validity of treating the communications industry as a natural monopoly. These doubts might be dismissed if the various attempts at entry were simply mistakes from the standpoint of the interests of the entrants themselves; but their great number and rapid expansion bely any such explanation as a general proposition.[94] Could it be that the Bell natural-emperor really has no clothes on? The answer to this question seems to have at least the following parts:

1. The most important explanation of the increased competitive challenges of recent years must be progress in communications technology. The attraction of microwave or of dealing directly with Comsat is that it promises service at costs lower than current AT&T rates. Since the Bell System has itself pioneered in the development of microwave, that technology is available to it as well as to its competitors. The problem is that its rates have to carry a very heavy and incompletely depreciated investment in a wide variety of communications technologies, new and old. We have, in short, the situation described in Chapter 4 of Volume 1: because traditional depreciation rates have been outrun by technological progress, the average total cost of service, including gross return on historic or book investment, exceeds average total costs under new technology. The emperor has a very heavy and expensive old wardrobe; his challengers are wearing light new clothing.

We have already discussed the knotty problems of efficient rate making

---

processing services by common carriers would involve them in unfair competition with the independent firms now providing these services. The reason for the latter concern is that the independent firms would, on the one hand, be competing with the common carriers and, on the other hand, be dependent on them for an essential part of their services; they might therefore be subjected to a "squeeze" in the margin they could earn between the competitive price they could charge and the prices they would have to pay for those services—a familiar problem in the competition between vertically integrated and nonintegrated companies. On the other hand, since the telephone company's electronic switching system is in effect a giant computer that can be programmed to provide data processing, storage, and retrieval services, it could well be inefficient to confine the company to the transmission and switching of voice messages.

And, once again, the foreign attachments rule must inescapably come under scrutiny, with the computer manufacturers and users demanding the right to furnish their own devices for attaching the computers to the telephone circuits. For a

general survey of these problems, see the Response of the U. S. Department of Justice in the above-mentioned Docket No. 16979, submitted March 5, 1968; Bernard Strassburg, "Competition and Monopoly in the Computer and Data Transmission Industries," *The Antitrust Bulletin* (Fall 1968), XIII: 991–997; Manley R. Irwin, "The Computer Utility: Competition or Regulation?" *Yale Law Jour.* (June 1967), LXXVI: 1299–1320; also Delbert D. Smith, "The Interdependence of Computer and Communications Services and Facilities: A Question of Federal Regulation," *Univ. of Penn. Law Rev.* (April 1969), CXVII: 829–859.

[94] Another possible explanation consistent with the natural monopoly hypothesis is that the incumbent companies were charging such extortionately monopolistic prices as to enable the entrants to profit in spite of their higher costs. While the relatively modest profit rate of the Bell System makes this explanation unconvincing too, as a general proposition, it comes much closer to the mark when the Bell System prices to particular users are compared with the costs of supplying those particular users with systems embodying the latest technology—as we shall see.

in these circumstances.[95] It may be argued, on the one hand, that this discrepancy between ATC_o and ATC_n should come out of the pockets of the stockholders, thus enabling all rates to be set at the latter, more nearly efficient level. As we have seen, a plausible case can be made, instead, for permitting a regulated company to recoup its average historic cost of service from current and future customers—in which case, since marginal costs are less than average total costs, price discrimination may be a justifiable means of doing so.[96]

In any event, to the extent that it is circumstances such as these that have made independent competitive entry profitable, that entry does not necessarily justify rejection of the natural monopoly hypothesis.

2. A second explanation of some of these instances of successful competition, again in principle consistent with the presence of natural monopoly, is AT&T's policy of pricing its communications services uniformly on the basis of national average or system-wide per mile costs rather than, differentially, on the basis of the varying average costs of different portions of the service.[97] As is suggested by our earlier discussion, the tendency to decreasing costs results most markedly from the increasingly intensive utilization of particular route capacities. This apparently means that AT&T's costs of service are far less than its system-wide average on the intensively utilized, heavy traffic routes and correspondingly far above that average on the thin routes. Yet, to take an example that the company itself cited in resisting the MCI application, its rates are the same between Booneville, Indiana, and Big Stone Gap, Virginia, as between Chicago and St. Louis, because the distances are the same. The consequence is that smaller competitors like MCI, confining themselves to the thickly traveled routes,[98] may enjoy lower average total costs than AT&T as a whole and may therefore be able to undercut the Bell rates on those routes.

3. Another way of saying this is that the Bell System has a very different product mix from that of its more specialized competitors. One of the FCC's witnesses in Docket 16258 has deprecated AT&T's demonstration of economies of scale by pointing to the entry of much smaller suppliers

---

[95] See pp. 120–122, 173–174, 176–177, in Volume 1.

[96] The case for price discrimination is admittedly weaker where the gap between LRMC and ATC results from inadequate past depreciation than when it reflects genuine economies of scale. In the short-run, a regulated company finding itself in this situation would probably have no choice but to argue for the right to engage in price discrimination, subject to the various limitations set forth in Chapter 6 of Volume 1. In the longer run, it presumably would be better off directing its efforts toward enhancing its ability to meet competition generated by new technology, by insisting on a more rapid amortization of inadequately depreciated assets, to the point where ATC_o came into line with ATC_n. At that point the artificial competitive handicap would be eliminated and value-of-service pricing would no longer be needed or justified. Such a policy

would, for a time, aggravate the competitive handicap: cost of service would in the short run be inflated by these higher depreciation allowances. But, in the longer run, the company would be in a far better position to justify its claim of natural monopoly in the marketplace, being better able to meet or forestall such competition as new technology spawned without the need for price discrimination.

[97] See the Hearing Examiner's Initial Decision in the *MCI* case, pars. 31–32.

[98] The numerous MCI-like applications to the FCC during the 1968–1970 period (see note 66a, above) all proposed service between major population centers—Chicago and New York City; Boston, New York, and Washington; Minneapolis-St. Paul and Chicago; San Diego and Seattle; Los Angeles, San Francisco, New Orleans and Houston; and so on.

and to the former company's insistence that it has to reduce rates discriminatorily down toward long-run incremental costs to retain the competitive business. Surely, he suggests, if the economies of scale are as great as AT&T says, that gigantic company ought to be able to hold its market against the entry of much smaller rivals even at rates uniformly equal to its average total costs:

"If more than one firm can exist in a market, this would tend to indicate that available economies of scale can be exhausted at a small level of output relative to the size of the market. . . .

"The conditions of extensive economies of scale and a competitive market are incompatible. If the market conditions permit competition, economies of scale should be readily exhausted, and the rate levels for *all* services should approximate long-run incremental cost as well as fully distributed costs. . . . On the other hand, the cost conditions that are prerequisite to the possibility of significant rate reductions in response to competitive necessity, i.e., economies of scale beyond the existing output level, should foreclose the market to competitors."[99] (Stress supplied.)

This is a telling argument and it may be borne out by the facts in this case. But it is not necessarily conclusive. It would be so if the competitors, large and small, were producing a single, homogenous product. But where the companies have widely divergent product mixes and cost structures, there may exist simultaneously both great economies of scale and very strenuous competition for some portions of the business. And, as we have particularly illustrated in discussing the competition between railroads on the one hand and trucking companies and barges on the other, or between electric and oil companies, one of the competitors, enjoying very considerable economies of scale, may have fully distributed costs on all its business that are much higher but marginal costs much lower than the others.[100] In the present context, it could well be that AT&T, serving all areas of the country, might have a lower *average* traffic *density*, and consequently a higher average cost, than its specialized competitors, concentrating on the high-density routes.

4. This leads to a dynamic explanation of the rash of entrants in recent years: these companies have in considerable measure been introducing different services from the ones offered by the Bell System. This has obviously been true of the suppliers of auxiliary equipment, from Hush-A-Phone through Carterfone (Bell companies offer the latter in certain parts of the country but not in others). One of the arguments used by the applicants in the *above-890* case was that private systems, directly integrated with their own operations, could provide them with a service better adapted to their own particular needs. We have already summarized the distinctive features of the proposed MCI service. To some extent these services are of lower quality than Bell's; this could explain their lower cost. These instances, as we have already noted, suggest the need for redefining the area of Bell's natural monopoly. Where the monopolist is not providing the full range and variety of services that customers desire

---

[99] Testimony of William H. Melody, FCC Docket No. 16258, November 25, 1968, mimeo., 22, 25–26.

[100] See, for example, pp. 156–157, and 161–163, Volume 1, and pp. 23–24 of this Volume.

and are willing to pay for, the implication could be that monopoly is not "natural" in these areas, even in the static sense. Or it could mean that monopoly would still be, statically, the most efficient mechanism for providing this range of services, but that it has in practice proved to be inferior to competition in the *dynamic* sense—that is to say, in actively developing and offering to customers the fullest possible range of services and quality-price combinations.

5. Finally, it is possible that the provision of these inferior services is commercially acceptable only on the basis of the assumption that the Bell System stands ready to make good any deficiencies that emerge, by providing backup facilities to which the customers may turn in the event that the competitive service breaks down or proves insufficient to their needs.

For all these reasons, competitive entry does not necessarily justify rejection of the natural monopoly hypothesis. But—and this is the relevant question for us—what kind of regulatory policy do they suggest? Does the possible survival of the natural monopoly thesis suggest, then, that entry ought in fact to be barred? Let the reader remember our admonition at the outset of this volume that there is no scientific or demonstrably correct answer to these essentially institutional questions. The following suggestions are inevitably based on the author's subjective interpretation of the lessons of regulatory experience; their value, if any, lies less in their substance than in the demonstration they afford of the interrelationships between the various facets of regulatory policy.

Above all, if this experience demonstrates anything, it demonstrates the virtue of freedom of entry and competition as a device for innovation—for encouraging the development of new and different services and for assuring the optimal development and exploitation of new technology.[101] The single-firm monopolist, even if a highly effective and energetic innovator, is unlikely to be able to perceive or vigorously to exploit all the possible unsatisfied kinds of demands or fruitful lines of innovation. As for the application of new technology, the way to get microwave radio or communications satellite put into use at the optimum rate is to see to it that prices charged *to the customers of the service that embodies or could embody them* reflect their respective lower costs. To insist, instead, that the lower ATC of the new mode be commingled with the higher ATC of the old, with all users of communication service paying at the resultant average cost, runs the serious risk of uneconomically retarding exploitation of the new. A company specializing in the application of the new technology, with a demand rendered elastic by virtue of its ability to take customers away from the established supplier, will have the maximum incentive to charge rates fully reflecting cost advantages over that competitor.

This is not to deny that even a monopolist supplier of communications

---

[101] For an exposition and partial documentation of the hypothesis that the Bell monopoly has discouraged innovation in areas where entry of competitors is foreclosed and led the company itself to put disproportionately great effort into innovation in areas where competitive entry threatens see Shepherd, *op. cit.*, in the Brookings Institution symposium on *Technological Change in the Regulated Industries*. For a documentation of the latter tendency in the case of another famous monopoly see Carl Kaysen, *United States v. United Shoe Machinery Company* (Cambridge: Harvard Univ. Press, 1956), 175, 200, 260, 264.

services would have an incentive to make the most economical use of the lowest-cost technology, regardless of the pattern of rates that it charged its customers. But, as we have suggested, the motivations of a regulated monopolist with a heavy investment in the old are inevitably mixed, and particularly when (1) the new is less capital-intensive than the old (see pp. 51–52, Chapter 2, above) or (2) the investment in the old has been depreciated at an uneconomically low rate (see pp. 118–119, Volume 1). Moreover, like any monopolist, it has a less elastic demand than one of a number of competitors, and therefore less of an incentive to reduce its rates to (the new) LRMC.[102]

On the other hand, to the extent that the competitive handicap of AT&T is attributable to inadequate past rates of depreciation on its historic investment, it is entitled to point out to the regulatory commissions that they cannot escape responsibility for its difficulties, since it has typically been they that have resisted requests for more rapid amortization. It would be particularly anomalous for the FCC to emerge from its deliberations with a decision that (1) ordered AT&T to put into effect large rate reductions, based on cost-of-service determinations containing unrealistically low, Commission-dictated depreciation allowances, (2) used the willingness of independent firms to enter the market because their ATC_n are below AT&T rates, based on ATC_o, as evidence of the desirability and feasibility of competition, while (3) refusing to permit AT&T the right to meet such competition by reducing rates selectively toward LRMC, on the ground that the company's demonstrated justification for such discrimination—the disparity between LRMC and ATC—is a reflection not of the economies of scale but only of inadequate past depreciation rates![103] To put it another way, it would clearly be inconsistent for the FCC (1) to continue to adhere to the old, unrealistically low depreciation rates, while then (2) permitting free competitive entry by companies able to take full advantage of the new technology while AT&T remains burdened with the cost of old, inadequately depreciated assets, and (3) refusing to permit the latter company to engage in competitive pricing down to full additional costs on competitive business, where this would permit an increased contribution to its remaining burden of overheads, with consequent benefit to all its customers.[104]

The fact that competitive entry has apparently been made possible in part by the Bell System's use of national average cost as the basis for its prices on

---

[102] Whether this last tendency produces only a statically higher price and correspondingly lower output or, additionally, a lower *rate* of introduction of new, cost-saving technology over time is a question too complex to consider here. See especially William Fellner, "The Influence of Market Structure on Technological Progress," in Amer. Econ. Ass'n, *Readings in Industrial Organization and Public Policy*, 277–296. I can only record my conclusion that a tendency of the latter kind as well can be demonstrated.

It is considerations like these that should make one skeptical about the recommendations of the President's Task Force on Communications Policy that the international communications business be turned over to a single chosen

instrument. See on this also note 76, p. 139, above and note 32, Chapter 6; also Peck, *op. cit.*, *Amer. Econ. Rev. Papers and Proceedings* (May 1970), LX: 199–203, and the comments by Kahn, *ibid.*, 219–220.

[103] Yet there is testimony in its Docket 16258—notably by Wein and Melody—that either specifically takes or is wholly consistent with all these positions.

[104] This discussion does not explicitly consider the possibly injurious effect of such discriminatory pricing on competition at the primary level—that is, between AT&T and its competitors. See on this point pp. 175–177, Volume 1, and pp. 247–250, below.

different routes, or by its providing the necessary backup in the event of breakdown, raises the issue of cream-skimming, which we discuss more fully in Chapter 6. Cream-skimming or not, however, the entry affords another example of the beneficial contribution of competition. The prices to different users *should*, on efficiency grounds, reflect differences in the respective cost of serving them;[105] and if users are willing, with full knowledge of what they are getting, to take an inferior or less reliable service, at lower prices, it is the function of the market to provide it to them. AT&T's failure to do so was remedied by competition.

Of course, economic efficiency is not the only socially appropriate goal of pricing. Perhaps there are good, noneconomic reasons for preferring uniform per mile rates regardless of differences in costs, tending as they do to treat all users equally regardless of their location.[106] It may indeed be that such rates are also economically efficient, taking into account externalities: the same (per mile) rates between rural as between urban areas, where the former are below and the latter above their respective *private* marginal costs, are a way of subsidizing living in the less populous areas of the country. To the extent that this slows down the movement of population into the cities, it reduces the congestion costs that would otherwise be imposed on the people already there. If on the other hand society places a high priority on the rehabilitation of its cities, it might well oppose a practice that involves urban subscribers subsidizing the communications rates charged companies that move out of city centers.

But it is not the function of AT&T as such to take these social or external costs into consideration. It is up to Congress or the regulatory commission to make up its mind which it prefers—either (1) enabling the chosen instrument to continue its internal subsidization, by prohibiting entry into the subsidizing markets, or (2) permitting it instead to relate its own rates for individual services more closely to their respective costs. Competitive entry has served a purpose if it forces the FCC to confront this question.

It seems unlikely that any of these considerations eradicates the case for natural monopoly at the core of the telephonic network. The provision of that network and the assumption of centralized responsibility for its planning and for the quality of the service it provides is still, it would seem, best left to a chosen instrument. But that a monopoly works best in certain aspects of the operation is not an argument for retaining its exclusive control over those aspects in which it has demonstrably not worked best. The economic ideal would clearly be for the area of natural monopoly to be defined as narrowly

---

[105] The case is actually more complicated: relative prices should be equated to relative *marginal* costs; and it is conceivable that the marginal costs on more and less densely used routes are equal even if their average costs are markedly different. On the other hand, if (as seems to be the case) it is only on the denser routes that employment of the newest, lowest-cost technology is economically feasible, this suggests that their marginal costs are lowest too and that uniform rates force them to subsidize users in less populous locations.

[106] The FCC members who dissented from the

MCI decision (Docket 16509, *Decision*, August 13, 1969) did so explicitly because they felt it was inconsistent with national-average cost pricing. But they offered no reasoned explanation of why they regarded that system as sacrosanct, except that under it "the small user in the hinterlands is afforded the same rates as the large users in the major cities." Dissent of Chairman Hyde. See also the dissents of Commissioners Lee and Wadsworth. But what, one might ask, about the discrimination against the small user in the center city, in favor of the wealthy company in the suburbs?

as possible, and for the chosen instrument to exercise its responsibility, to the greatest extent possible, by (1) efficient pricing, (2) vigorously anticipating all possible demands on it—thereby subjecting its claim of natural monopoly to the market test—and (3) setting rigorous quality specifications at the critical points—and not before—at which uncontrolled competition demonstrably poses a threat to the quality and efficiency of service.[107]

Natural Gas Transmission

The design of an efficient natural gas pipeline system involves many of the same considerations as the communications network. The local distribution of gas is generally recognized as a natural monopoly of the familiar type, with the same justification: economies of scale with increasing intensity of use of given distribution facilities. But with respect to the pipeline network that carries natural gas from the field to the city gate of the local distribution system, the question of the proper role of competition has come into increasingly intense contention in recent years. For at least a decade after World War II, the energies of the industry and of the Federal Power Commission were directed principally toward extending supply to areas of the country not as yet fully served. With the completion of something like a nation-wide network and with major pipelines crossing each other's paths with increasing frequency, the opportunities for growth in noncompetitive directions have declined and the possibilities of competition expanded cor-

---

[107] The intrusion of competition into the domain of what was previously a "natural monopoly" opens up another kind of intriguing possibility: why not remove the competitive areas entirely from regulation? Harold H. Wein, testifying on behalf of Western Union, and William H. Melody, testifying for the FCC staff, both in Docket 16258, have suggested that this separation be made. They would leave AT&T to make whatever returns it can on the competitive operation, subject only to the restraints of competition, and permit it to recover from its message toll telephone (MTT) customers only the separate costs of that service, determined on the basis of a full cost distribution. Their purpose is to protect the latter from exploitation: they contend that the company has been charging excessive rates on MTT in order to subsidize competitive rates on the business services.

It is impossible without more information to evaluate their proposal. The danger they describe cannot be assumed to be negligible, in view of the uncertainty, so far, that long-run incremental costs of the competitive operation can in fact be readily determined and fixed as a floor below which those rates may not be dropped. Indeed, it would appear at first that their suggestion of separating out the competitive from the noncompetitive operations could be only beneficial to the purchasers of the monopoly (MTT) service, since they have been contributing well in excess of the Company's average return on that portion of the total rate base that would be

allocated to them on a fully distributed basis (see p. 157, Volume 1).

But suppose, as it argues is indeed the case, AT&T can profitably obtain the competitive business at rates that more than cover long-run incremental costs but not at rates covering fully distributed costs. If the operations were "separated" in the manner here suggested, it would pay AT&T in the long run to get out and stay out of those competitive markets. The reason is that every sale there has the effect of reducing the MTT rate base—determined on the basis of relative use—and therefore justifying, under regulation, a reduction in the latter rates. The competitive business, that is to say, could be fully remunerative on a long-run incremental cost basis but unremunerative if to those incremental costs must be allocated a share of the total rate base determined on the basis of relative use. In the long run, therefore, AT&T would, under the above assumptions, find it in its interest to serve only the MTT customers. This outcome might be highly satisfactory to its competitor, Western Union, but it would not be in the interest of the purchasers of the monopoly service.

So the Wein–Melody proposal could have the effect of denying to all buyers the benefits of the great economies of scale in AT&T's Long Lines business. The MTT users, in particular, could lose the contribution to common costs made by the competitive business. Whether this possibility of loss outweighs the possible benefits of separation cannot be determined on an a priori basis.

respondingly. Pipeline companies may compete not only for the privilege of serving the incremental demand of existing markets but also for the patronage of existing customers, as contracts between distributors and pipelines come up for renewal.[108]

The analytical issues are familiar. To what extent do economies of scale call for a single chosen instrument to serve particular routes and markets? Are there cost savings that can be achieved only by a coordinated planning of investment and operations? Can the latter economies be achieved, while still leaving the field open to competition? Does competition raise the danger of cream-skimming or of excessive discrimination between those customers in a position to benefit from it and those who are not? To what extent, correspondingly, may customers properly be left free to shop around among competing suppliers? In contrast with oil pipelines and railroads, natural gas pipelines are not typically common carriers; to what extent might it be appropriate to make them so—requiring them to interconnect with others or to carry gas for them?

Economies of Scale. As far as the actual carriage of gas is concerned, economies of scale could not possibly require a single chosen instrument for the entire national market. Pipelines travel from one point to another; in consequence there is ample room for a large number of criss-crossing lines, with ample resultant possibilities of competition both in areas between lines and near their points of junction. The main potential economies of scale are to be found in employing pipe of the maximum diameter available and, to a lesser extent, of further increasing its capacity, within limits, by increasing pressure and by "looping," that is, by constructing parallel lines running through the same compressor stations.[109] But these economies taper off sharply once the largest possible pipe available is used and even more sharply when the limits of further expanding capacity in the manner indicated are reached.[110] Once the market has expanded to sufficient size, as a result, there

---

[108] Carl E. Bagge, "Regulated Competition: An Alternative to Antitrust," Address before the Independent Natural Gas Association of America, San Francisco, September 4, 1967, mimeo., 5. See the prediction of this development back in 1952:

"The Commission has had relatively few cases of these types [requests for competitive certification or competing requests for certification], possibly because so many areas of the country were, until recently, without any natural gas service that natural gas companies did not have to compete for territories. Intensification of the competition between companies to serve given areas may be expected in the future, for natural gas service has now been extended to all but one major area of the country." Koplin, *op. cit.*, 351–352.

[109] The *physical* principle is that whereas the cost of a pipeline, like its perimeter, is (roughly) proportional to its diameter, its capacity is proportionate to the square of the diameter. Whether it is *economical* to use the widest available pipe depends of course on the size and expected growth of demand. Against the lower potential costs of wider-diameter lines must be weighed the cost of building too far ahead of demand.

[110] Koplin computed costs per square inch of cross section per mile for pipelines of various diameters: these decline sharply from $436 for 4-inch line to $124 for a 16-inch and $105, $90, and $83.50, respectively, for 20-, 24- and 26-inch lines. He also found that pipeline and compressor station operating expenses, and supervision and engineering costs all tended to increase proportionately less than pipeline capacity. For later estimates, showing average total costs for a 1,000 mile carriage declining from 10.1¢ per mcf for a 16-inch to 6.0¢ for a 36-inch line, see Paul W. MacAvoy, *Price Formation in Natural Gas Fields* (New Haven: Yale University Press, 1962), 41. Koplin notes also the limitations of these economies to which we have referred. At the time of his writing, 1952, the maximum diameter pipe available was 36 inches, although no line of that size had as yet been constructed. *Op. cit.*, 352–357. The largest line under active discussion in this country today is 42 inches.

is often room, consistent with maximum efficiency, for more than one transmission line traversing roughly the same territory.

But for any particular project, designed to meet given increments in market demand, economies of scale can be extremely important. The possibility that they might counsel one large certification rather than a series of medium-sized and small ones played a central role in the FPC's decision in 1968 involving three separate applications to bring additional gas to the California market. The applications were not, strictly, competitive. The Pacific Gas Transmission Company (PGT) sought permission to import gas from Canada, for ultimate distribution in Northern California; the El Paso Natural Gas Company's application, like that of the Transwestern Pipeline Company, involved bringing additional West Texas gas into the southern part of the state, with each of the two supplying only a portion of the anticipated additional requirements. The Presiding Examiner, Seymour Wenner, made it clear at the outset that the important issue was whether the separate, piece-meal proposals represented the most efficient method of meeting the need:

"Viewed routinely, these applications are steps in a minuet whereby El Paso and Transwestern provide medium scale successive increments to the California market."

"The Transwestern proposal should be considered along with the instant El Paso proposal as a method of supplying California with additional gas over the years through piece-meal medium and small sized additions. Under these proposals the load will be split between the two companies; it will be split again within some four or five years when another round of looping is needed to carry the increased supply. The El Paso 36″ loop is not small. But in combination with the 30″ loops it would deny the market the economies of large diameter—42″—pipe."

"Viewed constructively, the underlying issue in this case is whether the Commission should take the opportunity to find out whether the use of large diameter—42″—pipe for additional supplies can substantially reduce the cost of California's future gas supply."[111]

The FPC staff proposed the substitution, for all three of the proposed projects, of a single, new 42-inch pipeline from West Texas to the California border, pointing out, additionally, that such a line would take the place also of future planned expansions of the El Paso and Transwestern lines through additional looping. The Examiner agreed with the basic intent of this "bold and constructive proposal . . . based on a sound engineering and economic concept" (p. 1182) but mainly because of inadequately resolved uncertainties about the need and adequacy of gas supplies for so large an addition to capacity at so early a time, proposed instead what he called a "minimax solution"—a compromise designed to minimize the risks attendant upon the Staff's proposal while taking maximum advantage of the potential economies of scale. This involved immediate certification of the PGT proposal and postponement of action on the other two (technically, the Transwestern application was not involved in this particular proceeding), in order to permit consideration of the 42-inch alternative.

[111] FPC, *Pacific Gas Transmission Company, El Paso Natural Gas Company*, Docket Nos. CP67–187 et al., Presiding Examiner's Initial Decision Upon Applications for Certificates of Public Convenience and Necessity, 40 FPC 1147, 1179–1182 (1968).

Wenner's conclusion contained an eloquent statement of the limitations of the regulatory device as traditionally employed and the case for stronger commission initiatives of the kind that he and the Staff had proposed here:[112]

"The major objection to the immediate approval of the El Paso proposal is that it forever forfeits the opportunity to evaluate and adopt a plan that is reasonably likely to reduce the cost of California's gas. In favor of giving up this chance is the consideration that immediate approval of the El Paso proposal is the easiest way. . . .

"A neglected field of administrative law is the relationship between licensing and rate making. The big opportunities for cost savings to consumers do not lie in the disallowing of particular costs in a rate case. Underlying costs are determined in the certificate case where the project is licensed.

"What is proposed here is that the opportunity be taken to find out—and adopt if the findings be favorable—whether the economies of large scale operation can be secured at minimum risk—economics that will benefit producers through greater sales of gas, pipelines through larger revenues over the long run, and consumers through price reductions." (p. 1189)

The FPC itself rejected the Wenner proposal, on the ground that the need for additional gas was too urgent to permit postponement, and therefore issued the certificates to PGT and El Paso as requested. Its chairman, Lee White, dissented from the latter part of the decision. He would have had the Commission force El Paso to put in a continuous 36-inch line, instead of one involving sections of smaller diameter; its failure to do so, he argued,

"saddles California consumers with a project which is considerably less desirable than an alternative project which would be far cheaper in the long run . . . and which could be certificated on the present record."[113]

It is unnecessary for us to attempt to judge whether the FPC majority was correct in declining to take up these initiatives.[114] The important lessons of the case for us have to do with, first, the limited possibilities of genuine competition between two or three pipelines serving a particular area and the possibility that they may, in such instances, merely take turns in capacity expansion with each retaining a tacitly accepted share of the market; second, the possible superiority of single-firm certification or coordinated planning of additions to capacity, as a means of more fully exploiting the potential economies of scale; and, third, the question of how, in such circumstances, competition can be preserved.[115]

---

[112] On this general problem, see pp. 47–48, 75–77, 86–88 and passim, Chapter 2, above.

[113] *Pacific Gas Transmission Company, El Paso Natural Gas Company*, Opinion and Order, 40 FPC 1147, 1167 (1968). The Commission majority rejected this alternative as well, on the ground that it had not been adequately considered in the record.

[114] It did, however, applaud the Staff's initiative and, in effect, promised to try to profit by its lesson:

"We wish to make clear that our rejection of the Staff's 42-inch line and the Examiner's minimax alternative does not indicate our approval of any practice by El Paso and Transwestern of seeking to meet the growing needs of the California market through relatively small scale facility increments to meet immediate market needs, which though initially less costly cannot hope to achieve available long range economies of scale. To the extent that any such tendency may reflect past actions of this Commission, the Staff's actions herein have forcefully brought to our attention the limitations of such a policy in providing optimum service to the growing California market." *Ibid.*, 1160–1161.

[115] In these circumstances it is possible to ask whether competition serves any social purpose at

On the third point, the dissenting Commissioner White offered an interesting suggestion: he would have certificated the single, more efficient project, but attached a condition that would permit the FPC, if it saw fit in the future, to require the favored applicant to carry gas at cost (perhaps even incremental cost) for its competitors:

"Transwestern, at present the only competitor of El Paso in the rich Permian Basin to California market, is afflicted with all of the ills which face any comparatively small company competing with a giant in an industry where economies of scale are important. The market in California . . . is controlled in effect, by very few buyers. While it is in the interest of those buyers to maintain some competition by keeping Transwestern alive, it is not in their interest to give Transwestern large contracts until it can sell gas as cheaply as El Paso, something it is presently not able to do. But this results in a vicious circle, for low unit gas transportation costs cannot be achieved without large pipelines, and large pipelines cannot be economically built or utilized without large contracts. The action of the majority today condemns Transwestern, or any new competitor, to a repetition of the same dreary cycle—a compromise by building a pipeline which, while too small for eventual use in reducing unit costs low enough really to compete, is initially too large for the small amounts of gas Transwestern will furnish. . . .

"The dilemma facing the Commission is a real one. On the one hand, any rational decision in this proceeding . . . must provide for expansibility at the lowest cost; on the other hand, provision of such expansibility can act to the detriment of El Paso's competitors. Stated differently, the problem is whether there is a way to preserve the fruits of competition and at the same time optimize the construction of pipeline facilities so as to achieve the benefits of scale. I am convinced there is.

---

all. One additional element in the equation, illustrated with particular force in the present instance, is the effect of interpipeline rivalry on the field price of natural gas. Transwestern was organized by gas producers, previously dependent almost exclusively on El Paso for their interstate sales, in hope of getting a better price. And, not surprisingly, Transwestern sharply increased its buying prices for gas in the field compared with the level theretofore paid by El Paso. The question of whether the resulting price increase was justified in terms of economic efficiency raises the whole complex question of whether the field market is or was effectively competitive. On the one hand, there can be little doubt that El Paso was using its monopsony power to hold the price below competitive levels and that the entry of competition on the buying side of the market was a salutary influence from the standpoint of economic efficiency. On the other hand, it is not clear that rivalry among pipelines, each attempting to sew up the large blocs of natural gas reserves that are prerequisite to their obtaining quasi-monopolistic certification to serve a particular market area, produces competitive equilibrium prices for those reserves either. This would be true even if the

pipelines were independent of producer interests: they would be unlikely to bargain hard over the contract price for the natural gas when their getting or not getting the certification was at stake, especially considering that, once certificated, they could confidently expect to incorporate that purchase price in their regulated cost of service. The social desirability of their competition was even more questionable where, as here, they were producers as well as buyers of the gas they proposed to carry. Their vertical integration could be expected to generate a strong incentive to pay above-competitive prices, which they could then incorporate in their cost of service and recover from consumers. For statements of these opposing points of view see MacAvoy, *Price Formation in Natural Gas Fields*, 101–145 and Kahn, "Economic Issues in Regulating the Field Price of Natural Gas," *Amer. Econ. Rev., Papers and Proceedings* (May 1960), L: 508–509, and for a fuller discussion Kahn, testimony before the FPC, *In the matter of Champlin Oil & Refining Co. et al.*, Docket Nos. G–9277 et al. (*Omnibus*), Vol. 38-LC, 4872-LC–5030-LC, and especially 4990-LC–5011-LC. See also the references in note 75, Chapter 1, above.

"While competition in the California market in the past has been less than perfect, it has been beneficial on occasion . . . and may be beneficial in the future. Therefore, considering El Paso's already dominant position in the market, its further expansion at this time must be conditioned to preserve competition and keep its competitors viable. Such a condition should, I believe, make it clear that should it develop in some future proceeding that utilization by some other person of the excess capacity or expansibility of the facilities which are the subject of this proceeding is required to ensure that optimum service is not at the expense of competition, such facilities will be available. This can be accomplished by a condition providing that, if the public interest is found to so require[,] any other person certificated to transport gas . . . will be able to utilize El Paso's cheap expansibility, and that any additional looping or other construction on the El Paso facilities necessary to transport such gas as we may certificate will be installed."[116]

Coordinated Investment Planning. As with the telephone network, the economies of scale that might make monopoly natural could flow not so much from the sheer size of individual production operations as from the centralized planning of investment. An apparently dramatic demonstration of these possibilities was provided by the application of a technique of "network analysis," developed by mathematicians at the United States Office of Emergency Planning, to the hypothetical problem of describing what would have been the optimal natural gas pipeline transmission system for the existing distribution of gas fields in the Gulf of Mexico.[117] The solution produced a system that could have cost less than half the cost of the network actually constructed.

It is not clear how much of this estimated savings reflected the mere advantage of hindsight—that is, of knowing more about the location of the various gas fields, ex post, than the people who designed the existing network knew when they had to make their plans—and how much the superiority of a coordinated application of the new technique. But the report of this exercise emphasizes the latter. It professes to demonstrate that "significant savings in network cost can be achieved even when only partial information is available," (p. 15) specifically considers the problem of designing networks when

---

[116] 40 FPC 1147, 1173–1175 (1968). This obligation would have had to be imposed in advance, as a condition of certification, because the FPC does not have the authority to require lines to serve others when this would necessitate expansion of their facilities (see note 85, Chapter 2, above; also pp. 166–177, Chapter 6, below). The Commission majority rejected this suggestion for several reasons, among them the fact that Transwestern itself had not expressed opposition to the El Paso proposal or requested any such condition. The fact that Transwestern had indeed "vigorously supported" the El Paso application is not necessarily conclusive, as any student of the antitrust literature will recognize; if, as Examiner Wenner suggested, each company was taking its turn in "a minuet" it was no more in the interest of any one of them to object

to the application of the other than it was for the competitors of U.S. Steel to complain of that company's alleged illegal monopolization of steel, since they too profited from the price umbrella that it held over the market. The FPC's citation of the absence of complaint from a competitor in this case could have been just as irrational as the similar contention by the U. S. Supreme Courts' controlling opinion in exonerating the steel company of an antitrust violation back in 1920. *U. S. v. United States Steel Corp. et al.*, 251 U.S. 417, 447–449 (1920).

[117] National Resource Analysis Center, Systems Evaluation Division, *Report R–1, Design of Economical Offshore Natural Gas Pipeline Systems* (A Study Prepared for the Federal Power Commission), Office of Emergency Preparedness, November 1968.

projections of future discoveries are taken into account and identifies as one important inefficiency of the present system the fact that

"separate portions of the gathering system were designed by different pipeline companies working independently. This independence often stems from the conflicting contractual arrangements between various pipeline companies and gas producers which make neighboring pipelines incompatible. Furthermore, pipeline routes from gas fields to onshore separation plants are often selected on the basis of constraints other than minimum network costs, such as interlocking interests between separation plants and pipeline companies." (p. 13)

"The results of this study indicate that increased cooperation among pipeline companies, including coordinated planning and integrated facilities, could yield great economic benefits." (p. 31)

The question is whether these economies of coordinated planning can be achieved under competition. And the solution, once again, would seem to be one of insisting on a chosen instrument approach for conducting the natural monopoly part of the operation—for example, by encouraging or requiring the several parties to organize themselves into a joint venture to perform these functions—while permitting or insisting on independent action in other parts. And the way to preserve the opportunities for competition where that is consistent with efficiency is, as Commissioner White urged in the *El Paso* proceeding, to force the chosen instruments in the naturally monopolistic area to behave like common carriers. For example, when confronted in 1969 with three separate applications by transmission companies to build individual pipeline facilities for bringing offshore Louisiana gas into land, the FPC was reportedly considering one of two alternatives: either to propose that the three companies combine to build one giant project, or to invite competing applications from new and entirely separate companies to build a single system that would serve the onshore facilities of the three applicants:

"These transport concerns ('they'd be like toll bridges,' one planner says) wouldn't be affiliated with either producers or transmission companies, and, in effect, would be a new industry."[118]

The Role of Competitive Considerations. That economies of scale need not preclude certification of competing pipelines seems clearly to have been demonstrated by the case involving the application of the Great Lakes Gas Transmission Company for permission to bring Canadian gas into the north-central portions of the United States.

In 1961, Trans-Canada Pipe Lines Limited decided that the increasing demand for gas in the eastern part of that country could best be served by construction of a new pipeline that would enter the United States in northern Minnesota and, running through northern Wisconsin and Michigan, reenter Canada at Sarnia, Ontario. The project would have the additional advantage, from its standpoint, of making possible expanded sales of Canadian gas in those states. Since this would involve selling gas to American distributors, Trans-Canada entered into discussions with several American companies to see whether any of them might be interested in a joint project. Unable to reach such an agreement, it applied for certification on its own, through

---

[118] *Wall Street Journal,* February 27, 1969, 8.

Great Lakes, its wholly owned subsidiary. Thereupon, the American companies most directly affected, the American Natural Gas and Midwestern Gas Transmission Companies, entered an alternative proposal to accomplish the same purposes. Before the FPC was able to act, the parties resumed negotiations, withdrew their separate, mutually exclusive applications and presented a proposal instead to have the project handled by Great Lakes, in which Trans-Canada would give American Natural a one-half interest. It was this joint venture that the FPC certificated in 1967, in preference to a competing application by the Northern Natural Gas Company. Northern appealed this decision in the courts, contending that the Commission had inadequately taken into account the deleterious effects of the joint venture on competition.[119]

The Court agreed with Northern, and therefore remanded the case to the FPC for further consideration.[120] Its reasoning was simple and convincing. American Natural supplies over 50 percent of all the gas consumed in Michigan and Wisconsin. Had Trans-Canada come in alone (via Great Lakes) it would have been a direct competitor. It obviously had intended to do so. Economies of scale made it sensible for any line planning to carry gas to eastern Canada to build capacity sufficient also to sell in Michigan. There were no economies of scale involved in American's participation in the project: all it did was buy a half-interest. To obtain this interest in a threatening competitor, American was willing to commit itself to take the Canadian gas, even though this would otherwise not have been in its interest or that of its customers:

> "these sales were agreed to, not because the Canadian gas was cheaper . . . but rather because American Natural, the parent of the buying subsidiaries, seemed willing to sacrifice the interests of its consumers in order to protect its markets and enhance economically the joint venture in which it owned a half interest. . . .
>
> "American Natural flatly stated that if the joint venture were not certificated it would have no desire to take this Canadian gas. . . ."[121]

---

[119] *Northern Natural Gas Company et al. v. Federal Power Commission*, 399 F. 2d 953 (1968). Northern contended that

"the joint venture resulted in an illegal division of the consumer market between Trans-Canada and American Natural, substantially lessened competition between United States distributors for the supply of Canadian gas, and illegally eliminated competition between independent applicants (Trans-Canada *versus* American Natural and Midwestern) in a Commission comparative proceeding." (*Ibid.*, 958).

[120] It did not agree specifically with Northern's charge (see the note immediately preceding) that the agreements were in violation of the antitrust laws and that the finding of such a violation would suffice to prevent the Commission from certifying the project. As the Court put it

"Although the Commission is not bound by the dictates of the antitrust laws, it is clear that antitrust concepts are intimately involved in a determination of what action is in the public interest, and therefore the Commission is obliged to weigh antitrust policy." *Ibid.*

[121] *Ibid.*, 970–971. On this motivation and consequence the Court accepts the comment of the FPC staff:

"American Natural's agreement to purchase this gas through its subsidiaries was part of the bargaining price it had to pay in order to obtain a half interest in the joint venture. This had an effect not only on those who market United States gas at its source, but ultimately on the consumers in the American Natural system. The staff of the Commission detected this and commented:

"'Thus the consumers . . . to whom service could be rendered more readily and more economically through the combined American Natural System, are the sacrificial pawns by which American Natural received (1) half ownership in Great Lakes and (2) Midwestern's quiet acquiescence in the withdrawal of their joint competitive proposal.'" *Ibid.*, 971.

For Trans-Canada, the quid pro quo was an insured market for their gas, without the need to compete with American-originating gas for that market: they made it clear that they would not have entered into the joint venture without the commitment on the part of American Natural's subsidiaries to take its gas. So the Court concluded:

"From the above it is clear that Trans-Canada will be able to market an additional 170,000 Mcf of gas per day in the United States without having to meet or beat the competition provided by United States source gas, and that American Natural's agreement to purchase this gas through its subsidiaries was part of the bargaining price it had to pay in order to obtain a half interest in the joint venture. . . .

"we believe that the joint venture substantially lessened competition among suppliers in the Michigan–Wisconsin consumer market and between Trans-Canada and suppliers of gas from United States sources. Unless the Commission finds that other important considerations militate in favor of the joint venture and that these considerations are more beneficial to the public than additional competition, the antitrust policies should be respected and the joint venture set aside." (p. 971)

Among the forms of competition that the Court was intent to preserve, and that it regarded as having been unreasonably eliminated in this instance, was the presentation of competing applications before the Commission itself.

"Petitioners have aptly noted that comparative proceedings before regulatory agencies are 'sensitive mechanism[s] for weighing the relative merits of . . . rival . . . projects' and one of the 'main competitive arenas' of the natural gas industry since it is there that the sellers challenge one another for the favor of the Commission. This process could easily be distorted if the Commission permitted potential applicants to get together to decide how a market would be divided before submitting their proposals to the Commission, for then private parties rather than the Commission would be determining what means of meeting a market demand is most closely in accord with the public interest. We cannot permit such an abrogation of administrative responsibility.

"The danger of allowing parties to agree among themselves prior to submitting their proposals to the Commission becomes all the more apparent when it is remembered that the Commission's power is largely a negative one; it must rely heavily on private initiative to propose projects to meet consumer needs. . . .

"There are few opportunities for consumers of natural gas to choose among the several suppliers offering a variety of services and prices. It is therefore extremely important that a competitive edge be maintained in Commission proceedings. This will increase the chance that the public will be given better service at a lower price. If the Commission determines, after reviewing individual proposals, that a joint project would be more advantageous, it can at that time refuse to certify the individual plans and itself suggest a joint application."[122]

---

[122] *Ibid.*, 971–972. It seems unlikely that it would always be practicable for the Commission to follow the Court's advice in this respect. It would seem unnecessarily wasteful, in those instances in which the private parties concerned saw the possibility of large economies achievable by joint operations, to require that they first prepare separate, uneconomic proposals, leaving it

The *Great Lakes* case is additionally interesting because of the excellent discussion it evoked from Judge J. Skelly Wright of the role of competition in this industry and in the regulated industries generally, and of the closely related question of the relationship between the antitrust laws and the regulatory statutes. These are worth quoting at length:

"The nature of the natural gas market was accurately described by Mr. Justice Douglas in *El Paso*:

'This is not a field where merchants are in a continuous daily struggle to hold old customers and to win new ones over from their rivals. In this regulated industry a natural gas company (unless it has excess capacity) must compete for, enter into, and then obtain Commission approval of sale contracts in advance of constructing the pipeline facilities. In the natural gas industry pipelines are very expensive; and to be justified they need long-term contracts for sale of the gas that will travel them. . . . Once the Commission grants authorization to construct facilities or to transport gas in interstate commerce, once the distributing contracts are made, a particular market is withdrawn from competition. *The competition then is for the new increments of demand that may emerge with an expanding population and with an expanding industrial or household use of gas.*' 376 U.S. at 659–660. . . .

"In this case the additional demand in the eastern Canadian market made a new pipeline feasible. . . .

"If a wholly-owned subsidiary of Trans-Canada would have become an actual competitor of suppliers in Michigan and Wisconsin, we believe that the effect would have been substantial and that the northern Wisconsin and Michigan markets could have expected significant benefits. This is so, in large part, because competition, even in a regulated industry, secures benefits which might otherwise be unattainable. Admittedly the Commission possesses a rate-making power and this power is designed to protect the consumers of natural gas. But it is clear that this power is largely a negative one. Thus the Commission may set a selling rate for a supplier only after it has been demonstrated that the present charge is unjust, unreasonable, unduly discriminatory or preferential, a heavy burden even for specialists as intimately familiar with the natural gas industry as is the Commission. On the other hand, if competition exists, albeit in a limited area, there would be

---

entirely to the Commission to see the advantages of joint action and to require it. At the same time, in the present instance, in which the collaboration apparently had nothing to do with cost savings, the Court's findings are persuasive.

On November 21, 1968, the FPC remanded the case to its Presiding Examiner, for hearings limited to the question of the appropriate ownership and operation of Great Lakes. The Examiner recommended that American Natural be required to divest itself of its interest in Great Lakes, unless Northern Natural was permitted to build the pipeline for which it was seeking authorization to bring Canadian gas into the Midwest. The Commission rejected this advice, concluding that the benefits flowing from American Natural's participation in the joint venture outweighed its anticompetitive effects. The record on remand, it found, showed no substantial possibility of competition between the two companies: Great Lakes was unsuited to sell gas directly to distributors, but would have to depend on pipelines like American, in an essentially symbiotic rather than competitive relationship. Its judgment was influenced by the condition of gas shortage that emerged in the United States during the late 1960's, which, it argued, meant that increasing imports of Canadian gas were required to supplement domestic supplies, rather than to supplant them. *Ibid.*, Opinion and Order on Remand Confirming Issuance of Certificates with Conditions, Opinion No. 580, July 10, 1970.

incentives for innovation by the regulated companies themselves and for their coming forward with proposals for better services, lower prices, or both. And once innovations or proposals are forthcoming by a supplier, the Commission could more easily act to universalize these benefits than it could have acted to extract them initially.

"Consider the types of natural gas markets which exist. There are some markets which are natural monopolies—that is, where the most efficient allocation of resources results in a single supplier. In such markets, competition is sacrificed to avoid wasteful duplication of services and investment, and hence regulation by the Commission is the only protection a consumer has. In virtually all other natural gas markets, there is a tight oligopoly or partial monopoly. In these markets the fortunes of the few sellers are highly dependent, and therefore there is an incentive for the sellers to arrive at a price which will offer the highest return to all of them. Such a uniform price, whether arrived at by formal agreements or merely through price leadership, is in essence a monopoly price and yields monopoly profits. . . .

"But in practice it appears that firms selling in such a market do not always seek a uniform monopoly price and, if sought, do not always attain it. Among the reasons why uniform monopoly prices are not sought or attained is that one seller may believe he can maximize his profits by expanding his total sales rather than taking a maximum profit on each sale. Also, even the mere addition of one seller to an oligopoly market makes the market more complex and less predictable. Therefore, there may be competitive actions and reactions in an oligopoly market.

"One instance of such activity in a tight oligopoly market within the natural gas industry was noted by the Supreme Court in *United States* v. *El Paso Natural Gas Co.*, *supra*, 376 U.S. at 654–655. There Pacific Northwest Pipeline Corporation, a potential supplier to the California natural gas market, sought, in an attempt to gain entrance to that market, to attract a major customer from El Paso. Pacific Northwest offered lower prices and an uninterruptible supply to this customer whose El Paso supply was then subject to interruption during peak demands. Although El Paso was able to hold this customer and thereby prevent Pacific Northwest from entering the California market, it was able to do so only by giving the customer a firm supply and by dropping its selling price 25 percent. It is significant that these benefits were initially the result, not of Commission regulation to which El Paso had always been subjected, but rather of the competition of a single potential entrant to the market. Thereafter, since Section 4(a) of the Natural Gas Act, 15 U.S.C. § 717c(b) (1964 ed.), prohibits suppliers of natural gas from maintaining preferential and unreasonable rates and Section 5(a), 15 U.S.C. § 717d(a) (1964 ed.), empowers the Commission to set reasonable rates after it has established that the prior rates were unjust, it is probable that at least a portion of the 25 percent drop in selling price enjoyed by this single customer who was the subject of the competition was subsequently extended to other customers of El Paso as well. Thus it appears that the competition and direct regulation would complement each other to the benefit of consumers generally.

"This example demonstrates the important role competition can play as a complementary force in regulated industries. . . .

"In sum, Congress, the Supreme Court, and this Court have concurred in the belief that competition has a role to play in the natural gas industry. Both courts have recognized specific instances where the goals of direct regulation and the antitrust laws have coalesced. This would seem to be increasingly true as the natural gas markets grow, often demanding new facilities because existing pipelines have reached their ultimate capacity. And when new facilities must be built, the competitive advantages afforded by a new entrant might often be more meaningful than any economies of scale which could be attained by permitting the present monopolist, or dominant market force, to construct the new facilities and fulfill the increased demand. Even limited competition would seem to encourage suppliers of natural gas to become more aggressive in proposing new rates and services, and thereby increase the effectiveness of regulation by the Commission."[123]

Here is Judge Wright's lucid, capsule account of the relationship of the antitrust to the regulatory statutes:

"Despite a continuing debate, it appears that the basic goal of direct governmental regulation through administrative bodies and the goal of indirect governmental regulation in the form of antitrust law is the same—to achieve the most efficient allocation of resources possible. For instance, whether a regulatory body is dictating the selling price or that price is determined by a market free from unreasonable restraints of trade, the desired result is to establish a selling price which covers costs plus a reasonable rate of return on capital, thereby avoiding monopoly profits. Another example of their common purpose is that both types of regulation seek to establish an atmosphere which will stimulate innovations for better service at a lower cost. This analysis suggests that the two forms of economic regulation complement each other.

"This theory of complementary regulation appears to be borne out by the Supreme Court cases holding that regulated industries must, to some degree at least, accommodate the antitrust laws. *F.M.C.* v. *Aktiebolaget Svenska Amerika Linien*, 390 U.S. 238 (1968) (ocean carriers); *United Mine Workers* v. *Pennington*, 381 U.S. 657 (1965) (labor union); *United States* v. *El Paso Natural Gas Co.*, 376 U.S. 651 (1964) (natural gas distributors); *United States* v. *Philadelphia National Bank*, 374 U.S. 321 (1963) (banking); *Silver* v. *New York Stock Exchange*, 373 U.S. 341 (1963) (stock exchange); *United States* v. *Radio Corporation of America*, 358 U.S. 334 (1959) (television communication); *Georgia* v. *Pennsylvania R. Co.*, 324 U.S. 439 (1945) (railroads); *United States* v. *South-Eastern Underwriters Ass'n*, 322 U.S. 533 (1944) (insurance); *McLean Trucking Co.* v. *United States*, 321 U.S. 67 (1944) (trucking); *United States* v. *Borden Co.*, 308 U.S. 188 (1939) (agricultural cooperatives). Moreover, the Court has held that even where there are specific statutory exemptions for regulated industries from the antitrust laws, such exemptions are to be very narrowly construed. *See, e.g., California* v. *F.P.C., supra*, 369 U.S. at 485–486; *Maryland & Virginia Milk Producers Ass'n* v. *United States*, 362 U.S. 458 (1960).

"The complementary regulation theory is also supported by congressional directives requiring certain regulatory agencies to enforce portions of the antitrust laws.* The Federal Power Commission, while not included on the

---

[123] 399 F. 2d 953, 963–966, 969–970 (1968). In these selections and in those that follow we have eliminated almost all the footnotes.

* "Section 11 of the Clayton Act, 15 U.S.C. § 21(a) (1964 ed.), vests authority to enforce compliance with § 7 by the persons subject thereto

list of enforcement agencies, has been instructed to 'transmit . . . evidence . . . concerning apparent violations of the Federal antitrust laws to the Attorney General.'** Congress has also explicitly advised certain agencies to consider basic issues of competition while regulating the industries within their jurisdiction.† For other agencies the obligation to act in favor of 'public convenience and necessity' has been construed as implying a duty to recognize and weigh traditional antitrust concepts.‡ For example, the Federal Maritime Commission has formulated a rule that acts of shipping conferences interfering with the policies of antitrust laws will be approved only if the conferences can ' "bring forth such facts as would demonstrate that the . . . [act] was required by a serious transportation need, necessary to secure important public benefits or in furtherance of a valid regulatory purpose of the Shipping Act." ' *F.M.C.* v. *Aktiebolaget Svenska Amerika Linien, supra*, 390 U.S. at 243. In approving this standard the Supreme Court noted that '[b]y its very nature an illegal restraint of trade is in some ways "contrary to the public interest." ' *Id.* at 244. And while the Supreme Court did not say that the F.M.C. was obliged to display the degree of deference for antitrust laws suggested by its rule, the Court did conclude that 'the antitrust test formulated by the Commission is an appropriate refinement of the statutory "public interest" standard.' *Id.* at 246.

"This is not to suggest, however, that regulatory agencies have jurisdiction to determine violations of the antitrust laws. *See California* v. *F.P.C., supra*, 369 U.S. at 490; *United States* v. *Radio Corporation of America, supra*, 358 U.S. at 350 n.18; *National Broadcasting Co.* v. *United States*, 319 U.S. 190, 223–224 (1943); *Mansfield Journal Co.* v. *F.C.C.*, 86 U.S.App.D.C. 102, 107, 180 F.2d 28, 33 (1950). Nor are the agencies strictly bound by the dictates of these laws, for they can and do approve actions which violate antitrust policies where other economic, social and political considerations are found to be of overriding importance.* In short, the antitrust laws are merely another tool which a regulatory agency employs to a greater or lesser degree to give 'understandable content to the broad statutory concept of the "public interest." ' *F.M.C.* v. *Aktiebolaget Svenska Amerika Linien, supra*, 390 U.S. at 244. But because competitive considerations are an important element of the 'public interest,' we believe that in a case such as this the Commission was obliged to make findings related to the pertinent antitrust policies, draw

---

"'in the Interstate Commerce Commission where applicable to common carriers subject to the Interstate Commerce Act, as amended; in the Federal Communications Commission where applicable to common carriers engaged in wire or radio communication or radio transmission of energy; in the Civil Aeronautics Board where applicable to air carriers and foreign air carriers subject to the Civil Aeronautics Act of 1938; in the Federal Reserve Board where applicable to banks, banking associations, and trust companies; and in the Federal Trade Commission where applicable to all other character of commerce . . .'."

** Section 20(a) of the Natural Gas Act, 15 U.S.C. § 717s(a) (1964 ed.).

† Savings and Loan Holding Company Amend-

ments, *supra* Note 4; Bank Merger Act, 12 U.S.C. § 1828(c) (1964 ed.); Civil Aeronautics Act, 49 U.S.C. § 488(b) (1964 ed.); Interstate Commerce Act, 49 U.S.C. § 5(2)(c) (1964 ed.).

‡ *F.M.C.* v. *Aktiebolaget Svenska Amerika Linien*, 390 U.S. 238, 243–246 (1968); *California* v. *F.P.C.*, 369 U.S. 482, 484–485 (1962); *United States* v. *Radio Corporation of America*, 358 U.S. 334, 351–352 (1959); *National Broadcasting Co.* v. *United States*, 319 U.S. 190, 222–224 (1943).

* *See Seaboard Air Line R. Co.* v. *United States*, 382 U.S. 154 (1965); *Pan American World Airways, Inc.* v. *United States*, 371 U.S. 296 (1963); *McLean Trucking Co.* v. *United States*, 321 U.S. 67 (1944). Also note the exceptions mentioned above which the F.M.C. has written into its policy.

conclusions from the findings, and weigh these considerations along with other important public interest considerations. *Johnston Broadcasting Co.* v. *F.C.C.*, 85 U.S.App.D.C. 40, 46, 175 F.2d 351, 357 (1949). *See also Baltimore & Ohio R. Co.* v. *United States*, 386 U.S. 372, 402–403, 436–437 (1967) (Mr. Justice Brennan concurring); *Scenic Hudson Preservation Conference* v. *F.P.C.*, 2 Cir., 354 F.2d 608 (1965), *cert. denied*, 384 U.S. 941 (1966)."[124]

Competition for Existing Business Versus Protectionism. In the pipeline cases discussed so far, the question at issue concerned the proper role of competition in meeting the incremental needs of growing markets. A series of recent cases, involving attempts by one pipeline to take particular customers away from another and by distribution companies or industrial customers to shift from one supplier to another, has posed with even greater clarity the question of whether the FPC ought to protect its chosen instruments from direct invasions of their thitherto exclusive domains. In general, the Commission has in recent years been increasingly sympathetic to such applications, emphasizing that it recognizes no right of pipelines to protection against competition in their geographic markets.[125]

For example, in 1966 the Commission certificated the Southern Natural Gas Company to supply additional requirements of the Chattanooga Gas Company, over the objections of its existing supplier, the East Tennessee Natural Gas Company, on the ground that East Tennessee's competing proposal would have been insufficient to meet the customer's requirements and Southern's rates were the lowest of the several applicants. In so doing, it also invalidated an exclusive-patronage provision in the Chattanooga-East Tennessee contract, to the effect that

"buyer agrees that it will not purchase gas, natural or manufactured, from any source other than Seller, and also that it will not manufacture gas for use or sale, except as expressly authorized by this contract."[126]

Some years earlier, in the *Lynchburg Gas Company* case, the Commission had taken the opposite position, when it upheld the Atlantic Seaboard Corporation's "partial requirements" (PR) rates, imposing a penalty on customers that did not buy exclusively from it. The FPC had justified that policy on the ground that when customers desert their historic suppliers they leave a heavier burden of fixed charges to be recovered from the ones that remain. The Circuit Court of Appeals overturned that decision, pointing out that there was no evidence in the record of the extent to which the full requirements customers of the Columbia Gas System (of which Atlantic Seaboard is a part) lacked access themselves to second sources of supply; and that the Commission had not considered to what extent any loss of sales to partial requirements customers might be made up by additional sales to others, thus rendering higher rates to the residual patrons unnecessary.[127]

---

[124] 399 F. 2d 953, 959–961 (1968). See also Sections 7(e) and 7(g) of the Natural Gas Act, p. 113, note 1, above.
[125] For earlier illustrations of a similar attitude, see Koplin, *op. cit.*, 359, 361–403; Nelson Lee Smith, "Federal Power Commission and Pipeline Markets: How much Competition?" *Columbia Law Rev.* (April 1968), LXVIII: 667–676.

[126] *Chattanooga Gas Company v. East Tennessee Natural Gas Company*, Opinion No. 494, 35 FPC 917 (1966). See also *Transcontinental Gas Pipeline Corporation et al.*, Opinion No. 493, 35 FPC 902 (1966) and Smith, *op. cit.*, 678–679.
[127] *Lynchburg Gas Co. v. F.P.C.*, 336 F. 2d 942 (1964).

On remand, the Commission took its newer, more clearly procompetitive line, holding that Columbia had not provided substantial evidence of its need for such a rate.[128] In upholding this later decision, the Circuit Court emphasized the appropriateness of the effort to obtain some of the benefits of competition "as an important and effective tool in increasing economic efficiency and quality of service."[129] Judge Harold Leventhal's judicious decision recognized the possibility of offsetting considerations—"a cross-current appears when cheap gas to one group of consumers results in higher prices to another" (*Ibid.*)—but pointed out that it was the function of the Commission to consider

"the nature and extent of economic consequences that may warrant protection of a historical supplier, and full requirements customers dependent on it, from the impact of competition, from a second source of supply—from competition that the Commission must determine serves the public interest. . . .

"The point is, however, that a policy favoring effective competition necessarily brings with it the reality of economic pinch, present or threatened. The presence of a second seller means that the historic supplier loses out on sales it would have otherwise had—assuming the same ardor in promoting sales in a non-competitive setting. It is through the enhanced efforts made by the supplier in response to such pressure that competition reaps its benefits. The hard problem then is not whether competition may hurt but rather where and how to draw the lines of acceptable range of competition and hurt, in response to the economic characteristics and interrelationships of the industry that require regulation in the first place." *Ibid.*

Similarly, in 1967 and 1968, the FPC certificated a second pipeline to serve distribution companies in the District of Columbia, Maryland and Virginia, which had turned to the new entrant in order to take advantage of its lower commodity rates;[130] permitted the City of Hamilton, Ohio, Municipal Gas Distribution System to shift its purchases to a new supplier, at a markedly lower price;[131] and acceded to the request of the Municipal Distribution System of the City of Corinth, Mississippi, that it order a reluctant Tennessee Gas Pipeline Company to establish a direct physical connection with the City's facilities and supply it with gas at rates more favorable than the ones charged by its previous supplier.[132] All of these decisions were upheld in the Courts.

---

[128] One factor making it easier for the Commission to justify its new determination was that the Columbia companies had in the interim filed restructured tariffs, drastically tilting rates from the old Atlantic Seaboard formula in such a way as to impose the preponderant portion of the System's fixed costs on the demand charge. This meant that the losses of revenues from *commodity* charges when partial requirements customers shifted their patronage would no longer force the pipeline to increase its rates to the remaining customers in order to recover all of its fixed costs. See the discussion of the Atlantic Seaboard formula at pp. 98–100, Volume 1.

[129] *Atlantic Seaboard Corporation et al. v. Federal Power Commission, et al.,* 404 F. 2d 1268, 1272 (1968).

[130] *Atlantic Seaboard Corporation v. Federal Power Commission et al.,* 397 F. 2d 753 (1968).

[131] The *Cincinnati Gas & Electric Company et al. v. Federal Power Commission, et al.,* 389 F. 2d 272 (1968). Cert. was denied by the U. S. Supreme Court, October 14, 1968.

[132] *Alabama–Tennessee Natural Gas Company et al.,* Opinion No. 534, 38 FPC 1069 (1967), sustained in *Alabama–Tennessee Natural Gas Company v. Federal Power Commission,* 417 F. 2d 511 (1969). Certiorari denied February 24, 1970. This case had the interesting feature that the customer's application was opposed by the new supplier as

In view of our repeated emphasis on the importance of competition as a supplement to regulation, it might appear churlish to express some dissatisfaction with the foregoing series of decisions. And yet it is difficult to emerge from reading them with full confidence that they have adequately appraised the limited ways in which competition can function in this industry and the secondary consequences of permitting it to do so in the selective manner that they authorize. Its benefits are almost invariably identified with the fact that particular customers—the Washington Gas Light Company or the Cities of Hamilton, Corinth or Lynchburg—will be able to obtain gas at lower rates. (It should be pointed out, however, that the competition between Atlantic Seaboard on the one hand and Transco on the other for the patronage of the first of these apparently produced another important benefit: "As a result of Transco's proposals, Seaboard reduced its rate and introduced a winter service that afforded pipeline storage."[133]) These savings to the successful customers have been great: they presumably would have to have been, to justify the effort of finding another supplier, investing, as was required in some instances, in additional facilities to connect up with him and contesting their right to shift before the Power Commission and in the Courts.[134]

But the FPC has not typically set forth convincing general economic rationalizations of its decisions, taking into account all their relevant effects, direct and indirect. To be sure, it was required in each case to weigh the injuries that the aggrieved pipelines claimed they would suffer from the loss of business and the possibility that this would force higher rates on their remaining customers. But in most instances, it rather lightly dismissed these countervailing considerations by pointing out that only a small percentage

---

well as the supplanted one. The City's previous exclusive supplier, Alabama–Tennessee, had been buying the gas in question from Tennessee Gas. So the City was asking the FPC to force the latter company thereafter to supply it directly rather than indirectly, so as it give it substantially more favorable rates. The Commission acceded, ordering Tennessee to supply the City's incremental requirements until January 31, 1970, when its contract with Alabama–Tennessee was to expire, and all its requirements thereafter. The basic issue here was the same as in the historic *Shrewsbury* decision (see note 85, Chapter 2, above). In both instances, the FPC ordered a private supplier to render service to a municipal distribution company directly rather than, as previously, through an intermediary.

[133] *Atlantic Seaboard Corporation v. FPC, et al.*, 397 F. 2d 753, 757 (1968). Both the Washington Gas Light Company and Commonwealth Natural Gas contended before the Commission that, because of the extremity of the seasonal fluctuation in demand for their gas and their inability to sell large quantities of interruptible gas because of the absence of heavy industrial users in their market area, they had urgent need for storage service, which Seaboard had been unwilling to supply. *Columbia Gulf Transmission*

Company, et al., Opinion No. 512, 37 FPC 118, 128–130 (1967). An important inducement for Washington to turn to Transco was that the latter company offered it winter sales of gas from its storage capacity. Competition seems to have played an important role here in overcoming the alleged reluctance of pipelines to substitute storage for pipeline capacity. See pp. 99–100, Volume 1 and p. 51, Chapter 2, above.

[134] The demand charge from Alabama–Tennessee to the City of Corinth was $2.69; the corresponding rate at which the Commission directed Tennessee to provide the city service was $1.95; the respective commodity charges were 24.29¢ and 20.44¢ per Mcf. 38 FPC 1069, 1073 note 2 (1967). In the case of the City of Hamilton, Texas Gas Transmission, the successful applicant, had offered the city a commodity charge of 22.22¢ per Mcf; the best counter offer by Cincinnati Gas & Electric, from whom Hamilton proposed to cease purchasing, was 30.5¢ In consequence, the City demonstrated that it would be able to generate substantial additional industrial sales, attracting new industry into the community, and raise its load factor from 33 to an estimated 57 percent. 389 F. 2d 272, 273–274 (1968).

of the pipelines' total sales would be lost and that loss would readily be made good by growth in other sales. But this was hardly a sufficient appraisal of the total consequences: as the Commission itself recognized in the *City of Corinth* case, for example,

"We are not unmindful of the fact that A–T's growth would be even greater were it allowed to keep the Corinth load and that, as a result, its customers might enjoy some additional economies. But we would be derelict in our duty if we were to ignore the immediate and measurable benefits to Corinth on such a theoretical and speculative loss to other A–T customers. Such a rationale would inevitably bind a customer to its existing supplier, thus effectively preclude the realization of the fruits of competition."[135]

This reasoning is not necessarily incorrect. But a satisfying economic appraisal would clearly attempt to answer such questions as: how did it happen that one supplier was able to offer rates on this particular business so much more favorable than its competitors? To what extent was it because one line happened to traverse market territories that gave it a much more favorable load factor than the other?[136] Or because a large customer (like the cities of Corinth and Hamilton) was simply circumventing an intermediary supplier? In these events, what was the net, ultimate effect of the loss of this particular business likely to be on all remaining customers of the deserted supplier—not just absolutely (would their rates have to be raised?) but relatively (how would their rates behave over time relative to those secured by the customers that succeeded in shifting)? What are the merits of permitting certain customers, who happen to be in a position to shift their patronage, to receive the benefits of competitively reduced rates and not others? Do we have here an illustration of the inescapably, and perhaps undesirably, discriminatory character of the kind of limited price competition that alone is possible among public utilities? If not, what will be the

---

135 38 FPC 1069, 1076 (1967).
136 This is the explanation offered by the Trial Examiner of Transco's ability to offer the lower rates that seduced Washington Gas Light and Commonwealth Natural away from Atlantic Seaboard. Apparently the difference was attributable principally to differences in (1) company policy—

"whereas Seaboard had traditionally restricted boiler fuel sales in order to protect its firm service (particularly for domestic use), the newer Transco system had promoted large interruptible loads, including boiler fuel gas for electric generation"—

and (2) rate structure, reflecting once again the historic Atlantic Seaboard formula, which arbitrarily inflated the commodity charge. Smith, *op. cit.*, 685. The Examiner would have denied the Transco application on this account, as would have Smith himself. See the note immediately following. But, as we shall conclude, these facts would not necessarily justify this conclusion. On the contrary, whatever the reasons for the difference in costs of pipelines A and B,

the economic presumption would be in favor of having the business go to the lower-cost supplier. See pp. 170–171, below.

In a private communication Mr. J. David Mann has argued eloquently the infeasibility and irrelevance of the Commission's investigating the causes of the higher rates of the pipeline losing the business:

"I shudder to think what kind of record an imaginative and obstructive lawyer or group of lawyers might compile on that subject. . . . I would hate to undertake the task of proving any pipeline to be inefficient and unreasonably 'high-cost' in its operation and then also prove that its present plight was not of its own doing before I could get a less expensive supply of gas from some other pipeline. . . . If his rates are high and apt to remain so, what real weight should the reason for their being high have in a case involving someone's efforts to obtain gas at the lowest reasonable rates? I should think little or none."

I am much indebted to Mr. Mann for his criticisms of this section.

position of the Commission when the other large customers come around whenever their long-term supply contracts expire, and insist on being accorded the same privilege of shifting?[137] The Commission seems to have given little formal consideration to these possibilities, at least as far as its written opinions show.[138] On the other hand, the position of the critics of these decisions seems also lacking in clarity. Smith points to the estimate that Atlantic Seaboard's loss of some of the business of its Maryland, District of Columbia, and Virginia distribution companies would cut its projected growth rate from 7 percent to 2 percent a year; but this would impose a burden on the remaining customers only if it could be demonstrated that it would result inescapably in a sacrifice of economies of scale in future capacity expansions by the entire Columbia System of which it is a part. As we have already suggested, economies of scale in pipeline transmission taper off sharply after a point; and against any loss of future potential economies, if the increments to one system's capacity are smaller rather than larger, would have to be weighed the corresponding benefit accruing to the successful competitors. Smith also emphasizes Atlantic's competitive handicaps stemming from its poorer load factor; but he recognizes that this was at least in part because the commodity rate in the company's pre-1965 rate schedules contained a substantial contribution to fixed charges. Not surprisingly, therefore, it was base-load sales that the pipeline lost to Transco; it was to take advantage of that supplier's much lower commodity charges that the distribution companies proposed to transfer their patronage. They planned

---

[137] The one strong objection, along these lines, was formulated by the Presiding Examiner in the *Columbia Gulf Transmission* (and *Atlantic Seaboard*) case (*op. cit.*, note 133, above). Here is the way his views are seen by former Commissioner Smith, who agrees strongly with them:

"He characterized Transco's position as an 'attempted foray directly into Atlantic Seaboard's market with a lower unit cost of service due primarily to its relatively high load factor operations, with which Atlantic Seaboard, which necessarily carries on substantially lower load factor business, cannot compete'. . . . He continued:

"'Although there still may be room in the natural gas business for competition, the rates of pipelines must continue to be based on cost of service tied to a depreciated original cost base, not competition. This means the greater the loss of business by one pipeline to another, the higher will be the unit cost of service of the pipeline having its business syphoned away.'

"The Examiner saw this as resulting in a vicious circle, with the customers playing off one pipeline against another, to their immediate advantage but to the detriment of Seaboard and its other customers. Looking to the future, he noted (i) that since 'Transco can now undersell Atlantic Seaboard, there is every reason to believe that it will always be able to do so' and (ii) that '[t]he Commission would, to be con-

sistent, have to let other customers of Atlantic Seaboard, able and desiring to do so, also obtain their future requirements from Transco'. . . ." *Op. cit.*, 684–685. See also the Concurring Opinion in this case of Commissioner Carver and his concurrence also in the *City of Corinth* case, *op. cit.*, raising similar questions.

[138] "As to long-term effects, Seaboard contends that the loss of sales in view of its lack of storage will result in converting Columbia Gulf to a winter design system with idle capacity and higher costs. As costs increase, it argues, a vicious circle will develop by which Seaboard's customers will try to obtain an increasing proportion of their requirements from Transco. There is nothing in the record to support these speculations. We have already noted how Seaboard's lower rates make sales expansions likely. In any case, however, these problems are not before us. We shall consider any future proposals to divert load from the Columbia system on the basis of the record then before us. Such a record will show the proposed diversion in the light of the most recent information on Columbia's markets. Here the possible losses of market, which are subject to our control, should not prevent us from approving Transco's present proposal with immediate benefits accruing to Washington, Commonwealth and their customers." *Columbia Gulf Transmission Company*, 37 FPC 118, 128 (1967).

no reduction in their purchases from Atlantic Seaboard under its demand charges. As long, therefore, as that charge was framed to follow peak-responsibility principles, this loss of business would involve no loss in the contribution to the pipeline's fixed, capacity costs that would have to be recouped from its other customers. There seems no economic justification for protecting an economically inefficient rate structure against the competitive inroads that it itself invited. On the contrary, it was the prospect of competition itself that forced Seaboard to introduce the above mentioned corrections in its rates.[139]

If a regulated company loses some business that has been bringing in revenues greater than its directly avoidable costs, it is important to bear in mind, that the burden falls, at least in the first instance, on its own profits, not on its other customers. Under what circumstances will or should that burden be passed on to the remaining customers? It would be necessary, first, that the pipeline fail to make good the deficiency in contribution to its fixed charges before its next general rate investigation—that it fall so far short of earning a minimum necessary return on equity as to make a persuasive case for rate increases that would not otherwise be justified. In view of the fact that the return on equity of natural gas pipelines has been running above 11 percent recently,[140] in view of the obstacles posed by long-term supply contracts to quick departures of other customers, and in view of the FPC policy of certificating competitive applications only when it appears existing suppliers would suffer no absolute decline in sales, this danger would seem to be remote. The second possibility would be that the line losing the business would on that account be less able to take advantage of scale economies in its subsequent expansions of capacity. We have already offered some reasons for deprecating this possibility, while recognizing, as in the El Paso–Pacific Gas Transmission Company case, that the Commission might well, in such cases, require competing pipelines to plan their capacity expansions jointly, in order to permit them most fully to achieve the available savings.

In view of the danger that competing pipelines may take on business at unremunerative rates in order to expand their rate bases, it is of course necessary for the FPC to satisfy itself that proposed competitive extensions of service are in fact remunerative. But once it has done so and satisfied itself, additionally, that the additions to capacity are taking the fullest possible advantage of potential economies of scale, it would seem it has sufficiently fulfilled its responsibilities. It is of course possible that captive customers will then pay a higher price for their gas than others in a position to take advantage of competitive offers—perhaps because their pipeline suppliers are paying a higher price for their gas, perhaps because they are using higher-cost, inadequately depreciated plant. But as long as they are not additionally injured by the competitive certifications, it would seem that these can have only desirable effects on balance.

---

139 *Ibid.*, 126.
140 The median return of 11 leading natural gas pipeline companies sampled by the author was 13.5 percent in 1966 and 13.3 percent in 1967; since some of these companies were diversified, the return on the pipeline business alone could have been somewhat lower. According to the National City Bank, the return of the 233 companies in its general category of electric power, gas, and others was 11.5 and 11.6 percent in these years (see note 76, p. 52, Volume 1, above).

If pipeline A has higher costs than pipeline B, even if for reasons beyond its control, that is surely not a reason for protecting A against B's competition. On the contrary. The efficient price is the marginal cost of the lowest-cost available alternative. Where competition is feasible it is the most effective device for producing that result. And even if it fails to reduce A's rates, it serves the social function of transferring as much as possible of the business to the company that can do it at the lowest social cost. True, problems are created when competition is feasible only in some markets and not in others. But that may merely reflect the fact that it is, truly, more costly to serve the captive customers of A than those to whom B's services are available.[141] Even in unregulated markets, competition is typically selective and discriminatory. But the dissatisfactions to which it gives rise among customers who are not immediate beneficiaries, raising the possibility that others of them, as well, will try to shift to other suppliers and creating opportunities for competitive entry are the instrument by which its benefits are generalized.

In short, the FPC's instincts have probably been sound in opening up gas wholesale markets to a greater measure of competition in these cases. It would seem appropriate to place on the objectors the burden of proof that the remaining captive customers, rather than merely the stockholders of the pipelines that lose business, will in fact be unjustifiably injured. We have seen reason to doubt that this is the usual case.

---

[141] Consider, for example, the case on efficiency grounds for permitting lower rail rates to shippers who can also be served by lower-cost water carriers than to others lacking this alternative, pp. 166–168, Volume 1.

CHAPTER 5

Destructive Competition and the Quality of Service

All economic regulation involves a limitation or suppression of competition, whether by control of entry or of price rivalry or both. This is true of the natural monopolies, as we have seen,[1] as well as of industries where monopoly is far from natural. And in principle all such regulation has the avowed purpose, among others, of assuring a satisfactory quality of service.

But the economic logic and consequences among the industries that were the subject of Chapter 4 are fundamentally different from those that are the subject of the present chapter. The overwhelming consideration among the natural monopolies is the presence of economies of scale and the omnipresent threat of monopolistic exploitation. Among the industries we propose now to examine, it is competition that is the natural state. Economies of scale are sufficiently limited relative to the extent of the market and entry sufficiently easy in the absence of governmental restraints as to make competition entirely feasible. And the preponderant case for regulation is that such competition tends to be excessively intense and it is for *that* reason, rather than the presence of excessive monopoly power, that the quality of service has to be protected by the imposition of governmental restraints.

In this discussion, as throughout our study, the focus is on avowedly *economic* regulation—that explicitly seeks to supplant competition at the core of the market process. We are not directly concerned, that is, with the mere specifications of product standards or the occupational licensure that purport only to set objective or physical standards of performance or qualification for practice, without determining how many suppliers there ought to be or who they should be or at what price they should sell.[2]

---

[1] See especially pp. 116–119, Chapter 4, above.
[2] We have already referred to the widespread use of occupational licensing as a means of protecting unwary buyers; and we have also described its perversion into an instrument for raising barriers to entry and protecting practitioners of a wide variety of trades from unwanted competition. And we have distinguished that kind of regulation in principle—however close they may come in practice—from the economic regulation that is the subject of these volumes. See pp. 1–2, 8–9, Volume 1, and 5–6, above. On the other hand, we shall draw on that experience as well as that of the regulated industries proper, where it helps illuminate the applicable economic principles and tendencies.

THE THEORY AND PREREQUISITES OF DESTRUCTIVE COMPETITION

What is the theory here? Why might competition prove to be excessive *from the standpoint of the consumer?*[3]

The major prerequisites are fixed or sunk costs that bulk large as a percentage of total cost; and long-sustained and recurrent periods of excess capacity. These two circumstances describe a condition in which marginal costs may for long periods of time be far below average total costs.[4] If in these circumstances the structure of the industry is unconcentrated—that is, its sellers are too small in relation to the total size of the market to perceive and to act on the basis of their joint interest in avoiding competition that drives price down to marginal cost—the possibility arises that the industry as a whole, or at least the majority of its firms, may find themselves operating at a loss for extended periods of time.

Actually, the history of the industries that are generally believed to be subject to destructive competition in the absence of government intervention has not been one of continuous depression. On the contrary, it has been a record of unusually great instability of prices and producer incomes, in both the long and the short-run. And the fundamental cause of this instability is the inelasticity of supply of most of these products.[5] As demand has increased —for example, in wartime or in the upswing of a business cycle—supply has been unresponsive in the short run: it takes several years to develop a coal mine; expanded exploratory effort for crude oil does not instantly produce

---

[3] It is obvious that it could be—indeed typically is—excessive from the standpoint of the seller. This distinction, while obvious, is worth emphasizing in the present context. All competition is "destructive" of the equity of the individual businessman who is subjected to it. That is why businessmen who will rarely (at least in the United States) declare opposition to competition as a general practice will ordinarily hasten to express their objection to competition that is "destructive," "excessive," or "cutthroat," and it is ordinarily difficult to see what price competition they would not so characterize.

[4] As J. M. Clark has pointed out, the feasibility and stability of pure competition depend on the circumstance of increasing marginal costs, both short- and long-run. The latter means that the presence of numerous firms is consistent with efficiency. And the former, that industry demand will ordinarily be intersecting a rising industry marginal cost curve at a point that will for most, or for a sufficiently large number of firms be at or above their average total costs as well (see Figure 1, p. 74 of Volume 1.) But if, as he argues is typically the case in manufacturing, the average variable cost curve (hence the marginal cost) is horizontal up to 90 or even 100 percent of capacity operations and demand fluctuates widely over the cycle, pure competition would drive price below average total cost for most producers most of the time. Moreover, as we

pointed out in Chapters 3 and 4 of Volume 1, it would subject price to wide fluctuations as demand alternately reached and fell short of the limits of capacity—which would tend to be restricted sufficiently to insure such a result, in order that minimum necessary profits were earned over the cycle. This entire discussion draws heavily on the writings of Clark, notably his *Studies in the Economics of Overhead Cost* (Chicago: Univ. of Chicago Press, 1923), Chapter 21; "Toward a Concept of Workable Competition," in Amer. Econ. Ass'n., *Readings in the Social Control of Industry*, 452–475; and *Competition as a Dynamic Process* (Washington: The Brookings Institution, 1961), 32–34, 58–60, and 120–123.

[5] The demand for some of them has been subject to unusually great fluctuation as well, in transitions from peace to war and back again, or over the business cycle. This has been true of copper, tin, and perhaps bituminous coal. But the demand for these products has been no more unstable than for steel, automobiles, or the services of the construction industry; and the demand for cotton textiles, sugar, coffee, tea, milk, and agricultural products generally—all of which have been subject to violent price fluctuations over time—has surely been more stable than the average, not less. The fundamental cause of price instability in all these cases, therefore, must be sought on the supply side.

additional production capacity; several years must elapse before newly planted rubber trees begin to add to supply; and there is no way of speeding up the biological processes on which expansion of milk supplies depends. In consequence, output of most of these products tends to expand far less than the average in periods of increasing demand—for example, during wartime—and their prices tend therefore to rise much more, as demand rises along a sharply upwardly sloping short-term supply curve. But entry into most of these industries is easy and capacity does finally respond to the incentive created by sharply increasing prices, though with a long delay reflecting the long incubation period between the decision to expand capacity and its emergence.

The "problem" of bituminous coal, agriculture, natural rubber, sugar, oil, milk, coffee, copper, and tin then emerges when the additional capacity becomes available and demand either ceases to grow as rapidly as before or declines; and the industries find themselves with excess capacity. This excess has been inflated, in many cases, by unusually great technological progress, as in the case of agriculture; by the rapid expansion of output in new, lower-cost areas, as in the case of rubber and sugar in the 1920s and 1930s; by the emergence of substitutes—oil for coal, synthetic fibers, plastics, and rubbers for the products of agriculture and plantations; by the growth of output in lower-income areas—textiles and coal in the U. S. South, textiles in the underdeveloped countries of the world. All of these make it possible for entry to continue and the supply curve to move to the right even in the presence of substantial excess capacity and declining incomes experienced by existing firms.

It is the long-delayed expansion of capacity, accentuated by the factors just described, that makes for a "sick industry." The other necessary ingredient is independent competitive behavior. If producers were few or were made to act in concert by government regulation, they would cut back their utilization of capacity (as well as refrain from adding to it), in order to avoid "spoiling the market"—unless, that is, they thought total industry demand was sufficiently price-elastic to make lower prices more profitable than sustained prices for all of them. That is to say, it is competition and a steeply inclined marginal cost function that makes supply inelastic down to the level of each individual firm's out-of-pocket costs, in the face of declining prices and shrinking profit margins; and it is this inelasticity of supply, in the presence of excess capacity, that makes the industry "sick"—in the sense that all or the preponderant proportion of firms in it are failing to cover their total costs, including a "normal" return on investment.[6]

Since a reduction of price below ATC of a sufficient number of firms is

---

[6] Thus, interestingly, aggregate capacity in a "sick industry" is typically not *idle*, and it is the failure to keep it idle that makes it sick. In what sense, then, is it excessive? In the sense that it is more capacity than can be supported at "normal" rates of return. See Lloyd G. Reynolds, "Cut-throat Competition," *Amer. Econ. Rev.* (December 1940), XXX: 736–738. It should be obvious that there is no clear, objective boundary line between a sick and a well industry. Even in the most prosperous of times, there will be firms in competitive industries that earn far less than "normal" returns; and even in the depths of an industry's depression, there will be efficient operators earning entirely acceptable profits. Indeed, as we have already suggested, one of the continuing sources of the "agricultural problem" in the United States (as it was of the textile or bituminous coal industry problems in the 1920s and 1930s) has been the continued expansion of investment and capacity by new and highly successful firms, using the most modern technology.

precisely the way in which a competitive market is supposed to operate in the presence of excess capacity,[7] why might such a circumstance, admittedly injurious to the profits of the sellers in the industry, also pose any threat to the welfare of its customers?

One possible reason is that the pressures of declining or inadequate revenues might force the curtailment of many postponable expenditures that the consumer would in the long run be better off having continued. This might be true of the repair, maintenance, and keeping-in-being of capacity that the market will in the long run wish to have retained and that can be retained at lower cost than it can be resurrected when demand justifies it;[8] research;[9] and the continued offer of temporarily unremunerative services. The economist would entertain some skepticism about this general argument. If, in fact, the capacity will eventually be required and can be maintained more cheaply than eventually resurrected, on proper discounting of the future costs of following the latter course, then, it might be anticipated, it would pay the businessmen to make these investments, for that is what they would be—present outlays in anticipation of the future income. The same should be true of research activities; if the anticipated future benefits, properly discounted, exceed the current outlays, it will pay the business to continue making those outlays, no matter how bad his current income statement looks. And if he lacks the necessary funds, it ought to pay him to turn to the capital markets to obtain them. This danger reduces, then, to the possibility either that, because of imperfect foresight, the producer might not see the desirability of maintaining the temporarily unprofitable operations or, because of imperfections of the capital market, he may not be able to raise the funds necessary to sustain the socially desirable investments. But these possibilities are not necessarily to be dismissed. Managers are likely to be much more willing to use internally generated funds for purposes like these than to go to the capital markets, and investors less reluctant to provide funds—or see them provided—in the first way than in the second.[10]

Indeed, destructive competition would be inconceivable except for the presence of market imperfections. In particular, it is the inability of capital

---

[7] Economic efficiency requires that price be set at short-run marginal cost, not average total cost, not only because this gives buyers the correct signals about the marginal opportunity costs of what they are buying, but also because it will tend automatically to restore the proper balance between capacity and demand. It will do so, first, because only as price falls below the variable costs of the higher-cost producers will they be induced to shut down their inefficient plants; and, second, because a reduction in price below the average total cost of new plants will discourage the entry of new capital—except where it *should* enter because its average total costs are less than the average variable costs of plants required to meet the market demand.

[8] For example, the temporary closing of coal mines may result in flooding if pumping is not continued. Simon N. Whitney, *Antitrust Policies* (New York: Twentieth Century Fund, 1958), I: 395. And the abandonment of pumping on marginal or stripper oil wells may result in permanent loss of their reserves. See, for example, Erich W. Zimmermann, *Conservation in the Production of Petroleum* (New Haven: Yale Univ. Press, 1957), 73–76.

[9] *The Wall Street Journal* periodically has survey articles describing how business firms react to a period in which their profits are being squeezed. These reactions include such diverse remedies as use of the mail in place of the long-distance telephone, travel by tourist instead of first-class, and curtailment of research and development activities. Just like other production, dismantling and later reassembling a research operation may in the long run be more costly than continuing it.

[10] See Dennis C. Mueller, "A Theory of Conglomerate Mergers," *Q. Jour. Econ.* (Nov. 1969), LXXXIII: 644–645, drawing on James S. Duesenberry, *Business Cycles and Economic Growth* (New York: McGraw-Hill, 1958), 87–97.

readily (that is, in the short run) to move out of a situation of excessive capacity, once it has become embodied in that capacity, that creates the possibility of gross returns on investment remaining for extended periods of time below the minimum required in the long run to maintain it.[11]

Another reason why unregulated competition might not in these circumstances be desirable is that, as we have pointed out earlier in considering the ideal behavior of public utility rates, wide fluctuations in price may be no more in the interest of consumers than sellers; they make long-range planning difficult and force a shift in attention from productive efficiency to buying and selling, to speculating and avoiding speculating on price. Price fluctuations are a product of market imperfections and they, in turn, promote uncertainty and inefficiency.

The other prominent imperfection that may make unrestricted competition particularly injurious to consumers is their own limited ability to judge the quality of products and hence to keep it at acceptable levels even when they have a wide range of competitive suppliers to choose from. The quality of service in public utility industries has many dimensions: not just its physical specifications but its reliability, safety, regularity, frequency, and the financial responsibility of its purveyors. A good deal of the case for regulation is the importance of assuring that these services meet acceptable standards in these various respects in the presence of monopoly: consider the extreme importance of having an assured and regular supply of electricity meeting fairly precise voltage requirements, of gas during the heating season, of regular, reliable, and safe telephone and transportation service and honest security brokers and stock exchanges protected against manipulation by insiders at the expense of outside investors. This kind of consumer protection can be equally necessary when price competition is very intense. The decline in price to average variable costs can lead to a skimping on safety, reliability, and frequency of service that consumers may have difficulty in detecting promptly.[12] The greater that difficulty, the greater the temptation of competitors to cut corners, since the competitor that skimps does not at once lose all his customers, while the one that scrupulously maintains quality may be inadequately rewarded for the higher costs of doing so.[13]

---

[11] As we shall see, the same role may be played by the immobility of labor. In fact, the most familiar historic instances of destructive competition for extended periods of time were situations in which it was the inelasticity in the supply of labor to the industry in question, consequent on labor immobility, that made the depression of the industries so deep, so extended and so injurious to the people dependent on it.

[12] That is, the consumer may be deceived when he turns to what looks like a cheaper source of supply: a discount house may turn out to give inadequate service on the appliance he buys from it; the tramp freighter or motor carrier turns out after the fact to be unreliable, to carry inadequate insurance against loss of cargo, and so on. For justifications of restrictions of competition essentially on the ground that uncontrolled rivalry would be highly imperfect, see Marx, *International Shipping Cartels*, Chapters 2, 12, 14;

and P. W. S. Andrews and Frank A. Friday, *Fair Trade, Resale Price Maintenance Re-examined* (London: Macmillan, 1960), 17–22.

[13] It might appear that, if consumers cannot indeed detect deteriorations in quality, it would pay even a monopolist, not just an unethical competitor, to try to cut costs in this manner. But monopolists who expect to be in that line of business for a long time and whose long-run profitability is dependent on the industry's general reputation with consumers will have greater means and incentive to maintain quality than individual smaller competitors, with a shorter time perspective and less of a concern about the industry's continuing reputation with consumers. What we have here, in the competitive case, is the possibility of a deterioration of performance because of (1) imperfections of the capital market—that is the real meaning of the "shorter time perspective" of smaller firms—and

Even if there is a danger of unregulated competition producing an unwanted deterioration in the quality of service, it does not necessarily follow that direct restraints on entry and price competition are the proper remedy. Legally prescribed quality standards could conceivably give consumers sufficient protection without the necessity for suppressing competition in other respects as well. Still, the suppression of competition may make it easier to enforce these other standards, for a number of reasons. First, the fewer the number of sellers, the easier it is to inspect them and to enforce whatever rules are set. Second, if entry is curtailed, the license itself is a valuable privilege, as we shall see. The firms permitted to operate will therefore have a sufficient financial stake in keeping their licenses to make them hesitant about risking cancellation for failure to perform adequately.[14] Third, because the license is valuable, regulatory commissions can require the favored licensees to assume financially burdensome service obligations that would otherwise be unprofitable for them. The protected franchisee becomes a chosen instrument for serving public purposes—maintaining regular schedules in the off-season, or serving unprofitable routes, or assuming the risks of maintaining an orderly market.[15] Finally the mere limitation in the number of firms and reduction in their turnover will itself give each of

---

(2) externalities: since the monopolist *is* the industry, any consumer discontent that results from an adulteration in the quality of service will eventually reflect injuriously on himself; individual competitors, in contrast, may in effect be passing some of those costs of consumer dissatisfaction off to the other firms in the industry.

Another way in which destructive competition may produce deterioration of service is by promoting labor unrest, as the pressures of declining prices and shrinking profits force companies to try to cut corners on wages, safety precautions, and other conditions of employment.

[14] Obviously, the more perfunctory and routine the renewal of licenses, the less effective this particular incentive will be. See the discussion of the policies of the Federal Communications Commission respecting the renewal of broadcast licenses, pp. 89–91, above.

[15] The fixing of minimum commission rates by the membership of organized security exchanges is defended on this last ground. See pp. 199–200, below. We consider at various points elsewhere the question of whether imposition of these unprofitable service obligations is economically justified.

One ironic illustration of this kind of rationalization is provided by New York State's former alcoholic beverage control law, which was supposed, it asserted, "to promote both temperance in the consumption of alcoholic beverages and respect for and obedience to law," by limiting the number of retail outlets and imposing compulsory retail price maintenance. [Quotation from the statute by Anthony M. Radice, "The New York State Liquor Market: The Rocky Road to Competition," *Cornell Law Rev.* (November 1968), LIV: 113–114.] Between 1950 and 1958, a period of sharply increasing state income and population, the State Liquor Authority issued no new licenses. In consequence, the median purchase price of transferred stores rose from $19,490 to $39,503: the store carried the license with it, provided the SLA approved the transfer. Harvey J. Levin, *Some Economic and Regulatory Aspects of Liquor Store Licensing in New York State: A Summary of Research,* (New York: State Moreland Commission on the Alcoholic Beverage Control Law, 1963), 17. It is probably true that the penalty of losing such valuable franchises made licensees hesitant about violating such regulations as the prohibition of sales to minors. But giving government employees the privilege of issuing them was a strange way of promoting "respect for and obedience to law": the predictable result was that some officials accepted bribes for issuing licenses or approving transfers. See *New York Times,* April 19, 1963, 1, and *ibid.,* May 24, 1963, 1. As for the compulsory resale price maintenance, it would probably occur only to an uncouth economist that the effectiveness of a prohibition of retail price competition in promoting temperance would depend on the elasticity of demand and that there was something questionable about using a device that would probably be much more effective for the poor than for the rich.

them a stronger incentive to take the long view of its profit-increasing activities and cultivate the consumer goodwill that would be jeopardized by skimping on service quality.[16]

THE THEORY APPLIED

The possibility must be conceded, then, that competition may in certain circumstances be excessively strong and that restrictions on it can produce an improved performance. The questions that must be asked in each regulatory situation are (1) to what extent those circumstances actually prevail or would prevail if controls were removed, (2) to what extent deterioration of service could instead be prevented merely by imposing standards of quality, safety, financial responsibility, and the like, and (3) whether such additional benefits as might be secured by limitations on entry and price rivalry are greater than the benefits that freer competition brings.

The Case of Trucking

The reader will recognize that arguments like the ones just summarized were used to justify passage of the Motor Carriers Act of 1935.[17] There seems no reason to doubt that the results of unregulated competition had not been satisfactory up to that time. The following is a representative appraisal:

"there was then a surplus of transportation of all kinds. Competition became destructive. Large numbers of small operators were engaging in motor transportation. Their rates were not published. Many of the smaller operators were not aware of the costs of doing business and they made such rates as seemed required to secure traffic. Many of them failed and went out of business, but others promptly took their places. There was no rate structure, variations in individual rates were wide, rates were constantly changing, charges to various shippers using the same carrier were often different, and the service was neither stable nor reliable. Shippers found it increasingly difficult to do business with motor carriers because of the unreliability of service and the financial irresponsibility of many of the carriers, and they were distressed at fluctuating rates and differential treatment."[18]

Does Trucking Pass the Tests? But—following our outline of the proper questions to ask—does trucking have the economic attributes of an industry subject to destructive competition? It would be difficult to find one less qualified. The first requirement is a low ratio of variable to total costs for extended periods of time (recall that in the indefinitely long run all costs are variable): since it is variable costs that fix the floor below which price cannot go (at least not for very long), a low ratio of variable to total costs

---

[16] See note 13, this chapter, above.

[17] See pp. 5–6, 14, Chapter 1, above. He will recall that there were other motives as well, notably the desire to protect the railroads and their value-of-service freight rate structure from increasingly intense motor competition, and the desire of the truckers themselves, backed by the Teamsters' Union, for protection against the competition that had become increasingly intense during the Great Depression.

[18] Marvin L. Fair and Ernest W. Williams, Jr., *Economics of Transportation*, rev. ed. (New York: Harper & Bros., 1959), 488. For a similar view, see Donald V. Harper, *Economic Regulation of the Motor Trucking Industry by the States* (Urbana: Univ. of Illinois Press, 1959), 27–28, 39, 40. For a contemporary view, see the report of the Federal Coordinator of Transportation, op. cit., note 8, Chapter 1, above.

means that price can for extended periods of time fall far enough below average total costs for a large enough proportion of firms in the industry to threaten its ability to provide continued service. In the case of railroads, costs that vary over even as long as five years with the volume of traffic are probably less than half of the total; and even over the much longer run, a period long enough to permit changes in the physical plant, they amount perhaps to 70 to 75 percent of the total.[19] For the motor-carrier industry, in contrast, variable costs amount to at least 90 percent of total costs in the very short run and close to 100 percent over a very short span of years. This same sharp contrast is reflected also in the respective operating ratios of the two industries—the ratio of operating expenses to total revenues: these have since World War II run between 75 and 80 percent for the railroads and between 95 and 97.5 percent for trucks.[20]

These differences are attributable, primarily, to the fact that the railroads have had to construct and maintain their own roadbeds, bridges, and rights-of-way, as well as their elaborate and expensive terminal facilities. The trucks, in contrast, pay for the roads they travel only as they use them—in excise taxes for motor fuel, annual license fees, tolls, and the like. They pay for them also in excises on their vehicles and tires, but these costs, too, vary largely with the rate at which they are used: the depreciation of trucks and tires is essentially a variable cost. Moreover, the trucks that constitute their principal investment thave three other characteristics that tend to reduce the fixed and increase the variable costs associated with them and diminish the possibilities of persistent excess capacity, which constitute the second major prerequisite of destructive competition. They are short-lived. This makes their depreciation far less subject to obsolescence, which is a function only of time and a fixed cost, and far more a function of the rate of their use, hence a variable cost. It also means that motor-carrier companies are within very short periods of time constantly facing the decision of whether to replace their capital equipment and are in a position therefore to do so only if prices cover average total cost (including, as always, a necessary return on investment). Second, the investment involved in each is comparatively small. The consequence is that truckers can increase their capacity in small increments, thereby greatly diminishing the pervasiveness of excessive capacity. Contrast their situation with that of industries where producers are few and the economies of scale are such that they must build capacity ahead of demand in large lumps.[21] Third, they are mobile. The capacity can, without any

---

[19] These are the authoritative estimates of Ford K. Edwards, and include a 4 percent return on investment as part of the capital costs. For references, see the next footnote. As Locklin points out, the earlier, generally accepted estimate, placing variable costs at only about one-third of the total, was much shorter run in perspective and assumed lower rates of capacity utilization than became common in the World War II and postwar periods. These various ratios of variable to total costs are in some measure arbitrary, since obviously, by definition, the ratio of fixed or variable costs to the total will change with different levels of operation.

[20] This last comparison tends to minimize the difference between the two kinds of carriers. Not all operating expenses are truly variable costs; and total rail revenues have not typically provided a return on the industry's extremely heavy fixed investment even remotely comparable to the return enjoyed by the motor carriers. These various cost data are summarized in Locklin, *op. cit.*, 131–135, 154–156, 318–319, 646–648; Dudley F. Pegrum, *Transportation: Economics and Public Policy* (Homewood: Richard D. Irwin, 1968), 138–142.

[21] See note 25, pp. 135–137, Volume 1.

difficulty at all, be transferred from one market to another; there is no reason, therefore, for excess capacity to hang over any one part of the market for extended periods of time, as long as demand in other markets is growing.

It is difficult to disagree with Pegrum, when he says, flatly: "Competition among motor carriers cannot be ruinous."[22] How, then, could it have been so in 1935? There are at least two ways of explaining. First, the mere fact that variable costs are a high proportion of the total does not necessarily protect an industry against the severe compression of prices and incomes characteristic of destructive competition. Variable costs put a stable floor under prices only if that floor is itself immobile. Suppose, however, that the principal component of those variable costs is the industry's wage bill; and suppose that the workers hired by the industry have no possibility of alternative employment, so that the supply of labor to the industry is completely inelastic on the downside within a wide range. The result will be that the burden of competition will be transmitted directly to wage rates: decreases in final product demand will result in the derived demand for labor moving vertically downward along the rigid labor supply curve, with the industry's depression in this case being transmitted directly into declining wages.[23] The long-extended downward wage-price spiral, with its accompanying labor

---

[22] *Public Regulation of Business* (Homewood: Richard D. Irwin, 1959), 531. An even more striking example is provided by the freight forwarders. The forwarder is a common carrier that contracts with shippers for transporting freight between two points and itself handles the shipment by making its own arrangements with the other common carriers. Generally, forwarders handle small shipments, which they pick up, consolidate, and ship at carload or truckload rates, then break down and distribute to their several destinations. Forwarders utilizing the services of common carriers that are regulated by the ICC are themselves subject to this regulation: in particular, they must be licensed by the Commission. Until 1958, these licenses were freely granted. But in 1957, Congress deleted from the original Enabling Act a provision that prohibited the ICC from denying permits on the sole ground that the applicant would compete with other forwarders. Thereafter, the ICC has subjected such applications to the same kind of stringent tests as it applies to would-be common-carrier truckers (see pp. 14–18, Chapter 1, above). The purported justification for such stringent regulation is the belief that free entry would result in "improvident and wasteful duplication of transportation services and facilities." See Comment, "Intermodal Transportation and the Freight Forwarder," *Yale Law Jour.* (June 1967), LXXVI: 1374, quoting from both the Senate and the House Reports on the 1957 Amendment. As this Comment makes quite clear, the alleged

danger of destructive competition is extremely difficult to credit: it points out, for example, that the capital-output ratio of the ICC-regulated forwarders is less than $\frac{1}{200}$ of that of the railroads. (*Ibid.*, 1375; see also pp. 1367–1368.) The CAB, in contrast, imposes no economic restrictions on entry into the air freight forwarding business, possibly because of its strong statutory commitment to the promotion of air transport. (*Ibid.*, 1369–1371, 1376.) But see note 50, Chapter 6, below.

[23] This was in large measure the way in which the "sickness" of the United States bituminous coal industry in the 1920s and 1930s manifested itself. Even though the variable wage costs accounted for over 60 percent of the total (James B. Hendry, "The Bituminous Coal Industry," in Walter Adams, ed., *The Structure of American Industry, Some Case Studies*, 3rd ed., New York: The Macmillan Co., 1961, 86), it was possible for the average value of bituminous coal at the mine to decline from $3.75 a ton in 1920 to $1.78 in 1929 (U. S. Bureau of the Census, *Historical Statistics of the United States, Colonial Times to 1957*, Washington, 1960, 356), because these variable costs themselves proved to be compressible: between 1923 and 1929, a generally prosperous period in the economy at large, the average hourly wage of coal miners declined from 84.54 to 68.14 cents. *Ibid.*, 93.

To the extent that the labor supply is equally inelastic on the upside, increases in final product demand will of course be similarly converted into corresponding increases in wages.

unrest, a typical feature of destructive competition, thus finds its explanation in the inelasticity of the industry's labor supply.[24]

A similar role was played in the motor-carrier industry during the Depression by the large stock of used trucks overhanging the market. The supply of used machinery (as of scrap metal) tends to be highly inelastic above the cost of reclaiming it or its scrap value. As the Depression wore on, the price of used trucks declined sharply, with the result that anyone who could drive could enter the business in the early 1930s with a minimal investment.[25] Part of the brunt of the destructive competition was therefore borne by the used truck market.

Second, a very large percentage of the economic cost of providing trucking service in those early days of the industry consisted in the return for the labor of the owner-operator, exactly as in the case of the family farm. The return on that labor, like the return on the investment in the truck itself, was a residual; it could be high if the industry was prosperous and could be compressed indefinitely, as long as the owners had no alternative employment, if the industry were depressed. During the Depression, these men had no alternative employment to which to turn; so the supply of their labor to this industry was, once again, completely inelastic. Indeed, with the sharp reductions in industrial employment, large numbers of workers moved into the owner-operation of service stations, farms, trucks, and small grocery stores, so that the supply of labor in these industries actually expanded in the face of declining remuneration.[26]

So the supply of the major inputs into the trucking industry was during the early 1930s either inelastic or even negatively elastic—with decreases in demand being either accompanied by or actually inducing an expansion in the quantity of service offered. This tended to produce the same inelasticity of supply as is imparted in other industries subject to destructive competition by a heavy investment in fixed capital.

There was probably another contributing factor—the overly optimistic anticipations that typically induce excessive entry into a young industry. There is every reason to believe that this condition would have been temporary. As G. Shorey Peterson wisely observed in 1929:

"The unusual intensity and irresponsibility of competition, upon which the whole argument rests, is more the outgrowth of the youth of the industry

---

[24] See Reynolds, *op. cit., Amer. Econ. Rev.* (December 1940), XXX: 744–745. Reynolds explains this downward movement in terms of a failure of these industries fully to exploit their monopsonistic power in labor markets in times of comparative prosperity and their progressive exploitation of that power under the downward pressure of competition on their selling prices in periods of excess capacity. Monopsony is not a necessary part of the process, however; the process could have occurred even in purely competitive labor markets, as the simple consequence of declining end-product demand and the inelasticity of labor supply to the industries affected.

[25] See Note, "Federal Regulation of Trucking:

The Emerging Critique," *Columbia Law Rev.* (March 1963), LXIII: 461.

[26] J. M. Clark contrasts interestingly the organization of the major portion of the economy, in which labor is one hired input and its costs are therefore variable, with the self-employment sector, in which its wage, like the return on capital, is a residual. In the latter circumstance, it is possible for the supply of the product to be not merely inelastic but actually backwardly sloping: decreases in price and in remuneration may induce the owners to put in even longer hours, in hope of maintaining their total income, a situation particularly conducive to destructive competition. See his *Competition as a Dynamic Process,* 174–175.

than of any permanent characteristics which it possesses. Competition is not cut-throat in the same sense as in the other public utility fields; it is rather the result of ignorance and of exaggerated ideas of possible profits. Mortality is high in most new industries. Quite obviously it cannot be permanently true that a field of service is unusually seductive in its appeal to new entrants and exceptionally harsh with those who enter it."[27]

These depressing and destabilizing influences have become greatly attenuated since 1935 and would surely have done so without regulation. The capital investment required to enter the industry, while still low, has increased markedly. Although economies of scale in trucking are comparatively slight, still

"the extremely small firm with the owner, his brother-in-law, and son can no longer compete with the twenty-man firm."[28]

Full employment in the economy generally has cut off the large and inelastic supply of labor to the industry. The workers have organized into a powerful union, which has the effect not only of raising wages but of making the labor supply completely elastic at the established wage level, thereby eliminating the downward compressibility of the most important component of the variable cost floor under price.

Yet, it is often asserted, there remains another possible source of destructive competition in trucking. This is the prevalence of joint costs, arising from the fact that the provision of capacity for transportation in one direction inescapably involves the provision of similar capacity, in fixed proportion, for the return haul. The marginal cost of the return haul, if the trucks are going out in the first direction anyway, are virtually zero, since the trucks must come back in any event, loaded or unloaded. This is another way of saying that even if all the costs of motor carriage were variable in the sense that they varied in direct proportion with mileage, the cost of picking up freight for half of the business—the return haul—are really not variable at all but sunk and have to be incurred whether or not transportation service is actually performed. This means that under competition—so the argument goes—rates on "the" back haul will tend to be driven down toward zero. But what, several observers have asked, if the back haul of carrier A is the front haul of carrier B? Competition between the two of them, with each willing to drop rates on *his* back-haul journey rather than return empty, can

---

[27] "Motor Carrier Regulation and Its Economic Bases," *Q. Jour. Econ.* (August 1929), XLIII: 618.
[28] Meyer *et al.*, *op. cit.*, 216. The authors cite the decline in the number of extremely small firms as an indication of this change: in 1935, 81 percent of the intercity trucking firms had annual revenues below $5,000; in 1951, in contrast, only 28 percent had revenues below $25,000. *Ibid.*, 216–217. On the presence or absence of economies of scale, see *ibid.*, 86–88, and for a survey of other studies, see Locklin, *op. cit.*, 644–645. While accepting the assertions of others that there are no marked economies of scale, George Wilson emphasizes the considerable importance of product differentiation in this industry—of speed, dependability, safety, and responsibility—and points out that "many of these qualitative elements tend to correlate positively with carrier size." "The Nature of Competition in the Motor Transport Industry," *Land Econ.* (November 1960), XXXVI: 388–389. Locklin agrees that large firms may have advantages in this respect over smaller ones. Wilson therefore suggests that there may even be a natural tendency to oligopoly in the industry—an additional reason for doubting the likelihood of destructive competition.

have the effect of pushing the rates on the *other's* "front haul" as well down toward unremunerative levels.[29]

This problem can be characterized in terms that we have used earlier in discussing the implications of the joint and common costs that are prevalent among public utilities: that, characteristically, the unit of production in these industries is greater than the unit of sale.[30] In the present context, the unit of production, almost all of whose costs are variable, would be the round trip; the unit of sale, even assuming that a single transaction would suffice to fill the truck, would be the trip in one direction from one point to another. The variable costs associated with the individual sale, assuming that the round trip was in any case going to be made, could be close to zero.

But the implication that the wide gap between the avoidable costs of the individual sale (for example, the return haul) and the average total costs of the unit of production (the round trip) creates a necessary tendency for unregulated competition to be destructive is unjustified. What we have here, in the simple case of trucks moving only from point A to point B and back, is a pure case of joint product. As we have seen in Chapter 3 of Volume 1, there is a determinate, competitive solution to the prices of two joint products; each of them does have a competitive supply price and the sum of those two marginal cost curves will equal the joint marginal production cost. Where the two prices settle that is, how the joint costs are distributed—will depend on the respective intensities and elasticities of the two demands; and those equilibrium prices will be equal to the respective marginal *opportunity costs* of the two products.[31] Where one of the products, because of the relatively low elasticity and level of its demand, is definitely a by-product (Figure 2, Chapter 3, Volume 1) that marginal opportunity cost will be zero and the other product will cover all the joint costs. But what if C's by-product is D's principal product and vice versa? To this there are two answers. First, what determines for each company which of its hauls is "back" and which "front"? Clearly, it must be the preponderant flow of traffic. But surely that will tend under competition to be the same direction for all competing sellers.[32]

Second, and more fundamentally, if C's trucks are all going out full in a westward direction and either coming back empty or having to charge less than one-half of the round-trip cost in order to return full, while D's trucks are coming eastward full and have to charge less than average total costs in the return direction, and if competition between the two to fill their trucks pushes their aggregate revenues for the round trip below joint costs, it can only mean that their combined capacities are greater than the combined demands for the joint services justify. The critical question, then, is not the presence or absence of joint costs but whether there is sufficient flexibility

[29] See Howard W. Nicholson, "Motor Carrier Costs and Minimum Rate Regulation," *Q. Jour. Econ.* (February 1958), LXXII: 150; also Wilson, *op. cit., Land Econ.* (1960), XXXVI: 389.

[30] See p. 77, Volume 1.

[31] See also note 11, pp. 93–94, Volume 1.

[32] If it were not, competition would tend to make it so. If supplier C obtained a greater contribution to joint costs from A to B traffic and supplier D from B to A traffic, obviously it would pay C to undercut D in order to get more of the B to A customers and D to do the same thing to get more of the shipments going in the opposite direction. Customers would have corresponding incentives to shift to the carrier accepting the lower rates on their particular service. The end result would be that both carriers would end up with the same "front" and "back" hauls—that is, with their peak and off-peak demands falling at the same times or locations.

in the decision of investors to supply capacity for the joint production to assure that capacity will be properly adjusted to the combined demand so as to permit the combined prices for the joint services to cover joint costs over time. The critical question about the feasibility of competition, in short, remains the elasticity of supply.

After all, certain important parts of the "unit of production" always exceed the unit of sale in every production process involving capital investment. A unit of X produced today is, as far as the cost of providing production capacity is concerned, a joint product with the unit of that product produced tomorrow. Yet, they are typically sold separately. The back-haul problem is therefore in no sense unique. Whether those units sold on different days together make a contribution over and above their separate variable costs sufficient to cover their joint cost depends on the adjustment and adjustability of capacity, over time, to their combined demand. Chronic excessive capacity is by no means inevitable.

The ability of truckers to assure a profitable adjustment of capacity to demand is enormously accentuated by the versatility of this mode of transportation—that is, the versatility it would enjoy if it were not for regulation. Not only can the same trucks carry a variety of items; in addition, a truck that moves from point A to point B is of course in no sense constrained to return to A by the same route. The A–B and B–A services are therefore not truly joint; they need not be supplied in fixed proportions. If rates on one leg of the journey fall, the trucker can vary his product mix by moving along alternative routes. It is only, then, if one can demonstrate some reason to expect chronic excessive capacity in the entire industry, over all routes, that the problem of the back haul could create an inherent tendency toward destructive competition.

The ready adjustability of aggregate trucking capacity, because of its comparatively short life and its ability to increase and decrease in small increments, would seem to make far less likely for this industry than most others such chronic overinvestment in "front-haul" capacity as to force joint revenues below total costs.[33]

There is one other characteristic of the industries one thinks of as having tendencies to destructive competition: their products are typically standardized, standardizable, or homogeneous. The reader can satisfy himself on this point by looking over our earlier list of examples.[34] The consequence of this

---

[33] "a trucker would not undertake a trip unless his expected revenue for the round trip would at least equal expected cost. The revenue from the first leg of the trip is usually known at the start . . . the return trip, however, may yield various amounts. . . . Since a trucker is faced with a probability function of revenue on his return trip, his realized revenue on any particular round trip may not cover his variable (out-of-pocket) costs. Thus, the situation visualized by Nicholson implies a continuing error in estimating return-trip revenue. Although occasional errors will be made, learning is expected to eliminate the source of error which would cause truckers continually to overestimate their return-trip revenues. In the long run, the market entry and exit of firms has to be relied upon for the movement toward joint-supply equilibrium." W. Miklius and D. B. DeLoch, "A Further Case for Unregulated Truck Transportation," *Jour. Farm Econ.* (November 1965), XLVII: 937. Nicholson recognizes this corrective tendency, but is not convinced of its sufficiency. *Op. cit.*, 148–152.

[34] On the case of coal, however, see Jacob Schmookler, in Walter Adams, ed., *The Structure of American Industry*, rev. ed. (New York: The Macmillan Co., 1954), 79–81.

Another possible exception is gasoline retailing, where there is important product and service differentiation. But the principal source of price wars here is the sale of surplus gasoline, unis that competition can center only on price; and, the product of each firm being completely substitutable for those of other firms, any and all price reductions must be met instantaneously by all competitors. Product differentiation, in contrast, has the effect of insulating firms in some degree from immediate loss of all their customers if they do not precisely meet a competitor's price; it gives them the kind of market niche, a partially protected and identifiable position, that Richard B. Heflebower has identified as the source of market stability or balance.[35] And correspondingly, it provides them with a focus for their competitive endeavors other than price.

As Wilson points out, "A truck journey by any particular carrier" is clearly not "equivalent to that of any other."[36] Because of the many important qualitative aspects of the service—dependability, safety and responsibility—an unregulated industry would almost certainly not be purely competitive; here, again, is a characteristic that diminishes the dangers of destructive competition.[37]

Would Quality Standards Suffice? The second question we said one ought to ask, when confronted with an argument for regulation in order to preserve the quality of service, is whether deterioration can be forestalled instead merely by imposing general quality standards on all suppliers. With respect to safety, for example

"The basic answer to the [Interstate Commerce] Commission's contentions regarding the need for comprehensive regulation to enforce safety standards is that the two underlying assumptions of its position, viz., that exempt or unregulated carriers have worse safety records than regulated carriers and that carriers with low earnings have inferior safety records, have never been proved."[38]

According to the Supreme Court,

"The conclusion that highway safety may be impaired [by permitting trucks exempt from economic regulation to travel the highways] rests . . . on

---

branded, largely by the very refiners that sell the identical products under their own brands. And the tendency to refine more products than they can sell through their own branded distributive channels is explainable by the pressures of truly extremely heavy fixed costs: the modern refinery is almost entirely automatic. The same is true at the service station level: the prime inputs of the service station operation are the labor of the owner-operator himself and the gasoline that comes to him, under price war conditions, at a price adjusted downward to enable him to meet competition.

[35] "Toward a Theory of Industrial Markets and Prices," reprinted from *Amer. Econ. Rev., Papers and Proceedings* (May 1954), XLIV: 121–139, in Amer. Econ. Ass'n, *Readings in Industrial Organization and Public Policy*, 297–315.

[36] *Op. cit., Land Econ.* (November 1960), XXXVI: 388.

[37] See the corroborating evidence of this in the Australian experience after deregulation, p. 191, below. As we have already observed (note 28,

above), Wilson concludes that this creates an inherent tendency toward oligopoly. He raises the question therefore of whether regulation may not have the effect, on balance, of keeping more firms in existence than would otherwise be the case. The much smaller average size of the truckers that are exempt from ICC regulation and the highly competitive character of their markets (as we will see below) casts doubt on this analysis; it seems much more likely that entry control has held down the number of truckers in the regulated part of the business (see James C. Nelson, "The Effects of Entry Control in Surface Transport," in *Transportation Economics, op. cit.*, 399–401). But even if Wilson is right, it would be a dubious defense of regulation that, by imposing artificial restrictions on the operations of motor carriers, it may have kept alive a larger number of firms than would otherwise have survived.

[38] Note, "Federal Regulation of Trucking: The Emerging Critique," *Columbia Law Rev.* (March 1963), LXIII: 505.

informed speculation rather than statistical certainty. A road check examination conducted by the Bureau [of Motor Carriers] did not indicate any significant difference in the number of safety violations [between exempt and regulated vehicles]. . . ."[39]

Further evidence is provided by the experience of Great Britain. Prior to the fall of 1969, Great Britain had a comprehensive licensing system for trucking comparable to the American one. A Report issued in 1965 by a Ministry of Transport committee chaired by Lord Geddes gave considerable attention to the question of whether quantitative or, as we have termed it, economic licensing was in fact a useful device for assuring safety of operations. It concluded that it was not, that the evidence indicated that "the present licensing system . . . has had no appreciable effect, directly or indirectly, on the prevailing safety standards." It specifically rejected the alleged necessity of regulating competition as a device for ensuring safety and concluded that the way to ensure these results was, instead, to issue revocable permits to all carriers, without any quantitative or economic limit, setting only the essential condition that the holder would abide by all safety regulations, and to enforce that condition vigorously by suspending or revoking permits for violations.[40]

The regulations imposed by the ICC with respect to safety, permissible hours of service, and equipment specifications are applied equally to private and exempt for-hire carriers, without subjecting them to the various economic controls that are applied to common and contract carriers generally. Public liability insurance standards could equally be required, as well as fitness and willingness-to-serve tests.

"The convenience of having the same agency administer both safety rules and economic regulation does not make a logical case for economic regulation. Limiting numbers and encouraging the growth of very large carriers may simplify enforcement of safety regulations, but that advantage hardly justifies the resulting market structures. . . .

"Aside from these . . . considerations, it is not at all certain that all regulated services conform to the high standards claimed by advocates of restrictive entry policies. Thus, in its recent annual reports, the Commission has reported about 15,000 informal complaints each year from shippers and receivers of freight, passengers, and others, alleging unsatisfactory service or unlawful practices. Numerous complaints of underestimating charges, slow payments for loss or damage, delayed deliveries, and other service deficiencies have long been levied against household goods carriers and have been the subject of ICC proceedings (during 1960, there were 2,338 shippers making such complaints)."[41]

The Effect on Industry Performance. The final and conclusive question is whether the advantages to the consuming public obtained by limiting competition outweigh the disadvantages. There is no conclusive way of

---

[39] *American Trucking Associations v. U. S.*, 344 U.S. 298, 305 note 7 (1953).

[40] Ministry of Transport, *Carriers' Licensing*, Report of the Committee, London, Her Majesty's Stationery Office, 1965, 44–56. This recommendation was incorporated in the mammoth Transport Act of 1968 (16 and 17 Eliz. 2 Law Reports Statutes, Chapter 73, 1968), although that Act did retain economic regulation of trucks over 16 tons in order to reduce highway congestion. See note 61, below.

[41] James C. Nelson, *op. cit.*, *Transportation Economics*, 416–417.

answering this question, since one cannot be certain how the industry would perform if regulation were completely removed. But there are a number of considerations and pieces of evidence strongly suggesting that the answer, as far as trucking is concerned, is that they do not.[42]

The most convincing is the eagerness of shippers to be served by unregulated companies. As we have already seen, something like two-thirds of all intercity truck traffic is carried in this way.[43] The simple fact of the matter is that most shippers who are in a position to do so "vote with their feet" for a competitive industry.[44]

The purported reason for exempting motor vehicles used to carry agricultural commodities from regulation[45] was that farmers need flexible transportation services, speedy in the case of perishables and adaptable to their seasonally fluctuating and not wholly predictable requirements. These needs of agriculture are special. But many other shippers doubtless have similar ones. It is competition and freedom of entry that provide the flexible adaptation of supply to demand, when and where and in what volume it appears; and it is regulation that, by interfering with the shifting of truckers from one route or product to another as required, introduces the inflexibilities that farmers are anxious to escape.

In this desire they are not alone. How else can one explain the more than 8,000 applications that the ICC receives from truckers each year, typically supported by shippers, requesting permission to enter the industry or to serve new routes?[46] Equally convincing is the phenomenal rise and preponderant role of private carriage. Private carriage recommends itself to companies with special needs that can best be served by their own facilities. But when this objective evidence of the preference of companies doing the major portion of all shipping for avoiding the regulated carriers is considered in conjunction with the evidence, to be mentioned presently, of the ways in which regulation raises costs, decreases flexibility, and holds up rates, it creates a strong presumption that most shippers regard regulation, on balance, as injurious to their interests.

The most important negative effects of regulation are the inefficiencies that it forces on both regulated and unregulated carriers by the detailed and intensive restrictions it places on their operations. A study of the certificates and permits of common and contract carriers as of 1942 by the Board of Investigation and Research (Nelson offers the opinion that "a roughly comparable pattern is in existence today")[47] disclosed that 62 percent of the regulated truckers were limited to special commodities; that 40 percent of these were limited to one commodity or commodity class and 88 percent to six or less; that 70 percent of the regular route common carriers had less than full authority to serve intermediate points, with more than one-tenth of them having no such authority at all; that about one-third of the intercity truckers had restrictions on their ability to carry return hauls and almost 10 percent

---

[42] The following appraisal draws heavily on the analysis of Nelson, *ibid.*, 395–422.

[43] P. 21, Chapter 1, above.

[44] See pp. 19–21, Chapter 1, for some of the efforts of shippers to avoid regulation.

[45] For a history of the agricultural exemption and its interpretation, see Fulda, *op. cit.*, 105–118.

[46] For one illuminating example, see the case study by David Welborn, *op. cit.*, 412–448.

[47] *Op. cit.*, *Transportation Economics*, 393; see pp. 390–393, on which this summary of the BIR report is based. On these restrictions see also pp. 15–18, above.

had no authority to transport any freight on the return trip. The regular-route common carriers must follow specified highways and in case after case have been turned down on applications to use a more direct routing between some of the cities they were authorized to serve. The BIR study found that these restrictions had caused large amounts of avoidable empty hauling, idle truck time, as well as additional mileage over circuitous routes. Among New England truckers surveyed 78 percent believed their operation would be more efficient if certificate restrictions were relaxed.[48] And paradoxically regulation subjects exempt operators to even more onerous restrictions and consequent inefficiencies, by making them confine themselves to exempt carriage. They may not, of course, solicit common- or contract-carrier business when and where they have excess capacity; the Commission has generally denied applications of private carriers for permits to engage in contract carriage on their return trips.[49]

Regulation gives rise to inefficiencies, also, by preventing the flexible response of price to temporary or local discrepancies between demand and supply. The efficient market solution for joint products, we saw in Chapters 3 and 4 of Volume 1, requires that their prices be adjusted to their respective demands, so as to be equated to their marginal opportunity costs. In an industry like trucking, where the geographic pattern of demand is highly complicated and changes from one day to the next, this kind of efficient pricing cannot possibly be prescribed, in advance, in regulatory proceedings. Fixed, regulated rate structures will therefore inevitably make it impossible to achieve the optimum utilization of capacity; and they will do so even more when, as in this instance, the general policy is to base them on average, fully distributed costs.[50]

To these sources of inefficiency must be added the expense and delay of the certification process itself. These costs may be worth incurring in situations of natural monopoly. They are doubly dubious in industries that seem to have all necessary attributes for effective performance without regulation.

The great virtue of the truck and of the competitive industry structure

---

[48] Meyer et al., *op. cit.*, 218–219 and Nelson, *op. cit.*, *Transportation Economics*, 408–409.

[49] See note 38, Chapter 1, p. 19, above, for a discussion of the circumstances under which farm cooperatives can carry nonfarm-related goods on back hauls. Also, ibid., for another illustration of the higher costs imposed by regulation on exempt carriers—the statutory limitations on the number of commodities barges may place on a single tow while retaining their exemption.

Because of these restrictions, it is difficult to interpret the evidence that common carriers tend to have larger average loads and a fuller average utilization of capacity than private or exempt for-hire carriers. That evidence alone might suggest that regulation promotes efficiency, by concentrating the business in the hands of fewer carriers. But to conclude from it that, on balance, regulation makes possible a more efficient utilization of plant in the entire industry, regulated and unregulated alike, would be highly questionable. See James C. Nelson, *op. cit.*,

Transportation Economics, 392, 410–412. For a finding that regulation imposes higher costs on regulated than exempt carriers, see Richard N. Farmer, "The Case for Unregulated Truck Transportation," *Jour. Farm. Econ.* (May 1964), XLVI: 398–409.

[50] See the very clear argument to this effect by Nicholson, *op. cit.*, *Q. Jour. Econ.* (February 1958), LXXII: 148–150. There is, we have already noted, a great deal of price discrimination in the trucking rate structure. But the general policy of the Commission—indeed, as Nicholson points out, the inevitable effect of any system of rate regulation—is to discourage differential contributions to overhead by different parts of the journey, and in particular between main and joint hauls even though in this, the true joint product case, this would *not* be discriminatory! On this last point, see note 11, pp. 93–94, Volume 1. On the evidence of a more flexible adjustment of price under nonregulated conditions, see p. 191, below.

with which its technology is so thoroughly compatible is precisely its flexibility and its versatility, both geographically and functionally—its ability to move on short notice to wherever it is needed and to pick up whatever kind of freight needs shipping. To take the fullest advantage of these attributes, operators must be free to move in these ways and to price flexibly, as market conditions demand. They cannot be free to do so under any regulation—least of all one with a strong protectionist inclination.[51]

There is another way in which regulation has an almost universal tendency to inflate costs. As we have already observed, the essential purpose of cartels is to raise price above the competitive level—that is, above marginal cost. If, as is usually the case, they succeed in holding price also above the average total costs of the most efficient producers and if they do *not* limit entry, the typical result is the entry of newer lower-cost firms, excess capacity, and the necessity for progressive cutbacks of output quotas.[52] If instead, as in trucking, entry is restricted but competition is not completely controlled, the firms within the industry will find it profitable, at the artificially maintained prices, to compete for business in other ways that increase cost. The ICC is not permitted, under the Motor Carriers Act, to place limitations on the amount of equipment and facilities or the schedules put into effect by certificated truckers. Consequently, there is a tendency for trucking companies to compete by offering greater frequency of service, at the cost of lower average utilization of capacity. This does, of course, mean improved service. The only way of testing whether the improvement is worth the higher costs it entails would be to offer shippers the choice between lower rates and less frequent operations, on the one hand, and the higher rates required for the more frequent scheduling, on the other. And it is precisely this choice that regulation prevents. The most convincing evidence that it is not worth the cost is the resort to private carriage by those shippers in a position to take advantage of this alternative.[53]

There is no room for doubt that, at least in the short run, regulation increases the price of transportation. The impact of this on shippers is necessarily very uneven, for two reasons. The first is, of course, that some shippers are in a position to escape by turning to private or exempt carriage. As far as the availability of this one escape-hatch is concerned, regulation would seem to bear most heavily on the small shipper or on the small, outlying community.[54]

---

[51] See especially pp. 14–28, Chapter 1, above.

[52] See pp. 28–29, Chapter 1, above.

[53] See the discussion of this phenomenon in Meyer et al., 219–220; Nelson, *op. cit.*, *Transportation Economics*, 391–392, 411–412.

[54] See, for example, the instance in which the Commission denied the Bee Line Express Company permission to provide direct service between the small town of Boaz and the cities of Birmingham and Chattanooga, even though (1) it was willing to do so and the motor carriers opposing its application were not and (2) shippers expressed dissatisfaction with the circuitous service they were currently getting. The ICC's justification was that the town's existing service was not "so inadequate as to justify a grant of additional authority." U. S. Senate, Select Committee on Small Business, *Competition, Regulation, and the Public Interest in the Motor Carrier Industry, op. cit.*, 6.

In 1956, shippers and carriers of fresh and frozen poultry succeeded in sustaining their position that these were agricultural products, entitled to exemption from ICC regulation; in 1958, the United States Department of Agriculture surveyed the experience in this industry after it became exempt. The results of the questionnaire were by no means unequivocal, but among the results that were consistent were the following: the major alleged disadvantages of regulated trucking included high rates, unwillingness to serve off-line points, slowness of

The second reason is that the restrictions on entry and price competition have helped—and, there is very convincing evidence, were intended to help—to preserve the discriminatory rate structure of the railroads from erosion by truck competition. The Federal Coordinator of Transportation, whose reports to Congress were influential in supporting what became the Motor Carriers Act of 1935, specifically justified this protection on the ground

"that railroad rates had traditionally been based on a formula that favored long hauls and low-value commodities, and that this practice of charging luxury goods relatively higher rates had generally been accepted as socially desirable."[55]

This was not a justification of price discrimination finely tuned, in accordance with the principles set forth in our Chapters 5 and 6 of Volume 1, to serve the interests of all rate payers; the avowed intention, rather, was to permit the continued subsidization of rates to certain shippers, notably farmers, at the expense of others.[56] There can be little doubt that regulation has the tendency to perpetuate these patterns of price discrimination and that the freer competition that is amply possible in truck transportation would go far to eliminate it [57]

These deleterious effects of regulation could well be a small price to pay, if the restraints on competition were necessary to prevent destructive competition and a serious deterioration of the quality of service. But there has been considerable experience with exempt carriage in the United States and with complete deregulation in Australia; and that experience casts considerable doubt on the reality of these dangers under freer competition. In general, it seems to demonstrate not only that competition produces lower rates, a larger number of suppliers, a wider range of alternatives, and more flexible service,[58] but also that it is compatible with efficiency,

---

delivery service, and the difficulties of obtaining service to distant markets. And among the advantages of exempt trucking frequently cited were lower rates and willingness to serve out-of-the-way points and distant markets. U. S. Department of Agriculture, "Interstate Trucking of Fresh and Frozen Poultry Under the Agricultural Exemption," Marketing Research Report No. 224, March 1958, 49, 51. I am indebted to my former students Charles R. Handy and Kenneth E. Kelly for some of these references to the literature describing the experience in the nonregulated sectors of the industry.

It is interesting to note that this evidence is the opposite of what we would expect if we accepted the case against free entry that it would result in cream-skimming and a deterioration of service on thin routes. See pp. 7–10, Chapter 1, above and pp. 220–246, below.

[55] Note, "Federal Regulation of Trucking: The Emerging Critique," *op. cit.*, 462.

[56] See *ibid.*, 462–463, note 17, and the references in note 27, p. 15, Chapter 1, above.

[57] W. Miklius and D. B. DeLoach present a regression analysis of the unregulated rates on California produce shipped to out-of-state points, which shows a high correlation between rate level and the distance of haul. This suggests little, if any, price discrimination. When rates on frozen poultry were under regulation, distance statistically explained only 56 percent of the rate variation; during 1956–1957, after this commodity was declared exempt (see note 54, above), distance explained 81 percent of the variations. *Op. cit.*, *Jour. Farm. Econ.* (November 1965), XLVII: 945.

[58] After it had been established that the carriage of poultry was exempt from regulation, the number of firms available for carrying it increased substantially and rates declined 33 to 36 percent in the period of a very few years; and they remained as stable as regulated rates. Of approximately 120 processors responding to the question of how they would react if poultry shipments were to be once again regulated, 46 of them said that they would turn to or increase their utilization of private trucking. U. S. Department of Agriculture, *op. cit.*, note 54, above, 1, 3; Clem C. Linnenberg, Jr., "Agricultural Exemptions in Interstate Trucking—Mend or End Them?", *Law and Contemporary Problems*

reasonable stability of rates, and continuity of service.[59] Cost comparisons between regulated and unregulated carriers in the United States have produced somewhat conflicting results;[60] but in view of the impediments and inefficiencies that regulation imposes on the exempt carriers, even these inconclusive results suggest that at worst deregulation would be unlikely to result in higher average cost of operation. And if it did, the burden of the higher costs of inefficient companies would be borne by their owners, not by the consuming public.

Australia's experience after it completely removed all regulations from the motor-carriage industry in 1954 has been studied by Stuart Joy; his conclusions are worth quoting at length:

"Immediately regulation was lifted, fierce rate wars ensued on all routes as established operators attempted to fight off intruders. Newcomers entered the industry as fast as new trucks could be purchased or released from other commitments, resulting in the operation of many vehicles which were unsuitable for long-distance haulage, being either too light in construction or having insufficient payload capacity. Overloading and excessive hours of driving were rife. . . . A combination of economic attrition and the stricter enforcement of load limits and driving-hour regulations slowly weeded out the weak, so that by late 1957, a state of uneasy equilibrium had been attained. . . . The rate stability from 1958 onward enabled the larger firms to consolidate their own positions, and by their influence in the industry as a whole, to establish a pattern of operation and administration which exists today. Sporadic attempts have been made to regulate minimum rates through hauliers' associations, but free entry has prevented the enlistment of a large enough proportion of hauliers to have a significant effect on rate levels. . . .

"The flexibility arising from having so many independent units in the market is ideal for a country extending 2,000 miles from the tropics to the cool temperate zone, in which the demand for road haulage varies from area to area throughout the year. Off the inter-capital routes, rates fluctuate freely, ensuring that seasonal demands are met with adequate capacity. This means that in the event of a shortage of work between Melbourne and Sydney, owner-drivers will look elsewhere for traffic rather than 'cut each other's throat' for the remaining inter-capital work. Next in importance are the nation-wide hauliers, a group of about ten firms, each offering comprehensive service, from smalls and parcels to full loads, between all capitals. . . . With their own fleets, and access to a large number of subcontractors, many of whom prefer to work exclusively for them because of their regular work and reliable payment, the larger firms can command higher rates from shippers than can

---

(Winter, 1960), XXV: 169. When frozen fruits and vegetables were added to the exempt list in 1956, according to studies of the U.S. Department of Agriculture, truck rates ranged 11 to 29 percent below their 1955 level; when an amendment to the Act restored them to regulation in 1958, their prices increased. See Ivan W. Ulrey, "Problems and Issues in Transportation Policy and Implications for Agriculture," *Jour. Farm. Econ.*

(December 1964), XLVI: 1284. These experiences are summarized also in James C. Nelson, *op. cit.*, *Transportation Economics*, 414. See also Friedlaender, *op. cit.*, 115–120.

[59] One study of a large sample of exempt carriers found that 75 percent had been in business for more than five years, 60 percent for over ten years. Farmer, *op. cit.*, 403–404.

[60] See p. 188, note 49, above.

owner-drivers or small vehicles having only a limited number of vehicles and customers. Such higher rates include a premium for the larger firms' ability to handle a widely fluctuating volume of traffic from each shipper, after the tradition of railway service. . . .

"The industry is now sufficiently mature to avoid competition at prices below short-run direct costs, largely because traffic gained at such sub-normal rates confers no immediate or future advantage, no good will attaching to panic rates. This was shown in the trade recession in 1960–1, when rates rarely fell below even long-run direct costs. . . .

"Free entry to interstate road haulage has not caused the demise of the railways. In fact, dynamic competition from the roads has been the cause of a vast improvement in the standard and cost of railway operations on competitive routes. But the most important conclusion to be drawn from the Australian experience is that freedom of entry and operation need not necessarily lead to chaotic conditions in the road haulage industry."

"the 'instability' and 'destructive and wasteful' competition so frequently forecast by established road haulage interests as being the inevitable outcome of free entry have not been apparent. Whilst there is an inevitable turnover of hauliers, the road haulage industry in its dealings with users is stable and efficient. It is considered that the availability of regular service at low cost is a more worthy policy objective than that of 'stability', where that term means a quiet life for established interests."[61]

There is no reason to doubt that regulation has produced improvements in the services provided by the motor-carrier industry, especially as compared with the situation before 1935. Dependability of service and the financial responsibility of regulated carriers for loss and damage has undoubtedly increased.[62] The experience with trip leasing did apparently demonstrate that it could be more difficult for the ICC to enforce its various safety regulations—having to do with the avoidance of overloading, equipment safety standards, maximum driving hours, and financial responsibility

---

[61] "Unregulated Road Haulage: The Australian Experience," *Oxford Econ. Papers*, n.s. (July 1964), XVI: 275–285. By permission of Clarendon Press, Oxford.

The British have an elaborate system of licensing controls similar to ours, and similarly introduced during the Great Depression to deal with what was regarded as the evils of excessive competition. The Geddes Committee, set up by the Ministry of Transport to examine these regulations (see note 40, above), concluded that they seriously reduced efficiency, by weakening the spur of competition, by imposing restrictions on the uses to which trucks could be put, and by impairing "the ability of hauliers to adapt quickly to the changing needs of their customers. . . . The haulage services required by trade and industry are ever-changing, often at short notice" (*Carriers' Licensing, op. cit.*, 59), and concluded for this reason, as well as because it conferred monopoly privileges, that economic licensing should be abolished. *Ibid.*, 6, 57–63, and *passim*.

According to the Committee, Sweden was persuaded in 1963 to abolish its comprehensive licensing, for similar reasons. *Ibid.*, 39–40.

The British Parliament did not accept these recommendations. The Transport Act of 1968 retains economic licensing, in an attempt to force the carriage of heavy loads over long distances on to the rails. See "Transport Act: So What is in it?" *The Economist* (November 2, 1968), CCXXIX: 50 and "Who Wants to Kill Transport Bill," *ibid.* (May 4, 1968), CCXXVII: 78.

[62] The survey of shippers of fresh and frozen poultry after carriage of this commodity became exempt (see p. 189, note 54, above) elicited, among the other opinions highly favorable to the new situation, the opinion that the main advantages of regulated carriers included "better service, financial responsibility and greater reliability."

On the other hand, we have already suggested several reasons for believing that the industry performance would have greatly improved in these respects after 1935 without regulation.

—on a large number of essentially unsupervised, uncertificated operators.[63]

Nor is there any reason to believe that a more highly competitive, unregulated motor-carrier industry would function perfectly. The removal of entry barriers would almost certainly lead to a heavy influx of new firms and a resurgence of price competition. Some of the firms would fail. Some of the service provided would be poor. Some rates would probably fall at least temporarily to unremunerative levels.

In the real world, our choices must always be between imperfect systems. The serious imperfections of competition before 1935 could clearly have convinced impartial observers of the necessity for regulation. But the economic conditions of today are vastly different from those of the depressed 1930s and the former conditions seem unlikely to recur. And the motor-carrier industry is a mature one. We now have had ample opportunity to observe the wastes, inefficiencies, and monopolistic consequences of regulation. That such improvements in quality as it may today provide are not deemed sufficient to justify the higher costs is strongly suggested by the general practice of shippers who have alternatives of dealing with nonregulated carriers. It is difficult for an economist to accept the notion that thorough cartelization of an industry is a necessary means of enforcing objective standards of safety and financial responsibility.

What is inconceivable, given the basic economics of this industry, is that deregulation could indeed usher in a long period of chronic sickness. Or that firms capable of providing reliable, efficient, and diversified service would be faced with the choice of either adulterating their product or going bankrupt. The industry simply lacks the essential prerequisites of destructive competition.

What is equally inconceivable is that performance would not improve in vital respects.

Stock Exchange Brokerage Commissions

In the United States all purchases and sales of securities, once they have been issued, are conducted either on the organized exchanges or in the so-called over-the-counter market. The New York Stock Exchange (NYSE) alone in 1962 accounted for 86 percent of the total dollar volume of stocks purchased on the 14 exchanges that are registered with the Securities and Exchange Commission; if one adds the 7 percent share of the American Stock Exchange (Amex) and the shares of the three leading regional exchanges, the Midwest, Pacific Coast, and Philadelphia-Baltimore-Washington, one has covered 99 percent of the total.[64] By 1968, the share of the

---

[63] See William J. Hudson and James A. Constantin, *Motor Transportation, Principles and Practices* (New York: Ronald Press Co., 1958), 553; also the basic Supreme Court decision, *American Trucking Associations v. U. S.*, 344 U. S. 298 (1953), upholding the validity of ICC rules imposing very stringent restrictions on the practice of trip leasing, 304–305. But see pp. 185–186, above.

The hard economic fact remains that trip leasing (see p. 19, Chapter 1, above) arose because it enabled exempt carriers of agricultural products to make use of what would otherwise

be empty capacity on return hauls, and certificated carriers, who were willing to lease the equipment, a means of performing the transportation function at lower cost. The ICC rule would simply have ignored the efficiency advantages of trip leasing; from the point of view of the cartelization of the industry, it could be regarded only as a disruptive practice.

[64] Securities and Exchange Commission, *Report of Special Study of the Securities Markets*, Washington, 1963 (hereinafter, SEC, *Special Study*), Part 1, Chapter 1, 11.

New York Exchange had dropped to 74 percent;[65] the reasons for this decline are an important part of the story that follows.

The NYSE was organized in 1792 as a private club and remains largely that, a voluntary association "owned" by its members, who hold "seats" on the exchange. The Securities and Exchange Act of 1934 conferred official recognition and status on it and the other exchanges, however. It required them to register with the SEC and conferred on them, subject to the surveillance of the Commission, the responsibility for regulating the activities of their members, assuring compliance by them and by companies whose securities they listed with the provisions of the Act, and in general serving the purpose of preserving the efficiency and integrity of the securities markets.[66]

From its very origination the NYSE had fixed the minimum commission rates that its members might charge, and the 1934 Act seemed to contemplate a continuation of this practice under the general heading of "self-regulation."[67] Until well into the 1960s this authority went essentially unchallenged and its exercise essentially unsupervised by the SEC.

"Between 1937 and 1958, the NYSE effected five changes in rate schedules—all increases and generally justified on the ground of rising costs. . . . Except for . . . occasional mildly negative reactions, the Commission, at least until the present [1965], has never interposed any serious objection. . . .

"Despite this history of consistent increases and the obvious importance of an appropriate schedule of rates for the protection of the investor, neither the self-regulatory agencies nor the Commission has formulated a program for determining and evaluating these charges."

"This void is surprising because any immunity from antitrust action in the securities field that may be brought on the grounds of price fixing by member firms presumably rests heavily upon the Commission's jurisdiction in this area. It is to be expected, therefore, that the Commission would have translated the statute's general reference to 'reasonableness' and the Exchange's vague references to such notions as 'fair return' into more meaningful guidelines of action. . . ."[68]

But like other cartel prices, these were at length subjected to a process of competitive erosion that finally forced first the practitioners, then the complaisant SEC and the general public into reexamining the logic and

[65] *Statistical Abstract of the U. S., 1969*, 457.
[66] See Sidney Robbins, *The Securities Markets, Operations and Issues* (New York: The Free Press, 1966), Chapter 4, "The Basic Securities Act and Self-Regulation—An Exercise in Government-Industry Cooperation." The recurring themes in the Act are that regulation and self-regulation are supposed to serve the "public interest" and the "protection of investors" by preventing unreasonable price fluctuations and ensuring "the maintenance of fair and honest markets." See *ibid.*, 125 and Chapter 5.
[67] This was generally inferred from the fact that the law gave the SEC the power "to alter or supplement the rules" of the Exchange "in respect of such matters as . . . the fixing of reasonable rates of commission. . . ." Section 19(b)(9) of the Securities Exchange Act, 15 U.S. Code 78s(b), 1964 ed. The authoritative statement of this position is in *Harold Z. Kaplan v. Lehman Brothers*, 250 F. Supp. 562 (1966), affirmed, 371 F. 2d 409 (1967), cert. denied, though with a written dissent by Chief Justice Warren, 389 U. S. 954 (1967).
[68] Robbins, *op. cit.*, 176–177, 70. See the fuller discussion of this problem in the SEC, *Special Study*, Part 2, Chapter V, 294–351.

validity of the price-fixing process.[69] The main reason for their vulnerability

---

[69] Various aspects of the Exchange's self-regulatory activities came also under antitrust attack in the 1960s. The first was launched by one Harold J. Silver, a nonmember over-the-counter broker in Dallas. Silver had enjoyed private wire connections with certain Exchange members, as well as ticker service from the Exchange itself; and then had them cut off, without explanation, by order of the Exchange, under its authority to regulate the dealings of members with nonmembers. The Supreme Court, in upholding the Silver suit against the NYSE for damages and injunction, pointed out that the action complained of would have been illegal *per se* as a group boycott under the antitrust laws but for the self-regulation provisions of the Securities and Exchange Act and the authority of the SEC to disapprove any such rules. But these provisions do not confer a blanket immunity under the antitrust laws. On the contrary, the court held that the failure to provide Silver with either explanation or opportunity for a fair hearing and the lack of SEC authority to review particular applications of its general rules (as in this case) deprived the Exchange of antitrust immunity. *Harold J. Silver v. New York Stock Exchange*, 373 U. S. 341 (1963).

The second attack was brought by one Harold Z. Kaplan and others, on behalf of five mutual fund investment companies of which they were stockholders. The plaintiffs charged that the practice of fixing minimum commission rates was a price-fixing conspiracy in violation of Section 1 of the Sherman Act, and sought treble damages and an injunction against the collective imposition of restraints on the rights of individual Exchange members to set their own commission rates. In this case, the Court held for the defendants, on the ground, already mentioned, that the 1934 Act by implication recognized this authority of the Exchange and immunized its exercise from the antitrust laws. See note 67, above. The New York Stock Exchange would have the SEC interpret the *Kaplan* decision as preventing the Commission ever, on its own discretion, from interfering with the authority of the Exchange to fix minimum rates (other than by approving or disapproving the specific rates set in this manner). The Department of Justice takes the position that *Kaplan* merely declares that such rate fixing is not illegal *per se* but does not preclude the SEC, in the exercise of its supervisory authority, from determining whether the fixing of minimum rates is indeed necessary to carry out the purposes of the 1934 Act. See its *Memorandum on the Fixed Minimum Commission Rate Structure* before the SEC, *In the Matter of Commission Rate Structure of Registered National*

Securities Exchanges, File No. 4–144, January 17, 1969, processed, 32–33.

Although our analysis here concentrates mainly on the fixing of minimum commission rates, it should be emphasized that the unrealistic character of the rates on large transactions and the successful efforts of large investors to circumvent them forced the stock exchanges generally and NYSE in particular to reexamine many of their other rules and practices as well. For example, it has led institutional investors to try to take over brokerage houses, to take out membership on the regional exchanges themselves and to demand a similar privilege of the NYSE as devices for participating in the excessive profits that were being extracted from them—thereby calling into question the NYSE's rules prohibiting public ownership of member firms and denying membership to institutional investors. It led nonmember brokers to demand an explicit sharing in the profits of the business they brought to members, thereby threatening the rules requiring members to charge the same, artificially sustained rates to nonmember brokers and ultimate customers alike.

This last rule, too, has been the subject of a continuing attack under the antitrust laws, by Thill Securities, which claims to act on behalf of 4,000 other nonmember brokers and security dealers. Their assertion that the NYSE's rules barring them from access to the floor for direct trading and prohibiting members' sharing commissions with nonmembers are in violation of the Sherman Act was initially rejected for the reasons set forth in the *Kaplan* decision. *Thill Securities Corp. v. New York Stock Exchange*, U. S. Dist. Ct., E. Wisc., Aug. 21, 1969. But the Circuit Court of Appeals denied "that the mere possibility of SEC review wraps the conduct of the Exchange in an impregnable shield of antitrust immunity." Rather, it held, following the *Silver* precedent, it must be demonstrated, first, that the Commission is in fact "exercising actual and adequate review jurisdiction," and, even so, second, that exemption of this particular rule—which would clearly constitute a group boycott *per se* in violation of the antitrust laws but for the partial exemption in the Securities and Exchange Act—is absolutely necessary for the discharge of the Exchange's responsibilities under the Act. In remanding the case to the District Court for a determination of these two points, the Court permitted itself

"the further observation, without prejudging the issue, that it is difficult to conceive how the Exchange can on remand argue that the anti-rebate rule is 'necessary to make the Act work'

was that the schedule of charges in effect until late in 1968 was grossly discriminatory and, unfortunately for its enforceability, the buyers most seriously discriminated against were those best able to invoke competition to protect their interests. Under that system, the commissions were based on both the value and the number of shares involved in the transaction. To illustrate the first basis, the commission on a purchase of 100 shares at prices of $1, $25, and $100 per share would have been $6.00, $31.50 and $49, respectively. As for the latter basis, the rates were uniform *per 100 shares*, no matter how large the actual transaction; for example, the commission on a purchase of 100 shares of a $25 stock would be $31.50, of 1,000 shares of the same stock, $315.[70] The critical defect was in the latter criterion: it obviously does not cost ten times as much to carry out an order to buy or sell 1,000 as 100 shares; if both purchases are made in a single transaction, the cost is likely to be the same for each. So this schedule of rates embodied a gross discrimination against large orders.

What made this discriminatory structure untenable was the enormous rise of institutional investing between 1958, the date of the last revision of commission rates, and the middle 1960s. Large institutional investors, especially the mutual funds, were able to escape exploitation, at least partially, in two major ways. First, since the schedule of minimum commission rates made their business unusually profitable, they were able to induce member brokers of the Exchange to give up a portion of the inflated commission in one way or another. The Exchange's rules prohibit rebates; so the customers could not demand any kind of direct reimbursement. But before 1969 those rules did permit commissions to be spread among member firms at the direction of the customer. So "give-ups" within the Exchange membership took the form of an order from, say, a mutual fund manager to the executing broker on a large trade to turn over some portion of his commission to another broker, as a reward to the latter for sales of the mutual fund's shares, research, and other services.[71] The extent to which commission rates on large transactions exceeded cost may be gauged from the fact that give-ups apparently ran between 40 and 80 percent of the commission, and some times higher. "Give-ups" to nonmember firms required somewhat more complicated arrangements, because of the NYSE's prohibition of cash payments to outsiders, but accomplished a similar purpose.[72]

---

when its members have gone to imaginative extremes to circumvent the rule when it serves their private economic purposes to do so. It appears from all we can read . . . that the rule is honored much more in its breach than in its observance, as through various devices, member firms routinely share commissions or the equivalent with favored non-member brokers." CCA, Seventh Circuit, August 27, 1970.

[70] SEC, *Special Study*, Part 2, Chapter VI, 296.

[71] It is necessary to distinguish three separate parties in these transactions—the managers of the mutual funds (M), the broker-dealers in their role as retailers of the shares of mutual funds to the investing public (R), and the brokers (B) through whom the funds conducted their own

security purchases and sales on the organized exchanges. In the give-up, M would direct B to pay a part of its commission to R, as a reward to R for selling M's shares.

[72] See Carol J. Loomis, "Big Board, Big Volume, Big Trouble," *Fortune* (May 1968), LXXVII: 221; Dept. of Justice, *Memorandum*, January 17, 1969, *op. cit.*, 75, 88–90; "Give-ups kickback on funds," *Business Week*, July 27, 1968, 97–99. The latter article estimates that the amount of give-ups could have been as much as one-half of the $233 million that Mutual Funds paid in broker commissions in 1967:

"Testimony about staggering amounts passing through the hands of individuals has led one

Second, they took their business, in increasing proportion, to the over-the-counter market and to regional exchanges, where they could negotiate commissions more closely related to the cost of serving them.[73]

The SEC itself began in the 1960s to put pressure on the stock exchanges to eliminate these practices, on the one hand by giving volume discounts and on the other by specifically prohibiting certain varieties of the give-up. Its objection to the latter practice was that the benefit of the rebates went not to the holders of mutual fund shares, on whose behalf the securities purchases were made, but to the managers of the funds themselves. The reason was that the typical recipient of the give-up was another broker, to compensate him for selling additional shares of the fund; and the larger the fund, the larger the management fees (typically $\frac{1}{2}$ percent of the net assets of the fund per year). In effect, thus, the give-up provided a means of channeling the cost-savings on commissions away from the funds themselves and their shareholders into additional selling effort, for the benefit not of those shareholders but of management and salesmen.[74]

The SEC therefore in January of 1968 proposed a rule 10b–10 to prohibit give-ups and to see to it that the savings from the excessive commission rates on large purchases would be returned to the benefit of the fund shareholders. During the remainder of 1968, hearings were held on the whole matter of the minimum commission rates; but as an interim measure, the NYSE in December put into effect a volume discount for large transactions and a rule abolishing customer-directed give-ups among its members.[75] It was into this set of hearings that the Department of Justice dropped its bombshell on April 1, 1968, when it argued, flatly, that the SEC ought to consider completely abolishing the collective fixing of minimum commission rates and in so doing set off an intense controversy about the entire future of this concerted restriction on price competition.[76]

SEC staff member to suggest wryly that give-up payments should be registered as securities and traded on exchanges." p. 99.

Robbins describes some of these indirect arrangements. For example, Exchange members would compensate nonmember brokers for their patronage by reciprocity—channeling other transactions through them. *Op. cit.*, 180–184. The American and various regional stock exchanges avoid many of these complications by offering special treatment to nonmember professionals.

[73] In addition, as we have already observed, many of them took out memberships in regional exchanges and did their transacting there. For one interesting example, note the acquisition of Jeffries & Co., a Los Angeles-based firm specializing in institutional brokerage, by Investors Diversified Services. On consummation of the agreement, Jeffries gave up its membership on the New York exchange and proposed to transact its business thereafter in the so-called third market, where the brokerage can be done at negotiated commission rates. *Wall Street Journal*, July 10, 1969, 2.

[74] See Loomis, *op. cit.*, *Fortune*, May 1968, 221; "Give-ups kickback on funds," *Business Week*, July 27, 1968, 97. The typical commission on sales of new mutual fund shares to the investing public is $8\frac{1}{2}$ percent. The competition among mutual fund managers (M—using the schematic representation of note 71, above) to sell additional shares, and in this way to increase the size of their funds, was so intense that they passed almost the entire $8\frac{1}{2}$ percent on to the retail salesmen (R)—themselves typically broker-dealers. The give-ups enabled M to give R an even larger inducement and reward, at no cost to themselves, instead of crediting the savings to the fund itself and hence to its shareholders. On most of the foregoing history, see David L. Ratner, "Regulation of the Compensation of Securities Dealers," *Cornell Law Rev.* (February 1970), LV: 348–389.
[75] *Wall Street Journal*, October 26, 1968, 2. The American Exchange made similar changes. *Ibid.*, November 4, 1968, 6.
[76] "The Commission should promptly take appropriate steps to determine the extent to which commission rate fixing by the NYSE is required by the purposes of the Securities

The NYSE did not respond by defending the existing commission rate structure. On the contrary, it moved to a recognition that rates to large buyers were unrealistic and indefensible and to an acceptance of a genuinely regulated level equated to cost plus a reasonable return and a structure of rates for different transactions more closely in line with their respective costs. To this end it commissioned the consulting firm National Economic Research Associates to analyze its members' costs and revenues and to recommend appropriate changes. In December it took a major step in this direction by introducing quantity discounts on large transactions. In February of 1970 it proposed to the SEC a new schedule, involving further cuts on these transactions, rate increases up to 100 percent on small ones, and a rise in the average sufficient to provide brokerage houses with an average return on invested capital of 15 percent.[77] It also indicated a willingness to consider offering discounts to nonmember brokers, who had theretofore under its rules been required to pay the same rates as the investing public.[78] But the issue remained unresolved as to whether any regulation at all was justified. Why not leave the determination of commissions to the forces of competition?

In October of 1970, the SEC responded with suggestions of its own that came down surprisingly hard on the side of freer competition. It proposed to free commissions on transactions of $100,000 or more (not a high cut-off point, by any means—2500 shares of a $40 security) from all control. In so doing, it in effect proposed to legitimize the actual state of affairs: the ban on give-ups had been subject to all sorts of circumvention—concealed discounts, free services, reciprocal deals—as was inevitable as long as the official rates remained far above cost; so that in fact commissions to institutional investors were already being individually negotiated under pressure of competition.[78a] For smaller transactions, it suggested a scale of rates somewhat lower than had been suggested by the Exchange; and it bade the membership adopt a uniform system of accounting and cost allocation to facilitate cost-based rate-making in the future. And it told the Exchange to bring to it by mid-1971 a plan to permit nonmember brokers some "reasonable access" to its facilities.[78b] This decision may make the issue of minimum rate control

Exchange Act. The Commission should then take action (a) to eliminate all rate fixing which is not found to be justified in the public interest; (b) to develop and promulgate standards governing the validity or reasonableness of any commission rates for which rate fixing is permitted to continue; and (c) to determine the proper means for assuring equitable and nondiscriminatory access by nonmember broker-dealers to the NYSE market." Before the Securities and Exchange Commission, *Inquiry into Proposals to Modify the Commission Rate Structure of the New York Stock Exchange*, SEC Release No. 8239, *Comments of the United States Department of Justice*, April 1, 1968, mimeo., 6. While expressing the opinion that minimum rate fixing was in fact unjustified, the Department raised the possibility that the setting of *maximum* rates might be warranted; it recognized the possible desirability, also, of the Commission's proposed rule requiring

that any give-ups that institutional investors were able to obtain go to the benefit of their companies.

[77] *New York Times*, February 15, 1970, sec. 3, 1. See the two Reports by National Economic Research Associates, Inc., to the Cost and Revenue Committee of the New York Stock Exchange, *Reasonable Public Rates for Brokerage Commissions*, 2 vols., February 1970, and *Stock Brokerage Commissions: The Development and Application of Standards of Reasonableness for Public Rates*, 2 vols., July 1970.

[78] "Pacific Coast Exchange Accuses Big Board of Trying to Kill Competition by Others," *Wall Street Journal*, June 10, 1969, 4.

[78a] Wayne E. Green, "Brokers and those Minimum-Fee Rules," *Wall Street Journal*, October 29, 1970, 10.

[78b] *New York Times*, October 23, 1970, 1, 69.

versus competition practically moot: since the SEC has the authority to approve or disapprove commission schedules, it is obviously in a position to have its way. But the issue of principle remains important, and by no means definitively resolved.

The major arguments, centering on the question of whether unregulated competition among brokers would be destructive, will have a familiar ring—reflecting either the essential similarity of the economic issues and conflicting interests involved in all proposed restrictions on competition or the fact that the contending parties all read the same economics textbooks. The distinctive aspect of the defense in this instance is attributable to the fact that there are two separate though related markets or industries involved. One is the market for securities, which, it is generally agreed, can be effectively competitive, provided the organized exchanges are regulated—as is the intention of the Securities and Exchange Acts—in order to prevent fraud, the use of information by insiders at the expense of outside investors, to insure financial responsibility of its agents, and so on. The prices here are the prices of the securities. The other market is for the *service of the brokers* who conduct the transactions in the first market. Those agents perform a variety of services for investors, but the essential one in the present context is effectuating purchase and sales orders. The price in question here is the commission rate.

The central defense of suppressing competition in the determination of that second price is that it is essential for the effective functioning of the first market—in the words of the antitrust laws, that the restraint at issue is "reasonably ancillary" or subordinate to the legitimate purpose of promoting the goals of the Securities and Exchange Act. According to this argument, the incentive of brokers to belong to the NYSE and to accept the numerous and costly restrictions imposed on members in order to protect the integrity of the securities markets[79] is dependent in considerable measure on the privileges of membership. One of these is that nonmember brokers must pay the same commission rates as public customers; when members turn to floor brokers to consummate a trade, in contrast, they pay only a fraction of that rate. The other is that the minimum commission rates are insulated from competition. If, instead, minimum rate regulation were removed, nonmember brokers could negotiate the commissions that members would charge them whenever they needed to buy or sell on the Exchange; and the attractions of membership would be correspondingly reduced. Brokerage

---

[79] These include the requirement that they make their trades in stock exchange-listed securities on the exchange floor, where specialists are under obligation to maintain an orderly market and forestall large price fluctuations by trading on their own account to fill temporary imbalances between demand and supply; submitting to pervasive stock exchange rules and surveillance (the NYSE estimates that compliance costs amounted to 15.3 percent on the average of the total costs their members incurred in their securities commission business); contributing to the Exchange's expenses in enforcing the self-policing rules (estimated by the NYSE as costing $6 million in 1968, or one-third of the budget of the SEC itself); and meeting the various qualifications—with respect to the training and background of their personnel, minimum capital requirements, issuance of reports, and the like—imposed by the Exchange. See the New York Stock Exchange, *Economic Effects of Negotiated Commission Rates on the Brokerage Industry, The Market for Corporate Securities, and the Investing Public*, August 1968 (hereinafter, *Economic Effects*, August 1968), 12, 21–22, 26–31, and Appendixes A and B, on which the following account draws heavily. See also its *The Economics of Minimum Commission Rates, Reply to Memorandum of the Antitrust Division of the Department of Justice dated January 17, 1969*, NYSE, May 1, 1969.

houses would be tempted to give up their membership, in order to avoid the onerous restrictions and costs above-mentioned. Where possible, they would avoid paying floor commissions to members by matching buy and sell orders in their own offices, or by trading in third markets wherever profitable, and they would negotiate commission rates for the execution of those orders on which they still needed access to the floor. In consequence, so the argument runs, fewer transactions would be conducted on the organized exchange itself and the result would be an attenuation of the enormous volume and continuity of trading operations that make it so effective a market; this continuity and depth give it a maximum ability to absorb purchase and sale orders with minimal price fluctuations and give investors the ready liquidity that makes them willing to hold securities instead of cash.

The Department of Justice, in contrast, attributes the continuity, depth, and liquidity of the centralized security exchanges not to the artificial incentives to membership provided by noncompetitive commission rates but to the fact that the security exchange—and the NYSE in particular—is a natural monopoly.[80] There is, it asserts, a

> "natural tendency of the securities market to centralize trading which is due to the economies and efficiencies associated with centralized markets. . . .
>
> "The economies and efficiencies of centralized trading are, of course, attested by the development of securities exchanges. To facilitate the bringing together of buy and sell orders, very early in the history of the industry brokers began to congregate in central locations. . . . Even today the chief function of a central securities market is to take advantage of such efficiencies, to provide what has been called space and time utility, to investors. . . .
>
> "In addition to scale economies in operating a market, the greater the number of trades conducted on a single marketplace in a given security the lower would be the per unit cost of trading. As far as stock exchanges are concerned, this evolutionary tendency toward a single marketplace is demonstrated by the near monopoly position now enjoyed by the NYSE in securities listed on the Exchange."[81]

It is undeniable that artificially maintained commission rates have had as at least one of their effects a weakening rather than a strengthening of that monopoly, encouraging the growth of trading in third markets and over the counter, precisely because traders sought in this way to obtain commission rates more closely reflecting the costs of executing their orders. On this ground, at least, competitive commission rates would tend to reverse this dissipation, bringing a greater proportion of the trading back to the stock exchange floor rather than, as the NYSE argument avers, in the opposite direction.[82] (But so would regulated rates more realistically related to costs.)

---

[80] *Memorandum,* January 17, 1969, *op. cit.*

[81] *Ibid.,* 47–49. The Department brief cites in support of this proposition Robert Doede, *The Monopoly Power of the New York Stock Exchange,* unpublished dissertation, University of Chicago, June 1967, and Harold Demsetz, "The Cost of Transacting," *Q. Jour. Econ.* (Feb. 1968), LXXXII: 33–53.

[82] So the Department deprecates the assertedly disincentive effects of competitive commission rates on stock exchange membership, contending that the speed and efficiency with which orders can be executed in the organized exchanges, at the best possible price and the lowest possible cost, would continue to recommend membership, with the advantages it carries of immediate

The Department argues, finally (note the analogy to trucking and occupational licensure generally), that the purposes of investor protection can be served by the direct imposition of rules directed to that end, without the need for suppressing price competition as an indirect inducement to member firms to accept such restrictions.[83]

It is not possible to make an absolute choice between these opposing views on purely a priori grounds. It is certainly arguable that, other things being equal, self-regulation, voluntarily induced by the advantages of membership, is preferable to the imposition of government controls. Conceivably, also, the pressures of price competition would indeed weaken the ties of brokers to the market in some respects—though it would clearly strengthen those of the investors that have fled the organized exchanges for more attractive commission rates. And, in so doing, it could create some incentive to execute orders without recourse to the Exchange; and if this happened small investors particularly might be unable easily to judge whether they had in fact obtained the best possible prices for their transactions. The question then is whether the cost to the public of noncompetitive commission rates is worth the benefits they help secure.

There is one objective and conclusive piece of evidence that the price the public pays is higher than the costs that self-regulation imposes on the members of the Exchange: seats on the New York Stock Exchange sold for around $500,000 in early 1969.[84] If new entrants are willing to pay this price for a ticket of admission, clearly the present value of the monetary benefits of membership exceeds that of the costs by something like this amount. As Harold Demsetz pointed out at the 1968 SEC hearings, the first impact of more competitive commission rates would therefore be not on the number of members in the Exchange but on the price of the seat. That

---

access to the floor and to the entire Exchange community, and of enhancing the reputation and attractiveness of member firms to investors.

"The importance to a firm's business of its reputation and ability to make efficient, timely execution of orders was emphasized by the testimony of a number of NYSE members. . . .

"It is, of course, the strength, 'thickness' and liquidity of the NYSE market which makes membership valuable, and will continue to do so (with or without fixed minimum rates)."

As for the burdens of membership, consequent on the self-regulatory functions of the Exchange:

"This is not to say that NYSE self-regulation is not a positive benefit to the investor. Of course it is. But the recognition of its value is an aspect of the value of NYSE membership. The NYSE in its institutional advertising continually refers to the higher standards of integrity imposed on member firms, and the members must be of the opinion that the public investor will recognize and reward the firm which subjects itself to this stricter form of self-regulation." *Memorandum*, January 17, 1969, 57, 67.

[83] If, for example, companies were moved to surrender their membership in order to escape burdensome regulations, this, it points out, could be counteracted "by raising the standard of regulation applicable to nonmembers" (*ibid.*, 176), something that would be desirable for its own sake in any event. Alternatively, or in addition, brokers might be *required* to become members of the Exchange, so that all would be subject to its discipline (pp. 177–178). Investors might be protected from the effects of the insolvency of brokerage firms by instituting a system of compulsory customer insurance (pp. 178–182). The NYSE instituted a similar plan in December of 1969, when its Board of Governors authorized a year-end transfer of $5 million out of its operating revenues into a special fund established to insure customers against such losses. *New York Times*, December 20, 1969, 45.

[84] It dropped some 50% in the following year. The main reasons for the change were apparently the drop in total trading volume, the reductions in commission rates put into effect the preceding December, and the prospect of a change in Exchange rules that would permit institutional investors to become members of the Exchange, the effect of which would be to take their business away from existing members.

price will fall to whatever extent necessary to make membership as attractive to new entrants after as it was before.[85] And as long as members continue to be required to bring their transactions to the floor of the Exchange, it is difficult to see how the introduction of more competitive rates could truly dilute the continuity or depth of the market. It is only if it can be predicted that the value of a seat will become negative that there is objective reason to anticipate an actual decline in membership.

This leads us to the central question: is the brokerage business inherently subject to destructive or cutthroat competition, in the absence of regulation? The industry model depicted by defenders of minimum rate fixing has these familiar components: a high ratio of fixed to variable costs, particularly in the short run;[86] substantial excess capacity much or most of the time, so that short-run marginal cost is typically below average total cost;[87] a demand for brokerage services that fluctuates sharply over time and is price-

---

[85] This testimony is quoted in the Department of Justice *Memorandum* of January 17, 1969, *op. cit.*, 63, note 25.

[86] It might appear anomalous that an industry with comparatively little investment in fixed capital could have a cost structure susceptible to destructive competition. But capital costs are not the only possible fixed costs. A firm's "capacity" may consist primarily in a pool of skilled personnel the size of which may not be readily responsive to changes in the demand for its services. Defining as variable those expenses that could be readily reduced within a period of a year in response to decreasing output, the NYSE placed in this category commissions and floor brokerage paid to others, clearing charges, commission fees, the compensation of registered representatives (typically a percentage of the volume of transactions), and employee bonuses and profit-sharing plans. It classified as fixed costs clerical and administrative salaries, communications costs, occupancy and equipment costs, and other expenses including promotion, licenses, dues and assessments. This classification produced a computation that 51 percent of total costs of brokerage houses are "overhead" and 49 percent variable; these ratios would shift to 44 percent and 56 percent, respectively, if one-fourth of the clerical and administrative salaries were shifted into the variable category. These fixed-cost ratios of 44 to 51 percent, the Exchange pointed out, are not far below those of electric utilities, are at least as high as those of railroads, and far above airlines and intercity freight motor carriers. *Economic Effects*, August 1968, *op. cit.*, 63–66. Clearly, the computation is highly sensitive to the classification of clerical and administrative salaries and to the use of one year as the relevant time period. It would be interesting to see by what percentage these staffs were in fact cut during the lean years immediately following the

issuance of the 1968 NYSE study. For an estimate that the ranks of job-seeking securities analysts increased 30 to 35% in the year from mid-1969 to mid-1970, see the *Wall Street Journal*, July 21, 1970, 1.

[87] The NYSE study supports this generalization, among other ways, by demonstrating that there was a clear tendency for the unit costs of various firms to move inversely with the number of their transactions between 1965 and 1966. Of the 57 firms, the number of whose transactions declined, one experienced decreased average total costs and 56 increases; among the 94 firms whose transactions rose by more than 25 percent, 62 experienced decreasing costs and 32 increasing. *Ibid.*, 54–58. This limited demonstration is not conclusive. The firms compared have various product- or output-mixes, and the figures for the average cost per "transaction" undoubtedly reflect allocations of common and joint costs the validity of which may be questionable. Also, it is not possible to tell to what extent the improved cost behavior of the firms experiencing an increase in output reflected the previous presence of excess capacity, to what extent economies of scale in the installation of additional capacity to meet the additional demand. At the same time, there is a strong inference here of the presence of excess capacity, at least in 1965, which means that short-run marginal costs were below average total costs in that year. For a criticism of these and other aspects of the NYSE's testimony, see "A Critique of the New York Stock Exchange's Report on the Economic Effects of Negotiated Commission Rates on the Brokerage Industry, the Market for Corporate Securities, and the Investing Public," prepared for the Department of Justice by H. Michael Mann, processed, 1968; and the NYSE's response, *The Economics of Minimum Commission Rates*, May 1, 1969, *op. cit.*, 37–38.

inelastic;[88] and a large number of sellers and low concentration ratios,[89] assuring that if price competition were permitted it would be keen. Such a model would, indeed, produce results of questionable desirability—extreme fluctuations in commission rates, with periods of deeply depressed earnings during which the industry would be reluctant to provide capacity sufficient for peak demands followed by sharp rate increases, as recovering demand pressed hard on the limits of capacity; and an inability of the industry, in the latter period, to provide the kind of instantaneous execution of orders that the public demands.[90]

The NYSE predicts, further, that the introduction of price competition would result in a serious deterioration in the quality of service. Brokerage firms, it asserts, would no longer be able to maintain the research and information-gathering activities in which they now widely engage or to provide this valuable information and advice to their customers, as they now do in large measure, at no extra charge. And this in turn would produce notably poorer investment decisions, particularly by the small investor:

> "The discount house concept, which ignores service, would probably become dominant in the securities business. Negotiated rates would force most firms to discontinue or reduce all services other than the execution of orders."[91]

---

[88] On the variability in demand, see the NYSE, *Economic Effects*, August 1968, *op. cit.*, 88–90. The contention that the demand for the services of brokers for executing transactions is price-inelastic is based on the consideration that the commission amounts to less than one percent of the cost of buying and selling securities, so that fluctuations in the former would have only a negligible effect on the decisions of buyers and sellers to engage in such transactions. On the other hand, Henry C. Wallich has pointed out that the commission could well bulk large relative to the prospective capital gains and losses that induce traders to buy and sell, and expressed the opinion that demand could well prove elastic. "Commission Rate Policy for a Large and Growing Auction Market," testimony before the SEC, Oct. 31, 1968, processed, 12–16.

The NYSE study might have recognized that the demand for the services of *NYSE members* had proved to have considerable price-elasticity, with large purchasers going outside the Exchange to consummate their transactions precisely in quest of lower commission rates. But it still could be true that the demand for the services of all brokers, inside and outside the Exchange, is inelastic, so that price competition could still be destructive in its effect on all brokers considered together.
[89] *Economic Effects*, August 1968, *op. cit.*, 70. For the full argument of the NYSE on the danger of destructive competition, see *ibid.*, 43–94.
[90] "Despite these fluctuations in demand, the public expects, and has a right to expect, almost instantaneous executions of its orders. Occasionally, when volume suddenly soars to new peaks

at an unforeseeable rapid pace, the securities industry may fall behind in its back-office work, as has occurred this year. Even at such times of peak volume, explanations and excuses for lack of capacity are unacceptable. . . .

"In some industries . . . it is possible to accumulate unfilled orders for three, six or even twelve months. . . . In the brokerage business, even relatively short delays are inconsistent with the concept of an orderly and efficient securities market. During periods of heavy demand, the industry *must* be prepared to meet peak load requirements.

"In a sense, the securities industry is like the power industry, which must have sufficient reserve capacity to run all air conditioners when temperatures reach an unexpected peak. . . .

"The securities industry must be prepared to handle peak volume, i.e., to carry 'excess' capacity during periods of average volume. In this industry, excess capacity is *not* redundant capacity." *Ibid.*, 89, 91.

One might accept this assertion with a certain amount of irony, coming as it does from an industry that had to close its doors regularly on Wednesdays during half of the year 1968 and was able to keep them open only from 10:00 A.M. to 2:00 P.M. for most of 1969, all in order to enable its back offices to catch up with the flood of paper work. In fairness it must be recognized that the volume of transactions had risen precipitately and unexpectedly in a very few years. On this, see note 93, below.
[91] *Ibid.*, 96.

Finally, it predicts, price competition is likely to be highly selective, centering on the patronage of the large, institutional purchasers, who have alternatives, and discriminating against the small investors, whose demand is more likely to remain exploitable. This is a somewhat ironic defense of a system that has, heretofore, discriminated *against* the large transaction; nevertheless, unless it can confidently be predicted that pure competition would prevail if all controls were removed, it must be taken into account.

The model of the industry that the proponents of greater price competition depict is, naturally, somewhat different. They see a cost structure dominated by the salaries of clerical and administrative personnel, the compensation of salesmen (typically set as a commission on sales), and brokerage and clearing charges related to individual transactions as primarily variable rather than fixed.[92] They see capacity that can be expanded or contracted primarily by hiring or letting go moderately skilled clerical and administrative staff as comparatively readily adaptable to changes in demand, over comparatively short periods of time.[93] Instead of an industry selling a standardized product, and able on this account to compete only in price,[94] they see one whose sellers make a great and successful effort to differentiate their services. The NYSE study itself points to this proliferation of services and the need of many investors for them in defense of noncompetitive rates; it fails to recognize that this differentiability of product

---

[92] See note 86, above. More than half of the costs included by the NYSE study as "overhead" were clerical and administrative salaries. If competition is to be truly destructive, the experience of other industries would seem to suggest, a much larger proportion of (fixed) costs would have to be of a kind that could not be readily adjusted downward in the space of, say, one to three years. There is no explanation in the NYSE study of why most of the clerical and administrative help could not be fired in a considerably shorter space of time than one year, if it seemed that the volume of business in the intermediate-term future did not justify their retention. This consideration does not eliminate the likelihood of firms having large amounts of excess capacity of this type, as demand fluctuates widely from one month or six-month period to the next, however. See also the footnote immediately following.

[93] The NYSE study provides statistics on the number of registered representatives and other personnel of its member firms during each of the years 1960 through 1967, compared with the average daily volume of security transactions. It points out that whereas the volume of trading had by 1964 fully recovered from its decline between 1961 and 1962 and far surpassed the volume of the former year, the number of employees other than registered representatives did not regain its 1961 level until five years later —in purported evidence "that firms respond only sluggishly to rising demand." *Ibid.*, 92. It may well be that they did respond "sluggishly." But their failure during the years 1962 through

1965 to hire as many "other personnel" as they had in 1961 would not seem to reflect any inherent inflexibility of their technology or cost structures. And their ability to increase their registered representatives from 28,000 to 42,000 and other personnel from 54,000 to 78,000 during the period covered by these statistics suggests no difficulty in expanding capacity, if they are willing to do so. True, average daily volume increased even more, from 3 million to 10 million shares; but in view of the NYSE's demonstrations, earlier, of the pervasive presence of excess capacity (note 87, above) and of economies of scale and in view, also, of the abundant opportunities for increasing the productivity of existing personnel by the use of automation, this discrepancy between the expansion in the number of employees on the one hand and the total volume of business on the other was to have been expected. These observations are not intended to suggest that the expansion of capacity was sufficient; there is evidence to the contrary (note 90, above). More directly relevant from the standpoint of the alleged dangers of destructive competition is the fact, demonstrated by these statistics, that between 1961 and 1962, when the average daily volume fell from 4,100,000 to 3,800,000 shares, the member firms reduced their other personnel from 64,000 to 57,500. On these matters, see the Department of Justice, *Memorandum*, January 17, 1969, *op. cit.*, 113–121.

[94] See pp. 184–185, this chapter, above.

is a prime defense against destructive competition. It is difficult to believe that these will not continue to be important methods of competition, that by no means all brokerage firms would find it either desirable or necessary to take the path of the discount appliance house. On the contrary, as in the appliance business itself, the industry would tend to differentiate itself as between firms competing principally on the basis of price and others continuing to emphasize research and other kinds of service, with a wide range of gradations in between.[95]

The counterpart of the NYSE's model of an industry prone to destructive competition is its picture of the industry's performance made possible by minimum rate controls: financially healthy, providing the investor with the benefits of its research and sound advice at no extra charge, encouraging the habit of stock ownership among small, individual investors (possibly subsidizing low commission rates to them by its discrimination against the large transactors), providing brokerage service in small and remote localities where it would otherwise be unprofitable.[96]

---

[95] It is impossible of course to be certain. As Dr. William C. Freund, economist for the NYSE, has reacted to the above in a private communication:

"One person's guess versus another's! One-hundred shares of GM are the same no matter where purchased and represent a highly standardized product. Undoubtedly, some firms could withstand the pressure of destructive price competition on the basis of unique services in a period of contracting volume. But the pressure to cut commission rates would, in general, probably be intense."

Still there is a contradiction between the Exchange's emphasis on the great need and desire of investors for these other services (*Economic Effects*, August 1968, *op. cit.*, 97–100) and its assumption that destructive price competition would be inevitable in the absence of regulation. A similar, at least partial contradiction exists between this prediction and another, to which we have already alluded, that competition would be highly discriminatory, particularly against small investors. This is indeed a possibility; but to the extent that it is, it means it would not be destructive. The more intense the price competition, the less it is possible for any purchaser, no matter how inelastic his demand, to be forced to pay a price higher than any other (in relation, of course, to their respective costs). Interestingly, the Report consistently refers to the rates that would emerge if minimum controls were eliminated as "negotiated," thereby suggesting not a general and uniform decline in prices to unremunerative levels, but a selective, negotiated reduction to some customers and not to others. What seems likely is that commission rates on large orders would, indeed, be negotiated; and that others would be at some published, administered price, relatively resistant to short-term fluctuations or to pressures down to the level of short-run marginal cost. As we have seen, this is in effect what the SEC proposed in October 1970 to legitimize.

Again, the Report predicts that uncontrolled competition would have a tendency to drive out those firms whose major source of revenue is from commissions, because they will be unable to compete with other, more diversified, brokerage houses that are dependent for only a fraction of their revenues on this business (*ibid.*, 73–83). But this very diversity in the character of brokerage firms could well diminish the likelihood that price competition among them would be destructive. They would not all feel an equal pressure immediately to match all price reductions. And since they undoubtedly vary widely in efficiency, commission rates might not have to fall very far before they would reach the average variable cost of the higher-cost firms, driving them out of business. Differences in the level of marginal cost of different firms impart an elasticity to an industry's supply schedule that is not present if one assumes that all firms are alike in their costs and product mixes and all of them have the *same level* of average variable costs, far below average total costs. On some of these considerations, see the Department of Justice, *Memorandum*, January 1969, *op. cit.*, 96–106. Moreover, the NYSE's solicitude for preserving all the existing firms in business conflicts with its purported evidence elsewhere of economies of scale. Even if its argument were correct that the process by which firms are eliminated would have no relationship whatever to their relative efficiencies, it would still follow, from its reasoning, that concentrating the remaining business in fewer hands would mean that it would be conducted at lower cost.

[96] *Economic Effects*, August 1968, *op. cit.*, 8, 83.

The counterpart of the opposing model, which predicts that competition would be effective and nondestructive, is a much less favorable appraisal of the industry's present performance. According to this model, the prohibition of price competition has been a shelter for inefficiency: the New York Exchange has been extremely sluggish in modernizing its methods, in particular in adopting automation and the computer to handle its geometrically growing volume of paper work.[97] Cartel pricing has driven away large investors, thereby dissipating, rather than reinforcing, the depth and continuity of the market. It has entailed price discrimination and internal subsidization—discrimination against large transactions and against investors (again, typically, the large ones) who wish to purchase only execution of orders and not all the auxiliary services the cost of which is provided in the single price package. These investors have succeeded in escaping this discrimination to some extent, by obtaining give-ups and reciprocal patronage; but these concessions, where mutual funds are involved, have accrued not to the owners but to their managers.[98]

And—to turn directly to one of the main proffered justifications of the present system—regulated, noncompetitive rates have uneconomically encouraged cost-inflating methods of competition. Nicholas Kaldor has pointed out that the inclusion of advertising cost in the price of advertised

---

[97] "In this age of automation, the Street has conspicuously failed to keep pace."

"it is clear that the industry in general, and some brokers in particular, did not get around to putting enough money and effort into the automation of facilities. . . . Besides that, the Street has always thought of sales first and all other things last. . . . [As we will observe presently, this is exactly what one would expect in an industry whose price is held at noncompetitive levels, but whose members are left free to compete in other ways.]

"The Exchange's own record with automation has been very uneven. Any expert studying the floor of the Exchange, and the process by which a trade is executed, would see many possibilities for automation; and indeed some of these are becoming reality. But the plain fact is that beyond a certain point, the members do not really wish to see the stock trade automated. For it is *they* who would be replaced by a computer." Loomis, *op. cit.*, 150–151. Courtesy of *Fortune Magazine*.

"'Characterized as the nerve center of American industry, the Exchange is really a glaring anachronism. . . .

"'The operating procedures of most brokerage houses . . . are in the green eye-shade era where Bob Cratchit would have no trouble fitting in immediately. . . .

"'. . . 'the technology is available . . . to solve most . . . security industry problems.'" William D. Smith, "Will Market Receive Massage?" *The New York Times*, March 30, 1969, Section 3,

1, 14. See the similar observation by M. J. Rossant, "Warning from S.E.C.," *The New York Times*, October 30, 1966, pp. 67, 73. On some of the respects in which the performance of the smaller exchanges has been superior to that of New York, see also Robbins, *op. cit.*, 266–273.

[98] It is important to recognize that many—but not all—of these defects would be eliminated by the more realistic and cost-related structure that the NYSE now advocates and that effective regulation would help to assure. It would eliminate the price discrimination and internal subsidization, eliminate give-ups, and bring the large institutional investors back to the Exchange. Likewise, contributing to this end would be a relaxation of the rules—currently under scrutiny of the SEC—that now prohibit publicly owned firms holding membership on the Exchange; the institutional investor could partially escape the discrimination against him by buying a seat. The NYSE approved public ownership in September of 1969. But those new regulations would still ban institutional investors from membership: its broker members understandably fear that otherwise the institutions would transfer their immense patronage to their own member subsidiaries. The proposed rules would prohibit any member firm from having as a customer any nonmember that shares in 5 percent or more of its profits—thereby eliminating any incentive of large investors to seek membership in order to share in the profits of handling their own transactions. See "Big Board Heads for a Showdown," *Business Week*, November 8, 1969. 120–125.

products carries an inherent tendency for more advertising to be produced than would be the case if customers had the choice of purchasing or not purchasing it directly. In unregulated markets generally, it is conceivable—although this writer would argue to the contrary—that "information" of this type is not overproduced, or would not be if buyers were well informed and had a fair choice between advertised and nonadvertised products, at prices corresponding to the respective costs of supplying them.[99] But in markets in which price competition is prohibited and consumers have no such choice, there can be no doubt that the Kaldor tendency prevails. As long as the artificially maintained price exceeds the marginal cost of some firms (and if it did not there would be no reason to regulate it), those firms, denied the ability to reach out for additional business by price reductions, will have an incentive to do so by providing "free" services of one kind or another, from salesmanship on the one hand to advice and research on the other. The customer who wants to buy execution of orders plus salesmanship, advice, and research pays the same price as the customer that wants only the first of these. The consequence is an inherent tendency to what might be termed service inflation, in which an equilibrium of cost and price is achieved not by reducing price to marginal cost but raising marginal cost to price.[100]

---

[99] See the references cited in note 103, p. 41, Chapter 1, above; also Telser, "Advertising and Competition," *Jour. Pol. Econ.* (December 1964), LXXII: 537–562.

[100] The NYSE Report offers two intriguing justifications of selling the auxiliary services and the order-execution in a package. The first is that information about securities is in one respect a public good: the marginal cost of making it available to additional customers is zero. Therefore, it contends, economic efficiency requires that its price be zero; and this is in fact accomplished if it is supplied at no additional cost along with the execution of orders. (The resultant higher commission rates, required to cover the cost of providing the services, might discourage the purchase of the joint package; but if the demand for brokerage services taken as a whole is inelastic, there is no offsetting economic inefficiency involved in selling the two together.) *Economic Effects*, August 1968, *op. cit.*, 105.

We have already encountered this reasoning in discussing the economics of free television. And, as we have pointed out there (pp. 40–41, Chapter 1, above) this reasoning is correct, as far as it goes. What it ignores is the fact that in another, equally important respect, the production of information has a marginal cost definitely above zero: the more research in which a company engages, the higher, of course, are the costs. And there is need for some pricing device to determine the proper flow of resources into this productive operation. As against the economic efficiency served by a zero price, of

encouraging the widest possible dissemination where the marginal costs of dissemination itself are practically zero, must be weighed the economic inefficiency of the zero price, in encouraging an excessive production of that information. (One may question, as well, the extent to which the single package price does in fact accomplish free distribution of the information; certainly brokerage houses confine some of it to their own customers.) This kind of calculation is impossible to make in a priori terms. But when one turns to the apparently larger expenditures of brokerage houses on selling expenses, the cost of which is likewise incorporated in the package, the inefficiencies of "service inflation" would seem definitely to outweigh the efficiencies. My student, Barbara Wiget, has in a paper "The Tyranny of the Big Exchange" supplied an amusing and not entirely unfair characterization of the Exchange's defense of the package-selling:

"Salesmanship and information have a way of confusing themselves in . . . [the] presentation. . . . The justification of what some have called a monopoly price on the basis of high selling costs . . . comes close to being a theoretical innovation. J. M. Clark is called on to buttress the argument. . . . Clark did not advocate government support of price fixing to maintain a level of advertising which free competition would reduce."

The other defense offered by the NYSE Report is an interesting adaptation of the present writer's demonstration, in another connection,

The industry provides an even more direct confirmation and illustration of this tendency. In 1969, under pressure of diminishing business and profit margins and in growing recognition of the fact that it was the large transactions that were highly profitable and the small ones that may not even have covered marginal costs, the brokerage firms instituted corresponding adjustments in their selling expenses. They began to cut salesmen's commissions on small transactions and to increase them on the large,[101] thereby once again demonstrating how costs get adjusted to price if price is not free to move.

The elimination of price competition in brokerage rates, then, has had some seriously deleterious effects on the performance of the market. These costs might nonetheless be worth paying—particularly if rates were effectively regulated henceforth, as the NYSE now proposes—if the industry's model of how competition would function in the absence of minimum rate regulation were realistic: as always, the real choice can only be between imperfect systems. There remains a possibility that free price competition would produce undesirable fluctuations in rates with the changing relationship of demand to capacity—fluctuations serving no economic purpose, if, as seems likely, the demand in the aggregate for brokerage services is inelastic. It is certainly possible, too, that price competition would be discriminatory. Product differentiation and an inadequate ability to shop around and obtain concessions could expose smaller customers to charges far in excess of the marginal cost of supplying them, while larger investors, seeking only the bare completion of transactions, could demand rates closely tied to cost.[102] Any such discrimination could produce a distortion in the choice by

that the operation of a competitive market can lead to the disappearance of certain, economically justified services, because it has no means of charging buyers what it is worth to them merely to have those services continuously *available*, regardless of whether they actually purchase it. For a fuller statement of the general thesis, see pp. 236–238, this chapter, below.

"individual investors might be unwilling to pay separately for research and advisory services each time they made a small decision to buy or sell stock. But if enough individuals decided against purchasing the information needed for better decision-making, the research and informational facilities of brokers would eventually dwindle, and perhaps disappear. The disappearance of the basic research facilities might constitute a genuine deprivation that customers would willingly have paid a considerable amount *in the aggregate* to avoid." *Economic Effects*, August 1968, *op. cit.*, 102–104.

The difficulty with this particular application of the argument is that there are already a large number of firms selling market information and advice, at a price; and, it must be presumed, there would be even more were it not that consumers already receive such advice "free" from brokerage houses in the commissions that

they pay for the execution of buy and sell orders. If, then, the introduction of competition in the setting of commission rates led some brokers to reduce their supply of these services, it seems almost certain they would not only remain available to customers for separate purchase but be available in greater quantity than theretofore. And even if some of the supply dried up, because buyers were unwilling to pay for it explicitly, there is no reason why it could not be expanded in the future, when and as economically justified.

[101] *Wall Street Journal*, December 9, 1969, 10. After a period in which it explicitly justified the packaging of order-execution and auxiliary services, the New York Exchange indirectly recognized the cogency of the argument against it when it suggested the possibility of a regulated rate structure that would permit separate charging for these services. *The Economics of Minimum Commission Rates*, May 1, 1969, *op. cit.*, 52. But its president later rejected the suggestion as "unrealistic." *Wall Street Journal*, November 24, 1969, 3.

[102] I am indebted to Joel B. Dirlam for emphasizing this side of the coin. And yet it is difficult to reconcile with the Exchange's emphasis on the extreme danger that competition would be destructive. The SEC's proposals of October 1970 would forestall this possibility by making the

small investors between investing on their own account and through the intermediary of mutual funds.

On the other hand, it is extremely difficult for an economist to accept the alternative system—a system of soft, nonprice, cost-inflating competition, grounded in the desire to protect competitors and having the effect of sustaining the capitalized monopoly profits that are reflected in the price of acquiring membership in a stock exchange. Effectively regulated rates—particularly if the auxiliary services were priced separately—could mitigate many of these inefficiencies and, if based on industry-wide cost averages, as is now proposed, could exert heavy pressure on inefficient brokers to mend their ways or to go out of business. But legally prescribed rates based on average industry costs are still not competitive rates; they still protect the relatively inefficient; they deny efficient firms the option of increasing their market shares by price reductions and still give them an incentive to compete by proliferating services.

The Regulation of Nonprice Competition: Air Transport

We have now seen two illustrations of an important economic principle: when limitations are placed on price competition, but market conditions are such as to make continued interfirm rivalry likely, the consequence will be an accentuation of service competition.[103] If the minimum rate regulation is effective, it will almost certainly hold price above the marginal costs of some producers, to which competition would otherwise drive it. (It could conceivably be confined to preventing sales *below* marginal costs, but since producers would not ordinarily make such sales except temporarily, in the hope of holding on to a share of the market in the expectation that prices would shortly improve,[104] it is rarely limited to this modest purpose.) But if competition is sufficiently strong, potentially, to drive price down to that level, it will ordinarily be sufficiently strong to induce these suppliers, confronting a price above their marginal costs, to seek other, nonprice methods of producing additional sales. Specifically, they will be inclined to improve service in one way or another, until their marginal costs, inflated by the service improvements, are equated to price.

Mark the general principle; it is an important one. If price is prevented from falling to marginal cost in the short run or to average total cost in the long run,[105] then, to the extent that competition prevails, it will tend to raise *cost* to the level of *price*. Only when, in this way, marginal cost is once again equated with price will the tendency to service inflation be halted.[106]

---

schedule of commissions on transactions of less than $100,000 maxima as well as minima. The greater danger seems to be that the ceilings on small transactions will not be compensatory.

[103] See pp. 189 and 206–207, this chapter, above.

[104] They might also do so with predatory intention, taking the out-of-pocket losses in order to drive rivals out of the market and in expectation of being able to charge monopoly prices thereafter; or for A–J–W kinds of reasons, in expectation of being permitted to recoup those losses in higher charges to customers with inelastic demand. But neither of these possibilities is typically applicable in minimum rate regula-

tion situations.

[105] To whose MC or ATC? To the costs of supplying just the quantity that customers will demand at the market price—to the marginal cost of producing that quantity (and under pure competition *all* producers will equate their marginal costs to that price) and to the ATC of the highest-cost producer that the market finds it necessary to draw into production in order to meet the demand.

[106] Precisely the same tendency prevails under government or cartel-imposed minimum price controls when entry is free or investment by existing firms is uncontrolled. See our illustration

If, therefore, regulatory commissions have the responsibility of keeping price rivalry from becoming destructive, they cannot escape the responsibility of deciding whether they ought to limit quality competition as well. As we have already pointed out in our discussion of the more traditional public utilities, in which the presumed danger is one of monopolistic exploitation, price regulation alone is meaningless except in terms of some specified unit and quality of service: a baker with a local monopoly can exploit his customers just as effectively by giving them only twelve rolls for some fixed price when in the presence of competition he would be likely to give them thirteen as by continuing to give them a baker's dozen but charging them $8\frac{1}{2}$ percent more than the competitive price. Similarly when regulation is introduced to keep competition from driving a price *down*: it will be futile to affix a minimum price for a dozen rolls if bakers remain free to decide how many rolls constitute a dozen.[107]

Regulation has heretofore shirked this responsibility in trucking and the security brokerage business, with consequences we have already observed. In air transportation, in contrast, the regulators have found it impossible to ignore it, possibly because airline companies, catering much more than the others to the whims of the ultimate consumer, have competed much more intensely in this way. Partly for the same reason, the airline case is more difficult to judge than the others, because there would doubtless be a great deal of service rivalry even in the presence of much sharper price competition than now prevails. Nor is there any reason to doubt that this kind of competition is, within limits that are difficult to define, just as important a contributor to consumer welfare as price rivalry. We return to this difficult problem of evaluation at a later point.

Price competition is discouraged in this industry, first, by the oligopolistic character of airline markets, itself attributable partly to the restrictions on entry imposed by the Civil Aeronautics Board. The oligopolists in this industry show the familiar reluctance to engage in direct price rivalry.[108]

---

of oil production control, pp. 28–29, Chapter 1, above. It is entirely consistent with this principle that when, in 1969–1970, airline profits turned to losses, the companies returned from full meals to sandwiches, stopped handing out macadamia nuts, began to charge for inflight movies, and started pruning their schedules. *New York Times*, October 13, 1970, 18C.

[107] This is not to suggest that the danger of what J. M. Clark has termed product (or service) inflation is confined to highly competitive industries. On the contrary, what Clark was referring to was the possibility that in highly concentrated industries—he referred particularly to American automobiles—competition may take the form principally of cost inflating and largely specious quality improvements. *Competition as a Dynamic Process*, 252–257. The restraint that oligopolists may feel it is in their joint interest to exercise with respect to price rivalry may not extend to improvements in their products or services. This is partly because a successful product variation is not as readily imitated as a

price cut, so that the firm that initiates it may feel that the advantages it may bring him, by way of larger sales or the ability to charge a higher price, will last for a while and so be worth the costs of competing in this manner. It may be true, also, because product rivalry—for example, frequent model changes—can move the entire industry demand curve to the right and so be in the interest of all producers; or because it may help cement the power of the oligopoly by raising additional barriers to entry and by being particularly difficult for smaller rivals to emulate. See the fuller discussion of this problem in Joe S. Bain, *Industrial Organization*, rev. ed. (New York: John Wiley & Co., 1968), 223–250, 348–357, 412–418, and this writer's *op. cit.*, *Kyklos* (January 1966), XIX: 39–44. It is cartelization that introduces the danger of service inflation in structurally competitive industries.

[108] See Caves, *Air Transport and its Regulators*, Chapter 1 and 15; Samuel B. Richmond, *Regulation and Competition in Air Transportation*, (New York: Columbia Univ. Press, 1961), 45–47.

Possibly contributing to this same restraint is the fact that they have agreed to notify the Air Transport Association of all proposed rate changes at least 15 days before filing them with the CAB, which undoubtedly gives the other companies an opportunity to put pressure on any one of them proposing to reduce rates.[109] Second, the CAB itself has tended quite consistently to discourage competitive rate reductions.[110] In the international field, price competition has been even more effectively contained by the International Air Transport Association (IATA), which, backed by the authority of governments to deny or withdraw landing privileges to airlines that refuse to adhere to its rate schedules, has imposed a particularly high and noncompetitive schedule of rates on international traffic.[111]

In part because the doors to price competition are closed, airline companies compete very strenuously among themselves in the quality of service they offer—most notably in adopting the most modern and attractive equipment and in the frequency with which they schedule flights, but also in providing comfort, attractive hostesses, in-flight entertainment, food and drink.[112] Among these, the one most closely approaching destructiveness in character is scheduling. There is a general belief that the airline with the most flights between any two points is the one to which customers will turn first in making their reservations. The result, where competition is strong and particularly in markets where new entry threatens, is a cumulative tendency to excess capacity, with each company vying with the other by increasing the number of daily flights on its schedule.[113] Ronald E. Miller attributes to

---

[109] Caves, *Air Transport and its Regulators*, 366; Richmond, *op. cit.*, 49–50.

[110] The Board has had to devote a good deal of attention to passing on requests for rate increases as well. See Caves, *Air Transport and its Regulators*, 142–154, 250. On the other hand,

"A red thread running through this narrative has been the Board's fear of any action that might, even indirectly, yield low rates of return for the carriers. There are many other instances of its nervousness about any fare proposals or situations that could lead to substantial general price competition among the carriers."

Ibid., 154; see also pp. 145, 155. The Board has also exercised its authority to prohibit undue or unreasonable rate discrimination generally in order to prohibit selective rate reductions incident to, or that threaten to accentuate, competition. *Ibid.*, 158–163, 167–168. It has imposed tight controls on the smaller, non-scheduled carriers that tend to compete more actively in price. See, for example, *ibid.*, 145, 149; and, on the restrictive policy toward irregular airlines, U.S. Senate, Select Committee on Small Business, *Future of Irregular Airlines*, 83rd Congress, First Session, Report No. 822, July 31, 1953.

[111] See Mahlon R. Straszheim, *The International Airline Industry* (Washington: Brookings Institution, 1969), 131–149, 170–172, 194–196; International Air Transport Association, "How International Airline Fares and Rates Are Made," Vladimir de Boursac, "The Raison d'Être of Traffic Conferences," and Lord Brabazon of Tara, "1962 IATA Paper," (the latter begins: "Coming to your organization, [International Air Transport Association] I must say about it right at the start that my admiration for it has never passed the bounds of moderation"), all reproduced in Stanley C. Hollander, *Passenger Transportation, Readings Selected from a Marketing Viewpoint* (East Lansing: Michigan State University, 1968), 539–560; also U. S. House of Representatives, Committee on the Judiciary, Antitrust Subcommittee, 85th Cong. 1st Sess., *The Airlines Industry*, April 5, 1957, 217–235, 275–276.

[112] The expenses in even the latter category alone are hardly negligible: one airline executive says that his company spends more than $30 for food and liquor for each transatlantic first-class passenger. *New York Times*, March 31, 1969, 39. Also "In Airlines' Battle, Every Inch Counts," *ibid.*, October 28, 1970, 1.

[113] See Caves, *Air Transport and its Regulators*, 333–348; Straszheim, *op. cit.*, 163–164, 168–170, 178–179; and, for example, "Which Cure for TWA?" *Business Week*, September 15, 1962, 48. According to this article, the president of TWA was trying to persuade his counterparts at American and United Airlines to ask the CAB for permission to discuss an agreed-upon reduction in capacity:

this competitive overscheduling the major part of the blame for the excessive capacity in the industry, showing up in load factors (ratios of revenue passenger miles sold to total available seat miles in scheduled service) typically running below 60 percent.[114]

This kind of competition, like persuasive advertising, is in considerable measure self-defeating. It may pay each individual company to advertise, whether aggressively or defensively—A having to advertise in order to keep from losing customers to B and B having to do the same for the same reason—but for all companies together the gain in revenue is probably typically less than the additional selling costs they have incurred. We shall have to take into account, before terminating this discussion, the fact that nonprice competition can mean an improvement in the quality of service: even persuasive advertising is not entirely unproductive, insofar as it provides some information and perhaps provides some assurance to customers of minimal standards of quality. The proliferation of scheduled flights, even more clearly, does mean greater convenience, offering the traveller a greater number of alternative times among which to choose in making any particular trip.[115] But where the scheduling is purely duplicative and the traffic actually generated could be carried in fewer flights, the competition has produced only waste.

The most thorough restrictions on the service competition among airline companies, as on price competition as well—as we have indicated, the latter accentuates the need for the former[116]—have been the ones imposed by the IATA, notably on the tourist flights of its members. Most notorious have been regulations prescribing the maximum allowable knee-room (commodious for midgets), dictating that meals be limited to sandwiches (which unruly competitors persisted in making more and more sumptuous) and requiring a uniform supplementary charge for in-flight motion pictures and other entertainment.[117] But these provide only a sketchy indication of the kinds of rules that are necessary if an agreement on prices is to stick:

> "Even a simple fare structure is meaningless unless a host of other matters is settled. Could this fare be sold by an agent? If so, at what rate of commission? . . .

"The chief drawback to this is that frequency of flight is one of the few competitive weapons that airline management has left. Prices are substantially the same, catering is about the same, speeds are almost identical, and though equipment is vastly different to the experts, it looks pretty much the same to the passenger walking out of the gate. Now Tillinghast is suggesting that numbers of flights be a matter not of management choice but of formula." Reprinted by special permission.

The subsequent sharp recovery in the profitability of the industry evidently took the steam out of the effort, at least temporarily. But sharply diminished profitability and declining load factors in the late 1960's led to a resumption of collective efforts, resulting in a formal request by TWA, United, and American Airlines to the CAB for permission to enter into a joint agreement to reduce flights. *New York Times*, August 29, 1970.

[114] *Domestic Airline Efficiency: An Application of Linear Programming* (Cambridge: M.I.T. Press, 1963), 108–114. Annual load factors can be computed from the CAB's *Annual Reports* to Congress.

[115] See Vickrey, *op. cit., Jour. Pol. Econ.* (June 1948), LVI: note 8 and p. 234. Miller explicitly ignores the welfare loss from diminished frequency of service, in calculating the extent of overscheduling. The objective of his model is to provide the same total amount of passenger trips at "minimum total direct cost." *Op. cit.*, 92 and 94, note 5.

[116] For an observation that the more stringent limitations on price competition internationally have led to more intensive service inflation in those markets, see Straszheim, *op. cit.*, 170–171.

[117] See *ibid.*, 105–107, 143–144.

"Would a stopover be allowed on this fare? If yes, and the stopover took place at night, would the airline be allowed to pay for his hotel accommodation . . .? How long could the stopover be and would he have to have a firm reservation on the next connecting flight? . . .

"How much baggage could he take? If he had his wife with him, could they pool this free baggage allowance? How much baggage could he himself carry over and above his free allowance? . . .

"There are very many more questions like this which have a substantial competitive impact and on which there must be agreement among the airlines to which the fare applies, if the agreement on the fare itself is going to stick. If there is no agreement there can be no fare because obviously if somebody is going to pay 20 percent commission to the agent or give the passenger free hotel accommodation, or let him carry as much luggage as he wants, that airline is going to get more passengers than the others."[118]

The attention paid by the CAB to service competition has been much more sporadic and, indeed, mixed in its intentions and effects.[119] For one thing, just as the Board has from time to time intervened to hold rates *down*, so it has frequently exerted its influence to *improve* the quality of service. Its primary device for doing so has been to grant certificates to competing companies on particular routes, something it has been especially willing to do when it could be demonstrated that the service previously provided was inadequate.[120] This would certainly seem the most efficient way of promoting that goal. It has also attempted to place limitations on overbooking, that is, the practice of accepting more reservations on a flight than there are actual spaces, in expectation that some of the reservations will be cancelled or the passengers will not show up. It has investigated the complaints of particular cities that they were receiving inadequate service and ordered certificated carriers to improve it.

In one important way, these policies have encouraged irrational service inflation. This, as Caves points out, has been the consequence of Board decisions denying carriers with older and less attractive equipment permission to charge correspondingly lower fares:

"the Board . . . . forbids the carrier with older or inferior equipment to set a differential to protect its market position. These policies create an overwhelming incentive for carriers to acquire equipment as modern or as appealing as any used by their direct competitors . . . . The carrier suffering equipment inferiority has all major avenues to protecting its market position blocked except that one."[121]

[118] de Boursac, in Hollander, *op. cit.*, 547–548. Reprinted by permission of the publisher, the Bureau of Business and Economic Research, Division of Research, Graduate School of Business Administration, Michigan State University.
[119] See Caves, *Air Transport and its Regulators*, Chapters 9–10, and Aaron J. Gellman, "The Regulation of Service Competition," in Hollander, *op. cit.*, 580–589, on which discussions the following summary draws heavily.
[120] On this policy, see also p. 16, note 29, above.
[121] *Op. cit.*, 241–242; see also 352–355. This is the conclusion, also, of A. J. Gellman's study, *The Effect of Regulation on Aircraft Choice*, unpublished Ph.D. dissertation, Massachusetts Institute of Technology, 1968, as cited by Almarin Phillips, "Technological Change in the Air Transportation Industry in the United States," a paper presented at the Brookings Institution Conference on Technological Change in the Regulated Industries, February, 1969. For a similar conclusion concerning the international market, see Straszheim, *op. cit.*, 170–171, 180–181.

When, for example, Alaska Airlines sought to introduce a lower fare for flights using DC-4's than Pan American was charging for its DC-6B equipment, the Board denied the request on the ground that, among other things, the latter planes were no more costly to operate than the former.[122] The reason has a superficial plausibility: it sounds as though the CAB was merely following the dictate of marginal-cost pricing. But airline rates are set not at marginal, but at variable costs plus a return on investment. If customers regarded service on the DC-4 as inferior, the consequence of uniform prices could have been to induce all of them to shift to the more attractive and modern Pan American equipment. This would obviously involve society in the necessity for bringing a larger number of these new planes into service, and scrapping more of the older ones, than would have been the case had passengers been presented with a choice between the two at prices reflecting their respective attractiveness. The marginal costs of the Pan American service would therefore have had to include the cost of purchasing additional equipment; the MC of the DC-4's would reflect variable costs alone.[123]

Indeed, the CAB specifically defended its rejection of the Alaska petition on the ground that "a fare differential would lessen the incentive of the carriers to introduce better equipment. . . ."[124] But of course as long as existing, "poorer" equipment can give service at prices in excess of variable costs, there is every economic reason to continue to use it; and to set obstacles in the way of its use in order to give carriers an incentive "to introduce better equipment" is to promote waste.

On the other hand, the Board has at times and in limited ways supplemented its efforts to hold price competition in check by placing collateral restrictions on the quality of service offered. When, after much foot-dragging, it permitted the introduction of coach fares, it took pains to assure that coach flights would be scheduled only at off-peak times and with much denser seating than on first-class trips.[125] So it denied the request of United Airlines that it be permitted to adopt a policy of selling only a portion of the seats available on coach flights, in order to improve passenger comfort, on the ground that this would constitute "an unfair method of competition."[126] Again, when TWA proposed to introduce "Siesta Sleeper Seats" on its transcontinental first-class flights—which would have reduced the number of seats that could be accommodated in the cabin—and United and American Airlines objected that they would have had to do the same if TWA were permitted to go ahead, the Board decided to permit the innovation only if the service was subjected to a 20 percent surcharge:

---

[122] Caves, *Air Transport and its Regulators*, 241, citing the *States-Alaska Fare Case*, Docket No. 6328 *et al.*, 21 CAB 354, 356–358 (1955).
[123] If the total costs of the two kinds of equipment seemed to be equal, it could only have been because the book value of the older equipment—and, consequently, the depreciation and return on investment components of the cost of using it—exceeded its market value. See pp. 117–122, Volume 1, above. This is on the assumption, of course, that Alaska Airlines' proposed lower rates would have covered at least the variable

costs of operating that equipment. If the variable costs of the DC–4's, including a return on the scrap or second hand sale price of the equipment, exceeded the rate necessary for them to get business in competition with the DC–6B's, the equipment should in fact have been withdrawn from service.
[124] Loc. cit., note 122.
[125] See note 110, above.
[126] *United Airlines, Inc.—Petition for Change in Coach Policy and for Exemption*, Docket No. 5884, January 6, 1953, as cited in Gellman, *op. cit.*, 583.

"TWA does not seek to justify the offering of sleeper-seat service at prevailing first-class fares on the ground that such service will promote new air traffic. Rather, it contends that it is offering such service almost exclusively because of competitive considerations. . . . The evidence shows that if all three carriers . . . were to operate a sleeper-seat service, the nonstop transcontinental market would be uneconomical for each."[127]

But these attempts have been comparatively few. One explanation, at least in the case of scheduling, is the limited authority of the Board; according to its enabling act,

"No term, condition, or limitation of a certificate shall restrict the right of an air carrier to add to or change schedules, equipment, accommodations, and facilities for performing the authorized transportation and service as the development of the business and the demands of the public shall require . . ."[128]

Another explanation of this permissiveness is its statutory mandate to promote the growth of air travel, which undoubtedly explains also its own enthusiasm for airlines adopting the most modern equipment. In any event, its controls over service competition have been mainly hortatory.[129] It took the airport congestion emergency of 1968 to induce the Board to authorize consultations among the airlines on the possibility of reducing the number of their scheduled flights during peak hours at the congested airports.[130]

---

[127] *Trans World Airlines Siesta Sleeper-Seat Service*, Docket No. 9063, et. al, Opinion, 27 CAB 788, 790 (November 1958).

[128] 49 U.S. Code 1371(c)(3), 1964 ed. See the similar limitation on the power of the ICC over motor carriers, at p. 189, this chapter, above. The CAB can exert indirect influence on scheduling, equipment purchases, selling, and other expenses of the *subsidized* airlines, because it can disallow costs that it deems excessive in determining the amount of subsidy. See G. E. Hale and Rosemary D. Hale, "Competition or Control IV: Air Carriers," *Univ. of Pennsylvania Law Rev.* (January 1961), CIX: 342. And it can exert similar pressures on the unsubsidized carriers, when they come in for fare increases. See Caves, *op. cit.*, 237–238.

[129] "While competing carriers are expected by the Board and the public to compete with vigor, a measure of scheduling self-discipline by individual carrier management is becoming increasingly imperative in the public interest and in the interest of a healthy industry. Although domestic airlines operate without a rate bureau, we seldom see any trace of what might be regarded as a rate war among competing airlines. Apparently, the industry has been successful in avoiding rate wars through carrier managements acting individually in their own interest. However, it is by no means clear why similar self-interest would not dictate a corresponding restraint against over-scheduling in competitive markets.

"This leads to another area where more and more industry officials have indicated informally that greater restraint by individual carrier managements, in connection with the level of advertising expenditures, may be required. I do not pretend to pass judgment on the proper level of advertising by each carrier in a competitive transportation system, but the questions raised within the industry, as to potential uneconomic advertising expense levels, may suggest an important area of potential economy that would be a worthwhile step towards at least curtailing the cost revenue squeeze." Address by Irving Roth, Director, Bureau of Economics, Civil Aeronautics Board, at the Wings Club Luncheon, New York City, September 18, 1968, processed.

[130] During the course of 1968, the overcrowding of flights during peak hours at several of the country's major airports resulted in delays of several hours in arrivals and departures. In this emergency, the CAB approved agreements between American and foreign air carriers to set up scheduling committees for five airports, for the purpose of instituting voluntary action to bring their combined number of scheduled flights within the safety limitations set up by the Federal Aviation Administration. The CAB, in announcing this approval on December 5, 1968, stated that it recognized that approval of the agreements represented "a departure from our customary policy with respect to so sensitive an area as scheduling."

Clearly, in general, the Board has discouraged price competition far more than service competition, with a strong resultant tendency for the industry to engage in cost-increasing service inflation.

> "While it is undeniably desirable that the level of service afforded the traveling public be raised continually, it is somewhat ludicrous to find virtually unrestricted service competition prevailing in this industry while prices are more or less rigidly controlled."[131]

Rivalry in improving service can obviously be just as productive of benefit to the traveling public as in price. How, then, can an economist presume to judge that it has gone too far? He may not, directly. All he can do is ask whether the service improvements have been subjected to the test of a competitive market. That test requires that customers be provided with a sufficient variety of price-quality combinations—consistent with efficient production—so that each can register a free and tolerably well-informed monetary appraisal of the quality differentials that are offered. By this test product inflation could be said to have occurred only if quality competition had operated in such a way as to eliminate, or to fail to develop, lower quality-price combinations that consumers would willingly have purchased in quantities sufficient to cover the cost of providing them. The reason why it is questionable that the service improvements produced by competition in the airline industry have been worth the cost is that the restrictions on *price* competition have denied consumers the alternative of less sumptuous service at prices reflecting its lower cost. They have therefore not had the opportunity to determine whether the better quality is in their collective judgment worth the higher cost of providing it.[132]

The objection is not necessarily that airlines have been forced by their competition to incur greater costs for denser schedules, advertising, meals, and in-flight entertainment than they would if they were able to get together and restrict such expenditures to the industry profit-maximizing level— although that certainly is what they have done.[133] To adopt any such criterion of industry performance would be to take the results of pure monopoly as the ideal: it is precisely the function of competition to force suppliers to do things that are not in their collective interest. The objection is, rather, that these cost-inflating service improvements have not been subjected to the test of having to compete with lower-cost, lower-price alternatives. The defect, in short, has not been the service competition, as such, but the inadequate play of *price* competition along with it.

The airline industry offers several evidences that price competition can, if it is given a chance, hold service inflation in check. Historically, passenger rates have been geared to first-class Pullman railroad fares, with a corresponding emphasis on luxurious service. "The first real break came when the irregular carriers introduced coach service at rates approximately 65 percent of standard trunk-line fares."[134] These nonscheduled airlines were

---

[131] Gellman, in Hollander, *op. cit.*, 587; see also pp. 585–589.

[132] See, for example, Straszheim, *op. cit.*, 114, 181, and *passim*.

[133] See, for example, the judgment of Caves, *Air Transport and its Regulators*, 347–348, 353.

[134] Horace M. Gray, "The Airlines Industry," in Adams (ed.), *The Structure of American Industry*, 3rd ed., 484. For a description of the similar role played by the irregular airlines in freight operations, driving air cargo down from about 60 to 16 cents per ton-mile, and a description of the efforts of the CAB to hold this competition in check, see *ibid.*, 485, 494–504.

for the most part companies that had come into the business, by the hundreds, after World War II, generally carrying passengers or freight on an irregular basis, when demand justified it, at rates lower than those charged by the regularly certificated trunk-line carriers.[135] For the first several years, coach service was offered only over high-density routes and during off-peak hours, with denser passenger seating than in first-class, and no meals were served. The enormous expansion of coach travel that followed, as the regular carriers introduced similar service of their own, clearly demonstrated that the majority of potential travelers preferred the lower price-quality combination to the one that had previously been available to them.[136] A similar illustration has been provided more recently by the popularity of the group charter flights, at rates substantially below those set by the IATA, and, later, the inclusive tour charters on scheduled North Atlantic flights. These, once again, were pioneered by the nonscheduled (later termed supplemental) air carriers and again subjected to various restrictions by the CAB and the IATA, in order to lessen their impact on the regular rate structures.[137]

Another, even more striking illustration is provided by the extraordinary impact that essentially unregulated price competition has had on the price

---

[135] *Ibid.*, 476.

[136] See the same conclusion of Straszheim, *op. cit.*, 119–120, and, with reference to the similar burgeoning of chartered flights, pp. 50, 181. Between the fiscal years ending June 30, 1952 and June 30, 1968, the share of total certificated revenue passenger miles accounted for by coach traffic rose from 15 to 45 percent. CAB *Annual Reports* for those years, pp. 13 and 4, respectively. Since coach service is not universally available, the statement that the majority of potential travellers prefer it seems reasonable. The emphasis on "potential" passengers is explained by the estimate, cited by Locklin, that as of 1950 about 70 percent of the coach travel was additional traffic to the airlines, and about 30 percent diverted from first class. *Op. cit.*, 777. On the price elasticity of demand for air travel, see also p. 103, above.

[137] The principal restriction is that the groups must have "affinity"—that is, they cannot have been formed merely in order to take advantage of the low group fares. See the CAB *Annual Reports* for 1949 and 1950, 24 and 25, respectively. For a description of CAB efforts to crack down on evasions of this requirement—"You see too many little old ladies getting aboard on the trips offered by the Far West Ski Association"—see *Wall Street Journal*, June 10, 1969, 1. In 1964 the Board for the first time certificated supplemental carriers to engage in the transatlantic charter business, stating that

"Historically, the Board has sought to encourage the development of a large mass international travel market . . . without undue

diversion from the regular route carriers." *Transatlantic Charter Investigation*, Opinion, 40 CAB 233, 253 (1964).

And it liberalized that policy in the subsequent years. See Straszheim, *op. cit.*, 216–220. The number of revenue passenger miles flown by the supplemental lines rose, in consequence, from 1.5 billion in 1963 to 8.7 billion in 1968. *Wall Street Journal*, July 30, 1969, 34.

In addition, travel agents can themselves charter flights and sell tickets to individuals, who need not be members of any cognizable group. But on such charters they may not offer bargain rates for air transportation alone. Instead, they and the airlines themselves can offer only "inclusive tour" packages that include a charge for a minimum of $70 worth of ground services—hotel accommodations, car rentals, and the like; this has the effect of bringing their quoted rates roughly up to the regular tourist fare. The governing U.S. statute requires that the operator of the inclusive tour must sell the package for at least 110 percent of the regular air fare; but the price he pays the airline can be negotiated.

A research report by the CAB's Bureau of Economics concluded there was no evidence that inclusive tour charters would have a materially adverse effect on the regularly scheduled service and recommended that the lower-price service be encouraged because it would open up to the airlines a "great, new, untapped source of potential customers." *Economic Impact of Inclusive Tour Charters on Scheduled North Atlantic Services*, January 1969, 21. See this Study also for a summary of the legal history of these plans.

and volume of air traffic between Los Angeles and San Francisco, California.[138] What made this possible was the fact that wholly intrastate air transport is free of CAB control and that the California Public Utilities Commission has no power to limit entry and has followed the practice, as far as rates are concerned, of approving virtually all changes. The results of this, the closest thing to a "controlled experiment" in public policy, have been summarized by Michael E. Levine as follows:

"Although the Los Angeles-San Francisco market has always been an important one, it was the fifth largest in the United States in 1948 (in terms of passenger miles), and became the largest only in 1961. Today, more revenue passengers travel between Los Angeles and San Francisco than between any pair of cities in the world. . . . The market has grown rapidly . . . and has been characterized by intense competition, a wide variety of marketing strategies, and the lowest overland air fares in the world.

"There are striking contrasts between the performance of this market and the performance of similar markets in the United States regulated by the CAB. For example, although the number of passengers traveling by air in the United States as a whole has increased between the years 1959 and 1964 by approximately 50 per cent, the number of travelers passing between Los Angeles and San Francisco by air has increased almost 300 per cent. Although the average jet coach fare level in the United States is approximately 5.5 cents per mile over stages considerably longer, and hence cheaper to operate, jet coach fare for the 350-mile trip from San Francisco to Los Angeles is approximately 3.9 cents per mile. Although the lowest fare between Boston and Washington, served only by CAB-certificated trunk carriers, is $24.65, Pacific Southwest Airlines, using the same modern turbo-prop equipment, carries passengers between Los Angeles and San Francisco, only 59 miles closer together, for $11.43. The jet fare is only $13.50. In other markets, obsolescent though economically viable aircraft have been rapidly retired as new aircraft have been introduced prematurely, because the fare structure has emphasized premium service and has not allowed the owner of obsolescent equipment to operate at a fare reflecting his lower capital costs. In Los Angeles-San Francisco, however, it has been common to see obsolescent equipment operated at fares reflecting the lower capital cost until replaced by new equipment so much more efficient that the capital cost charges could be amortized at fares which reflected customer demand for the new equipment."[139]

The significance of the 1959 point of comparison is that it was in that year that the Pacific Southwest Airlines (PSA), an intrastate carrier operating without a CAB certificate, first introduced modern turboprop aircraft,

---

[138] The following account is drawn from the very persuasive study of Michael E. Levine, "Is Regulation Necessary? California Air Transportation and National Regulatory Policy," *Yale Law Jour.* (July 1965), LXXIV: 1416–1447. See also the CAB, Research and Statistics Division, Bureau of Accounts and Statistics, *Traffic, Fares,* *and Competition, Los Angeles–San Francisco Air Travel Corridor,* Staff Research Report No. 4, Washington, August 1965.

[139] *Op. cit.,* reprinted by permission of the Yale Law Journal Company and Fred B. Rothman & Company from the *Yale Law Journal,* Vol. 74, pp. 1432–1433.

charging rates far below those charged by the three CAB-certificated carriers, United Airlines, TWA, and Western Airlines. In a scant three years, during which its competitors failed to respond, PSA increased its market share from 13 to 43 percent. United and Western eventually reacted by sharply reducing their fares and introducing jet service, beginning around 1962; but PSA likewise introduced jets and retained about 35 percent of the market, as of the early part of 1965. A particularly interesting additional fact is that despite the quintupled scheduling by United, the market leader, in introducing its new jets, load factors remained at a comfortable and profitable two-thirds, far above the national ratio;[140] and despite the drastic reduction in fares, from the $20 to the $11.43–13.50 range, PSA, with no other important source of income, was able to operate profitably:[141]

> "Lack of regulation has not caused chaos in California. Unregulated entry and price competition have not resulted in a multitude of tiny firms scrambling for passengers to the confusion of the general public. As the California market developed, advanced technology and effective marketing became essential to profitable operation; and it became increasingly difficult for a thinly-capitalized fringe operator to survive. Ultimately, no more than three important competitors remained, along with . . . periodically, a fringe operator trying to find a niche in the market. . . .
>
> "the California experience . . . indicates that the public has little to fear from unregulated entry. Participants in a market will be naturally limited to a number which ensures both competition and technical efficiency without chaos. The free-entry California market has and will have for the immediate future approximately the same structure—two to three major carriers—as most regulated routes. The important question is whether these carriers ought to be chosen administratively or by the competitive forces of the market. And the important difference is that transportation by air in the California unregulated market can be purchased for half to seven-tenths as much as it costs elsewhere."[142]

The experience with service inflation in air transportation suggests two possible alternative solutions. One is that if price competition continues to be restrained, service should likewise be subjected to much more consistent and effective controls than have hitherto been imposed on it—thus providing another illustration of the necessity for the regulatory net to be spread wider

---

[140] PSA's load factors ranged between 70 and 80 percent between 1961 and 1964 and were reported to exceed 80 percent on its single Boeing 727 in May of 1965, eight months after United introduced its jet shuttle service. CAB, *Traffic, Fares, and Competition, Los Angeles–San Francisco Air Travel Corridor*, 21.

[141] Except for 1960 and 1961, when it had some temporary difficulties, its return on stockholder equity consistently exceeded 30 percent in the 1959–1964 period. *Ibid.*, 15, 30. Levine describes a few interesting ways in which PSA has been able to hold its operating costs below those of its competitors. The one that is of direct relevance to our discussion of service inflation is:

"PSA has always managed somehow to squeeze a few extra seats into the aircraft it operates. Its 727's have 122 seats, compared to United's 114, because PSA ordered its equipment without full galleys, since meals are not served on this route. United, having ordered its 727's with its system needs in mind, carries the weight and space of the idle equipment." *Op. cit.*, 1439–1440, note 109. Reprinted by permission; see note 139, above.

[142] *Ibid.*, 1440–1441.

"Low fares, intensive advertising and constant innovation in service account for the spectacular growth of the Los Angeles–San Francisco market. This growth indicates that at least here there is elasticity of demand for air transportation." *Ibid.*, 1442.

and wider if it is to be effective.[143] The other would be to free the industry to provide low-price alternatives. Consideration of such a step would require a reexamination of the entire case for restricting competition in this industry. We make no such explicit assessment here, but the reader should by now be able to supply the relevant questions. Suffice it only to point out that many economists have concluded that passenger air transportation does not have the economic attributes of an industry prone to destructive competition, and that the public is entitled to enjoy the enormous potential benefits that freer competition—free entry and pricing—has demonstrated itself capable of providing.[144] One of those benefits would be that it would increase the variety of price-service combinations offered to the public and thereby tend to assure that cost-inflating service improvements were subjected to a fair market test. It would be pleasant if one could omit the "tend to." But how effective the test would in fact be would depend on how free was the competition that resulted from a removal of governmental restrictions. The notion of product inflation was originally developed with unregulated oligopolies in mind; the mere absence of government controls does not assure competition sufficiently keen and perfect to eradicate its possibility.[145]

THE ISSUE OF CREAM-SKIMMING

We have already, in Chapter 1, outlined the case that is frequently made for restrictions on entry or price competition in the interest of preventing cream-skimming; and we have encountered the argument from time to time elsewhere as well.[146] Here is clearly a way in which, allegedly, excessive competition can result in an eventual deterioration of the quality of service.

There are three possible approaches to an issue of this kind, all of which will be familiar to the reader. The first is the approach of the traditional, normative, microeconomic theory that underlies our Chapters 3–6 of Volume 1, and describes the "optimal" economic results that would issue from ideally perfect competition. The second would emphasize the institutional problems and considerations that are the subject matter of the present volume, which is concerned not with describing those "optimal" results but considering how they can be most closely approximated in the imperfect world of reality. This approach has to take into account the limitations of even a perfectly competitive market in serving the very purposes it purports

---

[143] See the judgment of Gellman, p. 216, above.
[144] See, for example, Caves, *Air Transport and its Regulators*, Chapter 18 and *passim*; Keyes, *Federal Control of Entry into Air Transportation;* also her "Reconsideration of Federal Control of Entry into Air Transportation," *Jour. Air Law and Commerce* (Spring 1955), XXII: 192–202; Richmond, *op. cit.*, 254–257; and Straszheim, *op. cit.*, 183–188, and the rest of Chapter 10. These authors recognize that to the extent that we insist on promoting such noneconomic goals as the provision of service on unremunerative routes subsidized by above-cost rates on remunerative routes, the possibilities of introducing more competition must necessarily be limited.

For particularly strong statements of the case for freer competition, see Levine, *op. cit.*, 1416–1447, and Kenneth W. Dam, in an excellent review of the Caves book, *Univ. of Chicago Law Rev.* (Autumn 1964), XXXII: 200–202.
[145] See note 107, p. 210, above. On the other hand, most observers and industry experience as well clearly suggest that freer price competition would in fact ensue and service inflation would, therefore, be held more effectively in check.
[146] Notably in Chapter 4, since the case for restrictions on entry into the market of a "natural monopoly" is often supported on cream-skimming grounds.

to serve—maximum efficiency in the presence of economies of scale, economic progress,[147] and optimum resource allocation in the presence of externalities.[148]

The third approach is to take into account the possibility that noneconomic goals may require qualification of the policy judgments that would flow from considerations of economic efficiency alone.

The Economic Case for Unrestricted Cream-Skimming

The economic case for free, cream-skimming competition is both static and institutional. The former aspect begins with the basic proposition that prices must be equated to marginal cost. Suppose, then, that under unrestricted competition there is a tendency for new firms to enter into particular portions of public utility markets or for existing firms to compete more strenuously for those markets, with the tendency to push down price. Assuming no errors of planning or judgment (we return to this assumption when we consider possible cases *for* restricting competition in circumstances like these), this must mean that prices in those markets are in excess of someone's marginal cost: either (1) existing firms are pricing above their own marginal costs or (2) their own marginal costs are higher than those of the entrants, or (3) price is being held above the marginal cost of some existing firms, but not necessarily of all. In any event, if there is in fact "cream" that some competitors are attempting to "skim," this is the best possible evidence that price in those markets is too high and should come down.

And experience indicates the superiority of competition as an institutional device for achieving this goal. The only forces that can hold price above someone's marginal cost are monopolistic or regulatory restrictions on output or price, conservatism or inertia. The most effective device for overcoming these obstructions is the freedom of individual businessmen to seek out and to exploit the market opportunities that these forces generate.[148a]

But what of the regulated common carriers, who are obliged by law to serve also the less remunerative markets and who may be unable to do so unless they can enjoy the protected profits on the creamy parts of their business? Here we encounter, first, a question of fact: the question is whether the carrying of the less remunerative business is a burden on the regulated company in its competition with allegedly cream-skimming interlopers. If it is not a burden, the cream-skimming case for protection can clearly be rejected. This will be the case as long as the less remunerative business covers its own marginal costs. The telephone company, for example, deserves no artificial protection against the entry of specialist firms seeking to take away its apparently more lucrative, daytime telephone business, in order to ensure

---

[147] See pp. xii and 114, above.

[148] Why do externalities involve "institutional" considerations? The problem of external costs and benefits may be regarded as issuing from defects in our property institutions—such as, for example, permitting one person to impose losses on another, without the latter necessarily being in a position to obtain compensation. A proper system of compensation and assessments would eliminate these distortions. See Morris A. Copeland, "Institutionalism and Welfare Economics," *Amer. Econ. Rev.* (March 1958), XLVIII: 1–17.

[148a] See the proposal by Milton Friedman for repeal of the law prohibiting private companies from carrying first-class mail:

"The resulting competition would not only improve postal service and reduce its cost. . . . It would also make starkly clear what categories of mail are more than paying their way and what categories are being subsidized." *Wall Street Journal*, March 11, 1970, 18.

its continued provision of nighttime service. Its rates for the former would have to be even higher than they are were it not also in a position, with the same equipment, to supply off-peak, nighttime service at rates in excess of incremental costs. The fact of its integration—it supplies both day and night service—gives it a competitive advantage in both of these markets against specialist competitors. Indeed, in such a situation it is in a sense impossible to say which part of the business is the cream, which part the skimmed milk, because the bulk of the costs are joint.

True, the contribution of the less remunerative business, though positive, may still not be sufficient to overcome other competitive handicaps of the regulated companies. They may be less enterprising or less ably managed than their competitors, or use an outmoded technology; or perhaps the competitors may, by virtue of the character of *their* integration, be able to take on the creamy business at rates covering *their* marginal costs but below those that the regulated company can charge. But none of these circumstances would justify imposing restrictions on that competition. Suppose, for example, that some firm outside the Bell System found a new way to transmit long-distance telephone messages using the rays of the sun—that is, during the daytime only—at total unit costs less than current daytime rates. Should the undermining of those high rates then be prevented on the ground that otherwise night telephone service would disappear? The correct economic answer is that no class of customers should be required to pay more than the total cost of serving it alone. Whether by competition or by regulation, the daytime rates should be brought down at least to the total unit costs under the new technology. If this requires higher nighttime rates for the joint service to continue, the night rate should go up, possibly to the point where that business covers the bulk of the joint costs. The advantages of integration may then still suffice to keep the old established telephone company in the day and night business, perhaps retaining its monopoly in both. Or they may no longer suffice, leaving it only in the latter business; and if that business will not bear the cost of continued service, night telephonic communication is no longer economically feasible and should disappear. In neither case is there economic justification for preventing the competition that brings about the equation of the two prices to their new, respective marginal costs.

But there may be a problem here arising out of the familiar difficulty of equating all prices to marginal cost when marginal costs are less than average. In general, the presumption—on institutional grounds—would still be in favor of competition. The fact that a competitor is willing to enter only the thick markets *suggests* that it is possible to supply them alone at costs lower than the rates previously charged; if his estimate proves wrong, it is he who will bear the costs of his error. On the other hand, we must recognize the possibility that while the rates that the entrant proposes to charge in the creamy market exceed his marginal costs, he may be enabled to take on that business only because he is charging rates in excess of MC on other parts of his business. We return below to this possible conflict between the dictates of economic efficiency (marginal-cost pricing for all) and the covering of total costs, as a possible consideration justifying restriction of cream-skimming competition.

The final possibility, of course, is that the skimmed-milk markets *are* a burden on the regulated company, because they do not cover their own separable, marginal costs. In this event those markets are being internally subsidized—a practice that is inacceptable on purely economic grounds.[149]

To summarize, then, the economic case against prohibitions of cream-skimming is that they are either unnecessary or a means of preserving an inefficient rate structure, and in either case an undesirable interference with the competitive pressures that provide the best possible guarantee of optimum performance, both statically and dynamically.

Possible Cases Against Cream-Skimming

The foregoing constitutes a very powerful argument for permitting competition the freest possible play even in public utility industries. It exerts its disciplinary influence where it actually occurs and where it does not. If a natural monopolist is producing and pricing as efficiently as possible, there is no need to bar competitive entry: it is economically unnecessary and will not take place anyhow. The legal barrier is effective only where customers in the creamy markets are being exploited; here competition will spring forth, if it is permitted, precisely because and to the extent that it is required. The burden of proof, and it is a heavy one, must be borne by those who advocate restrictions on competition in order to prevent alleged cream-skimming.

At the same time, it is possible to construct a checklist of possible bases for regulatory intervention on all three grounds suggested at the beginning of this discussion: (1) economic efficiency, (2) institutional inadequacies of competition, and (3) extraeconomic considerations. As we proceed to analyze these cases, we shall at an early point find it necessary to define "cream skimming" more carefully than is usually done. At times the term is used—typically by those seeking to ban the practice—when "competition" would be just as accurate, the more colorful designation being selected perhaps because it has a more negative connotation. Competition is always more or less selective; naturally it tends to focus on the more lucrative markets and to shun the others. Some items in our checklist will turn out, therefore, simply to be possible cases against competition generally; others will turn out to relate to cream-skimming as a special kind of competition that may indeed produce a special kind of undesirable result.

The Imperfections of Competition Case. Pure competition brings price into equality with short-run marginal cost. It is only under perfect competition that price will be equated continuously and costlessly to SRMC, LRMC and ATC, all at the same time, under conditions of long-run constant or increasing costs.[150] The very case for regulation is, in part, that in the real world competition is highly imperfect. This is really the kernel of the natural monopoly case for limiting entry. Why will not such monopolies arise "naturally" and without governmental assistance or protection—either as a result of the process of competition between existing firms or because no rational firm would choose to enter such an industry in the first place, since it could not hope to be able to survive in competition with that monopolist? The case for regulation must be that an uncontrolled

[149] See, for example, pp. 190–191, Volume 1, above.
[150] See note 25, Chapter 3 of Volume 1, p. 74.

On the problem of decreasing costs, see the following subsection of the present discussion.

market would not produce the monopoly result efficiently. Competitors might enter, if permitted to do, in expectation of being able to sell out. Or the several competitors might find it more profitable to live and let live, with rate payers bearing the burden of their excessive costs: there may exist no reliable institutional mechanism for driving out the excessive number of firms, concentrating production in the hands of the natural monopolist, and bringing costs and prices down to the minimum, technologically feasible level.

As we have already observed, the destructive competition argument, similarly, is grounded on alleged imperfections of competition—imperfect knowledge on the part of investors, which may result in excessive investment; immobility of capital and labor, which can produce destructive competition when capacity is excessive; and limited consumer knowledge, which can permit deterioration of service.[151]

So the presence of imperfections weakens the general case we have set forth in the defense of unrestricted cream-skimming. If competitors do enter a market, that case states, the presumption is that the customers were previously paying excessive prices; but this is so only if the entrants have correctly forecast their own costs and market prospects. If customers shift to the new suppliers, the presumption is they are better off with these new alternatives; but this is so only if customers correctly judge their respective qualities. And so on. If these conditions of perfection are not met or approximated, unrestricted cream-skimming can lead to waste, instability of rates, and deterioration of service.

There is no way of laying down general rules, a priori, for deciding whether imperfections of competition justify regulation to prevent cream-skimming. As against the possible imperfections of the competitive process must be weighed the corresponding imperfections of monopoly or regulation, which we have already amply observed. The burden of any mistakes that are made under competition is borne, in large measure, by the businessmen themselves; the burden of the mistakes of monopoly or of its ineffective regulation is borne principally by the consumer. For these reasons, most economists would incline to the competitive solution. The corollary of this rule is that the regulated companies themselves ought ordinarily to be permitted to meet competition by reducing their own rates toward long-run marginal costs. This would tend to forestall unjustified entry into the more lucrative market and give fullest possible recognition to the possible efficiency advantages of natural monopoly.[151a]

The Discrimination Problem. The central problem of cream-skimming is the problem of rate discrimination—of the relative remunerativeness of rates in the rich and the poor markets. If rates for all categories of service were at their respective marginal costs, there would be little purely economic basis for restricting competition. The difficulties arise when MC is below ATC, necessitating—or at least raising the possible desirability of—the kinds of discrimination described in Chapter 5 of our Volume 1.

The fact that most public utility rates must exceed marginal cost if average total costs are to be covered does not in itself constitute a sufficient case against competitive cream-skimming. On the contrary, it is the general

---

principle that no class of customers ought to be charged more than the total costs of serving them alone that justifies competition, as a means of preventing exploitation. But serious problems are raised by the fact that such competition is typically highly selective and hence discriminatory.

We have considered at length, in Chapter 6 of Volume 1, the applicable principles in circumstances like these and need only point out here their relationship to the cream-skimming problem. The first rule was that where a particular group of customers could in fact be supplied *alone* at rates lower than those currently charged them, it is appropriate to permit competition to drive rates down to that level, even though the consequent rate structure is discriminatory. The familiar example would be the case that we described of the two towns, A and C, connected by both a river and a rail line that passes through an intermediate town, B, that is not on the river. Here is a case for competitive entry by the water carriers, even if it threatens to "skim the cream" of the railroad's business, and for freedom of the railroad in turn to reduce its A to C rates as far down to marginal costs as necessary to keep the business.[152]

The important thing to notice about this case is that it is not cheaper for the *railroads* to carry the AC than the AB traffic. The "cost justification" for the discrimination is to be found in the fact that (1) AC can be served, by *water*, at an average total cost lower than that of the rail service, (2) its traffic can be retained by the rails at rates in excess of MC, and (3) permitting the discrimination will result in having the transportation function performed at lower total costs to society.

In the case of competition between two roundabout railroads, in contrast, we found no such "cost justification" and therefore no economic justification on grounds of static efficiency for permitting the discrimination.

Here, then, we have two models of competitive and discriminatory price reductions, one of them justifiable, the other not, on grounds of economic efficiency. (The latter is even less justifiable, it seems reasonable to state, on grounds of fairness.) Competition of both these kinds has, as we shall see, been criticized on the ground that it involves cream-skimming. But, strictly speaking, it need not. There is no necessity, in either of these cases, for the AC traffic to be more lucrative than the AB: what we have, merely, is one market in which competition is feasible and another in which it is not. The effect of competition, in these instances, is not to "skim the cream" but to *convert* the competitive market into skimmed milk, and in the proper circumstances to justify price discrimination where none need have prevailed before.

Of course, if one defines as "creamy" whatever business is worth competing for, whether nondiscriminatorily (as by the water carrier) or by the offer of selective rate reductions, then all competition is by definition cream-skimming. But if the latter term is to define an independent phenomenon it must apply to the competition for customers that are making a disproportionately large contribution to overheads.[153] It is for this reason that there is a general

---

[152] See pp. 167–168 and the ensuing pages in Volume 1, on which this discussion draws.

[153] The fact that if entry were free competitors would operate only when and where the traffic is heaviest does not at all demonstrate that these markets represent the "cream." As John Hibbs

points out, in assessing the argument for restricting allegedly cream-skimming competition in the passenger bus business,

"This argument fails to take into account that operation through the peak is likely to yield a presumption in favor of *true* cream-skimming; it tends to *eliminate* unjustified price discrimination. It is *noncream-skimming* competition that should be subjected to special scrutiny, because of the possibility that it may *introduce* unjustified price discrimination. In short, it is precisely because competition of this sort may *not* constitute cream-skimming that it may be economically undesirable.

What we have identified, then, is three distinct cases of what is often called cream-skimming—using that term to characterize any competition that reduces the contribution of some portions of a public utility business to joint or common costs and therefore either endangers the service to other customers or imposes on them a greater share of the burden:

1. True cream-skimming—competition for customers who are being discriminated *against*.[154] This was the case when the motor carriers took away the high value-of-service business of the rails and the nonscheduled airlines moved into the high-volume, peak-season traffic.[155] This competition is presumptively justified as a means of eliminating discrimination *against* the market on which the proposed competition would focus.

2. The rail-water carrier case. This is not a true case of cream-skimming. But competitive entry is justified, because the entrant is able to carry the contested traffic at an ATC below the rates of the existing supplier, and the latter in turn may for this reason be justified in discriminating in *favor* of customers in that market.

3. The rail-rail case, in which the introduction of discrimination in favor of customers in the competitive markets enjoys no such justification.[156]

---

lower net revenue to the monopolist, since that part of his fleet that is needed for peak operation alone and is idle the rest of the day is very costly. . . .

"The 'all day' operator should welcome his appearance [that is, that of the independent or 'pirate'] when traffic is heavy. If he is prepared to carry some of the peak traffic, while in no way reducing the off-peak loadings of the all-day operator, then the latter will find his net revenue increased." *Transport for Passengers*, Hobart Paper 23, Institute of Economic Affairs, London, 1963, 34–35.

[154] They may be the "victims" of discrimination in either of two different ways. (1) Existing suppliers may be practicing internal subsidization—charging rates above *their own* ATC of serving customers A alone in order to charge customers B rates below MC. The railroads have done this to some extent, as we have seen. The practice was economically indefensible even in the absence of the motor-carrier alternative; and one major objection to the Motor Carrier Act of 1935 is that it perpetuated it. (2) The discrimination may be economically justified in accordance with the principles summarized in

Chapter 5 of Volume 1: all customers pay at least their MC; the practice is therefore beneficial even to the customers who are being discriminated against. This was certainly originally true in large measure of rail value-of-service rates (see pp. 155–156, Volume 1, above). But the advent of the truck removed much of the economic justification, because the *new competitors* could serve the disfavored markets at an ATC lower than the rates previously charged them.

[155] See, however, the observation of Hibbs, note 153, above. But when the nonscheduled airlines invaded the New York to Miami market in the winter season and shifted to the transatlantic business in the summer, there was little reason to doubt that they *were* invading the more lucrative markets that had thitherto been subsidizing the low-density and off-season traffic. For evidence that airline costs decrease markedly with route density, so that the most heavily travelled routes are the most profitable, see Straszheim, *op. cit.*, 92–100, 110, 148, and Appendix B.

[156] As we have seen in Volume 1, pp. 168–170, there are instances of rail-rail competition in which such discrimination is justified, for reasons similar to those of the rail-water carrier case.

It will be useful to keep these three separate models in mind as we proceed to examine the three important recent cases in the field of communications in which cream-skimming was allegedly involved.

In the two major microwave cases (*above-890* and *MCI*),[157] one ground on which the common carriers asked the FCC to disallow the applications was that the applicants were would-be cream-skimmers:

> "They . . . argued that, if the Commission were to extend microwave eligibility to all those who seek it, the common carriers would stand to lose so much revenue that they would have to compensate for it by increasing their rates to the general public. . . . In this connection, Western Union claimed that . . . the addition of another competitive possibility, namely a private point-to-point communications system . . . might well destroy the ability of the telegraph company to operate at all."[158]

Similarly, in *MCI:*

> "possibly their principal complaint . . . is that, as Bell writes . . . 'Grant of the Applications Would Threaten The Integrity of The Nationwide Communications Rate Structure . . .' and Western Union . . . that 'MCI, by its own admission, seeks to enter a specialized and attractive market, with rate based on a particular microwave facility on a particular low cost route.' They assail MCI as a cream-skimmer, lapping up the profits on favorable routes and eschewing high-cost low-return service; accordingly, they say, on losing profitable routes (where expenses were relatively low) to a cream-skimmer, they would be compelled to reexamine their own rate structures, which distribute total costs for their undifferentiated service among customers favorably and unfavorably situated. They would have to saddle high charges then on high-cost users, instead of homogenizing the costs among all."[159]

It was partly for similar reasons that the FCC put tight restrictions on the ability of large users of communications services to deal directly with Comsat:

> "Sound policy indicates that . . . they [the terrestrial common carriers] should not be required to depend solely on ComSat for satellite circuits while ComSat is simultaneously allowed to syphon the most profitable part of the business from them. . . .

> "we find that revenues from leased circuits provide an important, if not indispensable, part of the carriers' total receipts. . . . Reports to the Commission show that in 1965 these carriers, as a whole, had net operating revenues, before Federal income taxes, of about \$20,300,000. Their revenues from leased circuit services for the same year were \$20,200,000. . . . Because of the relatively low nonfixed or variable costs associated with this service, the loss of such business could come close to wiping out completely the record carriers' earnings. . . .

> "The danger of the loss by the terrestrial carriers of existing or additional leased circuit business to satellite facilities is not merely theoretical. A recent complaint . . . and a press release issued by ComSat . . . indicate

---

[157] See our discussion of the natural monopoly aspects of these cases at pp. 129–136 and 146–152, above.

[158] FCC, *Above 890* Report and Order, 27 FCC

359, 390–391 (1959).

[159] FCC, *MCI* Initial Decision, *op. cit.*, note 58, Chapter 4, par. 93 (1967).

that ComSat would propose to charge both authorized users and carriers approximately the same amount for leased circuits and that the amount is substantially below current or recently proposed charges for leased cable circuits. Accordingly, the terrestrial carriers could reasonably be expected to lose a substantial share of their leased circuit revenues to ComSat. Under these conditions and in light of the data set forth above, it could very well be necessary to permit these carriers to increase rates charged other users in order to enable them to earn a fair return. Certainly such a detriment to the vast majority of users for the apparent benefit of a few large users would be in derogation of the objectives of the Act. The fact is that the Satellite Act requires the opposite result, namely, that the benefits of these lower rates be made available to all users."[160]

In part, genuine (and justified) cream-skimming of our type 1 was involved in these cases. That is, the proposed entry was into high-density, low-cost markets that the common carriers were, by their uniform rate policies, in effect forcing to subsidize the lower-density, high-cost traffic. On purely economic grounds, competitive entry in circumstances such as these should be not merely permitted but applauded.[161] As the Examiner remarked in *MCI:*

"The averaging method is embodied neither in the Decalogue nor in the Constitution. Without danger to the republic, there may be a weighing of the possible public benefits or disadvantages resulting from authorizing competition in selected areas . . .

"Clearly, if the averaging doctrine is sacrosanct (and 'cream-skimming' is an attendant horrific) to the extent the carriers claim, they have insulated themselves against private line competition except from carriers with unlikely initial operations as widespread as theirs. They are like courtiers who deign to accept challenges for duels only from those of equal rank. But the efforts of a relatively impoverished newcomer, proposing a novel if by no means faultless service, to give battle on his chosen ground, should not be impaled by this agency upon a principle devised by his opponents."[162]

There is another respect in which the microwave cases may fall within our first category. MCI proposed to perform no function other than the operation of the radio path, from one geographic point to another; and one reason it was able to do so cheaply was that its system was far less adequately protected against emergencies and outages than the facilities of the common carriers. It conceded that its commercial feasibility depended also on the ability of its customers to interconnect with the facilities of the common

---

[160] FCC, *Authorized Users* decision, 4 FCC 2d 421, 431–433 (1966).

[161] See pp. 147–148, 150–151, above. See, however, the possible externalities consideration mentioned at that point.

[162] *MCI* Initial Decision, pars. 110, 112. Herman Schwartz' defense of the Commission's Comsat *Authorized Users* decision offers support for the view that the users of leased channels who wanted to deal directly with the satellite cor-poration were victims of a system that forced them to subsidize the general message service:

"Such a policy [that is, that of the FCC] has obvious advantages, especially if Comsat's cost advantages were to be used only for 'cream-skimming' while the far less lucrative general message service, which accounts for most of the traffic, was left to the carriers and forced to support itself." *Op. cit., Yale Law Jour.* (January 1967), LXXVI: 471–472.

carriers, in order to give them end-to-end communications service. The carriers objected, therefore, that customers could subscribe to the MCI service only because they knew they could always call on the backup facilities of the common carriers if it broke down; that, by leaving it to the carriers to bear the financial burdens of providing backup and interconnection, MCI was improperly skimming the cream. It would seem that this problem, like the national average-cost pricing of the common carriers that helped create the opportunity for MCI's entry in the first place, is one of rate structure. If charges for the backup and interconnection services were high enough to cover the capacity costs of the common carriers' fulfilling, or standing ready to fulfill, those obligations, these responsibilities would not limit their ability to compete for the creamy part of the business. To put it another way, if the backup and interconnection services do represent the skimmed milk, the rates for which are subsidized by revenues from the portion of the business that MCI tried to serve, it would appear here as well that the latter's proposed cream-skimming represented a healthy competitive reaction to an improperly discriminatory rate structure.[163]

Apart from these specific instances of genuine cream-skimming in response to internal subsidization, the competition at issue in these cases seems to fall in our category 3. Customers in all three instances were attempting to get direct access to the benefits of new, lower-cost technology. These benefits would have flowed to them not because it was cheaper to serve them than the customers who would have remained dependent on the common carriers, but merely because they were in a position to take direct advantage of this new opportunity, whereas the general users of telephone and telegraph services were not. (It was only the large users of leased circuits who could afford to put in their own private microwave systems or would be served by MCI or could hope to deal directly with Comsat.) The problem was that the marginal costs of service by the most modern and efficient facilities were markedly below the carrier rates, based as they were on the composite costs of old and new facilities.[164]

Ideally, all users should have been charged only the lower ATC_n; but this would not have covered the company's total cost of service. In so far as there was no basis *on the cost side* for singling out some users as deserving that favorable treatment while leaving to others a disproportionate part of the

---

[163] But see also on this the discussion of option demand, pp. 238–240, below, which raises the possibility that adequate backup facilities cannot be provided or properly charged for in a competitive market.

[164] The rates Comsat was charging the common carriers for leased circuits, and that it proposed to offer direct, authorized users, were far below the rates that the carriers were in turn charging their customers. FCC, *Authorized Users* decision, 4 FCC 2d 421, 433 (1966). As one example, Schwartz cites the $4,000 per month per circuit that Comsat charged the Defense Department with the $7,100 per month proposed by the carriers. *Op. cit., Yale Law Jour.* (January 1967), LXXVI: 471, note 143. Claudia Goldin cites others: for example, in the early part of 1967

Comsat's rate to the carriers for a leased half-circuit (from the U.S. earth station to the satellite; the charge for the other half-circuit is set by the foreign agency or government) was $2,700 per month, for communication between New York and Europe, whereas the carriers' rate was $8,000. *The Economic Effects of the Introduction of Satellite Communications in the International Communications Industry,* honors thesis, Department of Economics, Cornell University, May 1967, 29–30. The carriers claimed, in the FCC proceedings, that they "transform . . . a 'raw channel' into a usable circuit." But the non-carrier users argued that they did not require these carrier services and pleaded for the right to deal directly with Comsat. *Ibid.,* 59.

burden of covering total, historic costs, it was indeed the responsibility of the FCC to question whether the selective competition proposed in these cases was economically justified.[165] In short, it appears that the situations fall partly within our category 3. To the extent that there was no inherent reason on the cost side to have the lower rates extended to the big rather than the small users (as in our cases 1 and 2), there is no basis for attributing to the FCC a policy of protecting a system of internal subsidization. (We consider presently whether there may have been a justification on the *demand* side.) The big users were no more subsidizing the small than the reverse.

To the extent that these factual assumptions apply, the FCC's *above-890* and *MCI* decisions were wrong and *Authorized Users* right. The Commission was to this extent justified, in the latter case, in trying to see to it that the benefits of satellite technology were passed on equally to small users and to large, to customers of the common carriers as well as to private users:

> "under unrestricted dealings between ComSat and noncarriers, large users might tend to contract directly with ComSat, while members of the general public are left to deal with the carriers. In such circumstances, it would be clearly impossible for the Commission to carry out its responsibility under Section 201(c)(5) to '. . . insure that any economies made possible by a communications satellite system are appropriately reflected in rates for *public* communications service.'"[166]

> "The foregoing considerations are thus consistent with the general concept pervading the Satellite Act of ComSat as . . . primarily a carrier's carrier, created to provide at least the space segment of international communications as part of an improved global communications network consisting of *all* means of providing such communications services, so that lower rates should be possible to all the using public."[167]

But there remain important reasons for holding to the opposite view: that *above-890* and *MCI* were on balance good decisions and *Authorized Users* questionable. There is the fact, first, that the system-wide average cost pricing by the carriers involves internal subsidization, which increased competition would in all cases have helped correct.

Second, the FCC's cost-averaging policy applies not just geographically but also to facilities embodying new and old technology:

> "rates for communications services are not to depend upon the facility used. Rather, 'composite rates' are to be charged which represent an average of the costs of *all* facilities, new and old, in order to prevent users of the new facility from receiving lower rates than users of the old."[168]

---

[165] It might appear, at first glance, that the situation here would fall into our category 2, the rail-water carrier case, with Comsat (and MCI and private microwave) playing the role of the water carrier—able to serve certain customers at an ATC lower than the ATC of the common carriers previously serving them and therefore properly permitted to do so. But to the extent that this lower ATC was the result not of any inherent advantage of the favored customers corresponding to the location of the AC towns on the river—that is, to the extent that increases in the demand for communications services by large and smaller users equally could have been satisfied by use of the new technology—the large users who happened to have direct access to it had no special claim on efficiency grounds to its lower costs.

[166] Stress supplied. *Authorized Users* Decision, 4 FCC 2d 421, 428 (1966).

[167] *Ibid.*, par. 24.

[168] Schwartz, *op. cit., Yale Law Jour.* (January 1967), LXXVI: 471.

This policy is the correct one where the marginal costs of supplying all users are in fact the same, regardless of which facilities happen to be serving them.[169] But if there are certain groups of customers whose demand is such that it can be satisfied only by the use of the higher-cost facility (and this would be true also if their demand grew and capacity had to be expanded to serve it), and other customers who, regardless of the particular facilities by which they are *actually* being served, could in fact be served by the newer, lower-cost technology, then they constitute two separate markets, with different marginal costs. To charge those two groups uniform rates, representing an average of the high and the low-cost facilities, would be economically inefficient, unduly subsidizing the former customers and discouraging purchases by the latter.

This was apparently the consequence of the FCC's cost-averaging policy. Averaging domestic and international line-haul costs together evidently forced the international users, who alone could benefit by the availability of the satellite, to subsidize domestic communications services. It also must uneconomically have retarded the application of that new technology, since its cost savings were not passed on fully in rates to those customers who alone were in a position to take advantage of it. To the extent that some of those customers could deal directly with Comsat, the latter's cream-skimming entry into competition with the common carriers would have helped eliminate these distortions.

The distortion was accentuated by the fact that the costs and revenues from the international operations of the communications common carriers are a tiny fraction of their system-wide totals. Any cost-savings that they obtain by leasing circuits from Comsat therefore would have been utterly submerged in their aggregate costs of service. The FCC was aware of this danger, however. And so, while it declined to permit Comsat to compete more freely and directly with the carriers, it did order the latter to reflect directly in their international rates the large cost savings made possible by the satellite:

> "Satellite circuits now becoming available should enable the carriers to secure facilities at lower costs in relation to terrestrial facilities and thereby permit them to reduce rates to reflect such cost reductions. We therefore expect the common carriers promptly to give further review to their current rate schedules and file revisions which fully reflect the economies made available through the leasing of circuits in the satellite system. Failure of the carriers to do so promptly and effectively will require the Commission to take such actions as are appropriate. Even though satellite circuits are not now and will not for some time be available to all points to which users presently lease circuits from terrestrial carriers, implementation of this policy by the carriers should also reduce charges to many points to which satellite circuits are not now available."[170]

---

[169] The fact that in a given community certain customers may be supplied electricity from an old plant, while adding the requirements of new customers will call for the construction of a new, lower-cost plant, provides no economic basis for charging the two groups different rates: their marginal costs are the same. See p. 140, Volume 1, above. And so would their average costs be equal, if economically correct depreciation were charged. See p. 121, Volume 1.

[170] *Authorized Users* Decision, 4 FCC 2d 421, 434–435 (1966). AT&T did in fact file substantially reduced rates in the latter part of that year. *Wall Street Journal*, December 29, 1966, 8.

Our analysis of the cream-skimming aspect of these decisions has concentrated thus far on the question of whether the customers who were or would have been favored by the proposed competition "deserved" the lower rates it would have brought, as far as the relative *costs* of serving them were concerned. We must inquire, additionally, whether differential treatment might have been justified because of differences on the demand side. Long-distance communication is, as we have seen, outstandingly characterized by increasing returns, which strongly recommend discriminatory price reductions to markets of elastic demand. And it is, indeed, likely that some portions of the markets that benefited by the microwave decisions and would have benefited by freer access to direct dealing with Comsat are highly elastic: witness the explosive growth in business use of communications services as the lower-cost opportunities have become available to them.[171] For this to justify differential rate reductions to these users, however, it is their total demand that must be relatively elastic and not the demand for the services of one source of supply (private microwave, or MCI, or Comsat) as against another (for example, AT&T). We simply do not know whether this condition obtains—whether, that is, the aggregate demand of these particular users of long-distance communications is any more elastic than the demand of patrons not in a position to set up their own microwave systems or deal directly with MCI or Comsat.

What we do know however is that competition—cream-skimming or not—is usually a more effective institutional mechanism than regulated monopoly for probing the elasticity of demand and encouraging the application of new technology. It is these dynamic, institutional considerations that provide the strongest support for the microwave decisions and the main reason for questioning *Authorized Users*. The principal and compelling demonstration of the numerous applicants in *above-890* was their desire and ability to provide lower-priced communications services than had thitherto been available to them, and what the Examiner proposed to give MCI was an opportunity to demonstrate that it could do the same thing. In *above-890*, the Commission explicitly recognized the potential advantages of the "competitive spur in the manufacturing of equipment and in the development of the communications art."[172] In *MCI*, the Examiner underlined the advantages of permitting the proposed competitive test of the elasticity of demand.[173]

What was disappointingly lacking in the *Authorized Users* decision was any

---

Again, when in its controversial TAT–5 decision, in 1968, the FCC authorized the carriers to lay a new transatlantic cable, it imposed the condition that they reduce charges for message telephone and private line voice-grade channel service by 25 to 30 percent. *TAT–5 Decision*, 13 FCC 2d 235, par. 10 (1968).

[171] In the *MCI* case, the Examiner was impressed by the possibility of a large, untapped demand for lower-cost communications services (see his *Initial Decision*, pars. 57, 80, 109, 113). On the other hand, it is of course difficult to ascertain to what extent this growth in business use has been a response to reduced price, to what extent a reflection of expanded demand.

[172] 27 FCC 359, 414 (1959).

"the private users uniformly took the position that, if the Commission were to restrict private microwave where there is available common carrier service, there would be a lessening of competition and a fostering of a monopoly in the manufacture, sale, and use of communications facilities contrary to the public interest. They claimed that such a policy would thwart the improvement and experimentation that accompany competition among manufacturers for the private users' market, and would kill the very incentive for common carriers to improve their service." *Ibid.*, 395.

[173] See pp. 134–135, above.

explicit recognition by the Commission of the similar, dynamic advantages that a less restrictive ruling would have provided. In view of the greater incentive of the established common carriers to use and expand their own terrestrial facilities than to lease additional circuits from Comsat,[174] it would seem particularly important to free the latter company for effective competition with the carriers rather than leave it in a position in which it would be the latter through whom it would have to deal and who would, therefore, be in a position to determine how rapidly use of the satellite would be pressed. That the Commission was not unaware of this danger is indicated by the condition it attached to its approval of the TAT-5, requiring the common carriers to use the new cable and satellite facilities proportionately.[175] It is important to recognize that in markets that are inevitably imperfect, the quest of strong competitors for purely strategic advantages, bearing no necessary relationship to their relative efficiency in serving the public, can be a very powerful force for improved market performance.[176] Even if the large prospective users of private communications systems did not, on efficiency grounds, "deserve" lower rates or costs than other less favorably situated customers, their pressure for such advantages and ability to take advantage of the lower costs promised by the new technology undoubtedly promoted its more rapid development and put corresponding pressures on the common carriers to improve their own service offerings.[177]

The Promotional Case. When a major purpose of regulation is to promote the growth of a new industry, regulators are tempted to prevent cream-skimmers from coming in too early, in order to give the original enterpriser an opportunity to reap the rewards of his pioneering efforts, as well as to hold down the subsidies that the Government may still be paying the industry. If the markets created by costly promotional endeavours can, once those efforts have produced the desired results, immediately be appropriated or invaded by free-loading competitors who have not themselves had to bear the cost of the original promotion, the efforts may never be undertaken in the first place. And if competitive entry is prevented, the monopoly profits that can be earned on the profitable parts of the business can cut down the amount of subsidy that the taxpayer has to contribute.[178] The point is that competition alone does not always necessarily cause an industry to do all the things we want it to do. We have already suggested the analogy to the case for a patent system and for the limitations on competition that it entails.

The purely economic aspect of the promotional argument (we set aside for the moment the possibility that government might wish to promote the development of an industry for such purposes as national defense) is based on alleged externalities: competition would prevent those who incurred the

---

[174] See our discussion of this problem in Chapter 2, pp. 51–52, above.

[175] See note 89, Chapter 2, p. 76, above.

[176] See Dirlam and Kahn, *Fair Competition*, 142–144, 150–152, 173–175, 182–184, 202–205, and *passim*.

[177] For a strong statement of this argument see the testimony of William Vickrey in FCC, *In the Matter of AT&T*, Dockets 16258 and 15011, Networks Exhibit No. 5, July 22, 1968, processed,

65–67. On AT&T's pricing response to the *above-890* decision, see Chapter 4, p. 132, above. In the international sphere, it was apparently only after the direct pressures by the FCC and the threat of direct Comsat competition that the carriers put into effect the substantial rate reductions reflected in Table 2 of our Chapter 3. *Wall Street Journal*, March 7, 1966, 7 and June 29, 1966, 4.

[178] See pp. 3–4, Chapter 1, above.

costs of promoting an industry's expansion from appropriating enough of the benefits to justify the effort. It could well be, for example, that the offering of regular airline service in thin markets and off-season promotes the demand for service generally. If some line runs a feeder service from remote cities in upstate New York to New York City, it will, in so doing, also promote more air travel between New York and Miami. Similarly, if there are regular flights between New York and Miami in the off-peak, summer season, this may help promote travel in the busy winter as well—for example, the summer tourists, by providing additional net revenues to hotels, make possible lower rates during the peak season. If, then, irregular airlines were permitted to enter only the New York to Miami route and only during the winter, they would be reaping where others had sown. This possible market failure would be prevented if one company enjoyed a monopoly in the peak business, in which case it would be the sole beneficiary of its off-peak promotional efforts, or if all airlines participating in the peak traffic were required to set up a joint venture to run the off-peak service, bearing its costs in proportion to their enjoyment of the external benefits.[179] Either arrangement would require denying access to the cream to any firm that did not bear its proper share of the skimmed milk.

Why, however, would any company wish to take on a losing operation merely because it generated additional business for other parts of its operation? There would seem to be only two possibilities, which we can best illustrate with the airlines example. The first and most obvious one is that the second service—the New York to Miami run during the winter—is supernormally profitable. If this is so, it clearly suggests that the purchasers of that service are subsidizing the other—passengers between Ithaca and New York City—in which event the argument against cream-skimming turns, once again, into an argument for the preservation of an economically indefensible internal subsidization.

The second possibility is that the New York to Miami business is not supernormally profitable but is subject to increasing returns. That is, its MC might be less than ATC, because of the presence of either excess capacity or incompletely exploited economies of scale. It could be, then, that the additional New York to Miami traffic generated by the Ithaca to New York run covers its marginal costs (including the losses on the feeder operation), without necessarily bringing in more than its ATC. In this event, the off-peak service would not be a burden on the peak customers, but would make a net contribution to covering some of their joint or overhead costs.

[179] This point is made, briefly, also by James R. Nelson, *op. cit.*, *The Antitrust Bulletin* (January–April 1966), XI: 29. One example of the latter remedy is the joint operation of unprofitable helicopter service between airports by the major airlines benefiting from it. For example, the CAB in 1968 permitted Pan American World Airways and Trans World Airways jointly to purchase the stock of New York Airways, which operates helicopters between Newark, Kennedy, and LaGuardia Airports. CAB Press Release, July 31, 1968. In another proceeding the same year, it issued a certificate for helicopter service between Washington and Baltimore airports to Washington Airways, which had been organized by ten of the 14 scheduled air carriers serving the area. It justified this "departure from our traditional selection of an independent operator to provide a proposed service" on the ground "that the problem of providing economically viable scheduled passenger helicopter service in our metropolitan areas has proven to be exceedingly complex," pointing out that the new service would require considerable financial assistance, which, presumably, only the interested lines would be willing to offer. Press release, November 21, 1968.

This seems a valid, hypothetical economic argument for opposing competitive entry into profitable business, since supply of the off-peak services might cease if the external benefits were skimmed off by competitors.

In fact, the latter case is probably not a good one as applied to the airlines. There is no reason, a priori, to expect that the additional traffic generated by the off-peak service would neatly fit into the airline schedules in such a way as to promote improved load factors; on the contrary, that demand, too, would doubtless have the same peak as the other and require a proportionate expansion in capacity. As for the possibility that it might eventuate in the fuller realization of potential economies of scale, the evidence does not suggest the continuing presence of long-run decreasing costs in airlines within the relevant range.[180] Moreover, if there were significantly increasing returns enjoyed by existing companies operating at the peak, it is difficult to see how new entrants could successfully challenge them.

These considerations do not destroy the promotional case for monopoly, on purely logical grounds. But it is important to emphasize that competition may be a much more effective and powerful promoter than monopoly. Consider, for example, the very important contribution made to the growth of the U.S. airlines industry by the nonscheduled carriers. They received no subsidy and were in varying degrees harassed by the CAB, but persisted in trying by one device or another to get into the lucrative parts of the business. And by their vigorous promotional efforts, not least of them the offer of lower rates, it was they who demonstrated how great and elastic was the potential demand for passenger air service. Moreover, as analyses of the patent system have made abundantly clear, the promotional argument is hardly one for unlimited monopoly, of unlimited duration. Innovation requires the proper combination of protection and competition.[181]

In most situations, external (that is, taxpayer-financed) subsidies are probably a far more efficient method than the protection of monopoly for promoting a more rapid industrial development, because they can directly provide such additional incentives as may be required while taking full advantage of the promotional effects of competition as well. Devising the optimal system of subsidies, whether external or internal, is an extremely difficult task and one that has rarely been done well—on the basis of a careful appraisal of the respective costs and benefits of alternative devices.[182]

---

[180] See Caves, *Air Transport and its Regulators*, 57–61; Locklin, *op. cit.*, 805–806 and the sources cited there; and Straszheim, *op. cit.*, 95–96. See also pp. 149–150 of Volume 1. This summary statement probably does not do justice to this complex question. There is evidence of economies of scale with increasing traffic density on particular routes (see note 155, this chapter, above). But there is evidence also of internal subsidization—that is, of unjustified discrimination against traffic on dense routes; and the question remains: if there are such economies of scale, why is it necessary to restrict entry artificially?

[181] See Kahn, "The Role of Patents," in John Perry Miller, ed., *Competition, Cartels and Their Regulation* (Amsterdam: North-Holland Publishing Company, 1962), 308–346; and Fritz Machlup, *An Economic Review of the Patent System*, U. S. Senate, Committee on the Judiciary, Subcommittee on Patents, Trademarks, and Copyrights, 85th Cong. 1st Sess. (1958).

[182] For a description of the various subsidies provided the United States airlines industry, see Locklin, *op. cit.*, 764–770, 784–787, 817–823. On some of the defects of the system, see Keyes, *Federal Control of Entry Into Air Transportation*, Chapter 8, and *op. cit.*, *Jour. Air Law and Commerce* (Spring 1955), XXII: 192–202; Gray, "The Airlines Industry," in Walter Adams, ed., *op. cit.*, 3rd ed., 487–490, and Caves, *Air Transport and its Regulators*, 403–418.

Externalities, Option Demand and the Tyranny of Small Decisions. Externalities are especially pervasive in the public utility sector, as we have already observed[183]—almost as a matter of definition, since one important reason for singling these industries out for special public supervision and subsidy is the wide spread of their effects. In particular, there exists a wide range of situations in these industries in which the total benefits that society derives, or thinks it derives, from the continued provision of their services exceeds what can be collected from their several customers at prices equated to marginal cost.

This kind of phenomenon is quite easy to see in cases where the provision of a service to some customers confers indirect benefits on others. The quality of life in New York, Chicago, and Los Angeles may be improved by the continued availability of plane, electricity, and telephone service in rural areas, because it helps keep other people happy to live there and so reduces urban congestion. These "external beneficiaries" might be willing, therefore, to pay something to keep rural areas pleasant and comparatively accessible places in which to live. Internal subsidization is one way of accomplishing this.[184] It is, of course, a highly imperfect device: it is not clear why air travelers or telephone subscribers in particular should bear the cost of the benefits of reduced congestion that accrue to entire localities; or why such other beneficiaries as the owners of real estate in the subsidized communities should not also bear part of the costs.[185] But it may be the best device practically available. And it is one that is undermined by cream-skimming entry into the markets that carry the burden of subsidy.

One instance of particular importance among the public utilities derives from the great value of having suppliers at all times ready and able to serve, on demand. Burton A. Weisbrod has described as one external benefit resulting from the actual supply of particular goods or services the mere *availability* of the service to *nonusers*: the service that they enjoy is the *option* to use the facilities whenever they wish. He points out that the competitive market may fail to satisfy this "option demand," when (1) the option is not in fact exercised (or not exercised with sufficient frequency), (2) revenues

---

[183] See pp. 193–195, Volume 1, above.

[184] Once again, the airline example is not a very good one. True, the CAB does to some extent require the certificated, trunk airlines to serve unremunerative markets as the price of their certification for the profitable ones. But once the major airlines stopped receiving governmental subsidies on the basis of financial need (all but one of them after 1957), they lost interest in continuing the unremunerative runs (the revenue deficiencies of which they had been able theretofore to have filled by the subsidy) and dropped them in large numbers. See Caves, *Air Transport and its Regulators*, 403. On the relation of externalities to the case for internal subsidization in communications, see pp. 150–151, Chapter 4, above.

Telephone service provides another interesting example of external economies, though one with little practical relevance to the question of cream-

skimming. The value of telephone service to any one subscriber depends on the number of other people who have phones. These benefits are of course mutual: as long, therefore, as each person with whom existing subscribers might conceivably wish to communicate rates the benefits to himself sufficiently high to justify his subscribing, no problem is raised by the fact that his doing so also confers benefits on others. But a case of genuine market failure could arise if any such person was either unable or, after comparing the costs and benefits to himself, unwilling to pay for the service: the resulting loss of benefits to other subscribers would not be reflected in his calculation. This possibility does suggest a valid basis for rate discrimination on the basis of relative elasticities of demand.

[185] This is part of the justification of local communities paying part of the costs of operating airports.

from *actual* purchasers are insufficient to cover the costs of continued operation, and (3) "expansion or recommencement of production at the time [in the future] when occasional purchasers wish to make a purchase . . . [is] difficult or impossible."[186]

I have characterized this possible instance of market failure as arising out of "the tyranny of small decisions"[187] The event that first suggested the phenomenon was the disappearance of passenger railroad service in Ithaca. The service was withdrawn because the individual decisions that travelers made, for each of their projected trips into and out of the various cities served, did not provide the railroad enough revenue to cover incremental costs. What reason was there to question the aggregate effect of those individual choices—withdrawal of the service? The fact is that the railroad provided the one reliable means of getting into and out of Ithaca in all kinds of weather; and I for one would have been willing to pay something to have kept alive this insufficiently exerted option. This suggests an at least hypothetical economic test of whether the service should have disappeared. Suppose each person in the cities served were to ask himself how much he would have been willing to pledge regularly over some time period, say annually, by purchase of prepaid tickets, to keep rail passenger service available to his community. As long as the amount that he would have declared (to himself) would have exceeded what he actually paid on that period—and my own introspective experiment shows that it would—then to that extent the disappearance of the passenger service was an incident of market failure.

The cause of the failure was the discrepancy between the time perspective of the choices that each traveler was given an opportunity to make—deciding, each time he planned a trip, whether to go by train—and that of the railroad, which was a long-run, virtually all-or-nothing and once-and-for-all decision, to retain or abandon passenger service. When each of us chose between the local airline or bus, his own automobile and the railroad, his individual choice had an only negligible effect on the continued availability of the last; it would therefore have been irrational to consider this possible implication of our individual decisions. The fact remains that each selection of x over y constitutes also a vote for eliminating the *possibility thereafter of choosing* y; if enough people vote for x, each time necessarily on the assumption that y will continue to be available, y may in fact disappear. And its disappearance may constitute a genuine deprivation, which customers might willingly have paid something to avoid. The only choice the market offered travelers to influence the longer-run decision of the railroad was thus shorter in its time perspective, and the sum-total of our individual purchases of railroad tickets necessarily added up to a smaller amount, than our actual combined interest in the continued availability of rail service. We were victims of "the tyranny of small decisions."

The railroad running through Ithaca provided service at peak seasons and off-peak, in fair weather and in foul. The airline and the automobiles may be said to have skimmed off the traffic in good weather, leaving to the

[186] *Op. cit.*, *Q. Jour. Econ.* (August 1964), LXXVIII: 471–477.
[187] *Op. cit.*, *Kyklos* (January 1966), XIX: 23–47. See the application of the same argument, above, to the potential disappearances under competition of local television broadcasters (pp. 36–37) and of research services provided by stock exchange brokers (note 100, this Chapter).

trains what they, with characteristic diplomacy, used to refer to as their "foul-weather friends" only. We have suggested earlier, in discussing the *MCI* case, that the problem may have been one merely of improper rate structure: the railroads might, for example, have reduced their rates substantially in good weather and charged much higher passenger fares on rainy or snowy days, when the airplanes were grounded, and in this fashion appropriated a share of the consumer surplus derived from their continued availability for just such emergencies. But this still would not have solved the inherent problem of trying to collect, in a price for individual journeys, the full value to passengers of keeping the service available. At each such time, the individual traveler would still be deciding whether to pay the higher price on the basis of the costs, pains, and benefits facing him in that particular instance. The higher fare might, for example, cause him simply to postpone the trip. He would still have no opportunity to convey to the railroad in cash—on the contrary, he would have an incentive to conceal—his full appraisal of the value to him of having the service available at all times.

It is this problem that is the most troublesome aspect of the *MCI* case and the others like it. If such ventures are economically feasible only on the assumption that when they break down or become congested subscribers may simply shift over to the Bell System for the duration of the emergency, they are indeed supplying an only partial service. If the common carrier is obliged to stand ready to serve and must carry the burden of excess capacity required to meet that obligation, it would seem that its average total costs would necessarily be higher than those of a private shipper or cream-skimming competitor who has no such obligation: the latter can construct capacity merely sufficient for operation at 100 percent load factors, with the expectation that it or its customers can turn to the common carriers in case of need.[188]

The fact that a competitor chooses to supply only service x while the common carrier is required to supply x plus y is not objectionable so long as customers know in each case what they are getting and, as we have already suggested, the separate charges for x and y reflect their respective costs.[189] So the first attempt at a solution to the MCI–AT&T problem (assuming the facts prove to be as we have been hypothesizing here) must be for the latter company to try to recover the costs of the service, the provision of backup capacity, separately from the x. The ideal way would be in the form of a lump-sum demand charge: those who retain the right to use the facilities should pay for the costs of standing by to honor that right, whether or not they actually exercise it. But merely to state this goal is to suggest the difficulties of attaining it. There is no way of determining a subscriber's capacity cost responsibility except in terms of the amount he actually uses it or will probably use it at the system's peak. A system of predetermined charges *per call* at peak hours works reasonably well for regular customers—although even for them it would be preferable to have rates that varied from one moment to the next depending on the degree of actual congestion present.[190] But such a system might not suffice to levy the proper charges on those who have the option but exercise it rarely or never—unless they could

---

[188] See the Doyle Report, 72; and Friedlaender, *op. cit.*, 117–118.

[189] See pp. 206–207, 216, above.

[190] See note 4, p. 88 and pp. 103–109, Volume 1, above.

be made to pay a special, higher charge per call than regular subscribers do, or their services were placed on an interruptible basis.

In short, AT&T might find itself in the position of the passenger railroad, incapable of devising charges for "rainy day" customers sufficient to cover the heavy capacity cost of standing ready to serve them. It is possible, thus, that the competitive market will not cover the costs of an infrequently exercised option that on purely economic grounds ought to be preserved. As in the case of the railroad, if the schedule of charges were high enough to cover the cost of capacity that was infrequently used but needed for emergency, it might pay no individual user to make use of it at such times, even though all, together, would obtain sufficient additional satisfaction from its availability to justify the requisite expenditure of society's resources.[191]

It is of course highly unlikely that this new, selective competition could actually destroy the AT&T alternative; unlike the passenger railroad, it is unlikely to disappear in the foreseeable future. But that is only because there are so many customers who do continue to exercise the option of using it. Therefore the more likely development is not that the option will disappear but that AT&T will be incapable of providing it except by levying unjustifiably high charges on its regular customers.

So, paradoxically, MCI's entry might well constitute cream-skimming, but cream-skimming with the effect of *introducing* internal subsidization where none existed before—subsidization of MCI's customers by AT&T's captive customers being forced to carry a disproportionate share of the back-up capacity costs.

This kind of market failure or discriminatory effect of selective entry could be avoided by protecting the public utility from competition. Observe again, however, that this solution would likewise be very imperfect. The customers who prefer the limited competitive service and place little value on the back-up capacity would be denied the former and would be forced to

---

[191] We mention but do not attempt thoroughly to analyze the analogous situation created by the competition of supplemental with regular airlines. The supplemental sells individual *flights* for charter to individuals or groups that can themselves assume the risks of filling them. The scheduled carriers offer the regular *availability* of service and sell individual *seats* on individual flights. The revenues from the latter sales must cover the costs of the former. The unit costs of the charter service *per passenger* per flight are necessarily lower than for scheduled operations— once a flight is scheduled all of its costs are fixed and the cost per passenger will vary in inverse proportion to the percentage of seats sold and their tickets can therefore sell at a much lower price.

By the kind of service they have chosen to offer, the supplementals skim the cream and their competition has the familiar justification: there are, they have proved, great numbers of travellers who want access only to the chartered flight, who can be served at unit costs much lower than the fares they would previously have had to pay

and who would otherwise have been forced to subsidize the less remunerative portions of the scheduled operations.

But those regular fares cover the costs also of the regular availability of scheduled service and to the extent that unrestricted competition of charter service jeopardizes the ability of the carriers to maintain that service, the travelling public—including the patrons of charter flights— could find itself the victim of the tyranny of small decisions. All travellers value in some measure the mere *availability* of service on a regularly scheduled basis, yet it pays none of them to support those operations when a cheaper charter flight is available. The regular airline might be unable to charge fares high enough for those flights for which competitive charter service is unavailable to cover the cost of standing by to serve for the same reason that railroads could not hope to do so on rainy or snowy days. The result could be the disappearance of an option of genuine value to travellers merely because there was no way of collecting what it was worth to them.

subsidize the continued availability of the latter to those who value it more highly.[192] This might conceivably be justified in the MCI type of situation, where the alternative, competitive policy would evidently involve the opposite distortion we have just described: as we have seen earlier, no system of customer grouping for rate making can avoid being discriminatory among the various members of the group.[192a] But such a "solution" would obviously be unthinkable in the case of railroad passenger service: the economic value of preserving that option between Ithaca and New York City would hardly have justified suppressing the cream-skimming airline, bus, and passenger automobile competition that were responsible for the railroad's financial plight. The preferable method of financing the provision of this back-up capacity, if its provision were economically justified,[193] would be to give it a direct subsidy, financed out of local real-estate taxes, as in the case of the local airports. But this too would be economically imperfect—unless the tax was on the rental value of land alone.[194]

There is one example of the possibly deleterious effect of competitive entry in jeopardizing the continued provision of service with important external benefits that is especially interesting because its relation to the cream-skimming issue has not to my knowledge been observed elsewhere. This is the competition between community antenna television (CATV) companies and the regular broadcasters, a problem we have already discussed at length elsewhere.[195]

Before the advent of CATV, program origination and the transmission of signals from broadcasters to viewers was a single, integrated function.[196] The CATV operators undertook to perform a more limited but important part of this function and for most viewers did it better than it had been done before. This proved to be extremely profitable. Like MCI, thus, they were in a sense cream-skimmers—doing only part of what had previously been a single job and in a sense getting a free ride on services or facilities provided by others. And, as we have seen, this competition did involve some threat to the continued provision of the auxiliary services—broadcasting by local stations and the origination of the programs that CATV operators picked off the air free of charge.

The first of these threats involved another possible external consequence: the loss of broadcasting signals to sparse rural areas, where cable service is uneconomical.[197] It is at least theoretically conceivable that this failure

---

[192] For a similar objection to fair trade laws, even though these too could be justified on the ground that they preserve economically valuable options —keeping in business the diversified book store, the prescription pharmacy, the liquor store that provides delivery service—see Kahn, *op. cit.*, *Kyklos* (January 1966), XIX: 34–39. And see the application of the same argument to the alleged case for fixing minimum brokerage commissions on security transactions, pp. 206–207, this chapter, above.

[192a] See pp. 189–190, Volume 1.

[193] Such an external subsidy would be economically justified only if the total discounted value of benefits to customers from the continued availability of this back-up capacity, though under-

stated by the revenues collectible from them, exceeded the present value of the costs of providing it.

[194] See note 15, pp. 130–131, Volume 1, above.

[195] See pp. 32–45, Chapter 1, above.

[196] The local station originated some of the programs it broadcast and made arrangements with the networks for the others.

[197] Indeed, as we also pointed out, the urban subscribers to the cable might by their individual decisions to subscribe have imposed an external cost on themselves as well, if the consequences were to drive out the local station, on which the FCC, in principle at least, had imposed a requirement that it originate some local programming. It would be difficult to ascribe this

could have been overcome without regulatory intervention. The threatened viewers might have approached the CATV operators and offered to pay them to carry the programs of the local stations and to avoid duplicating them with programs brought in from the outside, so as to diminish the competitive threat to the survival of the local station, on which they were entirely dependent. On the other hand, clearly, such a solution might not have been practical or sufficient. In any event, the FCC chose to intervene to give the local stations some protection against this competition. The intervention was clearly excessively protectionist in character; but in some respects it was, we found, an economically justifiable attempt to correct for possible market failure.

We have offered reasons for questioning the reality of the other possible external consequence of CATV's free ride—the discouragement of programming. But if the danger were a real one, it could presumably have been corrected by imposing charges on the CATV operators for use of the copyrighted material or by requiring them also to originate programs, rather than discouraging it, as was the FCC's original intention.

These external consequences are, in any event, to some extent required for economic efficiency in a dynamic economy. Recall our earlier fanciful hypothesizing that the introduction of sunlight-beamed telephone service might raise the price and threaten the viability of nighttime service. No group of customers has an inalienable right to the continued provision of service that has become uneconomic. If rural families have heretofore been receiving television programs as the free by-product of a system of local broadcasting that has lost its economic justification because small towns are better served by CATV, bringing in numerous signals from the outside, then they no longer have the right on purely economic grounds to that particular free ride. (I say this regretfully, as a rural dweller out of reach of any CATV system.) And there is no economic ground for insisting that they continue to enjoy it at the expense of urban dwellers, by denying the latter the benefits of CATV.

Offsetting Imperfections and the Problem of Second Best. We have already discussed the possible case for regulatory control stemming from the fact that competition in the real world is not perfect. In these circumstances, regulatory intervention may play the role of a kind of 'offsetting imperfection," producing a performance more nearly approximating the one that would be achieved by theoretically perfect but practically unachievable competition.[198] By the same token, unrestricted competition in particular markets or industries may produce poorer rather than better results if it is already distorted by the presence of (1) monopoly elements elsewhere in the economy, (2) differential taxes, or (3) subsidies, all of which have the possible

---

result to market failure, however, since if it paid the local station to originate broadcasts, it would presumably equally have paid the cable operators to do so; and if the latter were prevented from doing so by the Commission's rules as originally proposed, the failure would have been one resulting not from the tyranny of small decisions but from the foolishness of the FCC. The same would be true if the FCC had permitted the competition of the cable systems to drive local stations out of business and then failed to impose on the successor companies the same requirements respecting the origination of local programming as they had previously imposed on the local broadcasters.

[198] The case for offsetting imperfections was clearly expressed by J. M. Clark, in his "Toward A Concept of Workable Competition," *loc. cit.*, even though he does not actually use that term.

effect of producing a misallocation of resources between the market in question and all others. What we have, here, is a statement of the practical problem of the second best, to which we have already referred several times. There are some situations in which second-best considerations would seem to argue against unrestricted cream-skimming.

The most obvious illustrations come from the influence of taxes. For the most part, since these typically weigh with unusual severity on the public utilities and, therefore, their customers, they do not usually counsel restraints on competition in these areas. On the contrary, as we have suggested in Chapter 7 of Volume 1, they would seem to counsel the opposite policy, in order to minimize the effect of this distortion. On the other hand, those taxes that are levied only on the public utilities provide a possible case for regulatory restrictions on the operations of their less heavily taxed competitors. For a long time, for example, special excise taxes were levied on transportation and communications common carriers, and they continue to be levied in the latter case. Such taxes clearly distort the competition between common and private carriers—trucks, the private automobile, private microwave systems.

Distortions introduced by differential rates of government subsidy would in principle call for similar regulatory intervention to limit the competition of the favored suppliers. It seems clear, for example, that the large, heavy, diesel-fuel-burning motor trucks fall far short, in the registration fees and excise taxes that they pay, of reimbursing society for the incremental costs that they impose on it by virtue of the additional, wider and heavier-duty roads that they require.[199] Similarly, the usual practice in the United States has been to levy no charges on the carriers using the navigable waterways, on which very large expenditures of public funds are regularly made.[200]

An alternative policy would be to encourage or to permit the common carriers to meet this kind of competition freely by reducing their own rates to long-run incremental costs.[201] This expedient might well suffice, since common carriers do tend to be subject to increasing returns. Freeing the regulated carriers for more effective competition, rather than compounding one distortion issuing from government intervention by instituting yet another, would require loosening the numerous operating restrictions to

[199] See Lansing, *op. cit.*, 251–252, summarizing the incremental cost study made by the Bureau of Public Roads (BPR), *The Supplementary Report of the Highway Cost Allocation Study*, 89th Cong. 1st Sess., House Document No. 124 (1965).

[200] *Ibid.*, 60. The "first-best" solution to these distortions would, of course, be to eliminate the original taxes and subsidies. In his *Message on Transportation* to Congress, dated April 4, 1962, President Kennedy called for "consistent policies of taxation and user charges" and specifically for a repeal of the 10 percent passenger transportation tax (which "has undoubtedly discriminated against public transportation in favor of the automobile"), extension of the excise tax on gasoline to cover jet fuel, and adding a 5 percent tax on airline tickets and air freight weigh bills (all "as a minimal step toward recouping the heavy Federal investment in the airways"), a tax of 2¢ a gallon on all fuels used in transportation on the waterways, legislation "to make the domestic trunk air carriers ineligible for operating subsidies in the future," and "a step-by-step program with specific annual targets, to assure sharp reduction of operating subsidies to all other domestic airlines as well. . . ." *Op. cit.*, Part I(B). And in his 1965 message to Congress calling for the repeal or reduction of various excise taxes, President Johnson recommended additional user taxes on heavy trucks—and specifically an increase in the excise on highway diesel fuel from 4 to 7 cents a gallon. *New York Times*, May 18, 1965, 26.

[201] This was precisely the choice faced by the ICC in the *Southern Railway* grain decision; see note 12, p. 165, Volume 1, and p. 23, above.

which they have been subjected—something that is desirable on its own merits. It would have the crowning virtue, from the point of view of the consuming public, of extending to it the potential benefits of freer competition, rather than making the regulatory withdrawal of those benefits more uniform and complete.

In purely static terms, it is a matter of indifference whether the government corrects for a distortion introduced by a tax or subsidy in one place by introducing offsetting imperfections elsewhere, or by moving to eliminate the original distortion:

> "efficiency would be increased either by increasing the degree of control exercised over the uncontrolled sector or by relaxing the control exercised over the controlled sector. Both of these policies will move the economy in the direction of some second best optimum position."[202]

The preference that we have expressed for the competitive rather than the intensified regulatory correction is based largely on dynamic, institutional grounds.

Noneconomic Considerations. The economist may be betraying his parochialism when he relegates noneconomic considerations to a few summary comments, inserted long after the reader's concentration has begun to flag. It may instead be taken as an expression of the opinion that he has no particular expertise in this area. The reader must not construe the brevity of our treatment here as suggesting that these criteria of policy are unimportant. Such values as fairness, equality of opportunity, or national security are obviously potentially far more important than economic efficiency. Moreover, the criteria of efficiency implied by a market economy are based on highly restrictive assumptions with respect to the distribution of income and the superiority of consumer sovereignty—assumptions that obviously may be rejected by people with other values. The economist may object to internal subsidization on the grounds set forth in Chapter 7 of Volume 1: that it imposes sacrifices on others greater than the benefits to the subsidized customers; and that the poor would get more satisfaction, at less cost to the subsidizers, if they were given direct money grants instead. The noneconomist might well reject such an argument because it takes as its measure of satisfaction or welfare what consumers are willing and able to pay for particular goods and services. He might not only accept as a political fact of life but also approve, on noneconomic grounds, the possibility that society might be willing to help the poor by selling them electricity or telephone service below cost, or by giving their children free lunches, but be unwilling to do so by direct monetary transfers—even though the poor might prefer the latter.

On the other hand, the mere assertion by some interested party that a particular proposed policy is "fair," "just," or required in the interest of national security by no means justifies the accompanying implication that questions of economic efficiency can therefore be disregarded.[203] What the

---

[202] R. G. Lipsey and Kelvin Lancaster, "The General Theory of Second Best," *Rev. Econ. Studies* (1956), XXIV: 15.
[203] See this writer's colloquy with a staff member of the Subcommittee on Antitrust and Monopoly of the Committee on the Judiciary, U.S. Senate, Ninety-First Cong., 1st Session, *Hearings, The Petroleum Industry*, 1969, 147–149, as well as the testimony of other economic witnesses on this same subject.

economist must do is to insist that legislators or regulators (1) satisfy themselves that these other goals cannot equally well be achieved without the sacrifice of economic efficiency: after all, the economy that makes the most efficient use of its resources can then afford to make the greater outlays for national defense or free education; (2) explicitly confront the economic cost of achieving these other goals, in order to decide whether the benefits do indeed justify the costs: noneconomic decisions that involve the expenditure of resources, the sum total of which is limited, must still be made as rationally as possible, even if they are not made by economists; (3) openly decide who, appropriately, should bear the financial burden. This last requirement should conduce to the second as well: an explicit decision to have social welfare or national security programs paid for openly by taxpayers, rather than covertly by internal subsidization ought to produce not only a more just allocation of burdens but also a more rational appraisal of the balance between purported benefits and cost. On the other hand, democracies do not necessarily make their decisions rationally. It may well be argued, thus, that some particular, socially desirable ends would not be pursued if the costs were openly divulged; and that it is therefore a legitimate political strategy to have them financed covertly, even at the cost of considerable economic inefficiency.

The economist does have another kind of expertise to bring to policy questions like these. He is usually best equipped to trace the indirect consequences of proposed policies, in order to force those in the position to adopt or reject them to see whether they are in fact required for or do in fact contribute to the achievement of their avowed goals. Minimum wage laws are supposed to help the poor: the economist is obliged to ask to what extent instead they lead to unemployment at the lowest rungs of the labor ladder. A uniform flat monthly telephone charge for all local calls, or uniform subway fares within a metropolitan area may both strike the superficial observer as "fair" and perhaps particularly desirable because they keep down the cost of telephones or subway travel for the poor. The economist may be able to demonstrate whether such charges result instead in comparatively wealthy subscribers or commuters paying less and urban slum dwellers paying more than the respective marginal costs of serving them. On the other hand, it hardly requires the skills of an economist to question the national security justification of the policy that excludes Canadian ships as well as those of other countries from the United States coastal shipping business or that lumps petroleum imports from that country together with those that come from overseas in computing the proportion of total United States oil requirements that can be safely supplied from outside the country.

Considerations such as these obviously carry us well beyond the issue of cream-skimming alone. But they clearly do bear on that issue. For example, advocates of entry restrictions in the trunk airline business have justified the internal subsidization that they protect on the ground that small towns "deserve air service" as much as large.[204] It is not clear who, exactly, the people are in those towns who "deserve" such service: presumably, they are the relatively well-to-do who can afford to travel by air; nor is it immediately obvious by what morality they deserve to be subsidized in receiving such

---

[204] See p. 9, above.

service, either by general taxpayers or by regular travelers over the routes—like, say, New York to Puerto Rico—that can generate enough traffic to pay their way.[205]

The same questions must be asked about the FCC's attempts to protect local television stations against CATV competition on the ground that each town "ought" wherever feasible to have its own station and that this is the best way of getting diversity of programming. It is clearly worth asking whether such diversity might not be more effectively promoted by permitting CATV systems freely to bring in a maximum number of signals from the outside and to initiate their own programs; and whether cultural quality and diversity are not likely to be better achieved by more public service programming generated in a smaller number of producing centers or by encouraging the growth of educational television.

Again, encroachments by private carriers on common carrier companies in transportation and communications are often resisted on the ground that national security requires the preservation of strong, integrated common carrier systems, available for emergencies. The argument obviously commands respect. At the same time, it is by no means obvious that monopoly and cartelization are the best instruments for serving that purpose. It is the *total* of transportation facilities that is available in the case of military or other emergency, not just the common carrier component. To the extent that restrictions on competition in the interest of protecting the latter succeed in limiting the encroachments on their domain by unregulated carriers, the total national capacity is not necessarily enhanced at all. The argument is sometimes confined to the necessity for keeping in existence a strong railroad network as the backbone of the national communications system in the event of emergencies. But while there is little room for question that our transportation policy has been intended in part to protect the railroads, it is equally clear that minimum rate regulation by the ICC in recent decades has to some considerable extent had the opposite effect—preventing the railroads from regaining the larger share of the total transportation business to which they are entitled on grounds of pure efficiency.[206] There appears to be general agreement that if railroads were freer to compete for traffic, their profits would be larger, not smaller.[207] It is not clear in what way national security is served by preventing this.[208]

Similarly, in communications, national security might be most effectively served by our having the most widespread and diversified networks possible and—a particularly relevant consideration when the major communications companies obtain most of their equipment from their own manufacturing

---

[205] A more difficult case is presented by the increasing financial difficulties encountered in recent years by the Blue Cross hospitalization insurance companies. Blue Cross was founded and granted tax exemption on the expectation that it would offer group insurance at uniform rates, regardless of the age or infirmities of the members. Those uniform rates have naturally encouraged competing carriers to offer cost-related policies, with premiums based on actual hospitalization, to groups with below-average risks. This cream-skimming competition has left Blue Cross with progressively higher average-risk, average-cost subscribers, forcing it in turn to request sharp increases in premium rates. Richard Phalon, "Blue Cross Under Fire," *New York Times*, August 27, 1969, 39.

[206] See Meyer et al., *op. cit.*, 166–167 and *passim*.

[207] See the survey of the evidence by David Boies, Jr., *op. cit.*, 654–663, and in particular Peck, in Almarin Phillips, ed., *op. cit.*, 263–264.

[208] Boies, *op. cit.*, 658–659.

affiliates—by having the manufacturing experience distributed among the greater number of companies that would have the opportunity of acquiring it if the market were more fully open to them.

Conclusion: The Benefits and Dangers of Discriminatory Competition

It is hard to draw conclusions from these two long chapters, covering a wide diversity of situations, without simply rewriting them. What we have done is to identify the various possible cases for imposing regulatory restraint on free entry and unrestricted rivalry in the public utility industries. In the presence of economies of scale and numerous market imperfections, it is clear that competition can produce inefficiency, deterioration in the quality of service, and severe discrimination.

On the other hand, we have observed that regulation, too, has promoted and protected highly discriminatory rate structures, particularly in the industries considered in the present chapter, in which freer competition would otherwise have been feasible. It has also produced or sheltered immense inefficiencies— by interfering with the rational distribution of the public utility function among alternative media, by protecting conservative and inefficient operators from the pressures of competition and by encouraging service inflation—not to mention the costs of administering the regulatory system itself. And competition has made many important contributions to improved performance in these industries.

We have recognized that noneconomic purposes might justify some of these restrictions; but have pointed out how weakly the logical and evidentiary connection is usually made between those purposes and the restraints that are supposed to serve them. Moreover, there are also noneconomic considerations that argue strongly for competition—notably the value of having customers protected from monopolistic exploitation without the need for government intervention, the values of free entry and enterprise, and the values of *not* having businessmen dependent on grants of privilege for the right to enter this or that occupation, with its attendant risks of mutual corruption of both the political and economic processes.[209]

The strongest basis for regulatory limitation of competition is the presence of long-run decreasing costs. On the other hand, the welfare costs of regulation-enforced or protected inefficiency, or monopolistic pricing are particularly great in such situations because they deprive the consumer of the compounded benefit of a lower price that, by giving rise to additional sales and output, brings about a reduction in the average cost of production as well.[210] And this static welfare loss is far less important than the dynamic

---

[209] In a challenging article, Charles A. Reich cites the dispensation of valuable franchises— medallions to taxi companies, route permits to truck, bus, and airline companies, certificates to natural gas pipelines, licenses to liquor stores, allotments to growers of cotton or wheat and concessions in national parks—as one major category of government largesse, the enormous extension of which carries with it, as he very effectively demonstrates, a corresponding magnification of government power and an erosion of the security, independence and freedoms of the individual. "The New Property," *The Public Interest*, Number 3 (Spring 1966), 57–59.

[210] For an explanation of this same consequence of taxes that bear with unusual severity on public utilities, see p. 197, in Volume 1, above.

one: it seems a fair generalization that regulation has on balance been obstructive both of competition and of the innovation that it helps stimulate and justify. Aaron J. Gellman, Vice President of The Budd Company, argues persuasively, for example, that innovations in railroading have been thwarted not only because of the general discouragement to competition by the ICC, but specifically because of its minimum rate controls. By preventing rate reductions required to generate additional traffic, they have restricted the introduction of innovations that only a greater traffic volume would have justified.[211]

On the other hand, it is precisely in situations of decreasing costs that price competition is most likely to be discriminatory. Price discrimination can introduce serious inefficiencies at the secondary level. It can also *eliminate* competition at the primary level. Along with the possibility of injury to customers discriminated against, the principal rationalization for minimum rate regulation certainly is the alleged threat that large, integrated public utility companies, if free to reduce prices without limit, may drive competitors out of business, leaving only one or a few firms in full possession of the field.[212] The fear of predatory competition, or what Corwin Edwards has referred to as discriminatory sharpshooting, is one widely encountered

---

[211] Gellman cites the Southern Railway case, involving the introduction of "Big John" cars (see p. 23, above) as a classic illustration of this obstruction. "Economic Regulation and Innovative Performance in Surface Transportation," a paper prepared for the Brookings Institution Conference on Technological Change in the Regulated Industries, Washington, February 1969. See also p. 111, note 54, Chapter 3, above. Barber's conclusion, heavily influenced by the historical evidence of striking advances in productivity in transportation, is more equivocal:

"One crucial finding is that government regulation does not appear to have retarded the rate of technological advance in transportation so much as it has affected its composition and exploitation." *Op. cit.*, 883.

But while his own extensive account amply documents the ways in which regulation has frustrated as well as distorted the development and application of new technology, it offers very little persuasive evidence (except with respect to safety) of regulation's positive contributions to that admittedly very favorable record. See *ibid.*, 853–874. The conclusion seems inescapable that the productivity advance has occurred in spite of regulation.

For a view that regulation has had very little effect one way or another on the development of innovation in air transport, see Almarin Phillips, *op. cit.*, at the same Brookings Institution Conference. Phillips recognizes that the oligopolistic structure of passenger air transport and its avoidance of price competition both help explain the carriers' heavy emphasis on com-

petition through differentiation in the selection of aircraft (see our discussion of this point, pp. 211–214, this chapter, above); and that this kind of rivalry has contributed positively to the rapidity with which the industry has adopted the innovations of the aircraft manufacturing industry. But he suggests that the policies of the CAB have made very little independent contribution to this process:

"In a sense . . . the CAB has behaved much as would a reasonably far-sighted trade association operated by a group of oligopolistic carriers with partially overlapping but far from coincident market areas." *Ibid.*, 47.

Our own discussion suggests that the industry would be substantially more competitive in structure and more prone therefore to engage in price competition if it were not regulated. But Phillips' argument is in any event entirely consistent with the view that regulation has helped to implement what "a reasonably far-sighted trade association" would otherwise have wished to do (and would have been less able to do were the industry fully subject to the antitrust laws), and that its effect on the adoption of new equipment has therefore been far from neutral. Whether this influence has been economically sensible is, however, questionable, as we have already suggested.

On the proper regulatory response to technological change, see Adams and Dirlam, in Trebing, ed., *op. cit.*, 131–144.

[212] See, for example, the views of the Supreme Court majority in the *Ingot Molds* case, pp. 162–163, Volume 1.

in competitive industry generally, and was the principal original occasion for passage of Section 2 of the Clayton Act.[213]

Devotees of what they call "hard competition" scoff at the notion that it is necessary to limit price competition in this way in order to preserve it. There is, indeed, a risk of confusing the preservation of competition with the preservation of competitors. But the policy of protecting individual business-men from the kind of competition that may cause them to fail without regard to their relative efficiency, energy, or assiduity in serving customers is not necessarily paradoxical or inconsistent; and it is at least conceivable that hard competition that is discriminatory and selective might have this effect. And since discriminatory price competition is just about the only kind that is conceivable among public utility companies, the danger must be faced. It is accentuated in the regulatory context by the A-J-W tendency—by the fact that it could be in the long-run interest of a regulated monopolist to take on business at rates below even its SRMC, not merely temporarily, in quest of monopoly, but over longer periods of time—a danger further accentuated by the administrative difficulties of measuring the LRMC floor below which competitive rates ought not to be permitted to fall.

There is no easy solution to this dilemma. It is all very well to say that the only proper test of promotional rates is long-run marginal costs, and if rates that meet this test drive or keep competitors out of business, so be it. But even this principle is not unexceptionally correct: recall the undesir-ability of permitting rail-rail (or electricity-gas) competition to drive selected rates to marginal cost.[213a] Given the difficulties of measuring LRMC on specific, possibly small parts of a company's business, moreover, the possi-bility cannot be denied that competition may drive promotional rates too low. There is the additional, institutional consideration, which cannot be rejected out of hand, that even where on grounds of static efficiency only a single firm may "deserve" to survive, there may be dynamic benefits of maintaining a number of sources of initiative—to put it baldly, of keeping some competitors alive in the face of discriminatory competition. If it proved true, for example, that Western Union was incapable of competing with the Bell System in the provision of various business communications services when the latter set rates fully covering LRMC, it remains at least possible that preserving the competitor might in the long run contribute sufficiently to a greater and more varied innovation to outweigh the static welfare loss involved in holding up the Bell rates in order to keep it alive.

The question is not simply one of keeping undeserving competitors alive. The most difficult choices arise when it is the smaller competitor that actually does the pioneering, only to be met with a discriminatory response by the large incumbent firm. For example, in 1957 Sea-Land Service, a water carrier, altered four of its ships so that each could carry 226 truck trailers and announced rates 5 percent to $7\frac{1}{2}$ percent below competing rail rates for this efficient service. A number of railroads responded by cutting their own piggyback rates on competitive traffic to approximately the same level,

---

[213] "it shall be unlawful for any person engaged in commerce, in the course of such commerce, either directly or indirectly to discriminate in price between different purchasers of com-modities . . . where the effect of such discrimina-tion may be to substantially lessen competition or tend to create a monopoly in any line of commerce. . . ." 38 U.S. Stat. 730, Sec. 2 (1914).
[213a] See pp. 168–172, Volume 1, above.

which meant, since rail service is faster, that they would retain the lion's share of the business. Although the rail rates were compensatory, one sympathizes with the ICC's decision in 1960—overturned by the Supreme Court in 1963—ordering the railroads to cancel their rate cuts.[214]

On the other hand, the dangers of this kind of protectionism would certainly seem in most instances to outweigh any possible benefits. The foregoing considerations certainly do not justify the rigid limitations on price competition imposed, for example, by the ICC. Section 2 of the Clayton Act at least confines its prohibition to instances in which there is a threat to the continued vitality of competition; the ICC's rate regulation has no such limitation. Given the flexibility and mobility of trucking and water transportation, their ability to shift from one route to another and, therefore, to move back into any market out of which they may have been driven by temporary reductions in rail rates, the possibility of those reductions producing substantial and enduring increases in monopoly power would seem to be far weaker than the opposite one, which has in fact been realized: that minimum rate control will fasten a regime of thoroughgoing cartelization on these industries. We have, in Chapter 3, listed among the inducements to superior performance in public utilities such factors as the profit motive, managerialism, decreasing costs and elasticity of demand. But every one of them is strengthened by competition.

The likelihood of injury to competition at the seller's level would seem to be far more remote in the public utility area than in unregulated industry generally. The greater danger is not ordinarily that one firm may, by predatory pricing, drive out a host of smaller and weaker competitors but that sellers will be too large and too few and their competitive overlap too thin for effective competition. Where there are large numbers of competing sellers, as in the markets for transportation, energy, and private-line communication service, the chances are either (1) that the cost structures of the competitors are so different that it would be socially efficient to permit the firms with lower long-run marginal costs to prevail or (2) that the smaller firms will have large and powerful allies—like petroleum refiners or the producers of electronic equipment for private communications systems—fully capable of competitive survival as long as entry is free of regulatory blockage and is economically desirable.

It seems impossible to deny that in the regulation of competition in transportation we have gone too far in the direction of limiting price rivalry in order to keep competitors alive. If we must err, it would seem best to err in the opposite direction. If this direction of inclination is the correct one, regulatory commissions ought to be very restrained about disallowing promotional rates that do not cover fully distributed historical costs. Where utilities offer substantial reason to believe that particular categories of business can be expanded if offered rates that cover long-run incremental costs, the burden of proof of unremunerativeness ought to be placed on the Commission that would disallow the rates, rather than on the company that proposes them.

There is, of course, the danger that if the estimates prove to be mistaken, other customers may eventually have to pay higher prices in consequence.

---

[214] *ICC v. New York, New Haven & Hartford Railroad Co. et al.*, 372 U.S. 744 (1963). Cf. the brief reference to this decision at p. 23, Chapter 1, above.

But effective regulation can also ensure that they participate in the gains if the estimates are correct. Given regulatory lag, the burden of error will fall first on stockholders and management. In the presence of increasing returns, there are potential gains for all. In these circumstances, it would seem that the balance of public advantage lies on the side of permitting, indeed encouraging, rate experimentation of this kind. The argument in any particular instance that a restriction on competition is necessary in order to preserve competition ought properly to have to sustain a very heavy burden of proof.[215]

Whenever possible, most economists would probably conclude, competition should be permitted to do its job of bringing prices closer to cost, eradicating price discrimination, controlling tendencies to excessive service inflation, weeding out inefficient suppliers, stimulating improvements in efficiency and service. The ideal would be to reduce the scope of regulation, insofar as possible, to applying the LRMC test of remunerativeness, as a floor, and protecting from exploitation those many customers who, inevitably, will continue to lack access to sufficient competitive alternatives.[216] But there is no single best combination of regulation and competition, valid for all industries, in all times and places.

---

[215] This discussion draws heavily on my "Inducements to Superior Performance: Price," in Trebing, ed., *op. cit.*, 96–102.

[216] These are essentially the recommendations of Meyer *et al.* in the field of transportation, *op. cit.*, 196–202, 247–252. See also Wilson, *op. cit.*,

Jour. Pol. Econ. (August 1955), LXIII: 337–344, and Roberts, in *Transportation Economics, op. cit.*, 12, 29–36.

On the other hand, as we have seen, Wilson feels that minimum rate controls are required also in trucking. See note 29, this chapter, above.

CHAPTER 6

The Role and Definition of Competition: Integration

A business firm is said to be integrated when its activities embrace the production or sale of a number of products, or a single product in a number of markets, each of which either is or could conceivably be produced or served by companies that confined themselves to that single activity. It is horizontally integrated if it operates a number of establishments producing or selling the same product or group of products; geographic integration, thus, is one kind of horizontal integration. Obvious examples would be the chain store or the automobile manufacturer that operates a number of assembly plants in various parts of the country. Vertical integration means the carrying on by a single firm of a series of successive functions in the production and distribution process. Outstanding examples are to be found in the petroleum industry, where the largest firms produce crude oil, transport it in their own pipelines, refine it, transport it once again in their own tankers or product pipelines to their own terminals, and distribute it at least in part through service stations that they themselves own or control by long-term lease; the continued presence in the industry of nonintegrated operators, confining their activities to each of these individual strata, meets the second condition for the presence of integration, namely, that these activities are or could be performed by specialists. Conglomerate integration involves the production or sale of a variety of products or services, which may or may not (the term is used in varying ways) be closely interrelated technologically or commercially. Consider, at the two possible extremes of conglomerates, the steel company that produces thousands of varieties of steel products or the petrochemical refiner, the logic of whose product line is determined by the chemistry of petroleum and its derivatives, or the food processing company, that produces and distributes a wide line of merchandise to the grocery store, or the supermarket itself; and, at the other extreme, the textile company that manufactures aerospace equipment (Textron), the electrical equipment manufacturers (IT&T and RCA) that own car-rental agencies; the conglomerate that produces typewriters, nuclear submarines, and owns a restaurant chain and a book publisher (Litton Industries), or the one (Ling-Temco-Vought) with major interests in meat-packing, airlines, sporting goods, jet aircraft, electronics, and steel.[1]

Integration is usually understood as a characteristic of a single business firm or a group of financially affiliated firms. But some of its characteristics and consequences may be achieved by agreement among financially separate companies. Vertical integration is approximated, for example, by one company agreeing to supply the full requirements of another for a particular raw material; by a manufacturer agreeing to distribute his products exclusively through one distributor in each market territory; or by the independent distributor agreeing to handle exclusively the products of one supplier. Power pooling or the similar interchanges among natural gas pipeline companies achieve some of the same results as would the organization of the various participants into one larger, geographically integrated company; and the offer of piggyback rates by railroads for carrying truck trailers on flat cars can lead to the same kind of coordination as would the formation of a conglomerately integrated rail-motor carrier transportation company.

The treatment of integration in the public utility industries exhibits a wide range and variety of policies and attitudes, of which we can hope only to illustrate a few of the more interesting. With respect to financial integration, regulation is in some contexts permissive, even encouraging; in others hostile. Thus, although the link has been subject to almost continuous scrutiny and criticism, the vertical integration between Western Electric and the Bell System has been permitted to continue; railroads, airlines, and banks have been permitted to merge even when there had previously been some competition between them; single companies own a number of radio or television stations; in some states, so-called combination companies have been permitted, in the distribution of both electricity and gas; to a limited extent, railroads have been permitted to conduct auxiliary trucking operations; and producers of natural gas have held financial interests in, and in some cases have been permitted to organize, natural gas pipeline companies.

On the other hand, there is a tradition in the public utility industries that holds integration either obstructive of effective regulation or incompatible with effective competition. We have already described the breaking up of the great holding company empires under the Public Utility Holding

---

[1] As suggested, these terms are not always used in exactly the same way. The antitrust laws subject to particularly sharp scrutiny those instances in which firms integrate by either acquiring other firms or merging with them. Since Section 7 of the Clayton Act (as amended) prohibits such mergers or acquisitions only "where . . . the effect . . . may be substantially to lessen competition, or to tend to create a monopoly" (15 U.S.C. 18, 1964 ed.), in antitrust usage the concept of a horizontal merger is usually confined to a situation in which the two firms joined were previously selling the same product or group of products in the same geographic market—because only in that case could their union eliminate pre-existing competition. According to this usage, market-extension mergers, which join together similar companies operating in geographically separate markets, are generally considered as constituting a separate category of conglomerate, similar to those of the product-extension type, like the acquisition by Procter & Gamble, the leading manufacturer of soaps and detergents, of the Clorox Company, the leading manufacturer of liquid bleaches. See Willard F. Mueller, *Celler-Kefauver Act, 16 Years of Enforcement*, U.S. House of Representatives, 90th Cong. 1st Sess., Committee on the Judiciary, Staff Report to the Antitrust Subcommittee, 1967.

Company Act of 1935,[2] and the compromise embodied in the 1962 Communications Satellite Act between those senators who strongly urged that the development of international satellite communications be turned over to a government corporation and the established common carriers, who wanted to control it themselves.[3] The Panama Canal Act of 1912 amended the Interstate Commerce Act to prohibit railroads from holding "any interest whatsoever" in a water common carrier with which they do or may compete for traffic, though it permits exceptions to be granted by the ICC;[4] the Motor Carrier Act of 1935, as amended by the Transportation Act of 1940, directs the ICC to withhold its approval of railroad acquisition of or merger with a motor carrier,

> "unless it finds that the transaction proposed will be consistent with the public interest and will enable such carrier to use service by motor vehicle to public advantage in its operations and will not unduly restrain competition";[5]

and the ICC applies similar criteria in passing on railroad applications for motor-carrier certificates or permits even though no statute explicitly requires it.[6] Similarly, the consent decree settling the antitrust suit brought against the Bell System, while leaving undisturbed the challenged vertical relationship between AT&T and Western Electric, prohibited the System from engaging, either directly or indirectly, "in any business other than the furnishing of common carrier communications services."[7] The same distrust of integration underlies the Federal Communications Commission's "diversification policy" with respect to its awarding of licenses for radio and television stations:

> "When two or more candidates apply for the same outlet and when 'other things are equal,' the license should go to the non newspaper or to the candidate with no other media affiliations."[8]

The FCC also limits the number of television, AM and FM radio stations

---

[2] See pp. 72–73, Chapter 2, above. On the other hand, as we have seen, the Act does not abolish all holding companies, but directs the SEC to limit their operations "to a single integrated public-utility system, and to such other businesses as are reasonably incidental, or economically necessary or appropriate. . . ." 15 U.S. Code 79k (b) (1), 1964 ed. In a decision that seems certain to be appealed, the SEC in 1970 refused to extend the cover of the latter escape clause to the application of a natural gas company to diversify into financing the construction of low and moderate income housing — even though Congress had, in the National Housing Act, sought to encourage private industry to engage in such ventures. *In the Matter of Michigan Consolidated Gas Company* (70–4778), Administrative Proceeding, File No. 3–2111, Findings and Opinion, June 22, 1970. On this decision, see also note 21a, this chapter, below.
[3] See Chapter 4, pp. 136–137, above.

[4] 49 U.S. Code 5(14)–(16), 1964 ed.
[5] 49 U.S. Code 5(2)(b), 1964 ed.
[6] See Fulda, *op. cit.*, 381–382, and 402, citing the leading case *ICC v. Parker*, 326 U.S. 60 (1945) and his Chapter 12, for a thorough survey of the law; also Locklin, *op. cit.*, 846–853 and the *Doyle Report*, 138–144.
[7] *United States of America v. Western Electric Company Inc., and American Telephone & Telegraph Co.*, Final Judgment, Civil Action No. 17–49, U.S. District Court, District of N.J., January 24, 1956, section V. See also pp. 297, below and 145, note 93, above.
[8] Harvey J. Levin, *Broadcast Regulation and Joint Ownership of Media* (New York: New York Univ. Press, 1960), 173. Since the FCC has more often than not decided that "other things were not equal," Levin concludes that this policy "has exercised only a minor influence on the industry's actual structure," *ibid.*, 193.

that any single firm can own to a total of seven of each (no more than five TV stations can be VHF).[9]

---

[9] See Levin, "Competition, Diversity, and the Television Group Ownership Rule," *Columbia Law Rev.* (May 1970), LXX: 791–835.

On March 28, 1968, the Commission issued a Notice of Proposed Rule-Making, proposing in any future applications for new licenses or license transfers to prohibit common ownership of any two stations in the same market, even though in different media (AM radio, FM radio or TV). The Antitrust Division of the Department of Justice, documenting the pervasive multiple-media ownerships in major markets, urged the Commission to extend the prohibitions to license renewal proceedings as well, and to newspaper-broadcasting combinations. *In the Matter of Amendment of Sections 73.35, 73.240 and 73.626 of the Commission Rules*, Docket No. 18110, *Comments of the United States Department of Justice*, August 1, 1968. In early 1969 the Commission responded with a path-breaking decision that spread something close to panic through the industry, when it refused to renew the license of WHDH-TV in Boston on the ground that it was not sufficiently "free from media alliances": the owner of the station was the Boston Herald-Traveler Corporation, a newspaper company that also operated two local radio stations and held a controlling interest in a CATV company. The FCC turned the license over to a citizens group, Boston Broadcasters, Inc., composed of two Harvard professors and the Director of Massachusetts General Hospital. *Newsweek*, February 3, 1969, 65. Later in that year the Commission delayed renewal of the license of Station KRON-TV, in San Francisco, in order to consider whether the fact that it is owned by San Francisco's only morning newspaper constitutes an undue concentration of media control. *The New York Times*, April 27, 1969, 72. In 1970, in the afore-mentioned proceeding (Docket No. 18110), the FCC promulgated the rules it had earlier proposed, limiting ownership of broadcast stations of all kinds (whether AM, FM or TV) to one to each market (though permitting limited AM-FM radio combinations in small towns), so far as future licenses were concerned. It also proposed rules that would require present licensees, within five years, to reduce their holdings to either an AM-FM radio combination, a television station, or a newspaper in the same market. First Report and Order, and Further Notice of Proposed Rule Making, March 25, 1970. See also the submission in this proceeding by James N. Rosse, Bruce M. Owen, and David L. Grey, "Economic Issues in the Joint Ownership of Newspaper and Television Media," including the study by Owen, "Empirical Results on the Price Effects of Joint Ownership in the Mass Media," mimeo., Memorandum No. 97, Research Center in Economic Growth, Stanford University, May, 1970.

For similar indications of the determination of the Department of Justice to attack multimedia companies, see its *Complaint* under Section 7 of the Clayton Act in *U.S. v. Gannett Co., Inc., WREX-TV, Inc. and Rockford Newspapers, Inc.*, Civil Action No. 68 C 48, U.S. District Court, Northern District of Illinois, Western Division, filed December 5, 1968, contesting the acquisition by Gannett, the owner of WREX, of all the common stock of Rockford Newspapers, in 1967; and its submission to the Federal Communications Commission, *In the Matter of Amendment of Part 74, Subpart K, of the Commission's Rules and Regulations Relative to Community Antenna Television Systems et al.*, Docket No. 18397, *Comments of the United States Department of Justice*, April 7, 1969, recommending prohibition of any common ownership between CATV systems and either television stations or newspapers in the same community or market. The FCC complied, partially, in 1970, when it prohibited local cross-ownership of CATV systems by television broadcasters and all ownership of such systems by the TV networks; and it asked for comments on various suggestions for limiting multiple ownership of CATV systems on a regional and national basis, and on cross-ownership of CATV ventures with newspapers, magazines, advertising agencies, and others. *Ibid.*, Docket No. 18397, Second Report and Order, and Docket No. 18891, Notice of Proposed Rule Making and of Inquiry, June 24, 1970.

Separate but related developments, clearly illustrating the political aspects of multimedia ownership, were initiated in 1969, one by a Democrat and one by a Republican. In the first, Milton Shapp, defeated gubernatorial candidate, asked the FCC not to renew the license of WFIL-TV, in Philadelphia, one of the main properties in the publishing and television holdings of Walter Annenburg, whom President Nixon had previously appointed Ambassador to Great Britain. The Annenberg family, Shapp charged, enjoyed a "near news monopoly in the Philadelphia area" and had "conducted a personal vendetta against me," adding that "the news has been censored, omitted, twisted, distorted and used for . . . personal purposes." *New York Times*, July 4, 1969. The other incident was the highly publicized speech by Vice-President Agnew later that year, charging an excessive concentration of control over the news media and specifically singling out the newspaper and

With respect to vertical integration, airplane manufacturers must have the approval of the CAB to hold any ownership interest in airline carriers;[10] the Public Utility Holding Company Act prohibits affiliates from selling services or equipment to operating companies except under terms and conditions set by the SEC;[11] the Clayton Act prohibits common carriers from purchasing supplies without competitive bidding from companies with whom they have interlocking directors;[12] Comsat operates under a mandate to purchase all supplies by competitive bidding.[13]

With regard to the cooperation among unaffiliated companies aimed at achieving some of the benefits of integration, regulatory policies cover the whole range from prohibition to compulsion. As we have already indicated in Chapter 2, these companies have voluntarily sought to achieve the various advantages of collaboration, in which event regulation has been essentially permissive. But where the companies in question have also been actual or potential competitors, their zeal for collaboration has often been excessive rather than inadequate, and directed more to the suppression of competition than reduction in costs or improvement of service. In these circumstances, it has been necessary to police their agreements, in an attempt (though rarely with great assiduity, enthusiasm, or success[14]) to prevent their serving as instruments for the collusive suppression of desirable rivalry among the parties or for the exclusion of outside competitors.

On the other hand, for reasons that we have already examined, private companies do not always cooperate in all the ways that would be socially advantageous.[15] For these reasons, regulatory legislation and administration have from time to time essayed the more positive roles of persuasion, encouragement, and compulsion—though almost certainly far less than would have been desirable. And they have done so in the interest not only of efficiency but of preserving competition.

This combination of considerations and motives illustrates the major problems inherent in policies directed at maintaining competition. Effective competition calls for a balancing-off of considerations of efficiency on the one hand and purity of rivalry on the other. In the presence of economies of integration (as of scale), the balancing has to be between permitting firms large and integrated enough to enjoy these economies and firms numerous enough and with sufficient opportunity for effective rivalry. In the presence of potential economies of interfirm coordination, the balancing is one of cooperation on the one hand and independence of action on the other. At times, these goals coincide rather than conflict—when, for example, coordination is necessary both to save costs and to preserve the competitive opportunities of viable firms that would otherwise be excluded from a fair opportunity to compete. But in other circumstances they may conflict— where, for example, a merger of two competing railroads will reduce costs,

---

broadcasting properties of the (Democratic) *Washington Post* and *New York Times*.
[10] See the CAB proceeding on whether Howard Hughes should be permitted to retain control of Air West, a West Coast feeder line, despite his large interests in aircraft manufacture. *Wall Street Journal*, December 16, 1969, 38.
[11] 15 U.S. Code 79m (b), 1964 ed.

[12] 15 U.S. Code 20, 1964 ed.
[13] See Irwin, "Comment," in Trebing, ed., *op. cit.*, 156–160; but note from our descriptions of the relevant statutory provisions that Irwin's characterizations are not always accurate.
[14] See, for example, Boies, *op. cit.*; also pp. 69–70, above.
[15] See pp. 64–69, Chapter 2, above.

or where the integration of several public utility functions, in the interest of efficiency, gives rise to the danger that independent companies will be denied access to some complementary function on equal terms with their integrated competitors.

Manifestly, we cannot hope here to analyze all the policies we have just summarized, or any one of them thoroughly. The purpose of this chapter is to examine the implications of integration in the regulated industries, the contribution it can make to improved performance, the kinds of problems it raises, and its relationship to the broad yet central question of the proper role and requirements of effective competition in this sector of the economy.

FINANCIAL INTEGRATION

Although the merits of financial integration of public utility companies will differ from one kind of integration to another and from one industry to another, there are certain themes or considerations—both pro and con— that are more or less common to all. It would be efficient, therefore, to lay out the main ones at the outset, to provide a blueprint for the more detailed, individual illustrations that follow. In this way we illustrate, once again, the two parts of the task of devising the best possible institutional structure for any industry: on one side, the development and recognition of common principles and considerations; on the other, striking the best possible balance in the particular, and always in some degree unique, circumstances of each individual case.

The same observations apply equally to the unregulated sectors of the economy as well. What makes their application to the public utility situation in some degree unique is the typically greater degree of monopoly power prevalent in these industries; the greater external restraint on the full exploitation of that power imposed by regulation itself; and the special character of their technology. But these are differences of degree only. It is an open question whether the degree of monopoly power that exists or ought appropriately to be permitted in some of the regulated industries— most notably, transportation—is greater than prevails in such theoretically unregulated sectors of the economy as the production of automobiles or haircuts. It is also an open question how much greater a restraint is imposed on the exercise of monopoly by formal public regulation in these industries than by various informal influences and managerial self-restraint in some of the unregulated sectors of the economy.[16]

The simplest case for integration is that it may be a more efficient way of doing business. In the case of horizontal integration, the extreme situation is the one of natural monopoly. Vertical integration can make possible a closer synchronization of input and output flows, a closer control of quality, a better adjustment of capacity at the several stages of the production process than can be achieved by separate firms dealing with one another at arms length; and it may save enough, additionally, in reduced costs of selling and transferring materials or products from one level to the other to compensate firms for the limitation in their range of choice of suppliers

---

[16] In any event, since the focus of this book is on the formally regulated industries, we make no explicit effort as we go along to demonstrate consistently in which respects the argument applies equally to the unregulated sectors and in which respects it does not.

or customers that it usually involves. The possible efficiency advantages of conglomerate integration may be best conceived as arising from a fuller or better utilization of a firm's capacity, broadly defined—where its management, physical production plant, research laboratories, or distribution facilities can take on an additional product or market with a smaller increase in cost than if those products or markets were supplied by separate firms.

For these reasons alone, integration is potentially promotive of competition, not only because its cost savings may permit firms to compete more effectively, but also by virtue of the act of integration itself: it clearly contributes to competition if firms are free to undertake whatever new functions they choose, whenever they think they can perform them more effectively than they were previously being performed. The mere ability of firms to integrate thus constitutes a kind of potential competition that helps keep other firms on their toes.[17]

As far as vertical and conglomerate integration are concerned, this possible competitive contribution carries as a corollary a defense against the rather widespread supposition that integration is inherently dangerous because it increases business power and creates the threat of monopoly. The defense has two components. First, monopoly power, as the economist defines it, depends principally on the number of sellers of any given commodity or service: it is a horizontal phenomenon. Neither vertical nor conglomerate integration, as such, changes market structure in this respect, at least not for the worse. If accomplished by acquisition, all that changes is the identity of the firm in the market in question; if accomplished by internal expansion—that is, if the integrating firm enters the business by constructing its own facilities—the immediate effect is to increase the number of competitors in the market in question by one. (Clearly this defense does not apply to horizontal integration and particularly when accomplished by merger: in this event the number of competitors in any particular market is reduced by one.)

The second part of the defense is this: if a firm cannot increase its market power by vertical or conglomerate integration, what possible reason would it have to integrate except a belief that it can perform the new function at least as well or better than the firms already doing it? (Of course, if one felt that the possibilities of monopolistic exploitation in any market are increased by the mere fact that firms in it are large and integrated—a view that has adherents among economists[18]—this defense has diminished persuasiveness.)

---

[17] "Large businesses and integration are necessary agencies and inevitable manifestations of a free enterprise system. The firm that competes successfully must be permitted to grow; by the same token, businesses must ordinarily be free to expand if they think they can in this way enhance their ability to serve the customer. Competition requires also that business units be free, ordinarily, to take on new products, new functions, or enter new markets—in short, to integrate." Reprinted from Dirlam and Kahn, *Fair Competition*, 141. Copyright 1954 by Cornell University. Used by permission of Cornell University Press.
"The easiest curb on monopoly power, the

most effective cure for poor performance, and the one most consistent with free enterprise, is freedom of entry. And this includes, manifestly, the right of an existing business to extend its operations into any area its managers see fit to enter, i.e., to integrate." *Ibid.*, 151–152.
[18] A leading exponent of this position is Corwin D. Edwards. See, for example, his "Conglomerate Bigness as a Source of Power," *Business Concentration and Price Policy*, A Conference of the Universities–National Bureau Committee for Economic Research (Princeton: Princeton Univ. Press, 1955), 331–361, and his testimony before the Hart Committee, U.S. Senate, Committee on the Judiciary, Subcom-

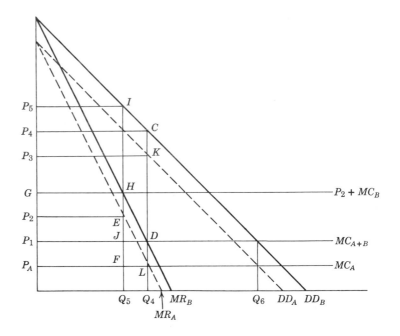

This defense has been developed with particular clarity for the case of vertical integration, but it has also been applied, with modifications, to conglomerate integration and to a host of competitive practices, like exclusive dealing, exclusive territorial distributorships, full-line forcing and tying-in,[19] that achieve some of the benefits of integration and are generally deemed to be at least potentially anticompetitive in effect. While this case must be substantially modified in the public utility context, it is nonetheless important that it be understood. Figure 1 provides the simplest possible explanation of the argument.

Vertical integration raises no problems whatever except in the event of some preexisting monopoly power. If all the horizontal strata of an industry, representing the successive stages of the production process, were purely competitive, there could be no possible effect on competition if some of the firms embraced two or more of these strata within their own spheres of

---

mittee on Antitrust and Monopoly, the 88th Cong. Second Sess., *Economic Concentration, Hearings*, Part 1, 1964, 36–56; see also the response by Jesse W. Markham, *ibid.*, Part 3,

1269–1281.

[19] See the writings of Bork and Bowman, cited note 21, below.

operation: the integrated firms would still be subject to the uninhibited checks of competition at whatever point they made their final sales. We therefore assume here the ultimate in monopoly—a single firm selling a final product, B, the demand for which is indicated in the figure. And we assume, for simplicity, that the industry has only two strata, one producing the input A and a second that transforms A into B, with respective marginal costs as indicated that we assume for simplicity to be horizontal. If the monopolist is unregulated and able to buy his input A at minimum cost (that is, at MC), he will maximize profit by producing up to the point where MC_{A+B} equals MR_B. His output will be Q_4, his price P_4, and his monopoly profit will be the rectangle P_1P_4CD.[20] As long as he can buy his input A at minimum cost, he has no incentive whatever to integrate vertically; he can extract all the possible monopoly profit there is to be extracted from the market by charging the markup CD over his own marginal costs. Clearly he would integrate backward only if he were paying a higher price for A than (he thinks) it would cost him to produce it himself—because the present suppliers are less efficient than he would be, or because they have monopoly power and are charging him more than MC, or if there were additional efficiencies in the combining of the operations.

Figure 1 illustrates one such possible occasion. Suppose that the suppliers of A do have some monopoly power and are therefore able to charge not P_A but, say, P_2, thus giving them monopoly profits designated by the rectangle P_AP_2EF. In this event, the downstream monopolist would find his own marginal costs elevated to the level $P_2 + MC_B$. In these circumstances, he would maximize his own profit by producing up to the point where this new, artificially elevated marginal cost curve equaled MR_B, or quantity Q_5. He would still be getting some monopoly profits, GP_5IH, but these would clearly be smaller than he had earned before, mainly because he would now have to share some of the potential monopoly profits from the industry with the suppliers of A. In this event, it would obviously pay him to go into the production of A himself, obtaining that input once more at cost, MC_A, increasing his output to Q_4, reducing his price to P_4 and in this way, once more, enjoying the monopoly profits P_1P_4CD. Notice that in this case, in which inputs are transferred from one stratum to another at prices in excess of marginal costs, the price to the ultimate consumer is raised even beyond the level charged by a single, integrated monopolist; and that, therefore, vertical integration is in the interest of the consumer as well as of the monopolist himself.[21]

---

[20] The reader might have some difficulty in accepting the difference between marginal cost and price as a measure of monopoly profits. Pure competition does equate price with marginal cost. But since there is no certainty that short-run marginal cost will in fact cover average total cost, it might be simpler for the reader to interpret the MC lines in the diagram as depicting long-run marginal cost, in an industry which produces under conditions of constant cost. This means that MC may be taken as equal to ATC, when firms operate at the lowest-cost point.

[21] It is in fact in the interest of suppliers at both levels, jointly. The two back-to-back monopolists do not succeed in maximizing their own aggregate profits when they operate independently in the manner indicated. The total of the profits earned by the suppliers of A and by the B monopolist, P_AP_2EF and GP_5IH, respectively, is less than P_1P_4CD, the profits earned by the latter when he is able to obtain his inputs at MC. The reason for this is quite simple. No matter what the arbitrary price at which A is transferred, the true marginal cost of the entire production process is still MC_{A+B}. The increase in output from Q_5 to Q_4 effected by vertical integration would add more to

So we have a simple illustration of the case for vertical integration on static grounds. Monopoly power is a horizontal, not a vertical phenomenon. It is in the interest of a (horizontal) monopolist to have all the other functions in his industry—the supply of his inputs, the processing, and distribution of his products—performed at minimum cost and charged for at the minimum price. As long as these two conditions prevail, he has no incentive to integrate vertically: he can appropriate the maximum profit available in the industry in the price that he charges for his own service, being assured that that price will be added to and will have added to it the minimum possible charge for all other services upstream and downstream from him. If those conditions do not prevail, it then does pay him to integrate; but in that event (if he made no mistake in doing so) the resultant lowering of the cost or price at which the associated function is performed can only be beneficial to consumers, if it affects them at all.

The possible benefits have a dynamic aspect as well. As we have suggested, the act of integration or the mere threat of entry into a market by this device can contribute the same stimulus as can other forms of direct, horizontal competition to continuing efforts at cost reduction and innovation by companies in that market. In addition, integration can encourage investment and innovation because of the special *incentives* to which it may give rise[21a], the particular *opportunities* it generates, and the additional *ability*

---

revenues than to costs: the sacrificed profit is represented by the triangle *JHD* (*JH* being the amount by which the cost of *A* to the *B* supplier is inflated by monopoly). The foregoing demonstration is taken essentially from J. J. Spengler, "Vertical Integration and Antitrust Policy," *Jour. Pol. Econ.* (August 1959), LVIII: 347. The argument has been developed at much greater length by Robert H. Bork, notably in his article, "Vertical Integration and the Sherman Act: the Legal History of an Economic Misconception," *Univ. of Chicago Law Rev.* (Autumn 1954), XXII: 157. Bork and Ward S. Bowman Jr. have also applied similar reasoning to conglomerate integration and various allegedly restrictive trade practices in "The Crisis in Antitrust," *Fortune*, reproduced along with exchanges with Harlan M. Blake and William K. Jones as "The Goals of Antitrust: a Dialogue on Policy," *Columbia Law Rev.* (March 1965), LXV: 363–466.

[21a] In refusing to permit the Michigan Consolidated Gas Co. to finance low and moderate income housing projects in the Detroit area (note 2, p. 253, above), the SEC held that the proposed operation lacked the requisite "operating or functional relationship" to the public utility business. The Act did, indeed, seem to envisage continued integration with "other businesses" only in the presence of direct, physical relationships between the several operations such that their integrated operation would result in lower costs of production or distribution. In so doing, it seemed to ignore the possibility of special *commercial* relationships such as might under integration give rise to an incentive to engage in socially desirable investments that might otherwise not be made. As Commissioner Smith argued, in his dissent:

"The fulcrum of any reasoned analysis of these questions is the term 'business.' Corporate business functions are becoming broader in concept than a strict limitation to operations.... Public utility companies in particular . . . have a basic commitment to the areas they serve.... It is not possible for a utility simply to pull up stakes and move to another area.... If large portions of the service area become dilapidated and unfit for habitation, the utility must face not only a possible reduction in revenue but the additional expense and burden of servicing areas that lie beyond....

"In light of the Congressionally recognized relevance of the present investments, I think it can readily be found that those investments are, under Section 11(b)(1), both reasonably incidental and economically necessary or appropriate to the operations of the utility system....

"The proposed housing projects involve modest commitments of capital and provide an economic return on those investments both to investors and consumers. For the same reasons the investments are likewise, under Section 9 (c) (3), 'appropriate in the ordinary course of business' under any construction of that term which takes into account the dynamics of contemporary corporate functions and responsibilities." *Loc. cit.*

that it may confer on a firm to mobilize resources for these purposes. A company will have unusual incentives to develop new equipment or other inputs that it needs in its own operations or better outlets or new uses for its product; it may have unusual opportunities, arising from its own operating experience, to perceive the need and possibilities for such an effort; and it might, by being able to assure successful innovations a market, be best able to justify the application of resources to their development.[22]

---

[22] Whether the superior ability of a large integrated company to raise capital is a reflection of imperfection of the capital market or, instead, a genuine efficiency advantage conferred by integration is a complicated question that cannot be resolved here. Certainly, if company A can raise funds in order to undertake an investment X because investors know that they will be protected by virtue of the wide span of A's operations and sources of income against any possible loss if that particular project proves a failure, whereas company B cannot raise capital for that very same investment, there is an element of imperfection in the capital market; the advantage of integrated company A over nonintegrated company B may be said to be essentially private and strategic. The proper test of whether a particular investment should be made is surely the risk of that investment, not the risk to the *investor*; the latter may be large or small depending on the mere size or diversification of the borrower. See the fuller discussion of this point at note 117, below. Arguing to some extent to the contrary, see George J. Stigler, "Imperfections in the Capital Market," *Jour. Pol. Econ.* (June 1967), LXXV: 287–292.

But where the advantage of A arises from the fact that it is in a better position to perceive the opportunity for the investment or to assure its success, this could be a genuine social, efficiency advantage of integration.

This whole area is one in which economists have not developed entirely satisfactory normative judgments. Because the present writer has grappled with the problem at some length (in collaboration with M. G. de Chazeau) he may be excused for quoting at some length from that earlier study:

"Economic theory has generally found the strongest case for market imperfection in the conditions needed for economic progress. . . . Here, if anywhere, the security of established position, conferred by size and integration, might be needed to balance the hazards of long and costly experimentation, of long-term expenditures on research and development for new products and processes, and of explorations to reveal new sources of crude oil and new ways of developing synthetics to take its

place. A logical case can be made for the proposition that the public benefits from these advantages of the large vertically integrated company—from its greater sensitivity to investment opportunities, ability to marshal funds, and willingness to use them at relatively low anticipated rates of return." *Integration and Competition in the Petroleum Industry* (New Haven: Yale Univ. Press, 1959), 278.

"The possible contributions [of integration to innovation] are varied but the basic one is to be found in the nature of the *incentives* inherent in integration itself—arising out of the mutual reenforcement and support that a company's separate operations lend to one another. The ownership of practically unusable sour crude in large amounts gave Standard Oil an urgent reason to seek a desulfurizing process and to apply it widely once it was found. The low, precarious margins of refiners provided strong incentives to minimize the costs of laying down crude oil at the refinery and distributing its products: they were practically forced to develop pipelines . . . to improve the efficiency of their barge and tanker transport, and to push forward the rationalization of their marketing. Heavy investments in refining and marketing facilities plus declining California output of crude oil undoubtedly spurred Union Oil to acquire oil shale lands and to study methods of using them. . . . One could go on; but the point is simply this: in a closely integrated operation, failure, irritation, need, or surplus at any one level or in any one process of the industry creates an imbalance which stirs up compensatory, socially beneficial activity at other levels. . . .

"The larger the exposure-front of a firm's commercial operations, the greater the probability that experts within its organization will recognize the potentialities of a new idea or product in commercial application; and the wider the firm's commercial interests, the more likely it is to apply its resources for the development of such an idea." Pp. 309–310.

"Imperfect knowledge and imperfect competition are characteristic of all real markets, including capital markets. It is because of these imperfections that the planning and budgeting of capital outlays are such vital management functions, and integration may contribute to

There are offsetting dangers even in unregulated industry, revolving around the possibility that integration may protect, reinforce, or extend preexisting (horizontal) monopoly power. The issue is much disputed and we make no effort further to analyze it here.[23] But these dangers are accentuated by monopoly and regulation. Backward vertical integration is a possible way of circumventing regulation in the exploitation of monopoly power.[24] Consider the situation illustrated in Figure 1, above. The ideal level of output is not Q_4 but Q_6; the efficient price, not P_4 but P_1. And that is the price that an effective regulatory commission would set (assuming, as before, that marginal cost suffices to cover average total cost as well), provided that the regulated company is able to buy input A at the competitive price or produces it itself. If, however, it (or its officers) were able to acquire control over the production of A or some beneficial share in its ownership, and this stratum of the industry were not itself regulated, the regulated company could appropriate all the potential monopoly gains from this industry in the price that it charged for A. That would be P_3—the price which, when there was added to it the marginal cost of performing the B function, would yield the industry profit-maximizing price to the final consumer, P_4. The utility commission would in this event be holding the company to its cost of service, P_4; but the only difference from the unregulated monopoly situation would be that the same total amount of profits, $P_A P_3 KL$, would now flow into the pockets of the affiliated unregulated producer of A rather than, in the form $P_1 P_4 CD$, into the coffers of the public utility company itself.[25]

---

their more effective performance. Firm A, which integrates several levels of production and processing, may know better than firm B, which operates at only one level, what investments will prove profitable for private investment and will meet a continuing public need. Or both A and B may recognize a socially profitable investment opportunity but, because the market for loanable funds is imperfect, only A may be able to effect the necessary financing on acceptable terms. . . . Such an advantage would be A's superior ability to reduce the real risks or realize the full benefits of investment by fitting a particular project into its integrated structure with consequent mutually sustaining or reenforcing advantages at more than one level of operation. For example, it might pay an integrated oil company, but not an outsider, to turn petroleum byproducts into synthetic detergents, carry them to market in its own trucks, and sell them in its own service stations, because the added costs of the project are slight and it already has facilities to do part of the job. . . .

"it seems impossible to doubt that because of the superior access to knowledge, opportunity, incentive, or resources, or because they already have part of the necessary capacity and it takes relatively little added capital to perform the new function, integrated firms

may make investments that would not otherwise be made—investments that may prove economically justifiable in the sense that they add to the social product a sufficient amount of goods and services to justify use of the savings here rather than elsewhere." (*Ibid.*, 260–261.)

For a similar argument, interpreting "Integration as an Adjustment to Risk and Uncertainty," which, by "increasing knowledge and control," promotes efficiency, reduces various insurancelike costs, and in certain circumstances makes commercially feasible the adoption of new cost-reducing technology, see the article by H. R. Jensen, E. W. Kehrberg and D. W. Thomas, *Southern Econ. Jour.* (April 1962), XXVIII: 378–384.

[23] See the Blake & Jones exchange with Bork and Bowman, note 21, above; also Fritz Machlup and Martha Taber, "Bilateral Monopoly, Successive Monopoly and Vertical Integration," *Economica*, n.s. (May 1960), XXVII: 101–119; Dirlam and Kahn, *Fair Competition*, 142–150 and *passim*; and de Chazeau and Kahn, *op. cit.*, 44–50 and *passim*.

[24] See p. 28, esp. note 20, in Volume 1.

[25] This same result can be demonstrated, as we have in the broken lines of Figure 1, by asking what it would be in the interest of a monopoly supplier of input A to charge, if he knew that the downstream function, B, would

A second danger peculiar to the public utilities is the A-J-W tendency: regulated companies might wish to integrate regardless of whether they can perform the added functions more efficiently than others are already doing so, in order to expand their rate bases and their total permitted profits.[26] This is only another way of making the more general point that the defenses of integration set forth above assume not only the absence of a possibility that it may increase monopoly power but also that firms attempt to maximize profits. Where they are prevented from doing so but are permitted to recover all additions to cost including a return on all additional investments, the taking on of losing operations may itself actually conduce to profit maximization. By the same token, these dangers of integration may prevail even in unregulated industries, to the extent that managers are willing to subordinate profit-maximization to the goal of increasing the size or growth of the firms they manage.

The third danger is one that exists also in unregulated industries, but it is accentuated by the greater monopoly power that typically prevails in public utilities: a firm may, by its integration, foreclose competitors from a fair opportunity to compete. This possibility arises, as we shall see, under conglomerate as well as vertical integration, but it can be most easily demonstrated in the latter situation. When a public utility monopolist provides its own input, it forecloses independent suppliers absolutely from selling at all to the entire industry. The typical defense of integration

---

be performed at a price of only MC_B. The derived demand for product A would be DD_A—the demand for the final product minus the marginal cost of performing the B function. In that event, the marginal revenue function for firm A would be MR_A, its profit maximizing point would be at the intersection of that marginal revenue function with its MC_A, its optimum output would be Q_4, its price P_3, to which would be added the MC_B, producing a final price of P_4. As this demonstrates, the possibility that the focus of monopolistic exploitation of the consumer would be simply transferred from the public utility phase, B, to the input-supplying stratum, A, is not itself dependent on vertical integration: it would pay suppliers of A in any event to organize themselves in order to extract such monopoly profits, if they possibly could. But it would not be in the interest of the nonintegrated public utility company to permit them to do so, because the higher price of A would mean lower sales, a smaller rate base, and therefore a smaller permissible total profit. It would therefore have a strong incentive to integrate backward in order to produce the input itself.

[26] An interesting illustration of both the competitive contribution of vertical integration and of its possible dangers is provided by one of the early cases in which the Federal Power Commission certificated a competing natural gas pipeline. The Michigan Consolidated Gas Company was originally almost entirely dependent for its supplies on the Panhandle Eastern Pipe Line Company. The relationship between the two was a stormy one, particularly during and immediately after World War II, when gas was in short supply and the Michigan company claimed that Panhandle was favoring its industrial users. When Panhandle seemed unwilling to expand its capacity sufficiently to meet the soaring demands of Michigan's market, the latter's parent, American Light and Traction organized a subsidiary, Michigan-Wisconsin Pipe Line Company, which applied to the FPC in 1945 for the right to lay a pipeline from the Southwest into the Michigan and Wisconsin market areas. Panhandle objected, seeking to reserve the market for itself. Since the Commission lacked the authority to require Panhandle to expand its capacity more rapidly, the backward integration by the local distribution companies proved an essential means of giving them the additional supplies that they required and freeing them from complete dependence on their reluctant supplier.

At the same time, the FPC was aware of the danger that those local distribution companies would thereafter give preference to their own affiliated suppliers, whose proposed prices, as it happened, were higher than those charged by Panhandle. It therefore attempted, in certificating the competing line, to protect the rights of Panhandle to share in the market. See Nelson Lee Smith, *op. cit.*, 668–673.

assumes that the integrated companies will continue at critical points to be subject to a market test—vertically integrated firms competing with one another and possibly also with nonintegrated firms at their various levels. In this event, their comparative efficiency is subject always to a test and their incentives to be efficient and progressive remain strong. But the vertically integrated monopolist is subject to no such check. Even, therefore, if it attempts to be as efficient as possible, there is no way of its knowing whether it is in fact succeeding in doing so.

These dangers, it might be argued, are the dangers of simple monopoly. It is monopoly that lacks the competitive spur and test; it is monopoly that is at least potentially subject to managerial stultification or pursuit of goals other than profit. But especially in the presence of regulation, vertical integration can *extend* both the *scope* of that monopoly and the ability to *exploit* it. When a public utility monopolist decides to produce its own equipment, it may (though it need not) by this act eliminate the pressures and tests of competition from the stratum of equipment manufacture as well. In this way it extends the danger of managerial conservatism untested and unspurred by competition to the manufacturing of inputs as well.

So what we have are the possible contributions of integration on the one hand and of competition on the other to efficient and progressive performance, with each institutional device in some ways potentially compatible, in some ways incompatible with the other. No wonder the marriage of competition and regulation is an uneasy one, with the terms of the contract subject to constant redefinition and the parties constantly rushing to their respective lawyers. No wonder, either, that no mere economist is capable of prescribing the ideal contract, ideal for all parties and all circumstances.

Combination Companies

There is one extremely strong case to be made for conglomerately integrated companies in any industry, wherever a service can be provided or performed by a number of alternative media: the company that is in a position to use any or all of the media will find it in its own interest to choose the combination in each case that performs the service at the lowest possible cost.

Figure 2 illustrates the general point. Here we assume an industry composed of three different plants (A, B, and C), with differing marginal cost curves, all capable of supplying a particular product or service. Part D of the figure is simply a (horizontal) summation of parts A, B, and C, representing the marginal cost for the industry as a whole: its horizontal or x-axis scale is smaller, simply in order to keep the size of the figure down. Assume first that the industry is a competitive one (to make this assumption more plausible, assume there are several hundred plants of each type, each separately owned.) Since under pure competition firms will produce up to the point at which marginal cost equals price, these various marginal cost curves will tell how much the various firms will provide at various prices and the horizontal summation of those marginal costs, in part D, is an industry supply curve. Assuming an industry demand curve, AR, the competitive price is P_c and its intersection with the various marginal cost curves for the individual plants specifies their respective outputs, Q_c. Notice, then, that the tendency of each company to produce up to the point at which marginal cost equals a uniform industry price has the effect of equalizing the cost

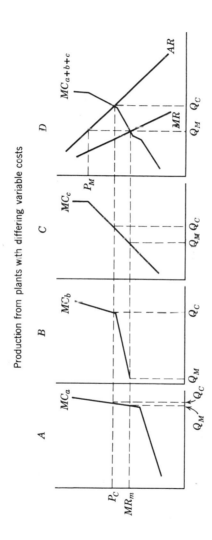

Production from plants with differing variable costs

at the margin of each, at P_c. And this results in the aggregate industry output being distributed among the various firms and plants in such a way as to produce it at the minimum cost. Any redistribution of output, for example, an increase in the production of C and a corresponding decrease by B, would involve a greater total utilization of resources, since the cost of the production cut back at B (moving downward to the left along its MC curve) would have been less than the additional cost of producing that quantity in C (moving upward to the right along its MC curve).

The same rule would be followed if all the plants were owned by a rational monopolist. In this event, marginal revenue for that company would be below average revenue, as shown in part D; the monopolist would therefore produce only Q_m, and sell it at the higher price, P_m. But in distributing that lesser output among his various plants, it would obviously be in his interest to do it in such a way as to minimize variable production cost, and that means equalizing the cost at the margin in the respective facilities. Since it is with MR rather than price that the monopolist equates his marginal cost, Figure 2 finds the proper levels of output of the individual plants by drawing the profit-maximizing MR_m leftward through parts A, B, and C of the diagram. The points of intersection between MR and the separate MC's determine the respective Q_m levels of output there indicated. Notice that the cutbacks from the Q_c levels differ greatly from one plant to another: the output of plant A is scarcely curtailed at all, whereas plant B is almost entirely shut down—and correctly so, because to produce any more from B would involve a larger incremental use of resources than would be saved by curtailing the output of plants A or C correspondingly. This is exactly how output would be distributed or redistributed by a cartel, if its several members were willing and able to behave in such a way as to maximize their joint profits;[27] and it is the way in which power pools allocate production from one moment to the next among the various elements in their interconnected network.[28]

It is easy to translate this demonstration into terms appropriate to an integrated transportation or communications company, by interpreting the various types of plants as describing the entire range of alternative media, over all the possible routes, that might be employed to handle a particular shipment. Assuming first, for simplicity, that what customers buy is transportation from one point to another, rather than rail, air, truck, ship, barge, or pipeline transportation over any particular routes as such, then an integrated transportation company would have an interest in supplying that

[27] See Don Patinkin, "Multiple-Plant Firms, Cartels, and Imperfect Competition," *Q. Jour. Econ.* (February 1947), LXI: 173–205. Typically, however, cartels have been unable to reach the necessary degree of understanding. Firm B, in our illustration, would be unwilling to curtail production and sales so drastically in the interest of maximizing industry-wide efficiency and profit, unless it obtained compensation from the others; industry profit-maximizing cartel behavior, in short, requires also an acceptable scheme for profit-sharing. More typically, cartels tend to behave in the opposite manner, curtailing output by the usually larger and lower-cost plants and firms in order to hold price high enough to permit continued production and survival of smaller, higher-cost producers—for the simple reason that the latter, being usually more numerous, have more votes. See Kahn, *op. cit.*, *International Encyclopedia of the Social Sciences*, Vol. II, 320–325 and *op. cit.*, U.S. Senate, Committee on the Judiciary, 137–138, reproduced in *Natural Resources Jour.* (January 1970), X: 58–60. Also Morris A. Adelman, "Efficiency of Resource Use in Crude Petroleum," *South. Econ. Jour.* (October 1964), XXXI: 101–122.

[28] See pp. 64–65, Chapter 2, above.

demand with the lowest-cost combination of media. In this manner, integration would eliminate the conflicts of interest that stand in the way of the wholehearted intermodal coordination required for maximum efficiency.[29] Without significant alteration the same expectations are applicable to companies that distribute both electricity and gas: we have already alluded to the example of a company that especially promoted sales of electricity in the winter and gas in the summer because these were their respective periods of off-peak demand.[30]

It would complicate but not alter this exposition to take into account the fact that the nature and quality of service provided by the various modes of transportation or sources of energy are not homogeneous, differing in such important respects as speed or susceptibility to door-to-door pickup and delivery in one case, cleanliness and cost of associated equipment in the other. It will still pay the integrated company, other things being equal, to provide the particular kind of service demanded by the lowest-cost combination of facilities and to offer higher quality service whenever its added value to customers exceeds the added costs of providing it.[31]

But surely, it will have occurred to the reader, this exposition has failed to take into account the A-J-W effect? Yes, this could well be a danger. Just as regulated companies might be reluctant to coordinate their operations and share some of the business with others, because they would prefer to keep as much of it as possible to justify their own rate bases (see p. 67, Chapter 2, above), so integrated companies, free from that particular constraint, might nonetheless prefer to use the media with the highest capital intensity rather than with the lowest marginal cost.

Whether this danger is important enough to counsel a prohibition of conglomerate integration depends on whether the A-J-W conditions are

---

[29] See pp. 66–69, above.

To be sure, such companies will define the relevant marginal costs in private terms and make no allowance for the possible discrepancies between private and social marginal costs that are so prevalent in transportation because of discriminatory governmental subsidies and taxes. It would be adding one illogicality to another, however, to try to compensate for these latter distortions by prohibiting integration—even though it happens that the railroads, who are the main victims of this discrimination, would presumably be more likely to insist on being permitted to reduce prices to marginal costs in order to win traffic back from their subsidized competitors if ownership of these competing facilities is kept separate than if the railroads too were able to take advantage of the subsidies by conducting their own motor carrier and barge operations.

[30] See note 16, Chapter 4, p. 95 of Volume 1.

[31] One is tempted to surmise, further, that it would be to the interest of such a company to set the price relationships among its various services efficiently—letting customers know exactly how much it would cost to provide them with different kinds of service by equating the rate differentials to the absolute differences in marginal cost, just as would happen under pure competition. (See pp. 174–175, Volume 1, on why this would be ideal.) In that event, the company or a competitive industry would in effect say to a customer: "You may have deliveries in one, two, or three days less time, or door-to-door, but it will cost you so many dollars extra because that is what it will cost me extra (incrementally) to give you this better service." But if the integrated company had monopoly power, it would not necessarily price in this way. If certain customers who required speed of delivery, for example, had inelastic demands *and* inadequate competitive alternatives, the price of the additional speed could be raised far above the incremental cost of supplying it, except to the extent that regulation prohibited it. But, of course, this kind of value-of-service pricing, limited only by the constraints of competition and regulation, prevails in the public utility industries today; conglomerate integration would be objectionable on this count only if it diminished the range of competitive alternatives available to customers with inelastic demand.

present or uncontrolled integration may bring them into being. This is a question that must be examined separately in each specific situation. The single most important condition is monopoly, incompletely exploited: the company has to be in a position in which it is *able* to use higher-cost methods of production when lower-cost methods are available, and to recoup by raising its charges correspondingly. So, to take two polar examples, Congress was obviously well advised to take this danger into consideration in judging whether to give the common carriers exclusive responsibility for developing and exploiting the communications satellite;[32] and, on the other hand, the danger seems a good deal less serious in the field of transportation today.

The efficiency advantages of permitting this kind of conglomerate integration will likewise vary markedly from one industry to another. In the simple model depicted in Figure 2, joining the plants together under common ownership produced no *improvement* in efficiency over the purely competitive outcome; and it resulted in a monopolistic reduction in output and increase in price. Manifestly, the introduction of multiplant or multimedia operations will improve an industry's social performance only if integration itself introduces cost savings or service improvements, or facilitates intermodal coordinations, that are unavailable to nonintegrated firms, or if the competition among nonintegrated companies is or would be seriously imperfect; *and* if the advantages thus achieved are not outweighed by the social disadvantages of increased monopoly power. The balance of social advantage will obviously vary from one industry to another.

Transportation. In the field of transportation the major issue has always been whether the railroad should be permitted to engage in other kinds of transportation. The Panama Canal Act of 1912 (p. 253, above) set the precedent of legislative opposition; and the national policy remains to this day in general one of disapproval except insofar as the proposed motor or water carriage is merely auxiliary and supplementary to the rail service.[33] The historic justification for this policy has been the danger of monopoly if the railroads were permitted to gain control of their major threatening competitors—in the first instance the ships that were about to use the new Panama Canal.

The danger is a real one for the simple reason that the proposed integration is not only conglomerate but at least partly horizontal: it involves joining

---

[32] See pp. 136–138, and note 102, p. 150, Chapter 4, above. On the other hand, as we have observed (note 76, p. 139, above), the President's Task Force on Communications Policy concluded that the possibilities of competition between cable and satellite are so limited in the international field—because the market is so small relative to available economies of scale—that the constitution of a single, multi-media chosen instrument offers the best hope of getting rational investment decisions made. *Op. cit.*, Chapter 2.

[33] According to the ICC interpretations, this means that the truck haul must be for only that portion of the total haul for which rail carriage is uneconomical—typically for picking up less than carload shipments and bringing them to the rail terminal, breaking up carload shipments and delivery to destination at the other end, and for carriage between points generating very small quantities of traffic. See *Pennsylvania Truck Lines, Inc., Acquisition of Control of Barker Motor Freight, Inc.*, 1 MCC 101 (1936), 5 MCC 9 (1937), and *Rock Island Motor Transit Co.— Purchase—White Line Motor Freight Co., Inc.*, 40 MCC 457 (1946), both as cited and described by Fulda, *op. cit.*, 386–391. The latter decision was sustained in *United States v. Rock Island Motor Transit Co.*, 340 U.S. 419 (1951). On the use of the requirement that the motor carrier handle only shipments that have a prior or subsequent movement by rail, see Fulda, *op. cit.*, 392–393.

together transport media that are not merely complementary (as when a truck picks up less than carload shipments and delivers them to a rail terminal) but also competitive or potentially so. So in its first decision under the Panama Canal Act, in which it demanded that various Eastern railroads give up their financial interests in water carriers on the Great Lakes, the ICC found that the railroads had

" 'a complete monopoly . . . over the lake line situation,' used their joint ownership to steadily advance rates and diverted from the lake routes to the all-rail lines some of the tonnage formerly moved by water,"

and concluded that financial separation of the two media would ensure

" 'a healthy rivalry and striving between such boat lines themselves and with paralleling railroads for all . . . traffic.' "[34]

Similarly, in its first decision under the corresponding provisions of the Motor Carrier Act of 1935, the Commission asserted:

"we are not convinced that the way to maintain for the future healthful competition between rail and truck service is to give the railroads free opportunity to go into the kind of truck service which is strictly competitive with, rather than auxiliary to, their rail operation. . . . Truck service would not, in our judgment, have developed to the extraordinary extent to which it has developed if it had been under railroad control. . . . The financial and soliciting resources of the railroads could easily be so used in this field that the development of independent service would be greatly hampered and restricted, and with ultimate disadvantage to the public."[35]

But it is precisely the fact that the various media are competing alternatives that constitutes the efficiency argument for permitting companies to sell not just rail or truck or air or water carriage but *transportation*—with freedom to select the least-cost methods of delivery.[36] This kind of diversification carries with it the possibility of dynamic as well as static benefits. Gellman contends that the greater freedom of Canadian than American railroads to operate extensively with other modes of transportation has spurred a great deal more innovation in developing multimodal shipping techniques in that country; it seems generally conceded that the exploitation of these possibilities has been unnecessarily slow in the United States.[37] Certainly the fewer the restrictions of this kind, the greater the possibility that each carrier could develop a range of alternative packages of services

[34] *Lake Line Applications Under Panama Canal Act,* 33 ICC 699 (1915) as described in Fulda, *op. cit.,* 378–379.
[35] *Pennsylvania Truck Lines-Barker Motor Freight,* 1 MCC 101 (1936), as quoted in the strong decision by the Supreme Court, *American Trucking Associations, Inc., et al. v. United States, et al.,* 364 U.S. 1, 8n. (1960). The main exception that the Court enunciated in this latter case to the general doctrine of confining trucking operations by railroads to "auxiliary and supplemental service" was in circumstances where the trucking service was not previously being performed adequately by independent companies. *Ibid.,* 11, citing its earlier decision in *American Trucking Assns. v. United States,* 355 U.S. 141 (1957).
[36] An early enthusiastic advocate was H. G. Moulton. See his "Fundamentals of National Transportation Policy," *Amer. Econ. Rev., Papers and Proceedings* (December 1933), XXIV: 33–46 and *The American Transportation Problem* (Washington: Brookings Institution, 1933), 889–890. For example, railroads have often been able to effect important economies by substituting trucking for more costly rail operations and buses for unprofitable passenger service. Locklin, *op. cit.,* 845.
[37] *Op. cit.,* 35–36, 47–48, and 74–75.

to meet the particular needs of each shipper, thereby relieving the latter of having to put the combinations together himself. The freer the railroads were to proceed along these lines, the freer they would be to compete with other transportation companies, some of them specialized, others as diversified as themselves. The restrictions imposed on the ability of carriers to adopt each other's technologies are at least in part protectionist in character: it is the trucks and water carriers that object to giving greater freedom to the railroads, and airlines that protest against similar efforts by motor carriers. What substance, if any, is there to the argument of these objectors that the public and not merely their own private interest is endangered by integration?

The traditional view has been that if railroads were free to go into water carriage and trucking, they would do so in order to control and suppress intermodal competition. With their preponderant investment in the rails, they would be interested not in promoting but in restricting these competitive media and diverting their traffic to the rails. This would require monopoly control over those rival media; it was feared railroads could achieve this because of their superior financial resources and the profits flowing from the traffic for which they still enjoyed a monopoly; these resources could be used to finance discriminatory sharpshooting, designed to drive their far smaller, nonintegrated rivals out of business.[38] In this unequal competitive combat the railroads would have the strategic advantage also of being able to divert to their own facilities—whether rail, water, or truck—whatever traffic they originated; and they could be expected to refuse to make their rail facilities available to their nonintegrated motor and water competitors on nondiscriminatory terms, so that the latter companies would be unable to offer shippers joint rates for multimedia service.[39]

---

[38] "Railroads, with large investments in fixed equipment . . . necessarily will try to keep as much traffic moving by rail as possible. Control of water or motor carriers would give them the opportunity to engage in destructive competition designed to force the competing water and motor carriers out of business. Once this was accomplished, the railroads could raise the water or motor rates well above the rail rates, thus diverting to the rails traffic normally moved by other modes. Indeed this was the practice of the railroads with respect to shipping on the Great Lakes before the Panama Canal Act." Note, "Coordination of Intermodal Transportation," *Columbia Law Rev.* (February 1969), LXIX: 271.

[39] As the Supreme Court put it, in sustaining ICC limitations on the trucking operations of railroads:

"Such limitation was in furtherance of the National Transportation Policy, for otherwise the resources of railroads might soon make over-the-road truck competition impossible. . . . Motor transportation then would be an adjunct to rail transportation, and hoped-for advancements in land transportation from supervised competition between motors and rails would not materialize. The control of the bulk of rail and motor transportation would be concentrated in one type of operation. Complete rail domination was not envisaged as a way to preserve the inherent advantages of each form of transportation." *United States v. Rock Island Motor Transit Company*, 340 U.S. 419, 432–433 (1951).

The Civil Aeronautics Board uses similar reasoning in barring surface carriers from engaging in air operations except those auxiliary or supplemental to their surface operations:

"the Board would not be justified in closing its eyes to the potential threat which the entry of surface carriers into this field would in many cases offer to independent air carriers or the effect which such participation might have upon the fulfillment of the policies of the Act. Surface carriers engaging in air transportation would at times be under a strong incentive to act for the protection of their investment in surface transportation interests. Again, by reason of their superior resources and extensive facilities for solicitation, such carriers would often be the possessors of powerful competitive weapons which would enable them to crush the competition of independent air carriers." *American President Lines, Ltd., et al.,* Petition, 7 CAB 799, 803 (1947).

The limited American experience with integrated transportation companies has not to my knowledge been analyzed with sufficient incisiveness for us to be able to judge to what extent the foregoing picture represents either an accurate historical diagnosis or a correct prognosis as of 1912 or 1935. It has some, at least, indirect, historical support. In truth, the railroads have shown little interest in collaborating with nonintegrated truck and water carriers, in order to permit shipments to be made with the lowest combination of media; instead, their typical posture has been one of obstruction and discrimination.[40] Of course this does not answer the case for integration— which is, precisely, that their attitude would be very different if the trucks and barges in question were their own. But their interest in the efficient allocation of the transport business has largely been confined, historically, to pressing for the intensification of regulatory protectionism rather than freeing them to compete more vigorously. As the *Doyle Report*, which is basically sympathetic to integration, points out, they have devoted all too little energy to determining the costs of handling different kinds of traffic on different media;[41] their past lethargy in this regard justifies little confidence

---

[40] It is always difficult to be certain whether the cases that have come to light are "typical": controversies arise only when one of the carriers is dissatisfied. But the frequency of these cases involving discrimination, exclusion, and refusal to cooperate with other carriers strongly suggests that this would be their typical behavior in the absence of regulation. See, for example, the section on piggybacking, later on in this chapter.

"Proponents of diversification make much of the possibility of offering a more complete service through that approach to coordination. It is claimed that, as a result of diversification, joint rates and through routes will be offered to shippers desiring service involving more than one mode. No attempt has been made by these proponents to explain why such joint rates and through routes have not been more generally established under present authority to do so but, rather, have been consistently avoided by many of these same proponents of diversification. Although the Interstate Commerce Act makes it the 'duty of rail carriers to establish reasonable through routes with common carriers by water and reasonable rates applicable thereto,' and equitable divisions, and reasonable facilities for the interchange of traffic, the rail carriers have not distinguished themselves for their zeal in fulfilling this duty." *Doyle Report*, 224–225; see also pp. 218 and 225, note 13.

For some examples of flagrant discrimination by the railroads against water carriers, with the rails setting much higher rates for a given portion of a journey when the shipment either originated with or continued by water carrier than if it were all-rail, see Fulda, *op. cit.*, 348–

350 and especially the leading case, *ICC v. Mechling*, 330 U.S. 567 (1947); also *Dixie Carriers, Inc. et al. v. United States*, 351 U.S. 56 (1956). In many of these cases, the ICC refused to eliminate the discrimination. See for example *Seatrain Lines, Inc. v. U.S.*, 233 F. Supp. 199 (1964). Despite its legal victory over the railroads and the Commission in this case, Seatrain went out of the coastal shipping business shortly thereafter; in part, it asserts, because it decided it was "hopeless to try to do business with people who were unwilling to do business with it." (Private communication.)

[41] "The truck is undoubtedly performing services which, in the interests of the best utilization of the economic resources of the country, the railroad should be performing, and the railroad is undoubtedly performing services which can be performed with greater economy by other means of transportation. . . . The arranging of through services, with each mode performing that part which it is best equipped to do, should also be easier if there is more than a vague notion of their respective economic capabilities." Jervis Langdon, Vice President and General Counsel, Baltimore and Ohio Railroad, as quoted in the *Doyle Report*, 214–215.

As the *Report* itself puts it,

"The rail carriers, and all carriers for that matter, have to get down to the business of finding out what their actual costs are on freight hauled in order to determine the proper role which each mode should play in the transportation economy of the country. To a large extent, this is a job which the transportation industry must do for itself." *Ibid.*, 217.

in the rationality with which they would distribute the traffic if permitted to integrate more freely.[42]

There is no reason to doubt the frequent allegations that the rails have at times used their affiliated carriers as "fighting ships" to drive competitors out of business.[43] Or, in view of their history of noncooperation in the development of joint rates and through routes, that they would divert such traffic as they could to their own trucking or barge affiliates and give them preferential access to their facilities—for such purposes as piggybacking—to the extent that the ICC permitted them to do so; and that the Commission has certainly been far from satisfactorily assiduous or effective in correcting such discriminations in the past.[44] This record suggests that any relaxation of the existing restrictions on integration must be accompanied by a broadening of the authority of the ICC to proscribe discriminations of this kind, and in particular to require the institution of intermodal joint rates, through routings and equipment interchanges by railroads with all other common carriers, on reasonable demand.[45]

On the other hand, any assessment of the alleged dangers of giving the railroads greater freedom to integrate conglomerately must center on the two questions of their *ability* and *incentive* to behave in the predicted fashion. As for the first, it seems unlikely that the integration would in fact produce the requisite monopoly power. In view of the ease of entry into trucking and water transport and the ability of existing carriers in these fields to move from one route to another, it is difficult to believe that the railroads would be able to gain control over these alternative media in such a way as to be able to retard their growth (any more than they are able to retard it now, by the discriminations and refusals to collaborate described above), or to raise their rates substantially above competitive levels. Of course, ICC regulation at

---

[42] "No evidence has been uncovered to show that the more powerful rail carriers are willing to abandon their identities to transportation companies; unless they do so there is no possibility of implementing the concept. . . .

"Even when allowed to do so, rail carriers are notorious for not diversifying. . . .

"It is because of this attitude which exists among many carriers that we have ventured the prediction that true transportation companies, as we view their role in the public interest, are still a far way off and that we do not anticipate a rash of grants of applications at a regulatory agency in the event our recommendation for dropping the special restrictions in this respect are enacted into law." *Ibid.*, 221, 224, 226.

For other references to the irrational conservatism of railroad managements, see pp. 14, 21, note 40, and 81–82, above. In fairness, much of the blame must be assessed, also, against the self-defeating obstructionism of the unions. For a specific illustration, see "A derailment at Last Chance Junction?" *Business Week*, March 28, 1970, 68–75.

[43] See for example, Fulda, *op. cit.*, 378–379;

Arne Wiprud, *Justice in Transportation: An Exposé of Monopoly Control* (New York: Ziff-Davis Publishing Co., 1945), 34–36.

[44] The ICC has the authority to require rail and water carriers to establish through routes and joint rates, but not rail and motor carriers or motor and water carriers. See Locklin, *op. cit.*, 867–868; the *Doyle Report*, 148–149. On the lack of assiduity on the part of the ICC, see *ibid.*, 218–229, 225, and President Kennedy's *Message on Transportation*:

"For many years some regulatory agencies have been authorized to appoint joint boards to act on proposals for inter-carrier services; but they have taken virtually no initiative to foster these arrangements which could greatly increase service and convenience to the general public and open up new opportunities for all carriers. I recommend, therefore, that Congress declare as a matter of public policy that through routes and joint rates should be vigorously encouraged, and authorize all transportation agencies to participate in joint boards." *N.Y. Times*, April 6, 1962, 18.

[45] See the specific recommendations to this effect by the *Doyle Report*, 228.

present thwarts these potentialities for competition as far as motor carriers are concerned; but the ICC would always have the power to admit new entrants, as needed. Much more important, a policy of freer competition in this industry, of which a removal of restrictions on conglomerate integration would be part, would surely have to embrace a removal of the economic barriers to entry in trucking. On the other hand, minimum rate regulation would probably have to be retained. Given this safeguard, it would be extremely difficult for the railroads even to undertake predatory competition. And the competitive viability of independent truckers and water carriers and the check on monopoly power that they exercise would be strengthened by adoption of the policies of compulsory interconnection, coordination, and nondiscrimination recommended above.

Equally questionable is the common assumption that it would be in the interest of integrated railroad companies discriminatorily to restrict the expansion of their trucking or barge affiliates. The fact that their principal investments are in the rail part of the operation should not give them any incentive to do so.[46] The larger investment in railroad facilities represents a sunk cost. It does not protect that investment, or enhance the return of the company as a whole, to divert to the rails traffic that the company's own affiliates can carry at lower incremental costs. The way to maximize profits would be to use the facilities with the lowest incremental costs; economic efficiency would require the same.

But would it not pay the company to give preference to the more capital-intensive medium, for A-J-W reasons? It would seem this danger could be dismissed in this instance. The 3.0 percent that the Class I railroads in the National City Bank sample earned on equity in 1967 can hardly be as high as the cost of capital.[47] In these circumstances it is inconceivable that it would pay them as a general policy deliberately to make use of higher incremental-cost media, in the expectation of obtaining rate increases sufficient to recoup the consequent losses, plus a return in excess of the cost of capital on the additional rate base thus justified.

The opponents of rail integration point out that the same efficiencies could be achieved by joint arrangements with nonintegrated motor and water

---

[46] See, for example, note 38, above and the *Doyle Report*, 225–226, citing the following testimony by the president of the Illinois Central Railroad as supporting the fear that

"the owned carrier would not be permitted to compete for traffic with parallel service of the owning carrier, this to the detriment of the user. . . .

"Question. Or if the line was not being operated to the best interests of the railroad, you would then interfere, would you not?

"Answer. To the best interests of the railroad, and to the bargeline, and to the public, we would then have to interfere. . . .

"Question. And the railroad interests would necessarily come first?

"Answer. Certainly, because that is where

our first interest is—

"Question. Your first responsibility, insofar as protecting investments, is the railroads' investment?

"Answer. That is right."

[47] The return is not high enough to justify them financing their capital needs to any appreciable extent by the sale of common stock. Although it is somewhat out of date, the picture of rail earnings and capital requirements in James C. Nelson, *Railroad Transportation and Public Policy*, Chapter 7, is still generally applicable. Of their gross capital expenditures for transportation property, totaling almost $11 billion in the period 1946–1955, the Class I railroads financed not quite $10 million, or less than one-tenth of one percent, by the sale of stock. *Ibid.*, 220.

carriers. There is no shortage of such companies who would be happy to carry the traffic that they are best equipped to do.[48]

The contention is basically correct. Intercompany cooperation can secure many of the same benefits as financial integration. Common ownership has the advantage that it eliminates the necessity for interfirm negotiations and profit-splitting, the obstruction created by the reluctance of one firm's management to give business to another and hence the need for external compulsion. Railroad companies would clearly have a greater incentive to distribute such business as they control most efficiently among alternative methods of carriage if they were integrated.[49] Financial integration, on the other hand, carries with it accentuated dangers of placing competitors at an unfair disadvantage vis-à-vis the affiliates of the integrated company, reducing the intensity of competition and, to the extent that monopoly is achieved, suppressing less capital-intensive alternatives.[50] The first of these

---

[48] So, in a case in which the ICC certificated a subsidiary of the Pennsylvania Railroad to extend the scope of its motor carriage, in order to permit a demonstrated cost-saving, the intervening independent trucking companies argued strenuously that the same cost savings could be achieved by requiring the railroad to coordinate with them, instead. The Supreme Court sustained the ICC action, partly on the ground that the Commission did not have the authority to compel the railroad to enter into such an arrangement with the truckers. *ICC v. Parker*, 326 U.S. 60 (1945).

[49] Their failure to do so sufficiently with non-affiliated carriers obviously does not demonstrate that they would be similarly backward with their own affiliates. Nor do the sordid episodes in which railroads have jointly mounted propaganda and political campaigns to harass their truck competitors. For an outstanding example of the latter, see *Noerr Motor Freight, Inc. v. Eastern Railroad Presidents Conference*, 155 F. Supp. 768 (1957), 166 F. Supp. 163 (1958), 365 U.S. 127 (1961).

Fulda observes

"the admitted policy of the railroads to eliminate the truckers from long-haul transportation appears to be irreconcilable with the recent efforts of the railroads to gain *for themselves* the right to engage in transportation diversification, that is to own or control truck lines, airlines and water carriers, and to operate them without restrictions. Putting it differently, the desire to recapture traffic from motor and water carriers shows confidence in the competitive strength of rail freight traffic; but the desire to expand into other fields seems to indicate the opposite." *Op. cit.*, 377.

Not at all. The efforts disclosed by the Noerr case, however reprehensible, were directed against competitors. They in no sense justify

the inference that the railroads would not make efficient use of those alternative media if they controlled them themselves. What should qualify any confident predictions of major changes if the railroads are given greater freedom to integrate is the demonstrated short-sightedness and conservatism of much railroad management.

[50] The problem is that if the carrier is not permitted to integrate it will often be reluctant to collaborate with other media and will instead try to divert traffic from them. If permitted to integrate, it is likely to be more willing to make use of those other media, through its own affiliates, but it also has a greater incentive to divert the business from competitors to those affiliates.

An interesting illustration of the problem of assessing these respective dangers is provided by the Civil Aeronautics Board's *Motor Carrier-Air Freight Forwarders Investigation* (Docket 16857, decided September 22, 1967). The question presented to the Board was whether long-haul motor carriers should be permitted entry into the air-freight forwarding business. The forwarder is a common carrier who operates no transportation equipment, as we have seen (p. 180, note 22); his major source of revenue is the usual spread in common-carrier schedules between less than carload and carload or truckload rates.

Historically, the CAB had prohibited entry by surface carriers into the air-freight forwarding field where it appeared that this would enable them to divert traffic to surface transportation. In the present case, the CAB majority voted to grant the authorization, largely on the ground that the truckers already had access to much of the potential air traffic "either along the applicants' own extensive motor carrier routes or along the routes of hundreds of regional motor carriers with whom

threats can be reduced by a much more forceful policy than has heretofore been followed of requiring intermedia coordination on equal and non-discriminatory terms, as well as by application of the antitrust laws. The latter dangers would seem to be minimal in this industry. In these altered circumstances of the last forty years or so, in which the scope of the railroads' monopoly has been enormously diminished and the greater need is to free them for more effective competition, it is not surprising that most economists now lean to a loosening of the restrictions on their conglomerate integration.[51]

But the balance of public advantage may have already been shifted away from freer intermodal integration by the railroad mergers of the 1960s.[52]

---

the applicants regularly interline traffic," and that the problem was one of giving them an incentive, in the spread between air-freight rates for small and large shipments, to turn it over to the airlines. The Commission recognized that the price it was paying to induce motor carriers to turn over for air carriage "shipments which are *already* being delivered into the hands of the truckers" was the enhanced danger that they might divert traffic away from the air:

"It is true that the competition of these applicants as air freight forwarders may divert some air freight gathering and consolidating activities from other air freight forwarders and from the direct air carriers themselves." (Stress supplied.)

But they evidently believed that the benefits from the former incentives would outweigh the additional dangers of diversion, and recognized that the latter threat could be diminished by expanding the authority of the nonintegrated air-freight forwarders to provide pickup and delivery services in connection with air transportation beyond their previously limited zones of operation.

The dissenting Commissioner Murphy emphasized the danger—that the interest of the motor carriers would lie in promoting their surface transportation business rather than air freight:

"Whether motor carrier-air freight forwarders would eventually dominate the air freight forwarding industry through their superior economic strength remains to be seen . . . . [I]n any event, I share an apprehension that through such entry by these and other surface carriers our direct air carriers would be made dependent upon their competitors for a major portion of their freight and cargo business."

He noted, in this connection, that no direct air carrier supported the truckers' entry as potential salesmen for their services and many opposed the applications.

The two opinions supply a nice summary of the two possible diversions that had to be weighed, the one in the presence, the other in the absence of integration. Commissioner Murphy was impressed with the former: "There is a great deal of wisdom in the old adage that one does not send a rabbit to market for lettuce." The majority responded,

"the rabbit is already getting the lettuce from the market. This decision will give him a reward for bringing it home instead of eating it himself along the way."

The majority considered its decision

"a real breakthrough in opening up the most hopeful avenue for increasing intermodal transportation of freight by surface and air. . . . [P]roviding this incentive for the truckers to utilize air carriage will make air transportation a stronger competitor for the movement of freight."

The president of the Emery Air Freight Corporation commented, instead, that

"successful coordination is possible only when it is accomplished by a forwarder who has no primary interest in either of the modes to be coordinated."

It may be, however, that he gave the game away when he went on to predict that the result of the decision would be "an excess of competition which will be difficult for all and ruinous for some." *The New York Times*, September 26, 1967.

Emery is a large, nonintegrated air-freight forwarder. Some of these companies tried to have the CAB's decision overturned in the courts, but were unsuccessful; see *Air Freight Forwarders et al.* v. *CAB*, 419 F.2d 154, *cert.* denied, 397 U.S. 1006 (1970).

[51] See, for example, Meyer et al., *op. cit.*, 261–263; Locklin, *op. cit.*, 853; and Friedlaender, *op. cit.*, 155–159. See, especially, the measured and cautious proposals of the *Doyle Report, op. cit.*, 222–229.

[52] See pp. 281–290, below.

As we have already observed, any threat that integration poses to the survival of competition or the welfare of customers diminishes the more integrated firms there are in competition with one another. The more railroad companies there are along major routes, the less is the possibility that any one of them will be in a position to suppress or rely inadequately on lowest-cost media; and the safer it is, therefore, to permit each to integrate freely. As the industry now approaches a structure in which only one or two giant railroads serve entire regions of the country, the greater is the threat of monopoly, the greater the power of a transportation company to deny nonintegrated carriers fair access to the market, to control the development of competing methods of carriage, and to exploit the consumer.[53]

In any event, it is well not to exaggerate the probable consequences, beneficial or harmful, of a greater freedom of railroads to integrate conglomerately. The possibilities of cost savings from a more rational distribution of the transportation business are enormous; but they can in principle be achieved by interfirm coordination and by more competitive pricing, along the lines outlined in our Chapter 6 of Volume 1. On the other hand, the alleged dangers of such a development—the danger that truckers, for example, will be driven out of business in great numbers and freight rates increased in consequence—are at least equally exaggerated.[54]

Electric and Gas. Trucking and water carriage are not easy industries to monopolize. It is this reason, above all others, that makes it difficult to see any menace in permitting railroad companies to extend their operations to competing media, *provided* the competitive opportunities of nonintegrated firms could be adequately protected. It is difficult to see, in those circumstances, that integrated railroad companies could possibly retard or discourage the utilization of trucks or water carriers, even if it were in their interest to do so; and the effect of financial integration would be to make any such retardation less in their interest, not more.

The distribution of electricity and gas, in contrast, are franchised, local monopolies. There is no room for doubt that an integrated company performing both of these services does have the power intentionally or unintentionally to restrict the sales of one product or the other product or both, by high pricing and sluggish promotion. Electricity and gas are substitutes or potential substitutes in large and important uses.[55] To this extent, the integration of the two is not really conglomerate but horizontal: it substitutes monopoly for duopoly.[56]

---

[53] "Thus the final Supreme Court approval of the Penn-Central merger has probably foreclosed the option of deregulation in conjunction with the formation of transportation companies. Now that a company with the potential monopoly power of the Penn Central has been formed, it is inconceivable that it would be permitted to acquire competing trucking and water lines to ensure a virtual transportation monopoly." Friedlaender, *op. cit.*, 168; see also pp. 157–159 and 166–167.

[54] This is also the general conclusion of Lansing, *op. cit.*, 217–218. For an interesting suggestion that the benefits of greater intercarrier coordination might be achieved, without integration, by "giving the wholesalers of the transportation industry, the freight forwarders, full freedom to operate in all modes of transportation," see Comment, "Intermodal Transportation and the Freight Forwarder," *Yale Law Jour.* (June 1967), LXXVI: 1360–1396.

[55] See pp. 102–104, Chapter 3, above.

[56] It does not remove all competition. Gas or electricity compete also with oil, for example in the home heating market or for use as boiler fuel. But the range of uses in which oil is competitive with the others would seem to be less than the range in which they compete with one another. In 1968, for example, 77 percent of all new homes sold were equipped to be heated

If the competition between financially separate gas and electric companies were in fact fruitful, it would seem that its effects could be measured by comparing their performance with that of the combination companies. Most of the evidence does point in that direction. Franklin H. Cook found that the total operating and maintenance costs per kilowatt hour for a sample of 48 to 51 straight electric companies averaged 0.76 cents in the period 1957–1961; the corresponding figure for 17 to 21 electric and gas combinations was 1.03 cents. He found, correspondingly, that their average revenues per kilowatt hour were 1.85 cents and 2.176 cents respectively.[57] A later comparison by National Economic Research Associates of the 47 straight electric companies with the 40 combination companies on Standard & Poor's Compustat tapes, for 1966, shows a similar result: the former had an average revenue in 1966 of 2.31 cents per kilowatt hour from residential electric sales as compared with 2.58 cents for the latter. Electricity consumption per residential customer averaged 5,744 kwh for the former and only 4,731 for the latter.[58]

Cook draws from these comparisons a presumption against combination companies.[59] But these apparent inferiorities in their performance could be reflective of extraneous factors having nothing to do with their integration. The lower rates and costs and larger average residential sales of the nonintegrated companies could, for example, have reflected the benefits of superior location—if, for instance, they happened on the average to have been located closer to coal mines or to sources of hydroelectric or publicly generated power, or in regions of the country where, because of the relatively mild climate, electric heating is more likely to be feasible.[59a] And their greater average sales per residential consumer could well, in view of the economies of increasing consumption per customer, have explained their lower unit costs and prices. The question would remain unanswered whether or to what extent their superior record could have been attributable also to their greater vigor in promoting the sale of electricity in competition with gas. More recently, however, Bruce M. Owen has done a more sophisticated statistical analysis, which attempts to take into account the independent effect of these other variables. And he finds that combination has a marked and statistically significant independent effect in producing a higher price of electricity and lower sales.[59b]

However, if combination itself tends to produce monopolistic retardation, the performance of the combination companies should compare unfavorably also with that of straight gas distribution companies. But the limited evidence available on this point is inconclusive.[60] It might be that there is some-

with gas, 16 percent with electricity and only 6 percent with oil. U.S. Department of Commerce, Bureau of the Census, *Construction Report: Characteristics of New One-Family Homes, 1968,* Table 24B. And the competition for the domestic cooking and clothes drying market is almost entirely between the first two.

[57] "Comparative Price Economies of Combination Utilities," *Public Utilities Fortnightly,* (January 19, 1967), LXXIX: 34–36.

[58] *Combination Companies: A Comparative Study,* processed, New York, November 1968. According to the NERA computations, the straight electric companies also showed greater average

growth rates from 1960 onward in both electricity consumption per residential customer and in the number of residential customers.

[59] *Op. cit.,* 38.

[59a] See note 69, below.

[59b] "Monopoly Pricing in Combined Gas and Electric Utilities," May 1970, to be published in the *Antitrust Bulletin.* See his similar demonstration of the effect of multi-media ownership on advertising rates, *op. cit.,* note 9, above.

[60] According to the NERA study, the same 40 combination companies realized an average revenue of 11.3 cents per therm of residential gas sales in 1966; for a sample of 13 straight

thing in the nature of combination that tends discriminatorily to restrict the sales of electricity alone; and we supply one possible reason for this below. But that is a plausible hypothesis only, nothing more; the objective evidence is still incomplete.

Combination undoubtedly produces some cost savings.[61] Customer expenses—meter reading and billing—are obvious possibilities.[62] The SEC, which, in enforcing the Public Utility Holding Company Act, has followed the general policy of requiring dissolution where there is common ownership of electric and gas properties, has in some instances found economies so significant as to require exceptions to that general policy.[63] But for the most part, these two operations must be essentially distinct. Their technologies, production, transmission, and distribution facilities are entirely separate. The few statistical comparisons that have been made show no evidences other than in customer expenses that the combination companies have lower unit costs than their rivals.[64]

Of course, a combination company would have an incentive, wherever there was a choice, to supply particular demands with the service involving the lower marginal cost. So, for example, we have earlier cited the case of one such company that promoted gas for summer sales (for example, for air conditioning) and electricity in the winter, in recognition of the fact that their respective peaks were at the opposite times. But such an efficient distribution of the business could be achieved also by aggressive competitive promotion and pricing, with a marginal cost floor. The question is whether the competition between duopolists would be sufficiently vigorous to produce

---

gas distribution companies the corresponding figure was 12.0 cents. Average sales per residential customer were 121 mcf for the former and only 108 for the latter. And while the average annual rate of growth in gas consumption per residential customer was the same for the two groups in the period 1961–1966, the number of residential gas customers served by the combination companies increased 27.2 percent in the 1960–1966 period as compared with 23.3 percent for the straight gas companies. Owen's analyses (note 59b, above) failed to discover a statistically significant relationship between combination and the price and volume of gas sales. See, however, note 70, below.

[61] See Emery Troxel, *Economics of Public Utilities* (New York: Rinehart and Company, 1947), 204–206.

[62] According to the NERA study, the customer costs per residential consumer of the combination companies were below those of both the straight electric and the straight gas companies. Either one of these comparisons alone might be suspect, since there must be some arbitrariness in the way in which combination companies allocate these expenses between their electric and gas divisions. But since they come out ahead in comparison with both of their nonintegrated rivals, the finding is persuasive.

This cost superiority of the combinations over the straight electric companies disappears

when the customer expenses are compared on a per kwh basis, because of the greater average consumption per customer of the latter than of the former. The significance of this alteration of the comparison depends on whether the larger sales per customer by the straight electric companies is in some way attributable to their independence. If it is merely the fortuitous result of some of the other factors suggested above, then it surely remains true that the combination companies have an efficiency advantage with respect to customer costs, even though that advantage is offset by the impact on costs *per unit of sales* of the electrics' greater sales per customer.

[63] For examples, see Ritchie, *op. cit.*, 135–191.

[64] In the NERA study, the straight electric companies showed slightly lower administrative, general, and sales expenses and markedly lower operating and maintenance expenses, per kwh, than the combination companies, but the latter in turn were markedly superior to the straight gas companies in both respects. On the other hand, Fred A. Tarpley is reported to have found "significant cost savings" enjoyed by a multiservice utility firm in *The Economics of Combined Utility and Transit Operations*, a dissertation submitted to Tulane University, 1967, as reported in *The American Economist*, Fall 1967 117–118.

this result in as full a measure as an integrated company, with an interest in minimizing cost. The likelihood of aggressive promotion of each product, it would seem, would be enhanced by financial separation—when there exists, side by side, rival companies, each of whose profit comes only from the successful promotion of its own product. But the recognition by both of their interdependence and mutual interest in not "spoiling the market" could lead them instead into a passive coexistence and market sharing. The evidence that straight electric companies do in fact spend more heavily on sales promotion than the combination companies (see note 68, below) tends to support the former rather than the latter hypothesis.

Furthermore, the incentive of the combination company to minimize costs surely must be reduced by the absence of competition and subject to modification by the A-J-W effect. The latter danger must be increased when the regulated monopolist is in a position to control the rate of exploitation of his major potential substitute; he then has both the incentive and the power to retard promotion of the less capital-intensive service.[65] So, it would seem, a combination company would be less likely than a straight electric company to offer promotional rates sufficiently attractive to induce builders to construct all-electric homes. The latter has the incentive of vastly increased sales, under circumstances of long-run decreasing costs. For the former, any increased sales of electricity are at the expense of sales of gas. Since all homes will be wired for electricity anyhow, it would seem not in its interest to try to cut gas out of the market entirely, thereby removing any justification for construction of the gas distribution facilities that would otherwise go into its rate base. On *a priori* grounds, it seems more likely that it would be straight gas and straight electricity companies that would make major efforts to promote total energy on the one hand or the all-electric home on the other, by the offer of discounts or other concessions that can only be at the expense (as *all* competition is indirectly at the expense) of their combined net revenues.[65a]

It is of course possible that the competition between separate electric and gas duopolists will have more of a cost-inflating than a price-reducing character.[66] Indeed, it seems likely that the separate companies would spend more on advertising, for example, than a single monopolist.[67] But these industries are not overly subject to this kind of rivalry. While selling expenses do seem to constitute a larger percentage of sales revenues for straight electric than for combination companies, the ratio for the former is still apparently below the economy average. Moreover, many of the sales promotional expenses incurred by public utilities really represent a form of price competition—for example, the losses they may take on sales of appliances, or the various cash and cash-equivalent allowances to builders described in

---

[65] See our earlier expression of concern on these grounds at the recommendation of the President's Task Force on Communications Policy for a single chosen instrument to control all media of international communications—both cable and satellite, p. 150, note 102, above.

[65a] See the much fuller analysis of these and other possibilities in John H. Landon and John W. Wilson, "An Economic Analysis of Combination Utilities," 1970, unpublished as of this writing.

[66] On the tendency of sellers in concentrated markets to compete in this way see note 107 Chapter 5, above.

[67] This is the view of Troxel, who considers the cost-saving possibilities of common ownership of greater promise than duopolistic competition. *Economics of Public Utilities*, 207.

Chapter 6 of Volume 1.[68] And, as we have already suggested, it seems much more likely that separate gas and electric than combination companies would engage in this kind of genuine, though imperfect, price competition—though here again, it would be good to see the hard evidence.[69]

Our tentative conclusion, based still on rather incomplete evidence, is that the efficiency advantages of combination are in this case outweighed by the advantages of preserving the only kind of competition that is feasible in these markets—competition between the two local, natural monopolists.[70]

---

[68] P. 177, Volume 1. According to computations by my former student, John H. Landon, the 122 electric companies listed in the FPC's *Statistics of Electric Utilities in the United States* spent an (unweighted) average of 1.96 percent of sales on selling expenses, whereas the 79 combination companies in the group spent 1.46 percent in their electric operations. These ratios may be compared with the 2.04 median ratio for the 44 consumer goods producers surveyed by Telser, *op. cit., Jour. Pol. Econ.* (Dec. 1964), LXXII: 543. These comparisons must be very rough. Consumer goods producers typically spend a larger percentage of their sales revenues on advertising than others; and only slightly more than 40 percent of the total revenues of electric companies represent sales to residential consumers. Edison Electrical Institute, *Statistical Year Book of the Electric Utility Industry for 1967*, September 1968, 2. On the other hand, it is possible that the selling expenses listed by the FPC, which include "demonstration, advertising, and other sales expenses," are more inclusive than those measured by Telser for the other industries. According to a survey, taken by the Dingell Committee, of utility company promotional payments, for example, only 25 percent of the total represented advertising allowances—payments to dealers, builders, or owners for advertising appliances, homes, or apartments; another 17.4 percent represented contributions to trade associations, for a variety of promotional activities, among other things; the remainder were direct payments to dealers, builders, or owners for the installation or conversion of equipment or appliances, installation of underground wiring, or assistance in financing. U.S. House of Representatives, Select Committee on Small Business, Subcommittee No. 5, 90th Congress, 2nd Session, *Promotional Practices by Public Utilities and Their Effect Upon Small Business*, House Report No. 1984, December 31, 1968, pp. 103–109.

[69] Abraham Gerber, of National Economic Research Associates, made a count for me of the relative use of special residential electric space heating rates by straight electric and combination companies in 1967. Again the evidence, culled from the Edison Electrical Institute rate book, is inconclusive. Of the 95 straight electrics, only 78 (or 82 percent) had such a rate, as compared with 51 of the 59 (86 percent) of the combination companies. On the other hand, he points out, of the companies in the first group with no such special rates, three had commercial space heating rates, one did not provide residential service at all (suggesting the desirability of a recalculation to omit *all* companies not in the residential market), and five are located in warm climates where electrical heating is in any event more feasible than in the country as a whole—more so than for any of the combination companies. A comparison adjusted for such factors, he surmises, would make the record of the straight electric companies look relatively better.

[70] This has been the general attitude of the SEC, as well, in enforcing the Public Utility Holding Company Act of 1935 (see p. 73, Chapter 2 and note 2, this chapter, above). The Commission has tended to interpret the proviso exempting holding companies from dissolution where this would result in "loss of substantial economies" as requiring the even more stringent showing that the "additional system cannot be operated under separate ownership without the loss of economies so important as to cause a serious impairment of that system." *Securities and Exchange Commission v. New England Electric System et al.*, 390 U.S. 207, 209 (1968).

In this last case, the SEC required the New England holding company to divest itself of a gas distribution system, in the face of an estimate by a management consulting firm that separation would result in a loss of economies amounting to 4.8 percent of the entire system's annual operating revenues. It did so partly because it concluded that the estimate was inadequately supported. But, it also asserted, even if that estimate were substantiated,

"it would not lead us to conclude that such a loss is so substantial, when compared with the loss of economies involved in prior divestment cases and viewed in the light of the objectives of the Act, as to warrant retention of the gas properties. . . ."

It pointed out additionally:

"that other nonaffiliated Massachusetts gas companies, all but one of them smaller than the

Horizontal and Geographic Integration

The electric power industry and the railroads have in recent years engaged in very intensive merger activities of a rather special kind. The merging partners have been essentially similar firms—as much as any such companies can be so characterized. The combinations have not been principally vertical, although the merging of any two railroads could hardly avoid involving some end to end operations. Nor have they been conglomerate, except again that in the nature of the case every railroad and every electric company offers a geographically distinct set of services. The integration can best be described as principally geographic and horizontal; the mergers have tended to produce more nearly integrated regional systems; they have also brought under unified control companies that had to some extent, at some geographic points, been in actual or potential direct competition.[71]

We have already alluded to the mergers in the electric power field, which during the decades of the 1950s and 1960s reduced the number of private systems from about 1,000 to less than 500 and which, according to the prediction of Donald C. Cook, president of American Electric Power Company, will continue until the number reaches something like 15.[72]

In terms of the results already accomplished, the consequent transformation of the railroad industry since the late 1950s—after almost four decades of virtual inactivity under the provisions of the Transportation Act of 1920[73]—has been even more dramatic:

"Even if no more mergers were to be proposed or approved, the effect

---

NEES gas system, are apparently able to operate successfully without electric utility affiliations; [and] . . . NEES did not establish that independent management devoted solely to promoting gas sales would not result in benefits to offset some of the projected losses." *Ibid.*, 213.

On the last point, the Commission was impressed by the fact that all seven of the independent Massachusetts gas distribution companies showed substantially higher gas sales per customer than NEES (83.7 mcf and 51.5 mcf. respectively), higher revenues per customer ($142.10 as compared with $104.49) and lower average prices ($1.70 and $2.03 per mcf).
[71] The same was true of the 1957 acquisition by El Paso Natural Gas Company of the Pacific Northwest Pipeline Corporation, both of which gathered gas in the San Juan Basin and had been involved in direct rivalry for the business of the largest industrial customer in California, in consequence of which the price had been driven down from 40 cents to 30 cents per mcf for a firm supply of gas—in contrast with El Paso's previous price of 32.5 cents for *interruptible* service. This merger was approved by the FPC, then, on the initiation of suit by the Antitrust Division of the Department of Justice, ordered dissolved by the United States Supreme Court,

in a series of landmark decisions concerning the applicability of the antitrust laws to the regulated industries. *California v. F.P.C.*, 369 U.S. 482 (1962); *U.S. v. El Paso Natural Gas Co.*, 376 U.S. 651 (1964); *Cascade Natural Gas Corp. v. El Paso Natural Gas Co.*, 386 U.S. 129 (1967); and *Utah Public Service Comm. v. El Paso Natural Gas Co.*, 395 U.S. 464 (1969). On some of these issues, see the opinion of Judge Wright in the *Northern Natural Gas* case, quoted at length in Chapter 4, pp. 161–165, above. On the competition between El Paso and Pacific Northwest in purchasing gas see also MacAvoy, *Price Formation in Natural Gas Fields*, Chapter 5 and esp. pp. 107–128.
[72] *Wall Street Journal*, January 30, 1969. See pp. 73–75, Chapter 2, above. Mr. Cook's company has sought permission of the SEC (under the Public Utility Holding Company Act of 1935) to acquire the Columbus & Southern Ohio Electric Co. The SEC's Division of Corporate Regulation filed a brief on March 17, 1969 opposing the application on the ground of adverse competitive effects, and the company made application on April 17, 1969 for a reopening of the Hearings for fuller consideration of the competitive issue. The case was still pending in mid 1970.
[73] See pp. 78–82, Chapter 2, above; also the *Doyle Report*, 247–257.

of the railroad merger wave on the nation's transportation network would be profound."[74]

"The current railroad merger wave amounts to the most complete, and the most significant, reorganization of any American industry since the turn of the century."[75]

For example, the series of mergers and acquisitions, beginning in 1959, that moved first the Virginian Railway Company,[76] then the Nickel Plate, the Erie-Lackawanna (itself the product of a merger of the Erie and the Delaware, Lackawanna & Western Railroads, approved in 1960),[77] and the Delaware & Hudson into the Norfolk & Western Railway Company;[78] that joined the Chesapeake & Ohio and the Baltimore & Ohio;[79] and, finally, that permitted the merger of the Pennsylvania and New York Central Railroads, on condition that they also include the New Haven[80]—reduced the provision of service to the entire Northeast and Middle Atlantic region of the country to three major railway systems; and the application of the Norfolk & Western to merge with the Chesapeake & Ohio group[81] would cut it to two. And while the experience of the 1920s justified a good deal of skepticism in assessing the prospects that grandiose nationwide consolidation plans would in fact be put into effect, the manifestly altered climate of the 1960s and the enormous steps that have already been taken lend immediate credibility to proposals of a decade or so ago to reduce the 500 operating railroads in the country to less than ten consolidated systems.[82]

In a sense, the issues in all these cases are the same and are basically simple. The preponderant case for the mergers is the expectation that they will improve efficiency. The preponderant case against them is their possible impairment of competition, for two reasons: first, the merging companies are typically actual or potential competitors in some parts of their business, and, second, they may be enabled by joining together to deny outside firms a fair opportunity to compete. The threshold question in all cases, therefore, is: how realistic are the expectations of important cost-savings? And the corollary question is to what extent the benefits can be achieved without full financial consolidation and with a lesser menace to competition, or to what extent, if the consolidation is permitted, the competitive opportunities of outsiders can be safeguarded.

[74] U.S. Department of Transportation, *Western Railroad Mergers*, a Staff Study by the Office of the Assistant Secretary for Policy Development and the Federal Railroad Administration, Washington, January 1969, 2.
[75] *Ibid.*, 1.
[76] 307 ICC 401 (1959).
[77] 312 ICC 185 (1960).
[78] 324 ICC 1 (1964), 330 ICC 780 (1967), 331 ICC 22 (1967), and *Penn Central Merger and N & W Inclusion Cases*, 389 U.S. 486 (1968).
[79] 317 ICC 261 (1962).
[80] 327 ICC 475 (1966), 328 ICC 304 (1966), finally affirmed by the U.S. Supreme Court, 389 U.S. 486 (1968).
[81] *Norfolk & Western Ry. Co.-Merger, etc.-Chesapeake & O. Ry. Co.*, ICC Finance Docket No. 23832. The ICC Hearing Examiner recommended approval of this last merger in a Report and Order served March 20, 1969. These cases are summarized in Carl Helmetag, Jr., "Railroad Mergers: The Accommodation of the Interstate Commerce Act and Antitrust Policies," *Virginia Law Rev.* (December 1968), LIV: 1505–1530.
[82] See the *Doyle Report*, 242; the influential article by Gilbert Burck, "A Plan to Save the Railroads," *Fortune*, August 1958, 82, proposing to consolidate all the railroads in the country into four noncompetitive regional systems; and the thoughtful Staff Study of the Department of Transportation, suggesting a number of hypothetical groupings for consolidating the Western railroads into four or five systems, *op. cit.*, 34–49.

We have already described the technological case for the regional integration of power company investments and operations.[83] The efficiency benefits are unquestionably great. The only question is how much more fully they are achieved by complete financial integration as compared with pooling and interconnection between financially separate systems. The related consideration is the possible impact of *either* device on competition. On this point, there are two opposing considerations. On the one hand, at the point of ultimate sale the "industry" is in any event a collection of regulated, local franchised monopolies. To the extent that this is the case, there can be no objection to regional or national groupings that reduce their several costs. On the other hand, there is nonetheless competition among its members, both actual and potential: the impact of various proposed integrations on this rivalry must therefore also be considered. Since these very questions arise with respect to power pooling as well, we reserve further consideration of these issues for pp. 314–323, below.

The cost savings that the railroad mergers are supposed to achieve are of a different character.[84] Here the overriding fact is the prevalence of excess capacity and duplication of facilities. Michael Conant, a strong proponent, estimated in the early 1960s that the capacity of the railroads was something like 2.8 to 3.5 times the actual amount of traffic they carried.[85] With the total freight ton-miles of the Class I railroads failing to regain their 1947 levels for the next sixteen years while technological changes were tending to increase capacity rather than reduce it; with passenger traffic continuing its dreary, long-run decline throughout the 1960s as well; with competition incapable of eliminating the excess capacity and with continuously low overall earnings, it is not surprising that there finally emerged among railroad executives as well as others the conviction that drastic rationalization was essential; and the only way to achieve it was through mergers.[86]

---

[83] See pp. 64–65, Chapter 2, above.

[84] They are similar in this one basic respect: that they come from concentrating traffic and investment on the lowest-cost routes or sources of supply—that is, from equalizing costs both short- and long-run continuously at the margin.

[85] *Railroad Mergers and Abandonments* (Berkeley: Univ. of California Press, 1964), 8, 11, 16. For a more selective estimate, identifying the very large year-round excess as being mainly in line, to a considerably lesser extent in terminal and passenger carrying and even less than that in freight car and motive power capacity, but concluding that

"It seems likely that the railroads could take on significant accretions of freight and passenger traffic without having to make proportionate additions of fixed capital facilities in all areas of railroading,"

see Nelson, *Railroad Transportation and Public Policy*, 148–171. Of course, freight cars and locomotives could be added readily if demand justified it. See pp. 184–185.

[86] See the *Doyle Report*, 229–230, 266; Conant,

op. cit., passim; Burck, *op. cit.* Burck later offered a similar proposal as "A New Flight Plan for the Airlines," *Fortune*, April 1969, pp. 98–101 and ff. We cannot appraise the latter proposals here. It is important to note, however, that the sentiment for large-scale mergers of airlines, rapidly mounting in 1969 and 1970, should be regarded with skepticism. As we have already suggested, economies of scale do not recommend them. And the advantages of better route patterns and a fuller utilization of equipment can be achieved also by permitting existing companies to diversify their own route structures and inducing them to pool equipment and equipment maintenance. See pp. 122–123 and 235, above.

There was no such general conviction about the essentiality of railroad mergers in the 1920s. The focus of the proposals for consolidation at that time was on the equalization of the profitability of weak and strong roads and the difficulty of authorizing rate increases such as were needed to provide adequate returns to the former without conferring supernormal profits on the latter. See pp. 79–81, Chapter 2, above.

The most important cost savings, it appeared, could be achieved by merger of parallel roads. This would permit the combining of terminal and repair operations, abandonment of parallel, underutilized track, consolidation of schedules and management, improved routing and utilization of equipment.[87] Gilbert Burck estimated, back in 1958, that annual savings of $1 billion, out of total operating expenses of $8 billion, were ultimately possible.[88] It was widely anticipated, also, that with costs reduced in this way, railroads would be in a better position to raise the large amounts of capital required for renovation and modernization of their facilities. The result of this, as well as of the merger itself, would be not only further reductions in cost, but, perhaps even more important, improvements in service because of the reduction of delays, utilization of modern equipment as well as selection of the most rapid routes and elimination of excessive freight interchanges.

It is probably too early to be certain whether estimates like those of Burck were realistic or wildly naive. The merging parties have had a strong incentive, naturally, to exaggerate the estimated savings. The limited experience since some of these major consolidations have gone into effect demonstrates a wide variation in the extent to which the promised savings were realized and most of the variations have been on the disappointing side:

"The conclusion of the economic evidence is that the cost savings arguments for large railroad mergers have to be very largely discounted, and must be applied to individual cases with very great circumspection."[89]

---

[87] See Conant, *op. cit.*, 87–88, summarizing the estimated annual cost savings of nine major mergers; also Department of Transportation Staff Study, *op. cit.*, 5. This generalization is supported by the opinion of most experts and the conclusion of most empirical studies that the economies of sheer scale in railroading are limited; that, for example, as far as sheer size is concerned, railroads like the Pennsylvania and New York Central were already large enough for maximum efficiency, and perhaps too large. The important economies of scale as yet incompletely achieved, if any, are economies of greater density of traffic. See note 6, Chapter 5, pp. 126–127, Volume 1. For example, the Department of Transportation Staff Study found a simple correlation of about 0.62 between the profit to sales ratios and the traffic density (net ton-miles per mile) in 1967 for 23 Western railroads. *Ibid.*, 20. Healy has even expressed skepticism about the remaining available economies of traffic density as well. "The Merger Movement in Transportation," *Amer. Econ. Rev., Papers and Proceedings* (May 1962), LII: 438–439; but see the comments of Merrill J. Roberts, *ibid.*, 445. Meyer et al. likewise tend to deprecate the evidence of unlimited economies of density but concede that the physical plant of railroads generally was excessive for current volumes of traffic:

"the rationalization of investment requires only management vigorous enough to pursue abandonment and sufficient funds to replace existing 'white elephants' with smaller and more efficient facilities." *Op. cit.*, 259–260.

Whether the available economies of rationalization are great or small, it would seem that they are not true economies of scale but manifestations of short-run decreasing costs, arising out of an admitted state of excess capacity. In this sense, it seems unquestionable, large portions of the American railroad system have chronically suffered from inadequate traffic density. Under whatever rubric the projected economies are best classified, it is difficult to escape the conclusion that railroad mergers have offered the opportunity for important savings in cost from rationalization; what remains subject to great uncertainty is the extent to which the management of the consolidated companies will in fact take advantage of it.

[88] *Op. cit., Fortune*, August 1958, 178. See also the *Doyle Report*, 244–246.

[89] U.S. Department of Transportation Staff Study, *op. cit.*, 13. The study nevertheless strongly supported mergers as an instrument for cutting costs:

"Nearly every transportation expert who has addressed himself to the subject has remarked on the critical need for rationalization of redundant rail facilities in this part of the country. Thus, the cost savings argument retains

There seems no reason to doubt that very important economies and improvements of service *can* be achieved or facilitated by mergers: this is not to say, however, that they *will*. The critical variable is the quality of management; the chief case for mergers seems at times to come down to the hope that the opportunities they create may impel some shaking up of unprogressive managements—an institutional consideration that is very difficult for an economist to evaluate.[90]

The dilemma from the point of view of public policy arises from the fact that these promised cost savings are greatest where the consolidation involves parallel, and therefore substantially competing, roads. In these circumstances, it is important to consider whether the benefits of coordination may be achieved by some other device more consistent with the preservation of competition. In principle, there are such alternatives here. One of the claimed advantages of the Pennsylvania-New York Central Railroad merger was that some traffic, originating with the former, could most efficiently be routed over the water level route of the latter, producing a considerable saving in mileage and cost and an improvement in speed.[91] As we have already suggested in Chapter 2, in principle there must have been a price, lying between the respective marginal costs of the two carriers, that it would have paid the Pennsylvania to offer the Central and the latter to accept to permit the one to use the other's tracks. Separate railroads have been known to enter into pooling agreements, limiting the number of trains

---

its appeal and its cogency for this portion of the Western merger problem." *Ibid.*, 5.

Its negative summary of the experience to date drew on Robert E. Gallamore, *Railroad Mergers: Costs, Competition, and the Future Organization of the American Railroad Industry*, unpublished Ph.D. dissertation, Harvard University, Cambridge, May 1968. The Staff Study quotes Gallamore:

"in most circumstances there have been difficulties in achieving merger savings. . . . [T]he overwhelming evidence is that size and complexity of a merger plan are the qualities that can lead to extra costs, rather than savings, in the wake of consolidation."

And, it points out, "Non-accomplishment of intentions and managerial diseconomies of scale are the biggest dangers." *Ibid.*, 10, 12.

An amusing consequence was that representatives of the Norfolk & Western and Chesapeake and Ohio railroads, in attempting to justify their proposed merger, felt it necessary to explain how their own situation differed from that of the Pennsylvania and New York Central companies, so as to justify their own expectations of cost saving and service improvement in the face of the failure of the latter's merger to have produced those promised results. "New York State Cites Pennsy in Opposing N. & W.—C. & O. Plan," *New York Times*, November 6, 1969, 67. The subsequent financial collapse of the Penn-Central further emphasized the almost

ludicrous gap between the merging parties' promises and their performance. See *Wall Street Journal*, June 12, 1970, 1, and the floor remarks of Senator Philip A. Hart, August 10, 1970.

[90] See, for example, Lansing, *op. cit.*, 213–214, and Meyer et al., who state and concede some validity to the

"subtler and more meritorious argument for the creation of four regional railroads . . . an application of the well-tested proposition of business administration—when in doubt, reorganize,"

although they conclude that these gains will be transitory. *Op. cit.*, 260. Still, there remains the probability that if new opportunities for gain are offered some response will on the average be forthcoming.

"The past decade has seen a continuous stream of innovations, but the quantum jump to containerization, new rolling stock, the avoidance of classification yards, and computerized traffic movement control systems that most experts visualize as essential to railroads achieving their full potential has not been realized. A new innovative spirit on the part of the industry's top management is a much hoped for result of the current merger wave." U.S. Department of Transportation Staff Study, *op. cit.*, 3–4.

[91] See *Pennsylvania Railroad Company-Merger-New York Central Railroad Company*, 327 ICC 475, 490–493 (1966).

or services offered by each, in order to save costs—the freight cars are a prime example of this kind of pool, used by all the roads in common, with each compensating the owner at a fixed rate. If two parallel roads have excess line or terminal capacity, they could enter into agreements to use some of the facilities jointly and abandon others.[92] And there is no doubt that these looser coordinations could fruitfully be much more widely used; Conant proposes that the ICC be given much broader authority than it now has to compel such arrangements.

But, as we have also suggested, these possible collaborations will always inevitably be limited by the continued divergences of interest between the potentially collaborating companies,[93] and, in consequence, such agreements have been comparatively few. As Conant points out,

> "such agreements are extremely difficult to negotiate. A railroad with a monopoly franchise on the most efficient route through an area is reluctant to share this route even though rentals would include a monopoly gain. A carrier is especially concerned not to lose its monopoly of the smaller towns solely on its route. . . . The carrier acquiring trackage rights and abandoning its own less-efficient route, runs the risk that the owner will refuse to renew the trackage agreement after the initial term expires. There is also the possibility that in times of heavy traffic, the owning carrier will give the right of way to its own trains and make the leasing carrier suffer all delays. Such uncertainties, when added to the barriers to abandonment of less-efficient routes, make carriers reluctant even to start negotiations for trackage rights on parallel lines."[94]

It must be conceded that mergers remove some of the obstacles and increase the likelihood of wholehearted collaboration.[95]

It is impossible to generalize about whether, or in which cases, the additional benefits of merger will offset the disadvantages of suppressed competition.[96] The general predisposition of the economist would be toward suspicion of mergers that reduce such competition as still prevails in industries like public utilities, where numbers of sellers are typically already few and entry is restricted.[97] This predisposition is intensified when mergers

---

[92] This discussion draws primarily on Conant, *op. cit.*, 91–112.

[93] See pp. 67–69, Chapter 2, above.

[94] *Op. cit.*, 100–101.

[95] Once again, appraising this likelihood must involve appraising the maddeningly elusive institutional consideration of whether the typically old management of the new company will in fact be moved to take advantage of the opportunities. See notes 87, 89, and 90, above.

[96] Incidentally, some of the interfirm collaborations short of merger would similarly suppress competition—for example, service pooling agreements.

[97] See, for example, Caves, *Air Transport and Its Regulators*, 444–445. The opposite view is, of course, that since it is not competition but regulation that is relied on to protect the public in the public utility industries, the presumption

is the other way. For example, in dismissing a suit brought by customers of one of two merging companies, challenging an FPC order permitting a merger, the U.S. Circuit Court of Appeals for the 7th Circuit stated:

> "Petitioners have shown, in general terms, that the merger will increase Edison's economic power and contribute to economic concentration in the electrical energy industry. They have not shown how such growth and concentration will aggrieve them. In a market characterized by competition a merger or other acquisition necessarily injures the consumer if it substantially lessens competition. In the electric utility industry, where restraints on competition are not only tolerated, but encouraged . . . and where rates are subject to federal or state regulation . . . injury to the consumer cannot be inferred from a merger, but must be demon-

are purportedly justified in order to eliminate the very deficiencies of industrial performance that have been accentuated by insulation from competition:

> "economic theory holds that competition will bring about good service to customers, and will stimulate technological improvements, efficient management, and appropriately aggressive marketing. One need not look very deeply into the railroad problem today in order to catalog its most outstanding deficiencies as precisely these: poor service, lack of technological progress, ineffective management, and poor marketing."[98]

It is intensified, similarly, when the mergers are of companies already evidently too large to be managed well.[98a] The fact remains that competition has fallen considerably short of achieving the economies that are apparently available, eliminating excess capacity, and concentrating traffic on remaining low-cost routes and terminals. The oligopolistic character of the intramodal rail market would even in the absence of regulation almost certainly have precluded the driving of rates down below the out-of-pocket costs of the higher cost carriers that would have been required to achieve this result. Nor would it be desirable, in view of the fact that interrailroad competition could only be highly discriminatory, and also given the very wide spread between out-of-pocket and average total costs, in situations of extensive excess capacity. The resultant impact of such destructive competition on the revenues of the surviving roads could on balance be to reduce rather than enhance the efficiency of the system as a whole. In such circumstances, merger is the obvious solution—offering benefits to both partners and promising to improve, rather than weaken, their ability to raise capital and hence to realize the promise of new technology.

It is at least conceivable that well-chosen mergers can invigorate excessively weak competitors and enhance the effectiveness even of intramodal rivalry. This is not the same as merely requiring that the merging partners

---

strated." *Utility Users League v. FPC*, 394 F. 2d 16, 19, 20 (1968).

It is the latter philosophy that is embodied in the Interstate Commerce Act. It sets up as the controlling standard of whether the ICC is to approve mergers merely that they be "consistent with the public interest." In this determination, it provides that,

"the Commission shall give weight to the following considerations, among others: (1) the effect of the proposed transaction upon adequate transportation service to the public; (2) the effect upon the public interest of the inclusion, or failure to include, other railroads in the territory involved in the proposed transaction; (3) the total fixed charges resulting from the proposed transaction; and (4) the interest of the carrier employees affected." 49 U.S. Code 5(2)(c), 1964 ed.

The desirability of preserving competition is not even mentioned, although the Supreme Court has insisted that the Commission explicitly take possible anticompetitive effects into account:

"In short, the Commission must estimate the scope and appraise the effects of the curtailment of competition which will result from the proposed consolidation and consider them along with the advantages of improved service, safer operation, lower costs, etc., to determine whether the consolidation will assist in effectuating the over-all transportation policy." *McLean Trucking Co. v. United States*, 321 U.S. 67, 87 (1944).

For a survey of the law of recent railroad merger cases, demonstrating that the Court has (under the Interstate Commerce Act) permitted mergers that would clearly have been held in violation of the antitrust laws, see Helmetag, *op. cit., Virginia Law Rev.* (December 1968), LIV: 1493–1530.

[98] Department of Transportation, Staff Study, *op. cit.*, 6.

[98a] See the references in note 89, above, especially to Senator Hart, and the evidence of diseconomies of sheer size cited in note 6, p. 126 of Volume 1.

agree, as a condition of ICC approval, to assume the burden of taking into their union weak roads that may be incapable even of covering their variable costs, as has happened in some cases[99]—a policy of enforced internal subsidization. But it is a consideration that argues strongly in favor of the regulatory agency itself proposing combinations

"which bring the unique advantages of given weak roads into a situation in which these advantages can be used to their greatest potential. . . . It is not as important assiduously to pair rich lines with poor (as was thought necessary under the 1920 Act) as it is carefully to consider linkages and rationalization of excess capacity."

"This process can be accomplished more efficiently in the context of an overall restructuring . . . since a decision can be made on the relative merits of merger with each other road, taking into consideration possibilities of abandonment, consolidation of duplicative facilities, extensions of territory, or short-cut routes."[100]

To recognize these possibilities in a well-planned merger program is of course not necessarily to approve of the particular programs of consolidation that have in fact been put into effect. The current merger movement suffers from the same defects as the efforts of the 1920s—notably the fact that the initiative continues to rest with the proposing lines, that the ICC is essentially confined to a quasi-judicial role of approving or disapproving proposals generated by private parties, in consideration of their own interests,[101] and that no one has assumed the responsibility for proposing integrated plans. Each individual merger has inevitable repercussions on other railroads and on the structure of the entire industry. Considering the need for a careful balancing off in each case of the benefits of cost-reduction and the dangers— the elimination of direct competition and diversion of traffic from excluded lines,[102] which gives rise, in turn, to the likelihood that they will then look

---

[99] The New Haven Railroad in the case of the Pennsylvania and New York Central. The ICC conditioned its approval of the Norfolk & Western-Nickel Plate acquisition on offering the Erie-Lackawanna, Delaware & Hudson and Boston & Maine Railroads the opportunity to be included. Helmetag, op. cit., 1514, 1519 note 149. These roads were in financial trouble; I do not know whether they were in fact incapable of covering variable costs.

[100] Department of Transportation, Staff Study, op. cit., 33, 8.

[101] The ICC can and does, however, impose conditions to protect outside parties. It has, for example, required the parties to take in railroads that were financially weaker or that might otherwise have suffered serious traffic diversion; it has inserted provisions to preclude such diversion (see, for example, Helmetag, op. cit., 1511)—requiring, for instance, that merging lines maintain certain existing routes and continue to solicit freight along them, in order to assure that traffic would continue to be available for interchange with excluded parties; it has

forced the merging parties to indemnify outside lines against losses of traffic (this was a condition imposed on the Penn Central merger, with respect to the Erie-Lackawanna, Delaware & Hudson and Boston & Maine Railroads, ibid., 1518); and it has compelled the consolidated carriers to cooperate with outsiders (for example, in the same case, it required the Penn Central to make certain trackage rights available to the Delaware & Hudson, in order to afford the latter a gateway to the New England line, ibid.). In the Pennsylvania-New York Central hearings, the management of the Erie-Lackawanna Railroad claimed that 80 percent of its traffic was subject to diversion if the merger were permitted to go into effect. W. N. Leonard, op. cit., Transportation Journal (Summer 1964), III: 13.

[102] This is not to suggest that all diversion of traffic resulting from mergers is necessarily inefficient. On the contrary, rationalization necessarily involves a considerable rerouting of traffic, which carries with it the high probability that excluded carriers will lose some of the business that they had previously inter-

for similar protection in other consolidations—most observers seem to agree, the proper approach has to be in terms of an integrated regional or national plan.[103]

It does not suffice, in taking account of these possible dangers, that the ICC merely satisfy itself that all railroads that might possibly be injured by any particular merger withdraw their opposition. They would presumably do so once their own interests had been taken care of—whether by promises of incorporation into the system under consideration, or of protections against diversion, indemnification for losses of business, or a promise that they in turn would be incorporated into some other system.[104] There remains the separate question of whether the interest of the consuming public, too, would be best served by the proposed combination.[105]

Ensuring this result requires a greater degree of regulatory planning than the ICC has heretofore been willing to undertake. In the words of the Department of Transportation's Staff Study:

"The current railroad merger wave amounts to the most complete, and the most significant, reorganization of any American industry since the turn of the century. This reorganization is progressing through the Interstate Commerce Commission and the courts even though a rational and coherent Federal policy toward rail mergers has never been developed and implemented by the ICC and the Executive Branch. Except in cases of conflicting applications, the ICC has been prone to approve each merger application largely as submitted to it, subject, however, to various conditions and to considerable delays—depending on the amount of opposition raised. The results of the rather random manner in which recent mergers have been proposed and approved are twofold. First, there has been no real overview of the public interest in rail mergers. Stated somewhat differently, the mergers proposed and approved were simply not the best of possible and more efficient alternatives. Second, the

---

changed with one or the other of the merging parties. It is to say, rather, that not all diversions that are in the interest of the merging parties are likely to contribute to efficiency in the national transportation system considered as a whole; and it is the function of the regulatory agency to attempt to devise solutions that contribute best to the latter goal. See, for example, Department of Transportation, Staff Study, *op. cit.*, 7–8, 27–31; also pp. 80–81, above.

[103] See, for instance, the *Doyle Report*, 269.

[104] The ICC at first disapproved the proposed mammoth merger of the Great Northern, the Northern Pacific, the Pacific Coast, and the Chicago, Burlington & Quincy Railroad Companies, largely on the ground that it would produce "a drastic lessening of competition," but also because it would adversely affect the Chicago, Milwaukee, St. Paul & Pacific and the Chicago & North Western Railway. 328 ICC 460 (1966). Between 1966 and 1967, the

Northern Lines reached an accommodation with those competitors, accepting certain conditions with respect to traffic diversions and agreeing, also, that it would not oppose their proposed merger if the Northern Lines merger were approved. The resulting withdrawal of opposition on the part of the competing roads was said to be largely responsible for the ICC's reversing its position and approving the merger just a year and a half later. *Great Northern Pacific & Burlington Lines, Inc.,-Merger, etc.-Great Northern Railway Company, et al.*, 331 ICC 228, 231 (1967); see also *Wall Street Journal*, November 15, 1967, 34. The ICC's decision was upheld by the U.S. Supreme Court in *United States v. Interstate Commerce Commission et al.*, 396 U.S. 491 (1970).

[105] It should be pointed out that there has been comparatively little shipper opposition to these proposed mergers, and in some cases substantial shipper support for them. See, for example, Helmetag, *op. cit.*, 1516, 1523–1524.

adversary process, far from resolving the merger issue in each case, has, if anything, created additional intra-industry conflict. Such conflict is especially notable in the phenomenon of 'defensive' mergers."[106]

Vertical Integration in Communications

The issue of the appropriateness of vertical integration has arisen in virtually all the regulated industries. In none has it been so long and intensely contested as in communications. The most famous and important case is the integration between the Western Electric Company and the Bell System. But the same issue is importantly involved in the question of how satellite communication, international and domestic, is to be organized. We have alluded also to the litigation over which companies should be permitted to own the ground stations that send signals to the satellites and receive signals from them. The proper role of independent manufacturers of communications equipment was central to the *Carterfone* case and an important consideration in *above-890* and *MCI* as well. Again, the International Telephone & Telegraph Corporation in 1967 filed an antitrust suit against the General Telephone & Electronics Corporation, contending that the latter's acquisition of a number of independent (that is, non-Bell) telephone companies in preceding years had excluded IT&T from the business of manufacturing and selling telephonic equipment to them.[107] In contrast, there seems to be no major push by the electric utility or railroad or airplane companies to be permitted to manufacture their own equipment, or by the natural gas pipelines, who are in any event not prohibited from doing so, to produce a substantially larger proportion of the gas that they transport.[108]

---

[106] *Op. cit.,* 1. The Staff Study is itself an exploratory effort to develop more satisfactory overall plans for the western part of the country, which would

"further the process of rationalizing uneconomic parallelism without depriving major shipping points of the inherent benefits of competition." *Ibid.,* 36.

For a similar strong and persuasive statement see W. N. Leonard, *op. cit., Transportation Jour.* (Summer 1964), III: 5–15 and see pp. 81–82, Chapter 2, above.

[107] *Wall Street Journal,* October 19, 1967, 2.

[108] Questions about vertical integration have, however, arisen in these industries as well. For example, there remains an important problem of reconciling the integration of electric power generation and transmission by large private companies with protecting the access of small municipal and cooperative distributors to the cheapest possible sources of energy—the very same problem that led to the imposition of common-carrier status on oil company pipelines. The pressure in electric power, similarly, is in the direction of requiring the integrated private companies' transmission systems to "wheel" (that is, transmit) power purchased by the nonintegrated distributors from third parties.

See pp. 316–317, below; also note 60, p. 68, above.

In the heated controversies all through the 1950s and 1960s over the propriety of regulating the field price of natural gas, proponents of regulation pointed out that some of the large jumps in the field price were posted by pipeline purchasers largely owned by producing interests, thus raising the familiar specter of cost-of-service regulation (in this case of the transmission lines) giving rise to an incentive to pay inflated prices for inputs purchased from financially affiliated companies. See note 115, p. 156, Chapter 4, above. And for even longer, pipeline companies have been insisting that their own gas-producing operations ought not to be regulated at all on an individual company cost-of-service basis or ought to receive the same treatment as (that is, the same area prices as are allowed) independent producers rather than being confined to the typically lower prices and rates of return typically permitted the transmission companies themselves. See, for example, *F.P.C. v. Hope Natural Gas Co.,* 320 U.S. 591 (1944); *City of Detroit v. F.P.C.,* 230 F. 2d 810 (1955), *cert.* denied 352 U.S. 829 (1956). See also the FPC's *Pipeline Production Rate Proceeding,* RP 66–24. A trial examiner's initial decision, issued March 3,

The ownership of Western Electric by AT&T raises two kinds of issues of public policy. The first and more fundamental is whether the manufacturer should be financially separated from the Bell companies. The other, raised in numerous rate cases since 1930,[109] concerns the propriety of the prices charged by the manufacturing company, since these enter the cost of service of the operating companies. The most prominent aspect of this controversy concerns the proper rate of return to be allowed Western Electric, in computing its allowable prices: should it be the same, low public utility type of rate allowed the operating companies, or should it be some higher figure reflecting the allegedly greater risks and demonstrably higher comparable earnings of capital goods manufacturing?

In practice these two issues are not easily separated; arguments about them overlap, coincide, and conflict in complicated and curious ways. Western has presented extensive and persuasive testimony, in various forums, defending both the level of its charges and its vertical integration with the operating companies as essential to the excellence of their collaborative performance.

The former demonstrations have been of two kinds. First, Western's prices to the Bell companies have run between 50 and 75 percent of the lowest prices available from all other manufacturers of similar products and, incidentally, far below the average price paid for such equipment by non-Bell telephone companies.[110] Second, its profits have consistently been markedly below those of comparable unregulated companies; and this clearly reflects restraint in pricing, a deliberate practice of charging less than the traffic would bear. According to Western's calculations, its return on the Bell investment in the period 1946 through 1967 averaged 9.3 percent compared with 12.3 percent for the 50 largest manufacturers; its profit per

---

1969, recommended that this production continue to be priced on a company-by-company cost of service basis but with one modification: that the tax-reduction benefits of the allowances for percentage depletion and the expensing of intangible well-drilling costs on newly acquired leases be divided equally between the pipeline-producer and its customers, rather than as theretofore, passed on 100 percent in correspondingly reduced rates. The FPC decision, Opinion 568, instead extended the general area rates to pipeline-produced gas from leases acquired in the future; the appeal from this decision was pending in the Circuit Court of Appeals for the District of Columbia as of November 1970.

[109] See *Smith v. Illinois Bell Telephone Co.*, 282 U.S. 133 (1930) and note 20, p. 29 of Volume 1. The same question is being examined in Phase 2 of the FCC's *In the Matter of AT&T*, Docket 16258.

[110] The Bell companies have been making systematic price comparisons of this kind on their own for several decades. More recently, Western commissioned a comprehensive investigation by McKinsey & Company, *A Study of Western Electric's Performance*, American Telephone and Telegraph Co., New York, 1969. This study compared Western's prices in 1966 with the lowest prices available from other manufacturers, and found ratios of 63 percent for central office, transmissions, and P.B.X. equipment, 48 per cent for telephone apparatus, 52 percent for exchange and toll cable and 74 percent for outside plant equipment (p. 93). This demonstration has in general been corroborated by studies of the FCC and the investigations by John Sheahan using much older data, "Integration and Exclusion in the Telephone Equipment Industry," *Q. Jour. Econ.* (May 1956), LXX: 255–260. On the other hand, Sheahan concludes that Western's costs and prices were not invariably the lowest available. *Ibid.*, 258. One familiar and striking comparison, frequently offered by the Bell companies, is the cost of the basic black telephone handset, for which Pacific Telephone and Telegraph Company paid Western $10.51 in the early 1960s, while the cost of a practically identical instrument from other manufacturers ranged from $23.16 to $27.90. *Pacific Telephone and Telegraph Company v. Public Utilities Commission of the State of California*, 401 P. 2d 353, 369 (1965), Supreme Court of California.

dollar of sales averaged 4.7 cents compared with 6.1 cents for the same 50 companies.[111]

Most states have accepted these demonstrations and approved the Western Electric charges.[112] But some have disallowed part of them. The strictest of these, California (before 1970), shrugged off the proffered evidence as inadequate and irrelevant, precisely because of Western's integration with the operating companies. Its view (before 1970) was that Western enjoys such enormous advantages from the guaranteed access to the huge market of the operating companies, advantages of economies of scale in manufacture and diminution of risk, as to render invalid all price and profit comparisons with other companies enjoying no such advantages.[113] On the same grounds, it rejected Western's contention that the capital goods manufacturing operation justifies a higher rate of return incorporated in the prices it charges to the operating companies than the commissions typically permit the operating companies themselves.[114]

---

[111] AT&T, "Vertical Integration in the Bell System," op. cit., 49. Comparisons with a more representative sample of manufacturing companies show a larger discrepancy: Western's return on beginning of year equity was 11.6 percent in 1966 and 9.7 percent in 1967 (Annual Reports, 1966 and 1967); returns for the sample of electrical equipment and electronics corporations surveyed by the First National City Bank of New York were 16.7 and 14.9 percent respectively. Monthly Economic Letter, April 1968, 46.

"When Western's returns are compared either to those of other electrical equipment producers, or to what it could earn with the objective a maximum short-run exploitation of its strong position, it seems clear that restraint is being exercised." Sheahan, op. cit., Q. Jour. Econ. (May 1956), LXX: 257.

[112] According to information from the Company, Western's charges were sustained in 13 of the 14 cases that went to the highest State courts in the period 1945 to 1966.

[113] "The commission states in its decision that Pacific, after establishing the inherent advantages of a single large market supplied by a single large supplier of telephone material and services, compared Western's prices with those of the 'much smaller non-Bell market of more than 90 manufacturers and suppliers for some similar equipment. Comparability of manufacturers and suppliers was not established and the reasonableness of other company prices, even assuming comparability, was not demonstrated. Moreover, the massive and unique market enjoyed by the nonoperating segments of American in the purchases by operating segments provides an advantage so great in volume alone in each of the fields of manufacturing, installation, purchasing and distribution that competition is effectively eliminated.

Western has a stable, assured and captive market. . . . We find [continues the commission] that little, if any, weight can be accorded such price comparisons in judging the reasonableness of Western's prices. It is the cost to Western that is significant'

"Further, according to the decision of the commission, Pacific 'attempted to justify the earnings of Western . . . by a comparison . . . of various financial ratios . . . for Western and for 47 selected utility suppliers. . . .' However, states the commission, Pacific's 'showing in this respect completely disregards the affiliation of Western with the Bell System and the unique conditions under which Western operates . . . and, even assuming comparability, does not demonstrate the reasonableness of earnings of the other companies. The advantage that the Bell System has in its integrated position . . . makes it impossible to compare one phase of its operations, that of Western Electric, with outside companies who have none of the same spread of operations and control. . . .'" The Pacific Telephone and Telegraph Company v. Public Utility Commission of the State of California, 401 P. 2d 353, 369 (1965). Stress supplied.

[114] In consequence,

"The [California] commission found and determined that Western's profit on sales to Pacific 'for rate-making purposes, should be adjusted' so as to result in a rate of return to Western not greater than the rate allowed Pacific. Accordingly, in arriving at Pacific's rate base the commission deducted $22,759,000 from payments made to Western which Pacific had included as original cost of plant, and in determining test-year expenses deducted the sum of $3,085,000 from payments by Pacific to Western. It is without question that 'for the purpose of fixing rates' the commission may

There is an element of plausibility in the California position—that is to say its former position, since it reversed itself in 1970.[115] To the extent that Western's evidently extremely efficient operation[116] is attributable to vertical integration, whether because of the economies of scale made possible by its preferential access to the huge Bell market or because of the intimate collaboration between manufacturing and operating companies, its superior performance constitutes a defense of the integration, lending support to the view that manufacturing is part of the "natural monopoly" of telephonic communications. The more "natural" and complete the integration, the less it would seem to make sense to claim that one part of the unit requires a higher rate of return than another. The more natural the monopoly, the more valid is the California Commission's conclusion that in judging the reasonableness of Western's prices, it is not the prices of its competitors but "the cost to Western that is significant."

The question remains: what is the proper measure of those costs? In particular, what is the proper measure of Western's cost of capital (k)? The company has presented extensive testimony documenting the greater variability of its sales than those of the operating companies, as an evidence of its greater risks, more nearly comparable with those of other suppliers of capital goods. The problem, once again, is one of reconciling this demonstration with the company's convictions about the essentiality and intimacy of its integration with the operating companies. It is unclear, in these circumstances, that its commercial risks or cost of capital can in any meaningful sense be said to be any different from those of the entire organization of which it is an integral part.

We make no effort to resolve the issue here. But even if one were persuaded on a priori grounds that it makes no sense to conceive of the Western part of the Bell System as having a k any different from that of the operating companies, it would still seem prudent, in attempting to *measure* it, to do so for the entire Bell System, *including* Western itself. This is not what the California Commission did. It simply assumed that Western's k was the same as that of the Pacific Telephone Co. and incorporated in the former's computed cost of service the same rate of return as it allowed the latter. Integration suggests the desirability of treating the entire enterprise as a unit

---

disallow excessive and unreasonable payments between affiliated corporations." *Ibid.*, p. 368.

For reference to an analogous but not identical practice in Michigan, see note 20, p. 29 of Volume 1.

[115] "The present record establishes that . . . the risks of the manufacturer, Western, are different and significantly greater than the utility, Pacific; that Western has risks of competition; that Western's prices are the lowest available; that . . . Western's cost savings have been passed on to its customer, Pacific; and that Western's financial characteristics are those of a manufacturer."

"Western's prices to Pacific and its earnings on its sales of manufactured products to Pacific have been fair and reasonable. . . ." Public Utilities Commission of the State of California, *Investigation on the Commission's own motion into the practices, contracts, service and facilities of The Pacific Telephone and Telegraph Co.*, Case No. 8858, Decision No. 76726, January 27, 1970, mimeo., 13a, 17.

[116] The McKinsey & Company study made some efforts to adjust the price comparisons between Western and independent manufacturers of telephone equipment for the differences in the size of their operations, attempting in this way to eliminate the advantages of the former of economies of scale made possible by its integration. Western Electric's costs, thus adjusted, still remained substantially below those of its competitors. *Op. cit.*, 21–25, 94–95. For a stern criticism of the entire McKinsey report, see Shepherd, *op. cit.*, in *Technological Change in the Regulated Industries*, mimeo, p. 45n.

in making cost computations; it does not justify doing so for only one part of the unit and then imputing the cost thus calculated to another part of the unit.[117]

---

[117] This procedure had the interesting consequence of imputing a return on Western Electric *equity* of only 7.05%, as compared with the 8.4% allowed Pacific Bell itself. The reason for this anomalous result is that the 6.9% return that the California Commission allowed the latter company on its *total* investment (and then imputed to Western) was based on its financing 35% of the total with debt, at an embedded cost of only 4.38% (and another 5% with preferred stock and advances). Western's capital structure, in contrast, had only 20% debt, with an embedded cost of 6.3%. (Information supplied by the company.)

The Bell System at one time argued for an enterprise-wide rate of return. It abandoned that position in favor of one arguing for a higher return for Western when it found commissions basing their findings of permissible rates of return solely on the needs of the operating companies and even at times justifying low returns on the ground that integration enabled those companies to shift many of the risks of the business *to* Western Electric!

There is also a reason of economic principle for considering Western's cost of capital separately. Risk, representing the degree of probability that individual expenditures of society's resources in capital investment will fail, in greater or lesser degree, to earn their opportunity costs, is a real, economic cost. And, as we have earlier contended (see note 22, this chapter, above), its proper measure is to be found in the spread of probable results of *particular investments*—not in the danger that the individual *investor* may fail to obtain a sufficient return on the *money* that he puts up to finance the project. The United States government, for example, can reduce the risk to the *lender* almost to zero, because, possessing sovereign power, it can always raise the funds necessary to service its debt by resort to taxation. It is not this minimal risk to the purchaser of government bonds that ought to determine the cost of capital, against which all government investment projects should be tested; rather, it is the opportunity cost of that capital—what it would add to national product in other uses—and the prospective returns of particular, proposed government investment projects, properly adjusted for the *risks of those individual projects*.

So it could well be that the economically proper k against which Western's own investments should be measured and that ought to be reflected in Western's prices is higher than the systemwide average—if indeed the real economic risks of the *projects* in which Western invests are greater than those of the operating companies.

What remains uncertain is the sufficiency of Western's proffered demonstration of those higher risks. True, fluctuations in sales over time are one commonly accepted indicator of risk, presumably because the more extreme the fluctuations in the success of particular categories of investments, the greater is the likelihood that any one of them will prove, ex post, to have been mistaken. This inference seems particularly justified in competitive markets, where fluctuations in sales may be construed as a reflection, among other things, of the special risks arising from competition itself. What is uncertain is whether a similar inference is justified, in the absence of competition, from the mere fact that the sales of Western Electric fluctuate more than those of the operating companies. If the latter could reliably be counted on to purchase all their requirements from the former, it seems doubtful that the mere fact that they purchase large quantities in some years and small quantities in others makes investment in one sector of the integrated operation any more risky than in the other.

"Western's . . . risk of failure is not distinctly of a different order than that of the Bell System as a whole. Cyclical fluctuations in earnings are more violent for Western than for the operating companies, but this is hardly a reason for a long-run average return significantly in excess of the range considered acceptable for the latter." Sheahan, *op. cit.*, Q. Jour. Econ. (May 1956), LXX: 257.

The foregoing discussion by no means exhausts the merits of this issue. The risks of Western's investments could still be greater than those of the operating companies in these circumstances *because* of regulation—if its profits fluctuate more than theirs but regulatory commissions do not permit it to earn the high profits in good years sufficient to compensate for the deeper decline of its earnings in bad ones. Again, its risks could be greater if the capital to output ratio of the operating companies—specifically, the arithmetic relationship between their purchases of inputs of the type supplied by Western Electric and their output—were subject to important fluctuation or change in the *long run*. This could take place if there occurred any marked secular change in the *rate* of growth of Bell output, since Bell's purchases from Western

In 1949, the United States Department of Justice filed a 73-page complaint against Western Electric and AT&T, the essence of which charge was that the two companies had monopolized

> "the production, manufacture, distribution, sale, and installation of telephones, telephone apparatus, telephone equipment, telephone materials, and telephone supplies,"

in violation of the Sherman Act.[118] The two essential instrumentalities of this alleged monopolization were said to be the patent policies of the Bell System and the vertically integrated relationship between the defendants, to both of which the government attributed Western's dominant position in the telephone equipment business.[119]

Note that what the government claimed was being illegally monopolized was the field in which Western Electric operates—the manufacture, distribution, sale, and installation of telephones, and telephone supplies and apparatus; and this was allegedly accomplished

> "(1) by vesting in Western the exclusive right to manufacture and sell such equipment to such operating companies and to the Long Lines Department of AT&T;

---

are a function not of its absolute *level* of sales but of their rate of expansion. Again, any decline in the automaticity with which the operating companies or their customers turn to Western for their equipment would have the same effect. Decisions like *Carterfone* weaken that link, hence increase Western's real risk. The rise of competition in communications in recent years has increased the risk of both the operating companies and Western, but not always equivalently.

[118] *United States of America v. Western Electric Company, Inc. and American Telephone & Telegraph Company*, Complaint, U.S. District Court, New Jersey, Civil Action No. 17–49, filed January 14, 1949, par. 59. This document and the Answer of the two defendants, as well as the Final Judgment, dated January 24, 1956, representing a consent settlement of the suit, are all reproduced in U.S. House of Representatives, Committee on the Judiciary, Antitrust Subcommittee, 85th Cong. 2d Sess., *Consent Decree Program of the Department of Justice*, Hearings, Part II—Volume I, Washington, 1958, pp. 1719–1795, 1800–1844, and 1845–1863. References to the paragraphs of the Complaint and Answer will be made directly in the text that follows.

[119] The defendants agreed with the government's charge (Complaint, Par. 45) that

> "virtually all of the Bell System requirements for telephones, telephone apparatus, equipment, materials, and supplies are purchased from Western, the only notable excep-

tion being building materials." (Answer, Par. 29)

And since both parties agreed also that the Bell companies owned approximately 85 percent of all the facilities used for rendering local telephone service in the country (Complaint, par. 42, Answer, par. 26), there was no essential dispute about the preponderant position of Western in the industry, thus defined. The government asserted, in addition, that AT&T owned and operated more than 98 percent of the facilities used in providing long-distance telephone service; the defendants responded that virtually all telephone facilities in the country are used from time to time for this purpose. (*Ibid.*) According to testimony by the U.S. General Services Administration, Western supplied about 90 percent of the equipment needs of the Bell companies and almost 80 percent of the U.S. market for telephone and telegraph apparatus in the early 1960s. (Irwin and McKee, "Vertical Integration and the Communication Equipment Industry: Alternatives for Public Policy," *Cornell Law Rev.* (February 1968), LIII: 447.) According to information supplied by the company and prepared for it by J. Fred Weston, it accounted in 1965 for 72.7 percent of total national value of shipments of such apparatus but, of the other products in its line, only 12.7 percent of the nonferrous wire drawing, 3.7 percent of microwave communication equipment, 3 to 7 percent of electron tubes, and 2 to 4 percent of various other instruments, hardware and types of equipment.

"(2) by requiring such operating companies and the Long Lines Department of AT&T to purchase their required equipment exclusively from Western. . . ." (Complaint, par. 60.)[120]

Two evils in particular, the government charged, flowed from this monopolization: excessive charges to the operating companies, on the one hand,[121] and delays in the introduction of cost-reducing innovations, on the other.[122]

---

[120] There are, however, interspersed throughout the Complaint various contentions also that the two defendants collaborated in such a way as to enhance and protect the monopoly positions of the Bell companies in *their* part of the business as well—the provision of telephone service. Under this heading would come the provision of the original contract between AT&T and Western Electric, covering the period 1882–1908, which prohibited the latter from selling telephone equipment to non-Bell companies (Complaint, Par. 56; Answer, Par. 54); the contention that

'Many types of equipment, particularly those essential to the successful operation of toll and long-distance lines, and all types of automatic switching equipment manufactured by Western have been consistently withheld from independent telephone companies" (Complaint, par. 56; see also Complaint, par. 74);

and that in those instances in which Western products are sold to non-Bell companies (through the Graybar Electric Company) the prices are 10 to 25 percent higher than those charged by Western to the Bell companies (Complaint, par. 120; the Answer admits the price differentials, but denies that Western fixes Graybar's prices or—"until recently"—controlled its management, par. 100).

So there are elements of a contention of mutual subsidization: that the operating companies use their monopoly to confer a monopoly in the manufacturing field on Western; and that Western to some extent uses its monopoly power to protect that of the operating companies. This double thesis is explicitly stated in Par. 74 of the Complaint. We make no effort to assess these allegations. There is some room for skepticism about the possibility of this kind of mutual magnification of monopoly. To the extent that Western is prevented by its Bell connections from making outside sales, its own market position and profits are contracted, not extended. To the extent that it either charges the operating companies lower prices or outside companies higher prices than it otherwise would choose to do, it is being forced to limit its monopoly and exploit it less than it otherwise would. (In unregulated markets one should be similarly skeptical about the other half of the model: to the extent that companies downstream make purchases from affiliates upstream that they would not otherwise make, in order to enhance the monopoly position of those affiliates, they do so at the expense of their own profits. But in regulated industries this kind of behavior could be a means of increasing the profits permitted on the combined operation.) And yet, though the obligations of each party to its partners may in some way restrict its own freedom of action, mutual support and benefit are clearly possible. Clearly, the Bell companies, with their overwhelming share of the telephone business, are in a position to confer on Western benefits large enough to outweigh the costs of its foregoing outside sales. And clearly also a policy of mutual exclusivity of patronage could well have seemed the most profitable one for the entire system.

[121] This contention really had several more or less separate aspects. One was, simply, that the absence of effective competition in the supply of equipment and materials to the operating companies resulted inescapably in the incorporation in the latters' cost of service of excessively high charges (Complaint, par. 124). Second was the contention that the prices of individual items of equipment were only remotely related to their respective costs (Complaint, par. 101). This was apparently a reference to the finding by the FCC, later corroborated by the careful investigations of Sheahan, that Western's computations of standard costs had been permitted to get seriously out of date in the 1930s—an understandable reflection of its comparative freedom from price competition. Sheahan, *op. cit.*, *Q. Jour. Econ.* (May 1956), LXX: 260–261. Third, the Department charged that higher profit margins were charged on items manufactured exclusively for the Bell companies than on items sold outside the system (Complaint, par. 101). This charge conflicts curiously with the opposite one, to which we have already referred, although the company's policy might of course have varied from one item of equipment to another. Sheahan concludes that it is the latter charge that has by far the greater validity: that the prices charged for Western equipment to non-Bell companies are substantially higher than to the Bell companies. See his *Competition*

For remedy, the Department of Justice asked for a long list of injunctions against continuation of the various alleged practices and agreements that it described. But the heart of its request was for two major remedies corresponding to the two major alleged instrumentalities for the illegal monopolization: compulsory licensing of all applicants under Bell System patents at reasonable royalties, and a dissolution of the tie between Western and the Bell System, with the requirement thereafter that the Bell companies be required to employ competitive bidding in all purchases of equipment, materials, and supplies.[123]

The case never went to trial. After seven years, during which considerable pressure was exerted on the Department of Justice to accept less drastic remedies,[124] a consent settlement was entered, the main relevant aspect of which for our present discussion is that it left the relationship between Western Electric and the Bell System essentially intact. The remedies in this part of the case were directed toward making regulation rather than competition more effective.[125]

The Bell System has, over many decades, developed a formidable defense of its vertical integration, the burden of which is that the financial link with manufacturing is essential to the provision of a low-cost, high-quality and ever-improving communications service. Central to this defense is the

---

Versus Regulation as a Policy Aim For the Telephone Equipment Industry, op. cit., 234–244. The final element is that

"Western's prices to Bell Operating Companies have been increased during periods of depression when prices in competitive markets have been reduced in an effort to retain business." (Complaint, par. 101.)

This charge was true, at least of the 1930s. Western's prices are based on anticipated full costs, which typically move inversely with volume. As a result it has at times reduced prices in boom periods after World War II; and it instituted a series of price increases in the early 1930s. Sheahan, *op. cit., Q. Jour. Econ.* (May 1956), LXX: 251, 255–256. The latter increases caused considerable difficulties with various State regulatory commissions, at least ten of which were moved to disallow some of them in computing operating company costs of service. The company is unlikely to repeat that venture; it has adopted the general policy of permitting its rates of return to fluctuate from year to year, rather than to resort to countercyclical pricing.
[122] "The purpose of such delayed introductions was to prevent existing plants from becoming obsolete." (Complaint, par. 102.) The Complaint goes on to document at some length six alleged instances of such retardation in the introduction of major equipment innovations. (Complaint, pars. 102–119.) The defendants answered at length (Answer, pars. 82–99); as we shall point out below, the evidence on this score is not very strong.

[123] The government asked, in addition, that Western Electric itself be broken up into three separate companies. (Complaint, Part VII, par. 11.)
[124] See the politically charged hearings by the Antitrust Subcommittee of the House of Representatives, covering almost 3,000 pages, in three volumes (note 118, p. 295 above) and the report subsequently issued by the same Subcommittee, 86th Cong., 1st Sess., *Consent Decree Program of the Department of Justice,* January 30, 1959, 29–120 and 290–323.
[125] See Kenneth E. Madsden, "Consent Decree: The History and Effect of Western Electric Co. v. United States," *Cornell Law Q.* (Fall 1959), XLV: 88–96.
Some eight years later, the Department of Justice brought suit to enjoin the acquisition of various independent telephone companies by General Telephone & Electronics Corporation, holding that these would violate Section 7 of the Clayton Act because they would tend to foreclose manufacturers of telephone equipment competitive with General from selling to the acquired operating companies. On November 15, 1966, the Department dropped this suit in consideration of the fact that it had earlier agreed to permit the "vastly greater" vertical integration of Western and Bell. See Manley R. Irwin and Robert E. McKee, *op. cit.,* 460–461. On the other hand, it was these and subsequent acquisitions by General that triggered the treble-damage suit by IT&T, referred to above (p. 290).

conception, already sketched in Chapter 4, of the integrated telecommunications network, "a web of millions of intricate and complicated mechanisms .... an ever-changing and delicately balanced machine," as a natural monopoly. Manufacturing, it adds, is an integral part of that monopoly.[126] This complex web of switching and transmission media, designed for an extremely high level of performance, necessitates, it is claimed, a continuous, intimate collaboration among all contributors to the service—research, development, manufacturing, installation, maintenance, and operations, a collaboration unconstrained by any divergencies of financial and managerial interests. The rapidity of technological change, it is asserted, calls for a similarly intimate collaboration both in the adaptation to it—the System is constantly offering new services, installing new equipment, adopting new technology, all of which must be integrated into the existing network—and, even more important, in fostering it. From a very early point, the scientists and engineers in Bell Laboratories, which does the fundamental research, collaborate continuously with their counterparts in Western and in the operating companies in the development process. Only in the presence of complete financial integration among the various parties, it is asserted, can collaboration be so intimate, continuous, and efficient—unhampered by conflict of financial interest or by the necessity of devising and perpetually redevising new collaborative relationships with financially separate companies, in arms-length negotiations. The role of vertical integration, in short, is to create a community of interest, making possible a free and open exchange of information and wholehearted collaboration in pursuit of the best interests of the telephone system as a whole.

More specifically, this means that the interest of the manufacturing organization is not separately pursued, but is subordinated to the efficient service of the ultimate customer; Western stands ready to meet the operating companies' needs, whatever they are: that is its function.[127] And this joining of manufacture and operations results in minimization of cost,

---

[126] AT&T, "Vertical Integration in the Bell System," 2.

[127] See *ibid.*, 19–20.

Other asserted aspects of this subordination of the interests of the manufacturer, as such, are the willingness of Western to invest promptly in the capacity needed to meet both normal and unanticipated increases in demand,

"even though conditions are not such as to induce the requisite expansion of capacity by an outside manufacturer of telephone equipment.... "Western has knowledge of estimated Operating Company requirements, organizes and tools up accordingly and begins production far in advance of actual orders and without assurance that the estimated requirements will materialize. Outside competing suppliers could not foretell the demand on them unless contractually assured of definite business, and would be reluctant to invest money to meet even predicted demands for the specialized equipment required for telephony without contractual protection." (*Ibid.*, 32–33.)

In consequence, it is said, Western can typically promise a one-year interval between the receipt of an order and the delivery of even its most complex equipment:

"Unaffiliated manufacturers, as for example in the electrical equipment industry, often wait for hard orders to materialize, and back orders of six years are now the general rule for generating equipment. As a result, the electric utilities must wait to have current needs met and must make hazardous estimates of their needs six years from now to be sure of the generating capacity adequate for customer demand," (*Ibid.*,35).

If this comparison is a fair one, it would seem to illustrate the tendency to which we have already referred for vertical integration, and particularly integration with a regulated monopolist who possesses some reserve of incompletely exploited monopoly power, to minimize risk (see pp. 260–262, this chapter and pp. 106–108, Chapter 3 [on the positive effect of A-J-W], above). Western, with its preferential access to the Bell market, and itself pricing like a public utility,

maintenance of the highest possible standards of service, and the most rapid possible improvement in both over time.

The argument is not merely hypothetical. It is buttressed with impressive evidence of good economic performance:

1. Although no definitive, objective comparisons have evidently been made, no one who has had occasion to use the telephone in a fair number of foreign countries would be likely to quarrel with the observation that the United States has a very good telephone system.[128]

2. Long distance telephone rates have dropped sharply in recent decades; the cost of intrastate telephone service has risen far less than the general price level. Correspondingly, the growth of productivity in communications has been markedly higher than in the economy generally, as we have already seen.[129]

3. The comparative performance of Western Electric alone in these respects is even more impressive. In the period 1950–1967, Western's prices for apparatus and equipment declined 16 percent; the Bureau of Labor Statistics price index for electrical equipment generally increased 53 percent in the same period. Again, during these same years, Western's prices for cable and wire rose 14 percent, compared with 95 percent in the BLS Index. Between 1948 and 1967, total factor productivity of Western Electric increased at an average 5.4 percent annually, compared with 3.5 for the entire electrical machinery and supplies industry and 2.5 for all manufacturing in the United States.[130]

---

may be able to afford to make investments in anticipation of demands that nonintegrated suppliers could not afford to make:

"If several manufacturers were competing for the business, and no one of them could be assured of any specified quantity of business over an extended period, they would be unwilling to risk major capital expenditures to meet peak demands." (*Ibid.*, 54.)

The McKinsey & Company study of Western Electric, cited above, repeats and documents many of these same arguments.

It is surely an overstatement to suggest that the nonintegrated manufacturers "would be unwilling" to do so: they do in fact do so, in industry after industry. But they would, presumably, require at least the prospect of a higher average rate of return, corresponding to their higher competitive risks. See our discussion of the ability of vertical integration to overcome the effects of market imperfections and the case of the reluctant nonintegrated supplier in notes 22 and 26 above. Here is another illustration of the possible conflict between the strong case that the Bell companies make for vertical integration and Western's asserted need for a rate of return comparable to that earned by nonintegrated equipment manufacturers. But the contradiction

is not inevitable: the integration, *per se*, reduces risk; but if because of the integration Western does indeed undertake commitments *more* risky than do unaffiliated manufacturers, it could still be that its prices should reflect a rate of discount of the probable returns on its projected investments, or a cost of capital, comparable with theirs.

128 It ought in principle to be possible to be more precise about this—to compare the average time it takes to complete a call, the percentage of busy circuits encountered, the record of breakdowns and the like. The Bell System regularly compiles such data for its own operations. An international comparison would provide some perspective on such obvious failures as the grossly inadequate capacity that turned up in New York City in 1969–1970 and the one to two years that company officials proclaimed at the time would be required to restore service of normal quality.

129 See pp. 99–100, Chapter 3, above.

130 McKinsey & Company, *op. cit.*, 14 and 92. These very substantial improvements in the pricing record after World War II may be regarded in some degree as a correction of what the FCC earlier found were overcharges in one form or another, after its comprehensive investigation of the industry. *Investigation of the Telephone*

This impressive improvement in Western's productivity no doubt reflects a correspondingly above-average research and developmental effort. According to figures supplied by the company, its R & D expenditures in the period 1960–1966 amounted to 5.2 percent of its Bell sales, a ratio that may be compared with less than 2 percent for all manufacturing and 3.5 percent for the communications and electronic equipment industry, excluding Western.[131]

4. As we have already seen, Western's prices are dramatically below those of other manufacturers of comparable supplies and equipment, reflecting a combination of managerial efficiency, the advantages of integration, and a policy of charging less than the traffic will bear.

It is extremely difficult for an economist or anyone else to make a decisive appraisal of the case just summarized. And yet a judgment has to be made by someone—a legislature, a court, or a regulatory commission—though, fortunately, not necessarily by us, here and now.

The factual evidence just summarized would certainly seem to reflect a "good"—perhaps an "excellent"—economic performance; and that must be our tentative verdict. The difficulty is that there is no objective yardstick against which to compare all these results. Comparisons with other companies and other industries must, of course, carry weight—indeed, heavy weight when the evidence shows much lower Western prices for the very products produced by the others and a much more progressive performance by Western than by other companies employing a similar technology. But these are decisive indicators only of a superior performance by Western Electric itself. The question before us is, rather, what the performance of the communications industry might have been if Western were not linked to Bell. And this is the comparison for which the objective facts are, in the very nature of the case, unavailable.

It is difficult, similarly, for an outsider to sift out the poetry from the objective facts in the Bell companies' defense of the financial linkage. On the one hand, it is difficult to credit to mere coincidence the fact that the company whose price and productivity record is so much superior to others with which it may reasonably be compared happens also to be integrated into the Bell System. It should be emphasized, also, that the defense of vertical integration in this industry is almost unique in its assertion of genuine managerial and technological benefits flowing from it.[132] Not in petroleum, steel, cement, aluminum, motion pictures, or grocery distribution, in all of which integration has been both widely prevalent and strenuously debated, have its protagonists based their arguments so directly on technological grounds. The financial union of crude oil production and refining, iron ore mining and steel-making, the production of ingot steel and the fabrication of steel products, electric power generation and aluminum reduction, the production, distribution, and exhibition of motion pictures,

---

Industry in the United States, Washington, 1939. This is the interpretation of Wilcox, *op. cit.*, 381–384. See also C. F. Phillips, *op. cit.*, 658–667. In any event, the improvements were real and very impressive.

[131] AT&T, "Vertical Integration in the Bell System," *op. cit.*, 46–47.

[132] "the case for a carrier-manufacturer tie is at its strongest in telecommunications." President's Task Force on Communications Policy, *The Domestic Telecommunications Carrier Industry*, Staff Paper 5, Part 1, Washington, June 1969, 193.

the manufacture of cement and of ready-mixed concrete, the synthesis of nitrogen compounds and the preparation of mixed fertilizers, coffee-roasting and food distribution have all been defended on such grounds as the necessity for assuring a sufficient and regular supply of vital inputs, more effective marketing, the circumvention of monopoly, the saving of selling costs and—it should be conceded—the possibilities it afforded for a closer specification and control of quality, but rarely or never on the ground that the technological interdependencies were so close that each operation had to be done by the same engineers and managers working in close collaboration.[133]

On the other hand, it is simply unclear how much would be lost if the responsibility for the management, development, and improvement of the communications network were vested exclusively in the operating companies, AT&T and the Bell Laboratories, the financial ties between which have not been subjected to serious question. It is surely they who must in any event bear it, ultimately. It is the Bell Telephone Laboratories that conduct the extensive as well as apparently first-class basic research,[134] systems engineering, and fundamental development work. It is AT&T, not Western Electric, that in the first instance foots the bill for these parts of the operation[135]: the ultimate payer is of course the user of telephone services. It is Bell Labs, AT&T, and the operating companies that play the preponderant role in the initiation and selection of new development projects;[136] it is they that must set the standards and assume the ultimate responsibility for both innovation and operations.

But these speculations do not address themselves to the most difficult and pertinent question. Most of the work of Bell Labs is in development, not research, in highly applied, not pure research. And it is here that the most intimate collaboration is with the manufacturing, not the operating company. The Bell System claims that without this intimate link, the Laboratories would be crippled in the preponderant part of their operations; that Western could similarly not survive without that collaboration; and that, hence, if Western were separated from the System most of the Labs would have to come away with it, thereby severing the vital tie with operations.[137] Once again, the impartial judge encounters the vexing problem of comparing the observable virtues of what is with the uncertain benefits of what might be.

---

[133] One limited exception—there may, of course, be others—apart from the case for closer quality control (which is, however, in none of these industries asserted with anything like the vigor shown in communications) would be the direct saving in fuel costs made possible by the transfer of pig iron in molten form from the blast furnace directly into the steel converter.

[134] Francis Bello "The World's Greatest Industrial Laboratory," *Fortune*, November 1958, pp. 148–150 and ff. An index of the quality of BTL that will appeal to university department chairmen and deans is provided by a count that the Bell System made of 2,703 papers published in 1967 in *The Physical Review*, in terms of the contributors' institutions. The University of California at Berkeley was first, with 150; Bell Labs tied for second with 101; the next industrial company

on the list was General Electric, in 26th place, with 33 papers. "Technological Innovation in the Bell System," Company Memorandum, undated, mimeo., 46–47.

[135] AT&T receives a flat percentage of the operating companies' annual revenues, in return for the various services it provides for them—research, planning, financial, and legal.

[136] McKinsey & Company, *op. cit.*, 243–246.

[137] "The most serious problem would be the disposition of Bell Laboratories . . . [T]he sections of Bell Labs concerned with development could become a part of Western Electric. This would help to eliminate Western's inside track to Bell orders, but it would also destroy the unity of Bell Laboratories." The Presidents' Task Force on Communications Policy, Staff Paper 5, Part 1, *op. cit.*, 191–192.

Clearly Western would, if separated, have to develop (or take with it) its own research and development operation. This could well expand the aggregate R & D effort, in the industry as a whole. What is unclear is how much would be lost if the operating companies abandoned this chosen and exclusive manufacturing instrument and were instead free to work with Western on some parts of the manufacturing and development process, and with companies like General Electric, International Business Machines or Radio Corporation of America on others, when and as it seemed in their interest to do so.

That there would be losses, it seems impossible to deny. The introduction of separate and to some extent conflicting financial interests means the introduction of bargaining, of divergent goals, divisions of loyalty; the substitution of possibly shifting contractual for financially integrated relationships must to some extent diminish the likelihood of continuous and completely open exchanges of information and collaboration.[138] There would be another important loss—the loss of one of the most important weapons a large user of purchased inputs has when confronting suppliers which do not give it good service: the threat to manufacture for itself. In light of the possibility that a nonintegrated telephonic equipment industry might be tightly oligopolistic, this defense ought not lightly to be surrendered.

The fundamental question is whether there would not be offsetting advantages. The fact that Western stands between the needs of the operating companies and other potential suppliers of equipment—even when they use non-Western equipment and materials, the Bell companies purchase them through that company—must severely discourage companies that might otherwise be interested and able to enter into competition for Bell patronage. There would be little point in their offering lower prices to get the business or making the investments that might put them in a position to do so, when the offer would in fact have to be made to Western itself, as purchasing agent for the operating companies. In these circumstances, the fact that Western's prices are consistently lower than those quoted for similar equipment by the much smaller manufacturing companies that must survive on sales to the independent telephone company market becomes considerably less than conclusive demonstration of the superior efficiency of the integrated relationship.[139]

---

[138] The case is not mainly one of a company buying standardized components, which can readily be let out for competitive bids. It is rather one of continuously developing new components for a total system whose design is never firmly set but subject to perpetual alteration, comparable in many ways to the procurement of complex new weapons or aerospace systems. The efforts of the Department of Defence to purchase such systems, to find means of cutting costs, preventing overruns, devising incentives for their efficient development and production are not encouraging in this regard. *Ibid.*, 182–185, 187–189.

[139] It should be recognized, however, that Western's prices are markedly lower also on such items as cable and switchboard lamps, of which it is not at all the largest producer. Its lower

prices are not explainable solely in terms of economies of scale made possible by integration. See notes 110 and 116, above. While agreeing that Western's prices "are almost always lower than outside market prices," so that "the Bell Companies are in effect nearly always buying in the cheapest market when they buy from Western," Sheahan also found "little indication of any tendency for Bell companies to buy from outside in the minority of cases where Western's individual prices are not lowest." *Op. cit., Q. Jour. Econ.* (May 1956), LXX: 259 and his *Competition versus Regulation as a Policy Aim*, 362. See also *ibid.*, 74—93.

"Savings might become more significant if there were an effective rule requiring Western

Most important of all is the likelihood that opening the market to a large number of other, technologically progressive companies, by offering them the opportunity of competing on equal terms for Bell company custom, would contribute powerfully to innovation. The result could well be even more rapid reduction in cost and proliferation of new services than has been accomplished thus far.[140]

"The benefits of freer entry could be considerable. The telephone equipment industry, with its high degree of automation and requirements for systematic design, once stood apart from the rest of the economy. But today those characteristics describe many industries. With the convergence of communications and computer technology, a number of the most progressive and dynamic manufacturers in American industry—firms like IBM, ITT, General Electric, Raytheon, and RCA—have significant potential as innovators and manufacturers of new communications equipment. So do the aerospace manufacturers, with their experience in electronics, materials, system design, and other relevant technologies and skills. . . . In an age where satellites, lasers, computers and other products of space-age industries are becoming increasingly important elements of communications technology, it would be parochial to assume that the carriers' affiliates had a complete monopoly of the ideas and techniques required to fulfill the promise held out to communications users by the course of technological advance."[141]

To a company that has not previously been directly exposed to it, competition represents a plunge into the unknown. It is not unreasonable for AT&T to argue that such a plunge represents a gamble for the ultimate consumer as well as for itself, and that it seems folly to give up a system that is producing efficiently, progressively and well, with demonstrable benefits, on the mere hypothesis that another kind of regime could do better. As Sheahan poignantly concluded:

"The telephone equipment industry could conceivably be termed workably competitive except for the semantical difficulty that its dominant Bell market exhibits practically no competition at all."[142]

On the other hand, the case for competition is not merely semantic or hypothetical. First of all, there is some historical evidence, though far from

---

to turn to outside suppliers in all such cases; a newly created possibility of selling to this gigantic market might lead to more favorable price quotations by outside companies hoping to build a market within the Bell System. As it stands, outside firms can have little reasonable hope of getting much Bell business, and no incentive to try through lower prices to expand their sales in this market." *Op. cit., Q. Jour. Econ.*, 259.

[140] This is the main conclusion of Sheahan's investigation: once the principle was established that the Bell companies were prepared to buy freely from the outside,

"production and research facilities in a good

many alert electrical equipment firms would become active supplements to those now in the Bell System.

"The difficulty now is not that Western is an inferior choice in the usual case; it is that Western is the best of an artificially restricted range of possibilities. Other firms realize quite correctly that they cannot break into this market on any significant scale, and therefore do not choose to invest money and skill in any actual attempt." *Ibid.*, 268.

[141] The President's Task Force on Communications Policy, Staff Paper 5, Part 1, *op. cit.*, 178–179.

[142] *Competition Versus Regulation as a Policy Aim*, 360.

overwhelming, that the Bell companies have at times been slow in adopting innovations originating outside of Western Electric, at least to the extent of waiting first to see whether Western might succeed in coming up with at least as good an alternative.[143]

Second, there are concrete evidences of the contribution competitive innovation can make in communications where it has had an opportunity to work—around the edges of the communications monopoly, as it has doubtless appeared to the independent manufacturers of equipment; uncomfortably close to the heart, in the view of the Bell System. The revolutionary development in the last decade of microwave and satellite communications, the burgeoning of user-owned attachments and in particular those associated with the use of shared computer facilities, the rapid introduction of CATV have, all of them, been vigorously pressed not only by large users and independent entrepreneurs in communications but also, at least with equal vigor, by competing manufacturers of equipment.[144]

[143] See the reference, note 122, above, to the much stronger statement in the 1949 antitrust complaint. Wilcox accepts some of these contentions without serious question:

"The company postponed the introduction of improvements such as the hand set and the dial system for many years so that its old equipment might wear out before it was junked." *Op. cit.*, 260.

Of course, this sort of retardation could be in the interest of a monopolist, regardless of whether it was vertically integrated. Sheahan's conclusions, based on a much more thorough appraisal, are much more moderate and qualified. See *Competition versus Regulation as a Policy Aim*, 148–170, and *op. cit.*, Q. Jour. Econ. (May 1956), LXX: 264–265.

[144] See especially pp. 129–131, Chapter 4, above. According to Manley R. Irwin, the main impulse for adopting the microwave radio relay technique came from independent equipment suppliers; the preponderant portion of the private systems, sanctioned by the *above-890* decision, were manufactured by Motorola, Collins Radio, RCA, and General Electric. The Bell System itself made a major contribution to the development of this innovation with a crash program in the 1946–1950 period that produced the TD-2. That intensive effort was evidently inspired in part by the fact that several competitors had entered or threatened to enter the field, it having become clear that microwave would be the logical technique for serving the rapidly growing needs of television. See Shepherd, *op. cit.*, in *Technological Change in the Regulated Industries*, mimeo., 56–58, drawing on, among other sources, F. M. Scherer, *The Development of the TD-X and TD-2 Microwave Radio Relay Systems in Bell Telephone Laboratories*, Weapons Acquisition Research Project, Harvard Univ. Graduate School of Business Administra-

tion, mimeo., October 1960.

In communications satellites, the proposals of the Bell System were for a global network of low- or medium-orbit satellites, approximately 50 in total, the large number required because each individual satellite, as it moved across the horizon, would be within radio range for only some 20 minutes; this required also very large capital outlays for the necessary ground stations. It was the aerospace industry and, in particular, Hughes Aircraft and Lockheed that pressed for and developed the synchronous satellites, which, orbiting at approximately 22,300 miles above the earth's surface, remain in a fixed position relative to that surface, thus vastly reducing the number and complexity of required satellites and ground stations.

Again, according to Irwin, it has been non-integrated firms that have taken the lead in introducing new switching techniques for message communications using computers and in devising a wide variety of "modems," devices that enable computers to transmit data via the telephone network. Not surprisingly, independent innovative activity was far more intense and productive in the 1965–1969 period in developing these and other devices for attachment to the private leased line network—where AT&T has permitted non-Bell attachments since 1965–1966—than for the dialed network, where until *Carterfone* the highly restrictive foreign attachment tariff prevailed. "Innovation and the Communications Industry," a paper presented at a Conference of the President's Task Force on Communications Policy, mimeo., 7; see pp. 5–8 and *passim*; also Irwin and McKee, *op. cit.*, 452–457; and Shepherd, *op. cit.*, in *Technological Change in the Regulated Industries*, mimeo., 50–51. On the role of independents in modems, see "A profitable way to translate computer talk," *Business Week*, May 16, 1970, 124. On the divergent assess-

But, in the last analysis, the plunge into competition is inescapably a plunge into the unknown. The essence of the case for competition is that the potential performance of an industry is unknowable; it is the rivalry of independent suppliers that offers the greatest possible assurance that all economically feasible avenues for cost reduction and service innovation will in fact be explored and their results subjected to the impartial test of the marketplace.

This is not, however, a sufficient guide to public policy in all times and places, as the institution of regulated public utility monopoly itself indicates. It remains possible that the manufacture of equipment for the central core of the natural monopoly, the communications network, is a "natural" part of that monopoly. This writer would find it extremely difficult himself, in the face of the objective record of good performance and the qualitative arguments that provide at least a highly plausible basis for attributing those results in important measure to vertical integration, to recommend the plunge into the unknown.

What does seem clear, as a matter not only of economic logic but of experience, is that the retention of such a vertical tie becomes less objectionable, the more it is possible to introduce competition into the communications business itself; or the more narrowly the area of natural monopoly is defined. What makes vertical integration possibly objectionable is its attachment to a regulated horizontal monopoly. What created the opportunity for independent entry into some portions of the business of manufacturing communications *equipment*, and therefore exposed Western Electric itself to indirect competition, was the entry of new purveyors of communications *service*. If the Bell System had from the outset been given complete control over communications satellites, if it had succeeded in persuading the FCC to deny large business users the right to set up private microwave facilities, and if its restrictive policies with respect to interconnection and alien attachments had been sustained, it seems most probable that the industry's performance would have been much less dynamic than it has been in the last decade. The defect would have been the defect of monopoly. But in those markets where the monopoly is and remains natural, the question must continue to be asked whether the foreclosure of competitive innovation in the supply of its major inputs that vertical integration entails may not be an excessive price to pay for the undoubted benefits flowing from it.[145]

---

ments of and contributions to the potentialities of satellite technology, see also Charles E. Silberman, "The Little Bird that Casts a Big Shadow," *Fortune*, February 1967, 108–111 and ff; also Lawrence Lessing, "Cinderella in the Sky," *Fortune*, October 1967, 131–133 and ff, both of these likewise clearly underlining the same conflict of interest between the common carriers and their affiliated manufacturing units, on the one hand, and nonaffiliated manufacturing innovators like Hughes Aircraft, on the other.

[145] There is a related issue that must be mentioned, even though we cannot pursue it at length here. If there is a strong case for permitting nonintegrated manufacturers fuller access to the communications market, is there not also a strong case for Western Electric competing more forcefully in making sales outside the Bell System? The question is intended to be essentially rhetorical. Partly as a result of historic company policy, partly as a result of the antitrust consent decree, which imposed various restrictions on the right of Western to sell in the open market and restricted AT&T and its operating companies from engaging in any business other than the furnishing of common-carrier communications services and related operations, Western has confined its sales almost exclusively to the Bell System and to the government. The large price differentials that it and the Bell companies proudly cite between Western and competitive equipment could not possibly be sustained if

Financial Integration: The Problem of Judgment

The reader may have observed how much more tentative our policy judgments have been so far in this chapter than in Chapter 5. It could be merely that the confidence shown in the previous chapter was misplaced and that only equally tentative conclusions should have been drawn there. But the difference between the two is instructive—illuminating not only the nature and limitations of economics but the important differences between the two situations under examination.

Chapter 5 was concerned with industries both structurally and behaviorally capable of much more effective competition than regulation has permitted. The institution of competition makes prediction possible: the competition of large numbers automatically enforces certain kinds of behavior and guarantees certain kinds of results from an *industry* no matter what the motivations and capabilities of individual members of the group.[146]

In this chapter, in contrast, we deal with small numbers in individual markets, and prediction becomes much more difficult. The economic performance of oligopoly is capable of much wider variation. It can be identical to that of monopoly, at one extreme; it can be intensely competitive; and it can be sometimes one and sometimes the other, in the same industry. When a proposal is under consideration to transform an industry from duopoly to monopoly and the latter offers certain efficiency advantages, as for example in the case of electric and gas distribution, it is very difficult to know how much of genuine competition would actually be surrendered. And one can no longer reliably predict, on the other hand, to what extent the opportunities for greater efficiency will in fact be grasped. The possible inhibiting influence of encrusted bureaucracy and its probable reactions to the new situation must be assessed.

Moreover, when numbers are few, some or all of those few are likely to have substantial monopoly power. And they may on that account be in a position to deny others access to the market on fair and equal terms. One must therefore assess the impact of financial integration on those opportunities for competition and try to determine to what extent can regulation *in practice* actually protect those opportunities.

Economists are understandably uneasy in prescribing policy for industries of small numbers.

Western competed freely in the open market.

No doubt, that company is restrained from doing so by a fear that it would be subject to antitrust attack, particularly if, as seems likely, some smaller telephone equipment suppliers would in consequence be put out of business; and no doubt, also, the consent decree itself reflects this same kind of ambivalence toward genuine competition. Finally, there would always be a danger, if Western and the Bell companies were free to compete in nonutility operations, that they might do so at non-remunerative prices, recouping any such losses in higher rates to their captive, utility customers; and it was to guard against any such possibility that some of the restrictions in the consent settlement were imposed. But even if the vertical tie between manufacturing and operating companies were retained, it would seem that sufficient protections could be devised against any such policy by requiring a strict separation of the accounts for Western's regulated and nonregulated activities; this additional impediment to regulation would, it would seem, be a small price to pay for the benefits that would be expected to flow—most obviously, lower costs for equipment and supplies purchased by independent telephone companies —from the entry of Western itself into direct competition in the electrical and telephonic equipment industries.

[146] See Arman A. Alchian, "Uncertainty, Evolution, and Economic Theory," Amer. Econ. Ass'n, *Readings in Industrial Organization and Public Policy*, 207–219.

INTERCOMPANY COORDINATION

We have alluded in many places to the great economies that can be achieved when public utility companies coordinate their activities in one way or another and have described numerous instances of such collaboration voluntarily undertaken. We have also described the obstacles to complete coordination. Regulatory compulsion has been required not only to ensure that the potential cost savings are more fully achieved but also because intercompany cooperation raises problems with respect to the preservation of competition. The dangers are either that the companies will cooperate not too little but too much—for example, to suppress competition among themselves—or that they will, either individually or collectively, use such power as they have or as they may achieve by cooperation to exclude independent firms from a fair opportunity to compete with them.

We shall consider only two cases in detail in this chapter. It might be useful therefore, in order to convey a fuller sense of the range and pervasiveness of these phenomena, to list a few examples, most of which we have already mentioned:

1. The establishment of joint rates and through routes by separate transportation companies. One problem is that railroads, in particular, have used their rate bureaus or conferences, whose ostensible justification is the need to plan such collaborations, as instruments also for the discouragement or suppression of price competition among themselves. Another is that they have often refused to coordinate on nondiscriminatory terms with water or motor carriers.[147]

2. The exchange of railroad freight cars, avoiding the necessity of transferring freight from the cars of one road to those of another on journeys requiring the facilities of both.[148] One problem has been the necessity of setting compensation rates high enough to induce the borrowing railroads to return cars promptly to their owners in time of shortage.[148a]

3. The requirement that the Bell companies interconnect with independent telephone companies[149], and then with any and all competitors.[149a]

---

[147] See pp. 271–272, above. There is an exellent survey of the railroad rate bureau phenomenon in Fulda, *op. cit.*, Chapter 9; his Chapter 10 is devoted to rate agreements in international shipping.

[148] The airlines similarly interchange equipment, subject to the approval of the Civil Aeronautics Board. For example, in February 1969, the CAB approved an interchange agreement between Northwest Airlines and Pan American World Airways, which will permit through-plane service between Minneapolis on the one hand and various points in Europe on the other. National Airlines has been able to justify purchase of several huge (350-seat) jet airplanes only because it plans to lease the planes to Pan American in its off-season. Gilbert Burck, "A New Flight Plan for the Airlines," *Fortune*, April 1969, 98–101 and ff.

[148a] See note 46a, p. 64, above.

[149] See p. 140, above. Section 766 of the California Public Utilities Code provides that:

"Whenever the Commission . . . finds that a physical connection can reasonably be made between the lines of two or more telephone corporations . . . whose lines can be made to form a continuous line of communication . . . and that public convenience and necessity will be served thereby, or finds that two or more telegraph or telephone corporations have failed to establish joint rates . . . for service by or over their lines, and that joint rates . . . ought to be established, the Commission may . . . require that such connection be made on the payment of such compensation . . . as it finds to be just and reasonable. . . ." As quoted in Public Utilities Commission of the State of California, *In the Matter*

4. The problems of independent manufacturers of communications equipment arising out of the historic Bell System policy of refusing to permit non-Bell equipment to be hooked up with the telephone network and the erosion of that policy by the FCC's *Hush-A-Phone* and *Carterfone* decisions.[150]

5. Voluntary purchases and sales of gas between pipeline companies.[151]

6. The FPC's periodic orders requiring particular natural gas pipeline or electric companies to interconnect with and provide service to municipal distributors at Commission-fixed prices.[152]

7. The attempt of the FPC staff to require competing applicants for certification to pool their plans in order to take fuller advantage of the economies of scale and the attempt of a dissenting Commissioner to attach to the certificate of the successful applicant a condition reserving the Commission's right at a later point to require him, if it saw fit, to carry gas for others.[153]

8. The running of a feeder helicopter service by a number of airline companies cooperatively, as a means of internalizing what would otherwise be the external benefits of that service.[154]

9. The requirement by the FCC that CATV companies carry the programs of local stations, and the problems created for those operators by the reluctance of the Bell Companies to let them use telephone company poles or ducts to carry their cables to subscribers.[155]

---

of the Application of the Pacific Telephone & Telegraph Company et al., Decision No. 74917, November 6, 1968 (mimeo.), p. 40.

The Commission points out that this statute was passed 55 years earlier when the Pacific Telephone Company refused to interconnect with the other companies.

"The Section has well served such purpose, as is evidenced by the fact that since its passage and early enforcement . . . the facilities of telephone companies in this State have become so interconnected that for many years the people of this State have had the public benefit of a wholly integrated toll network." *Ibid.*, 40–41.

"in fact every California independent company is a physical part of the nationwide toll network. The standards of quality for every part of such network, as a practical matter, are set by Bell System requirements. Both the statewide portion and the nationwide toll network have been developed as an integrated whole to allow full compatibility in dialing, signalling and transmission regardless of whether a call originates or terminates at a Bell System or an independent telephone station." *Ibid.*, 35–36.

Section 201 (a) of the Communication Act confers similar authority on the FCC:

"It shall be the duty of every common carrier engaged in interstate or foreign communication

by wire or radio to furnish such communication service upon reasonable request therefor; and . . . where the Commission . . . finds such action necessary or desirable in the public interest, to establish physical connections with other carriers, to establish through routes and charges applicable thereto and the divisions of such charges, and to establish and provide facilities and regulations for operating such through routes." 47 U.S. Code 201 (a), 1964 ed.

[149a] See note 60, p. 133, above.
[150] See pp. 140–145, Chapter 4, above.
[151] See p. 66, note 55, above.
[152] See note 85, pp. 75–76, above.
[153] See pp. 154–157, Chapter 4, above.
[154] See note 179 p. 234, above.
[155] See pp. 33–34, Chapter 1 and pp. 67–68, Chapter 2, above. In New York City, the problems of the cable operators are complicated by the fact that while the city has franchised some of them to lay cables under the streets, the duct space beneath Manhattan is controlled by the Empire City Subway Company, which is owned by the New York Telephone Company.

"Empire, the CATV people say, has not been too eager to furnish ducts—even at a rental of $1,350 a mile per year.

"Lack of cooperation from the Bell System is an increasing problem across the country, CATV men assert. The reason? CATV is highly profit-

Piggyback Service

The most important form of intermodal collaboration in the transportation field, in fact and in potential, is the use of truck trailers on railway flatcars (TOFC), popularly known as piggybacking. Piggybacking has the great attraction of combining the flexibility, the door-to-door pickup and delivery capacity of truck service with the far lower line haul costs of the rails (or water carriers) over long distances, while avoiding the often prohibitive costs of transferring freight from one medium to the other.[156] (These same observations apply to containerization generally, of which the use of the truck trailer itself as the container is only one form.) It offers the prospect of savings in cost and improvement in service if the companies operating the different modes can find one way or another of cooperating to offer it.

Piggybacking also greatly increases the likelihood that the rates for different kinds of freight will be based exclusively on costs. The elaborate system of price discrimination involved in the prevailing commodity rate structure requires identification of the commodities in order to assess what each will bear. Containerization lends itself instead to flat all-commodity rates per container or trailer (with appropriate modifications for weight, for example), regardless of its contents.[157] It was for this reason that the ICC in 1931 first rejected proposed piggyback rates: they would have undermined the commodity rate structure—the very structure that encouraged the inefficient transfer of so much traffic to higher-cost modes[158]—

able, and many phone companies think they should be in it." "CATV comes down from the hills," *Business Week*, September 16, 1967, 66. Reprinted by special permission.

In July 1969 the Department of Justice filed comments with the FCC, in connection with an inquiry involving certification of CATV systems, in which it maintained there was

"a serious danger that the existing local monopoly positions of the telephone companies as communications common carriers may prevent the development of an independent community antenna television industry."

It therefore recommended that the Commission require telephone companies to offer pole space or conduit space to all applicants on equal and nondiscriminatory terms and to forbid them offering CATV service in areas in which they themselves provide telephone service. *Telecommunications Reports* (July 28, 1969), XXXV: 9–10. The Commission adopted the recommendation (note 59, p. 68, above). Obviously there are possible efficiency advantages in permitting phone companies to offer CATV service integrated with their own; and they might have had superior incentives to innovate in this closely related field. The FCC therefore announced that its rule could be waived when, for example in sparsely populated areas, "CATV service would not exist without the affiliation of the telephone company." *Ibid*. But the historical fact is that CATV was pioneered by independent business-

men; and that the telephone companies had it in their power to hamper that competition and take over the business themselves. In these circumstances compulsory coordination may represent the optimum means of achieving the joint goals of efficiency, innovation, and competition.

[156] See Meyer *et al.*, *op. cit.*, 150–155, also 101–110 and Friedlaender, *op. cit.*, 38–43.

[157] The pioneering venture, the "ferry truck" service introduced in 1926 by the Chicago, North Shore & Milwaukee Railroad Company, at first used the traditional commodity rates; but in 1928 it shifted, with some exceptions, to a flat all-merchandise rate. ICC, *Ex Parte No. 230, Substituted Service—Charges and Practices of For-Hire Carriers and Freight Forwarders (Piggyback Service)* (hereinafter, *Ex Parte No. 230*), 322 ICC 301, 305 (1964). Under the so-called Plan I, in which the trucker merely substitutes rail haul on some part of the trip for traffic that he originates and controls, and Plan II, in which the railroad performs the entire service, door-to-door, freight continues to move under the regular tariffs. Under Plans III and IV, in which the rails' open tariffs impose a flat charge, regardless of the contents of the trailers or containers, those flat rates may apply only to mixed carloads; the ordinary rule is that not more than 60 percent of the weight of a total, two-trailer shipment may consist of any one commodity or article. *Ibid.*, 304–305, 311–312, 319, and 379–380.

[158] See pp. 14, 18–24, Chapter 1, above.

and discriminated against the shippers who would still have been subject to the value-of-service pricing that it embodied.[159]

But the 1931 decision could not indefinitely stave off a development that offered such great mutual benefits to the various carriers, not to mention the ultimate customers. In 1954 the ICC liberalized its rules. Thereafter, in the words of the Commission, the growth of piggybacking was "explosive" and its future appeared "almost unlimited."[160]

But the adoption of this extraordinarily promising device was, nevertheless, far too slow, simply because many railroads were unwilling to undertake the necessary cooperation and division of revenues with truckers. The Interstate Commerce Act requires railroads to establish joint rates and through routes with water carriers, but it imposes no such obligation with respect to motor carriers. The ICC therefore took the position that it lacked authority to compel piggybacking. Until 1964, and for the same reason, it took the position, also, that even if a railroad offered piggybacking service under its own open tariffs, it had the right to withhold it from contract or common-carrier truckers.[161]

So the ICC left the development of this promising innovation to the initiative of the railroads and insisted that their concurrence was necessary if truckers were to participate. In these circumstances, the lack of imagination and "intransigence of some railroad management" and the persistence of value of service rates, which failed to pass on to the shipper the cost savings of piggybacking, seriously retarded its utilization.[162] Most of the

---

[159] See the *Doyle Report, op. cit.*, 653–654, which also describes the first liberalization of that rule in 1936, in the case involving *Trucks on Flatcars Between Chicago and Twin Cities*, 216 ICC 435.

[160] In 1955, 32 railroads reported a total of 168,150 TOFC carloadings; in 1963, it was 63 reporting railroads and 797,500 such loadings. ICC, *Ex Parte No. 230*, 322 ICC 301, 309 (1964). By 1966, while the number of participating railroads had dropped to 56, the number of loadings had risen to 1,162,731. Note, "Piggyback Transportation and the ICC," *Southern Cal. Law Rev.* (1968), XLI: 391.

[161] These flat open-tariff rates were offered to private shippers and freight forwarders, who might supply their own trailers or loaded flatcars (under the so-called Plan IV) or use those of the railroads (Plan III), but not to common or contract-carrier truckers. See note 157, above. The Commission felt it could not require that such service be made available to the latter companies, as well, not only because it lacked the requisite authority but also because such arrangements would violate the principle that no person should be both a carrier and a shipper with respect to any given service: the trucking companies would be carriers *vis-à-vis* their shipper-customers and shippers vis-à-vis the railroads. See *American Trucking Associations, Inc., et al. v. Atchison, Topeka & Santa Fe Railway Co. et al.*, 387 U.S. 397, 403, 415 (1967).

[162] The *Doyle Report*, 659, 662–663.

"The end result of all this is that, although coordination has been regarded as vital for well over half a century, most joint rates are still the result of voluntary agreements between carriers and very little coordination exists except between railroad carriers." *Ibid.*, 653.

On the continued use of the traditional rate structures under Plans I and II, see note 157, above. In a sense, the excluded motor carriers also took an obstructionist position. They favored the use of substituted rail for truck service on traffic that they initiated and controlled (Plan I), a procedure that passed none of the cost savings on to shippers; and they opposed giving freight forwarders access to piggyback service, under Plans III and IV. *Ibid.*, 664–665. But this latter position was understandable, in view of the fact that they themselves were excluded from taking advantage of these open rates. More important, the unwillingness of individual truckers to cooperate could not in any event seriously have impeded the development of piggybacking, in view of the large numbers of truckers and the extreme likelihood that, if the option were open to them, at least some would take advantage of it. In contrast, the obstruction of the railroads, which continued to enjoy very substantial monopoly power over the development of the device over their own routes, ensured

growth of this kind of carriage until 1964 was therefore under all-rail rates and rail billings, with the railroads either picking up and delivering in their own trucks (Plan II) or doing the hauling under open tariffs for the account of private shippers or freight forwarders (Plans III and IV). Only in a minority of the cases were they willing to offer the service to contract or common-motor carriers who initiated the traffic and would in this way have shared in the revenues.[163] Without this kind of collaboration the development of piggybacking would always be impeded.

In 1964, finally, the ICC promulgated two important new rules, whose purpose it was to terminate the discriminatory exclusion of for-hire truckers and thereby also to encourage the more widespread utilization of this technique. Its Rule 2 required any railroad offering piggyback service under an open tariff to make it available at the same rate, without discrimination, to all parties, including competing carriers:

> "2 *Availability to all of TOFC service*—TOFC service, if offered by a rail carrier through its open-tariff publications, shall be made available to any person at a charge no greater and no less than that received from any other person or persons for doing for him or them a like and contemporaneous service in the transportation of a like kind of traffic under substantially similar circumstances and conditions."

And its Rule 3 authorized regulated carriers to take advantage of this opportunity, that is, to substitute piggybacking for all or any part of whatever transportation service they were authorized to perform:

> "3 *Use of open-tariff TOFC service by motor and water carriers in the performance of economically regulated transportation.*
>
> (a) Except as otherwise may be prohibited by these rules, motor common and contract carriers, water common and contract carriers, and freight forwarders may utilize TOFC service in the performance of all or any portion of their authorized service through the use of open-tariff TOFC rates published by a rail carrier."[164]

The Supreme Court, by a 6–3 vote, sustained these rules over the strenuous objections of railroads and freight forwarders and an adverse District Court decision.[165] It upheld Rule 2 on the basis of the fundamental, common-carrier obligation of the railroads to serve all customers ("any person") nondiscriminatorily:

---

its inadequate exploitation. In the mid-1960's, eighty percent of the railroads offering piggyback service offered Plan I. Friedlaender, *op. cit.*, 121 note 37, citing Merrill J. Roberts and Associates, *Intermodal Freight Transportation Coordination: Problems and Potential* (Univ. of Pittsburgh, Graduate School of Business, 1966), 62. Thus, the preponderant system still embodied value of service rate-making, and thereby discouraged the fullest development of piggybacking. It is Plans III and IV that offer the fullest promise of a rational redistribution of the transportation business, and they too continue to be hampered by ICC restrictions (see note 157, above). Friedlaender, *op. cit.*, 120–125.
[163] Ibid., 657; *American Trucking Associations v.*

Atchison, Topeka & Santa Fe Railway Co., 387 U.S. 397, 403–404 (1967).
[164] *Ex Parte No. 230*, 322 ICC 301, 336–337 (1964). These rules followed the recommendations of the *Doyle Report*, 667 and also of Meyer, *et al.*:

> "the maintenance of equal access for all to the rail piggyback facilities should take precedence over almost all other regulatory objectives." *Op. cit.*, 262–263.

On the other hand, as we shall see, the 1964 rules did not go as far as these authors recommended.
[165] *American Trucking Associations v. Atchison, Topeka & Santa Fe*, 387 U.S. 397 (1967), reversing 244 F. Supp. 955 (1965).

"The fact that the person tendering traffic is a competitor does not permit the railroad to discriminate against him or in his favor."[166]

As for Rule 3, it simply sustained the authority of the Commission, including its right to change its mind:

"in any event, we agree that the Commission, faced with new developments or in light of reconsideration of the relevant facts and its mandate, may alter its past interpretation. . . . In fact . . . this kind of flexibility and adaptability to changing needs and patterns of transportation is an essential part of the office of a regulatory agency. Regulatory agencies do not establish rules of conduct to last forever; they are supposed, within the limits of the law and of fair and prudent administration, to adapt their rules and practices to the Nation's needs in a volatile, changing economy."[167]

To which the economist can only say amen. As we have amply observed, regulatory commissions do not always justify the broad deference that courts usually accord to their "administrative expertise."

There are at least three reasons why ones rapture over these laudible decisions must be qualified. First, the ICC still lacks the authority to compel railroads to offer piggyback service to truckers; all it has done has been to require them to do so *if* they offer it also to private shippers and freight forwarders, under open tariffs. The rails might presumably respond by withdrawing their TOFC tariffs, in hope of keeping all use of the piggyback device to themselves.[168]

But this danger is probably remote. Practically all of the reporting railroads were offering TOFC service under open tariffs (under Plan III) at the time of the ICC decision[169] and had by this means attracted a very large amount of business from both for-hire truckers and private carriage.[170] It is unlikely that they could do as well if confined to their own limited abilities to perform door-to-door service (under Plan II). Nor is it clear that they would be permitted to discontinue their previous offerings of piggyback services, under the general regulation of abandonments in the Interstate Commerce Act:

"no carrier by railroad subject to this chapter shall abandon all or any portion of a line of railroad, or the operation thereof, unless and until there shall first have been obtained from the Commission a certificate that the present or future public convenience and necessity permit of such abandonment."[171]

---

[166] *Ibid.*, 407. The three dissenting judges "found it impossible," as Justice Harlan put it "to escape the impact" of the following proviso to the statutory prohibition of discrimination:

"*Provided, however,* that this paragraph shall not be construed to apply to discrimination, prejudice, or disadvantage to the traffic of any other carrier of whatever description." *Ibid.*, 422 and 411, quoting from 49 U.S. Code 3 (1).
[167] *Ibid.*, 416.
[168] This is on the assumption that they would still be permitted to offer Plan II, under which the railroad performs the entire service, door-to-door, using its own trucks and trailers, and charging shippers under its ordinary rate schedules. In any event, there is nothing in those rules to require any railroad to offer piggybacking at all, if it chooses not to do so.
[169] 387 U.S. 397, 404 (1967).
[170] *Ex Parte No.* 230, 322 ICC 301, 307–308 (1964).
[171] 49 U.S. Code 18, 1964 ed. This is the judgment of the author of the Note, "Piggyback Transportation and the I.C.C.," *Southern Cal. Law Rev.* (1968), XLI: 400.

The second reservation about the new rules is that they are silent about the level of TOFC rates, on which the rapidity with which this device is adopted heavily depends. It would of course be in the interest of the railroads to fix the rates somewhere between their own marginal costs and the line-haul costs of the motor carriers: if they were any higher, the latter would have no incentive to use the service. But within that range the railroads will have a strong temptation to exploit the monopoly power that they must inevitably continue to possess on this particular mode of transport, because of their cost advantage; any such tendency will necessarily mean that its exploitation will be uneconomically retarded. It is for this reason that Meyer *et al.* qualify their recommendations for substantial deregulation of transportation by calling for retention of regulatory control over maximum TOFC rates, with the strong recommendation that they be held closely to cost.[172]

Finally, the ability of truckers to take full advantage of this new opportunity continues to be restricted by the numerous limitations that the ICC imposes on their routes. In its 1964 decision, thus, the ICC adopted the following rule:

"5 *Circuity limitations*.

(a) Motor and water common carriers shall not participate in joint intermodal TOFC service which is to be provided in lieu of their authorized line-haul transportation . . . where the distance from origin to destination over the route including the TOFC movement is less than 85 percent of the distance between such points over the motor or water carrier's authorized service route; *provided, however,* that the Interstate Commerce Commission may grant relief from the provisions of this paragraph upon consideration of an appropriate petition."[173]

The fear was that without such a restriction motor carriers authorized to operate between two points by a circuitous route might now choose to substitute piggyback service over a more direct route, thus escaping the limitations in their certifications. The rule permits them to cut no more than 15 percent off the distance that their cargoes travel. The restriction is in itself, of course, a ridiculous prohibition of improved efficiency; but it is entirely consistent with, indeed required by, the routing restrictions in the carriers' certificates and the restrictions on competition that it is their purpose to impose.[174] A similar purpose underlay the Commission's rule that

---

[172] *Op. cit.,* 247.

[173] *Ex Parte No. 230*, 322 ICC 301, 364 (1964).

[174] An intriguing illustration of this kind of upside-down economics is provided by the Commission's description of its earlier decision, *Substituted Rail Service by Red Ball Transfer Co.,* 52 MCC 75 (1950) and 303 ICC 421 (1958), in which it had permitted Red Ball to substitute TOFC service on a particular route even though the rail route was somewhat shorter than its authorized highway route between Chicago and Kansas City, because

"it was found that using TOFC service would not enable Red Ball to provide an improved service and would not affect its competitive situation vis-à-vis motor carriers authorized to operate

directly between Chicago and Kansas City." *Ex Parte No. 230*, 322 ICC 301, 361–362 (1964).

The ICC explains this restriction in terms of its general policies in enforcing the Motor Carriers Act of 1935:

"To allow carriers to ignore the routing and gateway limitations in their operating authorities and to provide service between any points they serve, no matter how indirect their authorized operations, would be to allow them to provide totally new services for which no public need had been established, and would largely negate the certificate and permit requirements of the act. . . . It is obvious that this result would obtain from the indiscriminate substitution of direct TOFC service for indirect all-motor service." *Ibid.*

truckers and water carriers could put their trailers on rail flat cars and take them off only at geographic points that they were actually certificated to serve, thereby overriding the sensible suggestion of the Eastern railroads that it would suffice merely to require that motor carriers possess the authority for the entire freight movement from origin to destination:

> "4(d) Carriers participating in joint intermodal TOFC service shall interchange traffic only at a common point of service."

> "3(e) Motor and water common and contract carriers utilizing open-tariff TOFC service in the performance of authorized transportation shall tender traffic to and receive traffic from rail carriers only at points which the motor and water carriers are authorized to serve."[175]

Despite these reservations, the new ICC rules governing piggybacking should provide an important stimulus to intermodal cooperation consistent with the preservation of competition.

Power Pooling

The numerous power pooling and interconnection arrangements in which the majority of the country's electrical systems now participate likewise provide illustrations of the twin dangers of intercompany coordination: that the parties will cooperate too well and that they will do so too little, or with excessive selectivity.

In the typical power pool—in contrast with the simple purchase agreements by which the majority of the country's small distribution systems obtain their energy requirements—the collaborators are large, integrated private companies; they engage in the generation and transmission as well as local distribution of electricity. This is understandable, in view of the fact that very few of the pools involve complete integration of all the systems in an area: since most of them involve simpler *interchanges* of power between the partners, the participants tend to be companies that have something to exchange with one another, with a rough equivalence of contributions and benefits. There is no published study of the extent to which agreements have attached to them explicit provisions restricting competition among the partners. They could be rare: these companies for the most part stay within their respective service areas anyhow.[176]

On the other hand where there is competition, actual or potential, between participants in pools—or in simple purchase and sales agreements—there is a strong temptation for the participants to attach conditions that limit it.

"When systems from different segments of the industry attempt to organize

---

[175] *Ibid.*, 355.

[176] "Unquestionably the development of rate-making standards has tended to suppress competition for new service areas between investor-owned companies. The identity of cost characteristics, plus such rate-making, cast a serious damper on reaching for load by seeking to extend its service area boundaries. There is also greater recognition of the higher costs and the chaos which would be involved in the unlimited duplication of facilities. . . . [M]utual respect by investor-owned companies of their respective service area boundaries—even where ill-defined or where one company is large and the other small—is the rule, rather than the exception." Federal Power Commission, Report of the Legal Advisory Committee, *National Power Survey*, 1964, II: 366.

The Carva pool (which covers Virginia and the Carolinas) is, however, reported to have some such provision, to the effect that each member will refrain from using the joint facilities in a way adverse to the interests of any of the others.

a pool . . . all such systems may want to reach one or more formal agreements which have the effect of eliminating competition for loads. This is particularly the case wherever there is the possibility that a participant who is also a competitor may use the advantages derived from a pooling arrangement to undercut and take over the present or potential customers of one or more other participants. In such circumstances, there will necessarily be a hesitancy to enter into such a pooling arrangement unless there is assurance that it will not worsen established competitive positions."[177]

Restrictions of this kind are, thus, said to be prevalent in the very numerous contracts for the wholesale supply of power to municipal (that is, municipally owned) and cooperative distributors.[178] In such cases the seller, typically a large, integrated private company, imposes some such condition as that the buyer will confine its sales to a particular geographic area, or will not solicit the business of other wholesale customers of the supplying company, or simply will not resell any of the power at wholesale.[179]

The extent to which restrictions such as these are subject to the antitrust laws is still in large measure an open question that we cannot fully explore here. They certainly could be. In the *Pennsylvania Water* case, a Circuit Court of Appeals invalidated under the antitrust laws a division of markets agreement between integrated private utility companies incident to a power pooling arrangement.[180] In 1968, the Department of Justice filed a civil antitrust suit against two members of the Florida Power Interchange Pool, the Tampa Electric Company and the Florida Power Corporation, charging that they had conspired to divide up their respective geographic markets and consequently refrained from soliciting wholesale customers in each other's territory, in violation of the Sherman Act.[181] Representatives of the industry and the Federal Power Commission itself have in recent years supported bills introduced in Congress to give the Commission the power, which it does not now have, to exempt such restrictive arrangements from the antitrust laws.[182] In the absence of an explicit exemption, the legality of these restrictions would hinge on whether they might be found reasonably ancillary to (subsidiary to and necessary for the effectuation of) the power pooling arrangement, which is not itself illegal. The Department of Justice has been skeptical that they are: Donald Turner, the Assistant Attorney General in charge of the Antitrust Division, testified in opposition to the

[177] *Ibid.*, 367.

[178] This is felt to be particularly necessary in the case of the rural cooperatives, since these distributors are not typically confined to a specified service area.

[179] See, for example, the proceeding in which the Federal Power Commission disallowed a provision in the wholesale power supply contracts of the Georgia Power Company with its municipal customers, setting a limit to the amount of power that the latter could sell to any industrial companies within their franchised areas. *Georgia Power Company v. Federal Power Commission*, 373 F. 2d 485 (1967). See also *U.S. v. Northern Natural Gas Co.*, Civil No. 5–70–20, U.S. District Ct., District of Minnesota, Fifth Division, Stipulation,

March 31, 1970.

[180] *Pennsylvania Water & Power Company v. Consolidated Gas, Electric Light & Power Company*, 184 F. 2d 552 (1950). See, however, the subsequent history of that arrangement in *Pennsylvania Water & Power Co. v. Federal Power Commission*, 343 U.S. 414 (1952).

[181] Civil Action No. 68–297 CIV.-T., U.S. District Court, Middle Dist. of Florida, Complaint, July 8, 1968.

[182] See, for example, U.S. Senate, Committee on Commerce, *Amendment to Federal Power Act (Antitrust Review)*, *Hearing* on S3136, Serial No. 89–71, July 12–13, 1966. The same bill was reintroduced in the subsequent, 88th Congress (S683).

bill in question, pointing to the widespread adoption of pooling in preceding years without need for explicit exemption from the antitrust laws.[183] And so, apparently, is the FPC itself, at least as far as some of the more flagrant restrictions on competition are concerned.[184] In the absence of any such justification, it would seem that any agreement among pooling partners to stay out of each other's markets would be *per se* illegal under the antitrust laws. Moreover, recent decisions by the United States Supreme Court cast considerable doubt on the legality of restrictions on resale of wholesale power, even when not adopted collusively but imposed by a single supplying company.[185]

The other, and even more controversial, competitive issue has to do with the general tendency of the major pools to exclude from membership smaller, generally less fully integrated distribution companies—and particularly cooperative (coops) and municipally owned distributors ("munis"). As pooling has made possible the construction of larger and larger generating plants, with progressively lower unit costs, access to their supplies on terms not markedly inferior to those enjoyed by the pool participants themselves has become a matter of life or death to these distribution companies, who either lack generating facilities of their own entirely or whose facilities, smaller in scale, are at a progressive cost disadvantage. What is really at stake is the availability of supplies from the pooled facilities to these firms— their ability to purchase them and to have them transmitted ("wheeled") over the lines of the pool members—and the price they have to pay. The excluded companies have generally argued that only membership in the pool gives them the kind of assurance of equal and nondiscriminatory treatment that they require.[186]

The same kind of problem can arise even in the absence of pooling. A large integrated company could conceivably refuse to supply the needs of a local distributor or to "wheel" for it power purchased from some third party. Unless these transactions are effectively regulated, the big private systems that control transmission facilities adjacent to the coops and munis have power over the latter's very survival. Except in those areas in which federally generated electricity, to which they have statutorily preferential access, is available, the small distribution companies can typically hope to obtain economical supplies only from the big private companies. And since such a

---

[183] *Ibid.*, 57–71.

[184] See the reference to the *Georgia Power* case, note 179, above.

[185] See *U.S. v. Arnold, Schwinn & Co. et al.*, 388 U.S. 365 (1967).

[186] See, for example, Joseph A. Ruskay, "Power Play in the Electric Industry: Breaking the 'Birch Rod,'" *The New Leader*, Oct. 9, 1967, 16, describing "the ruthlessness displayed by the private utility combine trying to freeze out the municipal electric companies from access to low-cost, bulk . . . energy. . . ." Also Alex Radin, "The Role of Public Power in a Modern National Power Policy," paper presented at Fall Conference, Federal Bar Ass'n, Committee on Federal Utility and Power Law, October 16, 1967 (mimeo.). Radin emphasizes the advantages conferred by active participation in planning the installation of new facilities. The member

"is in a better position to know what opportunities are available to it and to propose a course of action which will serve its needs. . . . [A] utility which is privy to regional planning will usually have a better knowledge of where power might be bought and . . . sold. . . . [I]t will be able to propose changes in the design and location of the lines to its advantage, and it can more efficiently develop its own transmission system and schedule the installation of generation." *Ibid.*, 32.

company will usually refuse to wheel power from competing sources to whole-sale purchasers within its area, the latter will typically have only one large supplier from whom they can buy. It is this kind of situation that gives point to the authority asserted by the FPC to force the large private companies to interconnect and supply power to smaller distributors, and to fix the prices on these sales.[187] The great economies of scale in generation and transmission, and the control of transmission systems in each area by one or a few large private companies, together confer the same sort of power over the survival of nonintegrated competitors as did control over crude-oil pipelines by large, vertically integrated petroleum refining companies. In the latter case the remedy was amendment of the Interstate Commerce Act to make crude-oil pipelines common carriers and—after a long delay—effective ICC regulation of their rates and conditions of access.[188] As the oil experience suggests, one possible approach to protecting the competitive survival of the nonintegrated electricity distribution companies is to impose common-carrier status on the privately owned transmission lines.[189] The same result would in effect be accomplished in cases of pooling by seeing to it that the smaller companies were admitted to full membership.

The related issues of compulsory interconnection, wheeling, and the membership in power pools illustrate with great clarity the numerous facets of the question of the appropriate role of competition in the regulated industries, and the differences between the competitive and the regulated chosen instrument approach to the organization and control of industry. Consider the following composite outline of the responses that integrated private companies make to the foregoing statement of problems, along with our commentary on those responses:

1. Competition between electric systems is of minor importance and

[187] The antitrust laws too may be applicable in such situations. See the summary of the Department of Justice 1969 complaint against the Otter Tail Power Co., note 60, p. 68, above.

[188] See Roy A. Prewitt, "The Operation and Regulation of Crude Oil and Gasoline Pipelines," *Q. Jour. Econ.* (February 1942), LVI: 177–211; Eugene V. Rostow, *A National Policy for the Oil Industry* (New Haven: Yale Univ. Press, 1948), 57–66; de Chazeau and Kahn, *op. cit.,* 116–117, 332–341, 512–515; and George S. Wolbert, *American Pipelines* (Norman: Univ. of Oklahoma Press, 1952).

[189] See also note 192, below. The FPC has concluded that it has no such authority at present under its limited powers to require interconnection and service under Section 202(b) of the Federal Power Act (see pp. 75–76, Chapter 2, above). Following the instruction of *City of Paris, Kentucky v. Federal Power Commission,* 399 F. 2d 983 (1968), it concluded:

"If wheeling means the obligation of one public utility to make its transmission facilities available to 'facilitate' a power supply contract between two other unconnected electric companies, and nothing more, we think the Commission *lacks*

the power to order it. . . ." *City of Paris, Kentucky v. Kentucky Utilities Company,* Opinion and Order on Remand, 41 FPC 45, 49 (1969).

The case arose out of a supply contract between the City of Paris and the East Kentucky Rural Electric Cooperative Corporation, in consequence of which the City asked the FPC to require the Kentucky Utilities Company to transmit the power for it. Instead, the Commission approved a rate filing under which Kentucky Utilities would supply Paris directly.

Another possible solution to this particular problem—even farther beyond the FPC's statutory mandate—would be to divorce electricity generation and distribution, and to require the generating company or companies to serve all distributors nondiscriminatorily at cost-related rates. See the discussion at p. 74, Chapter 2, above. The proposals of the Department of Justice and FCC to force common carrier status on CATV systems are based on the same reasoning. See note 114, pp. 43–44, and note 122, p. 45, above; and *Comments of the United States Department of Justice* in FCC Docket No. 18397, September 5, 1969 (mimeo.), 5–6.

should in any event not be encouraged because it leads to wasteful duplication of facilities.[190]

It must be conceded that direct competition among electric companies is, indeed, quite limited; states rarely license more than one company to serve a particular locality or area. At the same time, as the restrictive provisions themselves suggest, there are certain areas and kinds of competition that could be significantly affected.

a. While most distribution companies typically stay within their own exclusive areas, this is not true of coops in most states. With the expansion of suburbs into previously rural areas, in consequence, the coops and the private companies frequently come into competition for new customers.[191] Is this kind of competition socially desirable? Large-scale duplication of distribution facilities would be inefficient. But rivalry at the edges of service areas, to determine which company is to take over a particular overlapping or adjacent market, could avoid serious inefficiency and at the same time, provided regulatory commissions were careful to prevent its taking the form of highly selective and local price cutting, could usefully exert considerable pressure on the affected companies to perform well for all their customers.

b. There is competition between separate utility systems to induce large industrial customers to locate in their respective territories, although its prevalence is disputed.

c. The very technological advances that have made wider and wider pooling desirable have also increased the likelihood of competition in wholesale power markets—by making it economical for distribution systems and companies with surplus generating capacity to reach out farther and farther, the one for supplies, the other for customers. The conception that freer competition should be permitted to prevail in wholesale markets clashes with the reliance on regulated chosen instruments: the latter model would emphasize the greater efficiency and opportunity for long-term investment planning if distributors obtain their wholesale energy under long-term contracts from a neighboring major integrated company, protected not by competition but by commission regulation of the wholesale price. Clearly, if the former conception is to prevail, compulsory wheeling or a common-carrier transmission system is a necessary part of the arrangement.[192] The issue is clearly joined,

---

[190] It is a possible defense to an antitrust proceeding against restrictive agreements that there was no competition for them to have suppressed. But where that was the clear purpose of the agreement, as in the case of simple price fixing or division of markets, the courts are likely to infer the necessary anticompetitive effect from the nature of the agreement itself: why would the parties take the trouble to enter into covenants like these if they did not fear that competition might otherwise break out between them?

[191] See "Competition for Loads between neighboring utility systems," FPC, *National Power*

Survey, 1964, Vol. II, 366–367.

[192] The more efficient alternative might be the one already mentioned (note 189, above)—divestiture of distribution and transmission, leaving the latter function to be performed, nondiscriminatorily for all comers, by nonintegrated common carriers. If the duplication of transmission facilities that would otherwise be necessary to create a competitive wholesale power market, in which power could be drawn from a variety of suppliers in various locations, would be inefficient, the obvious answer is that transmission is a natural monopoly and should be performed by regulated common carriers.

therefore, with respect to the sufficiency of regulated monopoly as a device for insuring optimum performance.

d. Yardstick competition. This is of course the principal kind of rivalry between the government–owned, cooperative, and privately owned utility system. It is a competition by example: each company is concerned that the way in which it treats its own customers compares favorably with the corresponding performance of its rivals, in the hope of a favorable political decision whenever the question arises of which kind of utility system is to be certificated for future service areas, or to serve the expanding needs or indeed the present requirements of existing ones. The competition is, in a sense, unfair; the public and coop "yardstick" is not a true measure of the achievable performance of private companies because the former pay less taxes and obtain their capital on more favorable terms; on the other hand, many of them suffer offsetting disadvantages from the smaller scale of their generating operations and their dependence on private companies for much of their energy. The rivalry is nevertheless real and has made an important positive contribution—Richard Hellman would say, far greater than regulation—to the improved performance of the electric industries.[193]

2. It is unfair to force private companies to share the benefits of their efficiency with competitors, and particularly with competitors that enjoy the unfair tax and capital cost advantages referred to above.

This is not an economic argument and will therefore not detain us long. The companies are franchised monopolists, enjoying valuable governmentally conferred privileges. Society has the right and duty to impose such corresponding obligations as it sees fit, as long as investors are then free to refuse the entire bargain. One economically justified obligation, in the presence of monopoly, is the acceptance of common-carrier obligations. Where, moreover, the companies achieve lower costs by collaboration in a pool, the issue is no longer one of depriving *individual* competitors of whatever advantages they may have achieved by their own prudence and efficiency but one of preventing a group of firms, by *combination*, from achieving decisive advantage over excluded rivals. It is an established antitrust principle that such combinations may not deny disadvantaged competitors access to those same opportunities on nondiscriminatory terms.[194] The only relevant question would be whether the imposition of such requirements and the prohibition of anticompetitive covenants would seriously diminish the incentive of the private companies to enter pools and avail themselves of these important economies.

3. It makes no sense to admit customers to membership in pools. This is, indeed, a puzzling and complex aspect of the issue. Power exchanges and pools are arrangements in which two or more similar companies, each with something to contribute, enter into a joint venture. In varying degrees they "pool" their generating facilities as well as their

---

[193] See pp. 104–106, Chapter 3, above.
[194] *U.S. v. The Terminal Railroad Ass'n*, 224 U.S. 383 (1912); *Associated Press v. United States*, 326 U.S. 1 (1945).

320 / Integration and Competition

requirements; they integrate their capital investments in generation and transmission as well as distribution. Each supplies reserve capacity that becomes available to the other in case of need; and both benefit from the resultant reduction in their combined reserve requirement. And they distribute the benefits to members in rough proportionality to their respective contributions. They provide for money payments only to the extent that there is a "balance of trade" in one direction or another—that is, when an individual member's flows of benefits and costs are unequal.[195]

Most municipalities, in contrast, have no generating capacity at all. Many or most of the remaining ones have only very high-cost generation facilities, access to which is of little or no benefit to the other members. Their interests and contributions are those only of buyers or customers, not of full participants in the pool.[196]

On the other hand, it must be recognized that as pools become more and more intensely integrated, and cover wider and wider areas, these same observations apply in increasing measure to all of their members. The contribution of each becomes decreasingly important relative to the size required to take full advantage of the available economies of scale; that is the reason for pooling in the first place. And—particularly when pools begin to make joint investments in additional facilities— all of the members may properly be regarded as contributors of capital on the one hand and customers on the other; possession of one's own generating facilities becomes a less and less relevant qualification for membership. Where excluded distribution companies have the legal authority to invest in generating facilities (and many do not), it is not clear why each dollar that they contribute to the joint investments represents any less of a contribution to the total benefits of scale economies than each dollar put in by their larger rivals.[197]

---

[195] See Abraham Gerber, "Power Pools and Joint Plant Ownership," *Public Utilities Fortnightly*, September 12, 1968, especially pp. 6–7.
[196] *Ibid.*, 7–10.
[197] See Roland W. Donnem, "Antitrust Aspects of Establishing Nuclear and Other Large-Scale Electricity Generation Facilities," an address before the Atomic Energy Committee, Federal Bar Ass'n, processed, Washington, October 15, 1969, 17 and, for a good survey of the subject, *passim*. In pools in which the members take turns in constructing plants, it would seem possible for the municipal companies to form a group to build a facility of economical size when their turn comes around. These considerations do not exclude the desirability of taking into account the varying contributions of the members of the pool in the apportionment of charges and joint benefits. Charles R. Ross, a former Federal Power Commissioner and a strong proponent of "the absolute necessity for small municipal systems to join the parade and become participants of the newly forming bulk power supply pools" and of "the requirement that membership to all pools be non-discriminatory," nevertheless concedes that non-discriminatory rules might provide for differential sharing of benefits in reflection of different contributions.

"I would be remiss, however, if I failed to point out that the basic principles of economics will have to be recognized in setting the ground rules of the pool agreements. In other words, some of the more well-endowed participants may be able to do better because of their contributions to the pool, such as lower-cost units, better types of load, etc. While this may be the case and a free ride is prohibited, nevertheless, the same general rules should apply to everyone." "Bulk Power Supply for Small Systems," an address before the 24th American Public Power Ass'n Conference, May 9, 1967 (mimeo.), 3–4.

In addition, the larger members typically provide back-up capacity for emergencies; smaller participants that made no such contribution ought clearly to bear their proper share of the costs. See note 200, below.

What then of municipal distributors who are not permitted to own their own generation capacity; if they too must be permitted equal access to membership in pools, why might not large private customers also request the privilege? The answer would seem to be that the distributors, even if nonintegrated, are also competitors or potential competitors of the pool members. If we would rely partly on their competition as a guarantor of good public utility performance, it may be necessary, in recognition of the ambivalent role they play, to treat them differently from other, possibly equally large customers.

4. The issue is really only one of proper public utility rate structures. What the small distribution companies want is to get their power at rates comparable with the costs borne by the pool members. The new pooled facilities may be expected to have lower average total costs than the entire systems of the separate integrated companies on whom the distributors depend for supplies.[198] Presumably the members of the pool obtain this incremental power at those lower costs; but they must recoup the higher average costs of their entire systems from their customers. If the small distributors were to obtain membership and then take all their power from the pool, they might end up getting their entire power supply at average costs lower than their competitors and former suppliers. It makes no economic sense to permit customers who happen to obtain all their supplies from a new facility lower rates than customers that happen to be served by a mixture of new and old facilities.[199] And it would constitute an inacceptable form of cream-skimming, subsidized competition for such customers—or pool members—who did not supply reserve, back-up generating and transmission capacity to obtain the same favorable rates as other members who bore those additional costs.[200] If, then, membership in the pool does not solve the question of the appropriate cost of power to the municipal companies, relative to the total costs borne by their private integrated competitors, it remains unclear why membership is so important, and why the problem could not equally be solved by effective FPC regulation of the wholesale rates charged by pool members to nonmember distribution companies. Even if the latter were members, they would in effect have to be charged rates that covered the costs of providing some of the benefits contributed by the other members and not by them.

[198] This is indeed the common assumption. None of the commentators seems to have explicitly raised the question of why this should normally be so—why ATC_0 should be higher than ATC_n —unless the old plant is chronically under-depreciated. See pp. 118–121, Volume 1, above. One possibility is the necessity of keeping older capacity available in reserve, against the possibility of outages. These plants could well have average variable costs in excess of the ATC of new plants *when fully utilized*, but still have value for occasional use, at times of peak demand (see pp. 97–98, Volume 1) or in emergencies when the marginal opportunity cost of current rises sharply.
[199] Donnem suggests that the small distribution companies are entitled simply to the same opportunities to get the low-cost power as the larger participants—for existing requirements or only for additional needs, for example, depending on how the latter are served. *Op. cit.*, 13.
[200] See the discussion of this problem in the case of alleged cream-skimming at pp. 238–239, Chapter 5, above. Differential charges for reasons of this kind would be entirely compatible with the recommendations of both Donnem and Ross (notes 197 and 199, above). See also Gerber, *op. cit.*, 10 and *passim*. This is one major outstanding issue in the *Gainesville* case (note 85, p. 76, above), which the Supreme Court agreed in October of 1970 to hear: is the Florida Power Co. entitled to charge Gainesville a portion of the fixed costs of maintaining reserve generating capacity?

5. In the last analysis, then, the issue is one of the effectiveness and adequacy of regulation. In principle, it would appear that there is nothing that membership in pools could contribute to giving munis and coops a fair competitive opportunity that could not be ensured also by effective FPC regulation.[201] The fact remains that it has been only in the last several years that the Commission has been vigorously asserting its authority over wholesale rates generally and compelling private integrated companies to interconnect with and supply smaller distributor-competitors. And as it has done so the private sector of the industry has importuned Congress to stop it.[202] It is obviously disingenuous for the private companies to argue on the one hand for the exclusion of the distributors from pools on the ground that they can receive all the reliability of service and protection with respect to price that they need from effective FPC regulation of wholesale sales, and at the same time to press for diminution of the Commission's authority over those sales.

In the last analysis, the issue is an institutional one and cannot be resolved in terms of economic principles. In fact such competition as exists—including the peculiar, essentially political competition of publicly owned "yardsticks"—does play an important role in exerting pressures on regulated monopolists to improve their performance; thus it becomes an important part of the task of public policy to keep it as effective as possible. This is the case for insisting on pool membership on reasonable and nondiscriminatory terms for companies now excluded, rather than relying completely on the regulated chosen-instrument device as the sole means of assuring efficient public service.[203]

But at a minimum it is the case for retaining in the FPC effective authority over wholesale power sales and rates. This is the real significance of the *City of Colton* and *Shrewsbury* decisions (notes 71, p. 30, and 85, p.75, above)—not so much that they make regulation of monopoly itself more effective, but that they make it possible to employ *regulation* to preserve the most effective *competition* possible in this industry—by guaranteeing municipal distributors and coops access to low-cost, pooled power at minimum rates.[204]

---

[201] See, however, note 186, above.

[202] Sec note 71, p. 30, Chapter 1 and pp. 75–76, Chapter 2, above. So Commissioner Ross urged the municipal power systems to support FPC authority to control the terms of wholesale power contracts,

"We won't be able to make that promise, however, if certain proposals to limit our jurisdiction are successful. Here again, we need your help." *Op. cit.*, 8–9.

On the resistance of the private companies to the extension of FPC authority, see Lister and Homan, *op. cit.*, IV, 2/23–2/25. On the Holland-Smathers Bill, to reduce the Commission's authority on primarily intrastate electric operations see U.S. Senate, Committee on Commerce, *Exemption of Certain Public Utilities from Federal Power Commission Jurisdiction, Hearings* on S. 218, 89th Cong. 1st Sess., Serial No. 89–38, May–June, 1965.

[203] See the similar reasoning of the Circuit Court of Appeals in *Municipal Electric Association of Massachusetts, et. al. v. Securities and Exchange Commission, Respondent, Vermont Yankee Nuclear Power Corporation, et. al, Intervenors*, March 26, 1969.

[204] This point is made forcefully by Hellman, who, as we have seen in Chapter 3, is a leading exponent of the view that government competition is the instrument on which we must place major reliance for assuring the best possible economic performance in this industry. He quotes Alex Radin, general manager of the American Public Power Association, on the ways in which the Association has taken advantage of these decisions, by showing their members when the price they pay for power is excessive and

The clearest summary of the case for this use of regulation to protect and promote competition is provided by the following two representative selections from the testimony, the first in opposition, the second in favor, on the Smathers-Holland bill, which would have at least partially reversed *City of Colton* and *Shrewsbury* by shifting jurisdiction partially to the States. They provide a fitting summary of these last three chapters, whose concern has been the proper role and definition of competition—and therefore also of regulation—in the regulated industries:

"the Sterling Municipal Electric Light Department testified that the Shrewsbury case in which the FPC ordered a lower wholesale rate to a municipality 'was the first price breakthrough that municipal plants in Massachusetts have ever had. Immediately following . . . practically every municipal plant was approached by their supplier and offered a lower rate. . . . We firmly believe that FPC is the best court of appeals that wholesale purchasers of electricity like ourselves have available.'"

And

"Edwin L. Mason, chairman of the Florida commission and a . . . [supporter of] S.218: 'The best regulation is very little regulation. This has been proven throughout the history of our country—the best regulation is little or no regulation.' . . . Asked by Sen. Bass how cost to the consumer could be regulated when the Florida commission had no jurisdiction over sales to municipality or REC, Mr. Mason replied: 'This is as I say an arm's length transaction between the municipality and the company.' Sen. Bass: 'That is a long arm. . . . What you are saying is that you have no jurisdiction and you don't want the FPC to have any jurisdiction?' Mr. Mason: 'That is correct.'"[205]

---

urging them to lodge complaints with the FPC. *Government Competition*, 59–60. His summary of the arguments for and against the Smathers-Holland Bill (note 202, above) is worth reproducing:

"Those for S.218 argued that the State commissions are effective . . . . *Colton* is said to produce duplication between Federal and State jurisdictions, and confusion. It is characterized as an FPC power grab. It was predicted that *Colton* will lead to public ownership.

"The key issue presented by S.218 according to Chairman Swidler of the FPC, is the survival of small and medium-sized municipal and REC [Rural Electric Coop] power systems. They depend on rate regulation under the Federal Power Act which he said the bill would 'destroy.' The companies for the bill, he declared, 'believe they have acquired a vested interest in non-regulation, and they want to preserve it.' Witnesses from the 'grass roots' characterized the State commissions as being ineffective usually and often friendly to companies. The only recourses of municipal and REC systems from company monopoly of wholesale power supply they testified, have been government competition,

and now the FPC. *Colton*, it was said, did not create regulatory duplication, and the jurisdiction to be removed from FPC by S.218 could not be exercised by the States.

"In the final analysis, what were the companies fighting through S.218? It was not regulation as such, for they have fully subscribed to the theory of the regulated natural monopoly. Why are they against FPC regulation of wholesale power rates, particularly after 1961? The answer . . . is that the companies are against regulation that is effective. Conversely, they favor the State commissions because they are inadequate. This is consistent with their actions and attitudes since 1905." *Ibid.*, 61–62.

The reference to 1961 is to the appointment that year of Joseph C. Swidler as the new Chairman of the FPC; thereafter the Commission began aggressively to assert its jurisdiction over wholesale rates.

Hellman cites the hearings on the Bill as having established that it was drafted by representatives of the private power companies.
[205] As reproduced *ibid.*, 99/10–99/12, notes 91b, 91i.

CHAPTER 7

The Institution of Regulated Monopoly: Reprise

Such are the major issues involved in trying to fashion institutional mechanisms for controlling the performance of industries for which competition seems an inappropriate regulator.

Integration, Coordination, and Competition as Partial Alternatives

Manifestly, financial integration, cooperation between separate companies, and freer competition are in large measure alternatives to one another. The first, by eliminating most of the obstacles to wholehearted collaboration between the parties joined together, offers the possibility of important gains in efficiency and innovation. Like interfirm cooperation, therefore, it may make for more effective competition. On the other hand, where associated with substantial monopoly power, it can in other ways seriously weaken the competitive regulator, first, by suppressing potential competition between the functions or modes it joins together and, second, by creating obstacles to the rivalry of outside parties. And competition itself can achieve many of the same benefits as integration without involving those dangers: if it is able to operate, it can produce the socially most efficient distribution of business among the various alternative media as well as supply powerful stimuli to dynamic improvements in efficiency and service.

But the three devices are far from perfect substitutes; and they are not mutually exclusive. The problem of social engineering is to devise the optimum combination of all three, as well as of direct regulation. And of course there are all kinds of regulation possible—of entry but not price (as in broadcasting and most instances of occupational licensure), or of price but not entry (as in oil and other cartels), private price-fixing but not public (as in maritime shipping or, until recently, stock brokerage commission rates), with or without the power to compel intercompany connection and coordination, and so on.

There is no single optimum pattern or combination for all situations. In the case of transportation, we tentatively concluded that the benefits of conglomerate integration outweighed the dangers—provided those dangers are also forestalled, as much as possible, by compelling integrated companies to coordinate their facilities and operations, on nondiscriminatory and closely regulated terms, with their nonintegrated competitors. But we recognized that the massive horizontal and geographic merger movement in railroading might already have tipped the balance the other way. In power pooling, too, it could well be that closer financial integration is once again appropriate, because of the new technology of electric generation and transmission. But it, too, must be subject to regulatory safeguards, not only against the abuses that led to the downfall of the public utility holding company but also in order to protect the competitive opportunities of nonintegrated companies. Conceivably, only vertical separation of electricity generation and transmission on the one hand from distribution on the other can provide the optimum balance. In communications, the case for unified control and centralized responsibility for the operation of the national switched network seems still secure. But it, too, is subject to the qualification of the need for freer entry in some markets, for a more fully guaranteed direct access to the ultimate consumer by the revolutionary new devices of the satellite, microwave transmission and CATV, and by a requirement that the monopolist operator of the switched network interconnect with other communications systems and with customer-purchased equipment, subject to proper safeguards. Here, as in transportation, freer price competition seems both possible and desirable—but must be subject to regulatory safeguards.

And many of the direct benefits promised by integration can in fact be achieved by freer competition. Airline companies can make fuller use of expensive equipment, in season and out, by merging or by interchange of equipment. But they can achieve it also by greater freedom of entry into different routes, with different seasonal patterns: if the carrier with a heavy investment in large, jet airplanes to serve the New York to Miami route in the winter were free to shift to the transatlantic routes in the summer, it would have far less need of joining with other companies in order to make the most efficient use of its equipment. Nothing could better promote a more efficient distribution of the transportation business than freer price competition.

But there is no point in attempting further summary. Two conclusions seem clearly to emerge. First, that competition has a vital role to play in the public utility industries. And, second, the proper balance between competition and monopoly, financial integration and intercompany coordination, voluntary and compulsory, will vary from one regulatory situation to the next and from one moment to the next—and must be the subject of constant regulatory attention and concern.

The Imperfections of Regulated Monopoly

Regulated monopoly is a very imperfect instrument for doing the world's work. It suffers from the evils of monopoly itself—the danger of exploitation, aggressively or by inertia, the absence of pervasive external restraints and stimuli to aggressive, efficient and innovative performance. Regulation itself tends inherently to be protective of monopoly, passive, negative, and unimaginative. The concentration by commissions on the rate base and rate of return has been far disproportionate to their importance compared with other dimensions of performance, has weakened incentive, and introduced distortions. Regulation is ill-equipped to treat the more important aspects of performance—efficiency, service innovation, risk taking, and probing the elasticity of demand. Herein lies the great attraction of competition: it supplies the direct spur and the market test of performance.

The possibility is by no means excluded that on balance regulation does more harm than good, or that such good as it does is not worth the cost. Against the limited gains from a control directed primarily at cutting a few points off the profit rate must be weighed the restrictions on competition with which it is typically associated—not to mention the direct costs of the regulatory process itself, which may run on the order of $1 billion annually.[1]

One inherent weakness of regulation is its inescapable involvement with the political process. It is an interesting exercise to try to discern the ways in which regulatory policy at the national level may be changed by the entry of the Nixon Administration. What will become of the new activism of the FPC, as demonstrated in its *Shrewsbury* decision, *National Power Survey*, or new-found energy in regulating the field price of natural gas? Will the spurt of initiative shown by the FCC in 1969 with respect to radio and television[2] subside, or give way to a more careful scrutiny of the way in which the networks permit commentary on the President's speeches? Again, the basic evil in transportation is not the policy of the ICC but the even balance of powerful interest groups that perpetually defeats effective reform.

This suggests in a way that the imperfections of regulation are inherent defects not of the institution itself but of the political process. Consider, for example, the mundane question of the salaries, prestige, and competence of the regulatory personnel and the adequacy of their budgetary support. Manifestly, elaboration of all the "correct" regulatory principles is of little avail if their interpretation and application are to be entrusted to incompetent and inadequately financed commissioners.[3] It should be clear from these volumes that the principles are far from clear-cut or self-enforcing, but require instead the exercise of the most complex judgments, both of economic analysis and in the reconciliation of economic and noneconomic objectives.

How well the regulation is actually performed, in practice, will depend, in the last analysis, on the fundamental factors that determine the distribution of political power in modern capitalism. This may seem a long jump in

---

[1] For a full—some will feel overly so—and powerful elaboration of this entire argument see Posner, *op. cit.* See also the discussion at pp. 108–112, Chapter 3, above.

[2] See pp. 89–90, Chapter 2, above.

[3] In February of 1969, the Subcommittee on Intergovernmental Relations of the Committee on Government Operations of the U.S. Senate began hearings on the "Utility Consumers' Counsel Act of 1969" (S.607), sponsored by Senator Metcalf. Information gathered by the Subcommittee showed that more than half of the state regulatory agencies had between zero and two lawyers and rate analysts; that 20 had only one or two accountants; that 26 did not have a securities analyst. A witness from Massachusetts described the responsibilities, staff and compensation of that state's Department of Public Utilities chief accountant, who is also a lawyer and who supervises the examination and audit of the accounting returns filed by 14 electric, 26 gas, 6 phone, 63 water companies, 88 bus and streetcar lines, 816 securities brokers, 2,599 moving firms and 15,055 truck carriers. For this work, he has a staff consisting of one other accountant and a clerk, and his own salary, after 22 years with the department, was $11,752 a year. "Senators Probe Power Rates," *The Washington Post*, April 13, 1969, F 1, 3.

logic—from the salaries of commission staff to the fundamental character-istics of modern capitalism—but it is a direct one. For what we are dealing with is a peculiar institution of American society, the private ownership and management of monopoly in essential industries—a combination of cir-cumstances that leads typically to socialization abroad—subject to govern-mental regulation. The regulatory power is in principle virtually unlimited. How vigorously and intelligently it will be exercised (and the rate of pay, financial support, and quality of administrative personnel is obviously one aspect of this same phenomenon) will depend on the basically political question of how power is distributed between producer and consumer interests, between public officials and private managers, and how aggressive are the interventions of public officials in asserting their conception of the public interest. These determining conditions will clearly vary from time to time and place to place: contrast, in the United States, the 1920s with the 1930s, the 1950s with the 1960s. Whether one regards these shifts in the balance of political power and of public versus private initiative as large or small, important or unimportant, is a matter, fundamentally, of ideology. The liberal or conservative will be inclined to feel that there was an im-portant difference between the New Deal of the 1930s and the "new era" of the 1920s, and possibly, even, between the administrations of Lyndon Johnson and Dwight Eisenhower; and will regard the accession to power of Richard Nixon with strong emotion. The radical—whether of the right or left—will tend to regard them all as minor variations on the same theme. The same will be true of their respective attitudes toward the efficacy and improvability of the institution of regulation.

The Choice Among Imperfect Systems

One's assessment of regulation, then, is closely determined by one's attitude toward American capitalism itself. At one extreme there will be the Marxist critics, who regard it, when they give it any thought at all, as a logical development of monopoly capitalism itself—involving the accumu-lation of economic power in private hands, subject to nominal control by a government that is itself the servant of that same economic power. Regula-tion, like political democracy itself, is for them a sham because it leaves undisturbed the locus of power. It serves the purpose of creating and pro-tecting monopoly, not of controlling it. The vagueness of the governing statutes, the "political" character of the administrative commissions, the ever-present threat of legislative intervention if regulation becomes too effective in serving the public interest, the tendency of agencies to become the captive agents of their industries—all are symptoms of that fundamental concentration of power in private hands.[4]

At another extreme are the representatives of what the economist would most readily recognize as "the Chicago school." For these eighteenth century liberals, regulation is unnecessary as far as doing good is concerned but very effective when it comes to doing harm. It is unnecessary because private monopoly power is always limited in size, scope, and duration: the self-interest of even monopolists, the possibilities of competitive entry into all industries if only the government would permit it, the presence of actual

---

[4] See, for example, Paul A. Baran and Paul M. Sweezy, *Monopoly Capitalism* (New York: Monthly   Review Press, 1966), 65–66.

competition even among the traditional public utilities all make regulation incapable of much improving matters and not worth its costs.[5] But in its association with the use of government power to protect monopoly, especially by restricting entry, regulation is, according to this view, productive of much more harm than good. Monopoly is enduringly dangerous only when conferred and protected by government.[6]

The fact that "right" and "left" converge in their dismissal of regulation does not mean that the truth necessarily lies in splitting the difference between them (a weak metaphor because on this particular point there is in a sense no difference.) It is of considerable interest that some of the intellectual predecessors of the present "Chicago school," equally dedicated to eighteenth century liberalism and the regime of competition and equally condemnatory of regulated monopoly, concluded that the proper solution instead was to socialize the natural monopolies. Their point was that the present institution embodies the worst of both possible worlds—monopoly without effective control, private enterprise without effective incentive or stimulus, governmental supervision without the possibility of effective initiative in the public interest.[7]

The virtual disappearance of this last proposal in the past twenty years is instructive. The experience with selective socialization during this period has demonstrated more clearly than could any *a priori* argument that there is no easy solution in changing the institutional form. The choice remains inescapably one between imperfect institutions. It is difficult to detect any significant improvement or even change in the functioning of the monopolistic industries that Western European governments have socialized. The comparison of American experience with TVA and, for instance, Consolidated Edison or the Pennsylvania Railroad, suggests the possible desirability of going in one direction; comparison of the Post Office with, say, AT&T suggests the opposite.[8] Socialization obviously does not eliminate the problems of monopoly, bureaucracy, inadequate incentives, and political interference.

In between are the great majority who regard the market economy much as they regard democracy—as a manifestly inefficient system that is better than any of the alternatives. To them there is available neither the comforting alternative of simple laissez-faire on the one hand or comprehensive socialization on the other. A politically free society will insist on exercising some control over its economic destiny. It is unwilling to rely on the beneficence or even long-run interest of private monopoly, particularly in the face of abundant historical evidence that the power is real and can be abused. To the pragmatist and twentieth-century liberal, competition is the preferred method for both restraining and prodding private management. To the

---

[5] See Stigler and Friedland, in Shepherd and Gies, *op. cit.*; and Posner, *op. cit.*
[6] See, for example, Friedman, *op. cit.*, Chapter 8; see also the echo of the same view in some of the early constitutional decisions concerning the power of government to regulate—notably the varying assessments of "monopoly of fact" and "monopoly of law," note 21, Chapter 1 of Vol. 1.
[7] See especially Henry Simons, *Economic Policy for A Free Society* (Chicago: Univ. of Chicago Press, 1948), Chapter 2; Frank D. Graham, *Social Goals and Economic Institutions* (Princeton: Princeton Univ. Press, 1944), Chapter 10; and Friedrich A. Hayek, *The Road to Serfdom* (Chicago: Univ. of Chicago Press, 1944), 36–42.
[8] See the widely applauded and persuasive recommendations of the Report of the President's Commission on Postal Organization, *Towards Postal Excellence*, Washington, D.C., June 1968, which were in large measure enacted in 1970.

extent that it can be relied on, the institution itself, rather than either political or managerial *policy*, takes over responsibility for the public interest. All competition is imperfect; the preferred remedy is to try to diminish the imperfections. Even when highly imperfect, it can often be a valuable supplement to regulation. But to the extent that it is intolerably imperfect, the only acceptable alternative is regulation. And for the inescapable imperfections of regulation, the only available remedy is to try to make it work better. That is the modest underlying assumption of these volumes.

Selected Bibliography

Adams, Walter, ed., *The Structure of American Industry*. 3rd ed. New York: The Mac-millan Co., 1961.

American Economic Association, *Readings in Industrial Organization and Public Policy*. Homewood, Illinois: Richard D. Irwin, Inc., 1958.

———, *Readings in the Social Control of Industry*. Philadelphia: The Blakiston Co., 1942.

American Telephone & Telegraph Co., *Vertical Integration in the Bell System: A Systems Approach to Technological and Economic Imperatives of the Telephone Network*. President's Task Force on Communications Policy, Staff Paper 5, Part 2, Appendix C, PB 184 418, June 1969.

Averch, Harvey, and Johnson, Leland, "Behavior of the Firm under Regulatory Constraint," *American Economic Review* (December 1962), LII: 1052–1069.

Barber, Richard J., "Technological Change in American Transportation: The Role of Government Action," *Virginia Law Review* (June 1964), L: 824–895.

Behling, Burton Neubert, *Competition and Monopoly in Public Utility Industries*. Urbana: University of Illinois Press, 1938.

Boies, David, Jr., "Experiment in Mercantilism: Minimum Rate Regulation by the Interstate Commerce Commission," *Columbia Law Review* (April 1968), LXVIII: 599–663.

Bonbright, James Cummings, *Principles of Public Utility Rates*. New York: Columbia University Press, 1961.

———, and Means, Gardiner C., *The Holding Company: Its Public Significance and its Regulation*. 1st ed. New York and London: McGraw–Hill Book Co., 1932.

Burck, Gilbert, "A Plan to Save the Railroads," *Fortune* (August 1958), LVIII: 82—86 and ff

Caves, Richard E., *Air Transport and its Regulators: An Industry Study*. Cambridge: Harvard University Press, 1962.

Clark, John Maurice, *Competition as a Dynamic Process*. Washington: The Brookings Institution, 1961.

———, "Toward a Concept of Workable Competition," in American Economic Association, *Readings in the Social Control of Industry*. Philadelphia: The Blakiston Co., 1942.

Clemens, Eli Winston, *Economics and Public Utilities*. New York: Appleton-Century-Crofts, Inc., 1950

Coase, Ronald H., "The Federal Communications Commission," *Journal of Law and Economics* (October 1959), II: 1–40.

Conant, Michael, *Railroad Mergers and Abandonments*. Berkeley: University of California Press, 1964.

Daggett, Stuart, *Principles of Inland Transportation*. Rev. ed. New York: Harper & Bros., 1934.

de Chazeau, Melvin G., and Kahn, Alfred E., *Integration and Competition in the Petroleum Industry*. New Haven: Yale University Press, 1959.

Dirlam, Joel B., and Kahn, Alfred E., *Fair Competition: The Law and Economics of Antitrust Policy*. Ithaca: Cornell University Press, 1954.

——, and ——, "The Merits of Reserving the Cost-Savings from Domestic Communications Satellites for Support of Educational Television," *Yale Law Journal* (January 1968), LXXVII: 494–519.

Donnem, Roland W., "Antitrust Aspects of Establishing Nuclear and other Large-Scale Electricity Generation Facilities," an address before the Atomic Energy Committee, Federal Bar Association. Processed. Washington, October 15, 1969.

Doyle Report. See U. S. Senate, Committee on Interstate and Foreign Commerce.

Farmer, Richard N., "The Case for Unregulated Truck Transportation," *Journal of Farm Economics* (May 1964), XLVI: 398–409.

Federal Coordinator of Transportation. See U.S. House of Representatives, Committee on Interstate and Foreign Commerce.

Friedlaender, Ann F., *The Dilemma of Freight Transport Regulation*. Washington: The Brookings Institution, 1969.

Friedman, Milton, *Capitalism and Freedom*. Chicago: University of Chicago Press, 1962.

Fulda, Carl F., *Competition in the Regulated Industries: Transportation*. Boston: Little, Brown and Company, 1961.

Garfield, Paul J., and Lovejoy, Wallace F., *Public Utility Economics*. Englewood Cliffs, N.J.: Prentice-Hall, Inc., 1964.

Gellman, Aaron J., "Economic Regulation and Innovation Performance in Surface Transportation," a paper presented at the Brookings Institution *Conference on Technological Change in the Regulated Industries*, February 1969. Processed.

Gerber, Abraham, "Power Pools and Joint Plant Ownership," *Public Utilities Fortnightly* (September 12, 1969), LXXXII: 23–31.

Glaeser, Martin Gustav, *Public Utilities in American Capitalism*. New York: The Macmillan Co., 1957.

Greenberg, Edward, "Wire Television and the FCC's Second Report and Order on CATV Systems," *Journal of Law and Economics* (October 1967), X: 181–192.

Hellman, Richard, *Government Competition in the Electric Utility Industry of the United States*. Unpublished dissertation, Columbia University, 1967. Processed.

Helmetag, Carl, Jr., "Railroad Mergers: The Accommodation of the Interstate Commerce Act and Antitrust Policies," *Virgina Law Review* (December 1968), LIV: 1505–1530.

Hollander, Stanley C., *Passenger Transportation, Readings Selected from a Marketing Viewpoint*. East Lansing: Michigan State University, Bureau of Business and Economic Research, 1968.

Hughes, William R., "Short-Run Efficiency and the Organization of the Electric Power Industry," *Quarterly Journal of Economics* (November 1962), LXXVI: 592–612.

Irwin, Manley R., and McKee, Robert E., "Vertical Integration and the Communication Equipment Industry: Alternatives for Public Policy," *Cornell Law Review* (February 1968), LII: 446–472.

Jaffe, Louis, "The Scandal in TV Licensing," *Harper's Magazine* (September 1957), CCXV: 77–84.

Johnson, Leland L., *The Future of Cable Television: Some Problems of Federal Regulation.* Santa Monica: The Rand Corporation, Memorandum RM-6199-FF, January 1970.

Jones, William K., *Cases and Materials on Regulated Industries.* Brooklyn: Foundation Press, 1967.

Kahn, Alfred E., "Cartels and Trade Associations," *International Encyclopedia of the Social Sciences.* New York: The Macmillan Co. and the Free Press, 1968, II: 320–325.

——, "The Combined Effects of Prorationing, the Depletion Allowance and Import Quotas on the Cost of Producing Crude Oil in the United States," U.S. Senate, Committee on the Judiciary, Subcommittee on Antitrust and Monopoly, 91st Cong., 1st Sess., *Government Intervention in the Market Mechanism,* Hearings, *The Petroleum Industry,* Part 1, Washington, 1969. Reproduced in *Natural Resources Journal* (January 1970), X: 53–61.

——, "The Tyranny of Small Decisions: Market Failures, Imperfections, and the Limits of Economics," *Kyklos* (January 1966), XIX: 23–47.

Kendrick, John W., *Productivity Trends in the United States.* Princeton: Princeton University Press, 1961.

Keyes, Lucile Shepherd, *Federal Control of Entry into Air Transportation.* Cambridge: Harvard University Press, 1951.

——, "Reconsideration of Federal Control of Entry into Air Transportation," *Journal of Air Law and Commerce* (Spring 1955), XXII: 192–202.

Koplin, Harry Thomas, *Natural Gas Act Certification Policy of the Federal Power Commission.* Unpublished Ph.D. dissertation, Cornell University, September 1952.

Landis, James M., *Report on Regulatory Agencies to the President-Elect.* U.S. Senate, Committee on the Judiciary, 86th Cong., 2d Sess., Committee Print, 1960.

Lansing, John B, *Transportation and Economic Policy.* New York: The Free Press, 1966.

Leonard, William Norris, "Issues of Competition and Monopoly in Railroad Mergers," *Transportation Journal* (Summer 1964), III: 5–15.

——, *Railroad Consolidation Under the Transportation Act of 1920.* New York: Columbia University Press, 1946.

Levine, Michael E., "Is Regulation Necessary? California Air Transportation and National Regulatory Policy," *Yale Law Journal* (July 1965), LXXIV: 1416–1447.

Lister, Louis, and Homan, Paul T., *Energy Industries and Public Policies in the United States.* Draft manuscript, Washington: Resources for the Future, Inc., 1968.

Locklin, D. Philip, *Economics of Transportation.* 6th ed. Homewood, Illinois: Richard D. Irwin, Inc., 1966.

Loomis, Carol J., "Big Board, Big Volume, Big Trouble," *Fortune* (May 1968), LXXVII: 146–151 and ff.

Lyon, Leverett S., and Abramson, Victor, *Government and Economic Life: Development and Current Issues of American Public Policy.* Washington: The Brookings Institution, 1940.

MacAvoy, Paul W., *Price Formation in Natural Gas Fields: A Study of Competition, Monopsony, and Regulation.* New Haven: Yale University Press, 1962.

Marx, Daniel, Jr., *International Shipping Cartels, A Study of Industrial Self-Regulation by Shipping Conferences.* Princeton: Princeton University Press, 1953.

McKinsey & Co., *A Study of Western Electric's Performance.* New York: American Telephone & Telegraph Co., 1969.

Meyer, John R.; Peck, Merton J.; Stenason, John; and Zwick, Charles, *The Economics of Competition in the Transportation Industries.* Cambridge: Harvard University Press, 1959.

Miklius, W., and DeLoch, D.B., "A Further Case for Unregulated Truck Transportation," *Journal of Farm Economics* (November 1965), XLVII: 933–942.

Morgan, Charles Stillman, *Regulation and the Management of Public Utilities*. Boston and New York: Houghton Mifflin Company, 1923.

Nelson, James C., *Railroad Transportation and Public Policy*. Washington: The Brookings Institution, 1959.

Nelson, James R., "The Role of Competition in the Regulated Industries," *Antitrust Bulletin* (January–April 1966), XI: 1–36.

New York Stock Exchange, *Economic Effects of Negotiated Commission Rates on the Brokerage Industry, the Market for Corporate Securities, and the Investing Public*. Processed, August 1968.

——, *The Economics of Minimum Commission Rates, Reply to Memorandum of the Antitrust Division of the Department of Justice dated January 17, 1969*. Processed, May 1, 1969.

Nicholson, Howard W., "Motor Carrier Costs and Minimum Rate Regulation," *Quarterly Journal of Economics* (February 1958), LXXII: 139–152.

Note, "Federal Regulation of Trucking: The Emerging Critique," *Columbia Law Review* (March 1963), LXIII: 460–514.

Olds, Leland, "The Economic Planning Function under Public Regulation," *American Economic Review, Papers and Proceedings* (May 1958), XLVIII: 553–567.

Peck, Merton J., "Competitive Policy for Transportation?" in Almarin Phillips, ed., *Perspectives on Antitrust Policy*. Princeton: Princeton University Press, 1965, 244–272.

——, "The Single-Entity Proposal for International Telecommunications," *American Economic Review, Papers and Proceedings* (May 1970), LX: 199–203.

Phillips, Almarin, "Technological Change in the Air Transportation Industry in the United States," a paper presented at the Brookings Institution *Conference on Technological Change in the Regulated Industries*, February 1969. Mimeo.

Phillips, Charles F., Jr., *The Economics of Regulation*. Rev. ed. Homewood, Illinois: Richard D. Irwin, Inc., 1969.

Posner, Richard A., "Natural Monopoly and its Regulation," *Stanford Law Review* (February 1969), XXI: 548–643.

Presidential Advisory Committee on Transport Policy and Organization. See U.S., Presidential Advisory Committee.

President's Task Force on Communications Policy. See U.S., President's Task Force.

Priest, A.J.G., *Principles of Public Utility Regulation: Theory and Application*. Charlottesville, Virginia: Michie Co., 1969.

Ransmeier, Joseph Sirera, *The Tennessee Valley Authority, A Case Study in the Economics of Multiple Purpose Stream Planning*. Nashville: Vanderbilt University Press, 1942.

Reynolds, Lloyd G., "Cutthroat Competition," *American Economic Review* (December 1940), XXX: 736–747.

Richmond, Samuel B., *Regulation and Competition in Air Transportation*. New York: Columbia University Press, 1961.

Ritchie, Robert F., *Integration of Public Utility Holding Companies*. Ann Arbor: University of Michigan Press, 1954.

Robbins, Sidney, *The Securities Markets, Operations and Issues*. New York: The Free Press, 1966.

Ross, Charles R., "Bulk Power Supply for Small Systems," an address before the 24th American Public Power Association Conference, May 9, 1967. Mimeo.

Schwartz, Herman, "Comsat, the Carriers, and the Earth Stations: Some Problems with 'Melding Variegated Interests,'" *Yale Law Journal* (January 1967), LXXVI: 441–484.

Schwartz, Louis B., "Legal Restriction of Competition in the Regulated Industries: An Abdication of Judicial Responsibility," *Harvard Law Review* (January 1954), LXVII: 436–475.

Seiden, Martin H., *An Economic Analysis of Community Antenna Television Systems and the Television Broadcasting Industry, A Report to the Federal Communications Commission* Washington: Government Printing Office, February 12, 1965.

Sharfman, I.L., *The Interstate Commerce Commission*. 4 vols. New York: The Commonwealth Fund, 1931–1937.

Sheahan, John B., *Competition versus Regulation as a Policy Aim for the Telephone Equipment Industry*. Unpublished Ph.D. dissertation, Harvard University, 1951.

——, "Integration and Exclusion in the Telephone Equipment Industry," *Quarterly Journal of Economics* (May 1956), LXX: 249–269.

Shepherd, William G., "Communications: Regulation, Innovation and the Changing Margin of Competition," a paper presented at the Brookings Institution *Conference on Technological Change in the Regulated Industries*, February 1969. Mimeo.

——, and Gies, Thomas G., *Utility Regulation. New Directions in Theory and Policy*. New York: Random House, 1966.

Smith, Nelson Lee, "Federal Power Commission and Pipeline Markets: How Much Competition?" *Columbia Law Review* (April 1968), LXVIII: 667–676.

Stelzer, Irwin M., "Rate Base Regulation and Some Alternatives: An Appraisal," a paper presented at a Brookings Institution *Symposium on the Rate-Base Approach to Regulation*, June 1968. Mimeo. Reproduced in *Public Utilities Fortnightly*, September 25, 1969, 3–11.

Straszheim, Mahlon R., *The International Airline Industry*. Washington: The Brookings Institution, 1969.

Telser, Lester G., "Advertising and Competition," *Journal of Political Economy* (December 1964), LXXII: 537–562.

Transportation Economics. See Universities-National Bureau Committee for Economic Research.

Trebing, Harry M., "Toward an Incentive System of Regulation," *Public Utilities Fortnightly* (July 18, 1963), LXXII: 22–37.

——, ed., *Performance under Regulation*. East Lansing: Institute of Public Utilities, Michigan State University, 1968.

Troxel, Emery, *Economics of Public Utilities*. New York: Rinehart and Company, 1947.

Twentieth Century Fund, *Electric Power and Government Policy*. New York: Twentieth Century Fund, 1948.

U.S. Department of Justice, *Memorandum on the Fixed Minimum Commission Rate Structure*, before the Securities and Exchange Commission, *In the Matter of Commission Rate Structure of Registered National Securities Exchanges*, File No. 4–144. Processed. January 19, 1969.

U.S. Department of Transportation, *Western Railroad Mergers*, A Staff Study by the Office of the Assistant Secretary for Policy Development and the Federal Railroad Administration, Washington, January 1969.

U.S. Federal Communications Commission, *In the matter of Amendment of Part 74, Subpart K, of the Commission's Rules and Regulations Relative to Community Antenna Television Systems, etc.* Docket No. 18397. Notice of Proposed Rule Making and Notice of Inquiry, December 12, 1968. First Report and Order, October 24, 1969. Second Further Notice of Proposed Rule Making, June 24, 1970.

——, *In the Matter of Establishment of Policies and Procedures for Consideration of Applications to Provide Specialized Common Carrier Services in the Domestic Public Point-to-Point Microwave Radio Service, etc.*, Docket No. 18920, Notice of Inquiry to Formulate Policy, Notice of Proposed Rule Making, and Order, July 15, 1970.

U.S. Federal Coordinator of Transportation. See U.S. House of Representatives, Committee on Interstate and Foreign Commerce.

U.S. Federal Power Commission, *National Power Survey*, Washington, 1964.

U.S. House of Representatives, Committee on Interstate and Foreign Commerce, 74th Cong., 1st Sess., *Report of the Federal Coordinator of Transportation, 1934*, House Document No. 89, Washington, January 30, 1935.

U.S. Presidential Advisory Committee on Transport Policy and Organization, *Revision of Federal Transportation Policy*. Reproduced in U.S. Department of Commerce, *Modern Transportation Policy*, documents relating to the report of the Presidential Advisory Committee on Transport Policy and Organization and implementing legislation, Washington, 1956.

U.S. President's Task Force on Communications Policy, *The Domestic Telecommunications Carrier Industry*, Staff Paper 5, Part 1. Washington, June 1969.

———, *Final Report*. Washington, December 7, 1968.

U.S. Securities and Exchange Commission, *Report of Special Study of the Securities Markets*. Washington, 1963.

U.S. Senate, Committee on Interstate and Foreign Commerce, 87th Cong., 1st Sess., *National Transportation Policy*, Preliminary Draft of a Report prepared by the Special Study Group on Transportation Policies in the United States (John P. Doyle, Staff Director). Washington, January 1961.

U.S. Senate, Select Committee on Small Business, 84th Cong., 2nd Sess., *Competition, Regulation and the Public Interest in the Motor Carrier Industry*, Senate Report No. 1693. Washington, March 19, 1956.

Universities-National Bureau Committee for Economic Research, *Transportation Economics*, A Conference of the Universities-National Bureau Committee for Economic Research. New York: National Bureau of Economic Research, 1965.

Vickrey, William S., "Some Objections to Marginal Cost-Pricing," *Journal of Political Economy* (June 1948), LVI: 218–238.

Weisbrod, Burton A., "Collective-Consumption Services of Individual-Consumption Goods," *Quarterly Journal of Economics* (August 1964), LXXVIII: 471–477.

Welborn, David M., "Trucking Service for Pittsburgh Plate Glass," in Edwin A. Bock, ed., *Goverment Regulation of Business, A Casebook*. Englewood Cliffs, N.J.: Prentice-Hall, Inc., 1965.

Westfield, Fred M., "Regulation and Conspiracy," *American Economic Review* (June 1965), LV: 424–443.

Wilcox, Clair, *Public Policies Toward Business*. 3rd ed. Homewood, Illinois: Richard D. Irwin, Inc., 1966.

Williams, Ernest, Jr., *The Regulation of Rail-Motor Rate Competition*. New York: Harper & Bros., 1958.

Wilson, George W., "Effects of Value-of-Service Pricing upon Motor Common Carriers," *Journal of Political Economy* (August 1955), LXIII: 337–344.

———, "The Effect of Rate Regulation on Resource Allocation in Transportation," *American Economic Review, Papers and Proceedings* (May 1964), LIV: 160–171.

———, "The Nature of Competition in the Motor Transport Industry," *Land Economics* (November 1960), XXXVI: 387–391.

Wilson, John William, *Residential and Industrial Demand for Electricity*. Unpublished doctoral dissertation, Cornell University, 1969.

Index

VOLUMES I & II

Above-890 decision, II: 129-132, 144, 148, 290
  cream-skimming aspects, II: 227-232
Adams, Walter, I: 8. II: 19, 30, 111, 247
Adelman, Morris A., II: 266
Adkins versus Children's Hospital, I: 5, 21
Administrative considerations; *see* Pricing, practical
  considerations
Adversary process; *see* Regulation, the adjudicatory
  role
Advertising, allocation of resources to, II: 41-42
  by AT&T, I: 28
  by electric companies, I: 28. II: 280
  incentives, I: 28
  see also Promotional expenditures
Affiliates, payments to, I: 28; *see also* Integration,
  vertical
Agnew, Vice-President Spiro, II: 254-255
Agriculture, fixed costs of, II: 121
  problems of, II: 173-174
Air Freight case, II: 46
Air Freight forwarders, II: 274-275
Airline fares, I: 65, 75-76, 95, 149-150, 153, 188-
  189. II: 217-219
  application of marginal costs, I: 75-77, 85
  see also Air transport regulation
Airlines, fare structure relative to cost, I: 153
  feeder helicopter service, II: 234, 308
  group charter flights, II: 217
  interchange agreements, II: 307
  mergers, II: 283
  non-price rivalry, II: 211-216
  non-scheduled (irregular), II: 216-217
  price competition, II: 216-219
  rates, trend, II: 100
  scheduling, II: 211-212, 215
  see also Air transport
Airplane landing fees, I: 100
Air transport, coach service, II: 217
  competition versus regulation, II: 216-220
  cost tendencies, I: 150. II: 226, 234-235
  demand diversity and economies of scale, II: 123
  service rivalry, II: 209-216
  subsidies, II: 235-236

  vertical integration in, II: 255
  see also Airlines
Air transport Ass'n, II: 211
Air transport regulation, II: 6, 9, 16, 91, 210-217,
  220; *see also* Civil Aeronautics Board
  allowable rate of return, II: 55
  and cream-skimming, II: 9, 226, 234-235, 239
  and equipment policy, II: 213-215
  and innovation, II: 213-215, 247
  of intermodal integration, II: 270, 274-275
  joint fares, II: 64
  of non-price competition, II: 212-216
  role of competition in, II: 113
Air transportation, promotion of, II: 4, 215
Air travel, elasticity of demand, II: 103, 217-219
"A-J-W effect," I: 25, 114, 120, 147-148, 171. II:
  49-59, 67, 101-102, 106-107, 138, 267-268,
  273, 279
  competition as safeguard, II: 56, 138, 167
  regulation as safeguard, II: 56, 76-77
Alabama versus Southern R. Co., II: 84
Alabama-Tennessee Natural Gas versus FPC, I: 34.
  II: 166-168
Alaska Airlines, II: 214
Alchian, Armen A., I: 30. II: 306
Alexander, Sidney S., II: 38
Aliber, Robert Z., I: 8
Aluminum, price control, I: 8
American Airlines versus CAB, II: 46
American Commercial Lines versus Louisville &
  Nashville R.R., I: 162. II: 23-24
American Electric Power Co., II: 281
American Light and Traction Co., II: 263
American Natural Gas Co., II: 159-161
American President Lines, II: 270
American Telephone & Telegraph Co., in the Matter
  of (Docket 16258), I: 51, 63, 101, 152, 157.
  II: 110, 132, 147-148, 150, 152, 291
American Telephone & Telegraph Co., advertising by,
  I: 28
  antitrust suits, II: 140, 144, 145, 253
  consent decree, II: 145, 253, 295, 297, 306
  innovation record, II: 296-304

patent policies, II: 295, 297
pricing policies, I: 156-158, 173-174, 176-177. II:
    132, 147, 150-152
see also Western Electric Co.; Communications;
    Telephone industry; Separations procedures;
    Transatlantic cable
American Tobacco Co. versus United States, II: 116
*American Trucking Associations versus Atchison,
    Topeka & Sante Fe R. Co.,* II: 311-312
*American Trucking Associations versus United
    States,* II: 193, 269
Anderson, Keith, II: 41
Andrews, P. W. S., II: 176
Annenburg, Walter, II: 254
Antitrust laws, I: 8, 31
    application to regulated industries, II: 76, 113,
        159-165, 194-196, 290, 295-297, 315-316
Area Rate Proceeding, Claude E. Aikman, et al., I:
    43, 68
Arnold, Schwinn, United States versus, I: 9. II: 316
Associated Press versus United States, II: 319
*Association of American Railroads, United States
    versus,* II: 69
Atlantic Coast Line Railroad versus North Carolina,
    I: 63, 142
Atlantic Seaboard formula, I: 98-100, 101-102. II:
    50, 98
Atlantic Seaboard versus FPC, I: 99. II: 165-170
Authorized users decision, II: 137-139
    cream-skimming aspects, II: 227-233
Averch, Harvey, II: 49; *see also* "A-J-W effect"

Bach, George L., I: 83
Bagge, Carl E., II: 12, 153
Bain, Joe S., II: 116, 210
Bandeen, R. A., I: 182
Banzhaf versus FCC, II: 91
Baran, Paul A., II: 327
Barber, Richard J., II: 100, 104, 247
Barges, exemption from regulation, II: 20-21, 26
Barlow, Robin, I: 131
Barnes, Irston R., I: 4, 21, 29, 37, 40. II: 61
Barnett, H. J., II: 33, 41, 42
Barrett, Edward M., I: 40
Barzel, Yoram, I: 126
Bator, Francis M., I: 190
Bauer, John, I: 40, 112-113. II: 107
Baumol, William J., I: 70, 144-145, 155, 164, 170,
    176, 180. II: 49, 59, 97, 101
Becker, Gary S., I: 29
Behling, Burton H., II: 117-118, 121-122
Bell Laboratories, II: 301
Bello, Francis, II: 301
Belsley, David, II: 33
Benishay, Haskel, I: 197
Ben-Shahar, Haim, I: 51
Bernstein, Marver H., II: 11
Blake, Harlan, M., II: 260, 262
Blank, David M., II: 42
Blue Cross, and cream-skimming
    competition, II: 245

Bluefield Water Works versus West Virginia, 43, 52
Bock, Edwin A., I: 26. II: 17
Boies, David B., Jr., II: 22, 78, 245, 255
Boiteux, Marcel, I: 85, 91, 97
Bonbright, James C., I: 28, 40, 68, 94, 98, 106-108,
    111, 113, 115-117, 132, 134-135, 137, 150,
    155, 173, 175, 185-186, 195, 197, 199. II:
    71, 72, 98, 103, 123-124
Bork, Robert H., II: 260, 262
Borts, George H., I: 126
Boston Herald-Traveler Corp., II: 254
Boston & Maine Railroad versus United States, II: 64
Boulding, Kenneth E., I: 83
Bower, Richard S., II: 58
Bowman, Mary Jean, I: 83
Bowman, Ward S., Jr., I: 195. II: 260, 262
Brabazon, of Tara, Lord, II: 211
Brady, Robert A., I: 10
Brand, Wallace E., II: 65
Brandeis, Justice Louis D., I: 3, 7, 28, 39, 112. II:
    104
Brass versus North Dakota, I: 4
Break, George F., I: 131
Brigham, Eugene F., I: 33-34, 117
Broadcasting, licensing of, II: 2, 32, 37, 89-92; *see
    also* Television
    multi-media ownership, II: 89, 253-255
Broadcasting commercials, regulation of, II: 92; *see
    also* Cigarette advertising
Brokerage business, elasticity of demand, II: 202-
    203
    elasticity of supply, II: 203-204
    fixed versus variable costs, II: 202-204
    product differentiation in, II: 204-205, 207-208
Brokerage commissions, and the antitrust laws, II:
    194-196
    charges to non-member brokers, II: 195-196, 198-
        199
    and discrimination, II: 196, 198, 204-206, 208
    give-ups, II: 28, 196-198
    regulation, by the SEC, II: 194, 197-199
        versus competition, II: 199-209
        and efficiency, II: 206
        and quality of service, II: 203, 207
        and selling costs, II: 207-208
        and service inflation, II: 206-208
        tendency to spread, II: 28-29
    under self-regulation, II: 194-209
Brown, Harry Gunnison, I: 111, 113, 142, 167, 170,
    175
Bryan, Robert F., I: 115, 117. II: 107
Budd versus New York, I: 5, 7
Bulk commodities transport, exemption from regu-
    lation, II: 20-21, 26
Bunker-Ramo Corp., II: 145
Burck, Gilbert, I: 8. II: 282-284, 307
Burger, Chief Justice Warren E., II: 90
Burns, Arthur Robert, I: 9-10
Businesses "affected with a public interest," I: 3-8
Bussing, Irvin, II: 61
Buyer ignorance, and regulation, II: 5, 176-178 *see*

also Competition, imperfections

California, Investigation of Pacific Tel. & Tel. Co.,
  II: 292-294, 307-308
California versus Lo-Vaca Gathering Co., II: 30
Capacity, excess, and destructive competition, II:
  173-176
  in relation to demand, I: 103-108; *see also* Cost,
    marginal, short-run, Cost, marginal opportun-
    ity, and Marginal cost pricing, short-run
  standby, II: 50, 149, 202-203, 236-241, 320-321
  in relation to cream-skimming, II: 229, 236-240
Capacity charge, *see* Two-part tariff
Capacity costs, distribution of, I: 87-103, 199. II:
  50
  under competition, II: 225-226, 228-229, 236-
    240, 321
  fixed peak, I: 90-91
  public utility practice, I: 95-100
  shifting peak, I: 91-95, 103, 107, 186, 199
  under strong regulation, II: 107-108
Capital costs, comparative, of public utilities, I: 35-
  36
Capital intensity of public utilities, I: 35-36; *see also*
  Costs, fixed
Capital markets, imperfections of, II: 175-176, 261-
  262
Capital outlays, control of, I: 26-35. II: 56, 76-77
Carlson, Marvin A. W., II: 4
Cartelization, I: 10
Cartels, economics of, I: 164. II: 19, 28-30, 189,
  209, 266
Carter Electronics Corp.; *see* Carterfone
Carterfone, II: 142-144, 290
Cary, William L., II: 92
Caves, Richard E., II: 16, 108, 210-211, 213-216,
  220, 235, 236, 286
Cedar Rapids Gas Light versus Cedar Rapids, I: 43
Certification; *see* Franchises, and Licensing
Chamberlin, Edward H., I: 9
*Chattanooga Gas Co. versus East Tennessee Natural
  Gas Co.,* II: 165
Chenery, Hollis B., I: 104
Chicago, Milwaukee & St. Paul versus Minnesota, I:
  37
*Chicago & N. W. versus Atchison, Topeka & Sante
  Fe,* I: 41
Cigarette advertising, regulation of, II: 90-91, 111
Cincinnati Gas & Electric versus FPC, II: 166
City of Colton case, II: 30, 322-323
City of Corinth case, II: 166-168
City of Detroit versus FPC, II: 290
City of Hamilton case, II: 166-168
City of Paris, Ky. versus FPC, II: 317
City of Shrewsbury case, II: 75-76, 167, 322-323
Civil Aeronautics Act, II: 113
Civil Aeronautics Board, authority over flight sched-
  uling, II: 215
  licensing policies of, II: 16, 46, 91, 180, 210
  policy on price competition, II: 211, 216;
  see also Air transport regulation

Clapham, J. H., I: 127
Clapp, Gordon R., II: 103
Clark, J. M., I: 9, 79, 84, 113. II: xi, 173, 181, 207,
  210, 241
Clayton Act, Sec. 7, II: 113, 163-164
Clemens, Eli Winston, I: 40, 47, 97, 130, 133, 136,
  142, 197. II: 72, 77
Cleveland, Frederick W., Jr., II: 54
Coal industry, destructive competition in, II: 173-
  175, 180, 184
Coal-Southern Mines to Tampa, I: 164
Coase, Ronald H., II: 3, 38, 109
Codes of "fair competition," I: 10
Collusion, II: 69
Colton, Cal.; *see City of Colton*
Combination companies, economics of, II: 264-268
  electric and gas, II: 276-280
  transportation, II: 253, 266-276
Commissions, regulatory, I: 10. II: 119, 326
  corruption and, II: 11; *see also* Corruption, political
  life cycles of, II: 11, 26
  resources of, II: 11, 326
  survey of, I: 10
Commodity charge; *see* Two-part tariff
"Common callings," I: 5-7
Common carriers, obligations of, I: 5-7
Common carrier status, imposition of, II: 43, 156-
  158, 317-318; *see also* Interconnection,
  compulsory
Communications, the case for network monopoly,
  II: 127-129, 143, 147-152, 298-300
  charging for back-up and interconnection, II: 228-
  229, 236-240
  competitive common carriers, II: 131-136, 146-
  152
  competitive issues in, II: 129-152, 248, 290-305
  cream-skimming in, II: 227-233, 238-241
  fragmentation of regulation, II: 87-88, 92-93
  full cost allocation, I: 152-153, 156-158. II: 152;
    see also Separations procedures
  innovations in, II: 144-145, 148-149, 299-305
  interconnection, II: 125-126, 133, 140-145, 307-
  308
  international, single-entity proposal, II: 117, 150
  long-run cost tendencies in, I: 125-126, 128-129.
    II: 147-152
  multi-media ownership, II: 89, 253-255
  pricing, nationwide average, II: 147-148, 150-151,
    228-231
    and technological progress, II: 146-147, 149-150,
    229-231
  private systems, II: 129-132, 142-144, 146-152
  productivity trends, II: 99-100, 299-300
  profitability of various services, I: 156-158. II: 132
  rates, long-run trends, II: 100
  regulation and national security, II: 245-246
  vertical integration, II: 130-131, 146, 290-305
    and national security, II: 245-246
  see also Transatlantic cable, Communications satel-
    lites, and Telephone industry
Communications Act of 1934, II: 32

Communications Policy, President's Task Force on, II: 33, 88, 93, 117, 145, 150, 300-303
Communications Satellite Corp. (Comsat), I: 113. II: 51-52, 76-77, 136-139, 227-233
Communications satellites, I: 122. II: 51-52, 56, 76-77, 136-139, 304-305
  domestic, II: 137, 139-140
  ground station ownership, II: 53, 138
Community antenna television (CATV); see Television, community antenna
Commutation rates, I: 100
Comparable earnings, standard for rate of return, I: 52-53, 198
Comparative proceedings, II: 136, 160; see also Licensing
Competition, in communications, I: 65, 156-158, 173-174, 176-177
  among customers, bearing on rate discrimination, I: 166-175
  destructive, I: 7, 9-10. II: 2, 5-6
    in air transport, II: 209-220
    and cream-skimming, II: 220-246; see also Cream-skimming
    and quality of service, II: 176-178; see also Service quality, inflation of
    and resource conservation, II: 175
    among stock brokers, II: 202-209
    theory of, II: 173-178
    in trucking, II: 6, 178-193
  and discrimination, I: 159-181. II: 7, 168-171, 221-233, 239, 246-250
  effective, prerequisites of, I: 18. II: 114
  exposure of public utilities to, I: 64-65, 159-181. II: 103-104
  as a factor in rate-making, I: 159-181
  fuel and energy, I: 64-65, 163, 177-180. II: 102-103, 276-277
  imperfections, in capital market, II: 175, 261
    and the case for regulation, II: 5-7, 114, 175-178, 223-224, 241-243, 329
    see also Imperfect competition
  in issuance of local franchises, II: 117-118
  with local industry and discrimination, I: 166-168
  non-economic values of, II: 246
  non-price, and regulation, II: 10, 185, 189, 204-208, 209-220
  perfect, defined, II: 114
  preservation of, by regulation, II: 255-256
  pure, defined, II: 114
    pricing under, I: 67
  and regulation contrasted, II: 12-13, 107, 114-115
  in regulatory statutes, II: 113-114
  restrictions on under regulation, II: 1-45, 111-112; see also Licensing
  role of under regulation, II: 1, 56, 103-104, 112, 113-119, 126, 149-152, 161-165, 232-233, 243, 246-250, 303-305, 324-325, 328-329
  in transportation, I: 64, 161-163, 164-166, 170-171
  wastes of, and natural monopoly, II: 121-122
  see also references to specific industries

Competitive bidding, in public utilities, II: 255
Computer industry, relation to communications, II: 145-146, 304
Computer services, pricing, I: 108-109
Conant, Michael, II: 283, 284, 286
Congestion costs, I: 87, 89, 197; see also Cost, opportunity, and Capacity costs, distribution of
Congress, interferences with effective regulation, II: 91-92
Conservatism, tendencies to of regulation, II: 11-45, 87-88
Consolidated Edison Co., I: 28. II: 50, 87
Constantin, James A., II: 193
Construction industry, and promotional competition in energy market, I: 177-180
Containerization; see Piggyback service
Continuing surveillance, II: 60
Contract carriers, regulation of, II: 18-19, 25
Cook, Donald C., II: 281
Cook, Franklin H., II: 277
Cookenboo, Leslie Jr., I: 126
Cooperatives, agricultural, exemption from regulation, II: 20
Copeland, Morris A., II: 221
Corinth, Miss.; see City of Corinth
Corruption, political, and regulation, II: 11-12, 91, 177, 246
Cost, of capital, attempts to measure growth expectations, I: 48-49
  effect of debt ratio, I: 50-51
  growth expectations as component, I: 47-48, 58-60
  problems of measuring, I: 45-51, 58-60
  and rate of return, I: 43, 45-51
  relation to operating ratio, II: 55-56
  slope of, II: 57-58
  incremental, specifying the increment, I: 66, 75-77
  joint, defined, I: 79; see also Joint products
  pricing under; see Joint products
  long-run incremental, I: 85-86, 107-108
  long-run marginal, and competitive rates, I: 160-166
  marginal, defined, I: 65-66
    problems of definition, I: 70-83
    relation of short-run and long-run, I: 136-137
    short-run, I: 70-71
    short-run increasing versus constant, I: 93-97. II: 173
    short-run in relation to average total; see Equilibrium, long-run and short-run
    specifying the time perspective, I: 70-75
    variability of, I: 84-85, 104
  marginal opportunity, and joint products, I: 79-83, 85, 90-95
  opportunity, I: 66, 72-73, 78, 85, 87-88, 93-94
  postponable, I: 71-73, 75
  of service, see Rate level
  structures, factor in competition, I: 161-163, 168-170, 173. II: 178-179
  user, I: 71-72
Costello, Peter, II: 107

Costs, average; *see* Costs, fully distributed, and Pricing, full-cost decreasing versus constant, I: 94, 96
  capital; *see* Capacity costs, distribution of
  common, assignability of, I: 78-79, 85, 134-137
    identifying marginal costs in the presence of, I: 77-83
    as an occasion for rate discrimination, I: 135-137
    pervasiveness of, I: 77-78
  of congestion; *see* Congestion costs
  decreasing; *see* Decreasing costs
  fixed, I: 12
    and destructive competition, II: 173-174
    as factor in natural monopoly, II: 119-122
    and marginal cost pricing, I: 70, 72-74
    in relation to replacement policy, I: 118
  fully distributed, I: 150-158, 198-199. II: 152
    in transport regulation, I: 162-166. II: 23-24, 85
  increasing, and natural monopoly, II: 123-125
  joint, in trucking, II: 182-184; *see also* Joint products
  marginal, short-run and long-run, I: 70-72, 75
  overhead, I: 9
  variable, I: 70-72
  see also entries for individual industries
Consumer sovereignty, I: 66-67
Cox, Commissioner Kenneth A., I: 122. II: 89
Coyle, Eugene P., II: 49
Cramer, Curtis A., II: 66
Cramton, Roger C., II: 112
Cream-skimming, II: 7-10, 221-246
  and back-up capacity, II: 228-229, 236-240, 321
  benefits of, II: 221-226
  categories of, II: 225-226
  in decreasing cost situations, II: 224-233
  impact on common carriers, II: 221-223, 238-239
  and industry promotion, II: 233-235
  in relation to peak demand, II: 225-226, 234-235
  and trucking, II: 8-9
Crew, M. A., I: 97
Crowley, William J., II: 58
Customer charge; *see* Two-part tariff

Daggett, Stuart, II: 79-81
Dam, Kenneth W., II: 220
Data Transmission Co., II: 135, 139
Davidson, Paul, I: 120
Davidson, Ralph K., I: 96, 98, 139, 187. II: 50
Davis, Otto A., I: 70
Dean, Joel, I: 83
deBoursac, Vladimir, II: 211, 213
deChazeau, Melvin G., I: 98, 115, 117, 155. II: 29, 107, 261-262, 317
Decreasing costs, long-run, I: 12, 123-130, 148-150; *see also* Natural monopoly
  and natural monopoly, II: 119-125
  overlap of long- and short-run, I: 126
  pricing implications, I: 130-132
  relation to technological progress, I: 12, 127-130
  short-run, I: 124, 126, 129-130, 135-137
Defense procurement, and cost control, I: 31.

II: 302
De Loch, D. B.; *see* Miklius, W.
Demand, diversity of and natural monopoly, II: 122-123, 127-128
  fluctuations of, and natural monopoly, II: 120
Demand charge; *see* Two-part tariff
Demand elasticity, as affected by competition, I: 159
  as a factor in pricing, I: 63-64, 93, 115, 141-142, 155-156, 188-189, 198-199. II: 102-103, 232
  problems of estimation, I: 185, 187-188
Demsetz, Harold, II: 200-201
Department of Justice, interventions in regulatory proceedings, I: 165. II: 45, 144, 146, 197, 200-202, 204-205, 254, 309
Depreciation, accelerated and treatment of income tax, I: 32-35
  adjustment for price level change, I: 34-35, 115; *see also* Rate base, reproduction cost
  and marginal cost pricing, I: 35, 71-73
  the proper time-pattern of recovery, I: 105-106, 117-122. II: 146-147, 150
  rates, typical, I: 118
  regulation of, I: 27, 32-35, 117-122. II: 152
  in relation to the A-J-W effect, II: 58-59
  in relation to gross return, I: 32, 34, 51, 111
  in relation to replacement policy, I: 118-120. II: 214
  and technological progress, I: 117-121. II: 146-147, 149-150, 321
  as a variable cost, I: 71-73
Depression, the Great, and spread of regulation, II: 18, 180-182
Destructive competition; *see* Competition, destructive
Dhrymes, Phoebus J., I: 126
Dilution of stockholder equity, I: 46-47
Dirlam, Joel B., I: 31, 68. II: 30, 36, 39, 41, 114, 208, 233, 247, 257
Discrimination, I: 63-64, 76, 123, 131-150, 155-181, 187-191, 199
  as affected by competition, I: 159-181. II: 221-233, 246-250
  communications rates, I: 156-158, 173-174. II: 132, 147-152, 228-231
  effect on competitors, I: 175-180, 188. II: 247-249
  identifying the marginal buyers, I: 140-142
  and the Interstate Commerce Act, I: 55, 145, 161-166, 170, 176. II: 14-15
  natural gas rates, I: 98-100. II: 166-171
  and the need for regulation, I: 147-148, 159-160, 166, 179. II: 7, 246-250
  occasions for, I: 123-137
  and peak-responsibility pricing, I: 93-94, 99-102, 146
  perfect, I: 131-133
  principles of, I: 137-150, 160, 172-175. II: 225
  problems of customer classification, I: 188-190
  the proper limits, I: 142-146
  under pure competition, I: 123

in transportation rates, II: 14-15; *see also* Inter-
    state Commerce Act, and Railroads, value of
    service pricing
in unregulated and regulated industry compared,
    I: 133, 159-160
see also Subsidization, internal
Distribution of income, consideration in pricing, I:
    67-69, 102-103, 144-147, 191. II: 243-245
Diversification, in communications, II: 139, 253-255
by gas distribution companies, II: 253, 260
Divestiture, vertical, II: 14, 301-305, 317-318
Dividends, pay-out ratios, investors' evaluation of,
    I: 47
Dividends to price ratios, and cost of capital, I: 47-
    48, 58-60
Dixie Carriers versus United States, II: 271
Dixie Express versus United States, II: 16
Dixie Highway Express versus United States, II: 16
Doede, Robert, II: 200
Donnem, Roland W., II: 320, 321
Doyle, John P. (*Doyle Report*), II: 15, 82, 85, 238,
    253, 271-273, 275, 281-284, 289, 310, 311
Duesenberry, James S., II: 175
Dunn, Robert M., I: 132
Dupuit, Jules, I: 87
Durand, David, I: 51

Earnings-price ratios, as evidence of cost of capital,
    I: 46-50, 58-60
East Ohio Gas Co., FPC versus, II: 30
Economic means and non-economic ends, I: 14-15
Economics, institutional, I: 18-19
    micro, principles, I: 16-19
    micro- and macro-contrasted, I: 16
    relation to public policy, I: 14-19. II: xi-xii; *see*
        also Non-economic considerations in policy
    science and prescription in, I: 14-17
Economies of scale, and competition, II: 114
    external, II: 119
    internal and natural monopoly, II: 119-125
    in regulated industries, I: 11-12, 124-130, 150
    see also Natural monopoly, and entries for indi-
        vidual industries
Edwards, Corwin D., II: 97, 247, 257
Edwards, Ford K., I: 156, 161. II: 179
Efficiency, regulatory appraisals of, II: 62-63
Electric companies, competition among, II: 317-
    319
Electric power industry, mergers, II: 75, 281, 286-
    287
    need for integration, II: 74-76; *see also* Power
        pooling
    organization, II: 70-76, 117-120, 124-126, 290
    problem of divided regulatory authority, II: 74-
        76; *see also* Jurisdiction, state versus federal
Electric Power Reliability Act, II: 76
Electric utilities, productivity trends, II: 99-100
Electrical equipment conspiracy, II: 53-54
Electricity, block rates, I: 96, 187
    compulsory interconnection in, II: 75-76, 317
    coops II: 74, 105, 316-323

demand elasticity, II: 102-103
discriminatory promotional rates, I: 148, 164
distribution, organization, II: 74, 117-119, 318;
    see also Combination companies
long-run cost tendencies, I: 125-126, 128, 163.
    II: 70, 73-75, 119-120, 124-125
municipally-owned companies, II: 50, 68, 70, 74,
    105, 316-323; *see also* Power pooling
Northeast power failure, II: 53
rates, England, I: 97-98
    France, I: 97
    impact of government competition, II: 105-106
    impact of regulation, II: 109-110
    long-run trends, II: 100
    straight electric and combination companies, II:
        277
    United States, I: 98
sales, straight electric and combination companies,
    II: 277
short-run marginal costs, I: 94, 96-97
standby capacity, adequacy, II: 50
see also Competition, fuel and energy, Nuclear
    fuel, Power pooling, Holding companies
Elkins Act, II: 27
Ellis, Howard S., I: 74. II: 119
El Paso Natural Gas Co., II: 86, 154-157
El Paso Natural Gas Co., United States versus, II:
    161-163, 281
Emergency Railroad Transportation Act, II: 79, 80
Emery Air Freight Corp., II: 275
Energy charge; *see* Two-part tariff
Entry, importance of, II: 116; *see also* Licensing
    restrictions of, *see* Licensing, and Franchises
Equilibrium, long-run and short-run, I: 56, 74
Excess capacity; *see* Decreasing costs, short-run
Expenses, control of, I: 26-35
Externalities, in communications, II: 142, 151
    and implications for regulatory policy, I: 69, 179,
        193-195. II: 87, 177, 221, 234-235, 236-241
    and internal subsidization, I: 190
    and railroad passenger service, I: 192. II: 84
    in telephone service, II: 236; *see also* Communica-
        tions

Fainsod, Merle, I: 28
Fair, Marvin L., I: 186. II: 178
Fairness, as a consideration in regulation, I: 31, 42-
    44, 100-102, 107, 115-116, 158, 190. II: 243-
    245
    under marginal cost pricing, I: 56, 100-102, 107,
        121-122
Fair shares, regulatory policies of, I: 56, 164-166.
    II: 22, 76-77, 87-88
Fair value; *see* Rate base, fair value
Farmer, Richard N., II: 188, 191
Farrell, M. J., I: 70
Federal Communications Commission, AT&T rate
    investigation, I: 156-158, 173. II: 60
    diversification policy, II: 253-254
    fragmentation of efforts, II: 87-88
    Investigation of the Telephone Industry, II: 296,

299-300
licensing policies; *see* entries under Licensing, Broadcasting, Communications, Television
see also Telephone industry, Broadcasting, Television, Radio, Communications, and AT&T
Federal Coordinator of Transportation, II: 6, 14
Federal Power Act, II: 30
Federal Power Commission, certification policies, II: 152-171
  jurisdiction and powers, II: 30, 31, 74-78, 317, 322-323
  see Atlantic Seaboard formula, Natural gas, Pipelines, gas, and Power pooling
Fellner, William J., I: 119, II: 150; *see also* Ellis, Howard S.
Felton, John R., II: 103
Ferrall, Victor E., Jr., II: 33
Financial markets, regulation of, II: 6; *see also* Stock exchanges, and Brokerage commissions
Fisher, Franklin M., II: 33, 37, 102-103
Fisher, L., I: 48
Florida Power Corp. versus FPC, II: 76, 321
"Flow through" of income tax savings, I: 33-34
Food and Drug Administration, I: 2
Fortnightly Corp. versus United Artists Television, II: 38, 42
Franchises, competitive, II: 117-118; *see also* entries under Licensing, and specific industries
  and corresponding obligations, II: 8, 128-129
  as a factor in public utility monopoly, II: 3, 117-118
  government, I: 3, 5
Freight forwarders, II: 180, 274-276
Freund, William C., II: 205
Friday, Frank A., II: 176
Friedlaender, Ann F., I: 197. II: 15, 21, 191, 238, 275, 276, 309, 311
Friedland, Claire; *see* Stigler, George J.
Friedman, Milton, II: 5, 221, 328
Friend, Irwin, I: 47, 49
Friendly, Henry J., II: 91
Fritz versus City of Edmond, I: 189
Froggatt, Albert M., I: 125-126, 155
Fulda, Carl H., II: 18, 187, 253, 269, 271, 272, 274, 307
Full-cost pricing; *see* Costs, fully distributed, and Pricing, full-cost

Gabel, Richard, I: 152
Gainesville Utilities Dept. versus Florida Power, II: 76, 321
Galambos, Louis, II: 27
Galbraith, John Kenneth, I: 2. II: xi
Gallamore, Robert E., II: 285
Gannett Co., United States versus, II: 254
Garfield, Paul, J., I: 11, 34-35, 42, 99-100, 109, 197. II: 120-124
Gas, compulsory interconnection in, II: 166-167
  distribution, franchise policies, II: 117-118
  long-run cost tendencies, I: 125. II: 120

  as a natural monopoly, II: 152; *see also* Combination companies
  pipelines; *see* Pipelines, gas
  productivity trends, II: 99
  rates, I: 95-100
    long-run trend, II: 100
    straight gas and combination companies, II: 277-278
  sales, straight gas and combination companies, II: 278, 281
  storage, and capacity cost responsibility, I: 98, 100
    incentives for providing, II: 51, 167
Gasoline retailing, price wars, II: 184-185
Geddes Report, II: 186, 192
Gelhaus, Robert J., I: 50
Gellhorn, Walter, II: 5
Gellman, Aaron J., II: 213, 214, 216, 220, 247, 269
General Motors Corp., United States versus, I: 9
General Passenger Fare Investigation, I: 26, 106
General Telephone Co., II: 144, 290, 297
George, Henry, I: 68
Georgia versus Pennsylvania Railroad, II: 69
Georgia Power Co. versus FPC, II: 315
Gerber, Abraham, I: 180. II: 280, 320, 321
German Alliance Insurance Co. versus Lewis, I: 3, 6
Gewirtz, Stanley, II: 9
Gies, Thomas G., I: 53. II: 60
Ginsberg, Eli, I: 1
Glaeser, Martin G., I: 11, 25, 108, 115. II: 118
Gold, Nathaniel, I: 40, 112
Goldin, Claudia, II: 229
Goldin, Hyman H., II: 42
Gordon, Lincoln, I: 28
Gordon, Robert Aaron, I: 29
Gorrell, Edgar, II: 4
Gort, Michael, I: 108
Gould, Jack, II: 33
Government enterprise, as alternative to regulated monopoly, II: 328
  competition of, II: 104-106, 118-119, 319
Graham, Frank D., II: 328
Graham, Willard J., I: 111
Grain in Multiple Car Shipments, I: 165. II: 23-24
Grampp, William D., I: 100
Gray, Horace M., II: 2, 107, 111, 216-217, 235
Graybar Electric Co., II: 296
Great Lakes Pipeline Co., II: 158-161
Great Northern Railroad-Northern Lines merger, II: 289
Green, Wayne E., II: 198
Greenberg, Edward, II: 33, 38
Greiner, William R., II: 15
Grey, David L., II: 254
Griliches, Zvi, I: 126
Gruening, Ernest, I: 28
Gujarati, Damodar, II: 103
Gulf Canal Lines versus United States, II: 21

Haber, William, II: 60
Hadley, Arthur T., I: 64
Hale, G. E. and Rosemary D., II: 215

Hamilton, Ohio; *see City of Hamilton*
Hamilton, Walton H., I: 10, 13
Handy, Charles R., II: 190
Harbeson, Robert W., I: 131
Harper, Donald V., II: 178
Harriss, C. Lowell, I: 197
Hart, Senator Philip A., II: 285
Hayek, Friedrich A., I: 2. II: 328
Healy, Kent T., I: 126. II: 284
Heflebower, Richard B., I: 84. II: 185
Hellman, Richard, II: 87, 105, 106, 110, 117-119,
    322-323
Helmetag, Carl, Jr., II: 282, 287-289
Hendry, James B., II: 180
Henry, Commissioner E. William, II: 89
Hepburn Act, II: 26, 27
Hibbs, John, II: 225-226
Hiestand, Dale L., I: 1
Hilton, George W., II: 27, 78
Hinshaw Amendment, II: 30
Hirshleifer, Jack, I: 83, 91, 93
Holding companies, I: 28. II: 30-31, 70-73
    regulation of, II: 51, 253, 260, 280-281
Hollander, Stanley C., II: 211
Homan, Paul T., II: 29; *see also* Lister, Louis
Hooley, Richard W., I: 118
Hoopes, Roy, I: 8
Hoover, Calvin B., I: 52
Hope Natural Gas, FPC versus, I: 38, 40, 42, 57.
    II: 290
Hopkinson, John, I: 95
Hotelling, Harold, I: 87. II: 35
Houthakker, H. S., I: 186. II: 103
Hudson, William J., II: 193
Hughes, Howard, II: 255
Hughes, William R., II: 50, 57, 66, 67, 74-75, 78
Hughes Aircraft Co., II: 304, 305
Huntington, Samuel P., II: 28
Hush-A-Phone, II: 141-142

Imperfect competition, implications for public
    utility pricing, I: 86, 104, 106-107, 112, 177-
    180; *see also* Second-best, problem of, and
    Competition, imperfections
Incentive plans, II: 59-63
Incentives, the problem of, I: 53-54. II: 47-70
Increasing returns; *see* Decreasing costs and Econ-
    omies of scale
Industries "affected with a public interest," I: 3-8
Inflation, implications for pricing; *see* entries under
    Rate base, reproduction cost; Depreciation;
    Return on investment, gross
Ingot Molds case, I: 162-165. II: 23-24
Innovation, prerequisites of, II: xii, 103-104, 114,
    148-150, 303-305, 246-247
Institutions, role of, I: 18-19. II: xi-xiii
Insurance, savings bank life, II: 104
Integration, and competition, II: 257, 260, 262,
    264, 324-325
    conglomerate, II: 251-252, 257, 264-280
    economics of, II: 256-268

geographic, II: 251, 252, 281-290; *see also* Power
    pooling, Interconnection, and Transportation,
    joint rates
    horizontal, II: 251, 252, 256, 268-269, 281-290
    in regulated and unregulated industries compared,
    II: 256
    treatment under regulation, II: 252-255
    vertical, II: 251, 256-264, 290-305, 316-318
Intercompany coordination, benefits of, II: 34, 64-
    65, 70-71, 73-76, 80, 252, 273-274
    dangers, II: 69-72
    obstacles, II: 50-52, 66-69, 73-76, 81-82, 271-272,
    274, 286
    regulation of, II: 256, 272-275, 307-308
Interconnection, compulsory, II: 75-76, 166-167,
    317; *see also* Communications
Internal subsidization; *see* Subsidization, internal
International Air Transport Ass'n., II: 211-212, 217
*International Business Machines, United States
    versus,* I: 9
International Telephone & Telegraph Corp., II: 290,
    297
Interruptible service, I: 95, 106-107. II: 239
Interstate Commerce Act, legislative intent, I: 55.
    II: 23, 26-28
Interstate Commerce Commission, authority over
    intercompany coordination, II: 78-79, 81, 272,
    274, 288, 310-312
    authority over scheduling, II: 189
    policies on intermodal competition, I: 164-166,
    170. II: 14-15, 21-24
    rate regulation by, II: 18, 22-24
    see also entries under Freight forwarders, Motor
    carrier regulation, Transportation, and Rail-
    roads
ICC, *Reduced Seasonal Household Goods Rates,* I:
    95
Investment planning, coordinated, II: 126-129, 152-
    158
Irwin, Manley R., II: 129, 145, 146, 255, 295, 297,
    304
Isbrandtsen Co., FMB versus, II: 69
Iulo, William, I: 125. II: 63

Jaffe, Louis L., II: 28, 88, 91
Jensen, H. R., II: 262
Johnson, Commissioner Nicholas R., I: 122. II: 77,
    89, 92
Johnson, Leland L., I: 77, 88, 94, 126, 147, 162.
    II: 32, 33, 43, 44, 139; *see also* "A-J-W effect"
Johnston, J., I: 126
Joint products, efficient pricing of, I: 79-83, 134.
    II: 182-183; *see also* Costs, joint
Joint ventures, in air transport, II: 234
    electricity, II: 74, 319-320; *see also* Power pooling
    gas pipelines, II: 158-161
Jones, William K., I: 30. II: 6, 17, 18, 21, 37, 91,
    260, 262
Joskow, Jules, I: 188
Joy, Stuart, II: 191-192
Jurisdiction, state versus federal in regulation, II:

30-32, 72, 74-75, 322-323

Kafoglis, Milton Z., II: 101
Kahn, Alfred E., I: 31, 43, 68, 197. II: 8. 28, 29, 36, 37, 97, 100, 106, 150, 156, 235, 237, 240, 243, 250, 266; *see also* entries under Dirlam, J. B., and deChazeau, M. G.
Kain, J. F.; *see* Meyer, J. R.
Kaldor, Nicholas, II: 41, 206-207
Kaplan versus Lehman Brothers, II: 194
Kaysen, Carl, II: 102-103, 149
Keezer, Dexter M., I: 4
Kehrberg, E. W., II: 262
Kelly, Kenneth E., II: 190
Kendrick, John W., II: 58, 99-100, 104
Kennedy, President, Message on Transportation, II: 25-26, 242, 272
Kessel, Reuben A., II: 5; *see* Alchian, Armen A.
Kestenbaum, Lionel, II: 145
Keyes, Lucile S., II: 4, 220, 235
Keynes, John Maynard, I: 71
KHJ-TV, license renewal, II: 90
Kingsbury Commitment, II: 140
Klevorick, Alvin K., II: 49
Knappen, Lawrence S., II: 55
Knight, Frank H., I: 74
Kolko, Gabriel, II: 27, 78
Kolsen, H. M., I: 98, 187
Komiya, Ryutaro, I: 126
Koplin, H. T., I: 132. II: 65, 153, 165
Kosh, David A., I: 48
Kreps, T. J., I: 83
KRON-TV, II: 254
Kurz, Mordecai, I: 126

Lake, Isaac B., I: 63
Lancaster, Kelvin; *see* Lipsey, R. G.
Landis, James M., II: 12, 89, 91
Landon, John H., II: 279, 280
Langdon, Jervis, Jr., II: 22, 271
Lansing, John B., II: 17, 18, 21, 242, 276, 285
Larner, Robert J., I: 29
Laughlin, James C., I: 68
Leasing, lack of incentive, II: 51-52, 54, 76
Leiter, Robert D., II: 28
Leonard, William N., II: 79-82, 88, 288, 290
Lerner, Abba P., I: 68
Lerner, Max, II: 1
Lessing, Lawrence, II: 51, 305
Leventhal, Judge Harold, II: 166
Levin, Harvey J., I: 88. II: 38, 40, 91, 137, 177, 253, 254
Levine, Michael E., II: 218-220
Lewis, Ben W., I: 15, 37, 39, 41, 53, 112, 115-117. II: 103, 107, 110
Lewis, W. Arthur, I: 85, 96
Licensing, in air transport, II: 4, 16, 112
  in broadcasting, II: 2, 32, 37, 89-92
  competitive, II: 117-119, 126-171
  of freight forwarders, II: 180
  natural gas pipelines, II: 152-171

occupational, I: 2, 8-9, 13. II: 5, 172, 177-178
in public utilities, I: 20. II: 112, 117-118; *see also* Franchises, and entries for particular commissions and industries
of taxis, effect, II: 111
in trucking, II: 15-18
Linnenberg, Clem C., Jr., II: 190
Lipsey, R. G., I: 69. II: 243
Liquor stores, licensing of, II: 177
Lister, Louis, II: 30, 32, 73-75, 322
Little, I, M. D., I: 70, 98, 131, 199
Load factor, and pricing, I: 96; *see also* Capacity costs, distribution of
Load factors, and competition, II: 168-170, 211-212; *see also* Demand, diversity of; Capacity, standby
Lochner versus New York, I: 4
Locklin, D. Philip, II: 9, 69, 79-81, 179, 182, 217, 235, 253, 269, 272, 275
Loevinger, Lee, I: 2, 122. II: 29, 60, 114
Loomis, Carol J., II: 196, 197
Lorie, J. J., I: 48
Louisville & N. R. Co., ICC versus, I: 95
Lovejoy, Wallace F., I: 177. II: 29; *see also* Garfield, Paul J.
Lynchburg Gas Co. versus FPC, I: 99. II: 165-170

MacAvoy, Paul W., I: 68. II: 27, 108, 111, 153, 156, 281
McConnell, Grant, I: 8
McDonald, John, II: 137
McDonald, Stephen L., II: 29
McGowan, John, J., II: 36
Machlup, Fritz R., II: 235, 262
McKee, Robert E., II: 295, 297, 304
McKenzie, Lionel W., I: 145
McKie, James W., I: 180
McKinsey & Co., II: 291, 293, 299, 301
McLean Trucking Co. versus United States, II: 287
Madsden, Kenneth E., II: 297
Main, Jeremy, II: 67
Management, compensation, II: 99
  motivations and incentives, I: 29-30, 44, 147. II: 62, 101-102
  separation of from ownership, I: 28-29
Mann, H. Michael, II: 202
Mann, J. David, II: 168
Mann-Elkins Act, II: 26, 27
Mansfield, Edwin, II: 100
Marginal cost, problems of embodying in rates, I: 186, 188-189; *see* Cost, marginal
Marginal cost pricing, economic rationale, I: 65-67
  long-run versus short-run, I: 83-89, 103-109, 176
  short-run, I: 56, 76, 104-109
Markham, Jesse W., II: 97, 258
Marshall, Alfred, I: 79
Marx, Daniel, Jr., II: 9, 69
Mason, Alpheus T., II: 104
Massé, Pierre, I: 97
Matthews, A. Bruce, I: 114. II: 52
May, Stacy; *see* Keezer, Dexter M.

Means, Gardner C., I: 28. II: 71, 72
Measuring costs and demand elasticities, problems
    of, I: 184-188
Mechling, ICC versus, II: 271
Meek, Ronald L., *I:* 91, 94-95, 97-98
Melody, William H., I: 121. II: 148, 150, 152
Mendelson, Morris, I: 116
Mergers, in regulated industries, II: 286-287; *see
    also* references to specific industries
  statutory provisions, II: 113, 253, 287
Messer, John S., II: 82-85
Metcalf, Senator Lee, I: 31. II: 93, 326
Meyer, John R., I: 110, 132. II: 97, 182, 188, 189,
    245, 250, 275, 284, 285, 309, 311, 313
Michigan Consolidated Gas Co., II: 253, 260, 263
Michigan-Wisconsin Pipe Line Co., II: 263
Microwave Communications, Inc., II: 132-136, 146-
    152, 290
  cream-skimming aspects, II: 227-232, 238-240
Microwave radio, II: 129-136, 146-152, 304
Midwestern Gas Transmission Co., II: 159-161
Midwestern Gas Transmission versus FPC, I: 34
Miklius, W., II: 184, 190
Miller, Merton H., I: 47-48, 51, 137, 139
Miller, Ronald E., II: 211-212
Minasian, Jora R., II: 42
Minow, Newton M., II: 38
Mishan, E. J., I: 145, 194, 196
Missouri versus Kansas Natural Gas Co., II: 30
Mitchell, Bridger M., II: 33
Modigliani, Franco; *see* Miller, Merton H.
Monopoly, association of regulation with, II: 1-45,
    111-112
  effect on public utility pricing, II: 107
  "of fact," I: 5
  "of law," I: 5, 7
  natural; *see* Natural monopoly
Monopsony, in capital markets, II: 58
Moore, Thomas G., II: 5, 109
Morgan, Charles S., I: 22-23. II: 28, 61-63, 86, 112
Morrisey, Fred P., I: 47
Morton, Walter A., I: 110, 115
Motor Carrier-Air Freight Forwarders Investigation,
    II: 274-275
Motor carrier, deregulation, Australian experience,
    II: 190-192
  rates, off-peak, I: 95. II: 182-183, 188
  regulation, II: 6, 8-9, 14-28, 186-193, 253, 269,
    272-273, 313-314
    agricultural exemptions, II: 15, 19-20, 26, 187-
      193
    effect on efficiency, II: 187-193, 313-314
    in Great Britain, II: 186, 192
    and price discrimination, II: 14-15, 188, 190
    and rate levels, II: 188-191
    and rate stability, II: 188-189, 191-193
    in relation to the Depression, II: 18, 180-182
    and service quality, II: 185-186, 187-193
Motor carriers, economies of scale, II: 182, 185
  elasticity of supply, II: 179-184
  fixed versus variable costs, II: 178-184

licensing of, II: 15-18, 187-188
problem of the back-haul, II: 182-184
product differentiation, II: 182, 185, 189
safety, II: 6, 185-186, 192-193
see also Transportation
Moulton, H. G., II: 269
Mueller, Dennis G., II: 175
Mueller, Willard F., II: 252
Municipal Electric Ass'n. of Mass. versus FPC, II: 70
Municipal Electric Ass'n. of Mass. versus SEC, II:
    322
Munn versus Illinois, I: 3-7, 36. II: 118
Musgrave, Richard A., I: 131

National Economic Research Associates, II: 55, 99,
    198, 277-278
National power survey, II: 78
National Recovery Program, I: 10
National security, as a consideration in regulation,
    II: 243-246
Natural gas, field price regulation, I: 40, 42-43, 68,
    151. II: 31-32, 156
  full cost allocation methods, I: 151; *see also Atlan-
    tic Seaboard* formula
  see also Pipelines, natural gas
Natural Gas Act of 1938, II: 30, 31, 113
Natural Gas Pipeline versus FPC, I: 34
Natural monopoly, I: 11-12, 124. II: 2-3, 113-171
  CATV as, II: 34
  evolution of, II: 117-119
  in radio, II: 2
  stock exchanges as, II: 200
  see also Economies of scale, and references to
    specific industries
Nebbia versus New York, I: 4-8, 13, 21
Nelson, James C., I: 64, 154, 170. II: 18, 22, 25,
    185-189, 191, 273, 283
Nelson, James R., I: 12, 53, 55, 73, 85, 106, 111,
    113, 145, 193. II: 3, 118, 234
Nelson, Robert A., II: 15
Nerlove, Marc, I: 126
Netschert, Bruce C., I: 65, 180. II: 102
Network analysis, II: 157-158
Netzer, Dick, I: 197
New Automobiles in Interstate Commerce, I: 165
New England Electric System, SEC versus, II: 280-
    281
New State Ice versus Liebmann, I: 3, 6-7
*New York, New Haven & Hartford Railroad, ICC
    versus,* II: 23, 248-249
New York Stock Exchange, II: 194, 201-202; *see
    also* Stock exchanges and Brokerage commis-
    sion rates
Nicholson, Howard W., I: 151. II: 183-184, 188
Noble State Bank versus Haskell, I: 3
*Noerr Motor Freight versus Eastern Railroad Presi-
    dents Conference,* II: 274
Non-economic considerations in policy, I: 14-15, 42,
    68-69, 100-103, 189-193. II: 151, 243-246;
    see also Fairness
Normalization of income tax liabilities, I: 33-34

Northern Natural Gas Co., II: 159-161, 315
Northwest Agricultural Cooperative Ass'n. versus ICC, II: 20
Northwestern Electric Co. (FPC, 1941), I: 28
Nuclear fuel, lease versus purchase, II: 52, 57

Obligation to serve, public utilities; *see* Common carriers, obligations of
  under antitrust law, I: 8
Obsolescence; *see* Depreciation
Off-peak demand; *see* Capacity costs, distribution of
O'Gorman & Young versus Hartford Fire Insurance, I: 3
Oil; *see* Competition, fuel and energy
Oil industry, regulation of, II: 29; *see also* Pipelines, oil
Olds, Leland, II: 74, 78
Oligopoly, competition under, II: 162, 210-220, 276-280, 287, 306
Operating ratio regulation, II: 54-56
Option demand, II: 37, 236-241; *see also* "Tyranny of small decisions"
Otter Tail Power Co. versus FPC, II: 76
Otter Tail Power Co., United States versus, II: 68
Owen, Bruce M., II: 254, 277-278

Pacific Gas Transmission Co., II: 154-157
Pacific Southwest Airlines, II: 218-219
Pacific Tel. & Tel. versus California, I: 31, 54-55. II: 292-293
Panama Canal Act of 1912, II: 253, 268-269
Panhandle Eastern Pipe Line Co., II: 263
Parke Davis and Co., United States versus, I: 9
Parker, ICC versus, II: 16, 253, 274
Parr, Arnold F., II: 49
Pastore, Senator John, I: 24
Pastore bill, II: 92
Patent system, II: 4
Patinkin, Don, II: 266
Peak, coincident versus non-coincident, I: 96-97
Peak responsibility pricing; *see* Capacity costs, distribution of
Peck, Merton J., I: 31, 110, 166. II: 18, 21, 51, 150, 245; *see also* Meyer, John R.
Pegrum, Dudley F., I: 161. II: 179-180
Penn-Central R.R., quality of service, I: 23-24
Pennsylvania-New York Central merger, II: 282, 284-285, 288
Pennsylvania R.R. Co.; discontinuance of Passenger Service, II: 83
Pennsylvania Truck-Lines-Barker Motor Freight, II: 269
Penn. Water & Power Co. versus Consolidated Gas, II: 315
Penn. Water & Power Co. versus FPC, II: 315
Performance, direct regulation of, II: 86; *see also* Service quality, regulation of
  industrial, problems of assessing, II: 95-97
  standards, absence of, II: 89-91
  see also Public utility performance

Permian Basin Area Rate Cases, I: 40, 42-43, 68, 151
Peterson, G. Shorey, II: 181-182
Phalon, Richard, II: 245
Phillips, Almarin, II: 18, 88, 213, 247
Phillips, Charles F., Jr., I: 4, 12, 21, 26, 31, 40, 42, 51, 55, 63, 96, 99, 113-114, 149, 154. II: 120, 132, 300
Phillips Petroleum Co. versus Wisconsin, II: 31
Piggyback service, II: 309-314
Pigou, Arthur C., I: 68, 94
Pipeline Production Rate Proceeding, II: 290-291
Pipelines, gas, coordinated investment planning, II: 65, 153-158
  cost allocation, I: 152; *see also Atlantic Seaboard* formula, Two-part tariff
  cost tendencies, I: 99. II: 153-155
  interconnection, compulsory, II: 166-167
  joint ventures in, II: 158-161
  profit rates, II: 170; *see also* Profit rates
  role of competition, II: 113, 152-171
  vertical integration of, II: 156, 263, 290-291
  oil, competitive problems created by, II: 317
  long-run cost tendencies, I: 124
Planning, regulatory, II: 77-86
Planning period, for long-run incremental cost computation, I: 108
Political economy, I: 14-15
Politics, and regulation, I: 31. II: 326-327; *see also* Corruption, political
Ponsonby, G. J., I: 101, 146
Posner, Richard A., II: 47, 77, 328
Post Office, II: 328
  cost ascertainment system, I: 155
Power pooling, II: 64-65, 314-323
  benefits, II: 64-65, 123
  obstacles, II: 50-51, 67-70, 73-76
  restrictive covenants, II: 314-316
Predatory competition; *see* Discrimination, effect on competitors
Presidential Advisory Committee on Transport Policy and Organization, II: 22, 24-25
President's Task Force on Communications Policy; *see* Communications Policy
Prewitt, Roy A., II: 317
Price discrimination; *see* Discrimination
Pricing, assessment of public utility performance, II: 97-101
  full-cost, I: 84, 106, 150-158
  marginal cost; *see* entries under Cost, marginal, and under Marginal cost pricing
  over time, I: 103-117, 121-122
  past versus future costs as basis, I: 88-89, 109-117, 121, 185
  peak responsibility; *see* Capacity costs, distribution of
  practical considerations, I: 83-86, 88, 104, 106-108, 182, 184-189, 198-199
  reactive, I: 109
  value-of-service; *see* Discrimination, and Railroads
  see also references to specific industries
Price regulation, central role of, I: 20-25

Priest, A. J. G., I: 7, 28, 30, 42. II: 30, 73, 124
Product differentiation; *see* Competition, non-price, and Service quality
Productivity trends, in public utilities, II: 58, 99-100
Profit rates, public utilities and others, I: 52, 170. II: 98-99, 170
Profits, regulation of, I: 20, 26, 30-31; *see also* Rate base and Rate of return
Promotion, as a purpose of utility regulation, II: 3-4, 10-11, 233-235
Promotional allowances, energy markets, I: 164, 177-180
Promotional expenditures, I: 95, 149, 164; *see also* Advertising
  straight versus combination companies, II: 279-280
Protectionism and regulation, II: 11-46, 87-88; *see also* Fair shares
Prudent investment, *see* Rate base, original cost
Public good, information as a, II: 207
  television as a, II: 40-41
Public Service Electric and Gas Co., I: 95
Public utilities, identified, I: 3, 10-11
Public Utility Holding Company Act, II: 30-31, 72-73, 78, 252-253, 255, 260, 278, 280
Public utility performance, assessment of, II: 95-101
  favorable influences, II: 101-111
  see also entries for specific industries and for specific aspects of performance
Public utility regulation; *see* Regulation
Puckett, Marshall; *see* Friend, Irwin
Pyramiding, in holding companies, II: 71

Quality of service, *see* Service quality

Radice, Anthony M., II: 177
Radin, Alex, II: 316, 322
Radio Acts of 1912 and 1927, II: 32
Radio, FCC licensing policy, II: 37
Radio spectrum, opportunity costs of, I: 88. II: 38
Radio stations, licensing of, I: 24
Railroad costs, common versus joint, I: 94
  management, conservatism of, I: 170-171. II: 21, 80-82, 85, 271-272, 285-287, 310
  rates, off peak (return hauls), I: 95, 164, 186
Railroads, box car exchanges, II: 64, 78-79, 307
  consolidation, under 1920 Act, II: 78-82
  danger of predatory competition by, II: 270-272, 274, 276
  discrimination against other carriers, II: 271-273, 275, 307, 310-312; *see also* Railroads, resistance to intermodal coordination
  excess capacity, II: 283-284
  freight rates, trends, II: 100
  full cost allocation, I: 150, 154-156. II: 85
  integration with motor and water carriers, II: 253, 268-276
  long-run cost tendencies, I: 126-127. II: 284
  mergers, II: 79-82, 281-290
    fragmented regulation of, II: 88, 288-290

passenger service, costs and profitability, I: 154-155. II: 85
  discontinuations, I: 192. II: 82-84
  regulation of quality, I: 23-24. II: 82-86
  productivity trends, II: 99-100, 104
  profitability, I: 170. II: 273
  rate bureaus; *see* Rate bureaus
  rate reductions by, II: 21-24
  recapture clause, II: 79
  resistance to intermodal coordination, II: 68, 80-82, 270-272, 274, 310-314
  share of freight traffic, United Kingdom, II: 21
  share of freight traffic, United States, I: 64
  small, competitive handicaps, II: 80-81, 288-289
  taxation of, I: 155, 197. II: 84
  value-of-service pricing, I: 155-156. II: 14-15, 21, 309-311
Ransmeier, Joseph S., II: 103
Rate base, I: 35-41, 109-117
  and depreciation, I: 32-33
  fair value, I: 37-38, 41
  incentive to inflate; *see* "A-J-W effect"
  original cost, I: 37, 39-41, 109-117
    and investment incentives, I: 110
  reproduction cost, I: 37-39, 41, 88-89, 109-117, 121
  valuation, survey of methods, I: 41-42
Rate bureaus, II: 69, 211, 307; *see also* Shipping conferences
Rate level, defined, I: 26
  regulation of, I: 26-54
Rates, industrial versus residential, I: 102
Rate structures, regulation of, I: 54-57; *see also* Discrimination, Marginal cost pricing, Peak responsibility, references to specific industries, etc.
Rationalization of industry, I: 9-10
Ratner, David L., II: 197
Raynor, Charles P., II: 69
RCA Communications, FCC versus, II: 46
Recoupment of discriminatory rate cuts, I: 170-171
Redford, Emmette S., I: 26
Red Lion Broadcasting Co. versus FCC, II: 90
Reed-Bulwinkle Act, II: 69, 113
Reel, A. Frank, II: 43
Rees, R., I: 197
Regulated industries, identified, I: 3, 10-11
Regulated sector, defined, I: 2-11
Regulation, the adjudicatory role, II: 86-92, 288-290
  association with monopoly, II: 1-45, 325-326, 328
  constitutional history of, I: 3-8
  and dynamic industry performance, I: 26. II: 13, 59
  economic rationale, I: 11-12. II: 2-11, 172
  efficacy of, II: 108-112, 325-329
  and efficiency, I: 29-32. II: 48-49, 51, 57, 58, 62-63
  fragmentation of, II: 87, 92
  inherent tendencies, II: 1, 11-13, 26-29, 46, 47, 87-88, 189, 209-210
  legal rationale, I: 3-8

limitations of, I: 18, 22-25, 29-32. II: 13, 47-48, 70, 77, 87-94, 107, 325-326
main characteristics, I: 2-3, 20-21. II: 12-13, 47
non-public utility, I: 2, 8-10. II: xiii
practical considerations, I: 37-39, 41, 83-86, 182-189; *see also* Pricing, practical considerations of price; *see* Price regulation
procedural reforms, II: 93
procedures, over-judicialization of, II: 87
of quality of service; *see* Service quality
role of economics in, I: 14-19
tendency of to spread, I: 24, 28-32
types of, I: 13
see also entries under the objects of regulation- e.g., rate levels, operating expenses, capital outlays, service quality, licensure of entry, price competition, etc.
Regulatory lag, I: 54. II: 48, 56-57, 59-60
Reich, Charles A., II: 246
Reinemer, Vic; *see* Metcalf, Lee
Rents, economic, I: 68
Reproduction cost; *see* Rate base, reproduction cost
Resale price maintenance, I: 8. II: 176-177
Research expenditures, capitalization of, II: 52
Return, on investment, gross, *see* Depreciation marginal versus average, I: 114
recovery over the cycle, I: 105-106, 110-112
rate of, I: 41-54, 105, 111-112
and ability to attract capital, I: 40, 42-43, 46-47
in air transport, II: 55
comparable earnings standard; *see* Comparable earnings
incentive function of, I: 44, 53-54. II: 48-49, 59-63
as a political bargain, I: 42-45
price level adjustment, I: 51, 115-116
sliding scale plans, II: 61
in trucking, II: 55
see also Profit rates
Reubens, Beatrice G., I: 1
Revenue requirements, I: 26, 111; *see also* Rate levels
Reynolds, Lloyd G., II: 174, 181
Ribnik versus McBride, I: 3, 9
Richmond, Samuel B., II: 210-211, 220
Ripley, William Z., II: 72, 79, 81
Ritchie, Robert F., II: 73, 278
Robbins, Sidney, II: 194, 197, 206
Roberts, Merrill J., I: 161. II: 28, 250, 287, 311
Robinson, Joan, I: 9, 133
Robinson-Patman Act, I: 148
Rock Island Motor Transit, United States versus, II: 270
Romnes, H. I., II: 145
Rose, Joseph R., I: 41, 51
Roseman, H. G., I: 48-49, 58, 60, 172
Rosenberg, Laurence C., I: 99-100
Ross, Charles R., II: 76, 87, 320-322
Ross, Homer, I: 100
Rossant, M. J., II: 206
Rosse, James N., II: 254

Rostow, Eugene V., II: 317
Roth, Irving, II: 215
Rothenberg, Jerome, II: 36
Ruggles, Nancy, I: 130, 145
Running charge; *see* Two-part tariff
Rural Electrification Administration, II: 105
Ruskay, Joseph A., II: 316

St. Louis & O'Fallon Ry. versus United States, II: 79
Samuels, Warren J., I: 195
Samuelson, Paul A., II: 40, 42
Sanders Brothers Radio Station, FCC versus, II: 37
Scanlon, John J., II: 52
Scenic Hudson Preservation Conference versus FPC, II: 87, 165
Schaffer Transportation Co. versus United States, II: 16
Scherer, Frederic M., I: 31. II: 304
Schmookler, Jacob, II: 186
Schumpeter, Joseph A., I: 15, 44
Schwartz, Herman, II: 53, 137, 138, 228-230
Schwartz, Louis B., II: 19, 46, 113
Scitovsky, Tibor, I: 145
Sea-Land Service, II: 248
Seatrain Lines versus United States, II: 271
Second-best, problem of, I: 44, 53, 69-70, 112, 195-198. II: 241-243
Securities Exchange Act, and self-regulation, II: 194-195, 199-200
Securities and Exchange Commission, II: 30, 73; *see also* Stock exchanges, Brokerage commission rates, Public Utility Holding Company Act
Securities markets; *see* Stock exchanges
Seiden, Martin H., II: 32, 38
Separations procedures, Bell System, I: 101, 152-153
Service, extension and discontinuation of, I: 22, 76-77, 154-155; *see also* Railroads, passenger service
Service quality, assessment of, II: 97
importance of, I: 21. II: 76
incentives to maintain, I: 24-25. II: 53, 176-178
inflation of, II: 10, 53, 189, 207-212
regulation of, I: 21-25. II: 82-86, 177-178, 185-186, 210-216
Seven-way cost study; *see* Communications, full cost allocation
Shapp, Milton, II: 254
Sharfman, I. L., II: 26-27, 79, 82
Sheahan, John B., I: 8. II: 53, 291-292, 294, 296-297, 302-304
Shepherd, William G., I: 30, 53, 56-57, 96, 98. II: 50, 58, 63, 99, 100, 107, 149, 293, 304
Shipping, dual rates, II: 69
Shipping conferences, II: 69, 164, 307
Shonfield, Andrew, I: 128
Shrewsbury Municipal Light Dept. versus New England Power Co., II: 75-76, 167, 322-323
Shultz, George P., I: 8
Silberman, Charles E., II: 305
Silver versus New York Stock Exchange, II: 195

Simons, Henry, II: 328
Sixty-two Cases of Jam versus United States, I: 2
Skinner & Eddy versus United States, I: 176
Sloss, James, II: 111
Smathers-Holland bill, II: 322-323
Smidt, Seymour, I: 106, 108
Smith, Adam, I: 1, 11, 14
Smith, Charles W., I: 113
Smith, Delbert D., II: 146
Smith, Nelson Lee, II: 165, 168-169, 263
Smith versus Illinois Bell, I: 29. II: 291
Smyth versus Ames, I: 37-39. II: 71
Socialization; *see* Government enterprise
Southern Bell Tel. & Tel., Florida, 1968, I: 23
Southern California Edison Co., FPC versus, II: 30
Southern Natural Gas Co., II: 165
*Southern Pacific Co., Passenger Service between
    California and Louisiana,* II: 82-85
Southwestern Bell Telephone Co. versus Missouri,
    I: 29
Southwestern Cable Co., United States versus, II: 33
Spengler, J. J., II: 260
Steel, price controls, I: 8
Steiner, Peter O., I: 91, 93, 138. II: 36, 41, 42
Stelzer, Irwin M., I: 65, 180, 188. II: 50, 55, 58,
    102
Stenason, W. J., I: 182; *see also* Meyer, John R.
Stern, Carl, II: 102
Stigler, George J., II: 109-110, 261, 328
Stock, market valuation of, I: 46-50, 58-60
Stock exchanges, and the antitrust laws, II: 194-196
    institutional membership, II: 28, 197, 206
    market shares, II: 193-194, 197, 200
    as a natural monopoly, II: 200
    regulation of, II: 6, 199-201; *see also* Brokerage
        commissions
Stocking, George W., I: 10
Stockpiling, I: 8
Strassburg, Bernard, II: 146
Straszheim, Mahlon R., II: 211-213, 216-217, 220,
    226, 235
Subsidies, to barges and trucks, I: 165-166. II: 242-
    243
    government, and marginal cost pricing, I: 130
    and restrictions on entry, II: 4
Subsidization, internal, I: 102-103, 143, 190-191.
    II: 236
    in airline rates, I: 153, 236, 244-245
    in communications, II: 151
    and cream-skimming, II: 221-223, 226, 228-229,
        234, 239
    in postal rates, II: 221
    in railroads, II: 15, 84
Subsidized competition alleged, in energy markets,
    I: 162-163
    in transportation, I: 162-163; *see also* entries
        under Discrimination and Communications
Substituted Rail Service by Red Ball Transfer Co.,
    II: 313
Surplus, consumer, producer, transaction, I: 131-
    132, 139, 144-145, 190-191

Swedish American Line, FMC versus, II: 69, 163-164
Sweezy, Paul M., II: 327
Swidler, Joseph C., II: 323

Taber, Martha, II: 262
Taff, Charles A., II: 18
*Tampa Electric and Florida Power Corp., United
    States versus,* II: 315
Tarif Vert, I: 97
Tarpley, Fred A., II: 278
Taussig, Frank W., I: 94
Taxation, of utility companies, implications for pric-
    ing, I: 197; *see also* Depreciation, accelerated
Taxes, neutrality of, I: 68, 130-131. II: 242-243
    property, and railroads; *see* Railroads, taxation
Taxi rates, impact of regulation, II: 111
Taylor, Lester D., II: 103
Teamsters Union, interest in regulation, II: 28
Technological progress, effect on natural monopoly,
    II: 10
    as an occasion for rate discrimination, I: 134
    public utility performance, II: 99-101
    in relation to regulation, II: 13, 29-30
    see Decreasing cost, long-run, and Depreciation
Telecommunications Policy, Office of, II: 93
Telephone, full cost allocation; *see also* entries under
    Separations procedures and Communications
Telephone companies, CATV operations, II: 68,
    308-309
    interconnections, II: 140, 307-308; *see also* Com-
        munications, interconnection
    rental of poles, II: 67-68, 308-309
Telephone industry, increasing cost tendencies, I:
    125. II: 123-124
    local, organization of, II: 117-118, 127
    relation to computers, II: 145-146
    see also Communications
Telephone rates, I: 95, 192-193. II: 132
    impact of regulation, II: 110
    trends, II: 100
Telephone regulation, continuing surveillance, II: 60-
    61
Telephones, foreign attachments, II: 6, 128, 140-146
Telephone service, demand elasticity, II: 102-103
    flat local charge, I: 192-193
    quality of, I: 23, 25. II: 53
Television, allocation of resources to, II: 40-42
    the censorship issue, II: 38, 90-91
    cigarette commercials, II: 90-91
    community antenna (CATV). II: 32-45
        carriage of local signals, II: 33-34
        collaboration with telephone companies, II: 67-
            68, 308-309
        as common carriers, II: 43
        the copyright problem, II: 42-45
        external costs, II: 36-37, 240-241
        FCC regulations, II: 33-34, 39-40, 43-45, 245,
            254
        impact on local stations, II: 32-33, 36-37, 39,
            42-43
        multi-media ownership, II: 254

program origination; *see* Television, local programming

prohibition of program duplication, II: 34

sale of advertising, II: 44-45

defects in industry performance, II: 35-36, 41

externalities, II: 34, 36

intercompany coordination, II: 34, 64

local programming, FCC policy on, II: 36, 37, 38, 43, 44, 45, 245

monopoly power in, II: 38-39

network programming, II: 38

pay- , II: 40-42, 44, 45, 92

pricing principles, II: 40-42

profitability, II: 38-39

program quality, II: 35-36, 41

public, II: 38

as a public good, II: 40

UHF stations, II: 35, 36, 39

see also Broadcasting

Television regulation, Congressional interference, II: 38

Television stations, licensure of, I: 24

numbers, II: 32

Telser, Lester G., II: 41, 207

Tennessee Valley Authority, cost allocation, I: 151

effect on electricity rates, II: 105-106

and elasticity of demand, II: 103

and electrical equipment conspiracy, II: 53-54

Terminal R. R. Ass'n. of St. Louis, United States versus, II: 125, 319

Test year, I: 26, 113-114

Theater, French, regulation of, II: 4

Thill Securities versus New York Stock Exchange, II: 195-196

Thomas, D. W., II: 262

Thompson, Edward T., II: 21

Three-part tariff, I: 95

Tipton, Stuart G., II: 9

Tobin, James, I: 52

Tolls on bridges, I: 87, 89, 109

Transatlantic cable, ownership of, II: 53

TAT-5, I: 122. II: 51, 76-77

Trans-Canada Pipe Lines, II: 158-161

Transcontinental Gas Pipeline Corp., II: 165, 167-170

Transportation Act of 1920, II: 27, 78-82

Transportation Act of 1958, I: 164-165. II: 23, 82-83

Transportation, common carrier share in total traffic, II: 21, 187

companies, II: 253, 266-276

competition, distortions of, I: 130, 161, 165-166, 192. II: 84, 242

reduced rates on back-hauls, I: 164, 175. II: 24, 182-184

and cream-skimming, II: 8-9, 225-226

diffusion of regulatory authority, II: 92

inefficiencies in, I: 166. II: 22, 84, 309; *see also* Motor carrier regulation

innovation in, II: 99-100, 104, 111, 247-248, 285

intercarrier coordination, benefits, II: 64, 66, 285-286

obstacles, II: 68-69, 286

joint rates, II: 64, 69, 271-272, 307

media, cost structures contrasted, I: 161-162. II: 178-180

inherent cost advantages of, I: 165. II: 23-24

service differences, I: 160-161

piggyback service, II: 309-314

Presidential Message on (1962), II: 25-26, 242, 272

private carriage, II: 19, 25, 187-189

productivity trends, II: 99-100, 247

protectionism in regulation of, II: 14-28

rail-rail competition, I: 169-173

rail-truck and rail-barge competition, I: 161-166, 168, 173. II: 14, 21-24, 248-249

rates, impact of regulation, II: 111

role of competition in, II: 24-28

see also Air transport, Motor carriers, Railroads, Interstate Commerce Commission, Shipping

Transport, Inc., Extension-Sioux Falls, II: 18

Transport Policy and Organization, Presidential Advisory Committee on, II: 24-25

Transport regulation, exempt carriers, II: 18-21, 24-26

fully distributed versus marginal costs in; *see* Transportation, rail-truck and rail-barge competition

of intermodal coordination, II: 272-275

and national security, II: 245

Transwestern Pipeline Co., II: 154-157

Trans-World Airlines, II: 211-212, 214-215

Trebing, Harry M., II: 30, 61, 87, 112

Trip leasing, II: 19, 192-193

Troxel, Emery, I: 4, 25, 29, 40, 51, 53, 55, 89, 114, 119, 147-149. II: 110, 278-279

Trucking; *see* Motor carriers, and Transportation

Turner, Donald, II: 315-316

Turvey, Ralph, I: 90, 125, 185-186, 190, 192, 196

Two-part tariff, I: 95-100, 152

Tyndall, David G., I: 125, 142, 187

"Tyranny of small decisions," in air transport, II: 239

and CATV regulation, II: 37, 240-241

in communications, II: 238-241

defined, II: 236-238

and deregulation of brokerage commissions, II: 207-208

and rail passenger service, II: 237-238, 240

Tyson versus Banton, I: 3-4, 6, 9

Ulrey, Ivan W., II: 191

United Artists Television versus Fortnightly Corp., II: 42

United Church of Christ versus FCC, II: 90

United Shoe Machinery Co., United States versus, I: 8

United States Steel Corp., United States versus, II: 157

United States versus; *see* entries for defendant companies

United Telephone of Florida, 1968, I: 23

Utility Users League versus FPC, II: 286-287

Value-of-service pricing; *see* Discrimination, also
    Railroads, value-of-service pricing
Van Dam, William C., II: 20
Veblen, Thorstein, I: 2. II: xi
Vickrey, William, I: 76, 100, 108-109, 121-122,
    127, 137, 144-146, 184-187, 199. II: 107,
    212, 233
Vidal, Gore, II: 41
Viner, Jacob, I: 74
Volotta, Alexander, II: 18

Wage-price guideposts, I: 8
Wallace, Donald H., I: 135
Wallace, Richard L., I: 98
Wallich, Henry C., II: 203
Walters, A. A., II: 21
Walton, Clarence C., II: 54
Washington plan, II: 61
Water carriers, exemption from regulation, II: 20-
    21, 25-26
Water supply, long-run cost tendencies, II: 124-125
Watkins, Myron W., I: 10
Wein, Harold H., II: 50, 64, 150, 152
Weintraub, Sidney, II: 59
Weisbrod, Burton A., II: 37, 236-237
Welborn, David M., II: 17, 187
Welch, Francis X., I: 41
Wellisz, Stanislaw H., I: 99-100. II: 49, 50; *see also*
    "A-J-W effect"
Wenner, Examiner Seymour, II: 154-157
Western Electric Co., Bell Co. payments to, I: 29.
    II: 291-294, 296-297, 299-300, 302
    productivity record, II: 299-300
    rate of return, II: 291-295
    research and development contribution, II: 300-
    302
    sales to non-Bell companies, II: 296, 305-306
    see also Communications, vertical integration and
    American Telephone and Telegraph Co.
Western Electric Co., United States versus, II: 253,
    295-297, 306
Western Union Telegraph Co., I: 23, 156-158, 166,

173, 176-177. II: 48, 248
Westfield, Fred M., II: 53, 54, 65
West Ohio Gas versus Public Utilities Commission,
    I: 30
Weston, J. Fred, II: 295
WHDH-TV, II: 254
Whinston, Andrew B.; *see* Davis, Otto A.
Whitaker, Gilbert R., Jr., I: 197
White, Commissioner Lee, II: 155-157
White Stephen, II: 33
Whitney, Simon N., II: 175
Wiget, Barbara, II: 207
Wilcox, Clair, I: 2, 10, 40-41, 168. II: 27, 92, 104,
    300, 304
Wildavsky, Aaron, II: 106
Wiles, P. J. D., I: 72
Williams, Ernest W., I: 186. II: 9, 21-22, 82, 178
Williams versus Standard Oil, I: 3, 6
Williamson, Oliver E., I: 30, 91
Wilson, Gary D., *see* Gelhaus, Robert J.
Wilson, George W., I: 77, 145, 156, 161, 170, 185.
    II: 14, 97, 111, 182, 183, 185, 250
Wilson, John W., II: 63, 103, 279
Wiprud, Arne, II: 272
Wisconsin versus FPC, I: 40
Wiseman, J., I: 68, 70
WLBT-TV, license renewal, II: 90
Wohl, M.; *see* Meyer, J. R.
Wolbert, George S., Jr., I: 6. II: 317
Wolff Packing Co. versus Kansas, I: 3, 6
Worcester, D. A., Jr., I: 133
WPIX-TV, license renewal, II: 89
Wright, Charles Alan, II: 54
Wright, David McCord, II: 13
Wright, Helen R., I: 10
Wright, Judge J. Skelly, II: 161-165

Yardstick competition; *see* Government enterprise

Zajac, E. E., II: 101
Zimmermann, Erich W., II: 175
"Zone of reasonableness" for rate of return, I: 42-43
Zwerdling, Daniel, I: 24. II: 89
Zwick, Charles; *see* Meyer, John R.